THE BIRDWATCHER'S
AND DIARY 2

Designed and published by
Hilary Cromack

Edited by
David Cromack

BUCKINGHAM PRESS LTD

In association with

SWAROVSKI
OPTIK

Published in 2009 by
Buckingham Press Ltd
55 Thorpe Park Road, Peterborough
Cambridgeshire PE3 6LJ
United Kingdom

(Tel/Fax) 01733 561 739
e-mail: admin@buckinghampress.com
www.buckinghampress.co.uk

© Buckingham Press Ltd 2009

ISBN 978-0-955033-98-8
ISSN 0144-364 X

Cover image: Kingfishers by Rob Cook. In addition to his freelance illustration work, Rob has for many years been a lecturer in scientific and natural history illustration in Lancashire.
To see more of Rob's work visit his website at: www.robcookart.com

Black and white illustrations: Dan Powell, who can be contacted at 01329 668 465 or dan.powell@care4free.net

Printed and bound in Great Britain by
Information Press, Oxford UK.

CONTENTS

CONTENTS

PREFACE

Author LP Hartley's opening sentence in his well-regarded novel *The Go Between* was "The past is another country, they do things differently there." That may be true in many spheres of life, but for the past 30 years *The Birdwatcher's Yearbook* has remained steadfast in its defence of the exacting standards set down by its founder John Pemberton.

In his preface for the first edition, John wrote: *"The Birdwatcher's Yearbook* (BYB) has been launched with the object of providing a comprehensive and convenient work of reference for all sections of the birdwatching community in Great Britain and for visitors from overseas.

He expressed the hope that the book would contribute to the advancement of birdwatching by publishing original articles by experts and encourage readers to widen their horizons, making them conscious of the constructive part they could play in conserving the nation's wildlife.

Since Hilary and I bought Buckingham Press in 2000 we have done our best to live up to those ideals, so that the *Yearbook* remains to birdwatching what *Wisden* is to cricket and the *Sky Sports Football Yearbook* is to the round ball game.

Can you remember what was happening in early November 1980 when the 1981 edition of *The Yearbook* went on sale? Ronald Reagan had just been elected for his first term as US president, while Jim Callaghan was stepping down as leader of the Labour Party. Trade union movement Solidarity had just been recognised by the Polish government and Blondie topped the UK hit parade with *The Tide Is High*.

Birdwatching at that time was not a mass-participation activity. It took the launch of *Bird Watching* magazine in 1986 and a boom in twitching around the same time to start to change birding's image. Suddenly it became an acceptable pastime and its growth in popularity has continued to the present day.

Providing today's audience with up-to-date and verified information is just as relevant as it was in the era before telephone hotlines, pager services and all the technological marvels we now take for granted, and that continues to be our mission when we publish each new volume.

We always strive to introduce new ideas to the *Yearbook's* contents and in this volume, Gordon Hamlett not only reviews the latest technological aides available to enhance your birdwatching, but also nominates his top bird books of the past 12 months.

I am sure you will enjoy reading Barbara Hall's account of the success of the Hawk and Owl Trust since it was founded 40 years ago, as well as Richard Facey's round-up of the most significant bird news in the past 12 months.

Of course all the most popular features are retained – as well as updating entries for many top reserves, we've added a number of new sites and the Checklists for both birds and dragonflies show the most recent additions to the lists.

So, *The Birdwatcher's Yearbook* should be able to answer all your information needs, but if it doesn't, please let me know. I am always keen to add new elements to ensure it remains an indispensible work of reference.

David Cromack (EDITOR)
editor@buckinghampress.com

Acknowledgements
We are indebted to many people, from club secretaries to reserve wardens, from county recorders to the press officers of the leading bird conservation organisations for their help in compiling up-to-date information. Special thanks go to Ieuan Evans and his colleagues at BTO.

A MESSAGE FROM THE SPONSORS OF THIS BOOK

ANNIVERSARIES are a time for celebration and I congratulate Buckingham Press Ltd for reaching a significant milestone with the publication of the 30th edition of *The Birdwatcher's Yearbook*.

The birdwatching community in Britain has grown in both size and complexity since the first edition made its debut, but the *Yearbook* has constantly evolved to meet the information needs of its readers.

Even in the age of the internet, the convenience of having so much information in one book and knowing that its accuracy has been assured by patient research and verification, ensures that the value of the book to bird conservation organisations, journalists, clubs and individual birdwatchers has been maintained year after year.

Swarovski's own experience in creating cutting-edge optical equipment makes us aware that British birdwatchers demand the very highest standards from each new product they buy – whether that be a binocular or a book.

Our goal is to continually improve our products through innovation and, having recognised that Hilary and David Cromack were driven by the same ideal in terms of book production, we were delighted to accept their invitation to become the sponsor of *The Birdwatcher's Yearbook* in 2002.

While regular buyers of the book need no introduction to its strengths, we feel confident that first-time readers will be impressed by its breadth of coverage. We feel confident it will meet all your needs – from detailing the country's best bird reserves, supplying that vital tide table information or simply putting you in touch with your local bird club. Put it to the test today – and for the rest of 2010. Happy birding.

Peter Antoniou
Managing Director, Swarovski Optik UK

SWAROVSKI
OPTIK

FEATURES

Mark Fisher

Today's Hawk and Owl Trust volunteers keep watch on Peregrines nesting on church towers or other high buildings in UK cities, like this one in Bath. The feature celebrating 40 years of the Trust starts on page 14.

KEY ORNITHOLOGICAL NEWS OF 2009

Richard Facey provides a digest of the most significant news stories relating to the world of birds, plus a selection of interesting snippets. Illustrations by Dan Powell.

Long-term Great Bustard plan starts to pay dividends

IT HAS BEEN a long road, but the pitter-patter of tiny Great Bustard feet are once again being heard on Salisbury Plain. The last time home-grown chicks roamed the area was in 1832, but thanks to the work of the Great Bustard Group the bird is back as a fully fledged UK breeding species.

British Great Bustards (*otis tarda*) became extinct by the 1840s, and on a global scale the species has not fared much better. A massive range contraction means the species' world population stands at roughly 35,000.

At last there are encouraging signs that Great Bustards may soon re-establish a population in Britain.

The Great Bustard Group has been releasing young chicks of Russian origin onto Salisbury Plain since 2004 but because the bird is slow to mature, it is only now that the birds have started to produce young. Eggs were laid in the summers of 2007 and 2008 but these turned out to be infertile, so the team had to wait another year to see if the results of their labours would be rewarded.

Success came in May of 2009 when, at a secret location, a female was seen incubating eggs; Britain's first two home hatched chicks were soon seen following their mother. A second female was seen a day later feeding another chick.

The team plan to carry on releasing Russian birds until 2013. In September 2008, 18 birds were released and benefited by being the first batch that could join a group of mature adults – a strategy that experience has shown greatly increases survival.

Source: *The Great Bustard Group* www.greatbustard.com

KEY ORNITHOLOGICAL NEWS OF 2009

Early success for Crane expansion plan

COMMON CRANE (*Grus grus*) has been missing from the East Anglian Fens for nearly four centuries, but in 2009 two pairs chose to rear young at the RSPB's Lakenheath Fen reserve.

Though a small population of Common Cranes set up camp in the Norfolk Broads in the early 1980s, this new record is thought to be the first breeding attempt by more than one pair at a single locality away from the original area.

The Fens was selected for a reintroduction programme as it was the region where the Common Crane made its last stand before becoming extinct as a breeding species. The Great Crane Project, run by the RSPB, Wildfowl & Wetlands Trust, Pensthorpe Conservation Trust and Viridor Credits Environmental Company, aims to re-establish a sustainable breeding population of the nominate species in the UK.

The project uses a similar technique to the Great Bustard scheme; taking surplus eggs from healthy populations, hatching them, and rearing the young before releasing them into the wilds of the UK.

Source: *Royal Society for the Protection of Birds*

BirdLife report gives cause for concern – and some hope for the future

IT IS A SALUTORY experience to discover that two centuries after Darwin's birth one of his celebrated Galapogos finches finds itself on BirdLife International's annual IUCN Red List of endangered species.

The annual update of the Red List can be a depressing read and the 2009 assessment was no different, with 1,227 (12%) of the world's birds now listed as Globally Threatened, with a further 192 in the highest threat category of Critically Endangered. This was just two species more than in 2008, but it is still a trend going in the wrong direction.

Though not the inspiration behind Darwin's seminal theory of evolution, the Medium Tree-finch (*Carmarhynchus pauper*)

A mere youngster in record-breaking terms

BECOMING a record-breaker at the age of six sounds unusual, but that is exactly what a Little Egret (*Egretta garzettta*) with the ring number GF09838 has become. It is officially the oldest member of species recorded in Britain and Ireland. Originally ringed in May 2003 at a site in Kent, the egret disappeared from the birding radar until its reappearance in July 2009.

This particular landmark reflects the fact that Little Egret is Britain's most recent colonist – in mainland Europe the longevity record belongs to a 22-year-old French bird.

Source: British Trust for Ornithology Ringing Office

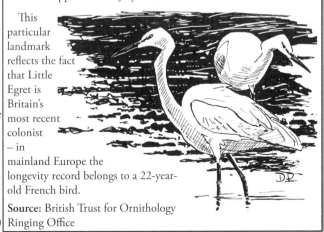

9

is among the Galapagos species that have become icons of natural selection. However, it is now rated as Critically Endangered as a result of falling prey to an introduced parasitic fly.

The recently discovered Gorgeted Puffleg (*Eriocnemis isabellae*), first featured in *The Birdwatcher's Yearbook* 2008, makes the List for the first time since its discovery because its specialised habitat, which stands at tiny 1,200 hectares, is being lost at the alarming rate of 8% annually.

Dramatic habitat loss is also responsible for the decline in the Sidamo Lark (*Heteromirafra sidamoensis*) and if action is not taken soon, it could earn the unwanted status of becoming the first bird to become extinct in mainland Africa since records started.

Previously the estimated population of 2,000 birds was distributed across a range of 760sqkm of the Ethiopian 'rangelands' of the Liben Plain. Unfortunately the Borana pastoralists are losing the use of their traditional rangelands, so that their livestock no longer keeps the encroachment of scrub at bay.

This factor, coupled with an increasing conversion to agricultural land and development, meant it was no surprise that a review of the Sidamo Lark in 2007-08 found the species' numbers were down by a staggering amount. Its global range, based on the availability of suitable habitat, now stands at an estimated 35sqkm and, more worryingly, the population is now estimated to be between 90-256 adults, possibly with a high male bias.

New White-eye species shows evolution in action

THE WHITE-EYE family is a geographically widespread family that enjoys a reputation for evolving new species faster than any other group of birds. And to maintain this reputation, a new species has been identified on the Solomon Islands.

The island chain already hold a dozen White-eye species, but a much longer bill and different leg and eye-ring makes the Vanikoro White-eye (*Zosterops gibbsi*) distinct. The new species' status appears secure on Vanikoro island, although introduced rats may be a problem waiting in the wings

Source: Duston. *Ibis, volume 150,* pages 698 to 706.

Though still listed as Critically Endangered, Slender-billed (*Gyps tenuirostris*) and White-rumped Vultures (*G. bengalensis*) did provide some hope for the future during 2009. Two Slender-billed and three White-rumped chicks have been reared at dedicated breeding centres, a first for the former species.

This is good news for the vultures; the Slender-billed's population stands at a meagre 1,000 individuals, while the annual 40% downturn in White-rumped's populations means it has the fastest rate of decline recorded for any species. Successful captive breeding, along with the banning of the drug Diclofenac in vetinary medicine, that led to decline of the species, are likely to be the key to conserving these species in the future.

The report offered more upbeat assessments for species such as Lear's Macaw (*Anodorhynchus leari*), which was down-graded from Critically Endangered to Endangered. Action from a raft of national and international non-governmental organisations, the Brazilian Government and local landowners has seen the macaw's numbers increase four times over.

Lear's Macaw was also joined on the Endangered list

by the recovering Mauritius Fody (*Foudia rubra*). This red-headed forest weaver had originally declined to around 100 pairs on mainland Mauritius between 1975 and 1993, mainly as a result of introduced predators.

To boost numbers, conservationists decided to establish a new population on a predator-free island, Ill aux Aigrettes, a 25 hectare island 625m off the Mauritius coast. Between November 2003 and March 2006, 93 Fodies, harvested from nests on the mainland threatened with predation and then hand reared, were released. The population soon established itself and the first wild fledglings were produced during the 2004-05 breeding season.

With the presence of each Mauritius Fody being monitored daily, the team report the island population stood at 47 breeding pairs and 142 individuals in December 2008.

Sources: *IUCN Red List Update*
– BirdLife International
Mauritius Fody introductions

Age will not wither them

BRITISH seabirds are in a class of their own when it comes to setting new age-related records. The Shaint Auk Ringing Group staged an expedition in 2009 to the Hebridean island that gives them their name, four miles or so off the coast of Lewis.

Among the birds they caught were two Puffins. On July 17 the group renewed its acquaintance with EX08155 who they originally ringed in June 1977, making the bird at least 32 years old. Not only that but the Ian Buxton who ringed this bird back in 1977 was there in 2009 for the reunion.

But five days later, the team beat their own record by two years when they refound

Two Puffins, caught by ringers within five days of each other, have set new longevity records for Britain.

EB73152, which was ringed in 1975. Not only did this bird take the British longevity honours, but also for Europe, by beating the existing record-holder by a year.

Source: British Trust for Ornithology Ringing Office

– Cristinacce, Handschuh, Switzer, Cole, Tatayah, Jones and Bell. *Conservation Evidence,* Volume 6, pages 1-5
Sidoma Lark - Spottiswoode, Wondafrash, Gabremichael, Dellelegn Abebe, Mwangi, Collar and Dolman. *Animal Conservation doi*:10.1111/j.1469-1795.2009.00246.x

Red danger signals for 18 more species in Britain

THE HEALTH of British bird populations is constantly changing, but sadly the latest report from our leading conservation bodies reveals more losers than winners. *Birds of Conservation Concern 3*, published in May 2009 updated the figures for the UK's avifauna last reported in 2002.

The publication assessed the fortunes of 246 species, of which 52 earned a place on the Red List (high conservation concern), 126 on the Amber List (medium conservation concern), while 68 species remain Green listed.

Eighteen species found themselves moved from Amber to the Red List, including six – Lapwing (*Vanellus vanellus*), Cuckoo (*Cuculus canorus*), Tree Pipit (*Anthus trivialis*), Yellow Wagtail (*Motacilla flava*), Wood Warbler (*Phylloscopus sibilatrix*) and Lesser Redpoll (*Carduelis cabaret*) — as the result of declines identified by the Breeding Bird Survey.

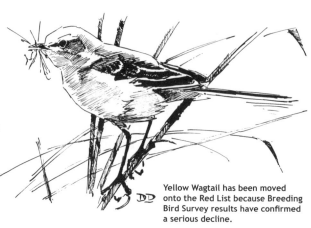

Yellow Wagtail has been moved onto the Red List because Breeding Bird Survey results have confirmed a serious decline.

The status of Balearic Shearwater (*Puffinus mauretanicus*) was assessed for the first time and it was placed straight on the Red List because its global status is Critically Endangered. Arctic Skua (*Stercorarius parasiticus*) was a dramatic loser, leap-frogging from the Green List straight to Red.

Not even the ubiquitous Mallard (*Anas platyrhynchos*) has an assured future — it was one of 23 species moved from the Green to the Amber List because of a decline in its non-breeding population of more than 25% in the last 25 years. The Pied Flycatcher (*Ficedula hypoleuca*) joined the ranks of declining long-distance migrants, and was accompanied in its move to the Amber List by the Swift (*Apus apus*).

Now to the good news. Red List regulars such as the Reed Bunting (*Emberiza schoeniclus*) and Bullfinch (*Pyrrhula pyrrhula*) were among the six species to move to the Amber List, as their population declines are now less than 50% over the long term.

One of the UK's smallest and the UK's fastest species were among the eight species that can celebrate a move from the Amber to the Green List; the rising fortunes of the Goldcrest are reflected in the results of the Breeding Bird Survey, while the Peregrine Falcon (*Falco peregrinus*) no longer finds itself listed as a Species of European Conservation Concern and therefore has found itself on the Green List.

Though still well short of their peak populations, Bullfinches have recovered enough to be moved from Red to Amber status.

Source: Eaton, Brown, Noble, Musgrove, Hearn, Aebischer, Gibbobs, Evan, Gregory. *British Birds*, volume 102, pages 296-341

KEY ORNITHOLOGICAL NEWS OF 2009

Tiny trio triumph in British Breeding Bird Survey

OF THE 221 species recorded in 2008's Breeding Bird Survey, UK trends were produced for 105 species. Among the winners were a trio formed by some of the smallest members of the UK's avifauna – Goldcrest (*Regulus regulus*), Long-tailed Tit (*Aegithalos caudatus*) and Chiffchaff (*Phylloscopus collibita*) – which increased by 28%, 17% and 14% respectively compared to 2207. The first two species reached their highest levels since the Breeding Bird Survey started.

In percentage terms, larger birds showed the greatest increases overall. Though the Red Kite (*Milvus milvus*) population dropped by 7% between 2007 and 2008, the massively successful re-introduction scheme has generated an outstanding 333% population increase between 1995 and 2008. But that increase has been eclipsed by a relative new, but now well entrenched, member to the UK's ornithological register. Although it showed a modest 2% increase between 2007 and 2008, the UK's Rose-ringed Parakeet (*Psittacula krameri*) population has increased by a staggering, show-stopping, 600% since 1995. Fruit farmers beware!

Sadly, the good news is balanced by the bad. While many of the medium distance migrants, such as the Chiffchaff, held their own or increased, several long-distance summer migrants have fared badly, with nine showing serious declines. Of these Turtle Dove (*Turtur turtur*), Cuckoo (*Cuculus canorus*), Whinchat (*Saxicola rubetra*) and Nightingale (*Luscinia megarhynchos*) all reached their lowest levels since 1994.

The rapid growth in the British population of fruit-eating Rose-ringed Parakeet (a staggering 600% increase since 1995) will concern farmers in SE England.

The Breeding Bird Survey is the main source of information about many birds of conservation concern. Recent amendments to the Red and Amber Lists (see above) now means that 20 Red-listed species are monitored by the annual BBS survey. Unfortunately 15 of these species continued their downward trend, with familiar species such as the House Sparrow still declining, at least in a UK context.

Song Thrush (*Turdus philomelos*) and Tree Sparrow (*Passer montanus*) seem to have turned the corner after a long period in decline. The latter species showed an increase of 50% between 2007 and 2008, with a 44% rise overall.

Although continuing a significant overall downward trend (-38%), the Spotted Flycatcher (*Muscicapa striata*) at least gave a glimmer of hope for the conservation minded by showing a 40% increase between 2007 and 2008.

No fewer than 34 Amber-listed species were also monitored by the 2,500 volunteers in more than 3,200 kilometre squares (the third highest total in the history of BBS) and there was an even split of increase and decrease for species in this category.

Source: *British Trust for Ornithology*

13

FORTY YEARS WORKING FOR WILD BIRDS OF PREY

The Hawk and Owl Trust has been in the forefront of the fight to protect Britain's most spectacular, but often maligned, bird species. Barbara Hall recounts the Trust's steady progress since 1969.

WITH PEREGRINES now nesting in city centres across the land, it is hard to believe that this iconic species once looked doomed in the UK. Yet in 1969 it was the desperate plight of Peregrines and other birds of prey endangered by organochlorine pesticides that inspired the birth of the Hawk Trust.

The charity, renamed the Hawk and Owl Trust in 1990 to reflect the breadth of its work for both nocturnal and diurnal species, has just celebrated its 40th anniversary.

Today it works, through conservation, research and education on its own reserves and in partnership with others, for wild birds of prey and their habitats so benefiting the whole web of life on which these top predators depend. With owls and other birds of prey continuing to face deadly threats, from drastic loss of habitat and nest sites to outright persecution, its work remains vital. Poisoning, trapping, shooting and theft of eggs or young made 2009 one of the worst years on record for crimes against Peregrines.

Current priority species for the Hawk and Owl Trust's work include the Marsh Harrier, now regularly breeding in the reedbeds of its Sculthorpe Moor reserve in Norfolk, and the Kestrel, which is thought to be declining.

The Trust recently launched a project to install a chain of nestboxes near selected stretches of highway around the country to see whether lack of natural nest sites is at the heart of the fall in Kestrel numbers. It is also backing PhD research into the Little Owl, a species declining across Europe.

An innovative polebox is manoeuvred into place in 1991 as part of a pilot nestbox project for Barn Owls in the Lincolnshire fens

Even in the early years, the Peregrine was far from the Trust's only concern, though it has always been its logo. A pioneering attempt to bolster the wild Red Kite population in 1971 by importing a continental male to enrich the gene pool was blocked by refusal of an import licence. Official policy has clearly changed since then. However the Trust didn't give up on kites – from 1972, its volunteers helped warden nest sites of the precious remnant population in Wales.

FORTY YEARS WORKING FOR WILD BIRDS OF PREY

Barn Owl crisis revealed

A critical point in the Trust's development came in the 1980s. In response to growing alarm about the Barn Owl's plight, the charity launched a mammoth research project to update 50-year-old data. The survey, co-ordinated by Colin Shawyer as a very dedicated volunteer, demonstrated a drop of about 70 per cent in the number of pairs in the British Isles, compared with 1932.

This was later reinforced by a joint survey with the British Trust for Ornithology, carried out between 1995 and 1997, which identified only about 4,000 breeding pairs in the UK.

Armed with the findings of the 1980s research, the Trust spearheaded the drive to save the species, drawing on a network of committed Barn Owl conservationists — largely volunteers identified and brought together by the project.

The Trust, with Colin as its first director of conservation and research, pioneered nestboxes and initiated habitat management projects to help farmers, other landowners and managers to attract Barn Owls back to their land.

Fieldworkers installed, and encouraged others to install, nestboxes in barns and trees and, where both of these were scarce, on poles, to allow populations to spread to prey-rich areas lacking natural nesting sites. It is estimated that today four in every five Barn Owl pairs now depend on nestboxes.

Research has long been at the heart of the Trust. In the 1970s it arranged for a student to undertake a PhD study of the feeding ecology of the Kestrel, while in the 1980s and 1990s there followed a detailed study of Merlin breeding in Scottish forests, research into the Long-eared Owl and the first international conference on small falcons.

The Trust's study for the Highways Agency of Barn Owl mortality on major roads presented a number of conservation recommendations to reduce the toll. This century has seen research on the growing phenomenon of urban Peregrines and their use of man-made structures for nesting and roosting.

The Trust has long supported the annual Hen Harrier Winter Roost

Jeff Pick

The Adopt a Box scheme was launched for the Trust by Chris Packham, who can date his long-standing support back to the early days of Red Kite wardening in Wales. He is pictured here some years later - in 1996 - helping to put up a Barn Owl nestbox in Berkshire.

15

Survey, launched more than 25 years ago by artist and author Donald Watson and Trust scientific adviser Dr Roger Clarke. Sadly both men have now died, but the Trust has joined with the BTO to continue what is thought to be the longest running non-breeding survey of a single bird species in the world. It has also backed a PhD study, finished in 2008, which has shed new light on the origins of Hen Harriers that winter in southern England.

For half its 40 years the Trust was essentially an organisation of volunteers and even today it employs only a small team of staff. Key to its way of working are its partnerships with others — individuals and like-minded organisations — and the dedication of its volunteers helping to monitor and conserve birds of prey and their habitats. Recently the Trust has been harnessing local community enthusiasm to find out more about the Long-eared Owl in the Mendip and Quantock Hills, Somerset.

New initiatives in land management

Staff and volunteers, often from local members' groups, continue to visit farmers and other landowners to advise on habitat management and install artificial nest sites. But the Trust also has a history of practical conservation under its own management. For a decade, up to 1982, it leased 700 acres of Shropshire woodland from the Forestry Commission to create habitat and improve knowledge about species such as Sparrowhawk and Goshawk.

In the early 21st Century this moved into a higher gear when the Trust, with the considerable help of volunteers, began to create two nature reserves open to the public: first Sculthorpe Moor Community Nature Reserve at Fakenham, north Norfolk, and then Shapwick Moor on the Somerset Levels.

It also began to manage Fylingdales Moor in North Yorkshire as a conservation area on behalf of its owner, The Strickland Estate. Despite all being 'moors' they are three very different habitats.

The Trust created the Sculthorpe Moor reserve on land mostly leased from a local parish charity. It includes the Wensum Valley's only example of saw sedge wetland, a priority habitat for conservation in Europe.

The reserve has become well known as one of the best places to view breeding Marsh Harriers. For the past two years (ie 2008 and 2009) images from a nestcam, believed to be the first installed for the species in the UK, have been shown on monitors on the reserve, the Trust's website and to viewers of *BBC Springwatch*. Other wildlife includes Barn Owl, Water Rail, Kingfisher, Willow Tit, many species of dragonfly and therefore Hobby and a host of plants.

Shapwick Moor Nature Reserve, on the Somerset Levels, was bought in 2007 with the help of an appeal to Trust supporters and funding from Natural England, Esmée Fairbairn Foundation, The Tubney Charitable Trust, Viridor Credits and the Bristol Port Company. Previously arable farmland, it forms part of the larger network of reserves known as the Avalon Marshes.

The Trust is restoring Shapwick Moor to flower-rich, semi-natural grassland with Natural England's support. Some land is being restored to fen. Rough grass margins will encourage owls and other birds of prey and the small mammals on which they feed. As well as Barn

FORTY YEARS WORKING FOR WILD BIRDS OF PREY

Owl, Kestrel, Buzzard and Hobby, the reserve is being created with a wide range of wildlife in mind, including Snipe, Lapwing and other wetland birds.

Natural England support is also playing a key role in the Fylingdales Moor conservation area – about 6,800 acres (2,750 ha) of heather moorland in the North York Moors National Park and a Special Protection Area (SPA) for Merlin and Golden Plover. The aim is to create a nationally important haven for wildlife, including Short-eared Owl and harriers.

A former grouse moor, the land is now managed to enhance wildlife, preserve archaeological remains and demonstrate the environmental benefit and sustainability of traditional moorland management techniques.

Education is a major strand of the Trust's work because of the importance of increasing knowledge and understanding of birds of prey and the impact we all have on the environment we share with them.

In 1988 it established the National Centre for Owl Conservation for visitors to the National Trust's

Graham Corney

The Sculthorpe Moor reserve was officially opened by HRH The Princess Royal in 2003, who is pictured here with the Trust's President, actor Liza Goddard, when she returned to open the education and visitor centre in 2007.

Blickling estate in Norfolk, later moving to nearby Wolterton Hall. Then in 1995, thanks to the support of the Whitley Animal Protection Trust, this was superseded by the Trust's new Conservation and Education Centre at the Chiltern Open Air Museum in Buckinghamshire. The model was extended with the establishment on the Sculthorpe Reserve of an environmentally friendly and accessible education and visitor centre, supported by Heritage Lottery and European Union funds.

The Trust offers schools a range of environmental programmes, geared to the National Curriculum, runs after-school Kestrel Clubs for 8 to 12-year-olds, and organises school holiday activities for children and their families. Outreach and adult education opportunities in various parts of the country range from owl prowls to one-day workshops tutored by acknowledged experts.

Helping to make all this work possible are the Trust's very supportive members and 'adopters'. In 1992 it launched a successful nestbox adoption scheme – Adopt a Box – and many people find this makes an excellent gift for Christmas and other special occasions, as well as for themselves. But, like so many conservation charities, the Trust's determined efforts to help some really special birds also depend very much on grants, sponsorship and legacies and it has many people to thank.

To find out more go to www.hawkandowl.org or email enquiries@hawkandowl.org. The Hawk and Owl Trust, PO Box 400, Bishops Lydeard, Taunton, Somerset TA4 3WH, tel: 0844 984 2824.

GOOD READS FOR BIRDWATCHERS

Avid bibliophile Gordon Hamlett runs the rule over scores of natural history books released in 2009 and recommends 14 titles to enhance your library.

B IRDWATCHING is a hobby that you can approach from a variety of viewpoints. You might be a photographer or artist, a dedicated local patch worker or avid twitcher, a ringer or even a humble hack reviewing bird books but we will all draw deep satisfaction from our activity.

The book trade is now catching up with this varied approach. Where once we were fed little more than a diet of new identification guides and fieldguides, there is now an explosion of subject matter, with many of the most interesting titles coming from mainstream publishers, rather than those specialising in natural history books.

Often taking a wider view of birds, many of the newcomers approach the hobby from angles not considered by mainstream ornithological publishers. Thus you can now find titles mixing birds with humour, history, geography, archaeology, biography, environmental science, culture etc…. and we are still getting new avifaunas and fieldguides as well. While there are mounting concerns about the world's biodiversity, the field of bibliodiversity is looking particularly healthy.

Bird books are arriving on the market at a rate of approximately one a week, so what qualities do my recommended choices possess? When it comes to evaluating a new work, I want the book to tell me something I hadn't known before: a new approach to identification perhaps or a fieldguide to somewhere that hasn't previously been covered. Yet another book on birds and gardening is going to have to be pretty special to elevate it above an already crowded field.

Books from smaller publishers or unexpected sources are usually interesting for two reasons. By their very nature they usually deal with quirky subjects. Also, they don't get a lot of coverage in the mainstream birding press. The editor remarked that he hadn't come across most of the titles on my list and that's good enough for me. If he hasn't heard of them, then probably you won't have either and I can suggest something new to get your juices going.

Personal bias comes into it too. We all have our favourite subjects. I'm a sucker for anything Scottish and I love the way we are seeing more and more books combining birds with other topics. As the Bible so nearly put it, 'Man cannot live by bird alone'.

If I don't like something, I will say so, but in a constructive way, I hope. Most publishers accept that their titles vary in quality. The bottom line always has to be 'would I have paid for that book with my own money and if so, would I have been pleased with my purchase?' Answer both of those with a 'yes' and you are going to be pretty close to making the shortlist. And before you ask, yes, I did buy several of the titles featured on the following pages.

GOOD READS FOR BIRDWATCHERS

Here are Gordon Hamlett's top 14 books from the
past 12 months, listed alphabetically by title:

A Field Guide to the Birds of South-East Asia second edition (Craig Robson, New Holland, 544pp. Hbk. £35. ISBN 978-1-84773-341-2)

Birds of East Asia (Mark Brazil, Helm, 528pp. Pbk. £29.99, ISBN 978-0-7136-7040-0).

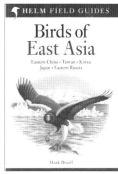

Travellers to Asia are particularly well catered for this year. The new edition of Craig Robson's guide has been totally updated to take in a plethora of taxonomic changes and new species. This guide covers Burma, Thailand, Malaysia, Singapore, Cambodia, Laos and Vietnam and includes 1,327 species. The only surprise is that there are no distribution maps.

Mark Brazil's guide is a completely new work and covers 985 species from eastern China, Taiwan, Japan, Korea and eastern Russia. Both books feature plates from an assortment of top artists, with a couple contributing to both volumes. Hefty, but luggable, each one becomes the undisputed number one guide for their particular region.

Birds of Ethiopia and Eritrea (John Ash and John Atkins, Helm, 463pp. Hbk. £45. ISBN 978-1-4081-0979-3).

Birds of the Horn of Africa (Nigel Redman et al, Helm, 496pp. Pbk. £29.99. ISBN 978-0-7136-6541-3).

And still the world continues to shrink.

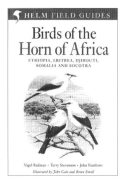

Not one but two books dealing with Ethiopia and surrounding areas, though how many tourists are likely to be visiting Eritrea, Somalia and Djibouti in the near future remains to be seen. The Horn of Africa fieldguide is a typical example of Helm's continuing excellence is this sector of the market. There are short descriptions and a distribution map opposite the 213 plates covering more than 1,000 species.

While you would obviously want the guide on holiday with you, the *Birds of Ethiopia and Eritrea* – an avifauna of the area — can probably stay at home for pre and post-tour analysis. There are 871 tetrad maps, assorted sections on the geography, habitats and conservation of the area, together with eight plates of photos of endemic species.

Birdscapes (Jeremy Mynott, Princeton UP, 368pp. Hbk. £17.95. ISBN 978-0-6911-3539-7)

Why do you like some birds more than others? What is the attraction of travelling to see a displaced bird in a country park when there are thousands on the coast nearby? Drawing on sources from a wide variety of literary, scientific and historical sources, Jeremy Mynott looks at the way we interact with birds and what that in turn tells us about ourselves.

You won't agree with everything written here – some of the theories culled from the Internet, such as the song 'The 12 Days of Christmas' being a codified version of the forbidden Catholic Mass have long been debunked as urban myths. But his breadth of knowledge is superb and this is easily the best book of its type that I have read.

Call of the Eagle (Dave Walker, Whittles Publishing, 164 pp. Pbk. £16.99. ISBN 978-1-9044-4582-1)

I have very fond memories in my formative years of discovering that I didn't have to travel to the Scottish Highlands to record one of the birds I had always dreamt of seeing. Not only were Golden Eagles breeding in England, but they were close to where we staying in the Lake District.

Dave Walker was an RSPB species protection officer for 25 years and the eagles were part of his remit. As well as unparalleled descriptions of eagle behaviour, there are also accounts of dealings with unhappy locals, unbending bureaucracy and egg collectors. Though one male still remains in Cumbria, he hasn't found a mate now for five years, so this book could well be the end of the story for England's eagles.

Harriers – Journeys Round the World (Don Scott, Tiercel Publishing, 200 pp hb, £39.99. ISBN 978-0-9532-0026-9)

The author's obsession with harriers started with his love of Hen Harriers in Northern Ireland 20 years ago and has subsequently taken him round the world. For anyone used to seeing the odd bird in the UK, descriptions of roosts of 1,100 Pallid and Montagu's Harriers in India are mind-blowing.

Published in a limited edition of just 700, and illustrated with a profusion of colour photos – the oddest being a pure albino Hen Harrier — and a few of Philip Snow's wonderful watercolours, this is sure to please both raptor lovers and book collectors alike.

The History of British Birds (Derek Yalden and Umberto Albarella, OUP. 263pp. Hbk/pbk, £55/£24.95. ISBN 978-0-1992-1751-9)

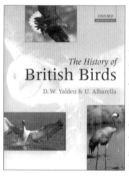

If you could travel back in time 500 years, what birds would you see? And what about 5,000 years? This book looks at evidence from a variety of sources as it tries to piece together our ornithological history. For the ancient evidence, this involves looking at bones found in archaeological digs, which include such records as Ptarmigan in Devon, Hazel Hen and Eagle Owl.

For more recent times, a study of place

names can provide useful clues; the numbers of villages referencing Cranes suggest how widespread this bird once was. For anyone with a combined interest of birds and archaeology/ancient history, this is a must-read volume.

Lars Jonsson's Birds (Lars Jonsson, Helm. 192pp. Hbk, £35. ISBN 978-1-4081-1014-0)

This was easily my favourite bird-art book of the last 12 months. No, cancel that. This is one of my favourite bird-art books of all time. As someone who struggles when drawing stick-men, I found the accompanying articles of how the various paintings are constructed to be a fascinating window into a previously closed world.

Not that the Swedish superstar painter is giving away all his secrets; he still sees further into the soul of a bird than most other artists. If you only know Jonsson's work from his best-selling fieldguide, then treat yourself and start exploring the bigger picture.

Rare Birds Where and When: Volume One (Russell Slack, £33.9 inc P&P from BirdGuides www.birdguides.com, 483pp. Hbk. ISBN 978-0-95628-230-9)

Covering Sandgrouse to New World Orioles, this book analyses the status and distribution of vagrants occurring in Britain and Ireland. Each of the 220-plus species covered details the bird's status, an historical review, a breakdown of where and when they turn up, plus a general discussion of the

records, including the rest of the Western Palearctic.

As well as the statistical analysis, there are also fascinating essays about the nature of vagrancy and the work of our two record committees – the BOURC and BBRC. The text is accompanied by observers' accounts of discovering a rare bird, line drawings of some of the species and plenty of histograms when there is sufficient data to illustrate a particular trend.

Say Goodbye to the Cuckoo (Michael McCarthy, John Murray. 244pp. Hbk. £16.99. ISBN 978-184854-063-7)

The day you get bored of watching Swallows or waiting for your first Willow Warbler to arrive back is the day you should take up train spotting. Migration has always fascinated us and Michael McCarthy writes a series of chapters about encounters with different species: he goes out with Mark Cocker looking for warblers in East Anglia for example, or visits Oxford, scene of David Lack's classic Swifts in a Tower.

Inexorably you get drawn in to the stories until you realise that things are not as they should be. Spotted Flycatchers are no longer at traditional sites. Cuckoos are no longer heard on local patches. This book is a total joy and should be required reading for all movers and shakers dealing with conservation. It will make you feel, by degree, fascinated, better informed, angry and, more than a little bit guilty.

Shorebirds of the Northern Hemisphere (Richard Chandler, Helm. 448pp. Pbk. £29.99. ISBN 978-1-40810-790-4)

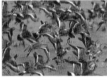

Photo-guides used to be awful; there was usually just one picture of a male in breeding finery and that was it. No flight shots, no juvenile plumages, nothing. Dull-looking birds didn't feature at all.

How things have changed. Here we have 850 colour photos covering 134 species. There are no less than 20 photographs of Dunlin, illustrating the different races and assorted plumages. A quick check in the best fieldguide currently available – *Collins Bird Guide* (Svensson et al, Collins) reveals only seven illustrations.

All the photos are well annotated and there is a full discussion of each species in the text. Whether you have a full-on loving relation with waders, or are struggling to cope with ID when the species you've studied changes into another plumage, this is a book that is well worth investigating further.

Skye Birds (Bob McMillan, skye-birds.com 176pp. Pbk. £11.95. ISBN 978-0-95502-530-3)

Skye has always been the poor relation when it comes to birding information for the islands off the Scottish west coast. Mull gets all the glory, yet the range of species is more or less identical to that of Skye. Star birds

on both islands are the eagles and with Skye now boasting 11 pairs of White-tailed Eagles and 29 pairs of Golden Eagles, you shouldn't be struggling for sightings.

This new edition details the status of all the birds recorded on the island. In addition, there are 12 pages detailing the best places to watch and sections on conservation, the geography of the island and a history of birding there. Eight plates of colour photos merely set off what is an essential purchase for visitors.

While Flocks Last (Charlie Elder, Bantam Press, 330pp. Hbk. £14.99. ISBN 978-0-59306-104-6)

This is part humorous travel book and part serious conservation story. The author decides to track down the 40 most endangered species on the British list, all in the space of a year. The so-called Red-list includes species such as Balearic Shearwaters, Water Rails and Red-necked Phalaropes. Some species such as House Sparrows aren't necessarily rare, but have declined dramatically and finding one in Central London proves far more difficult than anyone would have believed 25 years ago. This is a pleasant bedtime read with just enough meat to make you think and ensure that your dreams aren't as sweet as you might have hoped.

BIRDING TECHNOLOGY FOR THE 21ST CENTURY

For some people, developments in optics, digital and satellite technologies have revolutionised they way they go birdwatching, but as Gordon Hamlett explains, not all birders have rushed to embrace this brave new world.

IT USED to be so simple in the days when a pair of binoculars and a notebook equipped you fully for a day in the field. Today, there are any number of technological innovations, for use at home and in the field, to help you find, identify and record birds.

In terms of discovering news of rare birds, the advent of Birdline (a premium-rate telephone line with regularly updated recorded messages), in the late 1980s changed things radically so that thousands of birders now had access and could also pass on details of their own finds.

Today, the pager is the preferred method of information dissemination, with the keenest birders getting instant messages as soon as news of a scarce bird breaks. The sight of a hide full of birders simultaneously reaching for their pockets as the latest message arrives is one of the enduring images of modern birding.

Old habits die hard though. Every autumn, you can still see assorted birders waiting for news at Porthgwarra in Cornwall, scared to explore the valleys where pager reception is poor: imagine the horror of being stuck in Cot Valley when a major rarity turns up in nearby Nanquidno!

Optics innovations

Though the performance of binoculars and telescopes has improved immeasurably over the past few ways, it has happened in a gradual way rather than by massive leaps forward. New lens coatings have provided brighter images, close-focus is now de rigeur for top models and various alloys for body casings are deployed to reduce weight.

The real revolution has come in digital photography, which has enabled keen amateur snappers to achieve very acceptable results. You only have to look at the various bird magazines as recently as the 1990s to see blurred, grainy images of target species. Though autofocus lenses were a boon, especially when it came to taking flight shots, the top quality SLR cameras, and, especially, long lenses, were expensive and then photographers had to fork out for developing and printing costs.

Now, anyone can stick a small digital camera to the eye-piece of their telescope to produce a half-decent image, either directly, or with a judicious bit of tweaking on the computer when they get home. The use of the computer as a digital darkroom allows many a duff image to be salvaged by changing the exposure, sharpening up the image and removing distracting foliage from the final image etc.

Digiscoping brought photography to the birdwatching masses, not least because you could take hundreds of shots without incurring the cost of getting your film developed. This dramatically increased your odds of taking an acceptable image. However, not everyone found

BIRDING TECHNOLOGY FOR THE 21ST CENTURY

it easy to achieve the quality results they wanted and there has been an upsurge of interest in the more flexible digital single lens reflex cameras. Visit a bird reserve or twitch today and you are just as likely to see a long Nikon camera lens as you are to see a Nikon scope.

If there is to be one Holy Grail that revolutionises birding beyond measure, then I suspect that it will come in the field of optics. The limiting factor at the moment is the weight of the glass in your bins or scope. Yes, you can build bigger and brighter models but you wouldn't be able to carry them. Now imagine an optically pure plastic with the same light transmitting properties of glass but only a third of the weight. Well, we can all dream…

Computers and the internet

As computer technology developed, so did computerised learning aids. Companies such as BirdGuides produced a series of CD-ROMs and then DVD-ROMs. No longer were you restricted to learning your bird identification from the printed page. Now you could watch videos of your chosen species and listen to its songs and calls as well as reading all about it.

At the time of writing, two superb products show how far the technology has developed. *Birds of the Western Palearctic interactive (BWPi)* has all the content of the original nine volumes together with 20,000 multimedia clips.

Similarly, *British Birds interactive* puts 100 years of the definitive journal at your fingertips. The computer's search facility really adds value for the user by allowing you to find pieces of interest in a way that just wouldn't be feasible if you were doing it by hand.

Other computer programs that made an impact included the likes of Wildlife Recorder, a massive database which allowed birders to keep records of, and analyse their sightings in ways that would have been impossible manually.

As new versions of these programs appeared to match the increased processing power of home computers, the Internet came along to provide alternatives. Access to knowledge became global and instantaneous and you could opt for a casual bit of research rather than buying into the whole pre-packaged set of reference material.

If you want to read trip reports from birders visiting Bolivia (31 currently available) or find pictures of an Asian Paradise Flycatcher (5,840 listed), then you are only a few clicks of the mouse away. Identification problems can be solved in hours rather than months (if at all), simply by posting an image on a discussion group or e-mailing a picture to leading experts.

One unforeseen benefit of the net was the flow of information became two-way. More enlightened bird clubs started accepting bird records on an ad hoc basis, resulting in a massive increase in data to plug holes in our knowledge. It is noticeable that the British Trust for Ornithology allows you to input roving records to supplement all its survey work and clubs who haven't gone down this line yet are strongly encouraged to do so.

Social networking also came to prominence, with like-minded birders able to chat to each other, discuss sightings and swap hints and tips about the best binoculars, where to go on holiday or how to lobby your MP about the latest environmental outrage.

BIRDING TECHNOLOGY FOR THE 21ST CENTURY

The future

So where do we go from here? I predict there will be two main areas of development. Having access to all this information is one thing but it is of limited use if you are tied to a desk at home. Even though products such as the superb *Collins Bird Guide* are available for use on Personal Digital Assistants (PDAs – small handheld computers), the technology never really went mainstream.

That can't be said of two other devices though. Mobile phones and iPods are ubiquitous. Sound recordings and even video clips can be played on the latter and again, BirdGuides are leading the way with ten hours of footage, sounds and commentary for identifying British birds.

New mobile phone models appear constantly. Most now feature cameras, allowing you to take pictures through your telescope and e-mail them to other people. Internet access on the move is becoming increasingly available. While an MP3 facility (a digital format for sound files) is intended to let you listen to the latest pop songs, there is no reason why you can't download a selection of bird songs instead.

Bird songs and bird calls are destined to be the other major growth area. With the publication of the seminal book *The Sound Approach to Birding* (Constantine, The Sound Approach 2006), there is a growing realisation of just how much sound can contribute to bird identification. Indeed, you will only get a Scottish Crossbill past the records committees if you have a recording to back up your sightings.

As well as the ability to play recordings in the field (see above), new electronic products such as Remembird clip underneath your binoculars and allow you to take notes, play calls and make recordings of the birds you see and hear.

Certainly being able to play calls and songs in the field is useful; I know many birders who take advantage of this facility already. The trouble is the technology is often used solely to tape-lure difficult-to-see species such as crakes or Quail. And while one birder playing a quick burst of Lesser Spotted Woodpecker song in the woods to bring the bird closer might not cause any disturbance, hundreds of birders doing so in the early part of the year undoubtedly will. So we need to revisit the ethics of tape-luring.

Taking recordings of unidentified calls and analysing them back at home will undoubtedly produce some spectacular results, and increase the number of acceptable records of fly-over pipits and other difficult species, but will the average birder be prepared to go to those lengths?

Ultimately, all the products described involve companies adapting existing technology for a niche market. But where is the new technology going to come from? For that, you are likely to have to rely largely on the US military. As they develop their existing hardware, so the older versions are released to the public.

The most obvious example is satellite navigation. The army gets a bigger, better, more accurate version and we get the old one. Satellite tracking of migrant birds has now become widely adopted and added considerably to our knowledge base.

BIRDING TECHNOLOGY FOR THE 21ST CENTURY

I suspect that new site guides might well include instructions for your satnav to find each bird reserve; details for RSPB reserves can already be downloaded from their website. Similarly, various websites make use of Google Earth so that you can print out a walk route in advance.

And making life easier is what it's all about really. Technology can help you learn bird song, research a foreign trip, enhance your photos and pinpoint the latest rarity. But never forget, you can still have a damn good day out with just a pair of binoculars and a notebook…

And now the reality…

I have spent the last 12 months paying as much attention to the birders as the birds when out in the field, carrying out an informal survey of what equipment they were using.

Surprisingly for some gadgets, the answer was a surprising big fat zero. I didn't see anybody using mobiles for birding-specific purposes, other than phoning/texting friends and Birdlines.

Pagers still held sway as the preferred medium for receiving information. I found no-one using PDAs or Remembird to keep notes but then again, less than 5% of birders seemed to be keeping notes in a book either.

There have been some fancy new binoculars and scopes arriving on the scene, featuring water-repelling lenses, wide-angle zooms and flat-field eyepieces, but high prices and supply problems have restricted numbers in use.

So, where's the spare money going? New cameras and lenses, that's where. The photography bug has assumed pandemic proportions. Huge telephoto lenses are everywhere. The only problem that needs to be solved now is how do you carry scope, bins, camera, tripod, packed lunch and assorted accoutrements in the first place, and secondly, how do you unpack and assemble everything without upsetting everyone else in the hide?

Useful contacts

Pagers and phone information
Rare Bird Alert www.rarebirdalert.co.uk
Birdnet Optics www.birdnet.co.uk/pagers
Birdline 09068 700 222 (calls cost 60p/minute)

Computer programs
BirdGuides www.birdguides.com
Wildlife Computing www.wildlife.co.uk

Sound recording
Remembird www.remembird.com

Organisations
Royal Society for the Protection of Birds www.rspb.org.uk
British Trust for Ornithology www.bto.org

Other websites
Bird Forum www.birdforum.net
Google Earth http://earth.google.co.uk/

THE TOP 50 MOST USEFUL WEBSITES FOR BIRDWATCHERS

Gordon Hamlett worries that the initial enthusiasm for contributing information to the world-wide web is already waning, but he's still found plenty of bird-related sites you will find useful.

ARE BIRDWATCHERS losing their love of the Internet? There is still a gargantuan amount of information out there but (and it is a big but), what has changed over the last year or so is that fewer people seem to be contributing their individual little bits and pieces that go to make up the bigger picture.

These diminishing inputs are very noticeable on e-mail and discussion groups, where the number of contributors has reduced to a hard core. Whereas a couple of years ago, there would be notes from someone saying that they had just had a Sparrowhawk over their house, or that they had just seen their earliest ever Spotted Flycatcher of the year, these casual observations have diminished greatly.

It is the same on Bird Forum, the site which claims to be the world's biggest forum for birdwatchers. Many of our top quality birders no longer post their messages or sightings and pass on their knowledge on this site. Active threads, such as Norfolk Birding, once attracted dozens of regular contributors which meant the thread was vibrant, the discussions interesting. Now we are reduced to the same half dozen and the posts are more of the nature 'I went to A and B and saw X, Y and Z'. Not that there is anything wrong with that but the vibrancy of 18 months ago has vanished.

Numbers of trip reports are down and fewer pictures are getting uploaded, an interesting paradox given that sales of cameras continue to boom. Small, interesting websites are falling by the wayside, their owners presumably having neither the time, inclination or money to keep them going. People are turning to writing blogs instead but even here, most entries are sporadic at best.

So what are the reasons for this decline? Is it all just part of an increasingly selfish society? Are we just getting lazier? Perhaps people are being deterred from going public after having bad experiences such as being shot down in flames for a misidentification or an inadvertently inappropriate posting.

There are other ways of shooting yourself in the foot too. One county birding society used to have an e-mail system in place in which everyone posted their sightings. Very good it was too, especially for people on the move who could pick up their e-mails as they went.

The club decided unilaterally to scrap the e-mail group in favour of a forum on their website. Regardless of the rights and wrongs of the new system, the way it was handled split the county birders asunder. A rival e-mail system was put in place, with opposing factions arguing this way and that and ending up not talking to each other. The result, not surprisingly, was that a lot of birders wanted nothing to do with either the new or old and gave up in disgust. The consequence is fewer birds being reported. Come on guys. We're all supposed to be on the same side here.

As the American satirist Tom Lehrer wrote, 'Life is like a sewer. What you get out of it depends on what you put into it.' So if you only do one thing this year, post details of your sightings, submit a trip report, upload a photograph, ask a question or start a discussion. Let's try to get everything moving again.

Despite these downbeat comments, we must not forget that there are still many great websites catering for the diverse needs of birdwatchers. Here are my recommended sites (listed alphabetically within individual topics), that I hope you will check out for yourself in 2010.

INDEX OF RECOMMENDED BIRDING WEBSITES

Bird populations	Passerines	Swifts
Books	Raptors	Taxonomy
Gamebirds	Record-keeping	Trip reports
Maps	Seabirds	Waders
Miscellaneous	Sights and sounds	Weather
Owls	Social networking and blogs	Wildfowl

BIRD POPULATIONS

www.bto.org/birdtrends2008/index.htm
www.stateofthebirds.org
It is important to monitor how well individual species are doing; which ones are declining, which ones are holding their own etc. These two sites give the latest reports on the state of their respective nation's birds. The first site is for Britain, the second for the USA.

www.rbbp.org.uk
The Rare Bird Breeding Panel monitors those species which usually breed in numbers small enough not to warrant a place in the reports above. Here, as well as reporting confidentially any of your own records, you can download full reports going back to 1973. The panel also monitors non-native species and escapes and there are downloadable reports on these too.

BOOKS

www.archive.org/stream/birdlifeoflondon00 dixorich/birdlifeoflondon00dixorich_djvu.txt
One of the things that we will see a lot more of in coming years is the digitising of books. The text of — usually out-of-copyright — titles is scanned in and becomes available either for reading online or for downloading onto one of the new electronic book readers such as Kindle. This link offers the text of the 1909 title *The Bird-life of London*.

www.nhbs.com/birds_cat_13.html
If you want to know what bird books are going to be released in the near future, and all bird-book lovers do, then try this site. Though the NHBS website is a commercial bookshop, one of the options you have is to sort the titles by publication date. This gives you the latest best date for when a new title is due to appear.

GAME BIRDS

www.blackgrouse.info
Surely our most charismatic game bird, the Black Grouse, gets the full works from this site, with information for birders and shooters, management strategies, downloadable newsletters etc. One section that needs updating is on Where to Watch Blackcock as none are listed, yet there are

several well publicised organised lek watches in e.g. the Highlands.

www.greatbustard.com
The Great Bustard reintroduction scheme has just seen the first chicks born in Britain for 177 years. This site follows the story of the reintroduction from Russia as well as pages on identification and conservation.

http://www.youtube.com/watch?v=nb1H_-S4Xjk
This is a sort of 'what happens next' video so I'm not going to give too much away. The photographer was filming two Capercaillies when...Place your bets and see if you guessed correctly.

MAPS

http://birdingmaps.webs.com/
This is still very much a work in progress but the idea is an interesting one. Anyone who writes a blog (online diary) about their local patch can put a pin onto a map showing the location of their patch. Anyone logging on to the site can then look at the map and find out if anyone is writing about the areas that interest them.

www.ordnancesurvey.co.uk/oswebsite/getamap
If you want a map, there is no better option than Ordnance Survey. This site allows you to get a 1:25,000 scale map of the area you are interested in and download the map for use in your own applications or website.
http://wtp2.appspot.com/wheresthepath.htm
'Where's the Path' offers a side-by-side display of an Ordnance Survey map and an overhead satellite image. Markers are correlated so that if you point to somewhere on the OS map, you can immediately see the same place on the satellite picture. You can plot a route and print it out — ideal for all those birding walks in the bird magazines. One hint is to use this site early in the day. The owners are limited to a set number of OS uses per day and if they exceed that, you get a 1940s map instead of the current one.

MISCELLANEOUS

www.birdingtop500.com
So which are the most popular birding websites? This site lists, despite its name, the top 1,000, sorted according to the number of visitors they receive. Of course, popular doesn't always mean the best. For those, you will just have to keep reading this article every year...

OWLS

www.owlpages.com
Owls have always been one of the most popular groups of birds and here you can find a comprehensive selection of photos and sound clips, together with a series of articles covering everything from physiology to mythology.

PASSERINES

www.blackredstarts.org.uk
There was a boom in the British population of Black Redstarts in the aftermath of the Second World War as birds found bombsites to be ideal habitat. This site looks at the fortunes of this charismatic bird since then, especially in London and Birmingham.

http://pinemuncher.blogspot.com/
The more we know about the status of crossbills in Scotland, the more confused the picture seems to become. Are they Parrot or Scottish or Common Crossbills? Why do they have such a bewildering range of calls, such that you can only identify them by analysing recordings? This blog is written by a crossbill fanatic.

RAPTORS

http://derbyperegrines.blogspot.com/
Study of the Peregrines on Derby Cathedral has produced plenty of interesting, and previously unknown, insights into the birds' behaviour. In particular, an examination of the birds' prey has revealed that they hunt night-flying migrants, using the city lights to see. Follow their progress on this blog.

ANNUAL WEBSITE SURVEY

www.goldeneagle.ie
The attempt to re-introduce various raptors into Ireland has not been an easy one with several birds being either poisoned or shot. This excellent site from the Golden Eagle Trust has videos, satellite tracking, sightings maps and articles about Golden and White-tailed Eagles plus Red Kites.

www.hawkandowl.org
The Hawk and Owl Trust is celebrating their 40th anniversary (see the feature elsewhere in this edition). As well as their involvement with conservation, the Trust also runs three reserves in Norfolk, Somerset and Yorkshire. There are details on all the wildlife seen on these reserve as well as information pages on all the British species of raptors.

http://raptorpolitics.org.uk
Raptors generate more emotions — both pro and anti — than just about all the rest of the world's birds put together. This site looks at raptor persecution — especially in the Lancashire area — those responsible for the persecution and those policing it. Be prepared for a full and frank range of opinions.

www.redkites.net
Though centred on the Chilterns release scheme, this site will appeal to Red Kite lovers everywhere, with a fine selection of photos, video clips of a nest site and a wealth of useful information.

www.roydennis.org
The Highland Foundation for Wildlife is involved with the satellite tracking of large raptors. Whether it is long-distance migrants such as Homey Buzzards and Ospreys, or following the meanderings of young Golden and White-tailed Eagles, this is totally fascinating. There are sections too on proposed plans for re-introducing assorted mammals such as beaver (already underway), wolf and lynx into Scotland.

www.scottishraptorgroups.org
This group is concerned with the monitoring of 14 species of raptor, four species of owl and Ravens across the whole of Scotland. There is plenty of additional information for those interested in birds of prey, including a fine set of links for further exploration.

RECORD KEEPING

www.bubo.org
Do you keep a list of the birds you have seen? Do you keep many separate lists such as life, year, British, Western Palearctic? Are you competitive? If you answered 'yes' to any of these questions, then take a look at this site which allows you to set up and maintain your lists online and compare them with other birders. There are over 3,600 lists to choose from so you should find something to fill in the hours when it is too dark to bird outside.

http://printablebirdchecklists.homestead.com/
If you want a checklist of the birds you are likely to see when you go on holiday, then this site allows you to print out a list for any country in the world. The lists are in the form of an Excel worksheet and can be arranged alphabetically or systematically to suit. Lists are constantly updated as new species are added to a country's avifauna.

www.brandonbirding.co.uk/download.asp
www.rb59.com/bwpro
If you are looking for a database rather than a mere checklist, then both these sites offer free downloadable programs. Databases are a very personal thing, so try them out before spending a lot of time entering data only to find that they don't do what you want.

http://www.sparroworks.ca/bigby.html
You might not have come across BIGBYs before. It stands for Big Green Big Year and is a carbon-neutral form of year listing. There are currently 400 people across the world competing and you can share your experiences on the site's forum.

www.wildlife.co.uk
If you want a professional database, then this is one of the most popular. There are versions available for pocket PCs as well as desktops and you can choose from British, Western Palearctic plus Nearctic, and full world databases according to your needs. The packages also contain databases for moths, mammals, dragonflies and butterflies. A series of online tutorials show the package in action before you decide to buy.

SEABIRDS

www.seabirding.co.uk
For everyone who dreams of sailing the oceans, to seek out unusual species, there are enough trip reports here to fuel a thousand daydreams. Add in a hefty selection of identification articles, plenty of first class photos and even several recipes for 'chum' and you have an excellent seawatching site.

www.seawatch-sw.org
Operating from Gwennap Head in Cornwall, this is an ongoing project recording all sightings of Balearic Shearwaters round our coast. There are sections on identification, reports to be downloaded and a good selection of links. You can also submit your own sightings.

SIGHTS AND SOUNDS

www.arkive.org
Fronted by Sir David Attenborough, ARKive is a collection of videos, photos and fact files. Presentation is very slick and the standard extremely high, with many clips taken from top wildlife documentaries. The aim is to cover all 16,000 species currently threatened with extinction, covering mammals, fish, plants, fungi, invertebrates etc, as well as birds.

http://ibc.lynxeds.com
Want to see a video clip of a particular species? There's a good chance that you will find it here. The Internet Bird Collection currently boasts over 34,000 videos of some 6,000 species — about 60% of the world's total. There are also over 8,000 photos and 900 sound clips.

www.xeno-canto.org
This is a site where anyone can upload recordings of bird songs. Consequently there is a wealth of information, though at the moment, there is a heavy skew towards North and South America. Nevertheless, at the time of writing, there were 2,500 recordings of 350 species in Europe. A discussion forum allows you to ask/answer questions about all things vocal.

SOCIAL NETWORKING AND BLOGS

http://avibase.bsc-eoc.org/links/links.jsp?page=g_4
www.fatbirder.com/links/signpost_and_discussion/mailing_lists.html
Here are two selections of groups. Not as comprehensive as the Yahoo page (see below), but they do contain a lot of non-Yahoo groups as well and are a lot easier to use for a quick scan.

www.birdforum.net
This is easily the most popular site of its type, with over 82,000 members worldwide discussing anything and everything to do with birds, from taxonomy to digital photography, poetry to identification problems. Having said that, in common with many mailing lists, the number of people actively contributing to the threads seems to be falling.

www.birdingpal.org
If you are travelling to somewhere new and are looking for a bit of help in exploring the area, this site aims to put you in touch with locals who are prepared to show you round. The quid pro quo is that you in turn offer your services and help out visitors to your local patch should the need arise.

www.fatbirder.com/links/signpost_and_discussion/blogs.html
Reading other birders' online diaries is a very personal thing. Even when you find some you like and follow, they are ephemeral by nature and disappear at the drop of a hat. Rather than list a few of my favourites, here is Fatbirder's collection of several hundred to try. One advantage of blogs is that once you find some that you like, they usually have more links to other blogs that appeal to them and so are likely to appeal to you too.

http://uk.dir.groups.yahoo.com/dir/1600082988
Yahoo Groups currently list more than 3,600 bird-related groups, so you should be able to find some like-minded people whatever your interests. You can read previous messages and see how active a particular group is before signing up for it.

31

ANNUAL WEBSITE SURVEY

SWIFTS

www.londons-swifts.org.uk
Aimed at protecting old nest sites in the capital and creating new ones, there is plenty of general information about 'devil birds' and how to attract them, as well as a comprehensive set of links to related sites.

www.oum.ox.ac.uk/swifts.htm
This is a webcam on a Swift's nest (May-August). These Swifts at the Oxford University Museum of Natural History have been studied since 1947 and there are summaries of data for recent years as well as a leaflet about Swifts in general.

TAXONOMY

http://avibase.bsc-eoc.org/avibase.jsp
Pick a bird, any bird from the 10,000+ in the database. For each species, you get the bird's name in any number of languages and taxonomic variations. A series of links mean that you are then only a click away from searching all the main databases for maps, text, pictures, sounds etc. Avibase is an unbelievable resource.

www.worldbirdnames.org
It's attempting the impossible, trying to come up with a standardised list of English names but nevertheless, here are more than 10,300 species listed in systematic order. There are various downloads available if you want the information on your machine rather just online. The site is regularly updated with new lumps and splits.

TRIP REPORTS

www.travellingbirder.com/tripreports
This is by far the best place on the Net to find out where other birders have been and what they have seen. There are currently an amazing 6,400 trip reports listed. So, if you want to visit Nicaragua in November or Finland in February, this is the place to look first.

WADERS

www.waderstudygroup.org
The International Wader Study Group runs assorted shorebird projects and you can find details of colour-ringed birds that often crop up around our shores. Though the organisation is academic in nature, there are links to a site dealing with the satellite-tracking of Black-tailed Godwits and a wader discussion group as well as plenty of other useful resources.

WEATHER

http://www.xcweather.co.uk/
Wind speed and direction is all important for anyone planning to go seawatching and this is my favourite weather site, constantly updated and showing wind speed and direction over the whole country. You can also get five-day summaries for any number of locations — a great help for planning your weekend trips or seeing when there is going to be a fall of migrants along the east coast.

WILDFOWL

www.goose.org
This site from the International Goose Research Group acts as an umbrella organisation for all the various goose-related research projects around the world. There are some details of the various species but you have to work hard for your information; this site is as dry as a dehydrated duck in the desert.

www.oceanwanderers.com/CAGO. Subspecies.html
Identification of the various sub-species of Canada Geese has become increasingly important after recent taxonomic split into Canada Goose and Cackling Goose. Vagrant birds do turn up in the UK. This site looks at the various sub-species and has links to other identification sites.

DIARY 2010

This unusual action shot of a Yellow-legged Gull by Marek Walford caught the eye of judges in the annual Berkshire Ornithological Society photo competition.

EVENTS DIARY 2010

JANUARY

18 to Feb 1: RSPB Big Schools Birdwatch
Continuing the initiative to get children interested in wild birds – see RSPB website for local area events.

23: Sussex Ornithological Society annual conference
Clair Hall, Perrymount Road, Haywards Heath, West Sussex.

29-31: BTO Ringing Courses for Beginners
Kilbroney Centre, Rostrevor, Co Down.
Contact: ellen.walford@bto.org

30-31: RSPB Big Garden Birdwatch
Nationwide survey of garden birds.
Contact: RSPB on 01767 680 551.

FEBRUARY

2: World Wetlands Day
Various events at local level to raise awareness of wetland habitats and Ramsar sites in particular. www.wwd@ramsar.org

6-7: Building Bird Monitoring in Scotland national meeting
Stirling University, Stirling, Falkirk
Contact: ellen.walford@bto.org

19-21: BTO Bird Survey Techniques – residential course
Slapton Ley. South Devon.
Contact: ellen.walford@bto.org

MARCH

7: Berks & Oxon BTO members and bird club conference
Civic Centre, Britwell Rd, Didcot, Oxfordshire
Contact: ellen.walford@bto.org

17-20: MIGRES Foundation second bird migration and global change conference
Hotel Reina Christina, Algeciras, Spain.
Registrations on-line at:
http://www.fundacionmigres.org/congresos/globalchange/Presentation.html

18-25: Fourth Eilat migration festival
Bird tours, presentations and other bird-related events centred on Agamim Hotel in Eilat, southern Israel. www.eilatbirdsfestival.com

20: BTO/SOC Scottish birdwatchers conference
Culloden Academy, Inverness.
Contact: ellen.walford@bto.org

APRIL

6-8: BOU Annual Conference: Climate Change and Birds
University of Leicester. www.bou.org.uk

10: African Bird Club AGM
BTO, The Nunnery, Thetford Norfolk.
 Contact: contact@africanbirdclub.org

16-18: RSPB members weekend
York University.

20-22: BTO Bird Identification – residential course
Dale Fort, Pembrokeshire, South Wales.
Contact: ellen.walford@bto.org

30- May 2: BTO Bird Survey Techniques – residential course
Juniper Hall, Surrey
Contact: ellen.walford@bto.org

MAY

5-7: BTO Bird Identification – residential course
Malham Tarn, North Yorkshire.
Contact: ellen.walford@bto.org

7-9: BTO Bird Survey Techniques – residential course
Rhyd-y-Creuau, North Wales
Contact: ellen.walford@bto.org

15-16: Birdwatcher's Spring Fair and Digital Photofair
Middleton Hall (near Drayton Manor Park), Tamworth, Staffs.
Contact: Organiser Alan Richards on 0152 785 2357.

EVENTS DIARY 2010

TBA: Scottish Ornithological Club Spring Book Sale
Waterston House, Aberlady, East Lothian.
Contact: mail@the-soc.org

JUNE
5-13: Make Your Nature Count
New RSPB scheme to survey wildlife in summer.
Contact: RSPB on 01767 680 551.

JULY
9-11: BTO Ringing course for beginners
Flatford Mill, Suffolk.
Contact: ellen.walford@bto.org

10: AGM of OSME (Ornithological Society of the Middle East, the Caucasus and Central Asia)
BTO headquarters, the Nunnery, Thetford, Norfolk. Doors open 10am.
Contact: Ian Harrison on secretary@osme.org

16 to August 1: NEWA (National Exhibition of Wildlife Art)
Gordale Nursey, Burton, the Wirral. Preview evening July 15.
Contact: newa@mtuffrey.freeserve.co.uk or visit: www.newa-uk.com

AUGUST
6-8: BTO Ringing course for beginners
Slapton Fierld Studies Centre, Devon.
Contact: ellen.walford@bto.org

20-22: British Birdwatching Fair
Egleton Nature Reserve, Rutland Water, Rutland.
Contact: Call 01572 771 079 or e-mail: info@birdfair.org.uk

22-28: 25ᵗʰ International Ornithological Congress
Campos do Jordao, Sao Paulo, Brazil. http://www.acquaviva.com.br/sisconev/index.asp?Codigo=26

SEPTEMBER
7-10: 1ˢᵗ World Seabird Conference
Hosted by Pacific Seabird Group in the Victoria Conference Centre, British Columbia. www.pacificseabirdgroup.org

22-26: Annual meeting of Raptor Research Foundation
Fort Collins, Colorado. http://raptorresearchfoundation.org/conferences.htm

TBA: Scottish Ornithological Club annual weekend conference.
Contact club for date and venue details at mail@the-soc.org

OCTOBER
2: RSPB AGM & members day
Queen Elizabeth II conference centre, Westminster, London.

27-29: BTO Bird Survey Techniques - residential course
Flatford Mill, Suffolk.
Contact: ellen.walford@bto.org

30: Feed The Birds Day
A programme of events across the UK – check local press and RSPB website for details in your area.

NOVEMBER
20-21: North-West Birdfair
WWT Martin Mere, Burscough, Lancs.
Contact: Victoria Fellowes (marketing manager) on 01704 891 240 or victoria.fellowes@wwt.org.uk

DECEMBER
3-5: BTO Annual Conference
The Hayes Conference Centre, Swanwick, Derbyshire.
Contact: ellen.walford@bto.org

DIARY – JANUARY 2010

1	Fri	New Year's Day
2	Sat	
3	Sun	
4	Mon	Holiday (Scotland)
5	Tue	
6	Wed	
7	Thu	
8	Fri	
9	Sat	
10	Sun	
11	Mon	
12	Tue	
13	Wed	
14	Thu	
15	Fri	
16	Sat	
17	Sun	
18	Mon	
19	Tue	
20	Wed	
21	Thu	
22	Fri	
23	Sat	
24	Sun	
25	Mon	
26	Tue	
27	Wed	
28	Thu	
29	Fri	
30	Sat	
31	Sun	

DIARY – FEBRUARY 2010

1	Mon	
2	Tue	
3	Wed	
4	Thu	
5	Fri	
6	Sat	
7	Sun	
8	Mon	
9	Tue	
10	Wed	
11	Thu	
12	Fri	
13	Sat	
14	Sun	
15	Mon	
16	Tue	
17	Wed	
18	Thu	
19	Fri	
20	Sat	
21	Sun	
22	Mon	
23	Tue	
24	Wed	
25	Thu	
26	Fri	
27	Sat	
28	Sun	

DIARY 2010

1	Mon	
2	Tue	
3	Wed	
4	Thu	
5	Fri	
6	Sat	
7	Sun	
8	Mon	
9	Tue	
10	Wed	
11	Thu	
12	Fri	
13	Sat	
14	Sun	Mothering Sunday
15	Mon	
16	Tue	
17	Wed	St Patrick's Day (Bank Holiday N.Ireland)
18	Thu	
19	Fri	
20	Sat	
21	Sun	
22	Mon	
23	Tue	
24	Wed	
25	Thu	
26	Fri	
27	Sat	
28	Sun	British Summertime begins
29	Mon	
30	Tue	
31	Wed	

1	Thu	
2	Fri	Good Friday
3	Sat	
4	Sun	Easter Day
5	Mon	Easter Monday
6	Tue	
7	Wed	
8	Thu	
9	Fri	
10	Sat	
11	Sun	
12	Mon	
13	Tue	
14	Wed	
15	Thu	
16	Fri	
17	Sat	
18	Sun	
19	Mon	
20	Tue	
21	Wed	
22	Thu	
23	Fri	
24	Sat	
25	Sun	
26	Mon	
27	Tue	
28	Wed	
29	Thu	
30	Fri	

DIARY 2010

DIARY – MAY 2010

1	Sat	
2	Sun	
3	Mon	May Day
4	Tue	
5	Wed	
6	Thu	
7	Fri	
8	Sat	
9	Sun	
10	Mon	
11	Tue	
12	Wed	
13	Thu	
14	Fri	
15	Sat	
16	Sun	
17	Mon	
18	Tue	
19	Wed	
20	Thu	
21	Fri	
22	Sat	
23	Sun	
24	Mon	
25	Tue	
26	Wed	
27	Thu	
28	Fri	
29	Sat	
30	Sun	
31	Mon	Spring Bank Holiday

DIARY 2010

DIARY – JUNE 2010

1	Tue	
2	Wed	
3	Thu	
4	Fri	
5	Sat	
6	Sun	
7	Mon	
8	Tue	
9	Wed	
10	Thu	
11	Fri	
12	Sat	
13	Sun	
14	Mon	
15	Tue	
16	Wed	
17	Thu	
18	Fri	
19	Sat	
20	Sun	
21	Mon	
22	Tue	
23	Wed	
24	Thu	
25	Fri	
26	Sat	
27	Sun	
28	Mon	
29	Tue	
30	Wed	

DIARY – JULY 2010

1	Thu	
2	Fri	
3	Sat	
4	Sun	
5	Mon	
6	Tue	
7	Wed	
8	Thu	
9	Fri	
10	Sat	
11	Sun	
12	Mon	Bank Holiday N.Ireland
13	Tue	
14	Wed	
15	Thu	
16	Fri	
17	Sat	
18	Sun	
19	Mon	
20	Tue	
21	Wed	
22	Thu	
23	Fri	
24	Sat	
25	Sun	
26	Mon	
27	Tue	
28	Wed	
29	Thu	
30	Fri	
31	Sat	

DIARY – AUGUST 2010

1	Sun	
2	Mon	Bank Holiday Scotland
3	Tue	
4	Wed	
5	Thu	
6	Fri	
7	Sat	
8	Sun	
9	Mon	
10	Tue	
11	Wed	
12	Thu	
13	Fri	
14	Sat	
15	Sun	
16	Mon	
17	Tue	
18	Wed	
19	Thu	
20	Fri	
21	Sat	
22	Sun	
23	Mon	
24	Tue	
25	Wed	
26	Thu	
27	Fri	
28	Sat	
29	Sun	
30	Mon	Summer Bank Holiday
31	Tue	

DIARY – SEPTEMBER 2010

1	Wed	
2	Thu	
3	Fri	
4	Sat	
5	Sun	
6	Mon	
7	Tue	
8	Wed	
9	Thu	
10	Fri	
11	Sat	
12	Sun	
13	Mon	
14	Tue	
15	Wed	
16	Thu	
17	Fri	
18	Sat	
19	Sun	
20	Mon	
21	Tue	
22	Wed	
23	Thu	
24	Fri	
25	Sat	
26	Sun	
27	Mon	
28	Tue	
29	Wed	
30	Thu	

DIARY – OCTOBER 2010

1	Fri	
2	Sat	
3	Sun	
4	Mon	
5	Tue	
6	Wed	
7	Thu	
8	Fri	
9	Sat	
10	Sun	
11	Mon	
12	Tue	
13	Wed	
14	Thu	
15	Fri	
16	Sat	
17	Sun	
18	Mon	
19	Tue	
20	Wed	
21	Thu	
22	Fri	
23	Sat	
24	Sun	
25	Mon	
26	Tue	
27	Wed	
28	Thu	
29	Fri	
30	Sat	
31	Sun	British Summertime ends

DIARY – NOVEMBER 2010

1	Mon	
2	Tue	
3	Wed	
4	Thu	
5	Fri	
6	Sat	
7	Sun	
8	Mon	
9	Tue	
10	Wed	
11	Thu	
12	Fri	
13	Sat	
14	Sun	Remembrance Sunday
15	Mon	
16	Tue	
17	Wed	
18	Thu	
19	Fri	
20	Sat	
21	Sun	
22	Mon	
23	Tue	
24	Wed	
25	Thu	
26	Fri	
27	Sat	
28	Sun	
29	Mon	
30	Tue	

DIARY – DECEMBER 2010

1	Wed	
2	Thu	
3	Fri	
4	Sat	
5	Sun	
6	Mon	
7	Tue	
8	Wed	
9	Thu	
10	Fri	
11	Sat	
12	Sun	
13	Mon	
14	Tue	
15	Wed	
16	Thu	
17	Fri	
18	Sat	
19	Sun	
20	Mon	
21	Tue	
22	Wed	
23	Thu	
24	Fri	
25	Sat	Christmas Day
26	Sun	
27	Mon	Boxing Day
28	Tue	Bank holiday
29	Wed	
30	Thu	
31	Fri	

YEAR PLANNER 2011

January
February
March
April
May
June
July
August
September
October
November
December

LOG CHARTS

Peter Beesley

Corn Crake was fast disappearing as a breeding bird in mainland Britain, but a reintroduction scheme centred on the Nene Washes RSPB reserve in Cambridgeshire is starting to pay dividends.

A CHECKLIST OF BIRDS

Based on the British List formulated by the British Ornithologists' Union

NEWCOMERS to birdwatching are sometimes baffled when they examine their first fieldguide as it is not immediately clear why the birds are arranged the way they are. The simple answer is that the order is meant to reflect the evolution of the included species. If one were to draw an evolutionary tree of birds, those families that branch off earliest (i.e are the most ancient) should be listed first.

Previously the British Ornithologists' Union British List was based on Voous Order (BOU 1977), the work of an eminent Dutch taxonomist and many of the popular fieldguides for British and European birds follow this established order.

However, more than 26 phylogenetic studies, many using DNA analysis, have been published in recent years that togethe r form a large body of evidence showing that the order of birds in the British List did not properly reflect their evolution. A change in order was required to reflect these new findings, so that now swans, geese and ducks have replaced divers and grebes at the head of the list.

The British Ornithologists' Union's Records Committee (BOURC) is responsible for maintaining the British List and its recommended changes have been accepted by the British Ornithologists' Union, which has advised all book, magazine and bird report editors and publishers to begin using the new order as soon as possible and this is the fourth edition of *The Birdwatcher's Yearbook* to do so.

RECENT CHANGES TO THE LIST

Since the publication of the 2009 *Yearbook*, the BOURC has adjudicated on several species and made the following decisions:

Admitted to Category A
Pacific Diver *(Gavia pacifica)*. Juvenile found at Harrogate, N Yorks between Jan 12 and Feb 4, 2007. Until 2008 this was regarded as a sub-species of Black-throated Diver.

Yellow-nosed Albatross *(Thalassarche chlororhynchos)*. Immature bird found at Brean, Somerset, June 29-30, 2007).

Glaucous-winged Gull *(Larus glaucescens)*. Third-winter bird at Gloucester landfill site, Hempsted, Gloucestershire, December 15-16, 2006.

White Wagtail *(Motacilla alba leucopsis)*. Male seen at Seaham, County Durham, April 5-6, 2005. Colloquially known as Amur Wagtail, this taxon breeds in south-easternmost Russia, south through NE China, North and South Korea and SW Japan to Taiwan and eastern and southern China.

Asian Brown Flycatcher *(Muscicapa dauurica)* First-summer, Fair Isle, Shetland, 1-2 July 1992.

Hooded Merganser *(Lophodytes cucullatus linnaeus)*

One record: Immature or female, Oban Trumisgarry, North Uist, Outer Hebrides, from 23 October until November 1, 2000.

Wilson's Snipe *(Gallinago delicata)*. Juvenile on St Mary's Isles of Scilly, October 9, 1998. Formerly conspecific with Common Snipe.

Naumann's Thrush *(Turdus naumanni temminck)*. Split from Dusky Thrush.

Black-throated Thrush *(Turdus atrogularis jarocki)* and **Red-throated Thrush** *(Turdus ruficollis pallas)* were formerly considered as one species, Dark-throated Thrush.

Green Warbler *(Phylloscopus nitidus blyth)*. Formerly considered as conspecific with Greenish Warbler.

Removed from Category B
Madieran Storm-petrel *(Oceanodroma castro)*. The single record from Milford Haven in 1911 is no longer considered reliable due to missing evidence.

The British List now stands at 587 species (Category A = 568; Category B = 9; Category C = 10)

SPECIES, CATEGORIES, CODES – YOUR GUIDE TO GET THE BEST USE FROM THE CHECKLIST

Species list
The charts include all species from categories A, B and C on the British List, based on the latest BOU listing. Selected species included in categories D and E are listed separately at the end of the log chart.

Vagrants which are not on the British List, but which may have occurred in other parts of the British Isles, are not included. Readers who wish to record such species may use the extra rows provided on the last page. In this connection it should be noted that

separate lists exist for Northern Ireland (kept by the Northern Ireland Birdwatchers' Association) and the Isle of Man (kept by the Manx Ornithological Society), and that Irish records are assessed by the Irish Rare Birds Committee.

The commoner species in the log charts are indicated by the * symbol to help make record-keeping easier.

Taxonomic changes introduced in 2002 mean there is a new order of species (as outlined above). The species names are those most widely used in the current fieldguides and each is followed by its scientific name, printed in italics.

Species categories
The following categories are those assigned by the British Ornithologists' Union.

A Species which have been recorded in an apparently natural state at least once since January 1, 1950.

B Species which would otherwise be in Category A but have not been recorded since December 31, 1949.

C Species that, though originally introduced by man, either deliberately or accidentally, have established breeding populations derived from introduced stock that maintain themselves without necessary recourse to further introduction.

D Species that would otherwise appear in Categories A or B except that there is reasonable doubt that they have ever occurred in a natural state. (Species in this category are included in the log charts, though they do not qualify for inclusion in the British List, which comprises species in Categories A, B and C only. One of the objects of Category D is to note records of species which are not yet full additions, so that they are not overlooked if acceptable records subsequently occur. Bird report editors are encouraged to include records of species in Category D as appendices to their systematic lists).

E Species that have been recorded as introductions, transportees or escapees from captivity, and whose populations (if any) are thought not to be self-sustaining. They do not form part of the British List.

EU Species not on the British List, or in Category D, but which either breed or occur regularly elsewhere in Europe.

Life list
Ticks made in the 'Life List' column suffice for keeping a running personal total of species. However, added benefit can be obtained by replacing ticks with a note of the year of first occurrence. To take an example: one's first-ever Marsh Sandpiper, seen on April 14, 2008, would be logged with '08' in the Life List and '14' in the April column (as well as a tick in the 2008 column). As Life List entries are carried forward annually, in years to come it would be a simple matter to relocate this record.

First and last dates of migrants
Arrivals of migrants can be recorded by inserting dates instead of ticks in the relevant month columns. For example, a Common Sandpiper on March 11 would be recorded by inserting '11' against Common Sandpiper in the March column. The same applies to departures, though dates of last sightings can only be entered at the end of the year after checking one's field notebook.

Unheaded columns
The three unheaded columns on the right of the December column of each chart are for special

(personal) use. This may be, for example, to cater for a second holiday, a particular county or a 'local patch'. Another use could be to indicate species on, for example, the Northern Ireland List or the Isle of Man List.

BTO species codes
British Trust for Ornithology two-letter species codes are shown in brackets in the fourth column from the right. They exist for many species, races and hybrids recorded in recent surveys. Readers should refer to the BTO if more codes are needed.

In addition to those given in the charts, the following are available for some well-marked races or forms - Whistling Swan (WZ), European White-fronted Goose (EW), Greenland White-fronted Goose (NW), dark-bellied Brent Goose (DB), pale-bellied Brent Goose (PB), Black Brant (BB), domestic goose (ZL), Green-winged Teal (TA), domestic duck (ZF), Yellow-legged Gull (YG), Kumlien's Gull (KG), Feral Pigeon (FP), White Wagtail (WB), Black-bellied Dipper (DJ), Hooded Crow (HC), intermediate crow (HB).

Rarities
Rarities are indicated by a capital letter 'R' in the column headed BBRC (British Birds Rarities Committee).

EURING species numbers
EURING databanks collects copies of recovery records from ringing schemes throughout Europe and the official species numbers are given in the last column. As they are taken from the full Holarctic bird list there are many apparent gaps. It is important that these are not filled arbitrarily by observers wishing to record species not listed in the charts, as this would compromise the integrity of the scheme.

Similarly, the addition of a further digit to indicate sub-species is to be avoided, since EURING has already assigned numbers for this purpose. The numbering follows the Voous order of species so some species are now out of sequence following the re-ordering of the British List. For full details, visit: www.euring.org

Rare breeding birds
Species monitored by the Rare Breeding Birds Panel (see National Directory) comprise all those on Schedule 1 of the Wildlife and Countryside Act 1981 (see Quick Reference) together with all escaped or introduced species breeding in small numbers. The following annotations in the charts (third column from the right) reflect the RBBP's categories:

A Rare species. All breeding details requested.

B Less scarce species. Totals requested from counties with more than 10 pairs or localities; elsewhere all details requested.

C Less scarce species (specifically Barn Owl, Kingfisher, Crossbill). County summaries only requested.

D Escaped or introduced species. County summaries only requested.

64

SWANS, GEESE, DUCKS

BOU	Name	Scientific	Life list	2010 list	24 hr	Garden	Holiday	Jan	Feb	Mar	Apr	May	Jun	Jul	Aug	Sep	Oct	Nov	Dec	BTO	RBBP	BBRC	EU No
* AC	Mute Swan	Cygnus olor																		MS			0152
* A	Bewick's Swan	C. columbianus																		BS	A		0153
* A	Whooper Swan	C. cygnus																		WS	A		0154
* A	Bean Goose	Anser fabalis																		BE			0157
* A	Pink-footed Goose	A. brachyrhynchus																		PG	D		0158
* A	White-fronted Goose	A. albifrons																		WG	D		0159
* A	Lesser White-fronted Goose	A. erythropus																		LC	D	R	0160
* AC	Greylag Goose	A. anser																		GJ			0161
* A	Snow Goose	A. aerulescens																		SJ	D		0163
* C	Canada Goose	Branta canadensis																		CG	D		0166
* A	Barnacle Goose	B. eucopsis																		BY	D		0167
* A	Brent Goose	B. bernicla																		BG	D		0168
* A	Red-breasted Goose	B. ruficollis																		EB	D	R	0169
* C	Egyptian Goose	Alopochen aegyptiaca																		EG	D		0170
* B	Ruddy Shelduck	Tadorna ferruginea																		UD	D		0171
* A	Shelduck	T. tadorna																		SU			0173
* C	Mandarin Duck	Aix galericulata																		MN			0178
* A	Wigeon	Anas penelope																		WN	A		0179
* A	American Wigeon	A. americana																		AW			0180
* AC	Gadwall	A. strepera																		GA	B		0182
* A	Teal	A. crecca																		T			0184
* A	Green-winged Teal	A. carolinensis																			A		1842
* AC	Mallard	A. platyrhynchos																		MA			0186
* A	Black Duck	A. rubripes																		BD	A	R	0187
	Sub total																						

DUCKS Cont

BOU	Species	Scientific name	Life list	2010 list	24 hr	Garden	Holiday	Jan	Feb	Mar	Apr	May	Jun	Jul	Aug	Sep	Oct	Nov	Dec	BTO	RBBP	BBRC	EU No
* A	Pintail	A. acuta																		PT	A		0189
* A	Garganey	A. querquedula																		GY	A		0191
A	Blue-winged Teal	A. discors																		TB	D	R	0192
* A	Shoveler	A. clypeata																		SV	A		0194
* A	Red-crested Pochard	Netta rufina																		RQ	D		0196
A	Canvasback	A. valisineria																				R	0197
* A	Pochard	A. ferina																		PO	B		0198
A	Redhead	A. americana																		AZ		R	0199
A	Ring-necked Duck	A. collaris																		NG	A		0200
A	Ferruginous Duck	A. nyroca																		FD			0202
* A	Tufted Duck	A. fuligula																		TU			0203
* A	Scaup	A. marila																		SP	A		0204
* A	Lesser Scaup	A. affinis																		AY		R	0205
* A	Eider	Somateria mollissima																		E			0206
* A	King Eider	S. spectabilis																		KE	A	R	0207
A	Steller's Eider	Polysticta stelleri																		ES		R	0209
A	Harlequin Duck	Histrionicus histrionicus																		HQ		R	0211
* A	Long-tailed Duck	Clangula hyemalis																		LN	A		0212
* A	Common Scoter	Melanitta nigra																		CX	A		0213
A	Black Scoter	M. americana																				R	2132
* A	Surf Scoter	M. perspicillata																		FS			0214
A	Velvet Scoter	M. fusca																		VS	A		0215
A	Bufflehead	Bucephala albeola																		VH		R	0216
A	Barrow's Goldeneye	B. islandica																				R	0217
	Sub total																						

DUCKS, GAMEBIRDS, DIVERS, GREBES

BOU	Common name	Scientific name	Life list	2010 list	24 hr	Garden	Holiday	Jan	Feb	Mar	Apr	May	Jun	Jul	Aug	Sep	Oct	Nov	Dec				BTO	RBBP	BBRC	EU No
* A	Goldeneye	B. clangula																					GN	A		0218
* A	Smew	Mergellus albellus																					SY	A		0220
A	Hooded Merganser	Lophodytes cucullatus																							R	2190
* A	Red-breasted Merganser	Mergus serrator																					RM			0221
* A	Goosander	M. merganser																					GD			0223
* C	Ruddy Duck	Oxyura jamaicensis																					BY			0225
* A	Red Grouse	Lagopus lagopus																					RG			0329
* A	Ptarmigan	Lagopus muta																					PM			0330
* A	Black Grouse	Tetrao tetrix																					BK			0332
* BC	Capercaillie	T. urogallus																					CP	A		0335
* C	Red-legged Partridge	Alectoris rufa																					RL			0358
* AC	Grey Partridge	Perdix perdix																					P			0367
* A	Quail	Coturnix coturnix																					Q	B		0370
* C	(Common) Pheasant	Phasianus colchicus																					PH			0394
* C	Golden Pheasant	Chrysolophus pictus																					GF	D		0396
* C	Lady Amherst's Pheasant	C. amherstiae																					LM	D		0397
* A	Red-throated Diver	Gavia stellata																					RH	B		0002
* A	Black-throated Diver	G. arctica																					BV	A		0003
A	Pacific Diver	Gavia pacifica																							R	0033
* A	Great Northern Diver	G. immer																					ND	A		0004
A	White-billed Diver	G. adamsii																					IW	A		0005
A	Pied-billed Grebe	Podilymbus podiceps																					PJ	A	R	0006
* A	Little Grebe	Tachybaptus ruficollis																					LG			0007
* A	Great Crested Grebe	Podiceps cristatus																					GG			0009
	Sub total																									

ALBATROSS, FULMAR, PETRELS, SHEARWATERS, CORMORANTS

BOU	Species	Scientific	Life list	2010 list	24 hr	Garden	Holiday	Jan	Feb	Mar	Apr	May	Jun	Jul	Aug	Sep	Oct	Nov	Dec	BTO	RBBP	BBRC	EU No
*A	Red-necked Grebe	P. grisegena																		RX	A		0010
*A	Slavonian Grebe	P. auritus																		SZ	A		0011
*A	Black-necked Grebe	P. nigricollis																		BN	A		0012
A	Black-browed Albatross	Thalassarche melanophris																		AA	A	R	0014
A	Yellow-nosed Albatross	T. chlororhynchos																				R	0150
*A	Fulmar	Fulmarus glacialis																		F			0020
A	Fea's Petrel	Pterodroma feae																				R	0026
A	Capped Petrel	Pt. hasitata																				R	0029
A	Cory's Shearwater	Calonectris diomedea																		CQ			0036
*A	Great Shearwater	Puffinus gravis																		GQ			0040
*A	Sooty Shearwater	P. griseus																		OT			0043
A	Manx Shearwater	P. puffinus																		MX			0046
A	Balearic Shearwater	P. mauretanicus																					0046
A	Macaronesian Shearwater	P. baroli																			A	R	0048
*A	Wilson's Petrel	Oceanites oceanicus																					0050
B	White-faced Petrel	Pelagodroma marina																				R	0051
*A	Storm Petrel	Hydrobates pelagicus																		TM			0052
*A	Leach's Petrel	Oceanodroma leucorhoa																		TL	A		0055
A	Swinhoe's Petrel	O. monorhis																				R	0056
B	Madeiran Petrel	O. castro																				R	0058
A	Red-billed Tropicbird	Phaethon aethereus																				R	0064
*A	(Northern) Gannet	Morus bassanus																		GX			0071
*A	Cormorant	Phalacrocorax carbo																		CA			0072
A	Double-crested Cormorant	P. auritus																				R	0078
	Sub total																						

67

BITTERNS, HERONS, STORKS, SPOONBILL, RAPTORS

BOU			Life list	2010 list	24 hr	Garden	Holiday	Jan	Feb	Mar	Apr	May	Jun	Jul	Aug	Sep	Oct	Nov	Dec		BTO	RBBP	BBRC	EU No
* A	Shag	*P. aristotelis*																			SA			0080
A	Magnificent Frigatebird	*Fregata magnificens*																					R	0093
A	Ascension Frigatebird	*F. aquila*																					R	
* A	Bittern	*Botaurus stellaris*																			BI	A		0095
A	American Bittern	*B. lentiginosus*																			AM		R	0096
A	Little Bittern	*Ixobrychus minutus*																			LL	A	R	0098
A	Night-heron	*Nycticorax nycticorax*																			NT	D		0104
A	Green Heron	*Butorides virescens*																			HR		R	0107
A	Squacco Heron	*Ardeola ralloides*																			QH	A	R	0108
A	Cattle Egret	*Bubulcus ibis*																			EC	A		0111
A	Snowy Egret	*Egretta thula*																					R	0115
* A	Little Egret	*E. garzetta*																			ET	A		0119
A	Great White Egret	*Ardea alba*																			HW			0121
A	Grey Heron	*A. cinerea*																			H			0122
A	Great Blue Heron	*A. herodias*																					R	1230
A	Purple Heron	*A. purpurea*																			UR	A		0124
A	Black Stork	*Ciconia nigra*																			OS		R	0131
A	White Stork	*C. ciconia*																			OR	A		0134
A	Glossy Ibis	*Plegadis falcinellus*																			IB	A	R	0136
* A	Spoonbill	*Platalea leucorodia*																			NB	A		0144
* A	Honey-buzzard	*Pernis apivorus*																			HZ	A		0231
A	Black Kite	*Milvus migrans*																			KB	A		0238
* AC	Red Kite	*M. milvus*																			KT	A		0239
* A	White-tailed Eagle	*Haliaeetus albicilla*																			WE	A		0243
	Sub total																							

68

RAPTORS, RAILS AND CRAKES

BOU	Common name	Scientific name	Life list	2010 list	24 hr	Garden	Holiday	Jan	Feb	Mar	Apr	May	Jun	Jul	Aug	Sep	Oct	Nov	Dec	BTO	RBBP	BBRC	EU No
B	Egyptian Vulture	Neophron percnopterus																				R	0247
A	Short-toed Eagle	Circaetus gallicus																				R	0256
*A	Marsh Harrier	Circus aeruginosus																		MR	A		0260
*A	Hen Harrier	C. cyaneus																		HH	B		0261
A	Pallid Harrier	C. macrourus																			A	R	0262
*A	Montagu's Harrier	C. pygargus																		MO	A		0263
*AC	Goshawk	Accipiter gentilis																		GI	B		0267
*A	Sparrowhawk	A. nisus																		SH			0269
*A	Buzzard	Buteo buteo																		BZ			0287
*A	Rough-legged Buzzard	B. lagopus																		RF	A		0290
B	Greater Spotted Eagle	Aquila clanga																				R	0293
*A	Golden Eagle	A. chrysaetos																		EA	B		0296
*A	Osprey	Pandion haliaetus																		OP	A		0301
A	Lesser Kestrel	Falco naumanni																				R	0303
*A	Kestrel	F. tinnunculus																		K			0304
A	American Kestrel	F. sparverius																				R	0305
*A	Red-footed Falcon	F. vespertinus																		FV			0307
*A	Merlin	F. columbarius																		ML	B		0309
*A	Hobby	F. subbuteo																		HY	B		0310
A	Eleonora's Falcon	F. eleonorae																				R	0311
*A	Gyr Falcon	F. rusticolus																		YF	A	R	0318
*A	Peregrine	F. peregrinus																		PE	B		0320
*A	Water Rail	Rallus aquaticus																		WA	A		0407
*A	Spotted Crake	Porzana porzana																		AK	A	R	0408
	Sub total																						

GALLINULES AND WADERS

BOU	Common name	Scientific name	BTO	RBBP	BBRC	EU No
A	Sora	P. carolina	JC		R	0409
A	Little Crake	P. parva			R	0410
A	Baillon's Crake	P. pusilla	VC	A	R	0411
*A	Corn Crake	Crex crex	CE	A		0421
*A	Moorhen	Gallinula chloropus	MH			0424
A	Allen's Gallinule	Porphyrio alleni			R	0425
A	Purple Gallinule	P. martinica			R	0426
*A	Coot	Fulica atra	CO			0429
A	American Coot	F. americana			R	0430
*A	Crane	Grus grus	AN	A		0433
A	Sandhill Crane	G. canadensis			R	0436
A	Little Bustard	Tetrax tetrax			R	0442
A	Macqueen's Bustard	Chlamydotis macqueenii			R	0444
A	Great Bustard	Otis tarda	US	A	R	0446
*A	Oystercatcher	Haematopus ostralegus	OC			0450
*A	Black-winged Stilt	Himantopus himantopus	IT	A	R	0455
*A	Avocet	Recurvirostra avosetta	AV	A		0456
*A	Stone-curlew	Burhinus oedicnemus	TN	A		0459
A	Cream-coloured Courser	Cursorius cursor			R	0464
A	Collared Pratincole	Glareola pratincola			R	0465
A	Oriental Pratincole	G. maldivarum	GM		R	0466
A	Black-winged Pratincole	G. nordmanni	KW		R	0467
*A	Little Ringed Plover	Charadrius dubius	LP	B		0469
*A	Ringed Plover	C. hiaticula	RP		R	0470

Sub total

Column headers (recording columns, all blank): Life list, 2010 list, 24 hr, Garden, Holiday, Jan, Feb, Mar, Apr, May, Jun, Jul, Aug, Sep, Oct, Nov, Dec

BOU	WADERS Cont		Life list	2010 list	24 hr	Garden	Holiday	Jan	Feb	Mar	Apr	May	Jun	Jul	Aug	Sep	Oct	Nov	Dec			BTO	RBBP	BBRC	EU No
A	Semipalmated Plover	C. semipalmatus																				TV		R	0471
A	Killdeer	C. vociferus																				KL		R	0474
A	Kentish Plover	C. alexandrinus																				KP	A		0477
A	Lesser Sand Plover	C. mongolus																						R	0478
A	Greater Sand Plover	C. leschenaultii																						R	0479
A	Caspian Plover	C. asiaticus																						R	0480
*A	Dotterel	C. morinellus																				DO	B		0482
A	American Golden Plover	Pluvialis dominica																				ID			0484
A	Pacific Golden Plover	P. fulva																				IF		R	0484
*A	Golden Plover	P. apricaria																				GP			0485
*A	Grey Plover	P. squatarola																				GV			0486
A	Sociable Plover	Vanellus gregarius																				IP		R	0491
A	White-tailed Plover	V. leucurus																						R	0492
*A	Lapwing	V. vanellus																				L			0493
A	Great Knot	Calidris tenuirostris																				KO		R	0495
*A	Knot	C. canutus																				KN			0496
*A	Sanderling	C. alba																				SS	A		0497
A	Semipalmated Sandpiper	C. pusilla																				PZ		R	0498
A	Western Sandpiper	C. mauri																				ER		R	0499
A	Red-necked Stint	C. ruficollis																						R	0500
*A	Little Stint	C. minuta																				LX			0501
*A	Temminck's Stint	C. temminckii																				TK	A		0502
A	Long-toed Stint	C. subminuta																						R	0503
A	Least Sandpiper	C. minutilla																				EP		R	0504
	Sub total																								

WADERS Cont

BOU	Species	Scientific name	Life list	2010 list	24 hr	Garden	Holiday	Jan	Feb	Mar	Apr	May	Jun	Jul	Aug	Sep	Oct	Nov	Dec	BTO	RBBP	BBRC	EU No
A	White-rumped Sandpiper	C. fuscicollis																		WU			0505
A	Baird's Sandpiper	C. bairdii																		BP		R	0506
A	Pectoral Sandpiper	C. melanotos																		PP	A		0507
A	Sharp-tailed Sandpiper	C. acuminata																		VV		R	0508
* A	Curlew Sandpiper	C. ferruginea																		CV			0509
A	Stilt Sandpiper	C. himantopus																				R	5150
* A	Purple Sandpiper	C. maritima																		PS	A		0510
* A	Dunlin	C. alpina																		DN			0512
A	Broad-billed Sandpiper	Limicola falcinellus																		OA	A	R	0514
A	Buff-breasted Sandpiper	Tryngites subruficollis																		BQ			0516
* A	Ruff	Philomachus pugnax																		RU	A		0517
* A	Jack Snipe	Lymnocryptes minimus																		JS	A		0518
* A	Snipe	Gallinago gallinago																		SN			0519
A	Wilson's Snipe	G. delicata																				R	5192
A	Great Snipe	G. media																				R	0520
A	Short-billed Dowitcher	Limnodromus griseus																		DS		R	0526
A	Long-billed Dowitcher	Limnodromus scolopaceus																		LD		R	0527
* A	Woodcock	Scolopax rusticola																		WK			0529
* A	Black-tailed Godwit	Limosa limosa																		BW	A		0532
A	Hudsonian Godwit	L. haemastica																		HU		R	0533
* A	Bar-tailed Godwit	L. lapponica																		BA	A		0534
A	Little Whimbrel	Numenius minutus																				R	0536
B	Eskimo Curlew	N. borealis																				R	0537
* A	Whimbrel	N. phaeopus																		WM	B		0538
	Sub total																						

72

WADERS Cont, SKUAS, GULLS

BOU	Species	Scientific name	Life list	2010 list	24 hr	Garden	Holiday	Jan	Feb	Mar	Apr	May	Jun	Jul	Aug	Sep	Oct	Nov	Dec	BTO	RBBP	BBRC	EU No
A	Slender-billed Curlew	N. tenuirostris																				R	0540
*A	Curlew	N. arquata																		CU			0541
A	Upland Sandpiper	Bartramia longicauda																		UP		R	0544
A	Terek Sandpiper	Xenus cinereus																		TR		R	0555
*A	Common Sandpiper	Actitis hypoleucos																		CS			0556
A	Spotted Sandpiper	A. macularius																		PQ	A	R	0557
*A	Green Sandpiper	Tringa ochropus																		GE	A		0553
A	Solitary Sandpiper	T. solitaria																		I		R	0552
A	Grey-tailed Tattler	T. brevipes																		YT		R	0558
*A	Spotted Redshank	T. erythropus																		DR			0545
A	Greater Yellowlegs	T. melanoleuca																		LZ		R	0550
*A	Greenshank	T. nebularia																		GK	A		0548
A	Lesser Yellowlegs	T. flavipes																		LY		R	0551
*A	Marsh Sandpiper	T. stagnatilis																		MD		R	0547
*A	Wood Sandpiper	T. glareola																		OD	A		0554
*A	Redshank	T. totanus																		RK			0546
A	Turnstone	Arenaria interpres																		TT	A		0561
*A	Wilson's Phalarope	Phalaropus tricolor																		WF		R	0563
*A	Red-necked Phalarope	P. lobatus																		NK	A		0564
*A	Grey Phalarope	Phalaropus fulicarius																		PL			0565
*A	Pomarine Skua	Stercorarius pomarinus																		PK			0566
*A	Arctic Skua	S. parasiticus																		AC			0567
*A	Long-tailed Skua	S. longicaudus																		OG			0568
*A	Great Skua	S. skua																		NX			0569
	Sub total																						

73

GULLS AND TERNS

BOU	Species	Scientific name	Life list	2010 list	24 hr	Garden	Holiday	Jan	Feb	Mar	Apr	May	Jun	Jul	Aug	Sep	Oct	Nov	Dec	BTO	RBBP	BBRC	EU NO
A	Ivory Gull	*Pagophila eburnea*																		IV		R	0604
* A	Sabine's Gull	*Larus sabini*																		AB			0579
* A	Kittiwake	*Rissa tridactyla*																		KI			0602
A	Slender-billed Gull	*Chroicocephalus genei*																		EI	A	R	0585
A	Bonaparte's Gull	*C. philadelphia*																		ON		R	0581
* A	Black-headed Gull	*C. ridibundus*																		BH			0582
* A	Little Gull	*Hydrocoloeus minutus*																		LU	A		0578
A	Ross's Gull	*Rhodostethia rosea*																		QG		R	0601
* A	Laughing Gull	*Larus atricilla*																		LF		R	0576
A	Franklin's Gull	*L. pipixcan*																		FG		R	0577
* A	Mediterranean Gull	*L. melanocephalus*																		MU	A		0575
A	Audouin's Gull	*L. audouinii*																				R	0589
B	Great Black-headed Gull	*L. ichthyaetus*																				R	0573
* A	Common Gull	*L. canus*																		CM			0590
* A	Ring-billed Gull	*L. delawarensis*																		IN	A		0588
* A	Lesser Black-backed Gull	*L. fuscus*																		LB			0591
* A	Herring Gull	*L. argentatus*																		HG			0592
A	Yellow-legged Gull	*L. michahellis*																			A		5927
A	Caspian Gull	*L. cachinnans*																					5927
A	American Herring Gull	*L. smithsonianus*																				R	26632
* A	Iceland Gull	*L. glaucoides*																		IG	A		0598
A	Glaucous-winged Gull	*L. glaucescens*																				R	5960
* A	Glaucous Gull	*L. hyperboreus*																		GZ	A		0599
* A	Great Black-backed Gull	*L. marinus*																		GB	A		0600
	Sub total																						

TERNS Cont, AUKS, DOVES

BOU		Scientific name	Life list	2010 list	24 hr	Garden	Holiday	Jan	Feb	Mar	Apr	May	Jun	Jul	Aug	Sep	Oct	Nov	Dec	BTO	RBBP	BBRC	EU No
A	Aleutian Tern	Onychoprion aleutica																				R	0617
A	Sooty Tern	O. fuscata																				R	0623
A	Bridled Tern	O. anaethetus																				R	0622
*A	Little Tern	Sternula albifrons																		AF	B		0624
A	Gull-billed Tern	Gelochelidon nilotica																		TG		R	0605
A	Caspian Tern	Hydroprogne caspia																		CJ			0606
*A	Whiskered Tern	Chlidonias hybrida																		WD		R	0626
*A	Black Tern	C. niger																		BJ	A		0627
*A	White-winged Black Tern	C. leucopterus																		WJ			0628
*A	Sandwich Tern	Sterna sandvicensis																		TE			0611
A	Royal Tern	S. maxima																		QT		R	0607
A	Lesser Crested Tern	S. bengalensis																		TF	A	R	0609
A	Forster's Tern	S. forsteri																		FO		R	0618
*A	Common Tern	S. hirundo																		CN			0615
*A	Roseate Tern	S. dougallii																		RS	A		0614
*A	Arctic Tern	S. paradisaea																		AE			0616
*A	Guillemot	Uria aalge																		GU			0634
A	Brünnich's Guillemot	U. lomvia																		TZ		R	0635
*A	Razorbill	Alca torda																		RA			0636
*A	Black Guillemot	Cepphus grylle																		TY			0638
A	Long-billed Murrelet	Brachyramphus perdix																				R	6412
A	Ancient Murrelet	Synthliboramphus antiquus																				R	0645
*A	Little Auk	Alle alle																		LK			0647
*A	Puffin	Fratercula arctica																		PU			0654
	Sub total																						

75

DOVES Cont, CUCKOOS, OWLS, NIGHTJARS, SWIFTS,

BOU	Species	Scientific name	Life list	2010 list	24 hr	Garden	Holiday	Jan	Feb	Mar	Apr	May	Jun	Jul	Aug	Sep	Oct	Nov	Dec		BTO	RBBP	BBRC	EU No
A	Pallas's Sandgrouse	Syrrhaptes paradoxus																					R	0663
* AC	Rock Dove / Feral Pigeon	Columba livia																			DV			0665
* A	Stock Dove	C. oenas																			SD			0668
* A	Woodpigeon	C. palumbus																			WP			0670
* A	Collared Dove	Streptopelia decaocto																			CD			0684
* A	Turtle Dove	S. turtur																			TD			0687
A	Rufous Turtle Dove	S. orientalis																					R	0689
A	Mourning Dove	Zenaida macroura																					R	0695
* C	Ring-necked Parakeet	Psittacula krameri																			RI			0712
A	Great Spotted Cuckoo	Clamator glandarius																			UK		R	0716
* A	Cuckoo	Cuculus canorus																			CK			0724
A	Black-billed Cuckoo	Coccyzus erythrophthalmus																					R	0727
A	Yellow-billed Cuckoo	C. americanus																					R	0728
* A	Barn Owl	Tyto alba																			BO			0735
A	Scops Owl	Otus scops																					R	0739
* A	Snowy Owl	Bubo scandiacus																			SO	A	R	0749
A	Hawk Owl	Surnia ulula																					R	0750
* C	Little Owl	Athene noctua																			LO			0757
* A	Tawny Owl	Strix aluco																			TO			0761
* A	Long-eared Owl	Asio otus																			LE			0767
A	Short-eared Owl	Asio flammeus																			SE			0768
A	Tengmalm's Owl	Aegolius funereus																					R	0770
* A	Nightjar	Caprimulgus europaeus																			NJ			0778
B	Red-necked Nightjar	C. ruficollis																					R	0779
	Sub total																							

SWIFTS Cont, KINGFISHERS, BEE-EATERS, WOODPECKERS, LARKS

BOU	Species	Scientific name	Life list	2010 list	24 hr	Garden	Holiday	Jan	Feb	Mar	Apr	May	Jun	Jul	Aug	Sep	Oct	Nov	Dec	BTO	RBBP	BBRC	EU No
A	Egyptian Nightjar	C. aegyptius																				R	0781
A	Common Nighthawk	Chordeiles minor																				R	0786
A	Chimney Swift	Chaetura pelagica																				R	0790
A	Needle-tailed Swift	Hirundapus caudacutus																		NI		R	0792
*A	Swift	Apus apus																		SI			0795
A	Pallid Swift	A. pallidus																				R	0796
A	Pacific Swift	A. pacificus																				R	0797
A	Alpine Swift	A. melba																		AI			0798
A	Little Swift	A. affinis																				R	0800
*A	Kingfisher	Alcedo atthis																		KF			0831
A	Belted Kingfisher	Megaceryle alcyon																				R	0834
A	Blue-cheeked Bee-eater	Merops persicus																				R	0839
*A	Bee-eater	M. apiaster																		MZ	A		0840
A	Roller	Coracias garrulus																				R	0841
*A	Hoopoe	Upupa epops																		HP	A		0846
*A	Wryneck	Jynx torquilla																		WY	A		0848
*A	Green Woodpecker	Picus viridis																		G			0856
A	Yellow-bellied Sapsucker	Sphyrapicus varius																				R	0872
*A	Great Spotted Woodpecker	Dendrocopos major																		GS			0876
*A	Lesser Spotted Woodpecker	D. minor																		LS			0887
A	Eastern Phoebe	Sayornis phoebe																				R	0909
A	Calandra Lark	Melanocorypha calandra																				R	0961
A	Bimaculated Lark	M. bimaculata																				R	0962
A	White-winged Lark	M. leucoptera																				R	0965
	Sub total																						

77

LARKS, MARTINS, SWALLOWS, PIPITS,

BOU	Common name	Scientific name	Life list	2010 list	24 hr	Garden	Holiday	Jan	Feb	Mar	Apr	May	Jun	Jul	Aug	Sep	Oct	Nov	Dec		BTO	RBBP	BBRC	EU No
A	Black Lark	M. yeltoniensis																					R	0966
A	Short-toed Lark	Calandrella brachydactyla																			VL			0968
A	Lesser Short-toed Lark	C. rufescens																					R	0970
A	Crested Lark	Galerida cristata																					R	0972
*A	Wood Lark	Lullula arborea																			WL	B		0974
*A	Sky Lark	Alauda arvensis																			S			0976
*A	Shore Lark	Eremophila alpestris																			SX	A		0978
*A	Sand Martin	Riparia riparia																			SM			0981
A	Tree Swallow	Tachycineta bicolor																					R	0983
A	Purple Martin	Progne subis																					R	0989
A	Crag Martin	Ptyonoprogne rupestris																					R	0991
*A	Swallow	Hirundo rustica																			SL			0992
*A	House Martin	Delichon urbicum																			HM			1001
A	Red-rumped Swallow	Cecropis daurica																			VR			0995
A	Cliff Swallow	Petrochelidon pyrrhonota																					R	0998
A	Richard's Pipit	Anthus richardi																			PR			1002
A	Blyth's Pipit	A. godlewskii																					R	1004
A	Tawny Pipit	A. campestris																			TI			1005
A	Olive-backed Pipit	A. hodgsoni																			OV			1008
*A	Tree Pipit	A. trivialis																			TP			1009
A	Pechora Pipit	A. gustavi																					R	1010
*A	Meadow Pipit	A. pratensis																			MP			1011
A	Red-throated Pipit	A. cervinus																			VP			1012
*A	Rock Pipit	A. petrosus																			RC			1014
	Sub total																							

78

WAGTAILS, WAXWINGS, DIPPER, WREN, CHATS

BOU			Life list	2010 list	24 hr	Garden	Holiday	Jan	Feb	Mar	Apr	May	Jun	Jul	Aug	Sep	Oct	Nov	Dec	BTO	RBBP	BBRC	EU No
*A	Water Pipit	A. spinoletta																		WI			1014
A	Buff-bellied Pipit	A. rubescens																				R	1014
*A	Yellow Wagtail	Motacilla flava																		YW			1017
A	Citrine Wagtail	M. citreola																			A	R	1018
*A	Grey Wagtail	M. cinerea																		GL			1019
*A	Pied Wagtail	M. alba																		PW			1020
A	White Wagtail	M.a.leucopsis																			A		
A	Cedar Waxwing	Bombycilla cedrorum																				R	1046
*A	Waxwing	B. garrulus																		WX	A		1048
*A	Dipper	Cinclus cinclus																		DI			1050
*A	Wren	Troglodytes troglodytes																		WR			1066
A	Northern Mockingbird	Mimus polyglottos																				R	1067
A	Brown Thrasher	Toxostoma rufum																				R	1069
A	Grey Catbird	Dumetella carolinensis																				R	1080
*A	Dunnock	Prunella modularis																		D			1084
A	Alpine Accentor	P. collaris																				R	1094
A	Rufous Bush Chat	Cercotrichas galactotes																				R	1095
*A	Robin	Erithacus rubecula																		R			1099
A	Rufous-tailed Robin	Luscinia sibilans																				R	1102
A	Thrush Nightingale	L. luscinia																		FN	A		1103
*A	Nightingale	L. megarhynchos																		N			1104
A	Siberian Rubythroat	L. calliope																				R	1105
A	Bluethroat	L. svecica																		BU	A		1106
A	Siberian Blue Robin	L. cyane																				R	1112
	Sub total																						

79

BOU	CHATS Cont, WHEATEARS, THRUSHES		Life list	2010 list	24 hr	Garden	Holiday	Jan	Feb	Mar	Apr	May	Jun	Jul	Aug	Sep	Oct	Nov	Dec			BTO	RBBP	BBRC	EU NO
A	Red-flanked Bluetail	Tarsiger cyanurus																						R	1113
A	White-throated Robin	Irania gutturalis																						R	1117
*A	Black Redstart	Phoenicurus ochruros																				BX	A		1121
*A	Redstart	P. phoenicurus																				RT			1122
A	Moussier's Redstart	P. moussieri																						R	1127
*A	Whinchat	Saxicola rubetra																				WC			1137
*A	Stonechat	S. torquatus																				SC			1139
A	Isabelline Wheatear	Oenanthe isabellina																						R	1144
*A	Wheatear	O. oenanthe																				W			1146
A	Pied Wheatear	O. pleschanka																				PI		R	1147
A	Black-eared Wheatear	O. hispanica																						R	1148
A	Desert Wheatear	O. deserti																						R	1149
A	White-crowned Black Wheatear	O. leucopyga																						R	1157
A	Rock Thrush	Monticola saxatilis																				OH		R	1162
A	Blue Rock Thrush	M. solitarius																						R	1166
A	White's Thrush	Zoothera dauma																						R	1170
A	Siberian Thrush	Z. sibirica																						R	1171
A	Varied Thrush	Ixoreus naevius																				VT		R	1172
A	Wood Thrush	Hylocichla mustelina																						R	1175
A	Hermit Thrush	Catharus guttatus																						R	1176
A	Swainson's Thrush	C. ustulatus																						R	1177
A	Grey-cheeked Thrush	C. minimus																						R	1178
A	Veery	C. fuscescens																						R	1179
*A	Ring Ouzel	Turdus torquatus																				RZ		R	1186
	Sub total																								

BOU	THRUSHES Cont, WARBLERS		Life list	2010 list	24 hr	Garden	Holiday	Jan	Feb	Mar	Apr	May	Jun	Jul	Aug	Sep	Oct	Nov	Dec				BTO	RBBP	BBRC	EU No
* A	**Blackbird**	*T. merula*																					B			1187
A	**Eyebrowed Thrush**	*T. obscurus*																							R	1195
A	**Dusky Thrush**	*T. naumanni*																							R	1196
A	**Naumann's Thrush**	*T. naumanni*																							R	11960
A	**Black-throated Thrush**	*T. atrogularis*																								1197
A	**Red-throated Thrush**	*T. ruficollis*																							R	11970
* A	**Fieldfare**	*T. pilaris*																					FF	A		1198
* A	**Song Thrush**	*T. philomelos*																					ST			1200
* A	**Redwing**	*T. iliacus*																					RE	A		1201
* A	**Mistle Thrush**	*T. viscivorus*																					M			1202
A	**American Robin**	*T. migratorius*																					AR		R	1203
* A	**Cetti's Warbler**	*Cettia cetti*																					CW	A		1220
A	**Fan-tailed Warbler**	*Cisticola juncidis*																							R	1226
A	**Pallas's Grasshopper Warbler**	*Locustella certhiola*																								1233
A	**Lanceolated Warbler**	*L. lanceolata*																							R	1235
* A	**Grasshopper Warbler**	*L. naevia*																					GH			1236
A	**River Warbler**	*L. fluviatilis*																					VW	A	R	1237
A	**Savi's Warbler**	*L. luscinioides*																					VI	A	R	1238
A	**Aquatic Warbler**	*Acrocephalus paludicola*																					AQ			1242
* A	**Sedge Warbler**	*A. schoenobaenus*																					SW			1243
A	**Paddyfield Warbler**	*A. agricola*																					PY		R	1247
A	**Blyth's Reed Warbler**	*A. dumetorum*																						A	R	1248
* A	**Marsh Warbler**	*A. palustris*																					MW	A		1250
* A	**Reed Warbler**	*A. scirpaceus*																					RW			1251
	Sub total																									

WARBLERS Cont

BOU	Species	Scientific	Life list	2010 list	24 hr	Garden	Holiday	Jan	Feb	Mar	Apr	May	Jun	Jul	Aug	Sep	Oct	Nov	Dec		BTO	RBBP	BBRC	EU No
A	Great Reed Warbler	A. arundinaceus																			QW	A	R	1253
A	Thick-billed Warbler	A. aedon																					R	1254
A	Eastern Olivaceous Warbler	Hippolais pallida																					R	1255
A	Booted Warbler	H. caligata																				A	R	1256
A	Sykes's Warbler	H. rama																					R	12562
A	Olive-tree Warbler	H. olivetorum																					R	12580
*A	Icterine Warbler	H. icterina																			IC	A		1259
*A	Melodious Warbler	H. polyglotta																			ME			1260
*A	Blackcap	Sylvia atricapilla																			BC			1277
*A	Garden Warbler	S. borin																			GW			1276
A	Barred Warbler	S. nisoria																			RR			1273
*A	Lesser Whitethroat	S. curruca																			LW			1274
A	Orphean Warbler	S. hortensis																					R	1272
A	Asian Desert Warbler	S. nana																				A	R	1270
*A	Whitethroat	S. communis																			WH			1275
*A	Spectacled Warbler	S. conspicillata																					R	1264
A	Dartford Warbler	S. undata																			DW	B		1262
A	Marmora's Warbler	S. sarda																			MM	A	R	1261
A	Rüppell's Warbler	S. rueppelli																					R	1269
A	Subalpine Warbler	S. cantillans																				A		1265
A	Sardinian Warbler	S. melanocephala																				A	R	1267
A	Green Warbler	Phylloscopus nitidus																					R	12910
A	Greenish Warbler	P. trochiloides																			NP			1293
A	Arctic Warbler	P. borealis																			AP		R	1295
	Sub total																							

WARBLERS, FLYCATCHERS, TITS

BOU	Species	Scientific name	Life list	2010 list	24 hr	Garden	Holiday	Jan	Feb	Mar	Apr	May	Jun	Jul	Aug	Sep	Oct	Nov	Dec	BTO	RBBP	BBRC	EU No
A	Pallas's Warbler	P. proregulus																		PA			1298
* A	Yellow-browed Warbler	P. inornatus																		YB			1300
A	Hume's Warbler	P. humei																				R	1300
A	Radde's Warbler	P. schwarzi																					1301
A	Dusky Warbler	P. fuscatus																		UY			1303
A	Western Bonelli's Warbler	P. bonelli																		IW		R	1307
A	Eastern Bonelli's Warbler	P. orientalis																				R	1307
* A	Wood Warbler	P. sibilatrix																		WO			1308
* A	Chiffchaff	P. collybita																		CC			1311
A	Iberian Chiffchaff	P. ibericus																				R	1311
* A	Willow Warbler	P. trochilus																		WW			1312
* A	Goldcrest	Regulus regulus																		GC			1314
* A	Firecrest	R. ignicapilla																		FC	A		1315
A	Asian Brown Flycatcher	Muscicapa dauurica																					
* A	Spotted Flycatcher	M. striata																					1335
* A	Red-breasted Flycatcher	Ficedula parva																		FY			1343
A	Taiga Flycatcher	F. albicilla																				R	1343
A	Collared Flycatcher	F. albicollis																				R	1348
* A	Pied Flycatcher	F. hypoleuca																		PF			1349
* A	Bearded Tit	Panurus biarmicus																		BR	B		1364
* A	Long-tailed Tit	Aegithalos caudatus																		LT			1437
* A	Blue Tit	Cyanistes caeruleus																		BT			1462
* A	Great Tit	Parus major																		GT			1464
* A	Crested Tit	Lophophanes cristatus																		CI	B		1454
	Sub total																						

83

TITS, SHRIKES, CROWS

BOU			Life list	2010 list	24 hr	Garden	Holiday	Jan	Feb	Mar	Apr	May	Jun	Jul	Aug	Sep	Oct	Nov	Dec	BTO	RBBP	BBRC	EU No
* A	Coal Tit	Periparus ater																		CT			1461
* A	Willow Tit	Poecile montana																		WT			1442
* A	Marsh Tit	P. palustris																		MT			1440
A	Red-breasted Nuthatch	Sitta canadensis																				R	1472
* A	Nuthatch	S. europaea																		NH			1479
A	Wallcreeper	Tichodroma muraria																				R	1482
* A	Treecreeper	Certhia familiaris																		TC			1486
A	Short-toed Treecreeper	C. brachydactyla																		TH	A	R	1487
A	Penduline Tit	Remiz pendulinus																		DT	A	R	1490
* A	Golden Oriole	Oriolus oriolus																		OL	A		1508
A	Brown Shrike	Lanius cristatus																				R	1513
A	Isabelline Shrike	L. isabellinus																		IL		R	1514
* A	Red-backed Shrike	L. collurio																		ED	A		1515
A	Long-tailed Shrike	L. schach																				R	1517
* A	Lesser Grey Shrike	L. minor																				R	1519
* A	Great Grey Shrike	L. excubitor																		SR	A		1520
A	Southern Grey Shrike	L. meridionalis																				R	1520
A	Woodchat Shrike	L. senator																		OO			1523
A	Masked Shrike	L. nubicus																				R	1524
* A	Jay	Garrulus glandarius																		J			1539
* A	Magpie	Pica pica																		MG			1549
A	Nutcracker	Nucifraga caryocatactes																		NC			1557
* A	Chough	Pyrrhocorax pyrrhocorax																		CF	B	R	1559
* A	Jackdaw	Corvus monedula																		JD			1560
	Sub total																						

CROWS, VIREOS, FINCHES

BOU	Species	Scientific	Life list	2010 list	24 hr	Garden	Holiday	Jan	Feb	Mar	Apr	May	Jun	Jul	Aug	Sep	Oct	Nov	Dec			BTO	RBBP	BBRC	EU No
*A	Rook	C. frugilegus																				RO			1563
*A	Carrion Crow	C. corone																				C			1567
*A	Hooded Crow	C. cornix																							1567
*A	Raven	C. corax																				RN			1572
*A	Starling	Sturnus vulgaris																				SG			1582
A	Rose-coloured Starling	S. roseus																				OE			1594
*A	House Sparrow	Passer domesticus																				HS			1591
A	Spanish Sparrow	P. hispaniolensis																						R	1592
*A	Tree Sparrow	P. montanus																				TS			1598
A	Rock Sparrow	Petronia petronia																						R	1604
A	Yellow-throated Vireo	Vireo flavifrons																						R	1628
A	Philadelphia Vireo	V. philadelphicus																						R	1631
A	Red-eyed Vireo	V. olivaceus																				EV		R	1633
*A	Chaffinch	Fringilla coelebs																				CH			1636
*A	Brambling	F. montifringilla																				BL	A		1638
*A	Serin	Serinus serinus																				NS	A		1640
*A	Greenfinch	Carduelis chloris																				GR			1649
*A	Goldfinch	C. carduelis																				GO			1653
*A	Siskin	C. spinus																				SK			1654
*A	Linnet	C. cannabina																				LI			1660
*A	Twite	C. flavirostris																				TW			1662
*A	Lesser Redpoll	C. cabaret																				LR			1663
*A	Mealy Redpoll	C. flammea																					A		1663
A	Arctic Redpoll	C. hornemanni																				AL			1664
	Sub total																								

BOU	FINCHES, NEW WORLD WARBLERS		Life list	2010 list	24 hr	Garden	Holiday	Jan	Feb	Mar	Apr	May	Jun	Jul	Aug	Sep	Oct	Nov	Dec		BTO	RBBP	BBRC	EU No
* A	Two-barred Crossbill	Loxia leucoptera																			PD		R	1665
* A	Common Crossbill	L. curvirostra																			CR			1666
* A	Scottish Crossbill	L. scotica																			CY	A		1667
* A	Parrot Crossbill	L. pytyopsittacus																			PC	A		1668
A	Trumpeter Finch	Bucanetes githagineus																					R	1676
* A	Common Rosefinch	Carpodacus erythrinus																			SQ	A		1679
A	Pine Grosbeak	Pinicola enucleator																					R	1699
* A	Bullfinch	Pyrrhula pyrrhula																			BF			1710
* A	Hawfinch	Coccothraustes coccothraustes																			HF	A		1717
A	Evening Grosbeak	Hesperiphona vespertina																					R	1718
A	Black-and-white Warbler	Mniotilta varia																					R	1720
A	Golden-winged Warbler	Vermivora chrysoptera																					R	1722
A	Tennessee Warbler	V. peregrina																					R	1724
A	Northern Parula	Parula americana																					R	1732
A	Yellow Warbler	Dendroica petechia																					R	1733
A	Chestnut-sided Warbler	D. pensylvanica																					R	1734
A	Blackburnian Warbler	D. fusca																					R	1747
A	Cape May Warbler	D. tigrina																					R	1749
A	Magnolia Warbler	D. magnolia																					R	1750
A	Yellow-rumped Warbler	D. coronata																					R	1751
A	Blackpoll Warbler	D. striata																					R	1753
A	Bay-breasted Warbler	D. castanea																					R	1754
A	American Redstart	Setophaga ruticilla																			AD		R	1755
A	Ovenbird	Seiurus aurocapilla																					R	1756
	Sub total																							

BOU	NEW WORLD WARBLERS, SPARROWS, BUNTINGS		Life list	2010 list	24 hr	Garden	Holiday	Jan	Feb	Mar	Apr	May	Jun	Jul	Aug	Sep	Oct	Nov	Dec			BTO	RBBP	BBRC	EU No
A	Northern Waterthrush	S. noveboracensis																						R	1757
A	Common Yellowthroat	Geothlypis trichas																						R	1762
A	Hooded Warbler	Wilsonia citrina																						R	1771
A	Wilson's Warbler	W. pusilla																						R	1772
A	Summer Tanager	Piranga rubra																						R	1786
A	Scarlet Tanager	P. olivacea																						R	1788
A	Eastern Towhee	Pipilo erythrophthalmus																						R	1798
A	Lark Sparrow	Chondestes grammacus																						R	1824
A	Savannah Sparrow	Passerculus sandwichensis																						R	1826
A	Song Sparrow	Melospiza melodia																						R	1835
A	White-crowned Sparrow	Zonotrichia leucophrys																						R	1839
A	White-throated Sparrow	Z. albicollis																						R	1840
A	Dark-eyed Junco	Junco hyemalis																				JU		R	1842
A	Lapland Bunting	Calcarius lapponicus																				LA	A		1847
*A	Snow Bunting	Plectrophenax nivalis																				SB	A		1850
A	Black-faced Bunting	Emberiza spodocephala																						R	1853
A	Pine Bunting	E. leucocephalos																				EL			1856
*A	Yellowhammer	E. citrinella																				Y			1857
*A	Cirl Bunting	E. cirlus																				CL	A		1958
A	Rock Bunting	E. cia																						R	1860
A	Ortolan Bunting	E. hortulana																				OB			1866
A	Cretzschmar's Bunting	E. caesia																						R	1868
A	Yellow-browed Bunting	E. chrysophrys																						R	1871
A	Rustic Bunting	E. rustica																							1873
	Sub total																								

87

BUNTINGS Cont

BOU	Name	Scientific	Life list	2010 list	24 hr	Garden	Holiday	Jan	Feb	Mar	Apr	May	Jun	Jul	Aug	Sep	Oct	Nov	Dec	BTO	RBBP	BBRC	EU No
A	Chestnut-eared Bunting	E. fucata																				R	1869
A	Little Bunting	E. pusilla																		LJ			1874
A	Yellow-breasted Bunting	E. aureola																			A	R	1876
* A	Reed Bunting	E. schoeniclus																		RB			1877
A	Pallas's Reed Bunting	E. pallasi																				R	1878
A	Black-headed Bunting	E. melanocephala																				R	1881
* A	Corn Bunting	E. calandra																		CB			1882
A	Rose-breasted Grosbeak	Pheucticus ludovicianus																				R	1887
A	Indigo Bunting	Passerina cyanea																				R	1892
A	Bobolink	Dolichonyx oryzivorus																				R	1897
A	Brown-headed Cowbird	Molothrus ater																				R	1899
A	Baltimore Oriole	Icterus galbula																				R	1918
	Sub total																						

BOU	CATEGORY D & E SPECIES, PLUS SELECTED EUROPEAN SPECIES		Life list	2010 list	24 hr	Garden	Holiday	Jan	Feb	Mar	Apr	May	Jun	Jul	Aug	Sep	Oct	Nov	Dec	BTO	RBBP	BBRC	EU No
D	Ross's Goose	Anas Vosii																					
D	Falcated Duck	A. falcata																		FT		R	0181
D	Baikal Teal	A. formosa																		IK		R	0183
D	Marbled Duck	Marmaronetta angustirostris																				R	0195
EU	White-headed Duck	O. Leucocephala																		WQ			0226
EU	Rock Partridge	Alectoris graeca																					0357
EU	Barbary Partridge	A. barbara																					0359
EU	Pygmy Cormorant	P. pygmeus																					0082
D	Great White Pelican	Pelecanus onocrotalus																		YP		R	0088
EU	Dalmatian Pelican	P. crispus																					0089
D	Greater Flamingo	Phoenicopterus roseus																		FL		R	0147
EU	Black-winged Kite	Elanus caeruleus																					0235
D	Bald Eagle	H. leucocephalus																				R	0244
EU	Lammergeier	Gypaetus barbatus																					0246
D	Black (Monk) Vulture	Aegypius monachus																				R	0255
EU	Levant Sparrowhawk	A. brevipes																					0273
EU	Long-legged Buzzard	B. rufinus																					0288
EU	Lesser Spotted Eagle	Aquila pomarina																					0292
EU	Imperial Eagle	A. heliaca																					0295
EU	Booted Eagle	Hieraaetus pennatus																					0298
EU	Bonelli's Eagle	H. fasciatus																		FB			0299
EU	Lanner Falcon	Falco biarmicus																					0314
D	Saker Falcon	F. cherrug																		JF		R	0316
EU	Andalusian Hemipode	Turnix sylvatica																					0400
	Sub total																						

89

BOU	CATEGORY D & E SPECIES, PLUS SELECTED EUROPEAN SPECIES		Life list	2010 list	24 hr	Garden	Holiday	Jan	Feb	Mar	Apr	May	Jun	Jul	Aug	Sep	Oct	Nov	Dec				BTO	RBBP	BBRC	EU No
EU	Purple (Swamp-hen) Gallinule	*Porphyrio porphyrio*																								0427
EL	Crested Coot	*F. cristata*																								0431
FA	Greater Sand Plover	*C. leschenaultii*																					DP		R	0479
EU	Spur-winged Plover	*Hoplopterus spinosus*																					UW			0487
EU	Black-bellied Sandgrouse	*Pterocles orientalis*																								0661
EU	Pin-tailed Sandgrouse	*P. alchata*																								0662
EU	(Eurasian) Eagle Owl	*Bubo bubo*																					EO	bD		0744
EU	Pygmy Owl	*Glaucidium passerinum*																								0751
EU	Ural Owl	*S. uralensis*																								0765
EU	Great Grey Owl	*S. nebulosa*																								0766
EL	White-rumped Swift	*A. melba*																								0799
EU	Grey-headed Woodpecker	*Picus canus*																								0855
EU	Black Woodpecker	*Dryocopus martius*																								0863
EU	Syrian Woodpecker	*D. syriacus*																								0878
EU	Middle Spotted Woodpecker	*D. medius*																								0883
EU	White-backed Woodpecker	*D. leucotos*																								0884
EU	Three-toed Woodpecker	*Picoides tridactylus*																								0898
EU	Dupont's Lark	*Chersophilus duponti*																								0959
EU	Thekla Lark	*G. theklae*																								0973
EU	Black Wheatear	*O. leucura*																							R	1158
IA	Eyebrowed Thrush	*T. obscurus*																							R	1195
EU	Olive-tree Warbler	*H. olivetorum*																								1258
EU	Cyprus Warbler	*S. melanothorax*																								1268
D	Mugimaki Flycatcher	*F. mugimaki*																							R	1344
	Sub total																									

BOU	CATEGORY D & E SPECIES, PLUS SELECTED EUROPEAN SPECIES		Life list	2010 list	24 hr	Garden	Holiday	Jan	Feb	Mar	Apr	May	Jun	Jul	Aug	Sep	Oct	Nov	Dec				BTO	RBBP	BBRC	EU No
EU	Semi-collared Flycatcher	F. semitorquata																								1347
EU	Sombre Tit	P. lugubris																								1441
EU	Siberian Tit	P. cinctus																								1448
EU	Krüper's Nuthatch	Sitta krueperi																								1469
EU	Corsican Nuthatch	S. whiteheadi																								1470
EU	Rock Nuthatch	S. neumayer																								1481
EU	Masked Shrike	L. nubicus																								1524
EU	Siberian Jay	Perisoreus infaustus																								1543
EU	Azure-winged Magpie	Cyanopica cyana																								1547
EU	Alpine Chough	Pyrrhocorax graculus																								1558
D	Daurian Starling	Sturnus sturninus																							R	1579
EU	Spotless Starling	S. unicolor																								1583
D	(White-winged) Snow Finch	Montifringilla nivalis																							R	1611
D	Palm Warbler	D. palmarum																							R	1752
D	Yellow-headed Blackbird	Xanthocephalus xanthocephalus																								1911
EU	Cinereous Bunting	E. cineracea																								1865
D	Chestnut Bunting	E. rutila																							R	1875
D	Red-headed Bunting	E. bruniceps																								1880
D	Blue Grosbeak	Guiraca caerulea																							R	1891
	Sub total																								

91

BRITISH DRAGONFLY LIST

SPECIES	2010 list	Life list
DAMSELFLIES		
Calopterygidae (Demoiselles)		
Beautiful Demoiselle		
Banded Demoiselle		
Lestidae (Emerald damselflies)		
Emerald Damselfly		
Scarce Emerald Damselfly		
Southern Emerald Damselfly		
Willow Emerald Damselfly		
Winter Damselfly		
Platycnemididae (White-legged damselflies)		
White-legged Damselfly		
Coenagrionidae (Blue, blue-tailed & red damselflies)		
Large Red Damselfly		
Red-eyed Damselfly		
Small Red Damselfly		
Southern Damselfly		
Northern Damselfly		
Irish Damselfly		
Azure Damselfly		
Variable Damselfly		
Common Blue Damselfly		
Scarce Blue-tailed Damselfly		
Blue-tailed Damselfly		
Small Red-eyed Damselfly		
DRAGONFLIES		
Aeshnidae (Hawkers and Emperors)		
Azure Hawker		
Common Hawker		
Migrant Hawker		
Southern Hawker		
Brown Hawker		
Southern Migrant Hawker		

SPECIES	2010 list	Life list
Norfolk Hawker		
Emperor		
Lesser Emperor		
Green Darner		
Vagrant Emperor		
Hairy Dragonfly		
Gomphidae (Club-tailed Dragonflies)		
Common Club-tail		
Cordulegastridae (Golden-ringed Dragonflies)		
Golden-ringed Dragonfly		
Corduliidae (Emerald dragonflies)		
Downy Emerald		
Brilliant Emerald		
Northern Emerald		
Libellulidae (Chasers, Skimmers and Darters)		
Four-spotted Chaser		
Scarce Chaser		
Broad-bodied Chaser		
Black-tailed Skimmer		
Keeled Skimmer		
Common Darter		
Highland Darter		
Red-veined Darter		
Yellow-winged Darter		
Ruddy Darter		
Black Darter		
Vagrant Darter		
Banded Darter		
Scarlet Darter		
Wandering Glider		
White-faced Darter		
TOTAL		

BRITISH BUTTERFLY LIST

SPECIES	2010 list	Life list
Hesperiidae - Skippers		
Chequered Skipper		
Dingy Skipper		
Grizzled Skipper		
Lulworth Skipper		
Essex Skipper		
Small Skipper		
Silver-spotted Skipper		
Large Skipper		
Papilionidae		
Swallowtail		
Pieridae - The Whites		
Wood White		
Clouded Yellow		
Brimstone		
Large White		
Small White		
Green-veined White		
Orange Tip		
Lycaenidae - Hairstreaks, Coppers and Blues		
Green Hairstreak		
Brown Hairstreak		
Purple Hairstreak		
White-letter Hairstreak		
Black Hairstreak		
Small Copper		
Small Blue		
Silver-studded Blue		
Northern Brown Argus		
Brown Argus		
Common Blue		
Chalkhill Blue		
Adonis Blue		
Holly Blue		

SPECIES	2010 list	Life list
Large Blue		
Duke of Burgundy		
Nymphalidae - The Nymphalids		
White Admiral		
Purple Emperor		
Painted Lady		
Small Tortoiseshell		
Red Admiral		
Peacock		
Comma		
Nymphalidae - The Fritillaries		
Small Pearl-bordered Fritillary		
Pearl-bordered Fritillary		
High Brown Fritillary		
Dark Green Fritillary		
Silver-washed Fritillary		
Marsh Fritillary		
Glanville Fritillary		
Heath Fritillary		
Nymphalidae - The Browns		
Speckled Wood		
Wall		
Mountain Ringlet		
Scotch Argus		
Marbled White		
Grayling		
Gate Keeper		
Meadow Brown		
Ringlet		
Small Heath		
Large Heath		
TOTAL		

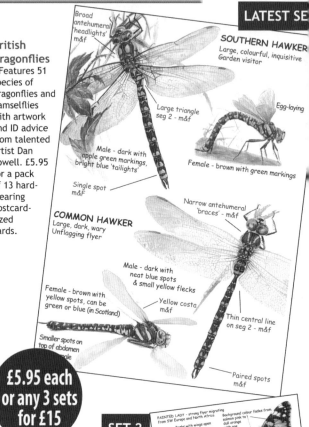

DIRECTORY OF ARTISTS, PHOTOGRAPHERS AND LECTURERS

Tony Bates, who took this photograph of a Steller's Jay during one of his visits to the United States, is listed in the Lecturer's Directory.

ART/PHOTOGRAPHY/LECTURERS

DIRECTORY OF
WILDLIFE ART GALLERIES

BIRDSBIRDSBIRDS GALLERY

Paul and Sue Cumberland opened Birds Birds Birds in June 2001. Now it is becoming one of the nation's leading bird art galleries. A steady increase in sales has encouraged professional wildlife artists to join the roster. Prints are now being produced and published in-house, using the giclee system. The gallery exhibits at Birdfair and various game fairs and county shows.
Address: 4, Limes Place, Preston St, Faversham, Kent ME13 8PQ; 01795 532 370;
email: birdsbirdsbirds@birdsbirdsbirds.co.uk
www.birdsbirdsbirds.co.uk

BIRDSCAPES GALLERY

Offers top quality bird art all year round, plus landscapes and other wildlife originals, sculptures, prints, wildlife art books and cards. More than 30 regular artists, including SWLA members, are represented, with new exhibitions each month.
Located next to the Cley Spy optical dealership and offering the opportunity of exploring the Farmland Bird Project on the Bayfield Estate.
Opening times: Mon-Sat, (10am-5pm), Sunday, (10am-4pm). The gallery may be closed for part of the day before a new exhibition.
Address: The BIRDscapes Gallery, Manor Farm Barns, Glandford, Holt, Norfolk. NR25 7JP. 01263 741 742. (Follow the brown signs to Cley Spy from Blakeney Church).

NATURE IN ART

The world's first museum dedicated exclusively to art inspired by nature. The collection spans 1,500 years, covers 60 countries and includes work by Tunnicliffe, Harrison, Thorburn, Scott and other bird artists. See work being created by artists in residence (see website for dates), plus a vibrant exhibitions programme. Sculpture garden, coffee shop, gift shop and children's activity areas.
Opening times: 10am-5pm (Tuesday to Sunday and bank holidays).
Address: Wallsworth Hall, Twigworth, Gloucester GL2 9PA (two miles N of city on A38). 01452 731 422. e-mail: enquiries@nature-in-art.org.uk
www.nature-in-art.org.uk

THE WILDLIFE ART GALLERY

Opened in 1988 as a specialist in 20th Century and contemporary wildlife art. It exhibits work by many of the leading European wildlife artists, both painters and sculptors, and has published several wildlife books.
Opening times: Mon-Sat (10am-4.30pm) and Sun (2pm-4.30pm).
Address: 97 High Street, Lavenham, Suffolk CO10 9PZ; 01787 248 562; (Fax) 01787 247 356.
E-mail: wildlifeartgallery@btinternet.com
www.wildlifeartgallery.com

DIRECTORY OF
WILDLIFE ARTISTS

ALLEN, Richard

Watercolour paintings, sketches and illustrations of birds, wildlife, flowers and landscapes, mainly based on extensive field sketching. Book work includes: *Sunbirds* (Helm) and *Guide to Birds of SE Asia* (New Holland). Stamp designs for The Solomons, Ascencion Island and Kiribati and murals, maps and interpretation boards for RSPB.
Exhibitions for 2010: British Birdfair, Rutland Water, August 2010.
Artwork for sale: Watercolour paintings, limited edition prints, original cover paintings from *Birding World* and header illustrations from *British Birds*. See website for details.
Address: 34 Parkwood Avenue, Wivenhoe, Essex, CO7 9AN; 01206 826 753.
e-mail: richard@richardallen31.wanadoo.co.uk
www.richardallenillustrator.com

APLIN, Roy

Born in Swanage, Isle of Purbeck now part of the Jurassic coastline. Lives in Wareham with easy access to Arne RSPB nature reserve (Dartford Warbler habitat). Self-taught artist, carpenter/

DIRECTORY OF WILDLIFE ARTISTS

joiner by trade, also involved in aviculture since the age of 9.
Exhibitions for 2010: Purbeck art weeks - end of May to first week of June; British Birdfair; Dorset Coppice Group country events.
Artwork for sale: Original watercolours plus goache paintings, limited edition prints, pencil sketches, cards.
Address: 11 Brixeys Lane, Wareham, Dorset BH20 4HL; 01929 553 742.
e-mail: roy.aplin@ukonline.co.uk
www.royaplin.com

BECKETT, Andrew

Worked as a freelance illustrator for 16 years represented by the agency Illustration Ltd. Exhibited as a wildlife artist at Birds in Art and NEWA (National Exhibition of Wildlife Art). Part-time lecturer of Scientific and Natural History Illustration at Blackpool & the Fylde College.
Formats: Original artwork, prints (mounted or framed).
Exhibitions for 2010: NEWA (see events diary for dates).
Artwork for sale: Contact the artist.
Address: 7 Buckingham Road, Lytham St Annes, Lancs FY8 4EU; 01253 730 167 mobile: 07946 820 156. e-mail: andysart@freeuk.com
www.illustrationweb.com/andrewbeckett

COOK, Robert A

Careful study, thoughtful composition and evocative light are the key elements in Rob's work. He has exhibited widely, including Birds in Art, NEWA and MIWAS. In 2009 his work was awarded *Wildscape* magazine 'Wildlife Artist of The Year' title and won *BBC Wildlife* Artist of the Year 'Animals in their Environment' award.
Formats: Oils, waterclour, pencil and charcoal.
Exhibitions for 2010: Please see website for details.
Artwork for sale: Original paintings, drawings and prints, commissions accepted and enquiries welcomed.
Address: 16 Beverley Avenue, Poulton-le-Fylde, Lancashire, FY6 8BN; 01253 884 849.
e-mail: info@robcookart.com
www.robcookart.com

DEMAIN, Michael

Started painting in 1992, turning professional in 2002. In his spare time he helps the RSPB monitor breeding raptors in the Bowland Fells.
Formats: Original paintings and limited edition reproductions.
Exhibitions for 2010: British Falconry Fair, Scottish Game Fair, CLA Game Fair, British Bird Fair.

Artwork for sale: A selection of gouache and oil paintings and limited edition prints.
Address: 175 Richmond Road, Accrington, Lancs BB5 0JB; 01254 237 378.
e-mail: mdemainwildart@aol.com
www.michaeldemainwildlifeart.co.uk

GALE, John

Bird illustrator and wildlife artist, concentrating on the Tropics and Antarctica
Formats: Oil paintings and bird illustration work.
Exhibitions for 2010: Major five week research trip to South Georgia, painting albatrosses and petrels in January 2010.
Products and services: Oil paintings and illustration work.
Address: 6 Underdown, Kennford, Exeter, Devon EX6 7YB; 01392 832 026.
e-mail: johngale@birdart.fsnet.co.uk
www.galleryofbirds.co.uk

GARNER, Jackie

Original paintings based on field sketches. Current projects: illustrations for Poyser Snowy Owl monograph, illustrations for research project on Egyptian wildlife. See website for details.
Exhibitions for 2010: Open Studio (June); British Birdwatching Fair (Aug); Nature in Art residency (28 Sept- 3 Oct); SWLA; exhibition WWT Slimbridge (Nov 7, 2010 to Jan 3, 2011).
Artwork for sale: Originals, limited edition prints, cards. Commissions accepted.
Address: The Old Cider House, Humphries End, Randwick, Stroud, Glos GL6 6EW.
01453 847 420/ 07800 804 847
e-mail: artist@jackiegarner.co.uk
www.jackiegarner.co.uk

GREENHALF, Robert

Fulltime painter and printmaker. Member of SWLA. Work features in many books including *Modern Wildlife Painting* (Pica Press 1998), Artists for Nature Foundation books on Poland and Extremadura and *Towards the Sea* (Pica Press 1999) - first solo book.
Formats: Watercolours, oils and woodcuts, available through galleries my website.
Exhibitions for 2010: SWLA (Mall Galleries, Sept).
Artwork for sale: Watercolours, oils and woodcuts, available through my website.
Address: Romney House, Saltburn Lane, Playden, Rye, East Sussex, TN33 7PH; 01797 222 381.
e-mail: robertgreenhalf@googlemail.com
www.robertgreenhalf.co.uk

DIRECTORY OF WILDLIFE ARTISTS

GRIFFITHS, Griff
Paintings of birds in the landscape mainly taken from field sketches around Cornwall but also drawing on his travels overseas and living around the UK coast. Recent experiments in oils have produced more abstract and spontaneous paintings alongside the more realistic acrylics.
Formats: Acrylics, oils and watercolours.
Exhibitions for 2010: WWT Slimbridge; Gallery Tresco, Isles of Scilly. Please see website for further details.
Artwork for sale: Commissions welcomed.
Address: Griffs Wildlife Studio, Creftow, 6 Church Street, Helston, Cornwall,TR13 8TG; 07971 678 464. E-mail: mail@artbygriff.com
www.artbygriff.com

HOOPER, Lisa
Artist/printmaker living and working in Dumfries and Galloway. Regular contributor to National Wildlife Exhibitions. Winner of *Birds Illustrated* prize (2008) for the most outstanding piece of avian art (NEWA).
Formats: Mixed print media (etchings, woodcuts etc).
Exhibitions for 2010: Programme available on website or phone for leaflet.
Artwork for sale: Work on display at address below, on website and at local outlets.
Address: Hoopoe Prints, Seymour House, 25 High Street, Port William, Newton Stewart, Dumfries DG8 9SL; 01988 700 392. www.hoopoeprints.co.uk

LEAHY, Ernest
Original watercolours and drawings of Western Palearctic birds, wildlife and country scenes. Also paints British mammals and butterflies. Illustrations for many publications including Poysers. Wide range of framed and unframed originals available. Commissions accepted and enquiries welcome.
Formats: E-mail for details of current work available and for quotations on commissioned work.
Exhibitions for 2010: Birdfair 2010, Rutland Water. Contact the artist for other forthcoming events.
Artwork for sale: See www.flickr.com/photos/ernsbirdart for latest work.
Address: 32 Ben Austins, Redbourn, Herts, AL3 7DR; 01582 793 144.
e-mail: ernest.leahy@ntlworld.com
www.flickr.com/photos/ernsbirdart
www.wildlifewatercolours.co.uk

LINGHAM, Steven
Fulltime wildlife and landscape artist, private collectors worldwide. First prize for the 'Best Bird Painting' in the MIWAS 2008 exhibition, plus 'Best British Wildlife Painting' award at MIWAS 2009 show.
Exhibitions for 2010: Please see website for details.
Artwork for sale: Originals, limited edition prints and greeting cards. All commissions undertaken.
Address: 07779 694 576;
e-mail: info@stevenlingham.com
www.stevenlingham.com
or www.natureartists.com

MILLER, David
David lives and works in the heart of west Wales in a wooded valley with the dramatic Pembrokeshire coastline on his doorstep. Well known for his underwater paintings of game, sea and coarse fish David also specialises in sea-birds and waders and regularly exhibits at the British Birdfair.
Artwork for sale: Original oils and prints of British wildlife, fish and birds.
Address: Nyth-Gwdi-Hw, New Mill, St Clears, Carmarthenshire SA33 4HY; 01994 453 545.
e-mail: david@davidmillerart.co.uk
www.davidmillerart.co.uk

NEILL, William
Watercolours and acrylics of the landscape and wildlife of the Outer Hebrides. Visit the Studio Gallery, Askernish, South Uist, for an update on what to see and where to go for everything from orchids and bumblebees to otters and birds.
Exhibitions for 2010: SWLA exhibition, Mall Galleries, London (Sep).
Artwork for sale: Watercolours, acrylics, limited editions and cards.
Address: Rannachan, Askernish, South Uist, Western Isles, HS8 5SY; 01878 700 237.
E-mail: bill_neill@hotmail.com
www.william-neill.co.uk

POMROY, Jonathan
Works in watercolour and oils, always from sketches, made on trips across the British Isles, most recently to the Isles of Scilly, Anglesey & Snowdonia, North West Scotland, Yorkshire Dales and coast and Slimbridge as well as around home in by the North York Moors. Work always on show at Birdscapes, Cley, Norfolk, Leverton Framers near Hungerford, Berkshire, The Wykeham Gallery, Stockbridge, Herriot Gallery, Hawes and at home in Ampleforth.
Exhibitions for 2010: February 27- March 14 at Wykeham Gallery, Stockbridge; April at the Herriot Gallery, Hawes; July 23- 27 at West Barn, Bradford on Avon; Autumn at Helmsley Arts Centre, North Yorkshire — See website for dates and further details of these and other exhibitions.

DIRECTORY OF WILDLIFE PHOTOGRAPHERS

Artwork for sale: Chiefly selling original watercolours and oils at one-man exhibitions and from website.
Address: Swift House, Back Lane, Ampleforth, North Yorkshire YO62 4DE;
www.jonathanpomroy.co.uk
e-mail: jonathan@pomroy.plus.com

ROSE, Chris

Originals in oils and acrylics of birds and animals in landscapes. Particular interest in painting water and its myriad effects. Limited edition reproductions available.
  In a Natural Light - the Wildlife Art of Chris Rose publised 2005. Illustrated many books including *Grebes of the World* (publ.2002) and *Handbook to the Birds of the World*.
Exhibitions for 2010: British Birdfair (Aug); SWLA (Mall Galleries, Sept 2010).
Artwork for sale: Original drawings and paintings, linocuts, illustrations, limited edition reproductions, postcards.
Address: 6 Whitelee Cottages, Newtown St Boswells, Melrose, Scotland TD6 0SH;
(Tel/Fax)01835 822 547.
e-mail: chris@chrisrose-artist.co.uk
www.chrisrose-artist.co.uk

SCOTT, Dafila

Trained as a zoologist then studied art under Robin Child at the Lydgate Art Research Centre UK. Has exhibited widely in the UK. Recent work includes both figurative and abstract paintings of wildlife, people and landscape.
Formats: Oil, acrylics and pastels.
Exhibitions for 2010: SWLA (Mall Galleries, Sept 2010).
Artwork for sale: Media: Oil, acrylics and pastels of birds, wildlife, people and abstract landscapes.
Address: White Roses, The Hythe, Reach, Cambridgeshire CB5 0JQ.
e-mail: dafilascott@yahoo.co.uk
www.dafilascott.co.uk

THRELFALL, John

Member of the Society of Wildlife Artists. Swarovski/Birdwatch Bird Artist of the Year 2007. Award winner at the NEWA Exhibition, 2001, 2004, 2006. Birdscapes Gallery award 2007.
Formats: Paintings in acrylic or pastel.
Exhibitions for 2010: 1) Scottish Ornithologists Club, Waterston House, Aberlady, East Lothian (April 3 - May 19). 2) The Rockcliffe Gallery, Rockcliffe, Kirkcudbrightshire (May 1-31).
Artwork for sale: Contact artist.
Address: Saltflats Cottage, Rockcliffe, Dalbeattie, Kirkcudbrightshire, DG5 4QQ; 01556 630 262.
www.johnthrelfall.co.uk

WARREN, Michael

Member of Society of Wildlife Artists (treasurer). President of Nottinghamshire Birdwatchers.
Exhibitions for 2010: Wildlife Art Gallery, Lavenham, Suffolk - June. Rutland bird fair - August. SWLA annual exhibition - September. See website for other information.
Artwork for sale: Original watercolour paintings of birds, all based on field observations. Books, calendars, cards and commissions welcomed..
Address: The Laurels, The Green, Winthorpe, Nottinghamshire, NG24 2NR; 01636 673 554; (Fax)01636 611 569.
e-mail: mike.warren@tiscali.co.uk
www.mikewarren.co.uk

WOODHEAD, Darren

Original watercolours of all aspects of the outside — birds, butterflies, mammals and other wildlife subjects, as well as landscapes and cloudscapes. All subjects painted direct in the field. Commissions undertaken.
Exhibitions for 2009/2010: Waterston House, The Headquarters of the Scottish Ornithologists Club, Aberlady (November 28, 2009 to February 3, 2010), Wildlife Art Gallery, Lavenham, Suffolk (Autumn), SWLA exhibition, Mall Galleries, London (Sept), others to be announced on the website.
Artwork for sale: Original watercolour paintings and brush drawings, sketches and pen drawings. Two solo books, *From Dawn Till Dusk* published by Langford Press in 2005, and *Up River, The Song of the Esk* published by Birlinn in August 2009. The latest book celebrates three years of work along a short stretch of river in the picturesque Scottish Borders.
Address: 36 Stoneybank Road, Musselburgh, East Lothian, EH21 6HJ; 0131 665 6802.
e-mail: darren.woodhead@virgin.net
www.darrenwoodheadartist.co.uk

WOOLF, Colin

Beautiful original watercolour paintings. The atmosphere of a landscape and the character of his subject are his hallmark, also the pure watercolour technique that imparts a softness to the natural subjects he paints. Owls, birds of prey and ducks are specialities. Commissions accepted.
Formats: Original paintings, limited edition prints and greetings cards.
Exhibitions for 2010: See website for exhibitions in 2010.
Artwork for sale: Please ring for personal viewing or visit website. *Daring To Fly* book, details Colin's artistic career and can be ordered via his website.
Address: Ardbeg, 2 Blairhill View, Blackridge, West Lothian EH48 3TR; 01501 751 796.
E-mail: colin@wildart.co.uk www.wildart.co.uk

ART/PHOTOGRAPHY/LECTURERS

99

DIRECTORY OF
WILDLIFE PHOTOGRAPHERS

BASTON, Bill
Photographer, lecturer.
Subjects: East Anglian rarities and common birds, Mediterranean birds and landscapes, UK wildlife and landscapes, Florida birds and landscapes, Northern Greece, Spain, western Turkey, Goa. General wildlife photography.
Products and services: Prints, slides, digital, mounted/unmounted.
Address: 86 George Street, Hadleigh, Ipswich, IP7 5BU; 01473 827 062. www.billbaston.com
e-mail: billbaston@btinternet.com

BATES, Tony
Photographer and lecturer.
Subjects: Mainly British wildlife, landscapes and astro landscapes.
Products and services: Prints (mounted or framed), original hand-made photo greetings cards.
Address: 22 Fir Avenue, Bourne, Lincs, PE10 9RY; 01778 425 137.
e-mail: tonybatesphotos@live.co.uk

BEJARANO, Santiago
An Ecuadorean naturalist and wildlife photographer who worked in the Galapagos for over a decade, with a great depth of knowledge and unique insight into these remarkable islands and their wildlife.
Subjects: Flora and fauna of Galapagos Islands and birds of Ecuador.
Products and services: Prints and posters of the wildlife of the Glapagos Islands and birds of Ecuador. Introductory classes to wildlife photography, including digital and basic Photoshop techniques.
Address: 25 Trinity Lane, Beverley, East Yorkshire HU17 0DY; 01482 872 716.
e-mail: info@thinkgalapagos.karoo.co.uk
www.thinkgalapagos.com

BELL, Graham
Professional ornithologist, photographer, author, cruise lecturer worldwide.
Subjects: Birds, animals, flowers, landscapes, all seven continents, from Arctic to Antarctic.
Products and services: Original slides for sale, £2 each.
Address: Ros View, South Yearle, Wooler, Northumberland, NE71 6RB; 01668 281310.
e-mail: seabirdsdgb@hotmail.com

BIRDS EYE VIEW PHOTOS
James Bird: Photographer, lecturer and former RSPB local group leader.
Subjects: Wildlife and worldwide travel images, having spent 23 years living abroad.
Products for sale: Prints, both mounted and unmounted, or framed for sale. Laminated cards in all sizes with free magazines and information leaflets given.
Address: Six Valentine Gardens, Kimbolton, Huntingdon, Cambridgeshire PE28 0HX; Tel/fax: 01480 861 955; (M)07914 633 355.
e-mail: jamesbird007@yahoo.co.uk

BOULTON, David
Professional nature photographer and lecturer.
Subjects: All types of flora and fauna including wild flowers, dragonflies, butterflies, fungi, trees, birds and animals and landscape photography (Norfolk and the Broads, Peak District, Yorkshire Dales and Lake District).
Products and services: 17 talks (audio/visual with relaxing music and sounds of nature). Photographic workshops, greetings cards, bookmarks and prints also available.
Address: 1 Mantle Close, Sprowston, Norwich, Norfolk NR7 8LD : 01603 415 610.
e-mail: dbp@ownersmail.co.uk
www.davidboulton.co.uk

BROADBENT, David
Professional photographer.
Subjects: UK birds and wild places.
Products and services: Top quality photographic prints. See website for details.
Address: Rose Cottage, Bream Road, Whitepool, St Briavels, Lydney, GL15 6TL; 07771 664973.
e-mail: info@davidbroadbent.com
www.davidbroadbent.com

BROOKS, Richard
Wildlife photographer, writer, lecturer.
Subjects: Owls (Barn especially), raptors, Kingfisher and a variety of European birds (Lesvos especially) and landscapes.
Products and services: Mounted and unmounted computer prints (6x4 - A3+ size), framed pictures, A5 greetings cards, surplus slides for sale. Limited edition calendars available.
Address: 24 Croxton Hamlet, Fulmodeston, Fakenham, Norfolk, NR21 0NP; 01328 878 632.
e-mail: email@richard-brooks.co.uk
www.richard-brooks.co.uk

DIRECTORY OF WILDLIFE PHOTOGRAPHERS

BUCKINGHAM, John
Worldwide bird and wildlife photographer
Subjects: Huge range of birds, botany and
wildlife in UK and Europe, plus great coverage
from Africa, Americas, Australia and worldwide..
Products and services: Original slides for lectures
and personal use.
Address: 3 Cardinal Close, Tonbridge, Kent TN9
2EN; (Tel/fax) 01732 354 970.
e-mail: john@buckingham7836.freeserve.co.uk

COSTER, Bill
Professional wildlife photographer, writer and
photographic tour leader. Author of *Creative Bird
Photography*.
Subjects: Wildlife and landscape from around the
world.
Products and services: Images for publication,
prints for sale. See my webite for details.
Stunning new digital shows (see Directory of
Lecturers).
Address: 17 Elm Road, South Woodham Ferrers,
Chelmsford, Essex CM3 5QB; 01245 320 066.
e-mail: billcoster@hotmail.com
www.billcoster.com

DUGGAN, Glenn
Specialist in tropical birding.
Subjects: Tropical birds, Trogons, Tanagers, Birds
of Paradise.
Address: 25 Hampton Grove, Fareham,
Hampshire, PO15 5NL; 01329 845 976, (M)07771
605 320.
e-mail: glenn.m.duggan@ntlworld.com
www.birdlectures.com

ELSBY, Kevin
General natural history with more than 30 years'
wildlife photography experience.
Subjects: All areas especially birds, mammals,
insects and plants.
Products and services: Images for sale via my
website, lecturer, tour guide.
Address: Wildlife on the Web, Chapel House,
Bridge Road, Colby, Norwich, NR22 8TB; 01263
732 839. e-mail: wildlife@greenbeelnet
www.wildlifeontheweb.co.uk

GALVIN, Chris
A birding photographer with passion for birds for
more than 30 years.
Subjects: Birds from the UK and abroad.
Products and services: Images for publication,
prints, mounted prints, commisions considered.
Address: 17 Henley Road, Allerton, Liverpool,
Merseyside, L18 2DN; 07802 428 385
or 0151 729 0123.
e-mail: chris@chrisgalvinphoto.com
www.chrisgalvinphoto.com

HAMBLIN, Mark
Freelance nature and landscape photographer and
writer.
Subjects: European wildlife and Scottish
landscapes.
Products and services: Photographic
commissions, books, greetings cards, fine art
prints.
Address: Ballinlaggan Farm, Duthil, Carr-bridge,
Inverness-shire, PH23 3ND; 01479 841 547.
e-mail: mark@markhamblin.com
www.markhamblin.com

HOBSON, Paul
Environmental science lecturer, photographer
for 20-plus years. Bias towards N.Europe, plus
conservation issues, particularly UK.
Subjects: Wildlife, UK and global, mainly UK, plus
N.Europe, including birds, mammals, invertibrates
and plants.
Products and services: Talks, workshops, 1:1
tuition, prints, tour leading.
Address: Sheffield. 0114 232 3699.
e-mail: paul.hobson6@virgin.net
www.paulhobson.co.uk

LANE, Mike
Wildlife photographer and lecturer.
Subjects: Birds and wildlife from around the
world, also landscapes and the environment.
Products and services: Website with instantly
downloadable online pictures. Talks and
workshops.
Address: 36 Berkeley Road, Shirley, Solihull, West
Midlands B90 2HS; 021 744 7988;
e-mail: mikelane@nature-photography.co.uk
www.nature-photography.co.uk

LANGLEY, John and Tracy
Wildlife photographers, workshop tutors and
lecturers.
Subjects: Birds, mammals, butterflies and other
wildlife. European, plus India (especially tigers).
Products and services: Digital images for
publication and commercial use. Mounted images,
framed images, greeting cards, bookmarks and
calendars.
Address: 16 Carrick Road, Curzon Park, Chester
CH4 8AW; 01244 678 781;
e-mail: little.owl@btopenworld.com
www.ourwildlifephotography.co.uk

DIRECTORY OF WILDLIFE PHOTOGRAPHERS

LANGSBURY, Gordon
Professional wildlife photographer, lecturer, author. Fellow of the Royal Photographic Society.
Subjects: Birds and mammals from UK, Europe, Scandinavia, N America, Gambia, Kenya, Tanzania, Morocco, Falklands and Spitzbergen.
Products and services: Digital and 35mm transparencies for publication, lectures and prints.
Address: Sanderlings, 80 Shepherds Close, Hurley, Maidenhead, Berkshire, SL6 5LZ; 01628 824 252.
e-mail: gordonlangsbury@birdphoto.org.uk
www.birdphoto.org.uk

LENTON, Graham
PhD Ornithology/Ecology. Former lecturer at Oxford University and Oxford Brookes University. Lifetime photographer of wildlife, plus publications of articles and photographs of birds and wildlife.
Subjects: Worldwide birds, mammals of Africa, wildlife, worldwide travel.
Products and services: Photos available for sale or reproduction.
Address: The Old School, 25A Standlake Road, Ducklington, Witney, Oxon OX29 7UR; 01993 899 033. e-mail: grahamlenton@btopenworld.com
www.gml-art.co.uk

LINGARD, David
Wildlife photographer, retired from RAF, now UK delegate to LIPU (BirdLife International partner in Italy).
Subjects: Birds and views of places visited around the world.
Products and services: 35mm transparencies and digital images.
Address: Fernwood, Doddington Road, Whisby, Lincs LN6 9BX; 01522 689 030. www.lipu-uk.org
e-mail: mail@lipu-uk.org

MAGENNIS, Steve
Steve Magennis Wildlife Photography, wildlife photographer, lecturer and workshop leader.
Subjects: British wildlife, bird life and landscapes.
Products and services: Commisioned photography, image library, framed and mounted prints, mounted prints (various sizes), greetings cards (cards can be personalised with personal or company details) and photo keyrings. Photographic workshops, half-day, full-day and holidays.
Address: 3 Chepstow Close, St James, Northampton, Northants, NN5 7EB; 01604 467 848; (M)07803 619 272.
www.stevemagennis.co.uk
e-mail: photos@stevemagennis.co.uk

McKAVETT, Mike
Wildlife photographer and lecturer.
Subjects: Birds and mammals from India, Kenya, The Gambia, Lesvos, N.America, Turkey and UK.
Products and services: 35mm transparencies and digital images for publication and commercial use plus lectures.
Address: 34 Rectory Road, Churchtown, Southport, PR9 7PU; 01704 231 358;
e-mail: mike.mckavett@btinternet.com.

MOCKLER, Mike
Safari guide, tour leader, writer and photographer.
Subjects: Birds and wildlife of Britain, Europe, Central and South America, India, Japan and several African countries. Africa a speciality.
Products and services: 35mm transparencies and digital images.
Address: Gulliver's Cottage, Chapel Rise, Avon Castle, Ringwood, Hampshire, BH24 2BL; 01425 478 103. e-mail: mikemockler@lineone.net
www.mikemockler.co.uk

NASON, Rebecca
UK, East Anglia-based bird and wildlife photographer.
Subjects: Wildlife photography. Specialising in birds from the UK, from Suffolk to Fair Isle..
Products and services: Large image stock library. Professionally printed images available, various sizes, mounts and frames. Acrylics and canvases, greetings cards.
Address: 8 Angel Lane, Woodbridge, Suffolk IP12 4NG; 01394 385 030; (M)07919 256 386.
e-mail: rebecca@rebeccanason.com
www.rebeccanason.com

OFFORD, Keith
Photographer, writer, tour leader, conservationist.
Subjects: Raptors, UK wildlife and scenery, birds and other wildlife of USA, Africa, Spain, Australia, India.
Products and services: Conventional prints, greetings cards, framed pictures.
Address: Yew Tree Farmhouse, Craignant, Selattyn, Nr Oswestry, Shropshire SY10 7NP; 01691 718 740. e-mail: keith-offord@virgin.net
www.keithofford.co.uk

PALMER, Phil
Wildlife photographer and tour leader.
Subjects: A variety of images from around the world.
Products and services: Images for publication available. Please send any requests. See also Lecturer Directory.

DIRECTORY OF WILDLIFE PHOTOGRAPHERS

Address: 43 Grove Coach Road, Retford, Nottinghamshire DN22 7HB; (Tel/fax)0113 391 0510. e-mail: info@birdholidays.co.uk www.birdholidays.co.uk

PARKER, Susan and Allan
Professional photographers (ASPphoto - Images of Nature) lecturers and tutors. Associates of Royal Photographic Society.
Subjects: Birds plus other flora and fauna from the UK, Spain, Lesvos, Cyprus, Florida and Texas.
Products and services: 35mm and digital images, mounted digital images, greetings cards and digital images on CD/DVD for reproduction (high quality scans up to A3+).
Address: Windhover Barn, 51b Kiveton Lane, Todwick, Sheffield, South Yorkshire, S26 1HJ; 01909 770 238. e-mail: aspphoto@tiscali.co.uk

READ, Mike
Photographer (wildlife and landscapes), tour leader, writer.
Subjects: Birds, mammals, plants, landscapes, and some insects. UK, France, USA, Ecuador (including Galapagos) plus many more. Behaviour, action, portraits, artistic pictures available for publication.
Products and services: Prints, greetings cards, books. Extensive stock photo library. More than 100,000 images in stock.
Address: Claremont, Redwood Close, Ringwood, Hampshire, BH24 1PR; 01425 475008.
e-mail: mike@mikeread.co.uk www.mikeread.co.uk

SMART, Oliver
Photographer and lecturer.
Subjects: All wildlife subjects, mainly UK-based, also Canada, Mediterranean, Madagascar, Seychelles and Europe.
Products and services: Bean bags, desk & wall calendars, greeting cards, digital files, mounted & framed prints (to A2 size), photographic workshops and digital slideshow lectures.
Address: 78 Aspen Park Road, Weston-super-Mare, Somerset BS22 8ER; 01934 628 888; (M)07802 417 810.
e-mail: oliver@smartimages.co.uk www.smartimages.co.uk

STEPHEN, Gerry
Subjects: Wildflowers and butterflies etc.
Address: 66 Northumberland Avenue, Thornton

Cleveleys, Lancs FY5 2LH; 01253 860 305, e-mail: melodystephen@hotmail.com

SWASH, Andy and Gill
Professional wildlife photographers and authors.
Subjects: Birds, habitats, landscapes and general wildlife from all continents.
Products and services: Images for publication and duplicate slides for lectures. Photographic library currently more than 3,000 bird species. High resolution images on CD/DVD. Conventional and digital prints, unmounted, mounted or framed. Greetings cards.
Address: Stretton Lodge, 9 Birch Grove, West Hill, Ottery St Mary, Devon EX11 1XP; 01404 815 383, (M)07767 763 670.
e-mail: swash@worldwildlifeimages.com www.worldwildlifeimages.com

TYLER, John
Subjects: Plants, fungi, insects and other invertebrates.
Products and services: Images for sale.
Address: 5 Woodfield, Lacey Green, Buckinghamshire, HP27 0QQ; 07814 392 335.
e-mail: johnclarketyler@gmail.com www.johntyler.co.uk

WARD, Chris
Lecturer, N Bucks RSPB Local Group Leader.
Subjects: Primarily birds (and some other wildlife) and landscapes from UK and worldwide (Spain, Mallorca, Cyprus, Americas, S. Africa, Goa, Australasia).
Products and services: Digital images and prints on request.
Address: 41 William Smith Close, Woolstone, Milton Keynes, MK15 0AN; 01908 669 448.
e-mail: cwphotography@hotmail.com www.cwardphotography.co.uk

WILLIAMS, Nick
Photographer, lecturer, author.
Subjects: W.Palearctic also Cape Verde Islands and Falkland Islands.
Products and services: Duplicate slides, some originals, prints also available..
Address: Owl Cottage, Station Street, Rippingale, Lincs, PE10 0TA; (Tel/Fax)01778 440 500.
e-mail: birdmanandbird@hotmail.com www.nickwilliams.eu

DIRECTORY OF LECTURERS

BASTON, Bill
Photographer, lecturer.
Subjects: East Anglian rarities and common birds, Mediterranean birds and landscapes, UK wildlife and landscapes, Florida birds and landscapes, Northern Greece, Spain, western Turkey, Goa, General wildlife photography.
Fees: Negotiable. **Limits:** Preferably within East Anglia.
Address: 86 George Street, Hadleigh, Ipswich, IP7 5BU; 01473 827062. www.billbaston.com
e-mail: billbaston@btinternet.com

BATES, Tony
Photographer and lecturer.
Subjects: Nine disolve projection shows (all include some music), 'A Woodland Walk', 'Seasons and Sayings', 'From a Puddle to the Sea', 'Favourite Places', 'USA, East and West', 'Folklore of Woodland and Hedgerow', The Hare and the Owls', 'A Wildlife Garden', 'Folklore of Ponds, Rivers and Seashore'.
Fees: £80 plus travel. **Limits:** None. **Time limitations:** To suit.
Address: 22 Fir Avenue,, Bourne, Lincs, PE10 9RY; 01778 425 137. e-mail: tonybatesphotos@live.co.uk

BEJARANO, Santiago
An Ecuadorean naturalist and wildlife photographer who worked in the Galapagos for over a decade, with a great depth of knowledge and unique insight into these remarkable islands and their wildlife.
Subjects: 'Galapagos Islands', 'Birds of Galapagos', 'Ecuador land of Mega Diversity', 'Hummingbirds'..
Fees: £40. **Limits:** None. **Limits:** None. **Time limitations:** None.
Address: 25 Trinity Lane, Beverley, East Yorkshire HU17 0DY; 01482 872 716.
e-mail: info@thinkgalapagos.karoo.co.uk
www.thinkgalapagos.com

BELL, Graham
Cruise lecturer worldwide, photographer, author, former BBRC member.
Subjects: Arctic, Antarctic, Siberia, Australia, Canada, Iceland, Seychelles, UK - identification, behaviour, seabirds, garden birds, entertaining

bird sound imitations, birds in myth and fact, bird names, taking better photos, etc..
Fees: £30 plus travel and B&B if required.
Limits: None. **Time limitations:** None.
Address: Ros View, South Yearle, Wooler, Northumberland, NE71 6RB; 01668 281 310.
e-mail: seabirdsdgb@hotmail.com

BIRD, James
Photographer, lecturer and former RSPB local group leader.
Subjects: 14 plus talks with humour on wildlife and worldwide travel, having spent 23 years living abroad, plus 'Garden Life'.
Fees: £45 within a 50-mile round trip from home, fuel inclusive. Between 50-100 miles is £60 inc fuel. Over 100 miles is £75 plus 25p per mile over 100. Overnight by arrangement. **Limits:** Nowhere too far. **Times:** Any time to suit.
Address: Six Valentine Gardens, Kimbolton, Huntingdon, Cambridgeshire PE28 0HX;Tel/fax: 01480 861 955; (M)07914 633 355.
e-mail: jamesbird007@yahoo.co.uk

BOND, Terry
Company Director, international consultant, ex-bank director, conference speaker worldwide, photographer, group field leader, lecturer on birds for more than 30 years.
Subjects: Six talks, including Scilly Isles, Southern Europe, North America, Scandinavia, 'Birdwatching Identification - a New Approach' (an audience participation evening).
Fees: By arrangement (usually only expenses). **Limits:** Most of UK. **Time limitations:** Evenings.
Address: 3 Lapwing Crescent, Chippenham, Wiltshire SN14 6YF; 01249 462 674.
e-mail: terryebond@btopenworld.com

BOULTON, David
Professional nature photographer and lecturer.
Subjects: 17 talks (audio/visual presentations with relaxing music), including 'Images of Nature', 'Wild Flowers', 'Broadland', 'Gardens', 'Lakeland', 'Butterflies and Insects', 'Fungi', 'Norfolk', 'Garden Wildlife', 'The Seasons' (four talks), 'Images of Tranquility'.
Fees: £50 plus 30p per mile (negotiable depending on size of group). **Limits:** None. **Time limitations:** Any.

DIRECTORY OF LECTURERS

Address: 1 Mantle Close, Sprowston, Norwich, Norfolk NR7 8LD: 01603 415 610.
www.davidboulton.co.uk
e-mail: dbp@ownersmail.co.uk

BOWDEN, Paul
Birdwatcher and nature photographer (hobby) for 30+ years. Takes both video and stills of birds and other wildlife.
Subjects: Birds of UK, Europe, USA or Australia (video on Powerpoint), butterflies and dragonflies of UK.
Fees: Travelling expenses and overnight accom. Where necessary. **Limits:** None, but longer trips will require overnight stay. **Time limitations:** Generally evenings and weekends.
Address: 4 Patmore Close, Gwaelod-y-Garth, Cardiff, CF15 9SU; 029 2081 3044.
e-mail: bowden_pe@hotmail.com

BRIGGS, Kevin
Freelance ecologist.
Subjects: General wildlife in NW England; specialist topics: Raptors, Oystercatcher, Ringed Plover, Goosander, Yellow Wagtail, Ring Ouzel, Lune Valley, 'Confessions of a Lunatic'.
Fees: £60 + petrol. **Limits:** None. **Time limitations:** None.
Address: The Bramblings, 1 Washington Drive, Warton, Carnforth,Lancs LA5 9RA; 01254 730 533.
e-mail: kbbriggs@yahoo.com

BROADBENT, David
Professional photographer.
Subjects: UK birds and wild places. In praise of natural places.
Fees: £70 plus travel. **Limits:** 50mls without o.n accom Anywhere otherwise. **Time limitations:** None.
Address: Rose Cottage, Bream Road, Whitepool, St Briavels, Lydney, Glos GL15 6TL. 07771 664 973.
e-mail: info@davidbroadbent.com
www.davidbroadbent.com

BROOKS, David
Freelance naturalist.
Subjects: Various talks on wildlife, principally birds. The UK talks concentrate mainly on Norfolk or on various islands around our coast and the overseas talks are largely about eastern Australia.
Fees: £50 plus travel expenses. **Limits:** Normally 50 mls without o.n. accom.
Time limitations: Any time.

Address: 2 Malthouse Court, Green Lane, Thornham, Norfolk PE36 6NW; 01485 512 548.
e-mail: brooks472@btinternet.com

BROOKS, Richard
Wildlife photographer, writer, lecturer.
Subjects: 12 talks (including Lesvos, Evros Delta, Israel, Canaries, E.Anglia, Scotland, Wales, Oman).
Fees: £75 plus petrol. **Limits:** None if accom provided. **Time limitations:** None.
Address: 24 Croxton Hamlet, Fulmodeston, Fakenham, Norfolk NR21 0NP; 01328 878632.
e-mail: email@richard-brooks.co.uk
www.richard-brooks.co.uk

BUCKINGHAM, John
Lecturer, photographer, tour leader.
Subjects: 60+ titles covering birds, wildlife, botany, ecology and habitats in UK, Europe, Africa, Australia, Indian sub-continent, North-South and Central America, including favourites such as 'How Birds Work', 'The Natural History of Birds' and 'Wonders of Bird Migration'.
Fees: £70 plus expenses. **Limits:** None. **Time limitations:** None.
Address: 3 Cardinal Close, Tonbridge, Kent, TN9 2EN; (Tel/fax) 01732 354 970.
e-mail: john@buckingham7836.freeserve.co.uk

BURROWS, Ian
Tour leader.
Subjects: Papua New Guinea, Cape Clear Island and 'Food from the Wild'.
Fees: £70 plus mileage over 100. **Limits:** Anything considered. **Time limitations:** Evenings preferable but other times considered.
Address: 60 Church Hill Cottages, Gayton Road, Grimston, King's Lynn, Norfolk PE32 1BG; 01485 601 328; (M)07789 118 355.
e-mail: Ian@explorenature.eu or Burrows8153@btinternet.com

CARRIER, Michael
Lifelong interest in natural history.
Subjects: 1) Birds in Cumbria, 2) The Solway and its Birds, 3) The Isle of May, 4) A Look at Bird Migration, 5) A Lifetime of Birds, 6)Some Remarkable Islands.
Fees: £20. **Limits:** None but rail connection helpful. **Time limitations:** Sept-March inc., afternoons or evenings.
Address: Lismore Cottage, 1 Front Street, Armathwaite, Carlisle, Cumbria, CA4 9PB; 01697 472 218. e-mail: m.carrier131@btinternet.com

DIRECTORY OF LECTURERS

CHARTERS, Roger

Experienced wildlife sound recordist and one-time professional photographer.

Subjects: Scandinavia with emphasis on the Arctic, Ukraine - a Birdwatcher's Paradise, Spain, including Coto Donana, The Australian Outback, Ecuador, its Rainforest, Cloud Forest and the Galapagos. Each talk last about one hour with extensive use of digital sound recordings and visual sequences.

Fees: £38 made payable to Warwickshire Wildlife Trust, + 28p per mile. **Limits:** None. **Time limitations:**

Address: 11 Eastnor Grove, Leamington Spa, Warwickshire CV31 1LD: 01926 882583.

e-mail: Roger.Charters@btinternet.com
www.roger-charters.co.uk

CLEAVE, Andrew MBE

Wildlife photographer, author, lecturer and tour leader

Subjects: More than 30 talks (including Galapagos, Iceland, Mediterranean birds and wildlife, Lundy, Shetland, ancient woodlands, dormice and seashore). Full list available.

Fees: £65 plus petrol. **Limits:** Approx. 60 mls without o.n accom. **Time limitations:** Afternoons and evenings, not school holidays.

Address: 31 Petersfield Close, Chineham, Basingstoke, Hampshire RG24 8WP; 01256 320 050. e-mail: andrew@bramleyfrith.co.uk

COOK, Tony MBE

35 years employed by WWT. Travelled in Europe, Africa and N. America.

Subjects: 22 talks from Birds of The Wash, garden birds to travelogues of Kenya, North America (both east and west), Europe (Med to North Cape).

Fees: £35 plus 20p per ml. **Limits:** 100 mls. **Time limitations:** None.

Address: 11 Carnoustie Court, Sutton Bridge, Spalding, Lincs PE12; 01406 350 069.

e-mail: cook1718@btinternet.com

COSTER, Bill

Professional wildlife photographer, writer and photographic tour leader. Author of *Creative Bird Photography*.

Subjects: Stunning new digital shows provide a unique look at subjects around the world, including: Pacific Northwest USA, Antarctica, Shetland, Birds and Landscape of USA Deserts, Florida, Britain and more. See my webite for full details (www.billcoster.com). Even if you have seen shows from the same location, my shows will be different.

Fees: £80, plus 30p per mile. **Limits:** None. **Time limitations:** None.

Address: 17 Elm Road, South Woodham Ferrers, Chelmsford, Essex CM3 5QB; 01245 320 066.

e-mail: billcoster@hotmail.com
www.billcoster.com

COUZENS, Dominic

Full-time birdwatcher, tour leader (UK and overseas), writer and lecturer.

Subjects: The Secret Lives of Garden Birds; Birds Behaving Badly (the trials and tribulations of birds through the year); Bird Sounds - As You've Never Heard Them Before; Have Wings Will Travel (the marvel of bird migration); Vive la Difference — a look at the unusual lifestyles of continental birds.

Fees: £90 plus travel. **Limits:** London and south. **Time limitations:** None.

Address: 3 Clifton Gardens, Ferndown, Dorset, BH22 9BE; (Tel/fax) 01202 874 330.

e-mail: dominic.couzens@btinternet.com
www.birdwords.co.uk

CROMACK, David

Former editor of *Birds Illustrated* magazine, co-publisher of Buckingham Press Ltd, former chairman of Peterborough Bird Club.

Subjects: Subjects: 1) Bird Magazines and the Art of Bird Photography (the inside story of how publications choose and use images); 2) Wild West Birding (Arizona and California); World Class Bird Images (Leading entries from International Wildbird Photographer competitions); 4) More World Class Bird Images (Outstanding entries from the 2007 IWP competition); 5) Asia's Teardrop - Birding in Sri Lanka (NEW TALK); 6) Contemporary Bird Artists (NEW TALK). All suitable for bird groups and photographic societies. Leaflet available on request.

Fees: £75 plus travel expenses (30p per mile). **Limits:** 150 miles from Peterborough. **Times:** All requests considered from January 2010.

Address: 55 Thorpe Park Road, Peterborough PE3 6LJ. 01733 566 815; (Fax) 01733 561 739; e-mail: editor@buckinghampress.com

DENNING, Paul

Wildlife photographer, lecturer.

Subjects: 15 talks, (birds, mammals, reptiles, butterflies etc, UK, western and eastern Europe, north and central America, Canaries).

Fees: £40 plus petrol. **Limits:** 100 mls. **Time limitations:** Evenings, weekends.

Address: 17 Maes Maelwg, Beddau, Pontypridd, CF38 2LD; (H)01443 202 607; (W)02920 673 243.

e-mail: pgdenning.naturepics@virgin.net

DIRECTORY OF LECTURERS

DUGGAN, Glenn
Ex-Commander Royal Navy, tour leader, researcher.
Subjects: Ten talks, subjects including, birds of paradise and bower birds, History of Bird Art (caveman to present day), Modern-day Bird Art, Famous Victorian bird artists (John Gould the Birdman and John James Audubon), Trogons and Tanagers.
Fees: £70 plus expenses. **Limits:** none with o.n accom. **Time limitations:** None.
Address: 25 Hampton Grove, Fareham, Hampshire PO15 5NL; 01329 845976, (M)07771 605320.
e-mail: glenn.m.duggan@ntlworld.com
www.birdlectures.com

ELSBY, Kevin
General naturalist with more than 40 years' experience. Tour Guide.
Subjects: A wide range of talks on many aspects of British and world wildlife.
Fees: £50 per talk plus 25p per mile. **Limits:** Anywhere considered. **Time limitations:** None.
Address: Wildlife on the Web,Chapel House, Bridge Road, Colby, Norwich NR22 8TB; 01263 732 839.
e-mail: wildlife@greenbeelnet
www.wildlifeontheweb.co.uk

EYRE, John
Author, photographer, conservationist and chairman Hampshire Ornithological Society.
Subjects: Many talks covering birding around the world (Europe, Africa, Australasia and the Americas), plus special Hampshire subjects. Examples include: New Zealand - Seabird Feast, Land Bird Famine; California Birds - Sea, Sage and Spotted Owls; Gilbert White's Birds; and The Changing Fortunes of Hampshire Birds.
Fees: £70, plus travel. **Limits:** Any location negotiable. **Time limitations:** None.
Address: 3 Dunmow Hill, Fleet, Hampshire, GU51 3AN; 01252 677 850.
e-mail: John.Eyre@ntlworld.com

GALLOP, Brian
Speaker, photographer, tour leader.
Subjects: 35 talks covering UK, Africa, India, Galapagos, South America and Europe - All natural history subjects. Made-to-measure talks available on request. 24hr emergency service.
Fees: £50 plus 25p per ml. **Limits:** None but overnight accommodation needed if over 100 mls. **Time limitations:** None.
Address: 13 Orchard Drive, Tonbridge, Kent TN10 4LT; 01732 361 892.
e-mail: brian_gallop@hotmail.co.uk

GALVIN, Chris
A birding photographer with passion for birds for more than 30 years.
Subjects: Northwest Year; Package Holiday Birding; Birds of Goa, Birding on the Doorstep and others.
Fees: £60-100. **Limits:** 100 miles.
Address: 17 Henley Road, Allerton, Liverpool, Merseyside L18 2DN;
07802 428 385 or 0151 729 0123.
e-mail: chris@chrisgalvinphoto.com
www.chrisgalvinphoto.com

GARCIA, Ernest
Writer/editor Gibraltar Bird Report
Subjects: Raptor and seabird migration at Gibraltar, birding in northern, southern and western Spain (Andalucia/Extremadura) and the northern coastal regions.
Fees: £50 plus expenses. **Limits:** None. **Time limitations:** None.
Address: Woodpecker House, 2 Pine View Close, Chilworth, Surrey GU4 8RS; 01483 539 053.
e-mail: EFJGarcia@aol.com

GARNER, David
Wildlife photographer.
Subjects: 20 live talks and audio-visual shows on all aspects of wildlife in UK and some parts of Europe. List available.
Fees: £40 plus 20p per ml. **Limits:** None. **Time limitations:** None.
Address: 73 Needingworth Road, St Ives, Cambridgeshire, PE27 5JY; (H)01480 463194; (W)01480 463194. e-mail: david@hushwings.co.uk
www.hushwings.co.uk

GARTSHORE, Neil
23-years working in nature conservation (National Trust, South Africa, RSPB) now a freelance contractor, writer, lecturer, tour guide & natural history book seller.
Subjects: Various talks including South Africa; Sub-Antarctic Prince Edward Islands; Japan; Farne Islands; Heathlands; and Poole Harbour.
Fees: Negotiable. **Limits:** Anything considered. **Time limitations:** Flexible.
Address: Moor Edge, 2 Bere Road, Wareham, Dorset BH20 4DD; 01929 552 560.
e-mail: neil@onaga54.freeserve.co.uk

GLENN, Neil
Author of *Best Birdwatching Sites in Norfolk*; regular contributor to *Birds Illustrated* and *Bird Watching* magazines; bird tour leader for Avian Adventures.
Subjects: Wildlife of the Lower Rio Grande

DIRECTORY OF LECTURERS

Valley, Texas. Birding the Arctic Circle. More to follow!
Fees: Negotiable. **Limits:** None.
Time limitations: Any day.
Address: 13 Gladstone Avenue, Gotham, Nottingham NG11 0HN; 0115 983 0946.
e-mail: n.glenn@ntlworld.com

GUNTON, Trevor
Ex.RSPB Staff, recruitment advisor, lecturer and consultant.
Subjects: 15 different talks, featuring places such as Shetland, other UK islands, Yorkshire from dales to coast, Viking lands (four different talks on Viking history). Two new talks on penguins plus A Norwegian Coastal Voyage; Wild Goose Chase (Holland and Romania); Starting Birdwatching; Great Gardens and Houses of East Anglia; Garden Birds. Other topics include wildlife on National Trust properties and gravel pits (Paxton Pits). Write/phone for full list.
Fees: Variable (basic £60 plus expenses). **Limits:** None. **Time limitations:** Anytime, anywhere.
Address: 15 St James Road, Little Paxton, St Neots, Cambs, PE19 6QW; (tel/fax)01480 473562.

HAMBLIN, Mark
Wildlife photographer and writer.
Subjects: Wild Scotland, Tooth & Claw - Living alongside Britain's Predators.
Fees: £250 plus actual costs. **Limits:** None. **Time limitations:** Lunchtime, afternoons and evenings.
Address: Ballinlaggan Farm, Duthil, Carr-bridge, Inverness-shire, PH23 3ND; 01479 841 547.
e-mail: mark@markhamblin.com
www.markhamblin.com

HAMMOND, Nicholas
Lecturer, author, former RSPB and Wildlife Trust staffer.
Subjects: More than 30 topics covering Art and Wildlife, History and Wildlife, Wildlife and Conservation. Popular topics include Modern Wildlife Painting; Hippos and Hoopoes; The Great Fen; Birds through Other People's Eyes. E-mail for full list of subjects.
Fees: From £75, **Limits:** 150 miles from Sandy.
Address: 30 Ivel Road, Sandy, Beds SG19 1BA; 01767 680 504.
e-mail: n.hammond4@ntlworld.com

HASSELL, David
Birdwatcher and photographer.
Subjects: Six talks (including British Seabirds, Shetland Birds, British Birds, USA Birds, including Texas, California, Florida etc.).
Fees: £45 plus petrol. **Limits:** None.

Time limitations: None.
Address: 15 Grafton Road, Enfield, Middlesex EN2 7EY; 020 8367 0308.
e-mail: dave@davehassell.com
www.davehassell.com

HOBSON, Paul
Wildlife photographer and lecturer.
Subjects: Birds, wildlife, wildlife photography, conservation.
Fees: £60-£100 plus 30p return mileage.
Limits: 200 miles. **Time limitations:** None.
Address: Sheffield. 0114 232 3699.
e-mail: paul.hobson6@virgin.net
www.paulhobson.co.uk

HOLT, Brayton
County Recorder since 1990, BTO rep. 1989-2003, co-writer of *Birds of Montgomeryshire* (2008).
Subjects: Birds of the Arctic to Antarctica and all continents between.
Fees: By negotiation. **Limits:** 75 miles from Welshpool - further with overnight accommodation provided.
Address: Scops Cottage, Pentre Beirdd, Welshpool, Powys SY21 9DL; 01938 500 266.
e-mail: brayton.wanda@virgin.net

LANE, Mike
Award-winning wildlife photographer, author and lecturer.
Subjects: Many talks with subjects drawn from the UK and abroad (see website for details).
Fees: Negotiable. **Limits:** None.
Time limitations: None.
Address: 36 Berkeley Road, Shirley, Solihull, West Midlands B90 2HS; 021 744 7988;
e-mail: mikelane@nature-photography.co.uk
www.nature-photography.co.uk

LANGLEY, John and Tracy
Wildlife photographers, workshop tutors and lecturers.
Subjects: Various talks on UK wildlife, wildlife photography and Indian wildlife (with special emphasis on tigers).
Fees: Variable. **Limits:** None.
Time limitations: None.
Address: 16 Carrick Road, Curzon Park, Chester CH4 8AW; 01244 678 781;
e-mail: little.owl@btopenworld.com
www.ourwildlifephotography.co.uk

LANGSBURY, Gordon
Professional wildlife photographer, lecturer, author.
Subjects: 12 talks - Africa, Europe, USA and UK.

DIRECTORY OF LECTURERS

Full list provided or visit website for details.
Fees: £95 plus travel expenses. **Limits:** None.
Time limitations: None.
Address: Sanderlings, 80 Shepherds Close, Hurley, Maidenhead, Berkshire, SL6 5LZ; 01628 824 252.
e-mail: gordonlangsbury@birdphoto.org.uk
www.birdphoto.org.uk

LENTON, Graham
PhD Ornithology/Ecology. Former lecturer at Oxford University and Oxford Brookes University. Lifetime photographer of wildlife, plus publications of articles and photographs of birds and wildlife.
Subjects: Barn Owls and rat control in Malaysia; Birds of the Seychelles; Wildlife and Birds of Antarctica; Birds of New Zealand; Birds of Namibia; Handa Island, Scotland.
Fees: £50. **Limits:** Preferably within 60mls.
Time limitations: 60 to 90-minute talks.
Address: The Old School, 25A Standlake Road, Ducklington, Witney, Oxon OX29 7UR; 01993 899 033. e-mail: grahamlenton@btopenworld.com
www.gml-art.co.uk

LINGARD, David
Photographer, retired from RAF, now UK delegate to LIPU (BirdLife International partner in Italy).
Subjects: Choice of talks on European birding and the work of LIPU.
Fees: £75 donation to LIPU, plus petrol costs.
Limits: None. **Time limitations:** None.
Address: Fernwood, Doddington Road, Whisby, Lincs LN6 9BX; 01522 689 030.
e-mail: mail@lipu-uk.org www.lipu-uk.org

LINN, Hugh
Experienced lecturer, photographer (Associate of Royal Photographic Society).
Subjects: 12 talks, covering UK, Europe, Africa and bird-related subjects. List available..
Fees: £45 plus travel. **Limits:** 100 mls without o.n. accom, 150 mls otherwise.
Time limitations: Flexible.
Address: 4 Stonewalls, Rosemary Lane, Burton, Rossett, Wrexham, LL12 0LG; 01244 571 942.

LOVELL, Stephen
Naturalist, RSPB lecturer, photographer.
Subjects: 18 topic including the natural history of several European destinations including Lesvos, Mallorca, Britain. Other talks available on New Zealand, Australia, St Lucia, Tanzania, Sri Lanka and Southern India.
Fees: According to distance - on request. **Limits:** None. **Time limitations:** None.
Address: 6 Abingdon Close, Doddington Park,

Lincoln LN6 3UH; 01522 689 456; (M)07957 618 684. e-mail: stephen.lovell7@btinternet.com

MAGENNIS, Steve
Wildlife photographer, lecturer and workshop leader.
Subjects: Wildlife photography, bird life and related subjects (see website for full details).
Fees: £85 plus travel @ 30p per mile over 40 miles. **Limits:** Up to 150 miles. **Time limitations:** Available all year round, day or evening.
Address: 3 Chepstow Close, St James, Northampton, Northants, NN5 7EB; 01604 467 848; (M)07803 619 272.
e-mail: photos@stevemagennis.co.uk
www.stevemagennis.co.uk

MATHER, Dr John Robert
Ornithologist, writer, tour guide, lecturer.
Subjects: Birds and other wildlife of: Kenya, Tanzania, Uganda, Ethiopia, South Africa, Costa Rica, Romania/Bulgaria, India and Nepal. Algonquin to Niagara (a tour around the Great Lakes); Landscapes, Flowers and Wildlife of the American West; Bird on the Bench (a fascinating account of bird biology); Wildlife and Scenery of Coastal Alaska, and the Canadian Rockies.
Fees: £75 plus 30p per mile. Overnight accommodation or £30 if over 75 miles.
Time limitations: Evenings.
Address: Eagle Lodge, 44 Aspin Lane, Knaresborough, North Yorkshire, HG5 8EP; 01423 862 775.

McKAVETT, Mike
Photographer.
Subjects: Six talks: Birds and Wildlife of India; North and Western Kenya and the Gambia; Bird Migration in North America; Birds of the Eastern Mediterranean.
Fees: £50 plus expenses. **Limits:** None. **Time limitations:** None.
Address: 34 Rectory Road, Churchtown, Southport, PR9 7PU; 01704 231358;
e-mail: mike.mckavett@btinternet.com.

MOCKLER, Mike
Safari guide, tour leader, writer and photographer.
Subjects: Birds and other wildlife of: Botswana, Kenya, Tanzania, Zambia, Spain, Finland, Norway, Costa Rica, Antarctica and South Georgia, India and Brazil.
Fees: Negotiable. **Limits:** None. **Time limitations:** Evenings.

DIRECTORY OF LECTURERS

Address: Gulliver's Cottage, Chapel Rise, Avon Castle, Ringwood, Hampshire BH24 2BL; 01425 478 103. e-mail: mikemockler@lineone.net www.mikemockler.co.uk

NASON, Rebecca
East Anglia-based bird and wildlife photographer. Subjects: Fair Isle (Working and birding at Britain's premier birding hotspot). Fees: Please e-mail for fee details. There is a set fee plus travel expenses. Limits: Within 2 hours drive of Woodbridge, Suffolk (negotiable). Time limitations: Flexible. Slideshow talks last from 1-2 hours. Address: 8 Angel Lane, Woodbridge, Suffolk IP12 4NG; 01394 385 030; (M)07919 256 386. e-mail: rebecca@rebeccanason.com www.rebeccanason.com

NOBBS, Brian
Amateur birdwatcher and photographer. Subjects: Wildlife of the Wild West, Israel, Mediterranean, Florida. Wildlife Gardening; Reserves for Birds (RSPB); Trinidad and Tobago; The Way Birds Feed. Fees: £40 plus 25p per ml. Limits: Kent, Surrey, Sussex, Essex. Time limitations: None. Address: The Grebes, 36 Main Road, Sundridge, Sevenoaks, Kent TN14 6EP; 01959 563530. e-mail: Brian.nobbs@tiscali.co.uk

OFFORD, Keith
Photographer, writer, tour leader, conservationist. Subjects: 16 talks covering raptors, uplands, gardens, migration, flight, woodlands, Australia, Texas & Florida, Gambia, Spain, S. Africa, Namibia, Costa Rica, Iceland. Fees: £90 plus travel @ 30p per mile. Limits: None. Time limitations: Sept - April. Address: Yew Tree Farmhouse, Craignant, Selattyn, Nr Oswestry, Shropshire SY10 7NP; 01691 718 740. e-mail: keith-offord@virgin.net www.keithofford.co.uk

PALMER, Phil
Tour leader for Bird Holidays and undertakes conservation-based expeditions e.g. breeding surveys for Spoon-billed Sandpiper in Russia. Subjects: Mostly birds, but includes mammals, insects, reptiles, whale watching etc. Many foreign trips including Alaska, Antarctica, Galapagos, Spitsbergen and the high Arctic. British birds; 'First for Britain' from Phil's book; The Secret Life of the Nightjar; Twitching in the UK; and bird photography. Fees: To suit all club budgets. Limits: None. Time limitations: None. Address: 43 Grove Coach Road, Retford,

Nottinghamshire DN22 7HB; (Tel/fax)0113 391 0510. e-mail: info@birdholidays.co.uk www.birdholidays.co.uk

PARKER, Susan and Allan
Professional photographers, (ASPphoto – Images of Nature), lecturers and tutors. Subjects: 16 plus talks on birds and natural history, natural history photography - countries include UK, USA (Texas, Florida), Spain, Greece, Cyprus. Fees: On application. Limits: Any distance with o.n accom or up to 120 mls without. Time limitations: None. Address: Windhover Barn, 51b Kiveton Lane, Todwick, Sheffield, South Yorkshire S26 1HJ; 01909 770 238. e-mail: aspphoto@tiscali.co.uk

READ, Mike
Photographer, tour leader, writer. Subjects: 12 talks featuring British and foreign subjects (list available on receipt of sae or via e-mail). Fees: £70 plus travel. Limits: 125 mls from Ringwood. Time limitations: Talks available 1st Sept to March 31 each winter. Address: Claremont, Redwood Close, Ringwood, Hampshire BH24 1PR; 01425 475008. e-mail: mike@mikeread.co.uk www.mikeread.co.uk

ROBINSON, Peter
Consultant ornithologist and former Scilly resident, author of Birds of the Isles of Scilly and bird lecturer. Subjects: Springwatch - The Real Story and various other subjects. See website for details. Fees: £85 plus petrol. Limits: None. Time limitations: None. Address: 19 Pine Park Road, Honiton, Devon EX14 2HR; 01404 549873 (M) 07768 538132. e-mail: pjrobinson2@aol.com

SMART, Oliver
Photographer and lecturer. Subjects: 1)Birds of Lesvos; 2) Grizzly Bears of Alaska; 3) Wildlife on Handa Island, NW Scotland; 4) Cameras and Creatures, from Cumbria to Canada. Fees: £75 plus 20p per mile. Limits: None but o.n. accom. may be required. Time limitations: None. Address: 78 Aspen Park Road, Weston-super-Mare, Somerset BS22 8ER; 01934 628 888; (M)07802 417 810. e-mail: oliver@smartimages.co.uk www.smartimages.co.uk

DIRECTORY OF LECTURERS

STEPHEN, Gerry
Subjects: More than 28 talks, mainly about wild flowers and their habitats but includes natural history of all types and cover areas of the USA, Canada, Europe and Africa.
All about 60 minutes duration but can be tailored to your needs.
Limits: £30 plus travel expenses at cost.
Time limitations: None - January/February by negotiation.
Address: 66 Northumberland Avenue, Thornton Cleveleys, Lancs FY5 2LH; 01253 860 305.
e-mail: melodystephen@hotmail.com

SWASH, Andy
Photographer, author, tour leader.
Subjects: Birds and general wildlife. Tales from travels in: the Andamans, Antarctica, Argentina, Australia, Brazil, Chile, China, Costa Rica, Cuba, Ethiopa, Galápagos, Kenya, Namibia, Peru, South Africa, Sri Lanka, USA or Venezuela.
Fees: £90 plus travel. **Limits:** None. **Time limitations:** Evenings.
Address: Stretton Lodge, 9 Birch Grove, West Hill, Ottery St Mary, Devon, EX11 1XP; 01404 815 383, (M)07767 763 670.
e-mail: swash@worldwildlifeimages.com
www.worldwildlifeimages.com

TAYLOR, Mick
Co-ordinator South Peak Raptor Group, photographer, ornithologist, writer.
Subjects: Several talks including Merlins; Peak District Birds; Peak District raptors; Alaskan Wildlife.
Fees: £60 plus petrol. **Limits:** Negotiable. **Time limitations:** Evenings preferred.
Address: 76 Hawksley Avenue, Chesterfield, Derbyshire, S40 4TL;01246 277 749.

TODD, Ralph
Lecturer & photographer, course tutor and former tour leader.
Subjects: 10 talks including: Galapagos Wildlife; On the Trail of the Crane; Polar Odyssey; Operation Osprey; Iceland & Pyrenees; Man & Birds-Travels through Time; A Summer in Northern Landscapes; Where Yee-haa meets Ole.
Fees: £70 plus expenses. **Limits:** None.
Time limitations: Any - also willing to act as substitute speaker at short notice.
Address: 9 Horsham Road, Bexleyheath, Kent, DA6 7HU; (Tel/fax)01322 528 335.
e-mail: rbtodd@btinternet.com

TYLER, John
Wildlife walks and talks.
Subjects: Life in a Nutshell (The world of small things); The Island of Crabs; Volcanoes and Dragons; Changing Wildlife of the Chilterns; The Ridgeway; The Glow-worm; The World of Fungi; Making Space for Wildlife.
Fees: £60 plus 40p per mile. **Limits:** 25 mile radius from Princes Risborough, Bucks.
Time limitations: None.
Address: 5 Woodfield,Lacey Green, Buckinghamshire HP27 0QQ; 07814 392 335.
e-mail: johnclarketyler@gmail.com
www.johntyler.co.uk

WARD, Chris
Photographer, N Bucks RSPB Local Group Leader.
Subjects: 20-plus talks on UK and worldwide topics (Spain, Mallorca, Cyprus, Americas, Africa, Goa, Australasia) - primarily birds, some other wildlife.
Fees: £50 plus petrol. **Limits:** 120 miles.
Time limitations: Evenings.
Address: 41 William Smith Close, Woolstone, Milton Keynes, Buckinghamshire MK15 0AN; 01908 669 448.
e-mail: cwphotography@hotmail.com
www.cwardphotography.co.uk

WILLIAMS, Nick
Photographer, lecturer, author.
Subjects: Several audio visual shows (including Morocco, Mongolia, Spain, Northern Germany, Camargue, Turkey, Northern Norway, Cape Verde Islands, Falklands and Birds of Prey).
Fee: £99-£125 depending on group size and distance. **Limits:** None.
Time limitations: None
Address: Owl Cottage, Station Street, Rippingale, Lincs, PE10 0TA; (Tel/Fax)01778 440 500.
e-mail: birdmanandbird@hotmail.com
www.nickwilliams.eu

WREN, Graham
Wildlife photographer, lecturer, tour guide.
Subjects: 25 talks - birds - UK 'Breeding Birds of Southern Britain' and 'Northern Britain', 'Bird Nesting Habitats - Past, Present and Future', Nest-boxes, plus Scandinavia. Detailed information package supplied on request.
Fees: £50-80 plus petrol. **Limits:** None.
Time limitations: None.
Address: The Kiln House, Great Doward, Whitchurch, Ross-on-Wye, Herefordshire, HR9 6DU; 01600 890 488.
e-mail: grahamjwren@aol.com

BTO SPEAKERS

BTO speakers can be contacted by post at BTO, The Nunnery, Thetford, Norfolk IP24 2PU.
Tel: 01842 750 050; Fax: 01842 750 030; www.bto.org

APPLETON, Graham (Director of Communications)
Subjects: Atlas 2007-11, The Work of the BTO, Flyway to Iceland, Time to Fly - Bird Migration, Yellowhammers, Buzzards and the next Atlas.
Fee: BTO fee (£40). Expenses: Negotiable. Distance: Dependant on expenses.
E-mail: graham.appleton@bto.org

AUSTIN, Dr Graham (Senior Research Ecologist)
Subjects: Wetland Bird Survey.
Fee: BTO fee (£40). Expenses: Travel.
Distance: By agreement.
E-mail: graham.austin@bto.org

BAILLIE, Dr Stephen (Science Director)
Subjects: BirdTrack, Population Monitoring.
Fee: BTO fee (£40). Expenses: Travel. Distance: By agreement.E-mail: stephen.baillie@bto.org

BAKER, Jeff (Head of Marketing)
Subjects: Atlas 2007-11, The work of the BTO, Little brown jobs - Warblers and how to identify them.
Fee: £40. Expenses: Travel expenses.
Distance: Dependent on expenses.
E-mail: jeff.baker@bto.org

BALMER, Dawn (Atlas Coordinator)
Subject: Atlas 2007-11.
Fee: BTO fee (£40). Expenses: Travel.
Distance: By agreement.
E-mail: dawn.balmer@bto.org

BARIMORE, Carl (Nest Records Organiser)
Subjects:Nest Record Scheme, Barn Owl Monitoring Programme.
Fee: BTO fee (£40). Expenses: Travel. Distance: By agreement. E-mail: carl.barimore@bto.org

BLACKBURN, Jez (Demography Team Licensing and Sales Manager)
Subjects: Bird Moult (suitable for ringers), Seabirds/Sule Skerry.

Fee: BTO fee (£40) (£70 for private talks).
Expenses: Travel. Distance: East Anglia.
E-mail: jez.blackburn@bto.org

CALLADINE, John (Senior Research Ecologist, BTO Scotland)
Subjects: BTO's work in the Scottish Uplands; Short-eared Owls; The Breeding Bird Survey (BBS) in Scotland; The Wetland Bird Survey (WeBS) in Scotland.
Fee: £40. Expenses: Petrol. Distance: Scotland and northern England.
E-mail: john.calladine@bto.org

CHAMBERLAIN, Dr Dan (Principal Ecologist and Head of Population Ecology & Modelling)
Subjects: Climate change, urban birds
Fee: BTO fee (£40). Expenses: Travel. Distance: By agreement. E-mail: dan.chamberlain@bto.org

CLARK, Jacquie (Head of Demography)
Subjects: Waders and Severe Weather, Why Ring Birds?, Ringing for Conservation, Migration.
Fee: BTO fee (£40). Expenses: Petrol. Distance: 100 mile radius of Thetford.
E-mail: jacquie.clark@bto.org

CLARK, Dr Nigel (Head of Projects Development Unit)
Subjects: Waders, Man and Estuaries, Horseshoe Crabs and Waders, Migration through Delaware in Spring.
Fee: BTO fee (£40). Expenses: Petrol. Distance: 100 mile radius of Thetford.
E-mail: nigel.clark@bto.org

CONWAY, Greg (Research Ecologist)
Subjects: Nightjars, Woodlarks and Dartford Warblers, Wintering Warblers.
Fee: BTO fee (£40). Expenses: Petrol. Distance: 100 mile radius of Thetford.
E-mail: greg.conway@bto.org

DIRECTORY OF LECTURERS

COOK, Mandy (Development Coordinator, BTO Scotland)
Subjects: Garden Birdwatch in Scotland; BirdTrack in Scotland; The Breeding Bird Survey (BBS) in Scotland; The Wetland Bird Survey (WeBS) in Scotland; Why record birds/making your birdwatching count.
Fee: £40. **Expenses:** Petrol. **Distance:** Scotland and northern England.
E-mail: mandy.cook@bto.org

ETHERIDGE, Brian (Scottish Raptor Monitoring Scheme Raptor Monitoring Officer)
Subject: The Scottish Raptor Monitoring Scheme.
Expenses: Petrol. **Distance:** Scotland and northern England. E-mail: brian.etheridge@rspb.org.uk

FULLER, Prof Rob (Director of Science)
Subjects: Atlas 2007-11, Woodland Management and Birds, Changing Times for Woodland Birds.
Fee: BTO fee (£40). **Expenses:** Travel. **Distance:** Negotiable. E-mail: rob.fuller@bto.org

GILLINGS, Dr Simon (Senior Research Ecologist)
Subjects: Atlas 2007-11, Winter Golden Plovers and Lapwings, Winter Farmland Birds.
Fee: BTO fee (£40). **Expenses:** Travel. **Distance:** Negotiable. E-mail: simon.gillings@bto.org

GOUGH, Su (BTO Training Officer and Editor, BTO News)
Subjects: Atlas 2007-11, The Work of the BTO, Urban Birds, Wildlife of Canada (non-BTO talk), Wildlife of Soutwestern USA (non-BTO talk), Wildlife of European Mountains (non-BTO talk).
Fee: BTO fee (£40). **Expenses:** Travel. **Distance:** Negotiable. E-mail: su.gough@bto.org

GRANTHAM, Mark (Demography Team Research Ecologist)
Subjects: A range of general talks on ringing, migration and Bird Observatories, Oiled sea-birds.
Fee: BTO fee (£40). **Expenses:** Travel. **Distance:** By agreement. E-mail: mark.grantham@bto.org

GREENWOOD, Professor JJD (former BTO Director)
Subjects: How to Change Government Policy by Counting Birds, Why Ring Birds?, The Future for Birds and People, Purposeful birdwatching around the world.
Fee: BTO fee (£40) (£50 for private talks).
Expenses: Public transport or 35p/mile.
Distance: 100 miles from Thetford (further by arrangement).
E-mail: jeremy.greenwood@bto.org

HENDERSON, Dr Ian (Senior Research Ecologist)
Subjects: Arable Farming and Birds.
Fee: BTO fee (£40). **Expenses:** Travel. **Distance:** By agreement. E-mail: ian.henderson@bto.org

HUMPHREYS, Liz (Research Ecologist, BTO Scotland)
Subjects: The Biodiversity in Glasgow (BIG) Project; The work of BTO (in Scotland)
Fee: £40. **Expenses:** Petrol. **Distance:** Scotland and northern England.
E-mail: liz.humphreys@bto.org

LACK, Dr Peter (Information Services Manager)
Subjects: Palearctic Migrants in Africa, On Foot in Rwanda and Zambia, Bird Ecology in East African Savannahs, General Natural History of Eastern Africa. (All are given as non-BTO talks).
Fee: Negotiable. **Expenses:** Travel. **Distance:** 60 miles from Bury St Edmunds.
E-mail: peter.lack@bto.org

LEWIS, Amy (Garden BirdWatch Development Officer)
Subjects: Garden Birds.
Fee: £40. **Expenses:** Petrol. 100 miles, further by arrangement. E-mail: amy.lewis@bto.org

MARCHANT, John (Monitoring Team Leader)
Subjects: Heronries, Waterways Breeding Bird Survey, Breeding Bird Trends in the UK.
Fee: BTO fee (£40). **Expenses:** Travel. **Distance:** By agreement. E-mail: john.marchant@bto.org

MORAN, Nick (BirdTrack Organiser)
Subjects: Migration: mapping movements with BirdTrack; 5 Years In The Desert: Birds and Birding in the UAE and Oman (non-BTO).
Fee: BTO fee (£40) (same for private talk).
Expenses: Travel. **Distance:** By agreement.
E-mail: nick.moran@bto.org

MUSGROVE, Dr Andy (Head of Monitoring)
Subjects: Monitoring the UK's Birds; Little Egrets in the UK
Fee: BTO fee (£40). **Expenses:** Travel. **Distance:** By agreement. E-mail: andy.musgrove@bto.org

ART/PHOTOGRAPHY/LECTURERS

113

DIRECTORY OF LECTURERS

NEWSON, Dr Stuart (Senior Research Ecologist)
Subjects: Tree Nesting Cormorants.
Fee: BTO fee (£40). Expenses: Travel.
Distance: By agreement.
E-mail: stuart.newson@bto.org

NOBLE, Dr David (Principal Ecologist – Monitoring)
Subjects: The Farmland Bird Indicator, Population Trends.
Fee: BTO fee (£40). Expenses: Travel. Distance: By agreement. E-mail: david.noble@bto.org

REHFISCH, Dr Mark (Director of Development)
Subjects: Wetland Work at the BTO, Water Quality and Waterbirds, Climate Change, Habitat Loss and Waterbirds, Monitoring Waterbirds, Sea Level Rise and Climate Change, Waterbird Alerts, Introduced Species including Golden Pheasants.
Fee: BTO fee (£40) (up to £40 for private talk).
Expenses: Travel. Distance: By agreement.
E-mail: mark.rehfisch@bto.org

RISELY, Kate (Breeding Bird Survey organiser)
Subjects: UK bird trends, BBS and other BTO surveys
Fee: BTO fee (£40). Expenses: Travel. Distance: By agreement. E-mail: kate.risely@bto.org

ROBINSON, Dr Rob (Modelling and Demography Group Principal Ecologist)
Subjects: Farming and Birds, House Sparrows.
Fee: BTO fee (£40). Expenses: Travel. Distance: By agreement. E-mail: rob.robinson@bto.org

SIRIWARDENA, Dr Gavin (Head of Land-use Research)
Subjects: Marsh and Willow Tits – Analysis of BTO Data; Evidence of Impacts of Nest Predation and, Competition, Quantifying Migratory Strategies, Winter Feeding of Farmland birds, general farmland talks (overview of BTO and other farmland bird research).
Fee: BTO fee (£40). Expenses: Travel. Distance: 50 miles (further with accommodation).
E-mail: gavin.siriwardena@bto.org

STANCLIFFE, Paul (Press Officer)
Subjects: Atlas 2007-11, The BTO Garden BirdWatch.
Fee: £40. Expenses: Travel. Distance: By agreement.
E-mail: paul.stancliffe@bto.org

SWANN, Bob (Scottish Atlas Organiser)
Subjects: Bird Atlas 2001-11
Fee: £40. Expenses: Petrol. Distance: Scotland.
E-mail: bob.swann@bto.org

TOMS, Mike (Head of Garden Ecology)
Subjects: Garden Birds.Birds in an urbanised landscape.
Fee: £40. Expenses: Petrol. Distance: 50 miles, further by arrangement.
E-mail: mike.toms@bto.org

WERNHAM, Dr Chris (Senior Research Ecologist and Head of BTO Scotland)
Subjects: The work of BTO (in Scotland); Why record birds/making your birdwatching count; BirdTrack in Scotland; The Breeding Bird Survey (BBS) in Scotland; The Wetland Bird Survey (WeBS) in Scotland
Fee: £40. Expenses: Petrol. Distance: Scotland and northern England.
E-mail: chris.wernham@bto.org

TRADE DIRECTORY

David Cromack

A male Eider indulges in a spot of wing stretching.

TRADE DIRECTORY

BIRD GARDEN SUPPLIERS

BIRD GARDEN SUPPLIES

ARK WILDLIFE LTD

Company ethos: Family-run garden wildlife mail order business offering a full range of high quality wild bird food produced on own premises in Hertfordshire.

Key product lines: Complete range of Ark® wild bird seed mixes with AdVit™ pro-biotics, along with premium grade straights such as sunflower seeds, peanuts and niger, supported by a full range of accessories including bird feeders, wildlife guides and more.

Other services: Mail order company, 24-hour shopping on-line, with fast next day delivery. Phone for a catalogue.

Opening times: Mon - Fri (8.30am-6pm), Sat (9am-2pm). Out-of-hours answer phone service.

Address: Dog Kennel Farm, Charlton Road, Hitchin, Hertfordshire SG5 2AB. 0800 085 4865; (fax)01462 420 022. e-mail: office@arkwildlife.co.uk www.arkwildlife.co.uk

BAMFORDS TOP FLIGHT

Company ethos: Family-owned manufacturing company providing good quality bird foods via a network of UK stockists or mail order. RSPB Corporate Member, BTO Business Ally, Petcare Trust Member.

Key product lines: A range of wild bird mixtures containing the revolutionary new 'Pro-tec Health Aid', developed by Bamfords, to protect and promote the welfare of wild birds. Vast array of other foods and seeds for birds.

Other services: Trade suppliers of bulk and pre-packed bird and petfoods. Custom packing/own label if required.

New for 2010: Bird foods in a handy 12.75kg bag. No VAT and great value.

Opening times: Mon - Fri 8.00 - 5.30pm; Sat 8.00 - 12.00 noon; Sunday 10.00 - 12.00 noon (mill shop only).

Address: Globe Mill, Midge Hall, Leyland, Lancashire PR26 6TN: 01772 456 300;(Fax) 01772 456 302. e-mail: sales@bamfords.co.uk www.bamfords.co.uk

BIRD VENTURES

Company ethos: A comprehensive stock of wildlife products for everyone from garden bird enthusiasts to keen birdwatchers. The business operates as an online shop and retail outlet based in Holt, Norfok. The business helps support Natural Surrounding, a wildlife centre with eight ecres of gardens and education facilities for all ages, which won Environmental Small Business of the Year for north Norfolk from the district council.

Key product lines: Nest box cameras, moth traps, butterfly nets, wildbird food, bird feeders, nest boxes, hedgehog homes, insect habitats, bat boxes, squirrel-proof feeders, wildflower seeds, children's nature study equipment and much more.

Other services: On-line 24 hours.

Opening times: Mon-Sat (9am-5.30pm).

Contact: Bird Ventures, 9B Chapel Yard, Albert Street, Holt, Norfolk NR25 6HG; 01263 710 203; (fax)01263 711 091. e-mail: paullaurie100@aol.com www.birdventures.co.uk

CJ WILDBIRD FOODS LTD

Company ethos: CJ WildBird Foods aims to make significant, recognisable contributions to the protection and welfare of wild birds and other wildlife.

Our ornithologists and wildlife advisors undertake research projects to ensure we are continually producing not only high quality products, but products designed specifically for the wildlife they are intended for.

We are proud to work in support of the RSPCA and RHS.

When buying products from us you are supporting the valuable wildlife conservation work of these charities.

Key product lines: CJ Wildlife bird feeders, bird food, nest boxes, bird tables and accessories, along with a broad range of wildlife care products, all available via our secure online web site or by mail order from our free catalogue.

Other services: Request a free *Handbook of Garden Wildlife* catalogue with advice, tips and products. CJ Wildlife brand products are also stocked widely in supermarkets, garden centres and pet shops. Sister company Subbuteo Natural History Books (www. wildlifebooks.co.uk)

New for 2010: Continuously adding new products to the range, call for a brochure or visit the website.

Opening times: Call our friendly and knowledgeable team on free-phone 0800 731 2820 Monday to Friday 9am - 5pm, Saturday 9am - 12pm.

Goods can be collected (10% discount). Website 24 hours. Next working-day delivery on orders by 1pm. Delivery just £1.99 and free on order over £50.

Address: The Rea, Upton Magna, Shrewsbury, Shropshire SY4 4UR; 0800 731 2820; (Fax) 01743 709 504. e-mail: enquiries@birdfood.co.uk www.birdfood.co.uk

BIRD GARDEN SUPPLIERS

CLOSEWATCH LTD

Company ethos: Nest box and bird feeder camera systems of the highest quality.
Key product lines: Cedarwood and marine grade ply nest boxes and feeder stations fitted with high resolution and HD cameras. HD infra-red wildlife cameras and pond cameras with built-in recording.
Other services: Made to order service.
Opening times:
Mon to Sat
(8am-8pm).

Address: 5
Crabtree Lane,
Bodmin, Cornwall PL31 1BL. 01208 790 00;
(M)07967 238 119.
e-mail: closewatch@btconnect.com
www.closewatchcameras.co.uk
www.wildlife-cameras.com

ERNEST CHARLES

Company ethos: Member of Birdcare Standards Assoc. ISO 9001 registered. Offering quality bird foods/wildlife products through a friendly mail-order service. Working in association with The British Trust for Ornithology.
Key product lines: Bird foods, feeders, nest boxes and other wildlife products.
Other services: Trade enquiries welcomed.
Opening times: Mon to Fri (8am-5pm).
Address: Stuart Christophers, Copplestone Mills, Crediton, Devon EX17 5NF; (Fax)01363 84 842; (Fax)01363 84 147. e-mail: stuart@ernest-charles.com
www.ernest-charles.com

foodforbirds.co.uk

Company ethos: Specialist mail order company supplying high quality wild bird foods via a fast and friendly next day service. Supporter of RSPB and BTO through parent company.
Key product lines: A great range of tried and tested, freshly made wild bird mixtures, together with a whole host of straight foods: peanuts, sunflowers, niger seed, fat foods etc.
Other services: Vast array of bird feeders for peanuts and seed, plus other wildlife foods, all of which can be ordered via a secure on-line website. Send for free catalogue.
New for 2010: Bird foods in a handy 12.75kg bag. No VAT and great value.
Opening times: Telesales (freephone) 8.00 - 5.30pm (order before midday for next day delivery). Answer phone outside these hours. On-line ordering and fax, 24 hours.
Address: Foodforbirds, Leyland, Lancashire PR26 6TN; (Freephone)0800 043 9022; (Fax)01772 456 302. e-mail: sales@foodforbirds.co.uk
www.foodforbirds.co.uk

GARDENATURE WILDLIFE CAMERA SYSTEMS

Company ethos: With more than 40 years experience within the manufacturing and sales industry, we offer the largest selection and highest quality of 'Nest box Camera Systems' available on the market today! We always aim to deliver a product and service that goes beyond customer expectations.
Key product lines: Nest box and feeder cam systems, general wildlife and pond camera kits, photography hides, camouflage clothing.

Other services: 24hr web shop. Free catalogue on request. Online camera streaming for your website. Trade supplier.
Address: Manor Farm Business Centre, Stutton, Ipswich, Suffolk IP9 2TD; 0844 351 0987; (fax)07092 879 406. www.gardenature.co.uk

JACOBI JAYNE & CO.

Company ethos: Market-leaders for more than 20 years, offering products and expertise to individuals and professionals alike. Conservation products of highest quality and proven worth.
Key product lines: Birdfeeders, next boxes, foods and accessories. UK distributor of Schwegler nest boxes, Droll Yankees feeders and Jacobi Jayne wildlife foods.
Other services: *Living with Birds* mail-order catalogue and online at www.livingwithbirds.com
New for 2010: Brand new Ring-Pullä easy-clean feeders.
Opening times: 24hrs (use websites or answering service when office is closed).
Contact: Clair Dance, Jacobi Jayne & Co, Wealden Forest Park, Canterbury, Kent CT6 7LQ; 0800 072 0130; (Fax)01227 719 235. www.jacobijayne.com
e-mail: enquiries@jacobijayne.com

VINE HOUSE FARM BIRD FOODS

Company ethos: Growing and selling wild bird food on a family-run farm. A full range of high quality bird foods and accessories direct to the customer through our mail-order service and farm shop.
Key product lines: A full range of bird food including home grown black sunflowers and a range of specialist mixes and feeder accessories.
Other services: A number of farm walks and open days in early summer for people to view our conservation award-winning farm. We also have a range of products available for wholesale customers.
New for 2010: The Wildlife Trust now recommend our bird seed to their members and also benefit from every sale we make.
Opening times: Mon to Fri (8am-5pm), Sat (8am-4pm), Sun (10am-4pm).

Contact: Nicholas Watts, Vine House Farm, Deeping St Nicholas, Spalding PE11 3DG; 01775 630 208; (Fax)01775 630 244.
e-mail:birdseed@vinehousefarm.co.uk
www.vinehousefarm.co.uk

BOOK PUBLISHERS

BUCKINGHAM PRESS LTD

Imprints: Single imprint company - publishers of *The Birdwatcher's Yearbook* since 1981, *Who's Who in Ornithology* (1997), *Best Birdwatching Sites* series covering Norfolk, Sussex, Highlands of Scotland, North Wales, Cornwall & Scilly. Plus sets of identification cards for British birds, dragonflies and butterflies.
New for 2010: *Best Birdwatching Sites in North East England.*

Address: 55 Thorpe Park Road, Peterborough, PE3 6LJ. Tel/Fax: 01733 561 739.
e-mail: admin@buckinghampress.com
www.buckinghampress.co.uk

CHRISTOPHER HELM PUBLISHERS

Imprints: *Christopher Helm:* the leading publisher of ornithology books in the world; includes many field guides, identification guides, family guides, county and country avifaunas, and a *Where to Watch Birds* series.
T & AD Poyser: an acclaimed series of respected ornithology monographs. Birds of Africa – the standard series of handbooks on African birds.
A & C Black: publisher of definitive natural history books.

New for 2010: *Birds of Argentina* by Mark Pearman, *Birds of the Middle East* (2nd edition) by Richard Porter and Simon Aspinall, *Birds of Mongolia* by S. Gombobaatar et al., *Birds of Ghana* by Nik Borrow and Ron Demey, *The Biggest Twitch* by Alan Davies and Ruth Miller.
Status of Birds in Britain and Ireland by David Parkin and Alan Knox, *Helm Dictionary of Scientific Bird Names* by James Jobling, *RSPB Gardening for Wildlife* by Adrian Thomas, *Where to Watch Birds in Britain* (2nd edition) by Simon Harrap and Nigel Redman, *Reed and Bush Warblers* by Peter Kennerley and David Pearson.
Address: 36 Soho Square, London, W1D 3QY; 020 7758 0200; (Fax)020 7758 0222.
e-mail: nredman@acblack.com
www.acblack.com/naturalhistory

COXTON PUBLICATIONS LTD

Company ethos: Logbooks connected with hobbies and pastimes.
Key product lines: *Bird Watcher's Logbook, Kitchen Gardener's Logbook.*
Opening times: Mail order, phone, e-mail.
Address: Eastwood, Beverley Road, Walkington, Beverley, East Yorks HU17 8RP; 01482 881 833.
e-mail@ jenny.macrae@virgin.net
www.coxton.alchemica.co.uk

HARPERCOLLINS PUBLISHERS

Imprints: *Collins Natural History:* the leading publisher of fieldguides to the natural world.
Collins New Naturalist Series: the encyclopaedic reference for all areas of British natural history.
HarperCollins: publisher of the best illustrated books.
New for 2010: *Collins Fungi Guide, Collins Bird Guide,* 2nd Edition large Format, *Collins Complete Garden Wildlife.*
Address: 77-85 Fulham Palace Rd, Hammersmith, London, W6 8JB; 020 8307 4998; (Fax)020 8307 4037.
e-mail: Myles.Archibald@harpercollins.co.uk
www.fireandwater.com www.collins.co.uk

NEW HOLLAND PUBLISHERS (UK) LTD

Imprints: *New Holland:* field guides, photographic guides, garden wildlife books and other illustrated titles on birds and general wildlife, plus personality-led natural history.
Struik: the world's leading natural history publisher on African wildlife.
New for 2010: *Atlas of Remarkable Birds; Bears in Space and 500 Other Amazing Animal Facts; Botanic Gardens - Modern Day Arks; Chris Packham's Back Garden Nature Reserve (new edition); Confessions of a Tabloid Twitcher; Field Guide to the Reptiles of South-East Asia; Kingfisher; Lizards of the World (Volume I); New Holland Advanced Bird Guide; New Holland Concise Bird Guide; New Holland Concise Butterfly and Moth Guide; New Holland Concise Wild Flower Guide; Watching Wildlife in London.*
Address: Garfield House, 86-88 Edgware Road, London W2 2EA; 020 7724 7773; (Fax)020 7258 1293.
e-mail: simon.papps@nhpub.co.uk
www.newhollandpublishers.com

WILDGuides LTD

Imprints; *WILDGuides:* natural history fieldguides covering butterflies, dragonflies, orchids, arable plants.
OCEANGuides: identification guides to marine wildlife covering Antarctic, Atlantic and Pacific titles.
Destination Guides: lavishly illustrated visitor guides to Galapagos, Seychelles, South Georgia, Falklands.
Crossbill Guides: regional heritage guides for walkers covering Spain, France, Poland, Hungary.
Recently published: *Britain's Reptiles and*

*Amphibians, Flowers of the New Forest, Crossbill
– Cevennes (France), Nightjars of the World.*
New for 2010: *Britain's Bees, Wildlife of South
Georgia, Britain's Butterflies* (2nd edition).
Address: PO Box 680, Maidenhead, Berkshire SL6 9ST;
01628 529 297; (Fax)01628 525 314.
e-mail: info@wildguides.co.uk
www.wildguides.co.uk

BOOK SELLERS

ATROPOS
Company ethos: Lively magazine for butterfly, moth
and dragonfly enthusiasts. Mail order book service
providing key titles swiftly at competitive prices.
Key subjects: Butterflies, moths, dragonflies and
other insects.
Other services: News of latest migrant insect
sightings provided on website.
Address: 36 Tinker Lane, Meltham, Holmfirth, West
Yorkshire HD9 4EX. 01326 290 287.
e-mail: atropos.editor@zen.co.uk www.atropos.info

CALLUNA BOOKS
Company ethos: We specialise in buying and selling
out-of-print natural history titles, with an emphasis
on quality stock at competitive prices.
Key subjects: Birds, mammals, flora, invertebrates
in the UK and worldwide, including the Poyser and
New Naturalist series, and general natural history,
conservation and countryside titles, including some
reports and journals. Stock of 2,500-plus titles
maintained.
Other services: Catalogues issued (usually 3 p.a) and
stocklist updated regularly on website. We exhibit at
some bird fairs including Rutland Water. Wants lists
welcomed with no obligation to buy.
Opening times: Mail order but viewing by
appointment possible.
Address: Moor Edge, 2 Bere Road, Wareham, Dorset
BH20 4DD; 01929 552 560. www.callunabooks.co.uk
e-mail: enquiries@callunabooks.co.uk

NHBS ENVIRONMENT BOOKSTORE
Company ethos: A unique natural history,
conservation and environmental bookstore.
The world's largest range of wildlife books and
equipment.
Key subjects: Natural history, conservation,
environmental science, zoology, habitats and
ecosystems, botany, marine biology, bat detecting,
entomology, GPS, birding.
Other services: Search
and browse our full
online catalogue
of more than
100,000 titles at
www.nhbs.com
New for 2010:
Expanded wildlife equipment range, including bat
detectors, butterfly nets, moth traps, head torches,
hand lenses and more.

Opening times: Mon-Fri (9am-5pm), for mail-order
service. Browse or order anytime at www.nhbs.com
Address: 2-3 Wills Road, Totnes, Devon TQ9 5XN;
01803 865 913. e-mail: customer.services@nhbs.co.uk
www.nhbs.com

PICTURE BOOK
Company ethos: General bookshop with specialist
interest in bird books and natural history.
Key subjects: Birdwatching, natural history, local
history.
Other services: Mail order, new and secondhand
books (easy-to-use on-line search facility).
Opening times: Tue-Fri (9.15am-4.30pm), Sat (9am-
4.30pm).
Address: Picture Book, 6 Stanley Street, Leek, ST13
5HG;01538 384 337; (Fax)01538 399 696.
e-mail: info@leekbooks.co.uk
www.birdbooksonline.co.uk

PORTLAND OBSERVATORY BOOK SHOP
Company ethos: To meet all the book needs of
amateur and professional naturalists.
Key subjects: Ornithology, botany, entomology,
marine biology, geology, ecology, general natural
history, conservation and local topography.
Other services:
Website and mail
order, discount
on new books and
increased discount for
observatory members.
All cards taken.
Opening times: Wed,
Sat and Sunday; (10am
to 4pm).
Address: Portland
Bird Observatory and Field Centre, Old Lower
Light, Portland Bill, Dorset DT5 2JT; Opening hours
01305 826 625, other times 01305 777 991. e-mail:
wright@churchknap.wanadoo.uk
www.portlandbirdobs.org.uk

SECOND NATURE
Company ethos: Buying and selling out-of-print/
secondhand/antiquarian books on natural history,
topography and travel.
Key subjects: Birds, mammals, flowers and all other
aspects of natural history.
Other services; Exhibits at bird/wildlife fairs.
New for 2010: A comprehensive website - www.
secondnaturebooks.com
Opening times: Mail order only.
Address: Knapton Book Barn, Back Lane, Knapton,
York YO26 6QJ; (Tel/fax) 01904 339 493.
e-mail: SecondnatureYork@aol.com
www.secondnaturebooks.com

SUBBUTEO NATURAL HISTORY BOOKS
Company ethos: Specialisation and careful selection
have allowed us to develop a fine reputation for
supplying & publishing natural history books, DVDs,

travel and field guides for those who enjoy bird watching and the natural world; while providing a fast, friendly and efficient service.
Key subjects: Natural History – Ornithology; UK, Europe & worldwide, mammals, reptiles & amphibians, aquatic fauna, butterflies & moths, plants & fungi, ecology & environmental science, wildlife art & photography.

Other services: Comprehensive online library, online book forum, gift wrap service, booklist service, worldwide book sourcing. Online ordering, with free delivery on orders over £50 (in-print titles & UK titles only), free catalogue, updates & monthly e-newsletter. Sister company CJ WildBird Foods Ltd - www.birdfood.co.uk
New for 2010: Continuously adding new titles to the range, call for a brochure or visit the website.
Opening times: Book shop: mon-fri (9am-5pm). Sat (9am-12pm). Online ordering 24 hrs.
Address: The Rea, Upton Magna, Shrewsbury, Shropshire SY4 4UR; 0870 010 9700; (Fax)0870 010 9699. e-mail: info@wildlifebooks.com www.wildlifebooks.com

WILDSOUNDS
Company ethos: Donates a significant portion of profit to bird conservation, committed to sound environmental practices, official bookseller to African Bird Club. BirdLife International species champion for the Spoon-billed Sandpiper.
Key product lines: Mail order, post-free books, multi-media guides and eGuides for PDAs - mobile versions of popular fieldguides complete with bird sounds and listing software. Publisher of *Birding in Eastern Europe* by Gerard Gorman; *Birds of Argentina vol 1 (Patagonia)* by Santiago Imberti, et al; *Sounds of Zambian Wildlife* by Bob Stjernstedt.
New for 2010: *Birds of Argentina* (vol 2).
Opening times: Weekdays (9.30am-5pm).
Address: Cross Street, Salthouse, Norfolk NR25 7XH; +44(UK) (0)1263 741 100; (Fax) +44 (0)1263 741 838. e-mail: sales@wildsounds.com www.wildsounds.com

WYSEBY HOUSE BOOKSHOP
Company ethos: We stock rare, out-of-print, second-hand and unusual titles which are on display in our shop or can be found on our website. Informed and friendly staff always ready to help personal shoppers or answer telephone and e-mail enquiries.
Key subjects: Bird books, gardening, forestry and natural history, art, architecture, design.
Other services: A well-designed website with easy-to-use search facility where books can be located by author, title, keyword or subject.
Opening times: Mon-Sat (9am-5pm), but we suggest

you ring beforehand just in case you are travelling some distance.
Address: Kingclere Old Bookshop, 2a George Street, Kingsclere, Nr Newbury, Berkshire RG20 5NQ; 01635 297 995; (Fax)01635 297 677. e-mail: info@wyseby.co.uk www.wyseby.co.uk

CLOTHING

COUNTRY INNOVATION
Company ethos: Specialists in clothing, footwear and accessories for the birdwatching market. Offering friendly advice by well-trained staff.
Key product lines: Full range of outdoor wear: jackets, fleeces, trousers, travel clothing, Ventile garments, Brasher footwear, Tilley hats, bags and accessories. Ladies fit available.
Other services: Mail order and website.
New for 2010: New Venture Waistcoat, Ladies Venture Waistcoat and Trousers, Plover range, Hawk Jacket, Buzzard Jacket.
Opening times; Mon-Fri (9am-5pm), Sat (9am-3pm).
Address: 1 Broad Street, Congresbury, North Somerset BS49 5DG; 01934 877 333. e-mail: sales@countryinnovation.com www.countryinnovation.com

PARÁMO DIRECTIONAL CLOTHING SYSTEMS
Company ethos: Innovators of technical mountain, birding and travel clothing using revolutionary Nikwax fabrics and functional design to provide performance and comfort for all outdoor enthusiasts and professionals, whatever their activity. Ethical manufacture. Eco-friendly.
Key product lines: Waterproof jackets and trousers, technical base layers and insulation overlayers. Of particular note: the Halcon and Pájaro birdwatching jackets, Torres insulating overlayers and the Andy Rouse Limited Edition range of Aspira smock, Cascada waterproof trousers and Mountain Vent pull-on.
Other services: Alterations to, repair and service of Páramo garments.

New for 2010: Men's and ladies Halcon Jackets, Torres overlayering sleeves and trousers. New Nature Professionals scheme – contact us on 00 44(0)1892 786 466. Online sales direct from Páramo at www. naturallyparamo.co.uk
Opening times; For independent retailers, consult our website or ring 01892 786 444 for stockist list and catalogue pack.
Address: Unit F, Durgates Industrial Estates, Wadhurst, East Sussex TN5 6JL, UK; 01892 786 444. e-mail: info@paramo.co.uk www.paramo.co.uk

EQUIPMENT SUPPLIERS AND SERVICES

ALWYCH BOOKS
Company ethos: The Bird Watcher's All-weather Flexible Pocket Book.
Key product lines: Alwych all-weather notebooks. All-weather sketchbook now available for artists.
Address: Janette Scott, Wishaw Printing Company, 84 Stewarton Street, Wishaw, ML2 8AG; 0845 270 2828; (admin)01698 357 223.

BIRD IMAGES
Company ethos: High quality products at affordable prices.
Key product lines: Bird DVDs filmed and narrated by Paul Doherty. A range of titles including identification guides and innovative guides to birdwatching places.
New for 2010: *The Birds of North America.*
Opening times: Telephone first.
Address: 28 Carousel Walk, Sherburn in Elmet, North Yorkshire LS25 6LP; 01977 684 666.
e-mail: paul@birdvideodvd.com
www.birdvideodvd.com

BIRDGUIDES LTD

BIRDGUIDES

Company ethos: Better birding through technology. The number one birder's website.
Key product lines: Software and video guides to British, European and American birds. Rare bird news services via e-mail, website and SMS. Books and an expanding range of natural history products for mobile phones.
New for 2010: *Breeding Birds of the Western Palearctic software. The Butterflies of Britain and Ireland* on DVD
Address: Birdguides Ltd, PO Box 4104, Sheffield S25 9BJ; 0114 283 1002;
order line (freephone) 0800 919 391;
e-mail: contact@birdguides.com
www.birdguides.com

GOLDEN VALLEY INSURANCE SERVICES
Company ethos: Knowledgeable, friendly insurance services. Free information pack on request. Freephone telephone number for all enquiries.
Key product lines: Insurance for optical/photographic/video/computer equipment for birdwatchers. Also, public liability for ornithological clubs and societies.
Other services: You can now apply online at www.photocover.co.uk or you can phone for instant cover. Call 01981 240 536 or 01981 241 062 or freephone 0800 015 4484.
Opening times: Mon-Fri (9am-5pm), answering machine at other times
Address: Sharron or Marion, Golden Valley Insurance Services, The Olde Shoppe, Ewyas Harold, Herefordshire HR2 0ES; 0800 015 4484; (Fax)01981

240 451. e-mail: gvinsurance@aol.com
www.photocover.co.uk

NEWART
Company ethos: Our company introduces innovative products in specialised fields.
Key product lines: 'Clipmate' was invented to prevent the swing and bounce of binoculars or other equipment when hung on a strap. The device is fitted to the binoculars which are then clipped to the user's coat, sweater or shirt. This gives the freedom of both hands, invaluable when walking with a dog lead, stick or nordic poles. The package retails at £10 + £2 p&p.
Address: Payment by cheque to 12 Verwood Drive, Barnet, Herts EN4 9TP; 020 8275 0018.

SRB-GRITURN
Key product lines: Photographic accessories and digiscoping solutions. Also retails binoculars, telescopes and tripods.
Other services: Specialist manufacture of camera adaptors and other engineered products.
Opening times: Mon to Fri (9am-5pm), and Sat (9am-12noon).
Address: SRB Griturn, Unit 21D Icknield Way Farm, Tring Road, Dunstable, Beds, LU6 2JX. 01582 661 878; (fax)01582 472 980;
e-mail: enquiries@srb-griturn.com
www.srb-griturn.com

WILDLIFE WATCHING SUPPLIES
Company ethos: To bring together a comprehensive range of materials, clothing and equipment to make it easier and more comfortable for you to blend in with the environment. Quick and friendly service.
Key product lines: Hides, camouflage, bean bags, lens and camera covers, clothing etc.etc.
New for 2010: More designs of camera, lens and scope covers.
Opening times: Mon to Fri (9am-5pm), Mail order. Visitors by appointment.
Address: Town Living Farmhouse, Puddington, Tiverton, Devon EX16 8LW; 01884 860 692(24hr); (Fax)01884 860 994.
e-mail: enquiries@wildlifewatchingsupplies.co.uk
www.wildlifewatchingsupplies.co.uk

WILDSOUNDS
Key product lines: Mail order, post-free books, multi-media guides and eGuides for PDAs - mobile versions of popular field guides complete with bird sounds and listing software e.g. *Collins Bird eGuide* and *Sasol eBirds of Southern Africa.* Publisher of *Birding in Eastern Europe* by Gerard Gorman; *Birds of Argentina vol 1 (Patagonia)* by Santiago Imberti, et al; *Sounds of Zambian Wildlife* by Bob Stjernstedt. Field recording equipment stockist.
New for 2010: *Birds of Argentina* (vol 2).
Opening times: Weekdays (9.30am-5pm).
Address: Cross Street, Salthouse, Norfolk NR25 7XH; +44(UK) (0)1263 741 100; (Fax) +44 (0)1263 741 838.
e-mail: sales@wildsounds.com   www.wildsounds.com

121

HOLIDAY COMPANIES

AVIAN ADVENTURES

Company ethos: Top quality, value-for-money tours, escorted by friendly, experienced leaders at a fairly relaxed pace. ATOL 3367.

Types of tours: Birdwatching, birds and wildlife photography and wildlife safaris, all suitable for both the first-time and the more experienced traveller.

Destinations: More than 70 tours worldwide.

New for 2010: Aragon, Spain: Colombia.

Brochure from: 49 Sandy Road, Norton, Stourbridge, DY8 3AJ; 01384 372 013; (Fax)01384 441 340.

e-mail: aviantours@argonet.co.uk
www.avianadventures.co.uk

BIRDFINDERS

Company ethos: Top-value birding tours to see all specialities/endemics of a country/area, using leading UK and local guides. ATOL 5406.

Types of tours: Birdwatching holidays for all abilities.

Destinations: Nearly 60 tours in UK, Europe, Africa, Asia, Australasia, North and South America and Antarctica.

New for 2010: Azores, Cape May USA, Croatia, Israel in Autumn, Mongolia, Russia's Ural Mountains, Sweden.

Brochure from: Vaughan Ashby, Westbank, Cheselbourne, Dorset DT2 7NW. 01258 839 066.

e-mail: info@birdfinders.co.uk
www.birdfinders.co.uk

Our office is open seven days a week (8am-8pm).

BIRD HOLIDAYS

Company ethos: Relaxed pace, professional leaders, small groups, exciting itineraries.

Types of tours: Birdwatching for all levels, beginners to advanced.

Destinations: Worldwide (40 tours, 6 continents).

New for 2010: Madagascar, Bhutan, Mongolia, Atlantic Odyssey.

Brochure from: 10 Ivegate, Yeadon, Leeds, LS19 7RE; (Tel/fax)0113 3910 510.

e-mail: info@birdholidays.co.uk
www.birdholidays.co.uk

BIRDWATCHING BREAKS

Company ethos: Birdwatching breaks and Black Isle birding, watching birds in their natural habitat and putting money into the local economy from green tourism.

Types of tours: Birding tours around the world to little-known destinations along with more traditional destinations using local guides in addition to our own. These tours are aimed at all abilities and, with the exception of one tour, we will not have more than 8 clients on a tour thus giving a better opportunity for all participants to see the birds and wildlife. We also specialise in Northern Scotland including the Highlands and Islands under the Black Isle Birding Banner. Our tours main interest is aimed at birds but

we also take in mammals and other wildlife. Many of our tours are suitable for photography.

Destinations: Canada, Chile, Colombia, Ethiopia, France, Guatemala, Iceland, India, Iran, Ireland, Jamaica, Japan, Lesser Antilles, Mallorca, Mongolia, Morocco,Nepal, Poland, Senegal, South Africa, Spain, Sri Lanka, Syria, Taiwan, Uganda, Vietnam and numerous in Scotland. Some of these tours are regularly featured others are old favourites that we have re-introduced for this year.

New for 2010: Colombia, Lesser Antilles, Iran and introducing short breaks within the UK & Europe.

Brochure from: Birdwatching Breaks, Cygnus House, Gordon's Mill, Balblair, Ross-shire IV7 8LQ; 01381 610 495. e-mail: enquiries@birdwatchingbreaks.com
www.birdwatchingbreaks.com

BIRD WATCHING AND WILDLIFE CLUB

Company ethos: To provide birdwatchers with high quality, reasonably priced accommodation, enabling them to make the best of their bird watching holidays in Scotland.

Types of tours: BWWC, based at the 3-star, 50-bedroom Grant Arms Hotel, is all about guests choosing what they want to do. The BWWC Resident Team provides advice, guides, maps, talks and briefings on wildlife-watching sites nearby.

Destinations: Cairngorms, Speyside and North East Scotland.

New for 2010: Special rates for birdwatching groups.

Opening times: (7am-10:30pm) seven days a week.

Brochure from: Grant Arms Hotel, 25 The Square, Grantown-on-Spey, Highlands PH26 3HF; 01479 872 526. e-mail: bookings@bwwc.co.uk
www.bwwc.co.uk

BRITISH-BULGARIAN FRIENDSHIP SOCIETY

Company ethos: To introduce people to the beauty of Bulgarian wildlife at exceptional value prices with expert leaders. ATOL 4465.

Types of tours: Birdwatching tours in winter, spring and autumn, also butterfly, wild flower and natural history tours. Groups size 12-14 persons.

Destinations: Specialists to Bulgaria, over 30 years experience.

New for 2010: Beginners Birdwatching, Nomansland Tour, Early and Late Summer Butterfly Tours.

Brochure from: Balkania Travel Ltd, Suite 3.40, Morley House, 320 Regent Street, London W1B 3BE; (Tel)020 7536 9400; www.balkaniatravel.com
e-mail:ognian@balkaniatravel.com
Or Dr Annie Kay 020 7237 7616 or
e-mail: annie.kay@btinternet.com
Website: www.bbfs.org.uk

DORSET BIRDING

Company ethos: To provide local knowledge and an expertise of Dorset's birds and wildlife, catering for all levels of experience and tailor-made to your requirements.

Types of tours: A guiding service for individuals and small groups aimed at providing an experience of Dorset's birds, wildlife and landscapes. Although there is a particular emphasis on birds, all species groups are covered. Half-day, full day, weekends or longer breaks are available. Local accommodation can be arranged.
Destinations: Dorset, New Forest.
Brochure from: Moor Edge, 2 Bere Road, Wareham, Dorset BH20 4DD;01929 552 560.
e-mail: enquiries@dorsetbirdingandwildlife.co.uk
www.dorsetbirdingandwildlife.co.uk

HEATHERLEA

Company ethos: Exciting holidays to see all the birds of Scotland and selected overseas destinations. Experienced guides and comfortable award-winning hotel offering great customer service.
Types of tours: Birdwatching and other wildlife watching tours.
Destinations: Scottish Highlands, including holidays from our base in Nethybridge, plus Outer Hebrides, Orkney, Shetlands and more. Selected overseas destinations include the Pyrenees, Lesvos, Kenya and Trinidad.
New for 2010: Our 20th season sees us add new destinations including Gambia and Nova Scotia.
Brochure from: The Mountview Hotel, Nethybridge, Inverness-shire PH25 3EB; 01479 821 248; (Fax)01479 821 515. e-mail: info@heatherlea.co.uk
www.heatherlea.co.uk

NORTH WEST BIRDS

Company ethos: Friendly, relaxed and unhurried but targetted to scarce local birds.
Types of tours: Very small groups (up to four) based on large family home in South Lakes with good home cooking. Short breaks with birding in local area. Butterflies in season.
Destinations: Local to Northwest England, including Lancashire, Morecambe Bay and Lake District.
Brochure from: Mike Robinson, Barn Close, Beetham, Cumbria LA7 7AL; (Tel/fax)015395 63191.
e-mail: mike@nwbirds.co.uk www.nwbirds.co.uk

ORIOLE BIRDING

Company ethos: Enhancing your ID skills and enjoyment of birding.
Types of tours: Norfolk and South Wales birding tours year-round, covering all the best sites and species, plus a selection of Britain's best destinations. Also a comprehensive range of international holidays and pelagics. ATOL protected 6839.
Destinations: Norfolk (20 tours), South Wales (four tours), Solway, North Wales, Speyside, Cornwall (three tours), Isles of Scilly pelagics, North-east England (two tours), Fair Isle, County Wexford, Mull and Iona, Mallorca, Extremadura, Romania, South Africa, The Gambia, Israel.
New for 2010: Armenia, Arizona, California, Texas, Hungary (two tours), Czech Republic, Bulgaria, Trinidad and Tobago, Turkey (three tours), Utsira,

Lesvos, Holland, Ebro Delta and Pyrenees, Madeira, China, India (two tours), Egypt, Kazakhstan, Outer Hebrides, Finland and Norway, Poland, Northern Cyprus, UAE and Morocco.
Brochure from: Oriole Birding, 84 Coity Road, Bridgend CF31 1LT; 01656 645 709.
e-mail: info@oriolebirding.com
www.oriolebirding.com

ORNITHOLIDAYS

Company ethos: Oldest bird tour company in the world (established 1965). Friendly and fun holidays led by full-time tour leaders. ATOL no 0743.
Types of tours: Escorted birdwatching and natural history tours.
Destinations: Worldwide including Trinidad and Tobago, Costa Rica, Bolivia, Australia, South Africa and Antarctica.
New for 2010: Ghana, Hawaii and Philippines.
Brochure from: 29 Straight Mile, Romsey, Hampshire SO51 9BB; 01794 519 445; (Fax)01794 523 544.
e-mail: info@ornitholidays.co.uk
www.ornitholidays.co.uk

SPEYSIDE WILDLIFE

Company ethos: Expert leaders, personal attention and a sense of fun - it's your holiday. ATOL no 4259.
Types of tours: Experts in Scotland and leaders worldwide - birdwatching, mammals and whale watching.
Destinations: Speyside and the Scottish Islands, Scandinavia, the Arctic, Europe, N and S America, Africa and India.
New for 2010: British Columbia.
Brochure from: Garden Office, Inverdruie House, Inverdruie, Aviemore, Inverness-shire PH22 1QH; (Tel/fax)01479 812 498.
e-mail: enquiries@speysidewildlife.co.uk
www.speysidewildlife.co.uk

SUNBIRD

Company ethos: Enjoyable birdwatching tours led by full-time professional leaders. ATOL no 3003.
Types of tours: Birdwatching, Birds & Music, Birds & History, Birds & Art.
Destinations: Worldwide.
New for 2010: Romania in winter, Cyprus, South Africa (Drakensberg and Kruger), Guatamala, Guyana, Bolivia, Colombia. Birds & Art in Tuscany. Birds & Music in Slovakia.
Brochure from: 26B The Market Square, Potton, Sandy, Bedfordshire SG19 2NP; 01767 262 522; (Fax)01767 262 916.
e-mail: sunbird@sunbirdtours.co.uk
www.sunbirdtours.co.ukcheck new destinations

THE TRAVELLING NATURALIST

Company ethos: Friendly, easy-going, expertly-led birdwatching and wildlife tours. ATOL no.3435. AITO 1124.
Types of tours: Tours include Birds and Butterflies, Bats, Butterflies and Flowers, Tigers, Arctic Cruises,

Whale-watching, Polar Bears.
Destinations: Worldwide.
New for 2010: Dragonflies in Spain & Hungary, Cacti
& Wildlife in Argentina, Birdwatching Latvia, Papua
New Guinea, Faroe Islands.
Brochure from: PO Box 3141, Dorchester, Dorset DT1
2XD; 01305 267 994; (Fax) 01305 265 506.
e-mail: info@naturalist.co.uk www.naturalist.co.uk

THE WILDLIFE GOURMET
Company ethos: To pass on our knowledge of wildlife
for future generations, through watching great birds
and wildlife that can be found around us, and to
enjoy good food and good wine in each area.
Types of tours: Birdwatching and general wildlife
trips including butterflies, wild flowers and mammals.
Destinations: Day trips to the Everglades, longer trips
to Texas, Alaska, Yellowstone, Rocky Mountain NP,
Florida and Europe.
Details from: Brett Hogan, P.O.Box 4, Islamorada,
Florida, U.S.A 33036. www.thewildlifegourmet.com
e-mail: thewildlifegourmet@yahoo.com

THINK GALAPAGOS
Company ethos: Specialists
in the Galapagos Islands, with
expert guides and personal
attention to ensure a once-
in-a-lifetime adventure travel
experience.
Types of tours: Friendly and relaxed holidays that
are educationally orientated for people with a keen
interest in wildlife and photography. Suitable for both
the first-time and more experienced traveller.
Destinations: Galapagos and mainland Ecuador.
New for 2010: Birding Special Trip to Ecuador and
Galapagos in May, led by top birding guides and
supporting the conservation work of RSPB in UK and
in Ecuador.
Brochure from: Rachel Dex, 25 Trinity Lane, Beverley
HU17 0DY; 01482 872 716. www.thinkgalapagos.com
e-mail: info@thinkgalapagos.karoo.co.uk

WILD INSIGHTS
Company ethos: Friendly, no-rush tours designed to
savour, understand and enjoy birds and wildlife fully,
rather than simply build large tick lists. Emphasis
on quality. ATOL no 5429 (in association with
Wildwings). No tape-luring or disturbance of wildlife.
Types of tours: UK workshops, Reader Breaks for *Bird
Watching* magazine and skills-building UK courses,
plus selected overseas tours.
Destinations: Various UK locations, plus USA, Costa
Rica, Africa, Northern India and Europe.
New for 2010: Iceland.
Calender brochure from: Yew Tree Farmhouse,
Craignant, Selattyn, Oswestry, Salop SY10 7NP. (Tel/
fax) 01691 718 740. e-mail: keith.offord@virgin.net
www.wildinsights.co.uk

WILDWINGS
Company ethos: Superb value holidays led by expert
guides.
Types of tours: Birdwatching holidays, whale and

dolphin watching holidays, mammal
tours and wildlife cruises worldwide.
Destinations: Europe, Arctic, Asia,
The Americas, Antarctica, Africa,
Australasia and the Pacific.
New for 2010: Birding Jamaica,
Birds and Wine (Spain), Indian Ocean
Seabird Expedition.
Brochure from: 577-579 Fishponds Road, Fishponds,
Bristol, BS16 3AF. e-mail: wildinfo@wildwings.co.uk
www.wildwings.co.uk

OPTICAL DEALERS

To assist readers in locating optics dealers in their
own area more easily, this section is devoted
into five regions, listed alphabetically as follows:
Eastern England, Northern England, South East
England, South West England and Western England.

EASTERN ENGLAND

BIRDNET OPTICS LTD
Company ethos: To provide the birdwatcher with
the best value for
money on optics,
books and outdoor
clothing.
Viewing facilities:
Clear views to distant hills for comparison of optics at
long range and wide variety of textures and edges for
clarity and resolution comparison.
Optical stock: Most leading binocular and telescope
ranges stocked. If we do not have it, we will
endeavour to get it for you.
Non-optical stock: Books incl. New Naturalist series
and Poysers, videos, CDs, audio tapes, tripods, hide
clamps, accessories and clothing.
Opening times: Mon-Sat (9:30am-5:30pm). Sundays,
see website for details.
Address: 5 London Road, Buxton, Derbyshire SK17
9PA; 01298 71 844. e-mail: paulflint@birdnet.co.uk
www.birdnet.co.uk

IN-FOCUS
Company ethos: The binocular and telescope
specialists, offering customers informed advice at
birdwatching venues throughout the country. Leading
sponsor of the British Birdwatchng Fair.
Viewing facilities: Available at all shops (contact
your local outlet), or at field events (10am-4pm) at
bird reserves (see *Bird Watching* magazine or website
www.at-infocus.co.uk for calendar)
Optical stock: Many leading makes of binoculars and
telescopes, plus own-brand Delta range of binoculars
and tripods.
Non-optical stock: Wide range of tripods, clamps and
other accessories. Repair service available.
Opening times: These can vary, so please contact
local shop or website before travelling.

NORFOLK
Address: Main Street, Titchwell, Nr King's Lynn, Norfolk, PE31 8BB; 01485 210 101.

RUTLAND
Address: Anglian Water Birdwatching Centre, Egleton Reserve, Rutland Water, Rutland, LE15 8BT; 01572 770 656.

LONDON CAMERA EXCHANGE
Company ethos: To supply good quality optical equipment at a competitive price, helped by knowlegeable staff.
Viewing facilities: In shop and at local shows. Contact local branch for details of local events.
Optical stock: All leading makes of binoculars and scopes.
Non-optical stock: All main brands of photo, digital and video equipment.
Opening times: Most branches open 9am to 5.30pm.

CHESTERFIELD
Address: 1A South Street, Chesterfield, Derbyshire, S40 1QZ; 01246 211 891; (Fax) 01246 211 563; e-mail: chesterfield@lcegroup.co.uk

COLCHESTER
Address: 12 Led Lane, Colchester, Essex CO1 1LS; 01206 573 444.

DERBY
Address: 17 Sadler Gate, Derby, Derbyshire, DE1 3NH; 01332 348 644; (Fax) 01332 369 136; e-mail: derby@lcegroup.co.uk

LINCOLN
Address: 6 Silver Street, Lincoln, LN2 1DY; 01522 514 131; (Fax) 01522 537 480; e-mail: lincoln@lcegroup.co.uk

NORWICH
Address: 12 Timber Hill, Norwich, Norfolk NR1 3LB; 01603 612 537.

NOTTINGHAM
Address: 7 Pelham Street, Nottingham, NG1 2EH; 0115 941 7486; (Fax) 0115 952 0547; e-mail: nottingham@lcegroup.co.uk

NORTHERN ENGLAND

CLEARVIEW BINOCULARS
Company ethos: Dedicated to serving the optical needs of naturalists, amateur astronomers and birdwatchers.

Viewing facilities: Retail outlet is situated on the edge of Newmillerdam country park.
Optical stock: Stockist of Visionary binoculars and telescopes, Optical Hardware binoculars, Olivon spotting scopes and Ostara binoculars.

Non-optical stock: Tripods, camera (especially digiscoping) adapters.
New for 2010: Ostara 10x42 and 8x42 'ED' binoculars due soon.
Opening times: Mon-Fri (9am-6pm), Sat-Sun (10am-5pm).
Address: The Old Coach House, Newmillerdam, Wakefield, Yorkshire WF2 6QG; 01924 229 787.
e-mail: sales@clearviewbinoculars.co.uk
www.clearviewbinoculars.co.uk

FOCALPOINT
Company ethos: Friendly advice by well-trained staff, competitive prices. No grey imports.
Viewing facilities: Fantastic open countryside for superb viewing from the shop, plenty of wildlife. Parking for up to 20 cars.
Optical stock: All leading brands of binoculars and telescopes from stock, plus many pre-owned binoculars and telescopes available.
Non-optical stock: Bird books, outdoor clothing, boots, tripods.
New for 2010: Growing range of photographic equipment & accessories.
Opening times: Mon-Sat (9:30am-5pm).
Address: Marbury House Farm, Bentleys Farm Lane, Higher Whitley, Warrington, Cheshire WA4 4QW; 01925 730 399; (Fax)01925 730 368.
e-mail: focalpoint@dial.pipex.com
www.fpoint.co.uk

IN-FOCUS
(see intoductory text in Eastern England).

LANCASHIRE
Address: WWT Martin Mere, Burscough, Ormskirk, Lancs, L40 0TA: 01704 897 020.

WEST YORKSHIRE
Address: Westleigh House Office Est. Wakefield Road, Denby Dale, West Yorks, HD8 8QJ: 01484 864 729.

LONDON CAMERA EXCHANGE
(see introductory text in Eastern England).

CHESTER
Address: 9 Bridge Street Row, CH1 1NW; 01244 326 531.

MANCHESTER
Address: 37 Parker Street, Piccadilly, M1 4AJ; 0161 236 5819.

PHOTO EXPRESS (LAKELAND) LTD
Company ethos: Friendly and independent advice, UK dealers for all top brands, competitive prices.
Viewing facilities: Full showroom facilities at Ulverston branch with expert advice.
Optical stock: Leica, Swarovski, Zeiss, Opticron, Vortex, Hawke, Bushnell to name a few.
Non-optical stock: Digital cameras, camcorders and accessories, tripods, digiscoping, hide clamps and cases.

New for 2010: Bigger range at the Bowness store.
Opening times: Mon-Sat (9am-5pm).
Address: 39 Market Street, Ulverston, Cumbria LA12
7LR ; 01229 583 050; (Fax)01229 480 135.
e-mail: Sales@Photo-express.net

WILKINSON CAMERAS

Company ethos: The widest range of photographic
and birdwatching equipment available at competitive
prices at all times.
Viewing facilities: Optical field days at selected
nature reserves in northern England. See website for
details of photographic courses and other events.
Optical stock: Binoculars from Bushnell, Canon,
Hawke, Leica, Nikon, RSPB, Steiner, Swarovski,
Vanguard and Viking. Spotting scopes from Bushnell,
Hawke, Leica, Nikon, Summit, Swarovski and
Vanguard. Wide range of bags, digital cameras, lenses
and video equipment.
Opening times: Branches open 9am to 5:30pm
Monday to Saturday. Sunday 11am to 4pm (Preston
only). e-mail: sales@wilkinson.co.uk
www.wilkinson.co.uk

BLACKBURN
42 Northgate, Blackburn, Lancs BB2 1JL: 01254 581
272; (Fax) 01254 695 867.

BURNLEY
95 James Street, Burnley, Lancs BB11 1PY; 01282 424
524; (Fax) 01282 831 722.

BURY
61 The Rock, Bury, Greater Manchester BL9 0NB;
01617 643 402; (Fax) 01617 615 086.

CARLISLE
13 Grapes Lane, Carlisle, Cumbria CA3 8NQ; 01228
538 583; (Fax) 01228 514 699.

KENDAL
19A The Westmorland Centre, Kendal, Cumbria LA9
4AB; 01539 735 055; (Fax) 01539 734 929.

LANCASTER
6 James Street, Lancaster, Lancs LA1 1UP; 01524 380
510; (Fax) 01524 380 512.

PRESTON
27 Friargate, Preston, Lancs PR1 2NQ; 01772 556 250;
(Fax) 01772 259 435.

SOUTHPORT
38 Eastbank Street, Southport, Merseyside, PR8 1ET.
01704 534 534; (Fax) 01704 501 546;
e-mail: southport@wilkinson.co.uk

SOUTH EAST ENGLAND

IN-FOCUS
(see introductory text in Eastern England).

ST ALBANS
Address: Bowmans Farm, London Colney, St Albans,
Herts, AL2 1BB: 01727 827 799:
(Fax) 01727 827 766.

SOUTH WEST LONDON
Address: WWT The Wetland Centre, Queen Elizabeth
Walk, Barnes, London, SW13 9WT: 020 8409 4433.

LONDON CAMERA EXCHANGE
(see entry in Eastern England).

FAREHAM
Address: 135 West Street, Fareham, Hampshire, PO16
0DU; 01329 236 441; (Fax) 01329 823 294;
e-mail: fareham@lcegroup.co.uk

GUILDFORD
Address: 8/9 Tunsgate, Guildford, Surrey, GU1 2DH;
01483 504 040; (Fax) 01483 538 216;
e-mail: guildford@lcegroup.co.uk

PORTSMOUTH
Address: 40 Kingswell Path, Cascados, Portsmouth,
PO1 4RR; 023 9283 9933; (Fax) 023 9283 9955; e-mail:
portsmouth@lcegroup.co.uk

READING
Address: 7 Station Road, Reading, Berkshire, RG1
1LG; 0118 959 2149; (Fax) 0118 959 2197;
e-mail: reading@lcegroup.co.uk

SOUTHAMPTON
Address: 10 High Street, Southampton, Hampshire,
SO14 2DH; 023 8022 1597; (Fax) 023 8023 3838; e-
mail: southampton@lcegroup.co.uk

STRAND, LONDON
Address: 98 The Strand, London, WC2R 0AG; 020
7379 0200; (Fax) 020 7379 6991;
e-mail: strand@lcegroup.co.uk

WINCHESTER
Address: 15 The Square, Winchester, Hampshire,
SO23 9ES; 01962 866 203; (Fax)01962 840 978;
e-mail: winchester@lcegroup.co.uk

SOUTH WEST ENGLAND

LONDON CAMERA EXCHANGE
(see introductory text in Eastern England).

BATH
Address: 13 Cheap Street, Bath, Avon, BA1 1NB;
01225 462 234; (Fax) 01225 480 334.
e-mail: bath@lcegroup,co.uk

BOURNEMOUTH
Address: 95 Old Christchurch Road, Bournemouth,
Dorset, BH1 1EP; 01202 556 549; (Fax) 01202 293 288;
e-mail: bournemouth@lcegroup.co.uk

BRISTOL
Address: 53 The Horsefair, Bristol, BS1 3JP; 0117 927 6185; (Fax) 0117 925 8716;
e-mail: bristol.horsefair@lcegroup.co.uk

EXETER
Address: 174 Fore Street, Exeter, Devon, EX4 3AX; 01392 279 024/438 167; (Fax) 01392 426 988. e-mail: exeter@lcegroup.co.uk

PAIGNTON
Address: 71 Hyde Road, Paington, Devon, TQ4 5BP;01803 553 077; (Fax) 01803 664 081.
e-mail: paignton@lcegroup.co.uk

PLYMOUTH
Address: 10 Frankfort Gate, Plymouth, Devon, PL1 1QD; 01752 668 894; (Fax) 01752 604248.
e-mail: plymouth@lcegroup.co.uk

SALISBURY
Address: 6 Queen Street, Salisbury, Wiltshire, SP1 1EY; 01722 335 436; (Fax) 01722 411 670;
e-mail: salisbury@lcegroup.co.uk

TAUNTON
Address: 6 North Street, Taunton, Somerset, TA1 1LH; 01823 259955; (Fax) 01823 338 001.
e-mail: taunton@lcegroup.co.uk

WESTERN ENGLAND

CLIFTON CAMERAS
cliftoncameras.co.uk

Company ethos: Specialists for binoculars & spotting scopes. Based near Slimbridge Wetland Centre in Gloucestershire. Sponsors of the Dursley Birding Club.
Optical stock: All top brands stocked. Nikon Premier Dealer, Swarovski Premier Dealer, Zeiss Authorised Dealer & Leica Optical Specialists. Come and try the New Leica Apo Televid 65 and Nikon Fieldscope EDG spotting scopes.
Non-optical stock: Professional camera and photographic supplier of Nikon, Sigma lenses and Gitzo tripods to name a few.
Opening times: Mon-Sat (9am-5.30pm).
Address: 28 Parsonage Street, Dursley, Gloucestershire GL11 4AA;01453 548 128.
e-mail: sales@cliftoncameras.co.uk
www.cliftoncameras.co.uk

FOCUS OPTICS
Company ethos: Friendly, expert service. Top quality instruments.
Viewing facilities: Our own pool and nature reserve with feeding stations.
Optical stock: Full range of leading makes of binoculars and telescopes.
Non-optical stock: Waterproof clothing, fleeces, walking boots and shoes, bird food and feeders.

Books, videos, walking poles, moth traps and accessories.
Opening times: Mon-Sat (9am-5pm). Some Bank-holidays.
Address: Church Lane, Corley, Coventry, CV7 8BA; 01676 540 501/542 476; (Fax) 01676 540 930.
e-mail: enquiries@focusoptics.co.uk
www.focusoptics.co.uk

IN-FOCUS
(see introductory text in Eastern England).

GLOUCESTERSHIRE
Address: WWT Slimbridge, Gloucestershire, GL2 7BT: 01453 890 978. 22314; (Fax) 01905 724 585; e-mail: worcester@lcegroup.co.uk

LONDON CAMERA EXCHANGE
(see introductory text in Eastern England).

CHELTENHAM
Address: 10-12 The Promenade, Cheltenham, Gloucestershire, GL50 1LR; 01242 519 851; (Fax) 01242 576 771;
e-mail: cheltenham@lcegroup.co.uk

GLOUCESTER
Address: 12 Southgate Street, Gloucester, GL1 2DH; 01452 304 513; (Fax) 01452 387 309;
e-mail: gloucester@lcegroup.co.uk

LEAMINGTON
Address: Clarendon Avenue, Leamington, Warwickshire, CV32 5PP; 01926 886 166; (Fax)01926 887 611;
e-mail: leamington@lcegroup.co.uk

WORCESTER
Address: 8 Pump Street, Worcester, WR1 2QT; 01905 22314; (Fax) 01905 724 585;
e-mail: worcester@lcegroup.co.uk

OPTICAL IMPORTERS AND MANUFACTURERS

CARL ZEISS LTD
Company ethos: World renowned, high quality performance and innovative optical products.
Product lines: Victory FL, Conquest, Stabilised, Victory and Classic compacts and Diascope FL telescopes.
New for 2010: Photoscope 85T* FL (combined digital camera and telescope).
Address: PO Box 78, Woodfield Road, Welwyn Garden City, Hertfordshire AL7 1LU; 01707 871 350; (Fax)01707 871 426. e-mail: binos@zeiss.co.uk
www.zeiss.co.uk

DEBEN GROUP INDUSTRIES
Company ethos: We design Hawke Sport Optics as a quantity range of binoculars and spotting scopes, which in-turn offer excellent value for money. Having established two market leaders within the range,

127

we will continue to create a simple but very popular range.

Product lines: Hawke Sport Optics consists of Frontier ED, Frontier PC, Endurance CF, Nature-Trek, Classic and Premier ranges. Each offers compacts, mid-size and full-size binoculars from £50 - £350. Also spotting scopes from £100 - £600 which also include models with ED glass.

New for 2010: New compact binocular range in both the Endurance CF and Frontier ED families, plus new ED spotting scope ranges in both the Endurance and Frontier families, all with a choice of eyepieces.

Address: Avocet House, Wilford Bridge Road, Melton, Woodbridge, Suffolk IP12 1RB; 01394 387 762.
e-mail: global@hawkeoptics.com

INTRO 2020 LTD

Company ethos: Experienced importer of photo and optical products.

Product lines: Steiner binoculars, Tamron lenses, Velbon tripods, Slik tripods, Kenko scopes, Summit binoculars, Hoya and Cokin filters. Tamrac and Crumpler bags and backpacks. Plus many other.

Address: Unit 1, Priors Way, Maidenhead, Berkshire SL6 2HP; 01628 674 411; (Fax)01628 771 055.
e-mail: sales@intro2020.co.uk
www.intro2020.co.uk www.cokin.co.uk,
www.metzflash.co.uk www.sliktripod.co.uk,
www.velbon.co.uk www.steiner-binoculars.co.uk,
www.sliktripod.co.uk www.tamrac.co.uk,

LEICA CAMERA LTD

Company ethos: A passion for developing innovative products of the highest quality which expand the natural limits of the human eye — bringing people closer to the outdoor world.

Product lines: Ultravid HD (High Definition) Binoculars - for the definitive full size viewing experience. Ultravid & Trinovid Compact Binoculars - small in size, big in performance.

Duovid - the world's first dual magnification binocular.

APO-Televid 82 and 65 Spotting Scopes with the world's first 25:50x wide angle zoom eyepiece.

Monovid -- convenient and versatile monocular with macro lens and outstanding close- focus length of only 10inches.

Premium range of compact digital cameras.

New for 2010: The only complete digiscoping solution from one brand - APO-Televid angled 82 & 65 Spotting Scopes with the world's first 25:50x wide angle zoom eyepiece & a new Digital Adapter for

digiscoping with Leica D-Lux 4 plus choice of two models of Leica tripod (carbon fibre or compact magnesium) plus tripod head DH1 for easy, precise operation.

New Monovid 8x 20 - allows observation of very small objects in the finest detail.

Address: Leica Camera Limited, Davy Avenue, Knowlhill, Milton Keynes MK5 8LB; 01908 256 400;(Fax)01908 671 316.
e-mail: enquiries@leica-camera.co.uk
www.leica-sportoptics.co.uk

NEWPRO UK LTD

Company ethos: Some very well-established and even old brand names with new company technology and attitude.

Product lines: Op/Tech straps, pouches and harnesses, Cullman tripods, hide clamps and monopods. LensPen optics cleaner.

New for 2010: New 'Dual Harness' from Op/Tech, new Nanomax and Magnesit tripods and monopods from Cullman.

Opening times: Mon-Fri (8.30am-5pm) plus many outdoor events.

Address: Old Sawmills Road, Faringdon, Oxon SN7 7DS; 01367 242 411; (Fax)01367 241 124.
e-mail: sales@newprouk.co.uk
www.newprouk.co.uk

OPTICRON

Company ethos: To continuously develop high quality binoculars, telescopes and accessories that are useful, ergonomically sound and exceptional value for money.

Product lines: Opticron binoculars,

monoculars, telescopes, telephotography/digi-scoping equipment and accessories.

New for 2010: New GS52 GA ED travelscopes (Oct 2009), new lightweight Verano BGA (Dec 2009) and new Countryman BGA (Spring 2010)

Address: Unit 21, Titan Court, Laporte Way, Luton LU4 8EF; 01582 726 522: (Fax)01582 273 559.
e-mail: sales@opticron.co.uk
www.opticron.co.uk

PYSER-SGI LTD

Company ethos: Our primary aim is customer/dealer care and satisfaction, achieved through technological leadership, quality technical assistance and post-sales service/support.

Product lines: Pyser-SGI quality binoculars at competitive prices, Kowa Prominar exceptional quality spotting scopes and binoculars including the new TSN-770 and TSN-880 series scopes and Prominar XD binoculars. Swift Sport Optics wide range of binoculars and spotting scopes, including the renowned original Audobon binoculars and New Reliant & Horizon ranges.

New for 2010: Continuing enhancements to the product ranges.

Address: Fircroft Way, Edenbridge, Kent TN8 6HA; 01732 864 111; (Fax)01732 865 544.
e-mail: sales@pyser-sgi.com
www.pyser-sgi.com

SIGMA IMAGING (UK) LTD

Company ethos: Sigma produces top quality, award-winning photographic equipment at affordable prices. All Sigma's lenses, flashguns and accessories are manufactured in Japan by fully trained Japanese craftsmen and are designed to work with all the popular SLR cameras.
Product lines: More than 40 lenses from 4.5mm to 800mm to fit all popular SLR cameras. Digital SLR and compact cameras. Flashguns to fit all popular SLR cameras.
Address: 13 Little Mundells, Welwyn Garden City, Hertfordshire AL7 1EW; 01707 329 999.
e-mail: sales@sigma-imaging-uk.com
www.sigma-imaging.uk.com

SWAROVSKI UK

Company ethos: Constantly improving on what is good in terms of products and committed to conservation world-wide.
Product lines: ATM and STM spotting scopes (both 65mm and 80mm objective lenses) offer lightweight bodies and complement the existing ranges of established ATS and STS SWAROVSKI telescopes. EL 8x32 and 10x32 binoculars are the latest additions to OPTIK a market-leading range of telescopes and binoculars. Swarovski tripods and Universal Camera Adaptor also available.
New for 2010: Lightweight Pocket Traveller range of binoculars (8x20 and 10x25 models).
Address: Perrywood Business Park, Salfords, Surrey RH1 5JQ; 01737 856 812; (Fax)01737 856 885.
e-mail: christine.percy@swarovski.com

VICKERS SPORTS OPTICS

Company ethos: To supply world-leading optical products to UK and Ireland birdwatchers, exclusively distributing brands Bushnell®, Tasco® and Premierlight® to retailers.
Product lines: The extensive Bushnell range offers cutting-edge binoculars, spotting scopes, nightvision equipment and more. Binoculars and spotting scopes by Tasco offer similarly high quality at entry-level. Premierlight LED lighting instruments perform exceptionally, from the hand-held torches to the lanterns.
Other services: UK and Eire returns service.
New for 2010: Innovative new products arriving frequently.
Opening times: Mon-Thu (8.30am-5pm), Fri (8.30am-4.30pm).
Address: Unit 9, 35 Revenge Road, Lordswood, Chatham, Kent ME5 8DW; 01634 201 284.
e-mail: info@jjvickers.co.uk
www.jjvickers.co.uk

OPTICAL REPAIRS AND SERVICING

OPTREP Optical Repairs

Company ethos: To give a speedy, economical and effective repair service.
Key services: Servicing and repair of binoculars, telescopes etc. Conversant with the special needs of birdwatchers.
Opening times: Mon-Thu (9am-5pm), Fri (9am-3pm)
Address: 16 Wheatfield Road, Selsey, West Sussex PO20 0NY; 01243 601 365.
e-mail: info@opticalrepairs.com
www.opticalrepairs.com

TRADE DIRECTORY

BIRD RESERVES AND OBSERVATORIES

Glastonbury Tor from the Hawk and Owl Trust's Trust's new Shapwick Moor Reserve, with its rhynes (ditches) that are characteristic of the Somerset Levels.

Why not widen your birdwatching horizons by visiting some new reserves in 2010? Here we detail more than 420 sites for you to explore — the information is updated each year, making it the most up-to-date guide covering the whole of Britain.

To reflect birdwatchers' growing interest in other flora and fauna, we have asked information providers for each site to highlight key mammal, insect and plant species – and elsewhere in this edition (pages 92 to 93) you can record your butterfly and dragonfly sightings.

Bedfordshire

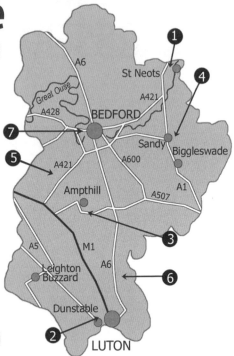

1. BEGWARY BROOK

Beds, Cambs, Northants and Peterborough Wildlife Trust.

Location: TL 169 564. 2 miles S of St Neots. From A1 S take A428 E and continue to Wyboston Lakes complex. Pass through complex and follow nature reserve signs to car park.

Access: Open all year. Partially suitable for wheelchairs.

Facilities: None.

Public transport: Bus, St Neots to Sandy, some stop in Wyboston (Saffords Coaches - 01767 677 395).

Habitat: Former gravel pit. Marsh and open pools next to Great Ouse.

Key birds: Wildfowl and wader species. *Spring*: Sedge, Reed and Willow Warblers, Blackcap. *All year*: Reed Bunting, Kingfisher, Goldcrest.

Other notable flora and fauna: Orange-tip and speckled wood butterflies, dragonflies and grass snakes. Plants include great burnet, common fleabane and marsh woundwort.

Contact: Beds, Cambs, Northants & Peterborough Wildlife Trust, The Manor House, Broad Street, Great Cambourne, Cambridgeshire CB23 6DH. 01954 713 500; Fax 01954 710 051. www.wildlifebcnp.org e-mail:cambridgeshire@wildlifebcnp.org

2. BLOW'S DOWNS

Beds, Cambs, Northants and Peterborough Wildlife Trust.

Location: TL 033 216. On the outskirts of Dunstable. Take A5065 from W of Luton, cross M1, take first exit at roundabout, park with care on verge. Can also walk half mile from Dunstable centre to W entrance at Half Moon Lane off A5.

Access: Open all year, not suitable for wheelchairs.

Facilities: None.

Public transport: None.

Habitat: SSSI, chalk downland, scrub and grassland, that is a traditional resting place for incoming spring migrants.

Key birds: *Winter*: Lapwing, Meadow Pipit, Sky Lark, Stonechat. *Spring/autumn*: Ring Ouzel, Wheatear, Whinchat, Black Redstart, Stonechat, Willow Warbler.

Other notable flora and fauna: Chalkhill blue, brown argus and marbled white butterflies. Plants include small scabious, burnet-saxifrage, squinancywort, great pignut, common spotted and bee orchids.

Contact: Trust HQ 01954 713 500; www.wildlifebcnp.org

3. FLITWICK MOOR

Beds, Cambs, Northants and Peterborough Wildlife Trust.

Location: TL 046 354. E of Flitwick. From Flitwick town centre (Tesco roundabout) on A5120, cross railway bridge, R at roundabout, immediately L into King's Road. After 500m, L into Moulden Road towards A507. After quarter mile R at Folly Farm, follow track to small car park. Also footpath to reserve from Moor Lane.

Access: Open all year.

Facilities: Car park. Please stick to public paths.

Public transport: Frequent buses (United Counties) from Bedford and Luton to Flitwick, or take train to Flitwick and then three quarter mile walk.

Habitat: SSSI. Important wetland for the area, blend of fen, meadow, wet woodland and fragile peaty soil. Supports mosses ferns and flowers.

Key birds: *Winter*: Siskin, Water Rail, Great Spotted Woodpecker. *Spring*: Lesser Spotted Woodpecker, Willow Warbler, Blackcap. *Summer*: Water Rail, Grasshopper and Garden Warblers, Cuckoo. *Autumn*: Brambling.

Other notable flora and fauna: Good variety of butterflies and dragonflies, plus chimney sweeper moth and conehead bush cricket. Plants include nine species of sphagnum moss, marsh pennywort, black knapweed, water figwort plus fly agaric and yellow brain fungus in autumn.

Contact: Trust HQ 01954 713 500; www.wildlifebcnp.org

4. LODGE (THE)

RSPB (Central England Office).
Location: TL 191 485. Reserve lies 1 mile/1.6km E of Sandy on the B1042 to Potton.
Access: Reserve is open daily 9am-9pm (or sunset when earlier); shop 9am-5pm weekdays, 10am-5pm weekends.
Facilities: Nature trails being extended to 5 miles. One bridleway (half mile) and gardens are wheelchair/pushchair accessible. One hide (wheelchair accessible), 50 yards from car park. Coach parking at weekends by arrangement.
Public transport: Buses to Sandy Market Square from Bedford, infrequent service. One mile walk or cycle from centre of Sandy or half mile from Sandy railway station, in part along trail through heathland restoration.
Habitat: This 180-hectare reserve is a mixture of woodland, heathland and acid grassland and includes the formal gardens of the RSPB's UK headquarters. New land being restored to heathland.
Key birds: *Spring/summer*: Hobby, Spotted Flycatcher. *All year*: Woodpeckers, woodland birds.
Other notable flora and fauna: Natterjack toads, rare heathland insects. Particularly good site for fungi, and lichens. Garden pools are good for dragonflies.
Contact: RSPB, 01767 680 541. www.rspb.org.uk e-mail: thelodgereserve@rspb.org.uk

5. MARSTON VALE MILLENNIUM COUNTRY PARK

Marston Vale Trust (Regd Charity No 1069229).
Location: SW of Bedford off A421 at Marston Moretaine. Only five mins from J13 of M1.
Access: Park and forest centre open seven days a week. Summer 10am-6pm, winter 10am-4pm. No dogs in wetlands reserve, rest of site OK for dogs and horses. Main 8km trail surfaced for wheelchair and pushchair access. All-terrain wheelchair available for free loan. Coach parking available.
Facilities: Cafe bar, gift shop, art gallery, exhibition. Free parking.
Public transport: Bedford to Bletchley line — trains to Millbrook and Stewartby station, 20 minute walk to Forest Centre.
Habitat: Lake - 610 acres/freshwater marsh (man-made), reedbed, woodland, hawthorn scrub and grassland.
Key birds: *Winter*: Iceland and Glaucous Gulls (regular), gull roost, wildfowl, Great Crested Grebe. *Spring*: Passage waders and terns (Black Tern, Arctic Tern), Garganey. *Summer*: Nine species of breeding warblers, Hobby, Turtle Dove, Nightingale, Bearded Tit. *Autumn*: Passage waders and terns. *Rarities*: White-winged Black Tern, Laughing Gull, divers, Manx Shearwater, Bittern.
Other notable flora and fauna: Dingy and grizzled skipper butterflies, excellent for dragonflies, red-veined darter in 2008. Also otter and brown hare, plus bee and pyramidal orchids and stoneworts.
Contact: Forest Centre, 01234 767 037.
e-mail: info@marstonvale.org www.marstonvale.org

6. PEGSDON HILL RESERVE

Beds, Cambs, Northants and Peterborough Wildlife Trust.
Location: TL 120 295. 5 miles W of Hitchin. Take B655 from Hitchin towards Barton-le-Clay. Turn R at Pegsdon then immediately L and park in lay-by. Reserve entrance across B655 via footpath.
Access: Open all year. Dropping off point for coaches only.
Facilities: None.
Public transport: Luton to Henlow buses (United Counties) stop at Pegsdon.
Habitat: Chalk grassland, scrub and woodland.
Key birds: *Winter*: Brambling, Stonechat, winter thrushes, raptors including Buzzard. *Spring*: Wheatear, Ring Ouzel, Tree Pipit, Yellowhammer. *Summer*: Turtle Dove, Grey Partridge, Lapwing, Sky Lark.
Other notable flora and fauna: Dark green fritillary, dingy and grizzled skippers, chalkhill blue, brown argus and small heath butterflies. Glow worms. Plants include pasqueflower in spring, fragrant and common spotted orchids.
Contact: Trust HQ 01954 713 500; www.wildlifebcnp.org

7. PRIORY COUNTRY PARK AND MARINA

Bedford Borough Council.
Location: TL 071 495. 1.5 miles SE from Bedford town centre. Signposted from A428 & A421. Entry point to new 'River Valley Park'
Access: Park and hides open at all times. No access to fenced/gated plantations.
Facilities: Toilets and visitor centre open daytime, all-year-round disabled access on new path around lake. Hides, nature trails, labyrinth, cycle hire, Premier Inn for meals, accomodation.
Public transport: Stagecoach (01604 676 060) 'Blue Solo 4' every 20 mins. Mon-Sat. Alight 1st stop Riverfield Drive (200 m). Rail station at Bedford (approx 2.5 miles)
Habitat: Lakes, reedbeds, scrub and woodland, meadows adjoining Great Ouse.
Key birds: Good numbers/variety of winter wildfowl, varied mix of spring passage species, with breeding warblers and woodpeckers, augmented by feeding terns, hirundines and raptors lakeside. *Winter*: Grebes, Pochard, Shoveler, Gadwall, Merlin, Water Rail, gulls, thrushes, Chiffchaff, corvids, buntings. *Passage*: Raptors, waders, terns, pipits. *Summer*: Hobby, Turtle Dove, Swift, hirundines, *acrocephalus* and *sylvia* warblers. *All year*: Cormorant, Little Egret, Heron, Stock Dove, woodpeckers, Kingfisher, Grey Wagtail, Treecreeper, Goldfinch, Bullfinch.
Other notable flora and fauna: 23 species of dragonfly, incl small red-eyed damsel & hairy hawker. 20 species of butterfly. Large plant list. Fox, muntjac and otter.
Contact: Jon Bishop, Wardens Office, Visitor Centre, Priory CP, Barkers Lane, Bedford, MK41 9SH. 01234 211 182.

Berkshire

1. DINTON PASTURES

Wokingham District Council.
Location: SU 784 718. Country Park, E of Reading off B3030 between Hurst and Winnersh.
Access: Open all year, dawn to dusk. Car parking charges apply 8am to 6pm each day. Dogs allowed.
Facilities: Three hides (one adapted for wheelchairs), information centre, car park, café, toilets (suitable for wheelchairs). Electric buggies for hire. Various trails between one and three miles in length.
Public transport: Not known.
Habitat: Mature gravel pits and banks of River Loddon. Sandford Lake managed for wildfowl, Lavell's Lake best for waders and scrub species.
Key birds: *All year:* Kingfisher, Water Rail. *Spring/summer:* Hobby, Little Ringed Plover, Common Tern, Nightingale, common warblers. *Winter:* Bittern, wildfowl (inc. Goldeneye, Wigeon, Teal, Gadwall), thrushes. Waders include Green and Common Sandpipers, Snipe, Redshank.
Other notable flora and fauna: Water vole, harvest mouse, great crested newt, Loddon pondweed and Loddon lily. Good range of dragonflies inc emperor, black-tailed skimmer, white-legged and banded agrion damselfies and migrant hawker.
Contact: Dave Webster, Ranger, Dinton Pastures Country Park, Davis Street, Hurst, Berks. 0118 934 2 016. e-mail:countryside@wokingham.gov.uk

2. HUNGERFORD MARSH

Berks, Bucks & Oxon Wildlife Trust.
Location: SU 333 687. On W side of Hungerford, beside the Kennet and Avon Canal. From town centre, go along Church Street past the town hall. Turn R under the railway. Follow public footpath over swing bridge on the canal near the church. The reserve is separated from Freeman's Marsh by a line of willows and bushes.
Access: Open all year. Please keep to the footpath. Dogs on leads please.
Facilities: Car park.
Public transport: Hungerford railway station half mile from reserve.

Habitat: An idyllic waterside site with unimproved rough grazing and reedbed.
Key birds: 120 species recorded. *Spring/summer:* Reed and Grasshopper Warblers. *Winter:* Siskin. *All year:* Mute Swan, Mallard, Little Grebe. Birds seen in the last ten years include Kingfisher, Yellow Wagtail, Water Rail.
Other notable flora and fauna: Water vole, grass snake.
Contact: BBOWT, The Lodge, 1 Armstrong Road, Littlemore, Oxford OX4 4XT. 01865 775 476. www.bbowt.org.uk

3. LAVELL'S LAKE

Wokingham District Council.
Location: SU 781 729. Via Sandford Lane off B3030 between Hurst and Winnersh, E of Reading.
Access: Dawn to dusk. No permit required.
Facilities: Hides.
Public transport: Information not available.
Habitat: Gravel pits, two wader scapes, although one congested with *crassula helmsii*, rough grassland, marshy area, between River Loddon, Emm Brook. To N of Lavell's Lake, gravel pits are being restored and attact birds. A lake is viewable walking N along River Lodden from Lovell's Lake over small green bridge. The lake is in a field immediately on R but is only viewable through hedge. No access is permitted.
Key birds: *All year:* Sparrowhawk. *Summer:* Garganey, Common Tern, Redshank, Lapwing, Hobby, Red Kite, Peregrine, Buzzard. Passage waders. *Winter:* Green Sandpiper, ducks (inc. Smew), Bittern.
Contact: See Dinton Lakes.

4. MOOR GREEN LAKES

Blackwater Valley Countryside Partnership.
Location: SU 805 628. Main access and parking off Lower Sandhurst Road, Finchampstead. Alternatively, Rambler's car park, Mill Lane, Sandhurst (SU 820 619).
Access: Car parks open dawn-dusk. Two bird hides open to members of the Moor Green Lakes Group (contact BVCP for details). Dogs on leads. Site can

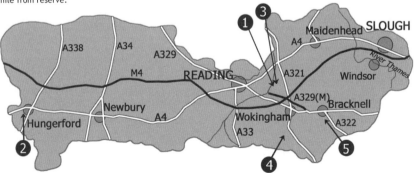

be used by people in wheelchairs, though surface not particularly suitable.

Facilities: Two bird hides, footpaths around site, Blackwater Valley Long Distance Path passes through site.

Public transport: Nearest bus stop, Finchampstead (approx 1.5 miles from main entrance). Local bus companies – Stagecoach Hants & Surrey, tel 01256 464 501, First Beeline and Londonlink, tel 01344 424 938.

Habitat: Thirty-six hectares (90 acres) in total. Three lakes with gravel islands, beaches and scrapes. River Blackwater, grassland, surrounded by willow, ash, hazel and thorn hedgerows.

Key birds: *Spring/summer*: Redshank, Little Ringed Plover, Sand Martin, Willow Warbler, and of particular interest, a flock of Goosander. Also Whitethroat, Sedge Warbler, Common Sandpiper, Common Tern. Dunlin and Black Tern on passage. Lapwings breed on site and several sightings of Red Kite. *Winter*: Ruddy Duck, Wigeon, Teal, Gadwall.

Contact: Blackwater VCP, 01252 331 353.
e-mail: blackwater.valley@hants.gov.uk
www.blackwater-valley.org.uk

5. WILDMOOR HEATH

Berks, Bucks & Oxon Wildlife Trust.

Location: SU 842 627. Between Bracknell and Sandhurst. From Sandhurst shopping area, take the A321 NW towards Wokingham. Turn E at the mini-roundabout on to Crowthorne Road. Continue for about one mile through one set of traffic lights. Car park is on the R at the bottom of the hill.

Access: Open all year. No access to woodland N of Rackstraw Road at Broadmoor Bottom. Please keep dogs on a lead.

Facilities: Car park.

Habitat: Wet and dry lowland heath, bog, mixed woodland and mature Scots pine plantation.

Key birds: *Spring/summer*: Wood Lark, Nightjar, Dartford Warbler, Tree Pipit, Stonechat.

Other notable flora and fauna: Dragonflies, slow worm, adder, grass snake, lizard. Bog plants inc sundews.

Contact: Wildlife Trust HQ, BBOWT, The Lodge, 1 Armstrong Road, Littlemore, Oxford OX4 4XT. 01865 775 476. www.bbowt.org.uk

Buckinghamshire

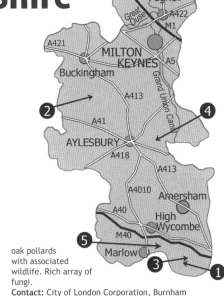

1. BURNHAM BEECHES NATIONAL NATURE RESERVE

City of London.

Location: SU 950 850. N of Slough and on W side of A355, running between J2 of the M40 and J6 of M4. Entry from A355 via Beeches Road. Also smaller parking areas in Hawthorn Lane and Pumpkin Hill to the S and Park Lane to the W.

Access: Open all year, except Dec 25. Main Lord Mayor's Drive open from 8am-dusk. Beeches Café, public toilets and information point open 10am to 5pm. Motorised buggy available for hire. Network of wheelchair accessible roads and paths.

Facilities: Car parks, toilets, café, visitor information centre. Easy access path network, suitable for wheelchairs, most start at Victory Cross. Coach parking possible, additional coach parking on request.

Public transport: Train: nearest station Slough on the main line from Paddington. Arriva, First and Jason Tours buses 40 and 74 stop at reserve. Call Traveline on 0870 608 2608.

Habitat: Ancient woodland, streams, pools, heathland, grassland, scrub.

Key birds: *Spring/summer*: Cuckoo, possible Turtle Dove. *Winter*: Siskin, Crossbill, regular large flocks c100 Brambling. Possible Woodcock. *All year*: Mandarin (good population), all three woodpeckers, Sparrowhawk, Marsh Tit, possible Willow Tit, Red Kite and Buzzard.

Other notable flora and fauna: Ancient beech and oak pollards with associated wildlife. Rich array of fungi.

Contact: City of London Corporation, Burnham Beeches Office, Hawthorn Lane, Farnham Common, SL2 3TE . 01753 647 358.
e-mail: burnham.beeches@cityoflondon.gov.uk
www.cityoflondon.gov.uk

135

2. CALVERT JUBILEE

Berks, Bucks & Oxon Wildlife Trust.
Location: SP 849 425. Near Steeple Claydon, NW of Aylesbury, Bucks.
Access: Access by permit (free) only. Apply to Trust who provide map and information with permit. Please keep to network of paths.
Facilities: Two hides, small car park.
Public transport: None.
Habitat: Ex-clay pit, railway and landfill site. Now with deep lake, marginal reedbed and scrub habitat.
Key birds: *Summer*: Nesting Common Tern, Kingfisher, warblers, occasional Nightingale, Lapwing. Passage migrants include Black-tailed Godwit, Greenshank. *Winter*: Bittern, Water Rail, Lesser Black-backed Gull roost. Wigeon. Rarer birds turn up regularly,.
Other notable flora and fauna: Rare butterflies, including dingy and grizzled skippers.
Contact: Wildlife Trust HQ, BBOWT, 01865 775 476. www.bbowt.org.uk

3. CHURCH WOOD

RSPB (Midlands Regional Office).
Location: SU 971 872. Reserve lies three miles from J2 of M40 in Hedgerley. Park in village, walk down small track beside pond for approx 200m. Reserve entrance is on L.
Access: Open all year. Not suitable for wheelchair users.
Facilities: Two marked paths with some inclines.
Public transport: None.
Habitat: Mixed woodland.
Key birds: *Spring/summer*: Red Kite, Buzzard, Blackcap, Garden Warbler, Swallow. *Winter*: Redpoll, Siskin. *All year*: Marsh Tit, Willow Tit, Nuthatch,Treecreeper, Great Spotted and Green Woodpeckers.
Other notable flora and fauna: Wood anenome, wood sorrel, bluebell and other woodland plants. Brimstone, comma, white admiral and peacock butterflies. Good range of fungi species.
Contact: RSPB central England Office, 01865 351 163. www.rspb.org.uk/wildlife/reserves

4. COLLEGE LAKE

Berks, Bucks & Oxon Wildlife Trust.
Location: SU 934 140. 2 miles N of Tring on B488, quarter mile N of canal bridge at Bulbourne turn L into gated entrance.
Access: Open Apr-Oct (10am-5pm); Nov-Mar (10am-4pm), closed Mondays. Wheelchair access to hides and disabled toilets.
Facilities: Large car park, coach park, many hides, interpretive buildings. Network of wheelchair-friendly paths, visitor centre, toilets.
Public transport: Tring railway station, 2 miles walk.
Habitat: Deep lake in former chalk pit, shallow pools, wet, chalk and rough grasslands, scrub.
Key birds: *Spring/summer*: Lapwing, Redshank, Little Ringed Plover, Sand Martin, Hobby, Common Tern, Sky Lark. *Winter*: Wildfowl (Wigeon, Shoveler, Teal, Gadwall), waders, inc. Snipe, Peregrine Falcon.
Other notable flora and fauna: Orchids including White helleborines, bee and gragrant. Chalk grassland flowers. Butterflies include small blue and skippers. Good numbers of dragonflies (16 species). Hares.
Contact: The Warden, College Lake, Upper Icknield Way, Bulbourne, Tring, Herts HP23 5QG. 01442 826 774; (M)07711 821 303. www.bbowt.org.uk

5. LITTLE MARLOW GRAVEL PITS

Lefarge Redland Aggregates.
Location: SU 880 880. NE of Marlow from J4 of M40. Use permissive path from Coldmoorholm Lane to Little Marlow village. Follow path over a wooden bridge to N end of lake. Permissive path ends just past the cottages where it joins a concrete road to sewage treatment works.
Access: Open all year. Please do not enter the gravel works.
Facilities: Paths.
Public transport: None.
Habitat: Gravel pit, lake, scrub.
Key birds: *Spring*: Passage migrants, Sand Martin, Garganey, Hobby. *Summer*: Reed warblers, Kingfisher, wildfowl. Autumn: Passage migrants. *Winter*: Wildfowl, possible Smew, Goldeneye, Yellow-legged Gull, Lapwing, Snipe.
Contact: Ranger Service, Wycombe District Council, Queen Victoria Road, High Wycombe, Buckinghamshire HP11 1BB.

Cambridgeshire

1. BRAMPTON WOOD

Beds, Cambs, Northants and Peterborough Wildlife Trust.
Location: TL 184 698. 4 miles W of Huntingdon. From A1 take A14 exit towards Huntingdon. Take first exit off A14 to Brampton (B1514). Go straight at first roundabout then R at second. Turn R at T-junction onto Grafham road, go through village, over A1, reserve is on N side of road 1.5 miles out of Brampton. Park in small car park.
Access: Open daily. Coaches able to drop passengers off but unfortunately not sufficient space available to park.
Facilities: Car park, interpretative shelter.

Public transport: Bus from Huntingdon to Brampton (H&D) then 2 mile walk.
Habitat: Ancient woodland, primarily oak, ash and field maple with hazel coppice.
Key birds: *Autumn/winter*: Marsh Tit, Woodcock, winter thrushes. *Spring/summer*: Common woodland birds, Green Woodpecker, Spotted Flycatcher.
Other notable flora and fauna: Brown argus, white admiral and black hairstreak butterflies, pine beauty and pine hawk moths. Dormouse, glow worms, smooth and great crested newts, plus various dragonfly species. Plants include meadow grasses, cowslip, yellow rattle, devil's-bit scabious, primrose, hairy and trailing St John's wort.
Contact: Trust HQ, 01954 713 500;
e-mail:cambridgeshire@wildlifebcnp.org
www.wildlifebcnp.org

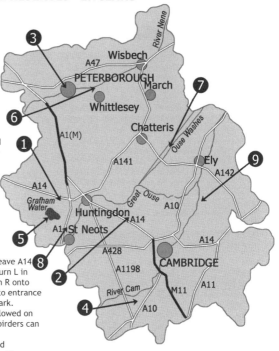

2. FEN DRAYTON

RSPB (Eastern England Office).
Location: TL 352 680. NW of Cambridge. Leave A14 at Junction 28; follow signs to Swavesey. Turn L in Boxworth End (signed to Fen Drayton). Turn R onto minor road (signed to Swavesey), then L into entrance to Fen Drayton Lakes. Follow signs to car park.
Access: Open at all times. Dogs are only allowed on public footpaths and bridleways. Disabled birders can get car access to one viewing screen.
Facilities: There are a number of public and permissive rights of way around the lakes and two open access fields. Information boards giving access details. Free trail guides and events leaflets are available from the Elney car park.
Public transport: Huntingdon: Stagecoach service 553 (with change to service 15 at St Ives), alight at Fen Drayton High Street. Cambridge: Stagecoach service 15 to Swavesey Middle Watch or Whippet No 15 to Fenstanton, alight in Fen Drayton High Street. Walk north (600 m) from Fen Drayton High Street onto Holywell Ferry Road, past recreation ground on left. Cambridgeshire Guided Bus service will have a request stop in reserve.
Habitat: A complex of lakes and traditional riverside meadows next to the River Great Ouse that used to be gravel workings.
Key birds: At least 213 species have been recorded in the area with some 65 species being regular breeders including Common Tern. Hobby, waders on passage. Rarities include Great White Egret, Purple Heron, Glossy Ibis, Common Crane, Red-Footed Falcon, Honey Buzzard and Whiskered Tern. Bitterns are now a regular sight, with Holywell Lake and Elney Lake being the favoured sites. *Winter*: Nationally important numbers of Gadwall and Coot.
Other notable flora and fauna: Good site for butterflies, dragonflies and mammals.
Contact: The Warden, RSPB Fens area office, The Grange, Market Street, Swavesey, Cambridge, Cambs CB24 4QG. 01603 661 662. www.rspb.org.uk

3. FERRY MEADOWS COUNTRY PARK

Nene Park Trust.
Location: TL 145 975. Three miles W of Peterborough town centre, signed off A605.
Access: Open all year, 7am to dusk (summer, 8am until sunset in winter. Electric scooters and wheelchair available for loan — call to book in advance. Coach parking free at all times. Car parking charges apply at weekends and Bank Holidays between April - Oct.
Facilities: Car park, visitor centre, toilets (inc disabled), café, two wheelchair-accessible hides in nature reserve area. Hard surface paths in park's central areas, but steep slopes in Bluebell Wood.
Public transport: Stagecoach X14 stops on A605 by Notcutts Nursey. Half mile walk to park entrance. Tel. Traveline 0870 6082 608 or www.traveline.org.uk
Habitat: Lakes, meadows, scrub, broadleaved woodland and small wetland nature reserve.
Key birds: *Spring*: Terns, waders, Yellow Wagtail. *Winter*: Grebes, Siskin, Redpoll, Water Rail, occasional Hawfinch. *All year*: Good selection of woodland and water birds, Kingfisher.
Other notable flora and fauna: Bluebell, wood anenome, wild garlic in woodland.
Contact: Visitor Services Officer, Nene Park Trust, Ham Farm House, Orton, Peterborough, PE2 5UU. 01733 234 443. www.nene-park-trust.org.uk
e-mail:visitor.services@nene-park-trust.org.uk

137

4. FOWLMERE

RSPB (Eastern England Office).
Location: TL 407 461. 7 miles S of Cambridge. Turn off A10 Cambridge to Royston road by Shepreth and follow sign.
Access: Access at all times along marked trail.
Facilities: One and a half miles of trails. Three hides, toilets. Space for one coach, prior booking essential. Wheelchair access to one hide, toilet and some of the trails.
Public transport: Shepreth railway station 2 miles.
Habitat: Reedbeds, meres, woodland, scrub.
Key birds: *Summer*: Nine breeding warblers. *All year*: Water Rail, Kingfisher. *Winter*: Snipe, raptors.
Other notable flora and fauna: Healthy population of water shrews. 18 species of dragonfly recorded.
Contact: The Warden, RSPB, Manor Farm, High St, Fowlmere, Royston SG8 7SH. Tel/Fax 01763 208 978.

5. GRAFHAM WATER

Beds, Cambs, Northants and Peterborough Wildlife Trust.
Location: TL 143 671. Follow signs for Grafham Water from A1 at Buckden or A14 at Ellington. Nature Reserve entrance is from Mander car park, W of Perry village.
Access: Open all year. Dogs barred in wildlife garden only, on leads elsewhere. Car parking £2 for day ticket.
Facilities: Five bird hides in nature reserve, two in the bird sanctuary area. Two in wildlife garden accessible to wheelchairs. Cycle track through reserve also accessible to wheelchairs. Visitor centre with restaurant, shop and toilets. Disabled parking. Use Plummer car park for lagoons and Marlow car park for dam area (good for waders and vagrants).
Public transport: Bus, St Neots to Bedford. Get off at Great Staughton then 2 mile walk.
Habitat: Open water, settlement lagoons ranging from reedbeds, open water, wet mud and willow carr, ancient and plantation woodland, scrub, species rich grassland.
Key birds: *Resident*: Common woodland birds, wildfowl. *Winter*: Waders including Common Sandpiper and Dunlin, Great Crested Grebe, Wildfowl including large flocks of Tufted Duck and Coot, Pochard, Shoveler, Shelduck, Goldeneye, Goosander and Smew, gulls (can be up to 30,000 roosting in mid-winter). *Spring/summer*: Breeding Nightingale, Reed, Willow and Sedge Warblers, Common and Black Terns. *Autumn*: Passage waders. *Rarities*: Have included Wilson's Phalarope (2007), Ring-necked Duck, Great Northern Diver, Glaucous, Iceland and Mediterranean Gulls.
Other notable flora and fauna: Bee and common spotted orchids, early purple orchid, common twayblade (in woods), cowslip. Common blue and marbled white butterflies, dragonflies including broad-bodied chaser, voles, grass snakes.
Contact: The Warden, Grafham Water Nature Reserve, 01480 811 075.

e-mail: matt.hamilton@wildlifebcnp.org
www.wildlifetrust.org.uk/bcnp

6. NENE WASHES

RSPB (Eastern England Office).
Location: TL 300 995. N of Whittlesey and six miles E of Peterborough.
Access: Open at all times along South Barrier Bank, accessed at Eldernell, one mile NE of Coates, off A605. Group visits by arrangement. No access to fields. No access for wheelchairs along bank.
Facilities: Small car park - one coach max. No toilets or hide.
Public transport: Bus and trains to Whittlesey, bus to Coates.
Habitat: Wet grassland with ditches. Frequently flooded.
Key birds: *Spring/early summer*: Corn Crake release scheme. Breeding waders (inc Black-tailed Godwit), duck (inc Garganey), Marsh Harrier and Hobby. *Winter*: Waterfowl in large numbers (inc Bewick's Swan, Pintail, Shoveler), Barn and Short-eared Owls, Hen Harrier.
Other notable flora and fauna: Water vole, otter, water violet, flowering rush and fringe water lily.
Contact: Charlie Kitchin, RSPB Nene Washes, 21a East Delph, Whittlesey, Cambs PE7 1RH. 01733 205 140.

7. OUSE WASHES

RSPB (Eastern England Office).
Location: TL 471 860. Between Chatteris and March on A141, take B1093 to Manea. Reserve signposted from Manea. Reserve office and visitor centre located off Welches Dam. Approximately ten miles from March or Chatteris.
Access: Access at all times from visitor centre (open 9am - 5pm every day except Dec 25/26). Welches Dam to public hides approached by marked paths behind boundary bank. No charge. Dogs to be kept on leads at all times. Disabled access to Welches Dam hide, 350 yards from car park. Track between Kingfisher and Stevens Hides very muddy following maintenance work. Groups welcome, but note that large coaches (36+ seats) cannot traverse final bend to reserve.
Facilities: Car park (inc 2 disabled bays) and toilets. Space for up to two small coaches. Visitor centre - unmanned but next to reserve office. Ten hides overlooking the reserve: nearest 350 yards from visitor centre (with disabled access) up to 1.8 miles from visitor centre. Boardwalk over pond — good for dragonflies in summer.
Public transport: No public transport to reserve entrance. Buses and trains stop at Manea — three miles from reserve.
Habitat: Lowland wet grassland — seasonally flooded. Open pool systems in front of some hides, particularly Stockdale's hide.
Key birds: *Summer*: Around 70 species breed including Black-tailed Godwit, Lapwing, Redshank, Snipe, Shoveler, Gadwall, Garganey and Spotted Crake. Also Hobby and Marsh Harrier. *Autumn*:

Passage waders including Wood and Green Sandpipers, Spotted Redshank, Greenshank, Little Stint, plus terns and Marsh and Hen Harriers. *Winter*: Large number of wildfowl (up to 100,000 birds) including Bewick's and Whooper Swans, Wigeon, Teal, Shoveler, Pintail, Pochard.
Other notable flora and fauna: Good range of dragonflies, butterflies and fenland flora.
Contact: Jon Reeves, (Site Manager), Ouse Washes Reserve, Welches Dam, Manea, March, Cambs, PE15 0NF. 01354 680 212. e-mail: jon.reeves@rspb.org.uk www.rspb.org.uk

8. PAXTON PITS NATURE RESERVE

Huntingdonshire District Council.
Location: TL 197 629. Access from A1 at Little Paxton, two miles N of St Neots.
Access: Free entry. Open 24 hours. Visitor centre open 7 days a week. Dogs allowed under control. Heron trail suitable for wheelchairs during summer.
Facilities: Visitors centre provides information about the surrounding area and light refreshments are available. Toilets available most days 9am-5pm (including disabled), two bird hides (always open), marked nature trails.
Public transport: Buses run from St Neots and Huntingdon to Little Paxton (enquiries 0845 045 5200). The nearest trans station is St Neots (enquiries 08457 484 950).
Habitat: Grassland, scrub, lakes. Site being expanded to include extensive reedbed.
Key birds: *Spring/summer:* Nightingale, Kingfisher, Common Tern, Sparrowhawk, Hobby, Grasshopper, Sedge and Reed Warblers, Lesser Whitethroat. *Winter:* Smew, Goldeneye, Goosander, Gadwall, Pochard.
Other notable flora and fauna: Wildflowers,

butterflies and dragonflies are in abundance. Along the meadow trail there are common spotted and pyramidal orchids. Bee orchids are found around the car park. Otters are known to use the reserve.
Contact: Kirsty Drew, The Rangers, The Visitor Centre, High Street, Little Paxton, St Neots, Cambs, PE19 6ET. 01480 406 795. www.paxton-pits.org.uk e-mail: paxtonpits@btconnect.com

9. WICKEN FEN

The National Trust.
Location: TL 563 705. Lies 17 miles NE of Cambridge and ten miles S of Ely. From A10 drive E along A1123.
Access: Reserve is open daily except Christmas Day. Visitor centre is open daily in summer. In winter visitor centre is open (10am - 4pm) but closed on Tuesdays.
Facilities: Toilets, visitor centre, café, hides, boardwalk, footpaths, cycle routes, coach and disabled parking.
Public transport: Nearest rail link either Cambridge or Ely. Buses only on Thu and Sun.
Habitat: Open fen, cut hay fields, sedge beds, grazing marsh, partially flooded wet grassland, reedbed, scrub, woodland.
Key birds: *Spring:* Passage waders and passerines. *Summer:* Marsh Harriers, waders and warblers. *Winter:* Wildfowl, Hen Harrier, Bittern.
Other notable flora and fauna: 7,800 species recorded: 22 species of dragonfly/damselfly, 27 species of butterfly and 1,000-plus species of moth. Water vole, otter.
Contact: Isobel Sedgewick, Wicken Fen, Lode Lane, Wicken, Cambs, CB7 5XP. 01353 720 274. e-mail: isobel.sedgewick@nationaltrust.org.uk www.wicken.org.uk

Cheshire

1. DEE ESTUARY (INNER MARSH FARM)

RSPB Dee Estuary Office.
Location: SJ 305 742. Located on the Wirral. From Chester High Road (A540) follow signs for Ness Botanical Gardens. At Burton turn into Station Road until it reaches Burton Point Farm.
Access: Open between 9am and 9pm (or dusk if earlier) each day except Tuesdays. £3 admission for non-RSPB members. Guide dogs only.
Facilities: 12-berth car park Single hide overlooks three pools and wetland area. Guided walks available.
Public transport: Trains stop at Neston. Buses between Neston and Hooton stop at Burton post office, from where it is a 1.5km walk to reserve. Contact Traveline on 0871 200 2233.

Habitat: Former farm now converted to wetland and meadow habitats.
Key birds: *All year:* Little Egret. *Spring/summer:* Avocet and Black-headed Gull colonies, Grasshopper and other commoner warblers, passage Black-tailed Godwit and regular Mediterranean Gulls. Hobby, Marsh Harrier. *Autumn:* Passage waders (inc Little Stint, Ruff, Spotted Redshank, Green, Curlew and Wood Sandpipers). *Winter:* Fieldfare, Redwing, Whooper and Bewick's Swans, Teal, Water Rail, Hen Harrier.
Other notable flora and fauna: Purple hairstreak recently added to extensive butterfly list. Pipistrelle and noctule bats, water vole, wide array of orchids. Red-eyed damselfly.
Contact: Colin E Wells, Burton Point Farm, Station Road, Burton, Nr Neston, Cheshire CH64 5SB. 0151 3367 681; e-mail: colin.wells@rspb.org.uk

NATURE RESERVES - ENGLAND

2. DEE ESTUARY (PARKGATE)

RSPB Dee Estuary Office.
Location: SJ 275 785. On W side of Wirral, S of Birkenhead. View high tide activity from Old Baths car park near Boathouse pub, Parkgate off B5135.
Access: Open at all times. Viewing from public footpaths and car parks. Please do not walk on the saltmarsh, the tides are dangerous.
Facilities: Car park, picnic area, group bookings, guided walks, special events, wheelchair access. Toilets at Parkgate village opposite the Square.
Public transport: Bus to Parkgate every hour. Rail station at Neston, two miles from reserve.
Habitat: Estuary, saltmarsh, pools, mud, sand.
Key birds: *Spring/summer/autumn*:Little Egret, Greenshank, Spotted Redshank, Curlew Sandpiper, Sky Lark. *Winter*: Shelduck, Teal, Wigeon, Pintail, Oystercatcher, Black-tailed Godwit, Curlew, Redshank, Merlin, Peregrine, Water Rail, Short-eared Owl, Hen Harrier.
Other notable flora and fauna: On very high tides, the incoming water displaces several mammal species inc pygmy shrew, water shrew, harvest mouse, weasel and stoat.
Contact: Colin E Wells, see Inner Marsh Farm above.

3. GOWY MEADOWS

Cheshire Wildlife Trust.
Location: SJ 435 740. Lies alongside River Gowy at Thornton-le-Moors, N of Chester, between A5117 and M56.
Access: Park next to church in Thornton-le-Moors and take public footpath opposite into reserve. Open all year.
Facilities: None.
Public transport: The Arriva bus service stops on the Thornton Green Lane opposite the church.
Habitat: 410 acres of lowland grazing marsh, rich in flora.
Key birds: Approx 100 species recorded, inc Barn Owl, Buzzard, Peregrine, Merlin, Hobby. *Spring/summer*: Wildfowl, warblers, Whinchat, Green Sandpiper, Lapwing, Jack Snipe, Snipe. *Winter*: Pintail, Shoveler, Reed Bunting. *Passage*: Stonechat, Wheatear.
Contact: Cheshire Wildlife Trust, 01948 820 728; e-mail: cheshirewt@cix.co.uk www.cheshirewildlifetrust.co.uk

4. MOORE NATURE RESERVE

Waste Recycling Group.
Location: SJ 577 854. SW of Warrington, via A56 Warrington-to-Chester road. At traffic lights at Higher Walton, follow signs for Moore. Take Moore Lane over

swing bridge to reserve.
Access: Open all year. One bird hide suitable for wheelchairs, other parts of site unsurfaced or gravel paths.
Facilities: Coaches by prior arrangement. Paths, bird hides, bird feeding area. Guided walks available on request. See website for wildlife events throughout the year.
Public transport: 62 and 66 buses from Warrington and Runcorn stop in Moore village, less than 1km from reserve. Call 0870 608 2608 for times.
Habitat: Wetland, woodland, grasslands, five pools.
Key birds: More than 130 species every year, inc. occasional rarities. *Spring/summer*: Breeding wildfowl and waders, Black-necked Grebe, warblers. *Autumn/winter*: Wide variety of wildfowl, Bittern. Also good for gulls, woodpeckers, owls and raptors. See website for list and latest sightings.
Contact: Paul Cassidy/Brian Webber, c/o Waste Recycling Centre, Arpley Landfill Site, Forest Way, Sankey Bridge, Warrington, Cheshire WA4 6YZ. 01925 444 689. e-mail: paul.cassidy@wrg.co.uk www.wrg.co.uk/moorenaturereserve

5. RUDHEATH WOODS

Cheshire Wildlife Trust.
Location: SJ 740 700. Located five miles S of Knutsford, at Allostock. From A50, turn W on to Wash Lane. Park in an unmade track which heads S after 0.25 miles. The track continues as a bridle path along the reserve, which is accessed over stiles and along various paths.
Access: Open all year.
Facilities: None. **Public transport:** None.
Habitat: Heathland, wet woodland.
Key birds: *Spring/summer*: Chiffchaff, other warblers, possible Hobby. Autumn: Waders, possible Greenshank, Green Sandpiper. Winter: Siskin, Redpoll, Snipe. All year: All three woodpeckers, Willow Tit.

Contact: Cheshire Wildlife Trust, Bickley Hall Farm, Bickley, Malpas, Cheshire SY14 8EF. 01948 820 728; (fax) 0709 2888 469, e-mail: cheshirewt@cix.co.uk www.cheshirewildlifetrust.co.uk

6. WOOLSTON EYES

Woolston Eyes Conservation Group.
Location: SJ 654 888. E of Warrington between the River Mersey and Manchester Ship Canal. Off Manchester Road down Weir Lane or from Latchford to end of Thelwall Lane.
Access: Open all year. Permits required from Chairman, £8 each, £16 per family (see address below).
Facilities: No toilets or visitor centre. Good hides, some elevated.

Public transport: Buses along A57 nearest stop to Weir Lane, or Thelwall Lane, Latchford.
Habitat: Wetland, marsh, scrubland, wildflower meadow areas.
Key birds: Breeding Black-necked Grebe, warblers (including Grasshopper Warbler), all raptors (Merlin, Peregrine, Marsh Harrier). SSSI for wintering wildfowl, many duck species breed.
Other notable flora and fauna: 19 mammal species recorded, plus 241 species of lepidoptera, four species of bat. Wide variety of butterflies and 22 species of dragonfly. Notable plants include marsh and bee orchids, helleborine, snakeshead fritillary and cowslip.
Contact: BR Ankers, Chairman, 9 Lynton Gardens, Appleton, Cheshire, WA4 5ED. 01925 267 355. www.woolstoneyes.co.uk

Cornwall

1. BRENEY COMMON

Cornwall Wildlife Trust.
Location: SX 054 610. 2.5 miles S of Bodmin. Take minor road off A390 one mile W of Lostwithiel to Lowertown. For Breney Common entrance, turn R at Reperry Cross, then L fork to Trebell Green and on towards Gurtla. The entrance track is on the left in Gurtla, after the Methodist church, opposite The Barn.
Access: Open at all times but please keep to paths. Disabled access from small car park at Breney.
Facilities: Wilderness trail. Boardwalk sections the only suitable surface for wheelchairs.
Public transport: None.
Habitat: Huge site (536 acres) includes wetland, grassland, heath and scrub.
Key birds: Willow Tit, Nightjar, Tree Pipit, Sparrowhawk, Lesser Whitethroat, Curlew.
Other notable flora and fauna: Royal fern, sundews and other bog plants. Butterflies (inc marsh and small pearl-bordered fritillaries, silver-studded blue).
Contact: Sean O'Hea, 01872 273 939.
e-mail: info@cornwt.demon.co.uk
www.cornwallwildlifetrust.org.uk

2. CROWDY RESERVOIR

South West Water.
Location: Follow signs from A39 at Camelford to Davidstow Airfield and pick up signs to the reservoir. On edge of the forestry plantation, park in pull-in spot near a cattle grid. A track leads to a hide via stiles.

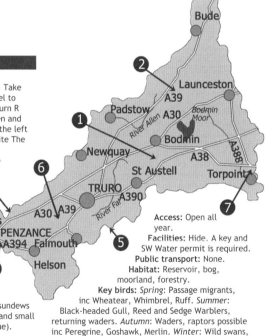

Access: Open all year.
Facilities: Hide. A key and SW Water permit is required.
Public transport: None.
Habitat: Reservoir, bog, moorland, forestry.
Key birds: *Spring*: Passage migrants, inc Wheatear, Whimbrel, Ruff. *Summer*: Black-headed Gull, Reed and Sedge Warblers, returning waders. *Autumn*: Waders, raptors possible inc Peregrine, Goshawk, Merlin. *Winter*: Wild swans, wildfowl, possible Smew. Golden Plover, Woodcock, Fieldfare, Redwing.
Contact: Leisure Services Dept, South West Water, Higher Coombe Park, Lewdown, Okehampton, EX20 4QT. 01837 871 565.

3. HAYLE ESTUARY

RSPB (South West England Office).
Location: SW 550 370. In town of Hayle. Follow signs to Hayle from A30.

Access: Open at all times. No permits required. No admission charges. Not suitable for wheelchair users. Dogs on leads please. Sorry — no coaches.
Facilities: Eric Grace Memorial Hide at Ryan's Field has parking and viewing, but birds here only at high tide. Nearest toilets in town of Hayle. No visitor centre but information board at hide.
Public transport: Buses and trains at Hayle. Call 0871 200 2233 for details.
Habitat: Intertidal mudflats, saltmarsh, lagoon and islands, sandy beaches and sand dunes.
Key birds: *Winter*: Wildfowl, gulls, Kingfisher, Great Northern Diver and waders. *Spring/summer*: Migrant waders, breeding Shelduck. *Autumn*: Rare waders, often from N America! Terns, gulls.
Contact: RSPB, 01392 432 691.

4. MARAZION MARSH

RSPB (South West England Office).
Location: SW 510 315. Reserve is one mile E of Penzance, 500 yards W of Marazion. Entrance off seafront road near Marazion.
Access: Open at all times. No permits required. No admission charges. Not suitable for wheelchair users. Dogs on leads please. Sorry — no coaches.
Facilities: No toilets or visitor centre. Nearest toilets in Marazion and seafront car park.
Public transport: First Group Nos 2, 7 and 8, plus Sunset Bay2Bay service 340 from Penzance. Call 0871 200 2233 for details.
Habitat: Wet reedbed, willow carr.
Key birds: *Winter*: Wildfowl, Snipe, occasional Bittern. *Spring/summer*: Breeding Reed, Sedge and Cetti's Warblers, herons, swans. *Autumn*: Large roost of swallows and martins in reedbeds, migrant warblers and Water Rail.
Other notable flora and fauna: Up to 22 species of dragonfly, plus 500 species of vascular plants, inc lawn camomile and yellow flag.
Contact: RSPB, 01392 432 691.

5. NARE HEAD

National Trust.
Location: Approx ten miles SE of Truro. from A390 head S on A307 to two miles S of Tregony just past the garage. Follow signs to Veryan then L signposted to Carne. Go straight over at crossroad, following Carne and Pendower. Turn L on a bend following NT signs for Nare Head. Bearing R, cross over a cattle grid to the car park. From the garage, Nare Head is about four miles.
Access: Open all year.
Facilities: Car park.
Public transport: None.
Habitat: Headland.
Key birds: *Spring/summer*: Razorbill, Guillemot, Sandwich, Common and Arctic Terns, possible Whimbrel, Fulmar. *Winter*: Black-throated and Great Northern Divers. Red-throated Diver possible. Scoter, Velvet Scoter, Slavonian, Black-necked and Red-necked Grebes.
Contact: National Trust, Lanhydrock House, Lanhydrock, Cornwall, PL30 4DE. 01208 432 691.

6. STITHIANS RESERVOIR

South West Lakes Trust.
Location: SS 715 365. From B3297 S of Redruth.
Access: Good viewing from causeway.
Facilities: New hide near main centre open to all.
Public transport: None.
Habitat: Open water, marshland.
Key birds: Wildfowl and waders (inc. rarities, eg. Pectoral and Semipalmated Sandpipers, Lesser Yellowlegs).
Contact: South West Lakes Trust, 01566 771930. www.swlakestrust.org.uk

7. TAMAR ESTUARY

Cornwall Wildlife Trust.
Location: SX 434 631 (Northern Boundary). SX 421 604 (Southern Boundary). From Plymouth head W on A38. Access parking at Cargreen and Landulph from minor roads off A388.
Access: Open at all times. Access bird hides from China Fleet Club car park, Saltash. Follow path alongside golf course — do not walk on course itself. Combination number for hide locks available at club reception.
Facilities: Two hides on foreshore, first (0.25 miles from car park) overlooks estuary, second (0.5 miles) has excellent views across Kingsmill Lake.
Public transport: None.
Habitat: Tidal mudflat with some saltmarsh.
Key birds: *Winter*: Avocet, Snipe, Black-tailed Godwit, Redshank, Dunlin, Curlew, Whimbrel, Spotted Redshank, Green Sandpiper, Golden Plover, Kingfisher.
Contact: Cornwall Wildlife Trust, 01579 351 155. e-mail: peter@cornwt.demon.co.uk www.cornwallwildlifetrust.org.uk

For a comprehensive survey of bird reserves in the county and The Isles of Scilly, see the latest, highly acclaimed *Best Birdwatching Sites in Cornwall and Scilly* book from Buckingham Press. See page 349 for details.

NATURE

Cumbria

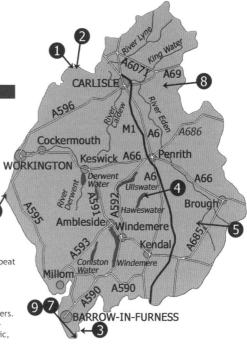

1. CAMPFIELD MARSH

RSPB (North of England Office).
Location: NY 197 615. At North Plain Farm, on S shore of Solway estuary, W of Bowness-on-Solway. Signposted on unclassified coast road from B5307 from Carlisle.
Access: Open at all times, no charge. Disabled visitors can drive to wheelchair-friendly hide to view high-tide roosts.
Facilities: Hide overlooking wetland areas, along nature trail (1.5 miles). No toilets or visitor centre.
Public transport: Nearest railway station at Carlisle (13 miles). Bus No 93 from Carlisle terminates at reserve's eastern end — 1.5 mile walk to North Plain Farm.
Habitat: Saltmarsh/intertidal areas, open water, peat bog, wet grassland.
Key birds: *Winter*: Waders and wildfowl include Barnacle and Pinkfooted Geese, Shoveler, Scaup, Grey Plover. *Spring/summer*: Breeding Lapwing, Curlew, Redshank, Snipe, Tree Sparrow and warblers. *Spring and autumn*: Passage waders such as Black-tailed Godwit, Whimbrel. Look for Pomarine, Arctic, Great and Long-tailed Skuas over the Solway. *Autumn/winter*: Up to 10,000 Oystercatchers among large roosting wader flocks. Hen Harrier.
Other notable flora and fauna: Roe deer, brown hare. Bog rosemary, bog asphodel, sundews and cotton grass. Large numbers of dragonflies (inc azure and emerald damselflies and four-spotted chaser).
Contact: North Plain Farm, Bowness-on-Solway, Wigton, Cumbria, CA7 5AG. www.rspb.org.uk
e-mail: dave.blackledge@rspb.org.uk

2. DRUMBURGH NATIONAL NATURE RESERVE

Cumbria Wildlife Trust.
Location: NY 255 586 (OS Landranger 85). From Carlisle city centre, head W on B5307 to Kirkbride. After about one mile, turn R to Burgh by Sands. Follow road for 7.5 miles to Drumburgh village. Turn L by post office, continue down track and park on R past Moss Cottage.
Access: Open all year. Difficult terrain, so it is best to walk on bunds built to re-wet the site.
Facilities: None.
Public transport: Bus service between Carlisle and Bowness-on-Solway stops in Drumburgh.
Habitat: Raised bog, woodland, grassland.
Key birds: *Summer*: Red Grouse, Curlew, Grasshopper Warbler. *Winter*: Geese from the Solway.
Other notable flora and fauna: Large heath butterfly, emperor moth, adder and lizards, roe deer, brown hare. Specialist plants include 13 species of sphagnum moss, sundews, cotton grass and bog rosemary.

Contact: Cumbria Wildlife Trust, Plumgarths, Crook Road, Kendal, LA8 8LX. 01539 816 300;
e-mail: mail@cumbriawildlifetrust.org.uk
www.cumbriawildlifetrust.org.uk

3. FOULNEY ISLAND

Cumbria Wildlife Trust.
Location: SD 246 640. Three miles SE of Barrow town centre on the A5087 from Barrow or Ulverston. At a roundabout 2.5 miles S of Barrow take a minor road through Rampside to Roa Island. Turn L into reserve car park. Walk to main island along stone causeway.
Access: Open all year. Access restricted to designated paths during bird breeding season. Slitch Ridge is closed at this time. No dogs allowed during bird breeding season. The island may be cut off for several hours around high-tide, so please consult tide tables.
Facilities: None.
Public transport: Bus: regular service from Barrow to Roa Island.
Habitat: Shingle, sand, grassland.
Key birds: *Summer*: Arctic and Little Terns, Oystercatcher, Ringed Plover, Eider Duck. *Winter*: Brent Goose, Redshank, Dunlin, Sanderling.
Other notable flora and fauna: Sea campion, yellow horned poppy. Six spot burnet and common blue butterfly.
Contact: Cumbria Wildlife Trust, 01539 816 300;
e-mail: mail@cumbriawildlifetrust.org.uk
www.cumbriawildlifetrust.org.uk

4. HAWESWATER

RSPB and United Utilities.
Location: NY 470 108. Golden Eagle viewpoint, near Bampton, 5 miles NW of Shap, off A6. Turn L in Bampton to car park at S of reservoir.
Access: The viewpoint is always open but only manned as below. Visitors are asked not to go beyond the viewpoint. There is no wheelchair access.
Facilities: Golden Eagle viewpoint, open Saturday and Sunday, plus bank holidays, Apr to end Aug (11am-4pm), telescopes available. There is no coach parking.
Public transport: None.
Habitat: Fells with rocky streams, steep oak and birch woodlands.
Key birds: *Upland breeders:* Golden Eagle, Peregrine, Raven, Ring Ouzel, Curlew, Redshank, Snipe. *Woodlands:* Pied Flycatcher, Wood Warbler, Tree Pipit, Redstart, Buzzard, Sparrowhawk.
Contact: 7 Naddlegate, Burn Banks, Haweswater, Penrith, Cumbria CA10 2RL.

5. SMARDALE GILL NATIONAL NATURE RESERVE

Cumbria Wildlife Trust.
Location: NY 727 070. NNR occupies a 6km stretch of the disused railway between Tebay and Darlington. Approx 2.5 miles NE of Ravenstonedale on A685 or 0.5 miles S of Kirkby Stephen station take turning signed to Smardale. Cross over railway and turn L to junction, ignoring turn to Waitby. Cross over railway and turn L at junction ignoring sign for Smardale. Cross disused railway, turn L immediately and L again to car park.
Access: Railway line is open to members and non-members but non-members should obtain a permit before visiting other parts of the reserve.
Facilities: None.
Public transport: Train: nearest station Kirkby Stephen. Buses from here to Kendal, Brough and Sedburgh.
Habitat: Limestone grassland, river, ancient semi-natural woodland, quarry.
Key birds: *Summer:* Redstart, Pied Flycatcher, Wood Warbler and commoner woodland species. *All year:* Usual woodland birds, Buzzard, Sparrowhawk.
Other notable flora and fauna: Scotch argus, northern brown argus, common blue and dark green fritillary butterflies. Fragrant orchid, common rockrose, bluebell and bloody cranesbill. Red squirrel.
Contact: Cumbria Wildlife Trust, 01539 816 300; www.cumbriawildlifetrust.org.uk

6. ST BEES HEAD

RSPB (North of England Office).
Location: NX 962 118. S of Whitehaven via the B5345 road to St Bees village.
Access: Open at all times, no charge. Access via coast-to-coast footpath. The walk to the viewpoints is long and steep in parts.
Facilities: Three viewpoints overlooking seabird colony. Public toilets in St Bees beach car park at entrance to reserve.

Public transport: Nearest trains at St Bees (0.5 mile).
Habitat: Three miles of sandstone cliffs up to 300 ft high.
Key birds: *Summer:* Largest seabird colony on W coast of England: Guillemot, Razorbill, Puffin, Kittiwake, Fulmar and England's only breeding pairs of Black Guillemot.
Contact: See Campfield Marsh above.

7. SOUTH WALNEY

Cumbria Wildlife Trust.
Location: SD 215 620. Six miles S of Barrow-in-Furness. From Barrow, cross Jubilee Bridge onto Walney Island, turn L at lights. Continue through Biggar village to South End Caravan Park. Follow road for 1 mile to reserve.
Access: Open daily (10am-5pm) plus Bank Holidays. No dogs except assistance dogs. Day permits: £2 adults, 50p children. Cumbria Wildlife Trust members free.
Facilities: Toilets, nature trails, eight hides (two are wheelchair accessible), 200m boardwalk, cottage available to rent - sleeps 10. Electric wheelchair for hire. Coach parking available.
Public transport: Bus service as far as Biggar.
Habitat: Shingle, lagoon, sand dune, saltmarsh.
Key birds: *Spring/autumn:* Passage migrants. *Summer:* 14,000 breeding pairs of Herring, Greater and Lesser Black-backed Gulls, Shelduck, Eider. *Winter:* Teal, Wigeon, Goldeneye, Redshank, Greenshank, Curlew, Oystercatcher, Knot, Dunlin, Merlin, Short-eared Owl, Twite.
Other notable flora and fauna: 450 species of flowering plants. Natterjack toad at North Walney.
Contact: The Warden, No 1 Coastguard Cottages, South Walney Nature Reserve, Walney Island, Barrow-in-Furness, Cumbria LA14 3YQ. 01229 471 066. e-mail: mail@cumbriawildlifetrust.org.uk www.cumbriawildlifetrust.org.uk

8. TALKIN TARN COUNTRY PARK

Carlisle City Council
Location: NY544 591. Twelve miles E of Carlisle. From A69 E at Brampton, head S on B6413 for two miles. Talkin Tarn is on E just after level crossing.
Access: All year. Wheelchair access around tarn, two kissing gates accessible. Tearoom has lift. Coaches welcome.
Facilities: Tearoom open all year (10.30am-4pm). Mondays takeaway only during winter. Dogs allowed around Tarn. Rowing boat hire at weekends and school holidays. Angling by day permit (with closed season).
Public transport: Bus: infrequent. Tel: 0870 608 2608. Train: nearest station is Brampton Junction. Tel: 0845 748 4950. One mile away by footpath.
Habitat: Natural glacial tarn, mature oak/beech woodland, orchid meadow (traditionally managed), wet mire and farmland.
Key birds: *Spring/summer:* Pied Flycatcher, Spotted Flycatcher, Redstart, Chiffchaff, Wood Warbler. *Winter:* Grebes, Smew, Long-tailed Duck, Goosander,

Gadwall, Wigeon, Brambling, swans.
Other notable flora and fauna: Common blue damselfly, common darter, small copper butterfly, otter, red squirrel.
Contact: Countryside Ranger, Talking Tarn Country Park, Tarn Road, Brampton, Cumbria CA8 1HN. 01697 73129, e-mail: fionash@carlisle.gov.uk

9. WALNEY BIRD OBSERVATORY

Location: Walney Island, Barrow-in-Furness, Cumbria.
Access: Several areas, notably the golf course and airfield, are restricted but the island's narrow width means most sites are viewable from the road or footpaths. Access to South Walney Nature Reserve (10am-5pm) is along permitted trails.
Facilities: Monitoring and ringing of breeding and migrant birds occurs across the island, with ringing opportunities for qualified ringers. For availability write to Walney Bird Observatory (address below).
Public transport: Barrow-in-Furness connects to the rail network and local bus routes serve Walney Island. Routes 1 and 1A cover the central area while 6 and 6A cover the north end of the island. No bus route is available for the southern end.
Habitat: Estuarine, maritime, dunes, freshwater and brackish pools, scrub and farmland.
Key birds: Renowned Eider and gull colonies at south end. The winter months provide a wildfowl and wader spectacular across the island. Migrants aplenty appear during both passage periods — the island has a proven pedigree for attracting rare and unusual species.
Other notable flora and fauna: Famed for Walney geranium, but also important for coastal shingle species such as sea holly, sea rocket and sea kale. Almost 500 species of moth recorded, inc sand dune specialities such as coast dart and sand dart.
Contact: Walney Bird Observatory, Coastguard Cottages, Walney Island, Barrow-in-Furness, Cumbria LA14 3YQ.

Derbyshire

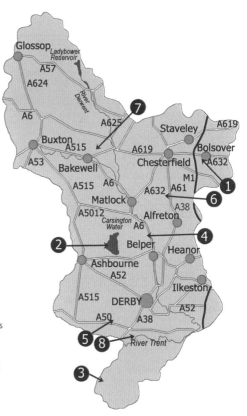

1. CARR VALE NATURE RESERVE

Derbyshire Wildlife Trust.
Location: SK 45 70. 1km W of Bolsover on A632 to Chesterfield. Turn L at roundabout (follow brown tourist signs) into Riverside Way. Car park at end of road. Follow footpath (waymarked) around Peter Fidler reserve.
Access: Open all year.
Facilities: Car park, coach parking on approach road, good disabled access, paths, viewing platforms.
Public transport: Various Stagecoach services from Chesterfield (Stephenson Place) all pass close to the reserve: Mon to Sat - 83 serves Villas Road, 81, 82, 82A and 83 serve the roundabout on the A632. Sun - 81A, 82A serve the roundabout on the A632.
Habitat: Lakes, wader flashes, reed bed, sewage farm, scrub, arable fields.
Key birds: Up to 150 species seen annually at this productive site. *Winter:* Large numbers of wildfowl including flocks of Wigeon and Teal, also wintering flocks of finches and buntings, Water Rail. Large skeins of geese fly over in early and late winter. *Spring/autumn:* Birds on migration including swallows, pipits and thrushes. In September Swallows gather in the marsh, in a gigantic roost of between 10-12,000 birds. They usually attract Hobbies. *Early summer:* Breeding birds, including Reed and Sedge Warblers, Whitethroat, Yellowhammer, Moorhen and Gadwall, plus Sky Lark. Long list of rarities.
Other notable flora and fauna: Dragonflies, mammals (hare, water vole, harvest mouse, water shrew).

Contact: Derbyshire Wildlife Trust, East Mill, Bridgefoot, Belper, Derbyshire, DE56 1XH. 01773 881 188. e-mail: enquiries@derbyshirewt.co.uk www.derbyshirewildlifetrust.org.uk

2. CARSINGTON WATER

Severn Trent Water.
Location: SK 24 51 (for visitor centre and main facilities). Off the B5035 Ashbourne to Cromford road.
Access: Open all year except Christmas Day. The car parks are open from 7am to sunset (Apr - end Oct) and 7.30am to sunset in winter. There are various access points. New lower track opened in spring 09 to improve access.
Facilities: Visitor centre with exhibition, restaurant, four shops (inc RSPB), play area and toilets. RSPB 'Aren't Birds Brilliant' project operates here twice a week. Four bird hides and three car parks (two chargeable, one free).
Public transport: TM Travel operates service 411 from Matlock and Ashbourne. The nearest train station is at Cromford. Call TM on 01142 633 890.
Habitat: Open water, islands, mixed woodland, scrub and grasslands, small reedbed.
Key birds: *Winter*: Wildfowl and a large gull roost plus possibility of divers and rare grebes. *Spring*: Good spring passage including Yellow and White Wagtails, Whimbrel, Black and Arctic Terns. *Summer*: Warblers and breeding waders. *All year*: Tree Sparrows and Willow Tits.
Other notable flora and fauna: Species-rich hay meadows, ancient woodlands with bluebells, three species of orchid, five species of bat, 21 species of butterfly and water vole.
Contact: Carsington Water, The Visitor Centre, Ashbourne, Derbyshire DE6 1ST. 01629 540 696. e-mail: customer.relations@severntrent.co.uk www.moretoexperience.co.uk and www.carsingtonbirdclub.co.uk

3. DRAKELOW NATURE RESERVE

E-ON, leased to Derbyshire Wildlife Trust.
Location: SK 223 204 (Landranger 128). Drakelow Power Station, one mile NE of Walton-on-Trent, off A38.
Access: Dawn to dusk for permit-holders only (plus up to two guests). Annual permit can be obtained from Derbyshire Wildlife Trust.
Facilities: Seven hides, no other facilities.
Public transport: None.
Habitat: Disused flooded gravel pits with wooded islands and reedbeds.
Key birds: *Summer*: Breeding Reed and Sedge Warblers. Water Rail, Hobby. *Winter*: Wildfowl (Goldeneye, Gadwall, Smew), Merlin, Peregrine. Recent rarities include Great White and Little Egret, Bittern and Spotted Crake, Ring-necked Duck and American Wigeon.
Other notable flora and fauna: Good for common species of dragonflies and butterflies.

Contact: Trust HQ, 01773 881 188. www.derbyshirewildlifetrust.org.uk

4. EREWASH MEADOWS

Derbyshire & Notts Wildlife Trusts
Location: SK 441 517. In three parts: Aldercar Flash, Brinsley Meadows and part of Cromford Canal. Ripley is nearest large town.
Access: Open all year — please keep to paths.
Facilities: None.
Public transport: Local bus services.
Habitat: The sites are now part of the largest floodplain grassland and wetlands in Erewash Valley.
Key birds: *Spring/summer*: Breeding Lapwing, Snipe, Reed Bunting and warblers. Raptors, waders and wildfowl seen on passage. *Winter*: Wildfowl species.
Other notable flora and fauna: Grass snake, amphibians, dragonflies, butterflies.
Contact: Trust HQ, 01773 881 188. www.derbyshirewildlifetrust.org.uk

5. HILTON GRAVEL PITS

Derbyshire Wildlife Trust.
Location: SK 249 315 (OS Langranger 128). From Derby, take A516 from Mickleover W past Etwall onto A50 junction at Hilton. Turn R at first island onto Willow Pit Lane. Turn L next to a large white house and park next to the gate. Follow track along S side of the pools.
Access: Open all year.
Facilities: Tracks and boardwalks, viewing screens.
Public transport: Local bus services from Derby.
Habitat: Ponds, scrub, wood, fen.
Key birds: *Spring/summer*: Great Crested Grebe, Common Tern, warblers. *Winter*: Wildfowl, Siskin, Goldcrest. *All year*: All three woodpeckers, Kingfisher, tits inc possible Willow Tit, Tawny Owl, Bullfinch.
Other notable flora and fauna: Dragonflies (15 species inc emperor, ruddy darter and red-eyed damselfly), Great crested newt, orchids, black poplar, fungi.
Contact: Trust HQ, 01773 881 188. e-mail: enquiries@derbyshirewt.co.uk www.derbyshirewildlifetrust.org.uk

6. OGSTON RESERVOIR

Severn Trent Water Plc.
Location: SK 37 60 (Landranger map 119). From Matlock, take A615 E to B6014, just after Tansley. From Chesterfield take A61 S of Clay Cross onto B6014, towards Tansley. Cross railway, the reservoir is on L after the hill.
Access: View from roads, car parks or hides. Suitable for coaches. Heronry in nearby Ogston Carr Wood (Derbyshire Wildlife Trust) viewable from road, W of reservoir.
Facilities: Three car parks (no charges), with toilets at N and W locations. Ogston BC members-only hide and public hide both wheelchair-accessible. Information pack on request.
Public transport: Hulleys 63 bus service (Chesterfield

to Clay Cross) and 64 service (Clay Cross to Matlock) both serves N end of reservoir (not Sundays).
Habitat: Open water, pasture, mixed woodland.
Key birds: All three woodpeckers, Little and Tawny Owls, Kingfisher, Grey Wagtail, warblers. Passage raptors (inc. Osprey), terns and waders. *Winter:* Gull roost attracts thousands of birds, inc regular Glaucous and Iceland Gulls. Top inland site for Bonaparte's Gull and also attracts Caspian/ Herring Gull complex. Good numbers of wildfowl, tit and finch flocks.
Contact: Malcolm Hill, Treasurer, Ogston Bird Club, c/o 2 Sycamore Avenue, Glapwell, Chesterfield, S44 5LH. 01623 812 159. www.ogstonbirdclub.co.uk

7. PADLEY GORGE

The National Trust (East Midlands).
Location: From Sheffield, take A625. After eight miles, turn L on B6521 to Nether Padley. Grindleford Station is just off B6521 (NW of Nether Padley) and one mile NE of Grindleford village.
Access: All year. Not suitable for disabled people or those unused to steep climbs. Some of the paths are rocky. No dogs allowed.
Facilities: Café and toilets at Longshaw lodge.
Public transport: Bus: from Sheffield to Bakewell stops at Grindleford/Nether Padley. Tel: 01709 566 000. Train: from Sheffield to Manchester Piccadilly stops at Grindleford Station. Tel: 0161 228 2141.
Habitat: Steep-sided valley containing largest area of sessile oak woodland in south Pennines.
Key birds: *Summer:* Pied Flycatcher, Spotted Flycatcher, Redstart, Wheatear, Whinchat, Wood Warbler, Tree Pipit.

Contact: National Trust, High Peak Estate Office, Edale End, Edale Road, Hope S33 2RF. 01433 670 368. www.nationaltrust.org.uk

8. WILLINGTON GRAVEL PITS

Derbyshire Wildlife Trust.
Location: SK 285 274. From A50 'Toyota Island' turn onto Repton Road towards Willington and Repton. Go through village towards Repton. Just before bridge over River Trent, turn R onto un-made track (Meadow Lane). Park on track and walk along lane.
Access: Access along Meadow Lane to viewing platforms all year. No access on site.
Facilities: Viewing platforms. Limited parking in lane.
Public transport: Local trains stop at Willington, local bus service from Derby.
Habitat: Open water, reedbed, shingle island, grassland.
Key birds: *Summer:* Breeding Lapwing, other waders, Common Tern, raptors, including Peregrine, Kestrel, Hobby and Sparrowhawk, Sand Martin, wildfowl. *Winter:* Waders and large flocks of wildfowl including Wigeon, Teal, Pochard and Shoveler. *Passage:* Large numbers of Curlew in spring, up to 20 species of waders in spring/autumn.
Other notable flora and fauna: Short-leaved water starwort. Several species of dragonfly, plus occasional otter signs, fox and other mammals.
Contact: Trust HQ, 01773 881 188. e-mail: enquiries@derbyshirewt.co.uk www.derbyshirewildlifetrust.org.uk

Devon

1. AYLESBEARE COMMON

RSPB (South West England Office).
Location: SY 058 897. Five miles E of J30 of M5 at Exeter, 0.5 miles past Halfway Inn on B3052. Turn R to Hawkerland, car park is on L. The reserve is on the opposite side of the main road.
Access: Open all year. One track suitable for wheelchairs and pushchairs.
Facilities: Car park, picnic area, group bookings, guided walks and special events. Disabled access via metalled track to private farm.
Public transport: Buses (Exeter to Sidmouth, 52a, 52b). Request stop at Joneys Cross (reserve entrance).
Habitat: Heathland, wood fringes, streams and ponds.
Key birds: *Spring/summer:* Hobby, Nightjar, Tree Pipit, Stonechat. *All year:* Dartford Warbler, Buzzard, Yellowhammer. *Winter:* Possible Hen Harrier.
Other notable flora and fauna: Good range of dragonflies and butterflies.

Contact: Toby Taylor, Hawkerland Brake Barn, Exmouth Road, Aylesbeare, Nr Exeter, Devon EX5 2JS. 01395 233 655. www.rspb.org.uk/reserves/guide/a/aylesbearecommon/

2. BOVEY HEATHFIELD

Devon Wildlife Trust.
Location: SX 824 765. On the outskirts of Bovey Tracey on SE edge of Dartmoor. From A382 Bovey Straight take Battle Road into Heathfield Industrial estate. Turn L into Cavalier Road, then Dragoon Close - the reserve is along a gravel path.
Access: Open all year. Dogs allowed on leads. Please keep to paths. Rough paths not suitable for wheelchairs. No coach access.
Facilities: Information hut open when warden is on site.
Public transport: Buses to Battle Road, Heathfield.
Habitat: Heathland.
Key birds: Breeding Nightjar, Tree Pipit, Stonechat and Dartford Warbler, plus commoner species.

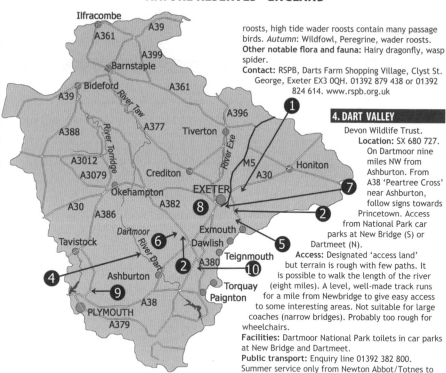

roosts, high tide wader roosts contain many passage birds. *Autumn*: Wildfowl, Peregrine, wader roosts.
Other notable flora and fauna: Hairy dragonfly, wasp spider.
Contact: RSPB, Darts Farm Shopping Village, Clyst St. George, Exeter EX3 0QH. 01392 879 438 or 01392 824 614. www.rspb.org.uk

4. DART VALLEY

Devon Wildlife Trust.
Location: SX 680 727. On Dartmoor nine miles NW from Ashburton. From A38 'Peartree Cross' near Ashburton, follow signs towards Princetown. Access from National Park car parks at New Bridge (S) or Dartmeet (N).
Access: Designated 'access land' but terrain is rough with few paths. It is possible to walk the length of the river (eight miles). A level, well-made track runs for a mile from Newbridge to give easy access to some interesting areas. Not suitable for large coaches (narrow bridges). Probably too rough for wheelchairs.
Facilities: Dartmoor National Park toilets in car parks at New Bridge and Dartmeet.
Public transport: Enquiry line 01392 382 800. Summer service only from Newton Abbot/Totnes to Dartmeet.
Habitat: Upland moor, wooded valley and river.
Key birds: *All year*: Raven, Buzzard. *Spring/summer*: Wood Warbler, Pied Flycatcher, Redstart in woodland, Stonechat and Whinchat on moorland, Dipper, Grey Wagtail, Goosander on river.
Contact: Devon Wildlife Trust, Cricklepit Mill, Commercial Road, Exeter EX1 4AB. 01392 279 244. www.devonwildlifetrust.org

Other notable flora and fauna: Heathers, wet and dry heathland plants, more than 60 endangered insect species, plus grayling and green hairstreak butterflies, slow worm, adder.
Contact: Devon Wildlife Trust, Cricklepit Mill, Commercial Road, Exeter, EX1 4AB. 01392 279 244. e-mail: devonwt@cix.co.uk

3. BOWLING GREEN MARSH

RSPB (South West England Office).
Location: SX 972 876. On the E side of River Exe, four miles SE of Exeter, 0.5 miles SE of Topsham.
Access: Open at all times. Please park at the public car parks in Topsham, not in the lane by the reserve.
Facilities: RSPB shop at Darts Farm, 1.5km from reserve, east of Topsham across River Clyst.
Public transport: Exeter to Exmouth railway has regular (every 30 mins) service to Topsham station (half a mile from reserve). Stagecoach Devon 57 bus has frequent service (Mon-Sat every 12 mins, Sun every half-hour) from Exeter to Topsham. Traveline 0871 200 2233.
Habitat: Coastal grassland, open water/marsh.
Key birds: *Winter*: Wigeon, Shoveler, Teal, Black-tailed Godwit, Curlew, Golden Plover. *Spring*: Shelduck, passage waders, Whimbrel, passage Garganey and Yellow Wagtail. *Summer*: Gull/tern

5. DAWLISH WARREN NATIONAL NATURE RESERVE

Teignbridge District Council.
Location: SX 983 788. At Dawlish Warren on S side of Exe estuary mouth. Turn off A379 at sign to Warren Golf Club, between Cockwood and Dawlish. Turn into car park adjacent to Lea Cliff Holiday Park. Pass under tunnel and turn L away from amusements. Park at far end of car park and pass through two pedestrian gates.
Access: Open public access, but avoid mudflats. Also avoid beach beyond groyne nine around high tide due to roosting birds. Parking charges apply. Restricted access for dogs (none allowed in hide).
Facilities: Visitor centre (tel 01626 863 980) open most weekends all year (10.30am-1pm and 2pm-5pm). Summer also open most weekdays as before, but can be closed if warden is on site. Toilets at entrance tunnel and in resort area only. Hide open at

all times — best around high tide.
Public transport: Train station at site, also regular bus service operated by Stagecoach.
Habitat: High tide roost site for wildfowl and waders of Exe estuary on mudflats and shore. Dunes, dune grassland, woodland, scrub, ponds.
Key birds: *Winter*: Waders and wildfowl – large numbers. Also good for divers and Slavonian Grebe offshore. *Summer*: Particularly good for terns. Excellent variety of birds all year, especially on migration.
Contact: Steve Ayres/Philip Chambers, Countryside Management Section, Teignbridge District Council, Forde House, Brunel Road, Newton Abbot, Devon, TQ12 4XX. Visitor centre: 01626 863 980. Teignbridge District Council: 01626 361 101 (Ext 5754).

6. EAST DARTMOOR NATIONAL NATURE RESERVE

Natural England
Location: SX 778 787. The NNR is two miles from Bovey Tracey on road to Becky Falls and Manaton. Road continues across Trendlebere Down, where there are roadside car parks and adjacent paths.
Access: Yarner Wood car park open from 8.30am-7pm or dusk if earlier. Outside these hours, access on foot from Trendlebere Down. Dogs welcome but must be kept under close control.
Facilities: Information/interpretation display and self-guided trails available in Yarner Wood car park also hide with feeding station (Nov-Mar).
Public transport: Nearest bus stops are in Bovey Tracey. Buses from here to Exeter and Newton Abbot (hourly).
Habitat: The reserve consists of three connected sites (Yarner Wood, Trendlebere Down and Bovey Valley Woodlands) totalling 365 hectares of upland oakwood and heathland.
Key birds: *All year*: Raven, Buzzard, Goshawk, Sparrowhawk, Lesser Spotted, Great Spotted and Green Woodpeckers, Grey Wagtail and Dartford Warbler (on Trendlebere Down). *Spring/summer*: Pied Flycatcher, Wood Warbler, Redstart, Tree Pipit, Linnet, Stonechat, Cuckoo, Whitethroat, Sky Lark. *Autumn/winter*: Good range of birds with feeding at hide, inc Siskin, Redpoll, plus Hen Harrier on Trendlebere Down.
Contact: Site Manager, Natural England, Yarner Wood, Bovey Tracey, Devon TQ13 9LJ. 01626 832 330. www.natural-england.org.uk

7. EXMINSTER MARSHES

RSPB (South West England Office).
Location: SX 954 872. Five miles S of Exeter on W bank of River Exe. Marshes lie between Exminster and the estuary.
Access: Open at all times.
Facilities: No toilets or visitor centre. Information in RSPB car park and marked footpaths across reserve.
Public transport: Exeter to Newton Abbot/Torquay buses — stops are 400 yds from car park. Traveline 0871 200 2233. No 2 buses Mon-Sat every 15 mins, Sun 1/2 hourly.

Habitat: Coastal grazing marsh with freshwater ditches and pools, reeds, scrub-covered canal banks, winter stubbles and crops managed for farmland birds.
Key birds: *Winter*: Brent Goose, Wigeon, Water Rail, Short-eared Owl. *Spring*: Lapwing, Redshank and wildfowl breed, Cetti's Warbler on canal banks. *Summer*: Gull roosts, passage waders. *Autumn*: Peregrine, winter wildfowl, finch flocks. There are also records of Cirl Bunting and Wood Lark.
Other notable flora and fauna: 23 species of dragonfly, including hairy and scarce chaser.
Contact: RSPB, 01392 824 614. www.rspb.org.uk

8. HALDON FOREST RAPTOR VIEWPOINT

Forestry Commission.
Location: Five miles W of Exeter.Turn off A38 at Haldon Racecourse junction, then follow signs for Dunchideock and Forest Walks. After just over 1 mile, turn L into Haldon Forest Park car park.Follow all-ability trail to the viewpoint.
Access: Open all year.
Facilities: Toilets in car park. Viewing point with benches. Path suitable for wheelchairs.
Habitat: Plantations, clearings.
Key birds: *Summer*: Hobby, Nightjar, Turtle Dove, Tree Pipit. *All year*: Goshawk, Sparrowhawk, Buzzard, all woodpeckers, Crossbill, Siskin.
Contact: Forestry Commission, Bullers Hill, Kennford, Exeter, Devon, EX6 7XR. 01392 832 262. www.forestry.gov.uk/england

9. PLYMBRIDGE WOOD

National Trust/Forest Enterprise.
Location: At the Estover roundabout, Plymouth (near the Wrigley company factory), take the narrow, steep Plymbridge Road. Park at the bridge area at the bottom of the hill. Coming from Plympton, pick up Plymbridge Road from either Plymouth Road or Glen Road.
Access: Open all year.
Facilities: Car park, woodland paths, picnic area.
Public transport: None.
Habitat: Mixed woodland, river, conifers.
Key birds: *Spring/summer*: Cuckoo, Wood Warbler, Redstart, Blackcap, possible Nightjar, Crossbill. *Winter*: Woodcock, Snipe, Fieldfare, Redwing, Brambling, Siskin, Redpoll, possible Crossbill. *All year*: Mandarin Duck, Sparrowhawk, Buzzard, Kestrel, Tawny Owl, all three woodpeckers, Kingfisher, Grey Wagtail, Dipper, Goldcrest, common woodland passerines, Marsh Tit, Raven.
Contact: National Trust, Lanhydrock House, Lanhydrock, Cornwall, PL30 4DE. 01208 432 691.

10. STOVER LAKE COUNTRY PARK

Devon County Council.
Location: Two miles N of Newton Abbot off A38 Exeter-Plymouth road. Follow the A382 L at Drumbridges roundabout, signed to Newton Abbot. After 0.25 miles follow the brown tourist sign L into

the car park (fee payable).
Access: Open all year. Wheelchairs available for visitor use.
Facilities: Car park, information centre, notice board display, site leaflets, maps, feeding station, 90 metre aerial walkway.
Public transport: From Newton Abbot, Exeter or Plymouth. Info from Traveline 0871 200 2233.
Habitat: Mixed woodland, lake and lowland heath. SSSI.
Key birds: *Spring/summer*: Sand Martin, Chiffchaff, Willow Warbler, Spotted Flycatcher, Nightjar, Great

Crested Grebe. *Winter*: Water Rail, Marsh Tit, Snipe. *All year*: Woodpeckers, Jay, Siskin, Kingfisher.
Other notable flora and fauna: More than 20 species of dragonfly and damselfly, including hairy dragonfly, downy, emerald and red-eyed damselflies. 34 species of butterfly have been recorded including white admiral, pearl-bordered and silver-washed fritillaries. A good site for bat watching with 10 species identified.
Contact: Rangers Office, Devon County Council, Stover Country Park, Stover, Newton Abbot, Devon TQ12 6QG. 01626 835 236.

Dorset

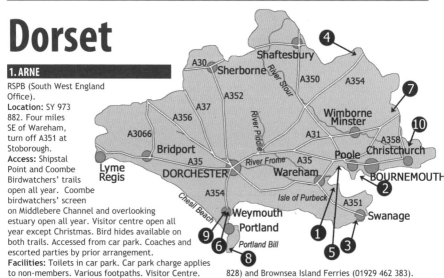

1. ARNE

RSPB (South West England Office).
Location: SY 973 882. Four miles SE of Wareham, turn off A351 at Stoborough.
Access: Shipstal Point and Coombe Birdwatchers' trails open all year. Coombe birdwatchers' screen on Middlebere Channel and overlooking estuary open all year except Christmas. Visitor centre open all year except Christmas. Bird hides available on both trails. Accessed from car park. Coaches and escorted parties by prior arrangement.
Facilities: Toilets in car park. Car park charge applies to non-members. Various footpaths. Visitor Centre.
Public transport: None to reserve. Nearest station is Wareham.
Habitat: Lowland heath, woodland reedbed and saltmarsh, extensive mudflats of Poole Harbour.
Key birds: *All year*: Dartford Warbler, Little Egret, Stonechat. *Winter*: Hen Harrier, Red-breasted Merganser, Black-tailed Godwit. *Summer*: Nightjar, warblers. *Passage*: Spotted Redshank, Whimbrel, Greenshank, Osprey.
Other notable flora and fauna: Sika deer, all six species of UK reptile, silver-studded blue and 32 other butterflies, 23 dragonflies, 850 moths and 500 flowering plants.
Contact: Alexia Hollinshead, Arne Nature Reserve, RSPB Work Centre, Arne, Wareham, Dorset BH20 5BJ. 01929 553 360.
www.rspb.org.uk/reserves/guide/a/arne/

2. BROWNSEA ISLAND

Dorset Wildlife Trust.
Location: SZ 026 883. Half hour boat rides from Poole Quay with Greenslade Pleasure Boats (01202 631

828) and Brownsea Island Ferries (01929 462 383). Ten minutes from Sandbanks Quay (next to Studland chain-ferry).
Access: Apr, May, Jun, Sept and Oct. Access by self-guided nature trail. Costs £2 adults, £1 children. Jul, Aug access by afternoon guided tour (2pm daily, duration 105 minutes). Costs £2 adults, £1 children.
Facilities: Toilets, information centre and shop, six hides, nature trail.
Public transport: Poole rail/bus station for access to Poole Quay and boats. Tel: 01202 673 555.
Habitat: Saline lagoon, reedbed, lakes, coniferous and mixed woodland.
Key birds: *Spring*: Avocet, Black-tailed Godwit, waders, gulls and wildfowl. *Summer*: Common and Sandwich Terns, Yellow-legged Gull, Little Egret, Little Grebe, Golden Pheasant. *Autumn*: Curlew Sandpiper, Little Stint.
Other notable flora and fauna: Red Squirrel, water vole, Bechstein's bat found 2007.
Contact: Dorset Wildlife Trust, The Villa, Brownsea Island, Poole, Dorset BH13 7EE. 01202 709 445.
e-mail: brownseaisland@dorsetwildlife.co.uk
www.wildlifetrust.org.uk/dorset

NATURE RESERVES - ENGLAND

3. DURLSTON COUNTRY PARK

Dorset County Council.
Location: SZ 032 774. One mile S of Swanage (signposted).
Access: Open between sunrise and sunset. Visitor centre open weekends and holidays during winter and daily in other seasons.
Facilities: Guided walks, visitor centre, toilets, hide, waymarked trails.
Public transport: Not available.
Habitat: Grassland, hedges, cliff, meadows.
Key birds: Cliff-nesting seabird colonies; good variety of scrub and woodland breeding species; spring and autumn migrants; seawatching esp. Apr/May & Aug/Nov.
Other notable flora and fauna: 34 species of butterfly and 500-plus species of flowering plants, inc nine species of orchid.
Contact: The Ranger, Durlston Country Park, Lighthouse Road, Swanage, Dorset BH19 2JL. 01929 424 443. e-mail: info@durlston.co.uk www.durlston.co.uk

4. GARSTON WOOD FOREST

RSPB (South West England Office).
Location: SU 004 194. SW from Salisbury. From A354 take turn to Sixpenny Handley then take Bowerchalke road (Dean Lane). Keeping R, proceed for approximately 1.5 miles. Garston Wood car park on L of road indicated by a finger post on R side of road.
Access: Pushchairs can be negotiated around all of the rides, though the terrain is best in dry weather. Dogs are only allowed on public footpaths and bridleways must be kept on a lead.
Facilities: Car park, reserve leaflet, picnic area, group bookings accepted, guided walks available, remote location, good for walking, pushchair friendly.
Public transport: The nearest train station is in Salisbury: from the bus station, take Wilts & Dorset 184 service to Sixpenny Handley (Roebuck Inn).
Habitat: Ancient woodland includes large area of coppiced hazel and maple. Other habitats include oak woodland, scrub and mixed plantation, with important features such as glades, rides and dead wood.
Key birds: Common woodland birds plus Turtle Dove and migrant warblers including Blackcap, Willow Warbler, Garden Warbler and Nightingale. Spotted Flycatcher. Raptors include Buzzard, Sparrowhawk and Goshawk. Winter thrushes.
Other notable flora and fauna: Butterflies, including silver-washed fritillary and elusive white admiral. Adders can be seen on the ride side. Good range of fungi. Fallow deer.
Contact: Alexia Hollinshead, see Arne NR.

5. HAM COMMON

Poole Borough Council.
Location: SY 99. W of Poole. In Hamworthy, take the Blandford Road S along Lake Road, W along Lake Drive and Napier Road, leading to Rockley Park. Park in the beach car park by Hamworthy Pier or Rockley Viewpoint car park, off Napier Road, opposite the entrance to Gorse Hill Central Park.
Access: Open all year. Not suitable for coaches.
Facilities: None.
Habitat: Local Nature Reserve consisting of heathland, scrub, reedbeds, lake. Views over Wareham Channel and Poole Harbour.
Key birds: *Spring/summer*: Stonechat, Dartford Warbler. *Winter*: Brent Goose, Red-breasted Merganser, occasional divers, rarer grebes, Scaup. Waders inc Whimbrel, Greenshank and Common Sandpiper. *All year*: Little Egret.
Contact: Poole Borough Council, Civic Centre, Poole, BH15 2RU. 01202 633 633. e-mail: information@poole.gov.uk

6. LODMOOR

RSPB (South West England Office).
Location: SY 686 807. Adjacent Lodmoor Country Park, in Weymouth, off A353 to Wareham.
Access: Open all times.
Facilities: One viewing shelter, network of paths.
Public transport: Local bus service.
Habitat: Marsh, shallow pools, reeds and scrub, remnant saltmarsh.
Key birds: *Spring/summer*: Breeding Common Tern, warblers (including Reed, Sedge, Grasshopper and Cetti's), Bearded Tit. *Winter*: Wildfowl, waders. *Passage*: Waders and other migrants.
Contact: Nick Tomlinson, RSPB Visitor Centre, Swannery Car Park, Weymouth, DT4 7TZ. 01305 778 313. www.rspb.org.uk

7. MOORS VALLEY COUNTRY PARK AND RINGWOOD FOREST

East Dorset District Council/Forestry Commission
Location: Two miles W of Ringwood, well-signposted from A31 between Ringwood and Three Legged Cross.
Access: Open every day (except Christmas Day) 8am-dusk. Visitor centre open 9am to 4.30pm daily. Many trails wheelchair friendly.
Facilities: Visitor centre, toilets, tea-room, country shop. Coach parking. Way-marked trails in good condition.
Public transport: Accessible by Wilts & Dorset No 36 service. Call 01988 827 005 or visit: www.wdbus.co.uk
Habitat: River, wet meadow, lakes, scrub, broad-leaved woodland, extensive coniferous forest, golf course.
Key birds: *Spring/summer*: Cuckoo, Nightjar, Sand Martin, Tree Pipit, Whitethroat. Occasional Wood Lark, Sedge Warbler. *Winter*: Teal, Pochard, Gadwall, Snipe, Redpoll. Occasional Brambling, Goosander. *Passage*: Whimbrel, Common Sandpiper, waders. *All year*: Buzzard, Lapwing, Woodcock, Little Owl, Grey Wagtail, Kingfisher, Dartford Warbler, Crossbill, usual woodland species.
Other notable flora and fauna: 27 species of dragonfly. Good numbers of butterflies and other

151

invertebrates. Roe deer, muntjac, badger, fox, rabbit, grey squirrel.
Contact: Moors Valley Country Park, Horton Road, Ashley Heath, Nr Ringwood, Dorset, BH24 2ET. 01425 470 721. e-mail: moorsvalley@eastdorset.gov.uk www.moors-valley.co.uk

8. PORTLAND BIRD OBSERVATORY

Portland Bird Observatory (registered charity).
Location: SY 681 690. Six miles S of Weymouth beside the road to Portland Bill.
Access: Open at all times. Parking only for members of Portland Bird Observatory. Self-catering accommodation for up to 20. Take own towels, sheets, sleeping bags.
Facilities: Displays and information, toilets, natural history bookshop, equipped kitchen.
Public transport: Bus service from Weymouth (First Dorset Transit Route 1).
Habitat: World famous migration watchpoint. Scrub and ponds.
Key birds: *Spring/autumn*: Migrants including many rarities. *Summer*: Breeding auks, Fulmar, Kittiwake. A total of 355 species recorded.
Contact: Martin Cade, Old Lower Light, Portland Bill, Dorset, DT5 2JT. 01305 820 553. e-mail: obs@btinternet.com www.portlandbirdobs.org.uk

9. RADIPOLE LAKE

RSPB (South West England Office).
Location: SY 677 796. In Weymouth. Enter from Swannery car park on footpaths.
Access: Visitor centre and nature trail open every day, summer (9am-5pm), winter (9am-4pm). Hide open (8.30am-4.30pm). Permit available from visitor centre required by non-RSPB members.
Facilities: Network of paths, one hide, one viewing shelter.
Public transport: Close to train station serving London and Bristol.
Habitat: Lake, reedbeds.
Key birds: *Winter*: Wildfowl. *Summer*: Breeding reedbed warblers (including Cetti's), Bearded Tit, passage waders and other migrants. Garganey regular in spring. Good for rarer gulls.
Contact: Nick Tomlinson, RSPB Visitor Centre, Swannery Car Park, Weymouth, DT4 7TZ. 01305 778 313. www.rspb.org.uk

10. SOPLEY COMMON

Dorset Wildlife Trust.
Location: SZ 132 975. Four miles NW of Christchurch near Hurn village.
Access: Open at all times. Permits required for surveying and group visits. Dogs under close control and on leads Apr to Aug. Limited disabled access.
Facilities: None. **Public transport:** None.
Habitat: Lowland heath (dry and wet) and deciduous woodland.
Key birds: *Summer*: Breeding Dartford Warbler, Nightjar, Wood Lark, Stonechat. Also Hobby. *Winter*: Snipe.
Other notable flora and fauna: Rare fauna includes sand lizard, smooth snake, green and wood tiger beetles, silver-studded blue butterfly. Wide range of dragonflies on many ponds.
Contact: Rob Brunt, Dorset Wildlife Trust, Brooklands Farm, Forston, Dorchester, Dorset, DT2 7AA. 01305 264 620. e-mail: rbrunt@dorsetwildlife.co.uk www.wildlifetrust.org.uk/dorset

Durham

1. BEACON HILL & HAWTHORN DENE MEADOW

Durham Wildlife Trust and National Trust
Location: NZ 427 458. Hawthorn Dene and Meadow located between Easington and Seaham on Durham Coast. Leave A19 at Easington or Seaham and join B1432, turn into Hawthorn Village. From N end of village, follow minor road E, signposted 'Quarry Traffic'. After quarter mile, road ends at two metal gates, with a cottage and farmhouse on the right. Park on grass verge on opposite side to cottage, taking care not to obstruct gateways. Access is by foot taking the right-hand path. Access to Beacon Hill (NZ 440 455) is along Coastal Footpath or through southern end of Hawthorn Dene.
Access: Open all year, dogs on leads in spring.
Facilities: Information point. Footpaths.
Public transport: Regular bus services from Durham to Hawthorn.
Habitat: Extensive area of semi-natural habitat situated on magnesian limestone escarpment. Steep-sided ravine woodland and limestone grassland.
Key birds: *Summer*: Sky Lark (important conservation site), Twite, Linnet, Yellowhammer, Goldfinch, Whitethroat, Blackcap, Wren, Long-tailed Tit, Grasshopper Warbler, Reed Bunting, Green Woodpecker, Kestrel, Sparrowhawk. *Winter*: Wide variety of waders inc Turnstone, Purple Sandpiper, Redshank, Curlew, Oystercatcher. Seabirds inc Red-throated Diver, Common Scoter, Guillemot, Cormorant and Great Crested Grebe. *Passage*: Wheatear, Fieldfare, Redwing, Waxwing, Buzzard, Ringed Plover, Dunlin, Knot, Lapwing.
Other notable flora and fauna: Good variety of butterflies. Snowdrops, bluebells and numerous species of orchid grow here, including early purple, bird's nest, lesser butterfly and bee orchids. Grassland plants include field scabious, greater knapweed, wild carrot, cowslip and bee, fragrant, common spotted and northern marsh orchids. Roe

deer, badger and brown hare.
Contact: Trust HQ, 0191 5843 112.
e-mail: durhamwt@cix.co.uk
www.wildlifetrust.org.uk/durham

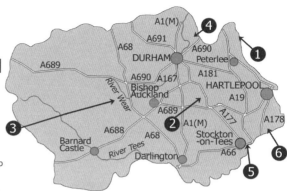

2. BISHOP MIDDLEHAM QUARRY

Durham Wildlife Trust.
Location: NZ 331 326. Half mile
N of Bishop Middleham Village, to
W of A177. Car parking restricted
to two lay-bys on the west side of
the road
adjacent to the reserve entrances.
Access: Open all year. Limited car
parking restricted to two lay-by's. Keep
footpaths, dogs on leads in spring.
Facilities: None
Public transport: Regular bus service from
Durham and Darlington to Coxhoe and Sedgefield.
Habitat: A large magnesian limestone quarry.
Key birds: Good range of farmland birds plus rare
breeding record of Bee-eater.
Other notable flora and fauna: Butterflies including
northern brown argus, dingy skipper, common blue,
small heath, ringlet and small and large skippers.
Internationally rare habitat, rich in orchid species
such as pyramidal, common spotted, fragrant and bee
plus large numbers of dark red helleborines. Other
plants include blue moor grass, moonwort, autumn
gentian and fairy flax.
Contact: Trust HQ, e-mail: durhamwt@cix.co.uk
0191 5843 112. www.wildlifetrust.org.uk/durham

3. HAMSTERLEY FOREST

Forestry Commission
Location: NZ 091 312. Eight miles W of Bishop
Auckland. Main entrance is five miles from A68, S of
Witton-le-Wear and signposted through Hamsterley
village and Bedburn.
Access: Open all year. Toll charge (£3). Forest drive
and car park close 8pm (dusk in winter). Visitor
centre open weekdays (10am-4pm) and weekends
(11am-5pm).
Facilities: Visitor Centre, tearoom, toilets, shop,
access for disabled. Visitors should not enter fenced
farmland.
Public transport: None.
Habitat: Commercial woodland, mixed and
broadleaved trees.
Key birds: *Spring/summer:* Willow Warbler,
Chiffchaff, Wood Warbler, Redstart, Pied Flycatcher.
Winter: Crossbill, Redwing, Fieldfare. *All year:* Jay,
Dipper, Green Woodpecker.
Other notable flora and fauna: Hay meadows have
wide variety of plants including globe flower.
Contact: Forestry Commission, Eals Burn, Bellingham,
Hexham, Northumberland, NE48 2HP. 01434 220 242.
e-mail: neil.taylor@forestry.gsi.gov.uk

4. MAZE PARK & PORTRACK MARSH

Tees Valley Wildlife Trust.
Location: Maze Park: NZ 467 191, Portrack Marsh:

NZ 465 194. Located midway between Middlesbrough
and Stockton. Access from A66 at Tees Barrage. Sites
are located on opposite banks of the River Tees, E of
the barrage.
Access: No permits required. National cycle route
passes through Maze Park. Surfaced paths at both
sites. Hide suitable for disabled users at Portrack
Marsh. Please keep to the permissive paths and public
rights of way.
Facilities: Hide at Portrack Marsh. No toilets or
visitor centre.
Public transport: Regular buses between
Middlesbrough and Stockton stop at the Tees Barrage
(Arriva, tel 0870 608 2608). Thornaby Station
one mile. Frequent trains from Darlington and
Middlesbrough.
Habitat: Freshwater marsh, scrub, post-industrial
grassland, riverside.
Key birds: *Winter:* Ducks, passage waders, Redshank,
Snipe and Jack Snipe, Lapwing, Grey Heron, Sky Lark,
Grey Partridge, Sand Martin, occasional Kingfisher
and Grasshopper Warbler.
Contact: Tees Valley Wildlife Trust,01287 636 382;
e-mail: teesvalleywt@cix.co.uk
www.wildlifetrust.org.uk/teesvalley

5. SALTHOLME WILDLIFE RESERVE AND DISCOVERY PARK

RSPB North West Office
Location: NZ506 231. From A19, take A689 north of
Stockton and then A1185. After four miles join A178
at mini roundabout. Take third exit and reserve is 250
yards on right.
Access: Open every day bar Dec 25. April 1 to Sept
30 (10am-5pm), Oct 1 to March 31 (10am-4pm). £3
per car, RSPB members, users of public transport and
cyclists free.
Facilities: Visitor centre with tearoom and shop,
large car park, including wheelchair-friendly and
coach parking, toilets (inc disabled), picnic area.
Crushed stone paths wheelchair users may need
assistance to reach bird hides. Walled garden
designed by TV gardener Chris Beardshaw.
Public transport: Stagecoach No1 bus from

Hartlepool stops at reserve entrance. Cycle track across reserve from Port Clarence; cycle storage at visitor centre.

Habitat: Wet grasslands, reedbeds, lakes with tern islands, wader scrapes.

Key birds: *All year:* Lapwing, Peregrine, Water Rail. *Spring/summer:* Snipe, Common Tern, Yellow Wagtail. *Autumn:* Varied waders inc Black-tailed Godwits and Green Sandpipers, occasional rarer species. *Winter:* Large numbers of wildfowl and waders.

Other notable flora and fauna: Hares, orchids, butterflies and dragonflies.

Contact: Saltholme RSPB, Seaton Carew Road, Middlesbrough. Tel: 01642 546 625 or e-mail: saltholme@rspb.org.uk

6. TEESMOUTH

Natural England (North East Region).

Location: Two components, centred on NZ 535 276 and NZ 530 260, three and five miles S of Hartlepool, E of A178. Access to northern component from car park at NZ 534 282, 0.5 miles E of A178. Access to southern part from A178 bridge over Greatham Creek at NZ 510 254. Car park adjacent to A178 at NZ 508 251. Both car parks can accommodate coaches.

Access: Open at all times. In northern component, no restrictions over most of dunes and North Gare Sands (avoid golf course, dogs must be kept under close control). In southern component, disabled access path to public hides at NZ 516 255 and NZ 516 252 (no other access).

Facilities: Nearest toilets at Seaton Carew, one mile to the N. Disabled access path and hides (see above), interpretive panels and leaflet. Teesmouth Field Centre (Tel: 01429 264 912).

Public transport: Half-hourly bus service (service 1) operates Mon-Sat between Middlesbrough and Hartlepool (hourly on Sundays), along A178, Stagecoach Hartlepool, Tel: 01429 267 082.

Habitat: Grazing marsh, dunes, intertidal flats.

Key birds: Passage and winter wildfowl and waders. Passage terns and skuas in late summer. Scarce passerine migrants and rarities. *Winter:* Merlin, Peregrine, Snow Bunting, Twite, divers, grebes.

Other notable flora and fauna: Northern component has large marsh orchid populations in damp dune grassland. Seal Sands supports a colony of 70 common seals.

Contact: Natural England, c/o British Energy, Tees Road, Hartlepool, TS25 2BZ. 01429 853 325. e-mail: northumbria@naturalengland.org.uk www.naturalengland.org.uk

Essex

1. ABBERTON RESERVOIR

Essex Wildlife Trust.

Location: TL 963 185. Five miles SW of Colchester on B1026. Follow signs from Layer-de-la-Haye.

Access: Open Tue-Sun and Bank Holiday Mondays (9am-5pm). Closed Christmas Day and Boxing Day.

Facilities: Visitor centre and reserve will move to the peninsula field during 2010 due to Essex & Suffolk Water raising water levels to meet increasing demand. Current facilities include toilets, nature trail, five hides (3 with disabled access). Ample parking, including coaches. Also good viewing where roads cross reservoir.

Public transport: Phone Trust for advice.

Habitat: 100 acres on edge of 1,200-acre reservoir.

Key birds: *Winter:* Nationally important for Mallard, Teal, Wigeon, Shoveler, Gadwall, Pochard, Tufted Duck, Goldeneye (most important inland site in Britain). Smew, Bittern and Goosander regular. Passage waders, terns, birds of prey. Tree-nesting Cormorant colony; raft-nesting Common Tern. *Summer:* Hobby, Yellow Wagtail, warblers, Nightingale, Corn Bunting; *Autumn:* Red-crested Pochard, Water Rail.

Other notable flora and fauna: Dragonflies including broad-bodied chaser, small red-eyed damselfly, butterflies including green and purple hairstreak, roesel's bush-cricket. Brown hare.

Contact: Centre Manager, Essex Wildlife Trust, Abberton Reservoir Visitor Centre, Church Road, Layer-de-la-Haye, Colchester CO2 0EU. 01206 738 172. e-mail: abberton@essexwt.org.uk

2. ABBOTTS HALL FARM

Essex Wildlife Trust.

Location: TL 963 145. Seven miles SW from Colchester. Turn E off B1026 (Colchester-Maldon road) towards Peldon. Entrance is 0.5 mile on R.

Access: Weekdays (9am-5pm). Two hides with wheelchair ramps. No dogs please. Working farm so please take care.

Facilities: Toilets, hides, guided walks, fact-sheets, information boards.

Public transport: None.

Habitat: Saltmarsh, saline lagoons, grazing marsh, farmland, woodland, freshwater lakes and ponds.

Key birds: *Winter:* Waders and wildfowl. Passage migrants and summer warblers.

Other notable flora and fauna: Range of butterflies, reptiles, newts and water vole.

Contact: Trust HQ, 01621 862 960. e-mail: admin@essexwt.org.uk

3. BRADWELL BIRD OBSERVATORY

Essex Birdwatching Society.

Location: 100 yards S of St Peter's Chapel, Bradwell-on-Sea. Mouth of Blackwater estuary, between Maldon and Foulness.

Access: Open all year.

Facilities: Accommodation for eight in hut; two rooms each with four bunks; blankets, cutlery, etc. supplied.

Public transport: None.

Habitat: Mudflats, saltmarsh.

Key birds: *Winter*: Wildfowl (inc. Brent Geese, Red-throated Diver, Red-breasted Merganser), large numbers of waders; small numbers of Twite, Snow Bunting and occasional Shore Lark on beaches, also Hen Harrier, Merlin and Peregrine. Good passage of migrants usual in spring and autumn. *Summer*: Small breeding population of terns and other estuarine species.

Other notable flora and fauna: A variety of dragonflies inc hairy dragonfly and scarce emerald damselfly.

Contact: Graham Smith, 48 The Meads, Ingatestone, Essex CM4 0AE. 01277 354 034.

4. FINGRINGHOE WICK

Essex Wildlife Trust.

Location: TM 046 197. Colchester five miles. The reserve is signposted from B1025 to Mersea Island, S of Colchester.

Access: Open six days per week (not Mon or Christmas or Boxing Day). No permits needed. Donations invited. Centre/reserve open (9am-5pm). Dogs must be on a lead.

Facilities: Visitor centre: toilets, shop, light refreshments, car park, displays. Reserve: seven bird hides, two nature trails, plus one that wheelchair users could use with assistance.

Public transport: None.

Habitat: Old gravel pit, large lake, many ponds, sallow/birch thickets, young scrub, reedbeds, saltmarsh, gorse heathland.

Key birds: *Autumn/winter*: Brent Goose, waders, Hen Harrier, Little Egret. *Spring*: 30 male Nightingales. Good variety of warblers in scrub, thickets, reedbeds and Turtle Dove, Green/Great Spotted Woodpeckers. *Winter*: Little Grebe, Mute Swan, Teal, Wigeon, Shoveler, Gadwall on lake.

Contact: Laurie Forsyth, Wick Farm, South Green Road, Fingringhoe, Colchester, Essex, CO5 7DN. 01206 729 678. e-mail: admin@essexwt.org.uk www.essexwt.org.uk

5. HANNINGFIELD RESERVOIR

Essex Wildlife Trust.

Location: TQ 725 972. Three miles N of Wickford. Exit off Southend Road (Old A130) at Rettendon onto South Hanningfield Road. Follow this for two miles until reaching the T-junction with Hawkswood Road. Turn R and the entrance to the visitor centre and reserve is one mile on the R.

Access: Open daily (9am-5pm) all year. Closed Christmas Day and Boxing Day. Disabled parking, toilets, and adapted birdwatching hide. No dogs. No cycling.

Facilities: Visitor centre, gift shop, optics, refreshments, toilets, four bird hides, nature trails, picnic area, coach parking, education room.

Public transport: Chelmsford to Wickford bus no 14 to Downham village and walk half mile down Crowsheath Lane.

Habitat: Mixed woodland (110 acres) with grassy glades and rides, adjoining 870-acre Hanningfield Reservoir, designated an SSSI due to its high numbers of wildfowl.

Key birds: *Spring*: Good numbers and mix of woodland warblers. *Summer*: Vast numbers of Swifts, Swallows and martins feeding over the water. Hobby and Osprey. *Winter*: Good numbers and mix of waterfowl. Large gull roost.

Other notable flora and fauna: Spectacular displays of bluebells in spring. Damselflies and dragonflies around the ponds. Grass snakes and common lizards sometimes bask in rides.

Contact: Bill Godsafe, Hanningfield Reservoir Visitor Centre, Hawkswood Road, Downham, Billericay, CM11 1WT. 01268 711 001. www.essexwt.org.uk

6. OLD HALL MARSHES

RSPB (Eastern England Office).

Location: TL 975 125. Approx eight miles S of Colchester. From A12 take B1023, via Tiptree, to Tolleshunt D'Arcy. Then take Chapel Road (back road to Tollesbury), after one mile turn L into Old Hall Lane. Continue up Old Hall Lane, over speed ramp and through iron gates to cattle grid, then follow signs to car park.

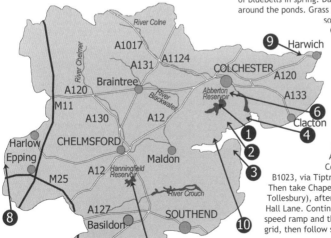

Access: By permit only (free in advance from Warden. Write to address below). Open 9am-9pm or dusk, closed Tues. No wheelchair access or facilities. No coaches.

Facilities: Two trails — one of three miles and one of 6.5 miles. Viewing screens overlooking saline lagoon area at E end of reserve. No visitor centre or toilets.

Public transport: Limited bus service to Tollesbury (one mile from reserve).

Habitat: Coastal grazing marsh, reedbed, open water saline lagoon, saltmarsh and mudflat.

Key birds: *Summer*: Breeding Avocet, Redshank, Lapwing, Pochard, Shoveler, Gadwall, Marsh Harrier and Barn Owl. *Winter*: Large assemblies of wintering wildfowl: Brent Goose, Wigeon, Teal Shoveler, Goldeneye, Red-breasted Merganser, all the expected waders, Hen Harrier, Merlin, Short-eared Owl and Twite. *Passage*: All expected waders inc Spotted Redshank, Green Sandpiper and Whimbrel. Yellow Wagtail, Whinchat and Wheatear.

Other notable flora and fauna: Brown hare, water vole, hairy dragonfly, scarce emerald damselfly, ground lackey moth, cream spot tiger, white letter hairstreak.

Contact: Paul Charlton, Site Manager, c/o 1 Old Hall Lane, Tolleshunt D'Arcy, Maldon, Essex CM9 8TP. 01621 869 015. e-mail: paul.charlton@rspb.org.uk

7. RAINHAM MARSHES

RSPB (South Eastern Regional Office).

Location: On N bank of River Thames, SE of Dagenham. From London take A13 to A1306 turn-off and head towards Purfleet for half a mile. At traffic lights, turn right, signposted A1090 and reserve entrance is 300 metres along this road.

Access: Open all year. Extensive programme of guided walks — check RSPB website for details. Approx 2.5 miles of boardwalks suitable for wheelchairs and pushchairs.

Facilities: Visitor centre, disabled toilets, car park on site, picnic area, shop, refreshments available. One bird hide.

Public transport: Route 44 (Ensignbus - 01708 865 656) runs daily between Grays and Lakeside via Purfleet. Arriva service (0870 120 1088) hourly Sundays and most public holidays.

Habitat: A former MoD shooting range, the site is the largest remaining expanse of wetland along the upper reaches of the Thames.

Key birds: *Spring*: Marsh Harrier, Hobby, Wheatear, hirundines and other migrants. *Summer*: Many waders, including Black-tailed Godwit, Whimbrel, Greenshank, Snipe, Lapwing, Avocet. Yellow-legged Gull. Merlin and Peregrine hunt among the gathering wader flocks. *Winter*: Waders, wildfowl, Water Pipit, Short-eared Owl, Little Egret.

Other notable flora and fauna: 21 species of dragonfly, including hairy hawker, scarce emerald and small red-eyed damselfly. Water vole, water shrew, fox, stoat, weasel, 28 species of butterfly and 13 species of orthoptera. Deadly nightshade.

Contact: The Warden, The Visitor Centre, Rainham Marsh Nature Reserve, New Tankhill Road, Purfleet, Essex RM19 1SZ. 01708 899 840. www.rspb.org.uk/reserves/

8. RIVER LEE COUNTRY PARK

Lee Valley Park

Location: Close to Waltham Abbey, Essex. Fishers Green entrance off B194.

Access: All hides open to public at weekends and Bank Holidays (excepting Christmas Day). Permit needed for weekday use — contact Lee Valley Park for details. Groups should also book with Info Centre. Hides and paths suitable for wheelchairs.

Facilities: Café, toilet and shop at Hayes Hill Farm. Information centre off A121 in Waltham Abbey. Bittern Watchpoint at Lee Valley Park.

Public transport: All sites served by buses — call Essex Bus Info on 0345 000 333 or Herts Travel Line on 01992 556 765.

Habitat: Former gravel pits now flooded, with wooded islands, reedbeds and marshy corners.

Key birds: *Winter*: Bittern at Fishers Green (best in winter - hide open every day). Wide variety of wildfowl inc Smew, Goosander, Shoveler and Gadwall. *Summer*: Breeding warblers, Nightingale, Little Ringed Plover, Turtle Dove. Wide variety of species on spring/autumn passage.

Contact: Lee Valley Regional Park Authority, Myddelton House, Bulls Cross, Enfield, Middlesex EN2 9HG. 01992 717711. www.leevalleypark.org.uk E-mail: info@leevalleypark.org.uk

9. STOUR ESTUARY

RSPB (Eastern England Office).

Location: Between Manningtree and Harwich. From Manningtree, stay on B1352 past Strangers Home pub in Bradfield, then look for brown sign to reserve.

Access: Open all year. Stour wood walk (1 mile) OK for wheelchairs in dry conditions. Walks to estuary and furthest hide not suitable, due to terrain and kissing gates. Dogs only allowed in Stour Wood.

Facilities: Two hides, one viewing screen. Two picnic tables.

Public transport: Nearest train station (One Railway) at Wrabness is 1 mile away. Hourly buses (Mon - Sat) running between Colchester and Harwich will stop at entrance to woods on request.

Habitat: Extensive woodland leading down to the River Stour estuary, saltmarsh at Deep Fleet and mudflats at Copperas Bay.

Key birds: *Spring/autumn*: Black-tailed Godwit, Dunlin, Ringed Plover. *Summer*: Nightingale and warblers. *Winter*: Brent Goose, plus nationally important numbers of wildfowl and waders.

Other notable flora and fauna: Woodland wildflowers in spring.

Contact: The Warden, RSPB Eastern England Office, Stalham House, 65 Thorpe Road, Norwich, Norfolk NR1 1UD. 01603 661 662. www.rspb.org.uk/reserves/

10. TOLLESBURY WICK MARSHES

Essex Wildlife Trust.
Location: TL 969 104. On Blackwater Estuary eight miles E of Maldon. Follow B1023 to Tollesbury via Tiptree, leaving A12 at Kelvedon. Then follow Woodrolfe Road S towards the marina. Use small public car park at Woodrolfe Green (TL 964 107), 500m before reserve entrance on sea wall. Car park suitable for mini-buses and small coaches.
Access: Open all times along public footpath on top of sea wall. The route is exposed to the elements so be prepared with adequate clothing and footwear. Motorised wheelchair access possible to Block House Bay.
Facilities: Public toilets at Woodrolfe Green car park.
Public transport: Hedingham bus services run to Tollesbury from Maldon, Colchester and Witham — call 01621 869 214 for information.
Habitat: Estuary with fringing saltmarsh and mudflats with some shingle. Extensive freshwater grazing marsh, brackish borrowdyke and small reedbeds.
Key birds: *Winter*: Large numbers of wintering wildfowl and waders, particularly Brent Geese and Wigeon, Lapwing and Golden Plover. Shoret-eared Owl, Hen Harrier and, increasingly, Marsh Harrier. *Summer*: Breeding Avocet, Redshank, Lapwing, Little Tern, Reed and Sedge Warblers, Reed Bunting, Barn Owl. *Passage*: Whimbrel, Spotted Redshank, Green Sandpiper.
Other notable flora and fauna: Plants include spiny restharrow, grass vetchling, yellow horned-poppy, slender hare's-ear. Hairy dragonfly, Roesel's and great green bush-crickets. Hares and occasional common seals can be seen from the footpath on top of the sea wall.
Contact: Jonathan Smith, Tollesbury, Maldon, Essex, CM9 8RJ. 01621 868 628.
e-mail: jonathans@essexwt.org.uk

Gloucestershire

1. ASHLEWORTH HAM

Gloucestershire Wildlife Trust.
Location: SO 830 265. Leave Gloucester N on A417; R at Hartpury and follow minor road through Ashleworth towards Hasfield.
Access: Access prohibited at all times but birds may be viewed from new hide in Meerend Thicket.
Facilities: Bird viewing hide and screen, interpretation panels.
Public transport: None.
Habitat: Low-lying grassland flood plain.
Key birds: *Winter*: Wildfowl (inc. 4,000 Wigeon, 1,500 Teal, Pintail, Goldeneye, Bewick's Swan), passage waders, Peregrine. *Summer*: Hobby.
Contact: Gloucestershire Wildlife Trust, Conservation Centre, Robinswood Hill Country Park, Reservoir Road, Gloucester, GL4 6SX. 01452 383 333. e-mail: info@gloucestershirewildlifetrust.co.uk
www.gloucestershirewildlifetrust.co.uk

2. COTSWOLD WATER PARK

Cotswold Water Park Society.
Location: The CWP comprises 140 lakes in the Upper Thames Valley, between Cirencester and Swindon. Many of these lakes are accessible by the public using public rights of way. Start from Cotswold Water Park Gateway Visitor Centre (SU 072 971). The Visitor Centre is immediately on L after A419. For Millenium Visitor Centre at Keynes Country Park (SU 026 957) from A419, take B4696 towards Ashton Keynes. At staggered crossroads, go straight over, heading towards Somerford Keynes. Take next R turn to Circencester. The entrance to Keynes Country Park is the second entrance on the R.
Access: Cotswold Water Park is open all year round. The visitor centres are open every day except Christmas Day.
Facilities: Paths are flat but with stiles and footbridges. Many are wheelchair accessible. Toilets, refreshments, car parking and information available from the visitor centres.

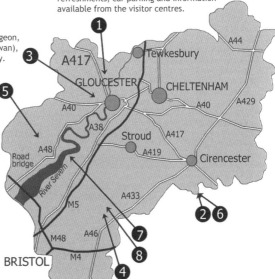

Hides available at Cleveland Lakes/Waterhay (lakes 68a and 68c), Shorncote Reed Bed (lakes 84/85), Cokes Pit (Lake 34) and Whelford Pools (Lake 111). Free copies of the CWP Leisure Guide are available from the visitor centres. These have maps showing the lake numbering. The guidebook *Wildlife in the Cotswold Water Park: Where to go and what to see* also available from centres.
Public transport: Bus: from Kemble, Cheltenham, Cirencester and Swindon. Tel: 08457 090 899. Train: nearest station is four miles away at Kemble. Tel: 08457 484 950.
Habitat: Gravel extraction has created more than 1,000ha of standing open water or 140 lakes, plus other associated wetland habitats, creating one of the largest man-made wetlands in Europe.
Key birds: *Winter:* Common wildfowl, Smew, Red-crested Pochard, Merlin, Peregrine. *Summer:* Breeding ducks, warblers, Nightingale, Hobby, Common Tern, Black-headed Gull colony, Reed Bunting, hirundines.
Contact: Cotswold Water Park Society, Cotswold House, Down Ampney Estate, Cirencester, Glos GL7 5QF. 01793 752 413. e-mail: info@waterpark.org www.waterpark.org

3. HIGHNAM WOODS

RSPB (South West England Office).
Location: SO 778 190. Signed on A40 three miles W of Gloucester.
Access: Open at all times, no permit required. The nature trails can be very muddy. Some limited wheelchair access. Dogs allowed on leads.
Facilities: One nature trail (approx 1.5 miles).
Public transport: Contact Traveline (public transport information) on 0871 2002 233 between 7am-10pm each day.
Habitat: Ancient woodland in the Severn Vale with areas of coppice and scrub.
Key birds: *Spring/summer:* The reserve has about 12 pairs of breeding Nightingales. Resident birds include all three woodpeckers, Buzzard and Sparrowhawk. Ravens are frequently seen. *Winter:* Feeding site near car park good for woodland birds.
Other notable flora and fauna: Tintern spurge in late June-early July. White-letter hairstreak and white admiral butterflies seen annually.
Contact: Barry Embling, Site Manager, The Puffins, Parkend, Lydney, Glos GL15 4JA. 01594 562 852. e-mail: barry.embling@rspb.org.uk www.rspb.org.uk

4. LOWER WOODS

Gloucestershire Wildlife Trust.
Location: ST 749 885. Reserve is about one mile E of Wickwar. Main parking is at Lower Woods Lodge, via a track off the Wickwar-Hawkesbury road. Public footpaths and bridleways cross the reserve.
Access: Open all year.
Facilities: Well-marked footpaths and bridleways. Walk leaflet available.
Public transport: None.
Habitat: Mixed woodland, mildly acidic or slightly

calcareous clay, grassland, river, springs.
Key birds: *Spring/summer:* Nightingale. *All year:* Usual woodland species including Tawny Owl, Jay, Nuthatch and Sparrowhawk. Kingfisher on river.
Other notable flora and fauna: 71 species of ancient woodland plants.
Contact: Gloucestershire Wildlife Trust, Conservation Centre, Robinswood Hill Country Park, Reservoir Road, Gloucester, GL4 6SX. 01452 383 333.
e-mail: info@gloucestershirewildlifetrust.co.uk www.gloucestershirewildlifetrust.co.uk

5. NAGSHEAD

RSPB (South West England Office).
Location: SO 097 085. In Forest of Dean, N of Lydney. Signed immediately W of Parkend village on the road to Coleford.
Access: Open at all times, no permit required. The reserve is hilly but there is limited wheelchair access. Dogs must be kept on leads during bird nesting season and under close control at all other times.
Facilities: There are two nature trails (one mile and 2.25 miles). Information centre, with toilet facilities (including disabled), open at weekends mid-Apr to end Aug. Schools education programme available.
Public transport: Contact Traveline (public transport information) on 0871 2002 233 (7am to 10pm each day).
Habitat: Much of the reserve is 200-year-old oak plantations, grazed in some areas by sheep. The rest of the reserve is a mixture of open areas and conifer/mixed woodland.
Key birds: *Spring:* Pied Flycatcher, Wood Warbler, Redstart, warblers. *Summer:* Nightjar. *Winter:* Siskin, Crossbill in some years. *All year:* Buzzard, Raven, Hawfinch, all three woodpeckers.
Other notable flora and fauna: Golden-ringed dragonfly seen annually. Silver-washed and small pearl-bordered fritillaries and white admiral butterflies present.
Contact: Barry Embling, Site Manager, The Puffins, Parkend, Lydney, Glos, GL15 4JA. 01594 562 852.
e-mail:barry.embling@rspb.org.uk www.rspb.org.uk

6. SHORNCOTE REEDBED (LAKES 84/85)

Cotswold Water Park Society.
Location: SU 026 957. Lakes 84/85 located adjacent to Keynes Country Park and most easily accessed from here. From A419, take B4696 towards Ashton Keynes. At the staggered crossroads, go straight over, heading towards Somerford Keynes. Take the next R turn to Cirencester. The entrance to Keynes Country Park is the second entrance on the R.
Access: Open at all times to walkers. Seasonal opening hours — check website for details. Per person charges apply. Paths are uneven with footbridges. No disabled access.
Facilities: Toilets, refreshments, car parking and information available from Keynes Country Park adjacent. A hide with log book is located on E shore.
Public transport: Bus: from Kemble, Cheltenham, Cirencester and Swindon. Tel: 08457 090 899. Train:

nearest station is four miles away at Kemble. Tel: 08457 484 950.

Habitat: Only lakes in Cotswold Water Park restored specifically for wildlife. Lakes with reedbed, marsh, ditches, islands and loafing areas.

Key birds: *Winter*: Common wildfowl, Smew, Peregrine, Merlin, Bittern, Stonechat. *Summer*: Breeding ducks, warblers, Hobby, Reed Bunting.

Contact: Cotswold Water Park Society, Cotswold House, Down Ampney Estate, Cirencester, Glos GL7 5QF. 01793 752 413.

7. SLIMBRIDGE

The Wildfowl & Wetlands Trust.

Location: SO 723 048. S of Gloucester. Signposted from M5 (exit 13 or 14).

Access: Open daily (9am-5.30pm or 5pm in winter) except Dec 25. Last entry 30 mins before closing. Wheelchair hire (book beforehand) — all paths wheelchair accessible. Free parking for cars and coaches.

Facilities: Restaurant, gift shop, gallery, cinema, discovery centre. Outdoor facilities inc 15 hides, tropical house, worldwide collection of wildfowl species, observatory and observation tower. Extensive events programme including Land Rover safaris (see website for calendar).

Public transport: Request bus service - contact www.stroud.gov.uk. Nearest train station at Cam and Dursley (4 miles).

Habitat: Reedbed, saltmarsh, freshwater pools, mudflats and wet grassland.

Key birds: *Winter:* Between 30,000 to 40,000 wildfowl esp. Bewick's Swan, White-fronted Goose, Wigeon, Teal, Pintail. Wader inc Lapwing, Golden

Plover, Spotted Redshank and Little Stint. Often there are large roosts of Starlings and gulls. *Breeding*: Kingfisher, Lapwing, Redshank, Oystercatcher, Common Tern, Reed Bunting and a good range of warblers. *Passage:* Waders, terns and gulls, inc Mediterranean and Yellow-legged Gulls. Yellow Wagtail and large passerine movements. Hobbies now reach double figures and there is an impressive list of rarities.

Other notable flora and fauna: Brown hare, otter, polecat and water vole. Scarce chaser and hairy dragonfly among 22 recorded species.

Contact: Marketing Manager, The Wildfowl & Wetlands Trust, Slimbridge, Gloucestershire GL2 7BT. 01453 891 900; e-mail: info.slimbridge@wwt.org.uk

8. SYMOND'S YAT

RSPB/Forestry Commission England.

Location: SO 563 160. Hill-top site on the edge of Forest of Dean, three miles N of Coleford on B4432, signposted from Forest Enterprise car park. Also signposted from A40, S of Ross-on-Wye.

Access: Open at all times. RSPB Information Officer on site daily, April to August.

Facilities: Car park, toilets with adapted facilities for disabled visitors, picnic area, drinks and light snacks. Environmental education programmes available.

Public transport: Very limited.

Habitat: Cliff above the River Wye and woodland.

Key birds: *Summer*: Peregrine, Buzzard, Goshawk, Raven and woodland species. Telescope is set up daily to watch the Peregrines on the nest.

Contact: RSPB, The Puffins, Parkend, Lydney, Glos L15 4JA. 01594 562 852.

Hampshire

1. BLASHFORD LAKES

Hampshire & Isle of Wight Wildlife Trust/Wessex Water/Bournemouth and West Hampshire Water/ New Forest District Council.

Location: SU 153 080. From Ringwood take A338 for two miles towards Fordingbridge/Salisbury, pass Ivy Lane R and take next R to Moyles Court / Linwood at Ellingham Cross, into Ellingham Drove. The main car park for hides is first L (entrance shared with Hanson works) after 400 yards. For Education Centre turn R opposite (entrance shared with Wessex Water and water-ski club) and straight on through gate and bear R between wooden pillars. Parking is just inside pillars or in front of centre.

Access: A network of permissive paths in the reserve link to New Forest and Avon Valley Long Distance footpaths. These paths and a number of wildlife viewing screens are always open. The six hides and Centre are open daily (9am-4.30pm). The Centre is also used for school and other organised visits, please

phone for further details. No dogs allowed. The paths are fully wheelchair accessible and kissing gates are RADAR key-operated to allow passage of disability buggies.

Facilities: Parking, footpaths, six hides, viewing screens, toilets and information including recent sightings board. Coach parking by arrangement. Picnic tables available beside the centre when not being used by booked groups.

Public transport: Bus service on the A338 Ringwood to Salisbury/Fordingbridge road stops just north of Ivy Lane, Ellingham Cross and Ibsley Church.

Habitat: Flooded gravel pits, areas of wet woodland, some of it ancient also dry grassland and lichen heath.

Key birds: *Winter*: Large number of over-wintering wildfowl, inc. Tufted Duck, Pochard, Wigeon, Shoveler, Goosander and internationally important numbers of Gadwall. Also a large gull roost. *Spring/ summer*: Breeding birds include Common Tern,

NATURE RESERVES - ENGLAND

Lapwing, Redshank, Oystercatcher, Kingfisher, Garden Warblers are especially common. *Autumn*: Waders on migration including Green and Common Sandpipers and Greenshank, also Hobby, Black Tern and passerines.

Other notable flora and fauna: Dragonflies (23 species recorded) including brown hawker, scarce chaser and large and small red-eyed damselfly. Roe deer are regular, also present badgers, otters, foxes, reptiles include adders and grass snakes.

Contact: Blashford Lakes Centre, Ellingham Drove, Ringwood, Hampshire BH24 3PJ. 01425 472 760. e mail: feedback@hwt.org.uk, www.hwt.org.uk

2. FARLINGTON MARSHES

Hampshire & Isle of Wight Wildlife Trust.
Location: SU 685 045. North of Langstone Harbour. Main entrance off roundabout junction A2030/A27.
Access: Open at all times, no charge or permits, but donations welcome. Dogs on leads only. Wheelchair access via RADAR gates. Short slopes up to sea wall. Paths around site are mostly level but the main path running along the sea wall can be uneven in places and muddy in wet weather. Groups — please book to avoid clash of dates.
Facilities: 2.5 mile trail. Information at entrance and shelter. No toilets.
Public transport: By bus: Several bus routes pass along the A2030 (Easter Road), close to the western entrance to the marsh. Contact First bus service on 023 8058 4321. By train: Hilsea station is one mile from reserve. Contact South West Trains on 0845 6000 650.
Habitat: Coastal grazing marsh with pools and reedbed within reserve. Views over intertidal mudflats/saltmarshes of Langstone Harbour.
Key birds: *Summer*: Breeding waders and wildfowl (including Lapwing, Redshank and Shelduck) also breeding Cetti's, Sedge and Reed Warbler, Bearded Tit. *Autumn to spring*: Waders and wildfowl, good numbers of migrating Yellow Wagtail among the cattle. *Winter*: Brent Goose, Wigeon, Pintail etc and waders (Dunlin, Grey Plover etc). On migration wide range of waders including rarities. Reedbeds with Bearded Tit, Water Rail etc, scrub areas attract small migrants (Redstart, Wryneck, warblers etc).
Contact: Mike Allen, Hampshire and Isle of Wight Wildlife Trust, Beechcroft House, Vicarage Lane, Curdridge, Hants SO32 2DP. 01489 774 439. www.hwt.org.uk - go to 'Reserves' and then 'news' for sightings, etc

3. FLEET POND LOCAL NATURE RESERVE

Hart District Council Service and Fleet Pond Society.
Location: SY 85. Located in Fleet, W of Farnborough. From the B3013, head to Fleet Station. Park in the long-stay car park at Fleet Station. Parking also available in Chestnut Grove and Westover Road. Pond car park off B3013.

Access: Open all year.
Facilities: Some surfaced paths, boardwalks in wet areas.
Public transport: Fleet railway station lies N of site.
Habitat: Lake, marshes, reedbeds, heathland, wet and dry woodland.
Key birds: *Spring/autumn*: Migrant waders incl. Little Ringed Plover, Dunlin, Greenshank, Little Gull, Lesser Spotted Woodpecker, occasional Kittiwake, terns, Wood Lark, Sky Lark, occasional Ring Ouzel, Firecrest, Pied Flycatcher. *Summer*: Hobby, Common Tern, Tree Pipit, occasional Red Kite and Osprey. *Winter*: Bittern, wildfowl, occasional Smew, Snipe, occasional Jack Snipe, Siskin, Redpoll.
Other notable flora and fauna: Dragonflies and damselflies in wet areas of marshes and heathlands. Butterflies, roe deer. Plants include ling and bell heather, phragmites reeds.
Contact: Hart District Council, Civic Office, Harlington Way, Fleet, Hampshire GU51 4AE. 01252 622 122. e-mail: countryside@hart.gov.uk

4. HAMBLE COMMON AND COPSE

Eastleigh Borough Council (Countryside Service).
Location: SU 48 09. Hamble Common is reached via Copse Lane from the B3397 Hamble Lane, which links with A27 and M27 (junction B) at Windhover roundabout near Bursledon.
Access: Open all year.
Facilities: Car parks are linked to each other and the rest of the site by a good network of footpaths. Ground conditions good in summer, but in winter/ after rain, stout waterproof footwear is advisable.

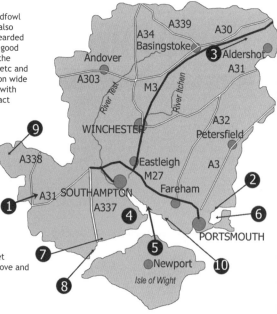

Public transport: None.
Habitat: Wet heathland, scrub, woodland, meadow, grassland overlooking Southampton Water.
Key birds: *Winter*: Wildfowl and waders. On the Southampton Water shore, Oystercatcher, Grey Plover, Ringed Plover, Dunlin, Turnstone, Curlew and Brent Geese common. In the creek wader numbers are lower, with Redshank, Lapwing and Dunlin, occasional Greenshank, Teal, Mallard, Shelduck, Grey Heron, Kingfisher most years.
Other notable flora and fauna: Grayling butterfly.
Contact: Eastleigh Countryside Service, Itchen Valley Country Park, Allington Lane, West End, Southampton, Hants SO30 3HQ. 023 8046 6 091.
e-mail: ivcp@eastleigh.gov.uk www.eastleigh.gov.uk

5. HOOK-WITH-WARSASH LOCAL NATURE RESERVE

Hampshire County Council.
Location: SU 490 050. W of Fareham. Car parks by foreshore at Warsash. Reserve includes Hook Lake.
Access: Open all year.
Facilities: Public footpaths.
Public transport: None.
Habitat: Shingle beach, saltings, marsh, reedbed, scrape.
Key birds: Winter: Brent Geese on Hamble estuary. Waders. Stonechat, Cetti's Warbler.
Contact: Barry Duffin, Titchfield Haven Visitor Centre, Cliff Road, Hill Head, Fareham, Hants PO14 3JT. 01329 662 145; Fax 01329 667 113.

6. LANGSTONE HARBOUR

RSPB (South East Region Office).
Location: SU 695 035. Harbour lies E of Portsmouth, one mile S of Havant. Car parks at Broadmarsh (SE of A27/A3(M) junction) and West Hayling LNR (first R on A2030 after Esso garage).
Access: Restricted access to ensure birds not disturbed. Good views from West Hayling LNR, Broadmarsh and Farlington Marshes LNR (qv).
Facilities: Mainline trains all stop at Havant. Local bus service to W Hayling LNR.
Public transport: See Farlington Marshes.
Habitat: Intertidal mud, saltmarsh, shingle islands.
Key birds: *Summer*: Breeding waders and seabirds inc. Mediterranean Gull and Little Tern. *Passage/ winter*: Waterfowl, inc. Black-necked Grebes, c5,000 dark-bellied Brent Geese, Shelduck, Shoveler, Goldeneye and Red-breasted Merganser. Waders inc. Oystercatcher, Ringed and Grey Plover, Dunlin, Black and Bar-tailed Godwits and Greenshank. Peregrine, Merlin and Short-eared Owl.
Contact: Chris Cockburn (Warden), RSPB Langstone Harbour, Unit B3, Wren Centre, Emsworth, Hants PO10 7SU. 01243 378 784.
e-mail: chris.cockburn@rspb.org.uk

7. LYMINGTON REEDBEDS

Hampshire & Isle of Wight Wildlife Trust.
Location: SZ 324 965. From Lyndhurst in New Forest take A337 to Lymington. Turn L after railway bridge into Marsh Lane. Park in the lay-by next to

allotments. The reserve entrance is on opposite side, to R of the house and over railway crossing. The footpath exits the reserve near the Old Ampress Works, leading to a minor road between the A337 and Boldre.
Access: Open all year. The best viewpoint over the reedbeds is from Bridge Road or from the Undershore leading from the B3054.
Facilities: None.
Public transport: Bus: at either end of the footpath through site, Marsh Lane and on the A337 (route 112). Five minutes walk from train station.
Habitat: One of largest reedbeds on S coast, fringed by alder and willow woodland.
Key birds: One of highest concentrations of Water Rail in the country; resident but most evident in winter. *Spring/summer*: Cetti's Warbler, Bearded Tit, Yellow Wagtail, Swallow, martins, Reed Warbler. *Passage*: Snipe, ducks. Otters are in the area.
Contact: Michael Boxall, Hampshire and Isle of Wight Wildlife Trust, Beechcroft House, Vicarage Lane, Curdridge, Hants SO32 2DP. 01489 774 400.
e-mail: feedback@hwt.org.uk www.hwt.org.uk

8. LYMINGTON-KEYHAVEN NATIONAL NATURE RESERVE

Hampshire County Council.
Location: SZ 315 920. S of Lymington along seawall footpath; car parks at Bath Road, Lymington and at Keyhaven Harbour.
Access: Open all year.
Facilities: None.
Public transport:
Habitat: Coastal marshland and lagoons.
Key birds: *Spring*: Passage waders (inc. Knot, Sanderling, Bar-tailed and Black-tailed Godwits, Whimbrel, Spotted Redshank), Pomarine and Great Skuas. Breeding Oystercatcher, Ringed Plover, Sandwich, Common and Little Terns. *Autumn*: Passage raptors, waders and passerines. *Winter*: Wildfowl (inc. Brent Goose, Wigeon, Pintail, Red-breasted Merganser), waders (inc. Golden Plover), Little Egret, gulls.
Contact: Hampshire County Council, Mottisfont Court, High Street, Winchester, Hants SO23 8ZF.

9. MARTIN DOWN

Natural England (Wiltshire Team).
Location: SU 05 19. Nine miles SW of Salisbury. Car park on A354.
Access: Open access, organised groups of 10+ should book in advance. Car park height barrier of 7ft 6 ins. Coaches only by prior arrangement. Hard flat track from A354 car park suitable for wheelchairs.
Facilities: Two car parks, interpretative boards.
Public transport: One bus Salisbury/Blandford. Call 01722 336 855 or visit www.wdbus.co.uk
Habitat: Chalk downland and scub.
Key birds: *Spring/summer*: Grey Partridge, Turtle Dove, warblers, Nightingale. *Winter*: Occasional Merlin, Hen Harrier.
Other notable flora and fauna: Species-rich chalk

downland with a variety of orchids. *The Times* online rates Martin Down in its Britain's Best 50 Days Out list.
Contact: South Wiltshire NNR Office, Parsonage Down NNR, Cherry Lodge, Shrewton, Nr Salisbury, Wilts SP3 4ET. 01980 620 485. www.naturalengland.org.uk email: wiltshire@naturalengland.org.uk

10. TITCHFIELD HAVEN

Hampshire County Council.
Location: SU 535 025. From A27 W of Fareham; public footpath follows derelict canal along W of reserve and road skirts S edge.
Access: Open Wed-Sun all year, plus Bank Hols, except Christmas and Boxing Days.
Facilities: Centre has information desk, toilets, tea room and shop. Guided tours (book in advance). Hides.
Public transport: None.
Habitat: Reedbeds, freshwater scrapes, wet grazing meadows.
Key birds: *Spring/summer*: Bearded Tit, waders (inc. Black-tailed Godwit), wildfowl, Common Tern, breeding Cetti's Warbler, Water Rail. Offshore seabirds include Gannet, Common Scoter, Yellow-legged Gull, Kittiwake and Little Tern. *Winter*: Bittern.
Contact: Barry Duffin, Titchfield Haven Visitor Centre, Cliff Road, Hill Head, Fareham, Hants PO14 3JT. 01329 662 145; Fax 01329 667 113.

Hertfordshire

1. AMWELL

St Albans Sand & Gravel.
Location: TL 375 128. Site lies between Hoddesdon and Ware, on the back road to Stanstead Abbotts near Great Amwell village.
Access: Open all year.
Facilities: Public hide and viewing area.
Public transport: None.
Habitat: Disused gravel pit with reedbeds and woodland.
Key birds: *Spring/summer*: Ringed Plover, Little Ringed Plover. *Winter*: Smew, ducks, Bittern. In process of becoming SSSI for wintering Gadwall and Shoveler.
Contact: Chief Ranger, Lee Valley Regional Park Authority, Head Office, Myddleton House, Bulls Cross, Enfield Middx EN2 9HG.

2. CASSIOBURY PARK

Welwyn & Hatfield Council.
Location: TL 090 970. Close to Watford town centre.
Access: Open all year.
Facilities: Car park, footpaths.
Public transport: Watford Metropolitan Underground station.
Habitat: Municipal park, wetland, river, alder/willow wood.
Key birds: *Spring/ summer*: Kingfisher, Grey Wagtail. *Winter*: Snipe, Water Rail, occasional Bearded Tit.
Contact: Welwyn & Hatfield Council, Council Offices, The Campus, Welwyn Garden City AL8 6AE. 01707 357 000. e-mail: council.services@welhat.gov.uk

3. KINGS MEADS

Herts & Middlesex Wildlife Trust/Thames Water/ Smith Kline Wellcome/East Herts District Council/ Environment Agency.
Location: Between Hertford and Ware, lying alongside A119 Ware Road. Park in Priory Street and Broadmeads (Ware) and streets in Hertford.
Access: Open all year.
Facilities: None.
Public transport: Bus stops on Hertford Road (A119). Trains to Ware station and Hertford East Station.
Habitat: Largest remaining area of grazed riverside flood meadow in Hertfordshire.
Key birds: *Summer:* Sky Lark, Reed Warbler, Reed Bunting,

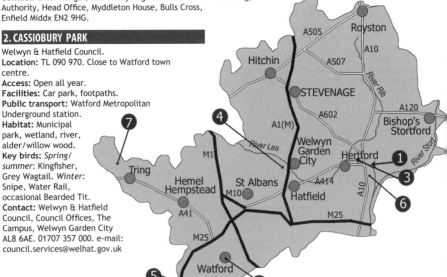

Sedge Warbler, Yellow Wagtail. *Winter/spring:* Gadwall, Shoveler, Wigeon, Teal, Snipe, gulls, waders.
Other notable flora and fauna: 275 species of wildflower, 19 species of dragonfly.
Contact: Herts & Middlesex Wildlife Trust, Grebe House, St Michael's Street, St Albans, Herts, AL3 4SN. 01727 858 901. e-mail: info@hmwt.org www.wildlifetrust.org.uk/herts

4. LEMSFORD SPRINGS

Herts & Middlesex Wildlife Trust.
Location: TL 223 123. Lies 1.5 miles W of Welwyn Garden City town centre, off roundabout leading to Lemsford village on B197, W of A1(M).
Access: Access, via key, by arrangement with warden. Open at all times, unless work parties or group visits in progress. Keep to paths. Dogs on leads. 150m earth path to hide. Wheelchair access ramp to hide. Coaches welcome and room to park on road, but limit of 30 persons.
Facilities: Two hides, classroom, chemical toilet, paths and bridges. Circular walk.
Public transport: Bus service to Valley Road, WGC & Lemsford Village No 366 (Arriva, Traveline 0871 200 2233). Nearest railway station Welwyn Garden City.
Habitat: Former water-cress beds, open shallow lagoons. Stretch of the River Lea, marsh, hedgerows. Nine acres.
Key birds: *Spring/summer:* Breeding warblers, Grey Wagtail, Kestrel, Green Woodpecker. *Autumn/winter:* Green Sandpiper, Water Rail, Snipe, Siskin, Little Egret, occasional Jack Snipe. *All year:* Mandarin Duck, Kingfisher, Grey Heron, Sparrowhawk.
Other notable flora and fauna: Muntjac, fox and stoat. Common butterflies and damselflies in summer.
Contact: Barry Trevis, Warden, 11 Lemsford Village, Welwyn Garden City, Herts AL8 7TN. 01707 335 517. www.wildlifetrust.org.uk/herts

5. MAPLE LODGE

Thames Water/Maple Lodge Conservation Society
Location: TQ 036 925. South of Ricksmanworth, close to village of Maple Cross. From M25 (Jt 17) turn left at traffic lights by The Cross pub. Drive down Maple Lodge Close and park in social club car park.
Access: Restricted to members of MLCS (combination locks on entrance gates). Visits by non-members and groups can be arranged in advance. Site can be boggy – please keep to designated paths.
Facilities: Information centre, toilets. Eight bird hides – two wheelchair-friendly. Winter feeding station.
Habitat: A man-made wetland habitat formed from two gravel pits and a sludge settlement area. Mixed broadleaf plantation on eastern side.
Key birds: Wildfowl throughout year, numbers building in winter. All three woodpeckers, plus variety of finches, thrushes and woodland species. Nesting species include Kingfisher, Tawny Owl, migrant warblers. Green, Common and Wood Sandpipers on passage.

Other notable flora and fauna: 170 species of moth recorded, plus many butterflies and aquatic insects. 125 species of wildflower recorded.
Contact: For membership of MLCS or to arrange visits, contact chairman Mrs Gwyneth Bellis on 01923 230 277.

6. RYE MEADS

RSPB/Hertfordshire & Middlesex Wildlife Trust.
Location: TL 387 099. Take Hoddesdon turn off A10 and follow brown duck signs. Near Rye House railway station.
Access: Open every day 10am-5pm (or dusk if earlier), except Christmas Day and Boxing Day.
Facilities: Disabled access and toilets. Drinks machine, staffed reception, classrooms, picnic area, car park, bird feeding area. Nature trails, hides. RSPB reserve has close-circuit TV on Kingfisher and Common Tern nests in summer.
Public transport: Rail (Rye House) 55 metres, bus (310) stops 600 metres from entrance.
Habitat: Marsh, willow scrub, pools, scrapes, lagoons and reedbed.
Key birds: *Summer:* Breeding Tufted Duck, Gadwall, Common Tern, Kestrel, Kingfisher, nine species of warblers. *Winter:* Bittern, Shoveler, Water Rail, Teal, Snipe, Jack Snipe, Redpoll and Siskin.
Other notable flora and fauna: Fen vegetation, invertebrates and reptiles.
Contact: RSPB Rye Meads Visitor Centre, Rye Road, Stanstead Abbotts, Herts SG12 8JS. 01992 708 383; Fax 01992 708 389.

7. TRING RESERVOIRS

All four reservoirs: British Waterways / Herts & Middlesex Wildlife Trust / Friends of Tring Res. WTW lagoon: Thames Water/FOTR.
Location: Wilstone Reservoir SP 905 134. Other reservoirs SP 920 135. WTW Lagoon SP 923 134 adjacent to Marsworth Reservoir. Reservoirs 1.5 miles due N of Tring, all accessible from B489 which crosses A41 Aston Clinton by-pass. NB: exit from by-pass only Southbound, entry only Northbound.
Access: *Reservoirs* – open at all times. Group visits need to be cleared with British Waterways. *WTW Lagoon* – open at all times by permit from FoTR. Coaches can only drop off and pick up, for advice contact FoTR. Wilstone Reservoir has restricted height access of 2.1 metres. Disabled access available for Startops and Marsworth from car park, as well as FoTR lagoon hide.
Facilities: Café and public houses adjacent to Startops Reservoir car park, safe parking for cycles. Wilstone Reservoir: Public house about 0.5 mile away in village. Cafe and farm shop about 0.25 mile from car park. Hides on all reservoirs and WTW lagoon.
Public transport: Buses from Aylesbury & Tring including a weekend service, tel. 0871 200 2233. Tring Station is 2.5 miles away via canal towpath.
Habitat: Four reservoirs with surrounding woodland, scrub and meadows. Two of the reservoirs have extensive reedbeds. WTW Lagoon with islands and

dragonfly scrape, surrounding hedgerows and scrub.
Key birds: *Spring/summer*: Breeding water birds and heronry. Occasional Black Tern. Regular Hobby, Red Kite, Marsh Harrier and Osprey. Warblers including Cetti's. *Autumn/passage*: Waders. *Winter*: Gull roost, large wildfowl flocks, bunting roosts, Bittern.
Other notable flora and fauna: Black poplar trees seen from banks, some locally rare plants in damp areas. 18 species of dragonfly include black-tailed skimmer, ruddy darter and emerald damselfly. Holly

blue and specked wood butterflies. Chinese water deer, Daubenton's, Natterer's and both pipistrelle bats.
Contact: Herts & Middx Wildlife Trust: see Directory entry. FoTR: see Peter Hearn in Bucks BTO entry, www.fotr.org.uk,
British Waterways, 510-524 Elder House, Eldergate, Milton Keynes MK9 1BW. 01908 302500, www.waterscape.com
e-mail:enquiries.southeast@britishwaterways.co.uk

Kent

1. BLEAN WOODS NATIONAL NATURE RESERVE

RSPB (South East Region Office).
Location: Location: TR 126 592. From Rough Common (off A290, one and a half miles NW of Canterbury).
Access: Open 8am-9pm for cars, open at all times for visitors on foot. No parking for coaches — please drop passengers off in Rough Common village. Green Trail suitable for wheelchair users.
Facilities: Public footpaths and five waymarked trails.
Public transport: No 27 from Canterbury hourly, stops at reserve entrance (ask for Lovell Road). No 4/4A every 20 minutes from Canterbury to Whitstable. Ask for Rough Common Road, 500m walk from site entrance. Local bus company Stagecoach 0870 243 3711.
Habitat: Mature oak woodland, plus birch, sweet chestnut, hazel and hornbeam coppice. Grazed and ungrazed heathland.
Key birds: Good for Woodpeckers, warblers and Nightingale in spring, fairly quiet the rest of the year. *All year*: Woodpecker (3 species), Nuthatch, Treecreeper, tits (5 species). *Spring*: Nightingale, Blackcap, Garden Warbler, Hobby, Nightjar.
Other notable flora and fauna: Badger, dormouse. Heath fritillary, white admiral, silver-washed fritillary. Common spotted orchid, wild service.
Contact: Michael Walter, Site Manager, 11 Garden Close, Rough Common, Canterbury, Kent CT2 9BP. 01227 455 972.

2. BOUGH BEECH RESERVOIR

Kent Wildlife Trust.
Location: TQ 49 64 89. Bough Beech is situated 3.5 miles S of Ide Hill, signposted off B2042.
Access: Confined to holders of permits granted for recording and study purposes only on application to the warden. The whole of the reserve may be viewed from the public road just S of Winkhurst Green (TQ 496 494). Park on roadside (one side only).
Facilities: Toilets and visitor centre open between Apr-Oct, Wed, Sat, Sun & Bank Holiday Mon (11am-4.30pm).
Public transport: Rail service to Penshurst Station (two miles south)

Habitat: Reservoir and adjacent woodland and farmland.
Key birds: Approx 60 species of birds breed in and around the reserve annually, with Mallard, Tufted Duck, Mandarin, Canada Goose, Coot and Great Crested Grebe notable among the waterfowl. Little Ringed Plover nest most years. Autumn especially good for numbers of waders like Green and Common Sandpipers and Greenshank. Many rarities have been recorded. Ospreys recorded most years. Winter wildfowl numbers are much higher than summer and include Goldeneye and Goosander.
Other notable flora and fauna: Great crested newt, toad, dragonflies (black-tailed skimmer, ruddy darter, emperor, southern aeshna, migrant hawker, red-eyed damselfly), common lizard, Roesel's bush cricket, long-winged conehead, dormouse, water shrew, white admiral butterfly, glow-worm, bats (pipistrelle, Daubenton, noctule, brown long-eared).
Contact: Kent Wildlife Trust, 01622 662 012.
e-mail: info@kentwildlife.org.uk
www.kentwildlife.org.uk

3. CLIFFE POOLS

RSPB (South East Region Office).
Location: TQ 722 757. On S bank of River Thames, N of Rochester. Take A289 off the A2 at Strood and follow B2000 to reserve. See RSPB website for more detailed directions.
Access: Free admission at all times, but donations welcome. Group bookings welcome. Monthly guided walks available. Dogs only on public footpaths.
Facilities: Six viewing points. Public rights of way encircle reserve and bisect it.
Public transport: Nearest bus stop at Six Bells pub in Cliffe.
Habitat: A mix of saline lagoons, freshwater pools, grassland, saltmarsh and scrub.
Key birds: Massed flocks of waders in winter, plus a wide range of wildfowl. A great variety of passage birds in spring and autumn. Breeding species include Lapwing, Redshank, Avocet, Ringed Plover, Shelduck. Also look out for Nightingale, Hobby and Turtle Dove.
Other notable flora and fauna: Good range of insects (rare bumblebees include shrill carder bee, brown-banded carder bee). Butterflies, including

NATURE RESERVES - ENGLAND

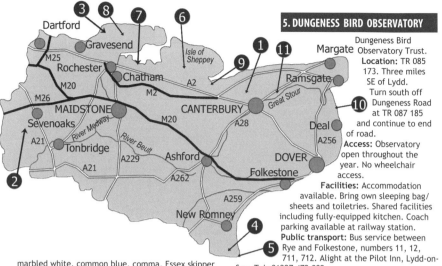

5. DUNGENESS BIRD OBSERVATORY

Dungeness Bird Observatory Trust. **Location:** TR 085 173. Three miles SE of Lydd. Turn south off Dungeness Road at TR 087 185 and continue to end of road. **Access:** Observatory open throughout the year. No wheelchair access.
Facilities: Accommodation available. Bring own sleeping bag/sheets and toiletries. Shared facilities including fully-equipped kitchen. Coach parking available at railway station.
Public transport: Bus service between Rye and Folkestone, numbers 11, 12, 711, 712. Alight at the Pilot Inn, Lydd-on-Sea. Tel: 01227 472 082.
Habitat: Shingle promontory with scrub and gravel pits. RSPB reserve nearby.
Key birds: Breeding birds include Wheatear and Black Redstart and seabirds on RSPB Reserve. Important migration site. Excellent seawatching when weather conditions are suitable. Power station outfall, 'The Patch' good for gulls and terns.
Other notable flora and fauna: Long Pits are excellent for dragonflies including small red-eyed damselfly. Moth trapping throughout the year.
Contact: David Walker, Dungeness Bird Observatory, 11 RNSSS, Dungeness, Kent TN29 9NA. 01797 321 309. e-mail dungeness.obs@tinyonline.co.uk www.dungenessbirdobs.org.uk

6. ELMLEY MARSHES

RSPB (South East Region Office).
Location: TQ 93 86 80. Isle of Sheppey signposted from A249, one mile beyond old Kingsferry Bridge. Reserve car park is two miles from the main road. **Access:** Use old bridge road – access road is one mile from bridge. Open every day (9am-9pm or dusk if earlier) except Tue, Christmas and Boxing days. No charge to RSPB members. Dogs are not allowed on the reserve. Less able may drive closer to the hides.
Facilities: Five hides. Disabled access to Wellmarsh hide. No visitor centre. Toilets located in car park 1.25 miles from hides.
Public transport: Swale Halt, a request stop is nearest railway station on Sittingbourne to Sheerness line. From there it is a three mile walk to reserve.
Habitat: Coastal grazing marsh, ditches and pools alongside the Swale Estuary with extensive intertidal mudflats and saltmarsh.
Key birds: *Spring/summer*: Breeding waders – Redshank, Lapwing, Avocet, Yellow Wagtail, passage waders, Hobby. *Autumn*: Passage waders. *Winter*:

marbled white, common blue, comma, Essex skipper and the migrant clouded yellow, plus large range of grasshoppers and bush crickets, including Roesel's bush cricket. Dragonflies include ruddy darters and migrant hawkers.
Contact: Paul Hyde, RSPB Nature Reserve, Northwood Hill, Bromhey Farm, Eastborough, Cooling, Rochester, Kent ME3 8DS. 01272 775 333.

4. DUNGENESS NATURE RESERVE

RSPB (South East Region Office).
Location: TR 063 196. SE of Lydd.
Access: Open daily (9am-9pm) or sunset when earlier. Visitor centre open (10am-5pm, or 4pm Nov-Feb). Parties over 12 by prior arrangement. Closed Dec 25 & 26.
Facilities: Visitor centre, toilets (including disabled access), seven hides, viewing screen, two nature trails, wheelchair access to visitor centre and six hides. Fully equipped classroom/meeting room. Coach parking available.
Public transport: Limited service. Bus 11 from Ashford stops at reserve entrance on request – one mile walk to visitor centre. Contact reserve for details.
Habitat: Shingle, flooded gravel pits, sallow scrub, reedbed, wet grassland.
Key birds: *All year*: Bittern, Marsh Harrier, Bearded Tit. *Spring*: Little Ringed Plover, Wheatear, Yellow Wagtail, Lesser Whitethroat. *Autumn*: Migrant waders and passerines. *Winter*: Smew, Goldeneye, Slavonian Grebe, Wigeon, Goosander and Bewick's Swan.
Other notable flora and fauna: Jersey cudweed, Nottingham catchfly, brown hare.
Contact: Christine Hawkins/Bob Gomes, Boulderwall Farm, Dungeness Road, Lydd, Romney Marsh, Kent, TN29 9PN. 01797 320 588/Fax 01797 321 962. e-mail: dungeness@rspb.org.uk www.rspb.org.uk

Spectacular numbers of wildfowl, especially Wigeon and White-fronted Goose. Waders. Hunting raptors – Peregrine, Merlin, Hen Harrier and Short-eared Owl.
Contact: Barry O'Dowd, Elmley RSPB Reserve, Kingshill Farm, Elmley, Sheerness, Kent ME12 3RW. 01795 665 969.

7. NOR MARSH

RSPB (South East Region Office).
Location: TQ 810 700. One mile NE of Gillingham in the Medway Estuary.
Access: No access as it is an island. It is viewable from Riverside Country Park (B2004) at the Horrid Hill Peninsula, giving overviews of the Medway Estuary saltmarsh and mudflats.
Facilities: None.
Public transport: Buses can be caught to Riverside Country Park. Phone Medway Council for the bus numbers, 01634 727 777.
Habitat: Saltmarsh and mudflats.
Key birds: *Winter*: Large numbers of wildfowl, including Brent Geese, Pintail, Knot and Avocets. *Spring and autumn*: Look out for Black-tailed Godwits.
Contact: RSPB, Bromhey Farm, Eastborough, Cooling, Rochester, Kent ME3 8DS. 01272 775 333.

8. NORTHWARD HILL

RSPB (South East Region Office).
Location: TQ 781 757. Adjacent to High Halstow, off A228, approx four miles NE of Rochester.
Access: Open all year, free access, trails in public area of wood joining Saxon Shoreway link to grazing marsh. Dogs allowed in public area on leads. Trails often steep and not suitable for wheelchair users.
Facilities: Four trails vary in length from half to 4 miles. New trail takes visitors to viewpoint overlooking heronry. Three nature trails in the wood and one joining with long distance footpath. Toilets at village hall. New car park at Bromhey Farm (Marshland car park) is signposted from High Halstow village. Information and public toilet in this car park.
Public transport: Buses to village of High Halstow. Contact Arriva buses (01634 283 600) for timetable details.
Habitat: Ancient and scrub woodland (approximately 130 acres), grazing marsh (approximately 350 acres).
Key birds: *Spring/summer*: Wood holds UK's largest heronry (between 150 and 200 pairs most years), inc growing colony of Little Egrets (50 pairs in 2007), breeding Nightingale, Turtle Dove, scrub warblers and woodpeckers. Marshes — breeding Lapwing, Redshank, Avocet, Marsh Harrier, Shoveler, Pochard. *Winter*: Wigeon, Teal, Shoveler. Passage waders (ie Black-tailed Godwit), raptors, Tree Sparrow, Corn Bunting. Long-eared Owl roost.
Other notable flora and fauna: Good range of dragonflies over the marsh, white-letter hairstreak butterfly in the woods.
Contact: Paul Hyde, RSPB, Bromhey Farm, Eastborough, Cooling, Rochester, Kent ME3 8DS. 01634 222 480.

9. OARE MARSHES LOCAL NATURE RESERVE

Kent Wildlife Trust.
Location: TR 01 36 48 (car park). Two miles N of Faversham. From A2 follow signs to Oare and Harty Ferry.
Access: Open at all times. Access along marked paths only. Dogs under strict control to avoid disturbance to birds and livestock.
Facilities: Three hides. Roadside viewpoint of East Hide accessible to wheelchairs. Those with pneumatic tyres can reach seawall path and hide. Small car park, restricted turning space, not suitable for coaches.
Public transport: Bus to Oare Village one mile from reserve. Arriva service (Mon-Sat), Jaycrest (Sun) - call Traveline on 0870 608 2608. Train: Faversham (two miles distance).
Habitat: Grazing marsh, mudflats/estuary.
Key birds: *All year*: Waders and wildfowl. *Winter*: Merlin, Peregrine. Divers, grebes and sea ducks on Swale. *Spring/summer*: Avocet, Garganey, Green, Wood and Curlew Sandpipers, Little Stint, Black-tailed Godwit, Little Tern, Marsh Harrier.
Contact: Tony Swandale, Kent Wildlife Trust, Tyland Barn, Sandling, Maidstone, Kent ME14 3BD. 01622 662 012. e-mail: info@kentwildlife.org.uk www.kentwildlife.org.uk

10. SANDWICH BAY BIRD OBSERVATORY

Sandwich Bay Bird Observatory Trust.
Location: TR 355 575. 2.5 miles from Sandwich, five miles from Deal. A256 to Sandwich from Dover or Ramsgate. Follow signs to Sandwich Station and then Sandwich Bay.
Access: Open daily. Disabled access.
Facilities: New Field Study Centre. Visitor centre, toilets, refreshments, hostel-type accommodation, plus self-contained flat.
Public transport: Sandwich train station two miles from Observatory.
Habitat: Coastal, dune land, farmland, marsh, two small scrapes.
Key birds: *Spring/autumn passage*: Good variety of migrants and waders, specially Corn Bunting. Annual Golden Oriole. *Winter*: Golden Plover.
Other notable flora and fauna: Sand dune plants such as lady's bedstraw and sand sedge.
Contact: The Secretary, Sandwich Bay Bird Observatory, Guildford Road, Sandwich Bay, Sandwich, Kent CT13 9PF. 01304 617 341. e-mail: sbbot@talk21.com www.sbbo.co.uk

11. STODMARSH NATIONAL NATURE RESERVE

Natural England (Kent Team).
Location: TR 222 618. Lies alongside River Stour and A28, five miles NE of Canterbury.
Access: Open at all times. Keep to reserve paths. No dogs allowed.
Facilities: Fully accessible toilets are available at the Stodmarsh entrance car park. Five hides (one

fully accessible), easy access nature trail, footpaths and information panels. Car park, picnic area and toilets adjoining the Grove Ferry entrance with easily accessible path, viewing mound and two hides.
Public transport: There is a regular Stagecoach bus service from Canterbury to Margate/Ramsgate. Alight at Upstreet for Grove Ferry. Hourly on Sun.
Habitat: Open water, reedbeds, wet meadows, dry meadows, woodland.

Key birds: *Spring/summer*: Breeding Bearded Tit, Cetti's Warbler, Garganey, Reed, Sedge and Willow Warblers, Nightingale. Migrant Black Tern, Hobby, Osprey, Little Egret. *Winter*: Wildfowl, Hen Harrier, Bittern.
Other notable flora and fauna: Nationally rare plants and invertebrates, including shining ram's horn snail.
Contact: Natural England, Coldharbour Farm, Wye, Ashford, Kent TN25 5DB. 07767 321 058 (mobile).

Lancashire

1. CUERDEN VALLEY PARK

Cuerden Valley Park Trust.
Location: SD 565 238. S of Preston on A49. Easy access from J28 and J29 of the M6, J8 and J9 on M61 and the end of M65.
Access: Open all year.
Facilities: Visitor centre, toilets.
Public transport: None.
Habitat: Mixed woodland, river, pond, lake, wildflower meadow, agricultural grassland.
Key birds: *All year*: Great Crested Grebe, Little Grebe, Kingfisher, Dipper, Great Spotted Woodpecker, Goldcrest, Little Owl and usual woodland and river birds.
Other notable flora and fauna: Dragonflies including emperor, emerald, black darter and migrant hawker. Butterflies including large and small skipper, holly blue, small copper, comma and gatekeeper. Roe deer and seven species of bat. Common spotted and marsh orchid, moschatel.
Contact: Cuerden Valley Park Trust, The Barn, Berkeley Drive, Bamber, Preston PR5 6BY. 01772 324 436. e-mail: rangers@cuerdenvalleypark.org

2. HEYSHAM NATURE RESERVE & BIRD OBSERVATORY

The Wildlife Trust for Lancashire, Manchester and North Merseyside/British Energy Estates.
Location: Main reserve is at SD 404 596 W of Lancaster. Take A683 to Heysham port. Turn L at traffic lights by Duke of Rothesay pub, then first R after 300m.
Access: Gate to reserve car park usually open 9.30am-6pm (longer in summer and shorter in winter). Pedestrian access at all times. Dogs on lead. Limited disabled access.
Facilities: Hide overlooking Power Station outfalls. Map giving access details at the reserve car park. No manned visitor centre or toilet access, but someone usually in reserve office, next to the main car park, in the morning. Latest sightings board can be viewed through the window if office is closed.
Public transport: Train services connect with nearby Isle of Man ferry. Plenty of buses to Lancaster from

various Heysham sites within walking distance (ask for nearest stop to the harbour).
Habitat: Varied: wetland, acid grassland, alkaline grassland, foreshore.
Key birds: Passerine migrants in the correct conditions. Good passage of seabirds in spring, especially Arctic Tern. Storm Petrel and Leach's Petrel during strong onshore (SW-WNW) winds in midsummer and autumn respectively. Good variety of breeding birds (e.g. eight species of warbler on the reserve itself). Two-three scarce land-birds each year, most frequent being Yellow-browed Warbler.
Other notable flora and fauna: Notable area for dragonflies, red-veined darter breeds at nearby Middleton Community Woodland main pond SD 418 592 (mid June - mid July). Bee orchid.
Contact: Reuben Neville, Reserve Warden, The

167

Wildlife Trust, The Barn, Berkeley Drive, Bamber Bridge, Preston PR5 6BY. 01524 855 030; 07979 652 138. www.lancswt.org.uk
http://heyshamobservatory.blogspot.com
Annual report from Leighton Moss RSPB shop.

3. LEIGHTON MOSS

RSPB (Northern England Office).
Location: SD 478 750. Four miles NW of Carnforth. Signposted from A6 N of Carnforth.
Access: Reserve open daily 9am-dusk. Visitor centre open daily 9.30am-5pm (9.30am-4.30pm Nov-Jan inclusive), except Christmas Day. No charge to RSPB members or those who arrive by public transport or bike. Dogs allowed on causeway only. Groups and coaches welcome — please book in advance.
Facilities: Visitor centre, shop, tea-room and toilets. Nature trails and five hides (four have wheelchair access), plus two hides at saltmarsh pools.
Public transport: Silverdale train station 150 metres from reserve. Tel: 08457 484 950.
Habitat: Reedbed, shallow meres and woodland. Saltmarsh pool approx 1 mile.
Key birds: *All year*: Bittern, Bearded Tit, Water Rail, Pochard and Shoveler. *Summer*: Marsh Harrier, Reed and Sedge Warblers. Avocet at saltmarsh pools.
Other notable flora and fauna: Common reed, otter, red deer.
Contact: RSPB Leighton Moss Nature Reserve, Myers Farm, Silverdale, Carnforth, Lancashire LA5 0SW. 01524 701 601. e-mail: leighton.moss@rspb.org.uk www.rspb.org.uk

4. MARTIN MERE

The Wildfowl & Wetlands Trust.
Location: SD 428 145. Six miles N of Ormskirk via Burscough Bridge (A59), 20 miles from Liverpool and Preston.
Access: Opening times: 9.30am-5.00pm (Nov-Feb), 9.30am-5.30pm (rest of year). Special dawn and evening events. Guide dogs only allowed. Admission charge. No charge for members. Fully accessible to disabled, all hides suitable for wheelchairs. Coach park available. Special rates for coach parties.
Facilities: Visitor centre with toilets, gift shop, restaurant, education centre, play area, nature reserve and nature trails, hides, waterfowl collection and sustainable garden. Provision for disabled visitors.
Public transport: Bus service to WWT Martin Mere from Ormskirk. Train to Burscough Bridge or New Lane Stations (both 1.5 miles from reserve). For bus times contact Traveline 0870 608 2608.
Habitat: Open water, wet grassland, moss, copses, reedbed, parkland.
Key birds: *Winter*: Whooper and Bewick's Swans, Pink-footed Goose, various ducks, Ruff, Black-tailed Godwit, Peregrine, Hen Harrier, Tree Sparrow. *Spring*: Ruff, Shelduck, Little Ringed and Ringed Plover, Lapwing, Redshank. *Summer*: Marsh Harrier, Garganey, hirundines, Tree Sparrow. Breeding

Avocets, Lapwing, Redshank, Shelduck. *Autumn*: Pink-footed Goose, waders on passage.
Other notable flora and fauna: Whorled caraway, golden dock, tubular dropwort, 300 species of moth.
Contact: WWT Martin Mere, Fish Lane, Burscough, Lancs, L40 0TA. 01704 895 181. www.wwt.org.uk e-mail: info.martinmere@wwt.org.uk

5. MERE SANDS WOOD

The Wildlife Trust for Lancashire, Manchester and North Merseyside.
Location: SD 44 71 57. 12 miles by road from Southport, 0.5 miles off A59 Preston – Liverpool road, in Rufford along B5246 (Holmeswood Road).
Access: Visitor centre open 9.30am-4.30pm - closed Fridays and Christmas Day. Car park open until 8pm in summer. Three miles of wheelchair-accessible footpaths. All hides accessible to wheelchairs.
Facilities: Visitor centre with toilets (disabled), six viewing hides, three trails, exhibition room, latest sightings board. Feeding stations. Booking essential for two motorised buggies.
Public transport: Bus: Southport-Chorley 347 and Preston-Ormskirk 2B stop in Rufford, 0.5 mile walk. Train: Preston-Ormskirk train stops at Rufford station, one mile walk.
Habitat: 40h inc freshwater lakes, mixed woodland, sandy grassland/heath.
Key birds: *Winter*: Regionally important for Teal and Gadwall, good range of waterfowl, Kingfisher. Feeding stations attract Tree Sparrow, Bullfinch, Reed Bunting, Water Rail. *Woodland*: Treecreeper, Nuthatch. *Summer*: Kingfisher. *Passage*: Most years, Osprey, Crossbill, Green Sandpiper, Greenshank.
Other notable flora and fauna: 18 species of dragonfly recorded annually.
Contact: Lindsay Beaton, Reserve Manager, Mere Sands Wood Nature Reserve, Holmeswood Road, Rufford, Ormskirk, Lancs L40 1TG. 01704 821 809. e-mail: meresandswood@lancswt.org.uk

6. MORECAMBE BAY (HEST BANK)

RSPB (Northern England Office).
Location: SD 468 667. Two miles N of Morecambe at Hest Bank.
Access: Open at all times. Do not venture onto saltmarsh or intertidal area, as there are dangerous channels and quicksands.
Facilities: Viewpoint at local council car park.
Public transport: No 5 bus runs between Carnforth and Morecambe. Tel: 0870 608 2608.
Habitat: Saltmarsh, estuary.
Key birds: *Winter*: Wildfowl (Pintail, Shelduck, Wigeon) and waders. This is an important high tide roost for Oystercatcher, Curlew, Redshank, Dunlin and Bar-tailed Godwit.
Contact: See Leighton Moss

7. RIBBLE ESTUARY

Natural England (Cheshire to Lancashire team).
Location: SD 380 240. W of Preston.

Access: Open at all times.
Facilities: No formal visiting facilities.
Public transport: None.
Habitat: Saltmarsh, mudflats.
Key birds: High water wader roosts (of Knot, Dunlin, Black-tailed Godwit, Oystercatcher and Grey Plover) are best viewed from Southport, Marshside, Lytham and St Annes. Pink-footed Geese and wintering swans are present in large numbers from Oct-Feb on Banks

Marsh and along River Douglas respectively. The large flocks of Wigeon, for which the site is renowned, can be seen on high tides from Marshside but feed on saltmarsh areas at night. Good numbers of raptors also present in winter.
Contact: Site Manager, English Nature, Ribble Estuary NNR, Old Hollow, Marsh Road, Banks, Southport PR9 8DU. 01704 225 624.

Leicestershire and Rutland

1. EYEBROOK RESERVOIR

Corby & District Water Co.
Location: SP 853 964. Reservoir built 1940. S of Uppingham, from unclassified road W of A6003 at Stoke Dry.
Access: Access to 150 acres private grounds granted to members of Leics and Rutland OS and Rutland NHS. All visitors should sign in at fishing lodge. Organised groups should contact Andy Miller on 01536 772 930.
Facilities: SSSI since 1956. Three bird hides. Fishing season March - Nov. Toilets and visitor centre at fishing lodge.
Public transport: None.
Habitat: Open water, plantations and pasture.
Key birds: *Summer:* Good populations of breeding birds, sightings of Ospreys and Red Kite. Passage waders and Black Tern. *Winter:* Wildfowl (inc. Goldeneye, Goosander, Smew) and waders. Tree Sparrow and Yellowhammer at feeding station. During winter months, Barn and Short-eared Owl can be seen hunting at dusk near Great Easton village (close to recycling centre).
Other notable flora and fauna: Otter, muntjac deer, red darter, demoiselles and blue damselfly. Cuckoo flower.
Contact: Andy Miller, Fishery Estate Manager. 01536 772 930. www.eyebrook.com

2. NARBOROUGH BOG

Leics and Rutland Wildlife Trust.
Location: SP 549 979. Reserve lies between River Soar and M1, 8km S of Leicester. From city, turn L off B4114 just before going under motorway, follow track to sports club. Park near club house and walk across recreation ground to reserve entrance.
Access: Open at all times, please keep to paths. Not suitable for wheelchairs. Dogs on short leads only.
Facilities: None. Small bus/coach could park in sports field car park
Public transport: Narborough train station. Buses X5, 140 to Narborough then 1km walk.
Habitat: Peat bog SSSI (the only substantial deposit in Leicestershire), wet woodland, reedbed, dense scrub and fen meadow.
Key birds: More than 130 species of birds have been recorded including all three species of woodpeckers,

six species of tit, Tawny Owl, Sparrowhawk and Kingfisher.
Other notable flora and fauna: Good varieties of butterfly including common blue, meadow brown, large and small skippers, small heath and gatekeeper. Banded demoiselles, also good for moths and beetles. Harvest mice and water voles recorded, also breeding grass snakes. In the meadow area, meadow saxifrage, common meadow-rue and marsh thistle.
Contact: Leicester and Rutland Wildlife Trust, Brocks Hill Environment Centre, Washbrook Lane, Oadby, Leicestershire LE2 5JJ . 0116 272 0444.
e-mail: info@lrwt.org.uk

3. RUTLAND WATER

Leics and Rutland Wildlife Trust.
Location: Two nature reserves 1. Egleton Reserve SK 878 075: from Egleton village off A6003 or A606 S of Oakham. Hosts British Birdwatching Fair every August. 2. Lyndon Reserve SK 894 058: south shore E of Manton village off A6003 S of Oakham. Follow 'nature reserve' signs to car park.
Access: 1. Open daily 9am-5pm, (4pm Nov to Jan). 2. Open winter (Sat, Sun 10am-4pm), Summer daily (9am-5pm). Day permits available for both. Reduced admission for disabled and carers. Closed Dec 25 and 26. Badger-watching hide can be booked from mid-April to July.
Facilities: 1: Anglian Water Birdwatching Centre has toilets and disabled access, mobility scooter to hides, conference facilities. Disabled access possible to 20 hides, incl three new hides on newly-created lagoon 4. Over three years it is planned to create nine new lagoons. 2: Interpretive centre now upgraded with new toilets, including disabled, new paths, use of a mobility scooter and new interpretive material, covers climate change and the impact to UK wildlife. Marked nature trail leaflet.
Public transport: None.
Habitat: Ramsar designated reservoir, lagoons, scrapes, woods, meadows, plantations, reedbeds.
Key birds: *Spring/autumn:* Outstanding wader passage, with up to 28 species recorded. Also wide range of harriers, owls, passerine flocks, terns (Black, Arctic, breeding Common, occasional Little and Sandwich). *Winter:* Up to 28 species of wildfowl (inc international important numbers of Gadwall and

Shoveler). Also Goldeneye, Smew, Goosander, rare grebes, all divers, Ruff. *Summer*: Ospreys among 70 breeding species.

Other notable flora and fauna: Otter, badger, fox, weasel, stoat. Up to 20 species of dragon and damselflies and 24 butterfly species.

Contact: Tim Appleton, Fishponds Cottage, Stamford Road, Oakham, Rutland LE15 8AB. 01572 770 651; Fax 01572 755 931; e-mail awbc@rutlandwater.org. uk; www.rutlandwater.org.uk www.ospreys.org.uk www.birdfair.org.uk.

4. SENCE VALLEY FOREST PARK

Forestry Commission
Location: SK 400 115. Within The National Forest. Ten miles NW of Leicester and two miles SW of Coalville, between Ibstock and Ravenstone. The car park is signed from A447 N of Ibstock.

Access: Open all year. Car park open 8.30am-dusk (precise times on noticeboard). Lower car park (2.2m height barrier) gives easy access to wheelchair-

friendly surfaced paths. Week's notice required for coach or minibuses visits.

Facilities: Two car parks, toilets (including disabled and baby-changing facilities), information and recent sightings boards, hide, surfaced trails.

Public transport: None.

Habitat: New forest (native broadleaf, mixed and pine), rough grassland, wildflower meadow, pools, wader scrape, river.

Key birds: *Spring/summer*: Artificial Sand Martin nesting wall, Wheatear, Whinchat, Redstart, Common and Green Sandpiper, Ringed and Little Ringed Plovers, Redshank. Dunlin and Greenshank frequent, possible Wood Sandpiper. Reed Bunting, Meadow Pipit, Sky Lark, Linnet, Yellow Wagtail. Possible Quail. Kestrel and Barn Owl seen occasionally. *Winter*: Stonechat, Redpoll, Short-eared Owl, Goosander and Wigeon possible.

Contact: Forestry Commission, Lady Hill, Birches Valley, Rugely, Staffs WS15 2UQ. 01889 586 593. website: www.forestry.gov.uk

Lincolnshire

1. DONNA NOOK

Lincolnshire Wildlife Trust.
Location: TF 422 998. Near North Somercotes, off A1031 coast road, S of Grimsby.

Access: Donna Nook beach is closed on weekdays as this is an active bombing range, but dunes remain open. Dogs on leads. Some disabled access.

Facilities: No toilets or visitor centre.

Public transport: None.

Habitat: Dunes, slacks and intertidal areas, seashore, mudflats, sandflats.

Key birds: *Summer*: Little Tern, Ringed Plover, Oystercatcher. *Winter*: Brent Goose, Shelduck, Twite, Lapland Bunting, Shore Lark, Linnet.

Other notable flora and fauna: The reserve has one of the largest and most accessible breeding colonies of grey seals in the UK. Other mammals include fox, badger, stoat and weasel and three species of shrew have been identified. Common lizard.

Contact: Trust HQ, 01507 526 667.
e-mail: lincstrust@cix.co.uk www.lincstrust.co.uk

2. EPWORTH TURBERY

Lincolnshire Wildlife Trust.
Location: SE 758 036. SW of Scunthorpe. Take A18 W from Scunthorpe then A161 S to Epworth. Turn R on High Street, continue onto Tottermire Lane then bear left onto Battle Green. Turn L onto Fieldside, R onto Carrside then L onto Turbary Road. The entrance is near bridge over Skyer's Drain. Parking available through gate, which should be kept closed, or on verge adjoining reserve. Park well away from corner.

Access: Open at all times. Keep to waymarked paths

and use hides when viewing open area. In order to avoid disturbing birds on the ponds, please do not climb on the banks.

Facilities: Car park, way-marked trail, two hides.

Public transport: None.

Habitat: One of the few relics of raised bog in Lincolnshire. Although extensively dug for peat in the past, areas of active sphagnum bog still exist. Areas of reed swamp and mixed fen vegetation, also fen and wet heath conditions and a considerable area of birch woodland of varying ages.

Key birds: Breeding birds include Tree Pipit, warblers, finches, Green and Great Spotted Woodpeckers and Woodcock. Greenshank, Green Sandpiper and Little Grebe are attracted to the wet area. Around Steve's Pond, occasional Hobby and Marsh Harrier, plus Teal, Little Grebe, Tree Pipit, Sparrowhawk and Buzzard. Willow Tit, Long-tailed Tit, Reed Bunting and Willow Warbler in the woodland areas. Occasionally Corn Buntings on the adjoining farmland. In the autumn and winter large flocks of Rooks, crows and Jackdaws fly into the reserve to roost. At Pantry's Pond in winter occasional Hen Harrier. Other birds include Yellowhammer, Linnet, Jay and Magpie. Sometimes in winter Long-eared Owls can be observed roosting close to the path.

Other notable flora and fauna: Eleven species of breeding dragonflies and damselflies have been recorded. Wood tiger moth is well established. Plants include sneezewort, yellow and purple-loosestrife, meadow-rue, and devil's-bit scabious.

Contact: Trust HQ, 01507 526 667.
e-mail: lincstrust@cix.co.uk www.lincstrust.co.uk

3. FRAMPTON MARSH

RSPB (Eastern England Office).
Location: TR 364 385. Four miles SE of Boston. From A16 follow signs to Frampton then Frampton Marsh.
Access: Visitor Centre open 10am-4pm each day except Dec 25. Three hides and 3.5km of wheelchair-accessible footpaths open at all times.
Facilities: Visitor Centre with hot drinks and snacks, three toilets (one with wheelchair access), footpaths, benches, viewpoints, 50-space car park (three for disabled visitors), bicycle rack, free information leaflets and events programmes.
Habitat: Saltmarsh, wet grassland, freshwater scrapes and developing reedbed.
Key birds: *Summer:* Breeding Redshank, Avocet, Lapwing, Sky Lark, Ringed Plover, plus passage waders (inc Greenshank, Curlew Sandpiper, Wood Sandpiper, Little and Temminck's Stints, Ruff and Black-tailed Godwit), Marsh Harrier and Hobby. *Winter:* Hen Harrier, Short-eared Owl, Merlin, dark-bellied Brent Goose, Twite, Golden Plover, Lapland Bunting.
Other notable flora and fauna: Water vole, muntjac and roe deer, stoat. Dragonflies inc emperor, hawkers, chasers and darters. Common butterflies plus wall brown, painted lady and speckled wood. Scarce pug, star wort and crescent striped moths on saltmarsh. Important brackish water flora and fauna includes nationally scarce spiral tassleweed and several rare beetles.
Contact: John Badley, Site Manager, Roads Farmhouse, Frampton Roads, Frampton, Boston, Lincs PE20 1AY. 01205 724 678.
e-mail: johnbadley@rspb.org.uk www.rspb.org.uk

4. FREISTON SHORE

RSPB (Eastern England Office).
Location: TF 397 424. Four miles E of Boston. From A52 at Haltoft End follow signs to Freiston Shore.
Access: Open at all times, free.
Facilities: Footpaths, two car parks, bird hide. Free information leaflets on site, guided walks programme. Bicycle rack, benches, viewpoints, seawatching shelter, reservoir viewing screen, wet grassland viewing platform.
Public transport: None.
Habitat: Saltmarsh, saline lagoon, mudflats, wet grassland.
Key birds: *Summer:* Breeding waders including Avocet, Ringed Plover and Oystercatcher, Corn Bunting and Tree Sparrow. *Winter:* Twite, dark-bellied Brent Goose, wildfowl, waders, Short-eared Owl and Hen Harrier. *Passage:* Waders, including Greenshank, Curlew Sandpiper and Little Stint. *Autumn:* Occasional seabirds including Arctic and Great Skuas.
Other notable flora and fauna: Water vole, muntjac and roe deer, stoat. Dragonflies inc emperor,

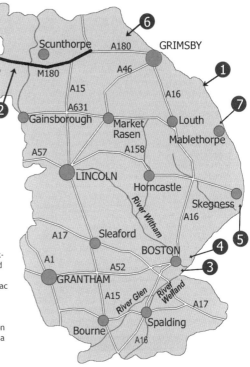

hawkers, chasers and darters. Common butterflies plus wall brown, painted lady and speckled wood. Scarce pug, star wort and crescent striped moths on saltmarsh. Important brackish water flora and fauna includes nationally scarce spiral tassleweed and several rare beetles.
Contact: John Badley, 01205 724 678 (See Frampton Marsh). e-mail: john.badley@rspb.org.uk

5. GIBRALTAR POINT NATIONAL NATURE RESERVE & BIRD OBSERVATORY

Lincolnshire Wildlife Trust.
Location: TF 556 580. Three miles S of Skegness on the N edge of The Wash. Signposted from Skegness town centre.
Access: Reserve open dawn-dusk all year. Charges for car parking. Free admission to reserve, visitor centre and toilets. Some access restrictions to sensitive sites at S end, open access to N. Dogs on leads at all times — no dogs on beach during summer. Visitor centre and toilets suitable for wheelchairs, as well as network of surfaced foot paths. Bird observatory and four hides suitable for wheelchairs. Day visit groups must be booked in advance. Access for coaches. Contact The Wash Study Centre for residential or day visits.
Facilities: Site also location of Wash Study Centre and Bird Observatory. Field centre is an ideal base

for birdwatching/natural history groups in spring, summer and autumn. Visitor centre, gift shop and cafe. Toilets open daily. Network of footpaths bisect all major habitats. Public hides overlook freshwater and brackish lagoons. Wash viewpoint overlooks saltmarsh and mudflats.

Public transport: Bus service from Skegness runs occasionally but summer service only. Otherwise taxi/car from Skegness. Cycle route from Skegness.

Habitat: Sand dune grassland and scrub, saltmarshes and mudflats, freshwater marsh and lagoons.

Key birds: Large scale visible migration during spring and autumn passage. Internationally important populations of non-breeding waders Jul-Mar (peak Sep/Oct). Winter flocks of Brent Geese, Shelduck and Wigeon on flats and marshes with Hen Harrier, Merlin and Short-eared Owl often present. Red-throated Divers offshore, peak Feb. A colony of Little Tern and Ringed Plover in summer. More than 100 species can be seen in a day during May and Sept. good passage of autumn seabirds in northerly winds.

Other notable flora and fauna: Pyramidal orchids occur in patches. Grey and common seal colonies, with porpoises offshore in most months. Butterflies include brown argus and green hairstreak.

Contact: Reserve and wildlife: Kev Wilson. Visit bookings: Jill Hardy, Sykes Farm, Gibraltar Point Nature Reserve, Gibraltar Road, Skegness, Lincs PE24 4SU. 01754 898 057. e-mail: kwilson@linwtrust.co.uk or gibpoint@btconnect.com www.lincstrust.org.uk

6. KILLINGHOLME HAVEN PITS

Lincolnshire Wildlife Trust.

Location: TA 165199 NW of Grimsby. Take A180 W, turn R on A1173 towards Immingham. Turn L at roundabout and continue to A160. Turn L then R onto Eastfield road. Turn R onto Chase Hill road then L onto Haven road. The reserve is situated to the S of Haven Road on the approach to North Killingholme Haven. Park carefully on the road.

Access: No general access to the reserve, but adequate viewing points are available from the public road and bank-top footpath.

Facilities: None.

Habitat: Marsh/wetland.

Key birds: A good site for water birds. Diving ducks, such as Pochard, Tufted Duck and, occasionally, Scaup. Breeding species include Little Grebe, and Reed, Sedge, Willow And Grasshopper Warblers. Ruddy Duck has also been known to breed here. The two large shallow pits, are of the greatest importance for birds, particularly for migrant waders

in spring and autumn. Spotted Redshank, Dunlin, Greenshank, Common Sandpiper, Little Ringed Plover, Ruff and Black-tailed Godwit, the latter often in large numbers, are regular visitors.

The list of scarce and rare species is long and includes Spoonbill, Avocet, Little Egret, Little and Temminck's Stints, Red-necked Phalarope, and Curlew, Pectoral, Baird's And White-rumped Sandpipers.

Contact: Trust HQ, 01507 526 667.

e-mail: lincstrust@cix.co.uk www.lincstrust.co.uk

7. SALTFLEETBY-THEDDLETHORPE DUNES NATIONAL NATURE RESERVE

Natural England.

Location: TF 465 924 - TF 490 883. Approx two miles N of Mablethorpe. All the following car parks may be accessed from the A1031: Crook Bank, Brickyard Lane, Churchill Lane, Rimac, Sea View.

Access: Open all year at all times. Keep dogs under close control. Easy access half mile trail suitable for wheelchair users starts adjacent to Rimac car park. Includes pond and saltmarsh viewing platforms.

Facilities: Toilets, including wheelchair suitability at Rimac car park. May to end of Sept events programme. Easy access trail at Rimac with viewing platforms.

Public transport: Grayscroft coaches (01507 473 236) and Lincolnshire Roadcar (01522 532 424) run services past Rimac entrance (Louth to Mablethorpe service). Lincs Roadcar can connect with trains at Lincoln. Applebys Coaches (01507 357 900) Grimsby to Saltfleet bus connects with Grimsby train service.

Habitat: 13th Century dunes, freshwater marsh, new dune ridge with large areas of sea buckthorn, saltmarsh, shingle ridge and foreshore.

Key birds: *Summer*: Breeding birds in scrub include Nightingale, Grasshopper Warbler, Whitethroat, Lesser Whitethroat, Redpoll.

Winter: Large flocks of Brent Goose, Shelduck, Teal and Wigeon. Wintering Short-eared Owl, Hen Harrier. Migrant birds in scrub and waders on Paradise scrape.

Other notable flora and fauna: Impressive show of sea lavendar in late summer, orchids in marsh and dunes including pyramidal, marsh and bee. Fourteen species of dragonfly including emperor. Water vole, roe and muntjac deer, foxes and badgers are common.

Contact: Reserve Manager, Natural England Workshops, Seaview, Saltfleetby St Clements, Louth, Lincolnshire LN11 7TR. 01507 338 611. www.naturalengland.org.uk

London, Greater

1. BEDFONT LAKES COUNTRY PARK

Continental Landscapes Ltd.
Location: TQ 080 728. OS map sheet 176 (west London). 0.5 miles from Ashford, Middx, 0.5 miles S of A30, Clockhouse Roundabout, on B3003 (Clockhouse Lane).
Access: Park open (7.30am-9pm or dusk, whichever is earlier), all days except Christmas Day. Disabled friendly. Dogs on leads. Main nature reserve only open Sun (2pm-4pm). Keyholder membership available.
Facilities: Toilets, information centre, several hides, nature trail, free parking, up-to-date information.
Public transport: Train to Feltham and Ashford. Bus – H26 and 116 from Hounslow.
Habitat: Lakes, reedbed, wildflower meadows, wet woodland, scrub.
Key birds: *Winter*: Water Rail, Bittern, Smew and other wildfowl, Meadow Pipit. *Summer*: Common Tern, Willow, Garden, Reed and Sedge Warblers, Whitethroat, Lesser Whitethroat, hirundines, Hobby, Blackcap, Chiffchaff, Sky Lark. *Passage*: Wheatear, Wood Warbler, Spotted Flycatcher, Ring Ouzel, Redstart, Yellow Wagtail.
Other notable flora and fauna: 140 plant species inc bee and pyramidal orchid. Nathusius pipistrelle bat, emperor dragonfly plus other butterflies and dragonflies.
Contact: James Herd, Ranger, BLCP, Clockhouse Lane, Bedfont, Middx TW14 8QA. 0845 456 2796. e-mail: bedfont.lakes@continental-landscapes.co.uk

2. CHASE (THE) LOCAL NATURE RESERVE

London Wildlife Trust.
Location: TQ 515 860. Lies in the Dagenham Corridor, an area of green belt between the London Boroughs of Barking & Dagenham and Havering.
Access: Open throughout the year and at all times. Reserve not suitable for wheelchair access. Eastbrookend Country Park which borders The Chase LNR has surfaced footpaths for wheelchair use.
Facilities: Millennium visitor centre, toilets, ample car parking, Timberland Trail walk.
Public transport: Rail: Dagenham East (District Line) 15 minute walk. Bus: 174 from Romford five minute walk.
Habitat: Shallow wetlands, reedbeds, horse-grazed pasture, scrub and wetland. These harbour an impressive range of animals and plants including the nationally rare black poplar tree. A haven for birds, with approx 190 different species recorded.
Key birds: *Summer*: Breeding Reed Warbler, Lapwing, Water Rail, Lesser Whitethroat and Little Ringed Plover, Kingfisher, Reed Bunting. *Winter*: Significant numbers of Teal, Shoveler, Redwing, Fieldfare and Snipe dominate the scene. *Spring/autumn migration*: Yellow Wagtail, Wheatear, Ruff, Wood Sandpiper, Sand Martin, Ring Ouzel, Black Redstart and Hobby regularly seen.
Other notable flora and fauna: 140 plant species, wasp spider, butterflies and dragonflies.
Contact: The Millennium Centre, The Chase, Off Dagenham Road, Rush Green, Romford, Essex RM7 0SS. 02085 938 096. e-mail: lwtchase@cix.co.uk www.wildlifetrust.org.uk/london/

3. LONDON WETLAND CENTRE

The Wildfowl & Wetlands Trust.
Location: TQ 228 770. Less than 1 mile from South Circular (A205) at Roehampton. In London, Zone 2/3, one mile from Hammersmith.
Access: Winter (9.30am-5pm: last admission 4pm), summer (9.30am-6pm: last admission 5pm). Charge for admission. Coach parking by arrangement.
Facilities: Visitor centre, hides, nature trails, discovery centre and children's adventure area, restaurant (hot and cold food), cinema, shop, observatory centre, seven hides (all wheelchair accessible), three interpretative buildings.
Public transport: Train: Barnes. Tube: Hammersmith then bus 283 (comes into centre). Other buses from Hammersmith are 33, 72, 209; from Richmond, 33.
Habitat: Main lake, reedbeds, wader scrape, mudflats, open water lakes, grazing marsh.
Key birds: *Winter*: Nationally important numbers of wintering waterfowl, including Gadwall and Shoveler. Important numbers of wetland breeding birds, including grebes, swans, a range of duck species such as Pochard, plus Lapwing, Little Ringed Plover, Redshank, warblers, Reed Bunting and Bittern.
Other notable flora and fauna: Large population of water voles. Slow worm, grass snake, common lizard. Seven species of bat inc soprano pipistrelle, noctule Daubenton's and serotine. 17 species of dragonfly and 25 species of butterfly. Notable plants inc cowslip, pyramidal and bee orchids.
Contact: London Wetland Centre, Queen Elizabeth Walk, Barnes, London, SW13 9WT. 020 8409 4400. e-mail: info.london@wwt.org.uk www.wwt.org.uk

4. SYDENHAM HILL WOOD

London Wildlife Trust.
Location: TQ 335 722. Forest Hill, SE London, SE26, between Forest Hill and Crystal Palace, just off South Circular (A205). Entrances as Crescent Wood Road and Coxs Walk.
Access: Open at all times, no permits required. Some steep slopes,so wheelchair access is difficult.
Facilities: Nature trail, information boards. No toilets.
Public transport: Train stations: Forest Hill (from London Bridge) or Sydenham Hill (from Victoria). Buses 363, 202, 356, 185, 312, 176, P4. Call Transport for London 0207 5657 299 for details.

Habitat: Ancient woodland, reclaimed Victorian gardens, meadow and small pond.
Key birds: Woodland and gardens species all year round. *All year:* All three woodpeckers, Tawny Owl, Kestrel, Sparrowhawk, Goldcrest, Nuthatch, Treecreeper, Stock Dove,. *Summer:* Blackcap, Chiffchaff, Willow Warbler. *Winter:* Fieldfare, Redwing.
Other notable flora and fauna: Five species of bat,

including noctule and brown long-eared. Bluebell, wood anemone, dog violet and primrose. Oak and hornbeam. Speckled wood, comma, painted lady and orange-tip butterflies.
Contact: London Wildlife Trust, Centre for Wildlife Gardening, 28 Marsden Road, London SE15 4EE. 0207 252 9186. e-mail: cbrown@wildlondon.org.uk www.wildlondon.org.uk

Manchester, Greater

1. ASTLEY MOSS

The Wildlife Trust for Lancashire, Manchester and North Merseyside.
Location: Lancs WT SJ692975. S of A580 at Astley; follow Higher Green Lane to Rindle Farm.
Access: Permit from Trust required.
Facilities: None.
Public transport: None.
Habitat: Remnant peat bog, scrub, oak/ birch woodland.
Key birds: *Spring/summer:* Breeding Tree Pipit. *Winter:* Raptors (inc. Merlin, Hen Harrier), finch flocks, thrush flocks; Long- and Short-eared Owls.
Other notable flora and fauna: Sphagnum mosses, 10 species of dragonfly recorded.
Contact: Trust HQ, Cuerden Park Wildlife Centre, The Barn, Berkeley Drive, Bamber Bridge, Preston PR5 6BY. 01772 324 129. e-mail: lancswt@cix.co.uk www.wildlifetrust.org.uk/lancashire/

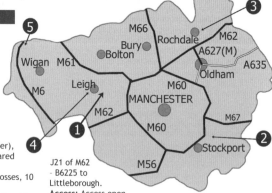

2. ETHEROW COUNTRY PARK

Stockport Metropolitan Borough Council.
Location: SJ 965 908. B6104 into Compstall near Romiley, Stockport.
Access: Open at all times; permit required for conservation area. Keep to paths.
Facilities: Reserve area has SSSI status. Hide, nature trail, visitor centre, scooters for disabled.
Public transport: None.
Habitat: River Etherow, woodlands, marshy area.
Key birds: Sparrowhawk, Buzzard, Dipper, all three woodpeckers, Pied Flycatcher, warblers. *Winter:* Brambling, Siskin, Water Rail. Frequent sightings of Merlin and Raven over hills.
Other notable flora and fauna: 200 species of plant.
Contact: John Rowland, Etherow Country Park, Compstall, Stockport, Cheshire SK6 5JD. 01614 276 937; e-mail: parks@stockport.gov.uk

3. HOLLINGWORTH LAKE

Hollingworth Lake / Rochdale MBC.
Location: SD 939 153 (visitor centre). Four miles NE of Rochdale, signed from A58 Halifax Road and

J21 of M62 - B6225 to Littleborough.
Access: Access open to lake and surroundings at all times.
Facilities: Cafes, hide, trails and education service, car parks, coach park by prior arrangement. Free wheelchair hire, disabled toilets and baby changing facilities, fishing. Visitor centre open 10.30am-6pm (Mon-Sun) in summer, 11am-4pm (Mon-Fri), 10.30am-5pm (Sat & Sun) in winter.
Public transport: Bus Nos 452, 450. Train to Littleborough or Smithy Bridge.
Habitat: Lake (116 acres, includes 20 acre nature reserve), woodland, streams, marsh, willow scrub.
Key birds: *All year:* Great Crested Grebe, Kingfisher, Lapwing, Little Owl, Bullfinch, Cormorant. Occasional Peregrine, Sedge Warbler, Water Rail, Snipe. *Spring/autumn:* Passage waders, wildfowl, Kittiwake. *Summer:* Reed Bunting, Dipper, Common Sandpiper, Curlew, Oystercatcher, Black Tern, 'Commic' Tern, Grey Partridge, Blackcap. *Winter:* Goosander, Goldeneye, Siskin, Redpoll, Golden Plover.
Contact: The Ranger, Hollingworth Lake Visitor Centre, Rakewood Road, Littleborough, OL15 0AQ. 01706 373 421. www.rochdale.gov.uk

4. PENNINGTON FLASH COUNTRY PARK

Wigan Leisure and Culture Trust
Location: SJ 640 990. One mile from Leigh town centre. Main entrance on A572 (St Helens Road).
Access: Park is signposted from A580 (East Lancs

Road) and is permanently open. Four largest hides, toilets and information point open 9am-dusk (except Christmas Day). Main paths flat and suitable for disabled. Coach parking available if booked in advance.

Facilities: Toilets (including disabled) and information point. Total of seven bird hides. Site leaflet available and Rangers based on site. Group visits welcome and guided tours or a site introduction can be arranged subject to staff availability.

Public transport: Only 1 mile from Leigh bus station. Several services stop on St Helens Road near entrance to park. Contact GMPTE on 0161 228 7811.

Habitat: Lowland lake, ponds and scrapes, fringed with reeds, rough grassland, scrub and young woodland.

Key birds: Waterfowl all year, waders mainly on passage in spring and autumn (14-plus species). Breeding Common Tern and Little Ringed Plover. Feeding station attracts Willow Tit and Bullfinch all year.

Other notable flora and fauna: Wide variety of butterflies and dragonflies.

Contact: Peter Alker, Pennington Flash Country Park, St Helens Road, Leigh, WN7 3PA. 01942 605 253 (Also Fax number). e-mail: pfcp@wlct.org

5. WIGAN FLASHES LOCAL NATURE RESERVE

Lancashire Wildlife Trust/Wigan Council.
Location: SD 580 035. Leave M6 at J25 head N on A49, turn R on to Poolstock Lane (B5238). There are several entrances to the site; at end of Carr Lane near Hawkley Hall School, one off Poolstock Lane, two on Warington Road (A573). Also accessible from banks of Leeds and Liverpool Canal.

Access: Free access, open at all times. Areas suitable for wheelchairs but there are some motorcycle barriers (gates can be opened by reserve manager for large groups). Paths being upgraded. Access for coaches - contact reserve manager for details.

Facilities: Six hide screens.

Public transport: 610 bus (Hawkley Hall Circular). Local timetable info - call 0161 228 7811.

Habitat: Wetland with reedbed.

Key birds: Black Tern on migration. *Summer*: Nationally important for Reed Warbler and breeding Common Tern. Willow Tit, Cetti's and Grasshopper Warblers, Kingfisher.
Winter: Wildfowl, especially diving duck and Gadwall. Bittern (especially winter).

Other notable flora and fauna: Interesting orchids, with the eight species including marsh and dune helleborine. One of the UK's largest feeding assemblage of noctule bats. Eighteen species of dragonfly which has included red-veined darter.

Contact: Mark Champion, Lancashire Wildlife Trust, Highfield Grange, Wigan, Lancs WN3 6SU. 01942 233 976. e-mail:wiganflashes@lancswt.org.uk

Merseyside

1. AINSDALE & BIRKDALE LOCAL NATURE RESERVE

Sefton Council.
Location: SD 300 115. SD 310 138. Leave the A565 just N of Formby and car parking areas are off the un-numbered coastal road.

Access: Track from Ainsdale or Southport along the shore. Wheelchair access across boardwalks at Ainsdale Sands Lake Nature Trail and the Queen's Jubilee Nature Trail, opposite Weld Road.

Facilities: Ainsdale Visitor Centre open summer and toilets (Easter-Oct).

Public transport: Ainsdale and Southport stations 20 minute walk. Hillside Station is a 30 minute walk across the Birkdale Sandhills to beach.

Habitat: Foreshore, dune scrub and pine woodland.

Key birds: *Spring/summer*: Grasshopper Warbler, Chiffchaff, waders. *Winter*: Blackcap, Stonechat, Redwing, Fieldfare, waders and wildfowl. *All year*: Sky Lark, Grey Partridge.

Other notable flora and fauna: Red squirrel.

Contact: Sefton Council, Southport Town Hall, Lord Street, Southport, PR8 1DA. www.sefton.gov.uk

2. DEE ESTUARY

Metropolitan Borough of Wirral.
Location: SJ 255 815. Leave A540 Chester to Hoylake road at Heswall and head downhill (one mile) to the free car park at the shore end of Banks Road. Heswall is 30 minutes from South Liverpool and Chester by car.

Access: Open at all times. Best viewpoint 600 yards along shore N of Banks Road. No disabled access along shore, but good birdwatching from bottom of Banks Road. Arrive 2.5 hours before high tide. Coach parking available.

Facilities: Information board. No toilets in car park. Wirral Country Park Centre three miles N off A540 has toilets, hide, café, kiosk (all accessible to wheelchairs). Birdwatching events programme on RSPB website.

Public transport: Bus service to Banks Road car park from Heswall bus station, or bus to Irby village then walk one mile. Contact Mersey Travel (tel 0151 236 7676).

Habitat: Saltmarsh and mudflats.

Key birds: *Autumn/winter*: Large passage and

winter wader roosts — Redshank, Curlew, Black-tailed Godwit, Oystercatcher, Golden Plover, Knot, Shelduck, Teal, Red-breasted Merganser, Peregrine, Merlin, Hen Harrier, Short-eared Owl. Smaller numbers of Pintail, Wigeon, Bar-tailed Godwit, Greenshank, Spotted Redshank, Grey and Ringed Plovers, Whimbrel, Curlew Sandpiper, Little Stint, occasional Scaup and Little Egret.
Contact: The Senior Ranger, Wirral Country Park Centre, Station Road, Thustaston, Wirral, Merseyside, CH61 0HN. 01516 484 371/3884.
e-mail: wirralcountrypark@wirral.gov.uk
www.wirral.gov.uk/er

3. HILBRE ISLAND LOCAL NATURE RESERVE

Wirral Country Park Centre (Metropolitan Borough of Wirral).
Location: SJ 184 880. Three tidal islands in the mouth of the Dee Estuary. Park in West Kirby which is on the A540 Chester-to-Hoylake road – 30 minutes from Liverpool, 45 minutes from Chester. Follow the brown Marine Lake signs to Dee Lane pay and display car park. Coach parking available at West Kirby but please apply for permit to visit island well in advance as numbers limited.
Access: Two mile walk across the sands from Dee Lane slipway. No disabled access. Do not cross either way within 3.5 hours of high water - tide times and suggested safe route on noticeboard at slipway. Prior booking and permit needed for parties of five or more - maximum of 50. Book early.
Facilities: Hilbre Bird Observatory. Toilets at Hilbre (primitive!) and Marine Lake. Permits, leaflets and tide times from Wirral Country Park Centre.
Public transport: Bus and train station (from

Liverpool) within 0.5 mile of Dee Lane slipway. Contact Mersey Travel, tel 0151 236 7676.
Habitat: Sandflats, rocky shore and open sea.
Key birds: *Late summer/autumn:* Seabird passage Gannets, terns, skuas, shearwaters and after NW gales good numbers of Leach's Petrel. *Winter:* Wader roosts at high tide, Purple Sandpiper, Turnstone, sea ducks, divers, grebes. Passage migrants.
Other notable flora and fauna: Nationally scarce rock sea lavender.
Contact: See Dee Estuary

4. MARSHSIDE

RSPB (North of England Office).
Location: SD 355 202. On south shore of Ribble Estuary, one mile north of Southport centre on Marine Drive.
Access: Open 8.30am-5pm all year. Toilets. No dogs please. Coach parties please book in advance. No charges but donations welcomed. Park in Sefton Council car park along Marine Drive.
Facilities: Two hides and trails accessible to wheelchairs. Two viewing screens and a viewing platform.
Public transport: Bus service to Elswick Road/Marshside Road half-hourly, bus No 44, from Lord Street. Contact Traveline (0870 608 2608).
Habitat: Coastal grazing marsh and lagoons.
Key birds: *Winter:* Pink-footed Goose, wildfowl, waders, raptors. *Spring:* Breeding waders, inc. Avocet and wildfowl, Garganey, migrants. *Autumn:* Migrants. *All year:* Black-tailed Godwit.
Other notable flora and fauna: Hares, various plants including marsh orchid, migrant hawker dragonfly.
Contact: Graham Clarkson, Warden, RSPB, 24 Hoghton Street, Southport, PR9 0PA. 01704 536 378.
e-mail: graham.clarkson@rspb.org.uk

5. NORTH WIRRAL COASTAL PARK

Metropolitan Borough of Wirral.
Location: SJ 241 909. Located between the outer Dee and Mersey Estuaries. From Moreton take A553 E then A551 N. Turn left onto Tarran Way South then R onto Lingham Lane. Parking available by lighthouse. Foreshore can be viewed from footpath which runs alongside.
Access: Open at all times.
Facilities: Visitor centre, several car parks, 3 toilet blocks (one summer-only), extensive footpath network and public bridleways, 4 picnic areas.
Public transport: The area being served by Grove Road (Wallasey), Leasowe, Moreton, and Meols Merseyrail Stations, and with bus routes along Leasowe Road, Pasture Road and Harrison Drive.
Habitat: Saltmarsh.
Key birds: Important as a feeding and roosting site for passage and wintering flocks of waders,

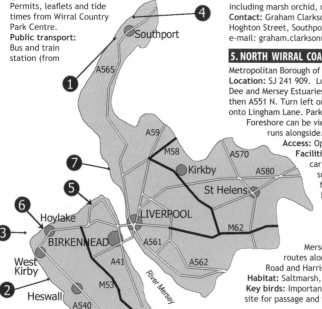

wildfowl, terns and gulls. Wintering populations of Knot (20,000+), Bar-tailed Godwit (2,000+) and Dunlin (10,000). Redshank (1,000+) and Turnstone (500+) feed on the rocky shore at Perch Rock and on the rocky sea walls. Oystercatcher (500+), Curlew, Grey Plover and Black-tailed Godwit also regularly roost here in relatively high numbers. Small populations of wildfowl, including Common Scoter, Scaup and Goldeneye, Red-throated Divers and Great Crested Grebes also frequently winter on this site.

Other notable flora and fauna: Sea holly, marram grass, storksbill, burnet rose and rarities like the Isle of Man cabbage can be found. This area is one of only two known sites in the world for the very rare British sub-species of the belted beauty moth.

Contact: Ranger Service, North Wirral Coastal Park, Leasowe Lighthouse, Moreton Common, Wirral CH46 4TA. 0151 678 5488. www.wirral.gov.uk e-mail: coastalpark@wirral.gov.uk

6. RED ROCKS MARSH

Cheshire Wildlife Trust.

Location: SJ 206 880. 9 km west of Birkenhead immediately W of Hoylake and adjacent to the Dee estuary.

Access: Open all year.

Facilities: Car park, hide.

Public transport: None.

Habitat: Sand dune, reedbed.

Key birds: *Spring/summer:* Wildfowl, warblers. *Passage:* finches, Snow Bunting, thrushes.

Other notable flora and fauna: The only breeding colony of natterjack toads on the Wirral Peninsula.

More than 50 species of flowering plant recorded, including parsley, quaking grass, Danish scurvy grass, wild asparagus and various orchid species.

Contact: Cheshire Wildlife Trust, Bickley Hall Farm, Bickley, Malpas, Cheshire SY14 8EF. 01948 820 728; (fax) 0709 2888 469.
e-mail: cheshirewt@cix.co.uk
www.cheshirewildlifetrust.co.uk

7. SEAFORTH

The Wildlife Trust for Lancashire, Manchester and North Merseyside.

Location: SJ 315 970. Five miles from Liverpool city centre. From M57/M58 take A5036 to docks.

Access: Only organised groups which pre-book are now allowed access. Groups should contact the reserve office (see below) at least seven days in advance of their planned trip. Coaches welcome.

Facilities: Toilets at visitor centre when open, three hides.

Public transport: Train to Waterloo or Seaforth stations from Liverpool. Buses to dock gates from Liverpool.

Habitat: Saltwater and freshwater lagoons, scrub grassland.

Key birds: Noted site for Little Gull on passage (Apr), plus Roseate, Little and Black Terns. Breeding and passage Common Tern (Apr-Sept). Passage and winter waders and gulls. Passage passerines, especially White Wagtail, pipits and Wheatear.

Contact: Steve White, Seaforth Nature Reserve, Port of Liverpool L21 1JD. 0151 9203 769.
e-mail: swhite@lancswt.org.uk

Norfolk

1. CLEY MARSHES

Norfolk Wildlife Trust.

Location: TG 054 441. NWT Cley Marshes is situated four miles N of Holt on A149 coast road, half a mile E of Cley-next-the-Sea. Visitor centre and car park on inland side of road.

Access: Open all year round, except Christmas Day. Visitor centre open Apr-Oct (10am-5pm daily), Nov-early Dec (10am-4pm Wed-Sun). Cost: adults £3.75, children under 16 free. NWT members free. Out of season, obtain permit from Watcher's Cottage, 400m along coast road towards Cley village.

Facilities: Brand new environmentally-friendly visitor centre incorporates an observation area, interactive interpretation including a remote controllable wildlife camera, a café, and sales area. Four hides (with excellent wheelchair access) provide birdwatching within metres of the pools where the birds congregate. Audio trail. Wildlife Detective Bumbags for children are free to hire. Boardwalk and information boards. Reserve leaflet.

Public transport: Coasthopper bus service stops outside, every two hours. Connections for train and bus services at Sheringham. Special discounts to visitors arriving by bus. Call Norfolk County Bus Information Line on 01603 223 800 for info.

Habitat: Reedbeds, salt and freshwater marshes, scrapes and shingle ridge with international reputation as one of the finest birdwatching sites in Britain.

Key birds: Bittern, Avocet, Marsh Harrier, Spoonbill, Bearded Tit and large numbers of wildfowl, including Wigeon, Teal, Pintail and Brent Goose. Migrating waders such as Ruff and Temminck's Stint. Many rarities.

Contact: NWT, Bewick House, 22 Thorpe Road, Norwich, Norfolk NR1 1RY. 01603 625 540.
e-mail admin@norfolkwildlifetrust.org.uk
www.wildlifetrust.org.uk.Norfolk

2. HICKLING BROAD NATIONAL NATURE RESERVE

Norfolk Wildlife Trust.

Location: TG 428 222. Approx four miles SE of

Stalham, just off A149 Yarmouth Road. From Hickling village, follow the brown badger tourist signs into Stubb Road at the Greyhound Inn. Take first turning L to follow Stubb Road for another mile. Turn R at the end for the nature reserve. The car park is ahead of you.
Access: Open all year. Visitor centre open Apr-Sep (10am-5pm daily). Cost: adults £3.25, children under 16 and NWT members free.
Facilities: Visitor centre, boardwalk trail through reedbeds to open water, birdwatching hides, wildlife gift shop, refreshments, picnic site, toilets, coach parking, car parking, disabled access to broad, boardwalk and toilets. Groups welcome. Water trips mid-May to mid-Sept (additional charge — booking essential).
Public transport: Morning bus service only Mon-Fri from Norwich (Neaves Coaches) Cromer to North Walsham (Sanders). Buses stop in Hickling village, a 25 minute walk away.
Habitat: Hickling is the largest and wildest of the Norfolk Broads with reedbeds, grazing marshes and wide open skies.
Key birds: Marsh Harriers, Bittern, warblers. From October to March the raptor roost at Stubb Mill, provides excellent views of raptors flying in to roost. Likely birds include Marsh Harriers, Hen Harriers, Merlins, Cranes and Pink footed Geese.
Other notable flora and fauna: Swallowtail butterfly, Norfolk hawker (rare dragonfly)
Contact: John Blackburn, Hickling Broad Visitor Centre, Stubb Road, Hickling, Norfolk NR12 0BW. e-mail johnb@norfolkwildlifetrust.co.uk www.norfolkwildlifetrust.org.uk

3. HOLKHAM

Natural England (Norfolk and Suffolk Team).
Location: TF 890 450. From Holkham village turn N off A149 down Lady Ann's Drive to park.
Access: Access unrestricted, but keep to paths and off grazing marshes and farmland.
Facilities: Two hides. Disabled access.
Public transport: Bus Norbic Norfolk bus information line 0845 3006 116.
Habitat: Sandflats, dunes, marshes, pinewoods.
Key birds: *Passage*: Migrants. *Winter*: Wildfowl, inc. Brent, Pink-footed and White-fronted Geese.
Summer: Breeding Little Tern.
Other notable flora and fauna: Seablite bushes,

attractive to incoming migrant birds, sea aster and sea lavender.
Contact: M. Rooney, Hill Farm Offices, Main Road, Holkham, Wells-next-the-Sea, NR23 1AB. 01328 711 183; Fax 01328 711 893.

4. HOLME BIRD OBSERVATORY

Norfolk Ornithologists' Association (NOA).
Location: TF 717 450. E of Hunstanton, signposted from A149. Access from Broadwater Road, Holme. The reserve and visitors centre are beyond the White House at the end of the track.
Access: Reserve open daily to members dawn to dusk; non-members (9am-5pm) by permit from the Observatory. Please keep dogs on leads in the reserve. Parties by prior arrangement.
Facilities: Accredited Bird Observatory operating all year for bird ringing, MV moth trapping and other scientific monitoring. Visitor centre, car park and several hides (seawatch hide reserved for NOA members), together with access to beach and coastal path.
Public transport: Coastal bus service runs from Hunstanton to Sheringham roughly every 30 mins but is seasonal and times may vary. Phone Norfolk Green Bus, 01553 776 980.
Habitat: In ten acres of diverse habitat: sand dunes, Corsican pines, scrub and reed-fringed lagoon make this a migration hotspot.
Key birds: Species list over 320. Ringed species over 150. Recent rarities have included Red Kite, Common Crane, Red-backed Shrike, Osprey, Yellow-browed, Pallas', Greenish and Barred Warblers.
Contact: Holme Bird Observatory, Broadwater Road, Holme, Hunstanton, Norfolk PE36 6LQ. 01485 525 406. e-mail: info@noa.org.uk www.noa.org.uk

5. LYNFORD ARBORETUM

Forest Enterprise.
Location: TL 821 943, TL 818 935. On the Downham Market-Thetford road on A134. At the Mundford roundabout, follow signs to Swaffham. Take the first R to Lynford Hall. Follow road past the hall to the car park on the L. Disabled drivers can turn R. Alternatively, from the roundabout head S towards Thetford. Take the minor road signed L almost immediately to Lynford Lakes. Follow the road to the L turn, signed to the lakes. There is a car park at the bottom of the track.
Access: Open all year.
Facilities: Two car parks, tracks. Suitable for wheelchairs. No dogs in arboretum.
Public transport: None.
Habitat: Plantations, arboretum, lake.
Key birds: *Spring/summer:* Possible Wood Lark, Tree Pipit, possible Nightjar and Firecrest, Kingfisher, waterfowl. *Winter:* Crossbill, possible Hawfinch. *All year:* Usual woodland species, woodpeckers.
Other notable flora and fauna: More than 200 species of tree.
Contact: Forest Enterprise, Santon Downham. Brandon, Suffolk, IP27 0TJ. 01842 810 271.

6. SCULTHORPE MOOR COMMUNITY NATURE RESERVE

Hawk and Owl Trust
Location: TF900 305. In Wensum Valley, just W of Fakenham, on A148 to King's Lynn, brown sign signposted 'Nature Reserve' opposite village of Sculthorpe. Follow Turf Moor Road to the Visitor and Education Centre.
Access: Open Tue-Sun plus Bank Holiday Mondays (except Christmas Day). April to September: Tues-Wed (8am-6pm), Thur-Sun (8am-dusk). October to March: Tues-Sun (8am-4pm). Free admission — donations requested. Car park at visitor and education centre. Guide dogs only. Wheelchair access to visitor centre, boardwalks and two hides.
Facilities: Visitor and education centre open 10am-4pm Tuesday - Sunday, with adapted toilets, hot drinks dispenser, interpretive displays and live CCTV coverage from around the reserve. Base for specialist courses, school visits and other events. One of three hides accessed by bark chipping path. Coach parking available.
Public transport: Norfolk Green (tel: 01553 776980 website: www.norfolkgreen.co.uk) bus X8 Fakenham to King's Lynn stops at the end of Turf Moor Road. Sustrans no.1 cycle route from Harwich to Hull runs within 200 metres of the end of Turf Moor Road.
Habitat: Wetland reserve, with fen containing saw sedge (a European priority habitat), reedbed, wet woodland, pools, ditches and riverbank.
Key birds: More than 80 species recorded, including breeding Marsh Harrier, Barn Owl and Tawny Owl, visiting Buzzard, Goshawk, Hobby, Kestrel, Osprey, Sparrowhawk, also Water Rail, Kingfisher, Marsh Tit and Willow Tit and Golden Plover.

Other notable flora and fauna: Mammals include otter, water vole and roe deer, 19 species of dragonfly/damselfly, butterflies including white admiral, glow-worms, fungi including scarlet elf cup and a host of plants including marsh fern and saw sedge.
Contact: The Hawk and Owl Trust, Sculthorpe Moor Community Nature Reserve, Turf Moor Road, Sculthorpe, Fakenham, Norfolk NR21 9GN. 01328 856 788. e-mail: leanne.thomas@hawkandowl.org

7. SNETTISHAM

RSPB (Eastern England Office).
Location: TF 651 330. Car park two miles along Beach Road, signposted off A149 King's Lynn to Hunstanton, opposite Snettisham village.
Access: Open at all times. Dogs to be kept on leads. Two hides are suitable for wheelchairs. Disabled access is across a private road. Please phone office number for permit and directions. Coaches welcome, but please book in advance as a height barrier needs to be removed.
Facilities: Four birdwatching hides, connected by reserve footpath. No toilets on site.
Public transport: Nearest over two miles away.
Habitat: Intertidal mudflats, saltmarsh, shingle beach, brackish lagoons, and unimproved grassland/scrub. Highest tides best for good views of waders.
Key birds: *Autumn/winter/spring:* Waders (particularly Knot, Bar and Black-tailed Godwits, Dunlin, Grey Plover), wildfowl (particularly Pink-footed and Brent Geese, Wigeon, Gadwall, Goldeneye), Peregrine, Hen Harrier, Merlin, owls. Migrants in season. *Summer:* Breeding Mediterranean Gull, Ringed Plover, Redshank, Avocet, Common Tern. Marsh Harrier regular.
Contact: Jim Scott, RSPB, Barn A, Home Farm Barns, Common Road, Snettisham, King's Lynn, Norfolk PE31 7PD. 01485 542 689.

8. STRUMPSHAW FEN

RSPB (Eastern England Office).
Location: TG 33 06. Seven miles ESE of Norwich. Follow signposts. Entrance across level-crossing from car park, reached by turning sharp R and R again into Low Road from Brundall, off A47 to Great Yarmouth.
Access: Open dawn-dusk. RSPB members free, adults £2.50, children 50p, family £5. Guide dogs only. Limited wheelchair access — please phone for advice.
Facilities: Toilets, reception hide and two other hides, two walks, five miles of trails.
Public transport: Brundall train station about one mile from reserve. Bus stops half a mile from reserve - contact NORBIC (0845 300 6116).
Habitat: Reedbed and reedfen, wet grassland and woodland.
Key birds: *Summer:* Bittern, Little Egret, Bearded Tit, Marsh Harrier, Hobby, Kingfisher, Cetti's Warbler and other reedbed birds. *Winter:* Bittern, wildfowl, Marsh and Hen Harrier.
Other notable flora and fauna: Rich fen flora inc marsh pea, milk parsley, marsh sowthistle, six species

of orchid, inc marsh helleborine and narrow-leaved marsh orchid. Otter, Chinese water deer and water vole. Norfolk hawker, scarce chaser and variable damselfly among 20 dragonfly species. Swallowtail, white admiral and small heath butterflies.
Contact: Tim Strudwick, Staithe Cottage, Low Road, Strumpshaw, Norwich, Norfolk, NR13 4HS. 01603 715 191. e-mail: strumpshaw@rspb.org.uk www.rspb.org.uk

9. TITCHWELL MARSH

RSPB (Eastern England Office).
Location: TF 749 436. E of Hunstanton, off A149.
Access: Wheelchairs available free of charge. All paths and trails suitable for wheelchairs. Reserve and hides open at all times. Coach parking — pre-booking essential. Access may be restricted between August and October 2010 because of coastal project work. Call 01485 210 779 before visiting.
Facilities: Visitor centre, shop with large selection of binoculars, telescopes and books, open every day 9.30am to 5pm (Nov 5 - Feb 10, 9.30 to 4pm). Tearoom open from 9.30am to 4.30pm every day (Nov 5 - Feb 10, 9.30 to 4pm). Visitor centre and tearoom closed on Christmas Day and Boxing Day.
Public transport: Phone Traveline East Anglia on 0871 200 22 33.
Habitat: Freshwater reedbed, brackish and fresh water lagoons, extensive salt marsh, dunes, sandy beach with associated exposed peat beds.
Key birds: Diverse range of breeding reedbed and wetland birds with good numbers of passage waders during late summer/autumn. *Spring/summer:* Breeding Avocet, Bearded Tit, Bittern, Marsh Harrier, Reed Sedge and Cetti's Warbler, Redshank, Ringed Plover and Common Tern. *Summer/autumn:* Passage waders including Knot, Wood and Green Sandpiper, Little Stint, Spotted Redshank, Curlew Sandpiper and many more. *Winter:* Brent Goose, Hen/Marsh Harrier roost, Snow Bunting. Offshore Common and Velvet Scoter, Long-tailed Duck, Great Northern and Red throated Divers.
Other notable flora and fauna: 25 species of butterfly, including all the common species plus Essex skipper and annual clouded yellow. 21 species of dragonfly, including small red-eyed damselfly. Good diversity of salt marsh plants including shrubby sea-blite *(suaeda vera)* and three species of sea lavender.
Contact: Centre Manager, Titchwell Marsh Reserve, King's Lynn, Norfolk, PE31 8BB. 01485 210 779.

10. WEETING HEATH

Norfolk Wildlife Trust.
Location: TL 756 881. Weeting Heath is signposted from the Weeting-Hockwold road, two miles W of

Weeting near to Brandon in Suffolk. Nature reserve can be reached via B1112 at Hockwold or B1106 at Weeting.
Access: Open daily from Apr-Sep. Cost: adults £2.50, children free. NWT members free. Disabled access to visitor centre and hides.
Facilities: Visitor centre open daily Apr-Aug, birdwatching hides, wildlife gift shop, refreshments, toilets, coach parking, car park, groups welcome (book first).
Public transport: Train services to Brandon and bus connections (limited) from Brandon High Street.
Habitat: Breckland, grass heath.
Key birds: Stone Curlew, migrant passerines, Wood Lark.
Contact: Bev Nichols, Norfolk Wildlife Trust, Bewick House, 22 Thorpe Road, Norwich NR1 1RY. 01603 625 540. e-mail: BevN@norfolkwildlifetrust.org.uk www.wildlifetrust.org.uk/Norfolk

11. WELNEY

The Wildfowl & Wetlands Trust.
Location: TL 546 944. Ten miles N of Ely, signposted from A10 and A1101.
Access: Open daily (10am-5pm) except Christmas Day. Free admission to WWT members, otherwise £5.95 (adult), £4.50 (senior), £2.95 (child). Wheelchair accessible. During wet winter, paths to remote hides may be flooded.
Facilities: Visitor centre (wheelchair-friendly), café open 9.30am-4.30pm) daily. Large, heated observatory, additional 6 hides. Free parking and coach parking. Provision for disabled visitors.
Public transport: Poor. Train to Littleport (6 miles away), but from there, taxi is only option or cycling — Welney is on the National Cycle route.
Habitat: 1,000 acres of washland reserve, spring damp meadows, winter wildfowl marsh (SPA, RAMSAR site, SSSI, SAC).
Key birds: Large numbers of wintering wildfowl are replaced by breeding waders, gulls, terns and warblers. *Winter:* Bewick and Whooper Swans, wintering wildfowl e.g. Wigeon. *Spring/summer:* Common Tern, Avocets, Lapwing, Black-Tailed Godwit, House Martin, occasional rarities.
Other notable flora and fauna: Key flora includes: purple loosestrife, meadow rue, mixed grasses. Dragonflies include emperor, scarce chaser, banded damselfly, small red-eyed damselfly. Approx. 400 species of moth including goat moth. Butterflies include brown argus.
Contact: Sarah Graves, Marketing and Learning Manager, WWT, Hundred Foot Bank, Welney, Nr Wisbech, PE14 9TN. 01353 860 711. www.wwt.org.uk e-mail: info.welney@wwt.org.uk

---

For a comprehensive survey of bird reserves in the county, see the highly acclaimed *Best Birdwatching Sites in Norfolk* (2nd edition) book from Buckingham Press. See page 349 for details.

Northamptonshire

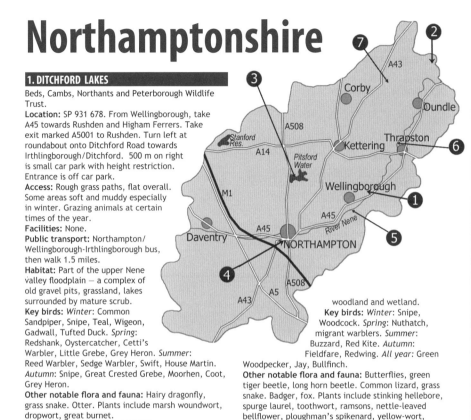

1. DITCHFORD LAKES

Beds, Cambs, Northants and Peterborough Wildlife Trust.
Location: SP 931 678. From Wellingborough, take A45 towards Rushden and Higham Ferrers. Take exit marked A5001 to Rushden. Turn left at roundabout onto Ditchford Road towards Irthlingborough/Ditchford. 500 m on right is small car park with height restriction. Entrance is off car park.
Access: Rough grass paths, flat overall. Some areas soft and muddy especially in winter. Grazing animals at certain times of the year.
Facilities: None.
Public transport: Northampton/ Wellingborough-Irthlingborough bus, then walk 1.5 miles.
Habitat: Part of the upper Nene valley floodplain — a complex of old gravel pits, grassland, lakes surrounded by mature scrub.
Key birds: *Winter*: Common Sandpiper, Snipe, Teal, Wigeon, Gadwall, Tufted Duck. *Spring*: Redshank, Oystercatcher, Cetti's Warbler, Little Grebe, Grey Heron. *Summer*: Reed Warbler, Sedge Warbler, Swift, House Martin. *Autumn*: Snipe, Great Crested Grebe, Moorhen, Coot, Grey Heron.
Other notable flora and fauna: Hairy dragonfly, grass snake. Otter. Plants include marsh woundwort, dropwort, great burnet.
Contact: Trust HQ, 01954 713 500
e-mail:cambridgeshire@wildlifebcnp.org
www.wildlifebcnp.org

2. OLD SULEHAY

Beds, Cambs, Northants and Peterborough Wildlife Trust.
Location: TL 060 985 Stamford seven miles. From A1 take exit to Wansford. In Wansford take minor road past church towards Fotheringhay, Nassington and Yarwell. After one mile turn right at crossroads in Yarwell onto Sulehay Road. From here access can be gained to nature reserve by various public rights of way. Limited parking in lay-bys along Sulehay Road.
Access: Main ride is surfaced in woodland although other paths can get muddy. Quarry has uneven paths and steep slopes. Grazing animals at certain times of the year
Facilities: Ring Haw section has surfaced track and grassed paths.
Public transport: Bus Oundle to Peterborough stops at Yarwell (Stagecoach).
Habitat: Mosaic of limestone quarries, grassland,

woodland and wetland.
Key birds: *Winter*: Snipe, Woodcock. *Spring*: Nuthatch, migrant warblers. *Summer*: Buzzard, Red Kite. *Autumn*: Fieldfare, Redwing. *All year*: Green Woodpecker, Jay, Bullfinch.
Other notable flora and fauna: Butterflies, green tiger beetle, long horn beetle. Common lizard, grass snake. Badger, fox. Plants include stinking hellebore, spurge laurel, toothwort, ramsons, nettle-leaved bellflower, ploughman's spikenard, yellow-wort, clustered bellflower, common spotted-orchid, woodland and limestone grassland fungi.
Contact: Trust HQ, 01954 713 500;
www.wildlifebcnp.org
e-mail:cambridgeshire@wildlifebcnp.org

3. PITSFORD RESERVOIR

Beds, Cambs, Northants and Peterborough Wildlife Trust.
Location: SP 787 702. Five miles N of Northampton. On A43 take turn to Holcot and Brixworth. On A508 take turn to Brixworth and Holcot.
Access: Lodge open mid-Mar to mid-Nov from 8am-dusk. Winter opening times variable, check in advance. Permits for reserve available from Lodge on daily or annual basis. Reserve open to permit holders 365 days a year. No dogs. Disabled access from Lodge to first hide.
Facilities: Toilets available in Lodge, 15 miles of paths, nine bird hides, car parking.
Public transport: None.
Habitat: Open water (up to 120 ha), marginal vegetation and reed grasses, wet woodland, grassland

and mixed woodland (40 ha).
Key birds: Typically 165-170 species per year with a total list of 250 species. *Summer*: Breeding warblers, terns, grebes, herons. *Autumn*: Waders if water levels suitable. *Winter*: Up to 10,000 wildfowl, feeding station with Tree Sparrow and occasional Corn Bunting.
Other notable flora and fauna: 31 butterfly species, 384 macro moths, 20 dragonfly species (including damselflies) , 377 species of flora and 105 bryophytes, 404 fungi species.
Contact: Dave Francis, Pitsford Water Lodge, Brixworth Road, Holcot, Northampton, NN6 9SJ. 01604 780 148. e-mail: dave.francis@wildlifebcnp.org

4. STORTON'S PITS LOCAL NATURE RESERVE

Beds, Cambs, Northants and Peterborough Wildlife Trust.
Location: SP 732 600. In Northampton. From junction of A45 with A43 west of town centre take A45 north to first roundabout and turn right. At next roundabout turn right and immediately left into Fisherman's car park. The two sites are either side of the track.
Access: Flat overall. Section of surfaced path to viewing platform, other paths soft and uneven in places with many steps on peninsula. The two reserves are adjoining.
Facilities: Viewing platform, paths, some surfaced.
Public transport: Train to Northampton then walk 1 mile or bus to St Giles and get off at Sixfields roundabout.
Habitat: One of a number of old gravel pits along the Nene valley.
Key birds: *Winter*: Water Rail, Snipe, Teal, Tufted Duck, Starling. *Spring*: Cuckoo, Green Woodpecker, Reed Bunting, Bullfinch, tits, Whitethroat, Blackcap. *Summer*: Reed Warbler, Sedge Warbler, Common Tern, Swift, House Martin. *Autumn*: Snipe, Great Crested Grebe, Moorhen, Coot, Grey Heron.
Other notable flora and fauna: Holly blue and green-veined white butterflies, water beetles. Grass snake. Bats. Cuckooflower, reed sweet-grass, marsh woundwort, purple loosestrife, water mint.
Contact: Trust HQ, 01954 713 500
e-mail:cambridgeshire@wildlifebcnp.org
www.wildlifebcnp.org

5. SUMMER LEYS LOCAL NATURE RESERVE

Northamptonshire County Council.
Location: SP 886 634. Three miles from Wellingborough, accessible from A45 and A509, situated on Great Doddington to Wollaston Road.
Access: Open 24 hours a day, 365 days a year, no permits required. Dogs welcome but must be kept on leads at all times. 40 space car park, small tarmaced circular route suitable for wheelchairs.
Facilities: Three hides, one feeding station. No toilets, nearest are at Irchester Country Park on A509 towards Wellingborough.
Public transport: Nearest main station is Wellingborough. No direct bus service, though buses

run regularly to Great Doddington and Wollaston, both about a mile away. Tel: 01604 670 060 (24 hrs) for copies of timetables.
Habitat: Scrape, two ponds, lake, scrub, grassland, hedgerow.
Key birds: Hobby, Lapwing, Golden Plover, Ruff, Gadwall, Garganey, Pintail, Shelduck, Shoveler, Little Ringed Plover, Tree Sparrow, Redshank, Green Sandpiper, Oystercatcher, Black-headed Gull colony, terns.
Contact: Chris Haines, Countryside Service, Northamptonshire Council, PO Box 163, County Hall, Northampton, NN1 1AX. 01604 237 227.
e-mail: countryside@northamptonshire.gov.uk

6. THRAPSTON GRAVEL PITS & TITCHMARSH LOCAL NATURE RESERVE

Beds, Cambs, Northants and Peterborough Wildlife Trust/Natural England.
Location: TL 008 804. Seven miles E of Kettering. From A14 take A605 N. For Titchmarsh turn L at Thorpe Waterville, continue towards Aldwincle. Take first L after church and continue to small car park on L. Take footpath to reserve.
Access: As well as the Aldwincle access point, there is a public footpath from layby on A605 N of Thrapston.
Facilities: Six hides.
Public transport: Bus service to Thrapston.
Habitat: Alder/birch/willow wood; old duck decoy, series of water-filled gravel pits.
Key birds: *Summer*: Breeding Grey Heron (no access to Heronry), Common Tern, Little Ringed Plover; warblers. Migrants, inc. Red-necked and Slavonian Grebes, Bittern and Marsh Harrier recorded. *Winter*: Good range of wildfowl inc Goosander and gulls.
Contact: Northants Wildlife Trust, Ling House, Billing Lings, Northampton, NN3 8BE. 01604 405 285; Fax 01604 784 835. www.wildlifebcnp.org
e-mail:northamptonshire@wildlifebcnp.org

7. TOP LODGE, FINESHADE WOOD

Forestry Commission
Location: SP 978 983. Off the A43 between Stamford and Corby. Follow brown tourist signs to Top Lodge Fineshade Woods.
Access: Visitor Centre (10am - 5pm), Car parking (7am - 7pm) always open except Christmas Day. Caravan Club site open Mar-Nov — please see CC website for more details. Visitor Centre is fully accessible — Smelter's Walk is an all-ability trail leading to the Wildlife hide.
Facilities: Visitor centre, toilets, Top Lodge Café, RSPB shop, with live footage of Red Kite nests in season. Guided walks and events throughout the year. Wildlife hide in wood. Three waymarked walking trails (one is for all abilities, two are surfaced), 1 horse trail, 1 family cycle trail, dedicated coach and horse box parking.
Public transport: None.
Habitat: Ancient woodland, coniferous woodland, beech woodland, open areas, small pond.

Key birds: Centre of Northants' Red Kite reintroduction scheme. A wide range of birds of mixed woodlands. *All year*: Red Kite, Great Spotted Woodpecker, Goshawk, Nuthatch, Crossbill, Marsh Tit, Willow Tit. *Summer*: Turtle Dove, warblers. *Winter*: Hawfinch.
Other notable flora and fauna: Adder, grass snake, slow worm, common lizard. Fallow deer, badger.

Orchids including greater butterfly, early purple and common spotted, other flora of ancient woodland.
Contact: Sarah Walker, Visitor and Community Services Manager, Forestry Commission Northants, Top Lodge, Fineshade, Nr. Corby, Northamptonshire NN17 3BB. 01780 444 920.
e-mail: sarah.walker@forestry.gsi.gov.uk
www.forestry.gov.uk/toplodge

Northumberland

1. ARNOLD MEMORIAL, CRASTER

Northumberland Wildlife Trust.
Location: NU255197. Lies NE of Alnwick and SW of Craster village.
Access: Public footpath from car park in disused quarry.
Facilities: Information centre (not NWT) open in summer. Interpretation boards.Toilets (incl disabled) and picnic site in quarry car park. Easy going access along path through site. Coach parking in adjacent public car park.
Public transport: Arriva Northumberland nos. 401, 500, 501.
Habitat: Semi-natural woodland and scrub near coast.
Key birds: Good site for migrant passerines to rest and feed. Interesting visitors can inc. Bluethroat, Red-breasted Flycatcher, Barred and Icterine Warblers, Wryneck; moulting site for Lesser Redpoll. Breeding warblers in summer.
Other notable flora and fauna: Spring flora including primrose and non-native periwinkle.
Contact: Northumberland Wildlife Trust, The Garden House, St Nicholas Park, Jubilee Road, Newcastle upon Tyne NE3 3XT. 01912 846 884;
e-mail: mail@northwt.org.uk www.nwt.org.uk

2. DRURIDGE POOLS - CRESSWELL POND

Northumberland Wildlife Trust.
Location: Two sites lying on coast between Newbiggin and Amble, off A1068. 1. Druridge Pools NZ 272 965. 2. Cresswell Pond NZ 283 945. Half mile N of Cresswell.
Access: Day permits for both reserves. Wheelchair users can view northern part of Cresswell Pond from public footpath or roadside.
Facilities: 1. Three hides. 2. Hide.
Public transport: None.
Habitat: 1. Deep lake and wet meadows with pools behind dunes. 2. Shallow brackish lagoon behind dunes fringed by saltmarsh and reedbed, some mudflats.
Key birds: 1. Especially good in spring. Winter and breeding wildfowl; passage and breeding waders. 2. Good for waders, esp. on passage.
Contact: Jim Martin, Hauxley Nature Reserve,

Low Hauxley, Amble, Morpeth, Northumberland. 01665 711 578.

3. EAST CHEVINGTON

Northumberland Wildlife Trust.
Location: NZ 265 985. Overlooking Druridge Bay, off A 1068 between Hauxley and Cresswell.
Access: Main access from overlow car park at Druridge Bay Country Park (signed from main road).
Facilities: Four public hides, café, toilets and information at Country Park. ID boards for coastal plants.
Public transport: Arriva 420 and 423 bus services.
Habitat: Ponds and reedbeds created from former open cast coal

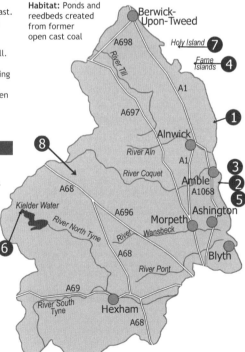

mine. Areas of scrub and grassland.
Key birds: Large numbers of wildfowl, including Greylag and Pinkfooted Geese in winter. Breeding Sky Lark, Stonechat, Reed Bunting, plus Reed, Sedge and Grasshopper Warblers. Capable of attracting rarities at any time of year.
Other notable flora and fauna: Coastal wildflowers.
Contact: Trust HQ. 01912 846 884; www.nwt.org.uk e-mail: mail@northwt.org.uk

4. FARNE ISLANDS

The National Trust.
Location: NU 230 370. Access by boat from Seahouses Harbour. Access from A1.
Access: Apr, Aug-Sept: Inner Farne and Staple 10.30am-6pm (majority of boats land at Inner Farne when conditions are calm). May-Jul: Staple Island 10.30am-1.30pm, Inner Farne: 1.30pm-5pm. Disabled access possible on Inner Farne, telephone Property Manager for details. Dogs allowed on boats but not on islands.
Facilities: Toilets on Inner Farne.
Public transport: Nearest rail stations at Alnmouth and Berwick. Hourly Travelsure buses between Budle and Beadnell Bays (Mon-Sat). Call 01665 720 955.
Habitat: Maritime islands – between 15-28 depending on state of tide.
Key birds: 18 species of seabirds/waders, four species of tern (including Roseate), 55,000-plus pairs of Puffin, 1,200 Eider, Rock Pipit, Pied Wagtail etc.
Contact: John Walton, 8 St Aidans, Seahouses, Northumberland NE68 7SR. 01665 720 651.

5. HAUXLEY

Northumberland Wildlife Trust
Location: NU 285 023. South of Amble.
Access: Day permit required. Access through High Hauxley village. Site is signposted off A1068.
Facilities: Reception hide open daily from 10am-5pm (summer) or 10am-3pm (winter) and five public hides. Toilets and information.
Public transport: Arriva 420 and 423 bus services.
Habitat: Ponds created from former opencast coal mine. Areas of woodland and grassland.
Key birds: Large numbers of wildfowl use the site in winter, waders use the site at high tide. Roseate Terns sometimes join commoner species in late summer. Waders and migrants on passage. *Winter:* Bewick's Swan, Shoveler, Lapwing and Purple Sandpiper.
Other notable flora and fauna: A variety of invertebrates, including butterflies, dragonflies and amphibians such as great crested newt.
Contact: Trust HQ. 01912 846 884;
e-mail: mail@northwt.org.uk www.nwt.org.uk

6. KIELDER FOREST

Forestry Commission
Location: NY 632 934. Kielder Castle is situated at N end of Kielder Water, NW of Bellingham.
Access: Forest open all year. Toll charge on 12 mile

forest drive and car park charge applies. Visitor centre has limited opening in winter.
Facilities: Visitor centre, exhibition, toilets, shop, access for disabled, licensed café. Local facilities include youth hostel, camp site, pub and garage.
Public transport: Bus: 814, 815, 816 from Hexham and seasonal service 714 from Newcastle.
Habitat: Commercial woodland, mixed and broadleaved trees.
Key birds: *Spring/summer:* Goshawk, Chiffchaff, Willow Warbler, Redstart, Siskin. *Winter:* Crossbill. *Resident:* Jay, Dipper, Great Spotted Woodpecker, Tawny Owl, Song Thrush, Goldcrest.
Other notable flora and fauna: Impressive display of northern marsh orchids at entrance to Kielder Castle.
Contact: Forestry Commission, Eals Burn, Bellingham, Hexham, Northumberland, NE48 2HP. 01434 220 242. e-mail: richard.gilchrist@forestry.gsi.gov.uk

7. LINDISFARNE NATIONAL NATURE RESERVE

Natural England (Northumbria Team).
Location: NU 090 430. Island access lies two miles E of A1 at Beal, eight miles S of Berwick-on-Tweed.
Access: Causeway floods at high tide, so check when it is safe to cross. Some restricted access (bird refuges). Coach parking available on Holy Island.
Facilities: Toilets, visitor centre in village. Hide on island (new hide with disabled access at Fenham-le-Moor). Self-guided trail on island.
Public transport: Irregular bus service to Holy Island, mainly in summer. Main bus route follows mainland boundary of site north-south.
Habitat: Dunes, sand, mudflats and saltmarsh.
Key birds: *Passage and winter:* Wildfowl and waders, including pale-bellied Brent Goose, Long-tailed Duck and Whooper Swan. Rare migrants.
Other notable flora and fauna: Butterflies include dark green fritillary (July) and grayling (August). Guided walks advertised for 9 species of orchid including coralroot and Lindisfarne helleborine.
Contact: Phil Davey, Senior Reserve Manager, Beal Station, Berwick-on-Tweed, TD15 2PB. 01289 381 470.

8. WHITELEE MOOR

Northumberland Wildlife Trust
Location: NT 700 040. Reserve located at head of Redesdale, south of A68 Newcastle to Jedburgh road where it crosses Scottish Border at Carter Bar.
Access: There is parking at tourist car park at Carter Bar and on laybys on forest track at reservoir end. A public footpath leads along old track to Whitelee Limeworks and then southwards. This footpath extends to southern boundary of site and eastwards along it to link up with a bridleway from White Kielder Burn via Girdle Fell to Chattlehope Burn. Additionally there is access on foot via Forest Enterprise road near eastern corner of reserve. reserve is remote and wild, and weather can change quickly. Visitors should have hill-walking experience if attempting long walks.
Facilities: Car park and laybys.

NATURE RESERVES - ENGLAND

Habitat: Active blanket bog and heather heath.
Key birds: The River Rede and its tributaries add to the habitat diversity. Notable breeding birds include Merlin and Stonechat. Black Grouse, Sky Lark, Meadow Pipit, Dunlin, Curlew, Golden Plover, Grey Wagtail, Dipper and Ring Ouzel regularly visit the reserve.

Other notable flora and fauna: Otters often hunt along the Rede and a herd of feral goats may be seen.
Contact: Northumberland Wildlife Trust, The Garden House, St Nicholas Park, Jubilee Road, Newcastle upon Tyne NE3 3XT. 01912 846 884; e-mail: mail@northwt.org.uk www.nwt.org.uk

Nottinghamshire

1. ATTENBOROUGH NATURE RESERVE

Nottinghamshire Wildlife Trust.
Location: SK 523 343. On A6005, seven miles SW of Nottingham alongside River Trent. Signposted from main road.
Access: Open at all times. Dogs on leads (guide dogs only in visitor centre). Paths suitable for disabled access. Coaches welcome by prior appointment.
Facilities: Education and visitor centre with café and shop, all accessible to wheelchair users. Nature trail (leaflet from Notts WT), one hide.
Public transport: Railway station at Attenborough - reserve is five mins walk away, visitor centre a further 10 minutes. Rainbow 5 bus service between Nottingham Broadmarsh and Derby bus station runs regularly throughout day. Alight at Chilwell Retail Park and walk 500m along Barton Lane.
Habitat: Disused, flooded gravel workings with associated marginal and wetland vegetation.
Key birds: *Spring/summer*: Breeding Common Tern (40-plus pairs), Reed Warbler, Black Tern regular (bred once). *Winter*: Wildfowl (including Bittern), Grey Heron colony, adjacent Cormorant roost.
Other notable flora and fauna: Smooth newt, dragonflies including four-spotted chaser and migrant hawker.
Contact: Attenborough Nature Centre, Barton Lane, Attenborough, Nottingham NG9 6DY. 01159 721 777. e-mail: enquiries@attenboroughnaturecentre.co.uk www.attenboroughnaturecentre.co.uk

2. BESTHORPE

Nottinghamshire Wildlife Trust.
Location: SK 817 640 and SK813 646 (access points). Take A1133 N of Newark. Turn into Trent Lane S of Besthorpe village, reserve entrances second turn on L and R turn at end of lane (at River Trent).
Access: Open access to two hides (one with disabled access from car park at present). No access to SSSI meadows. Limited access to areas grazed with sheep. Dogs on leads.
Facilities: No toilets (pubs etc in Besthorpe village), two hides, paths, nature trail (northern part).
Public transport: Buses (numbers 22, 67, 68, 6, S7L) run by Marshalls, Lincs, Road Car and Travel Wright along A1133 to Besthorpe village (0.75 mile away). Tel: 0115 924 0000 or 01777 710 550 for information.
Habitat: Gravel pit with islands, SSSI neutral

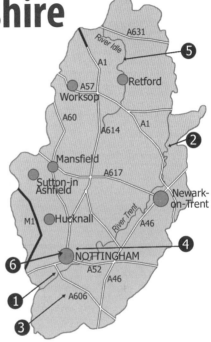

grasslands, hedges, reedbed, etc.
Key birds: *Spring/summer*: Breeding Grey Heron, Cormorant, Little Ringed Plover, Kingfisher, Grasshopper Warbler. *Winter*: Large numbers of ducks (Pochard, Tufted Duck, Pintail, Wigeon) and Peregrine.
Contact: Nottinghamshire Wildlife Trust, The Old Ragged School, Brook Street, Nottingham NG1 1EA. 01159 588 242. e-mail: info@nottswt.co.uk www.wildlifetrust.org.uk/nottinghamshire

3. BUNNY OLD WOOD WEST

Nottinghamshire Wildlife Trust.
Location: Limited parking off the A60 at SK 579 283. Please do not obstruct access. Further footpath access is at SK 584 293 off Wysall Lane.
Access: Open all year. No coach parking available.
Facilities: None
Public transport: None.

Habitat: Mixed woodland.
Key birds: *All year*: Usual woodland species, all three woodpeckers, Tawny and Little Owls. *Spring/summer*: Usual visitors, including Blackcap. Possible Brambling and Hawfinch.
Other notable flora and fauna: Bluebells, plus good selection of common woodland plants. Butterflies including white-letter hairstreak.
Contact: Trust HQ. 01159 588 242.
e-mail: info@nottswt.co.uk
www.wildlifetrust.org.uk/nottinghamshire

4. COLWICK COUNTRY PARK

Nottingham City Council.
Location: SK 610 395. Off A612 three miles E of Nottingham city centre.
Access: Open at all times, but no vehicle access after dusk or before 7am.
Facilities: Nature trails. Sightings log book in Fishing Lodge.
Public transport: Call park office for advice
Habitat: Lakes, pools, woodlands, grasslands, new plantations, River Trent.
Key birds: *Summer*: Warblers, Hobby, Common Tern (15+ pairs). *Winter*: Wildfowl and gulls. Passage migrants.
Other notable flora and fauna: Purple and white letter hairstreak butterflies.
Contact: Head Ranger, The Fishing Lodge, Colwick, Country Park, River Road, Colwick, Nottingham NG4 2DW. 01159 870 785.
www.colwick2000.freeserve.co.uk

5. IDLE VALLEY

Tarmac Ltd/ Hanson/ Nottinghamshire Wildlife Trust.
Location: SK 690 856. Formerly listed as Lound Gravel Pits. Two miles N of Retford off A638 adjacent to Sutton and Lound villages.
Access: Open at all times. Use public rights of way only (use OS Map Sheet No 120 - 1:50,000 Landranger Series).
Facilities: Two public viewing screens off Chainbridge Lane (overlooking Chainbridge NR Scrape) and two more overlooking Neatholme Scrape.
Public transport: Buses from Bawtry (Church Street), Retford bus station and Worksop (Hardy Street) on services 27/27A/83/83A/84 to Lound Village

crossroads (Chainbridge Lane).
Habitat: Working sand and gravel quarries, restored gravel workings, woodland, reedbeds, fishing ponds, river valley, in-filled and disused fly ash tanks, farmland, scrub, willow plantations, open water. Wildlife Trust has received nearly one million pounds (lottery grant) to transform site into a wetland reserve.
Key birds: 250 species recorded. *Summer*: Gulls, terns, wildfowl and waders. Passage waders, terns, passerines and raptors. *Winter*: Wildfowl, gulls, raptors. Rarities have inc. Ring-billed Gull, Caspian, White-winged Black, Gull-billed and Whiskered Terns, Manx Shearwater, Lesser Scaup, Green-winged and Blue-winged Teal, Richard's Pipit, Baird's, Pectoral and Buff-breasted Sandpipers, Long-billed Dowitcher, Killdeer, Spoonbill, Bluethroat, Nightingale, Snow Bunting, Shore Lark, Great Skua, Cattle Egret and Great White Egret.
Contact: Lound Bird Club, Gary Hobson (Secretary), 18 Barnes Avenue, Wrenthorpe, Wakefield WF1 2BH. 01924 384 419. e-mail: gary.lbc1@tiscali.co.uk
www.loundbirdclub.piczo.com

6. WOLLATON PARK

Wollaton Hall.
Location: Situated approx 5 miles W of Nottingham City Centre.
Access: Open all year from dawn-dusk.
Facilities: Pay/display car parks. Some restricted access (deer), leaflets.
Public transport: Trent Buses: no 22 and Nottingham City Transport: no's 31, and 28 running at about every 15 mins.
Habitat: Lake, small reedbed, woodland.
Key birds: *All year*: Main woodland species present, with good numbers of Nuthatch, Treecreeper and all three woodpeckers. *Summer*: Commoner warblers, incl Reed Warbler, all four hirundine species, Spotted Flycatcher. *Winter*: Pochard, Gadwall, Wigeon, Ruddy Duck, Goosander, occasional Smew and Goldeneye. Flocks of Siskin and Redpoll, often feeding by the lake, Redwing and occasional Fieldfare.
Contact: Wollaton Hall & Park, Wollaton, Nottingham, NG8 2AE. 01159 153 900.
e-mail: wollaton@ncmg.org.uk
www.wollatonhall.org.uk

Oxfordshire

1. ASTON ROWANT NATIONAL NATURE RESERVE

Natural England.
Location: SU 731 966. From the M40 Lewknor interchange at J6, travel NE for a short distance and turn R onto A40. After 1.5 miles at the top of the hill, turn R and R again into a narrow, metalled lane. Drive to car park, which is signposted from the A40.
Access: Open all year. Some wheelchair access, please contact site manager for more information.

Facilities: On-site parking, easy access path to viewpoint, seats, interpretation panels.
Public transport: Regular bus services to Stokenchurch, 2km S of reserve. Red Rose Travel bus goes to Aston Rowant village (call 01296 747 926).
Habitat: Chalk grassland, chalk scrub, beech woodland.
Key birds: *Spring/summer*: Blackcap, other warblers, Turtle Dove. Passage birds inc Ring Ouzel, Wheatear and Stonechat. *Winter*: Brambling, Siskin, winter

thrushes. *All year*: Red Kite, Buzzard, Sparrowhawk, Woodcock, Tawny Owl, Green and Great Spotted Woodpeckers, Sky Lark, Meadow Pipit, Marsh Tit.
Other notable flora and fauna: Rich chalk grassland flora, including Chiltern gentian clustered bellflower, frog, bee, pyramidal and fragrant orchids. Good range of less common butterflies, inc silver-spotted, dingy and grizzled skippers, chalkhill blue, green hairstreak and green fritillary.
Contact: Natural England (Chiltern and North Wessex Downs Team), Aston Rowant Reserve Office, Aston Hill, Lewknor, Watlington, Oxon OX49 5SG. 01844 351 833. www.naturalengland.org.uk

2. FOXHOLES

Berks, Bucks & Oxon Wildlife Trust.
Location: SP 254 206. Head N out of Burford on the A424 towards Stow-on-the-Wold. Take third turning on R. Head NE on unclassified road to Bruern for 3.5km. Just before reaching Bruern, turn L along track following Cocksmoor Copse. After 750m, park in car park on R just before some farm buildings.
Access: Open all year. Please keep to the paths.
Facilities: Car park, footpaths. Can be very muddy in winter.
Public transport: None.
Habitat: River, woodland, wet meadow.
Key birds: *Spring/summer*: Nightingale, Yellow Wagtail, possible Redstart, Wood Warbler, Spotted Flycatcher. *Winter*: Redwing, Fieldfare, Woodcock.
All year: Little Owl, all three woodpeckers, possible Hawfinch.
Other

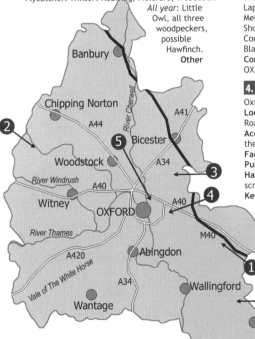

notable flora and fauna: Fantastic show of bluebells in May. Autumn fungi.
Contact: Trust HQ, 01865 775 476.
www.bbowt.org.uk

3. OTMOOR

RSPB (Central England Office).
Location: SP 570 126. Car park seven miles NE of Oxford city centre. From B4027, take turn to Horton-cum-Studley, then first L to Beckley. After 0.67 miles at the bottom of a short hill turn R (before the Abingdon Arms public house). After 200 yards, turn L into Otmoor Lane. Reserve car park is at the end of the lane (approx one mile).
Access: Open dawn-dusk. No permits or fees. No dogs allowed on the reserve visitor trail (except public rights of way). In wet conditions, the visitor route can be muddy and wellingtons are essential.
Facilities: Limited. Small car park with cycle racks, visitor trail (3 mile round trip) and two screened viewpoints. The reserve is not accessible by coach and is unsuitable for large groups.
Public transport: None.
Habitat: Wet grassland, reedbed and open water.
Key birds: *Summer*: Breeding birds include Cetti's and Grasshopper Warblers, Lapwing, Redshank, Curlew, Snipe, Yellow Wagtail, Shoveler, Gadwall, Pochard, Tufted Duck, Little and Great Crested Grebes. Hobby breeds locally. *Winter*: Wigeon, Teal, Shoveler, Pintail, Gadwall, Pochard, Tufted Duck, Lapwing, Golden Plover, Hen Harrier, Peregrine, Merlin. *Autumn and spring passage*: Marsh Harrier, Short-eared Owl, Greenshank, Green Sandpiper, Common Sandpiper, Spotted Redshank and occasional Black Tern.
Contact: RSPB, c/o Folly Farm, Common Road, Bexley OX3 9YR. 01865 351 163. www.rspb.org.uk

4. SHOTOVER COUNTRY PARK

Oxford City Council.
Location: SP 565 055. Approach from Wheatley or Old Road, Headington.
Access: Open all year, best early morning or late in the evening.
Facilities: Car park, toilets, nature trails, booklets.
Public transport: None.
Habitat: Woodland, farmland, heathland, grassland, scrub.
Key birds: *Spring/summer*: Willow Warbler, Blackcap, Garden Warbler, Spotted Flycatcher, Whitethroat, Lesser Whitethroat, Pied Flycatcher, Redstart, Tree Pipit. *Autumn*: Crossbill, Redpoll, Siskin, thrushes. *All year*: Sparrowhawk, Jay, tits, finches, woodpeckers, Corn Bunting.
Contact: Oxford City Council, PO Box 10, Oxford, OX1 1EN. 01865 249 811.

5. SYDLINGS COPSE

Berks, Bucks & Oxon Wildlife Trust.
Location: SP 559 096. 3.5 miles north-east of Oxford. From Headington roundabout, take

NATURE RESERVES - ENGLAND

Bayswater Road north through Barton; turn left on B4027; after 500 m, park opposite Royal Oak Farm and tea room; take bridleway for 600m, passing two small woods; reserve on right 100m from bridleway. Parking on soft verge, 600m.
Access: Open daily.
Facilities: Public footpath. Public hide.
Public transport: Not known.
Habitat: Reedbed, fen, a stream, ancient woodland, heath, limestone grassland and sandy soil are all packed into the steep valley.
Key birds: Summer warblers, woodpeckers and occasional Stonechat.
Other notable flora and fauna: Mammals such as badgers, deer, foxes and bats. More than 400 species of chalk grassland, woodland and heath plants. Common lizard, grass snake, slow worm.
Contact: Trust HQ, 01865 77 5476.
www.bbowt.org.uk

6. WARBURG RESERVE

Berks, Bucks & Oxon Wildlife Trust.
Location: SU 720 879. Leave Henley-on-Thames NW

on A4130. Turn R at the end of the Fair Mile onto B480. L fork in Middle Assendon. After 1 mile, follow road round to R at grassy triangle, then on for 1 mile. Car park is on R.
Access: Open all year — visitor centre opens 9am-5pm. Please keep dogs on a lead. In some areas, only guide dogs allowed.
Facilities: Visitor Centre, toilets, car park, two hides, one with disabled access, nature trail, leaflets. Visitors with disabilities and groups should contact the warden before visits. Car park not suitable for coaches, only mini-buses.
Public transport: None.
Habitat: Scrub, mixed woodland, grassland, ponds.
Key birds: *Spring/summer*: Whitethroat, Lesser Whitethroat. *All year*: Sparrowhawk, Red Kite, Treecreeper, Nuthatch, Tawny Owl. *Winter*: Redpoll, Siskin, sometimes Crossbill, Woodcock.
Other notable flora and fauna: Good for orchids, butterflies and mammals (roe, fallow and muntjac deer).
Contact: Warburg Reserve, Bix Bottom, Henley-on-Thames, Oxfordshire, 01491 642 001.
e-mail: bbowtwarburg@cix.co.uk

Shropshire

1. BUSHMOOR COPPICE

Shropshire Wildlife Trust
Location: SO 430 880. Head S from Church Stretton and take first R off A49 signed Bushmoor.
Access: Park in Bushmoor village and follow track leading from right-angled bend. Follow green lane to gate and carry onto wood along field margin. Appox half mile from road.
Facilities: None.
Public transport: Buses stop at Bushmoor village.
Habitat: Small mixed woodland and scrub.
Key birds: *Spring/summer*: Migrant warblers and flycatchers, plus common woodland species.
Other notable flora and fauna: Golden saxifrage, bluebells and yellow archangel. Dormouse.
Contact: Shropshire Wildlife Trust, 193 Abbey Foregate, Shrewsbury, Shropshire SY2 6AH. 01743 284 280. e-mail: shropshirewt@cix.co.uk www. shropshirewildlifetrust.org.uk

2. CLUNTON COPPICE

Shropshire Wildlife Trust.
Location: SO 343 806. From Craven Arms, take B4368 to Clunton village, go straight over bridge and up the hill to small car park just before reserve sign.
Access: Open at all times. Access along road and public rights of way only.
Facilities: Limited parking in small quarry entrance on R, or opposite The Crown pub.
Public transport: Buses between Craven Arms and

Clun stop at Clunton. One mile walk to reserve is steep.
Habitat: Sessile oak coppice. Good for ferns, mosses and fungi.
Key birds: Buzzard and Raven regular. *Spring/summer*: Wide range of woodland birds, inc. Redstart,

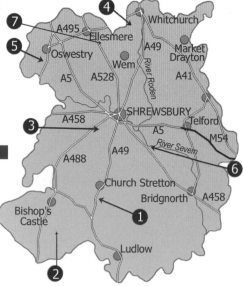

188

Wood Warbler and Pied Flycatcher, Woodcock.
Other notable flora and fauna: Dormouse, sessile oak woodland plants, bluebell, bilberry.
Contact: Trust HQ, 01743 284 280.
e-mail: shropshirewt@cix.co.uk www.
shropshirewildlifetrust.org.uk

3. EARL'S HILL

Shropshire Wildlife Trust
Location: SJ 409 048. Near Minsterley, SW of Shrewsbury. Turn off A488 at Pontesford along lane by Rea Valley Tractors. Car park 700 yards further on.
Access: Follow green route for easier walking. Purple route leads to summit. Car park at entrance.
Facilities: None.
Public transport: Buses to Bishops Castle and Minsterley stop at Pontesford.
Habitat: Steep-sided volcanic hill, scree slopes and crags, topped by Iron Age fort. Ancient woodland on eastern slopes.
Key birds: *Spring*: Migrants species such as Redstart, Pied Flycatcher and warblers. Dipper and Grey Wagtail on stream. Green Woodpecker common on open grassland.
Other notable flora and fauna: Dormouse. More than 30 species of butterfly recorded, plus bluebells and ash woodland plants. Yellow meadow ant.
Contact: Trust HQ, 01743 284 280.

4. FENN'S, WHIXALL AND BETTISFIELD MOSSES

Natural England (North Mercia Team).
Location: The reserve is located four miles SE of Whitchurch, ten miles SW of Wrexham. It is to the S of the A495 between Fenn's bank, Whixall and Bettisfield. There is roadside parking at entrances, car parks at Morris's Bridge, Roundthorn Bridge, World's End and a large car park at Manor House. Disabled access by prior arrangement along the railway line.
Access: Permit required except on Mosses Trail routes.
Facilities: There are panels at all of the main entrances to the site, and leaflets are available when permits are applied for. Three interlinking Mosses Trails explore the NNR and canal from Morris's and Roundthorn bridges.
Public transport: Bus passes nearby. Railway two miles away.
Habitat: 2,000 acres of raised peatland meres and mosses.
Key birds: *Spring/summer*: Nightjar, Hobby, Curlew, Tree Sparrow. *All year*: Sky Lark, Linnet. *Winter*: Short-eared Owl.
Other notable flora and fauna: Water vole, brown hare, polecat, adder, 2,000 species of moth, 27 species of butterfly, nationally important for dragonflies, inc white-faced darter.
Contact: Natural England, Attingham Park, Shrewsbury, Shropshire SY4 4TW. 01743 282 000; Fax 01743 709 303.
e-mail: north.mercia@natural-england.org.uk

5. LLYNCLYS COMMON

Shropshire Wildlife Trust.
Location: SJ 273 237. Five miles SW of Oswestry. Park in layby on A495 at SJ 277 242, opposite Dolgoch and walk up Turner's Lane or follow footpaths.
Access: Open at all times.
Facilities: None.
Public transport: Buses stop at Pont and Dolgoch.
Habitat: Old mixed limestone sward with some woodland and scrub, small pond.
Key birds: Sparrowhawk, Green Woodpecker, Goldcrest, large warbler population. Occasional Peregrine, Buzzard.
Other notable flora and fauna: Great crested, common and palmated newts in Oliver's Pond. More than 300 species of plant, including 12 species of orchid and limestone flowers. Bluebells and ramsons in woods. Good site for skippers and pearl-bordered fritillary butterflies, horned dung beetle and hairy-footed flower bee.
Contact: Trust HQ, 01743 284 280.
e-mail: shropshirewt@cix.co.uk www.
shropshirewildlifetrust.org.uk

6. VENUS POOL

Shropshire Ornithological Society.
Location: SJ 5478 0607. Site located 6 miles SE of Shrewsbury in angle formed by A458 Shrewsbury to Much Wenlock road and minor road leading S to Pitchford. Entrance is half a mile along minor road which leaves A458 half a mile (0.8 km) SE of Cross Houses.
Access: Public access to much of site, including four hides. Please keep to footpaths shown on notice boards at both entrances. Wheelchair-friendly paths to two public hides and Lena's Hide overlooking feeding station. Dogs not allowed anywhere.
Facilities: Car park with height restricting barrier. Five hides (one for SOS members only). Information boards.
Public transport: Shrewsbury-Bridgnorth buses stop at Cross Houses, which is one mile walk from Venus Pool, partly along busy main road.
Habitat: Site extends to almost 27 hectares (66 acres) and incorporates the pool itself, several islands and areas of open shoreline, fringing tall vegetation, marshy grassland, hedgerows, and areas of scrub and woodland. Species-rich meadows surround the pool, with an arable field growing bird-friendly crops.
Key birds: Venus Pool is noted for wintering wildfowl and passage waders, plus a sprinkling of county rarities, which have included Black-necked Grebe, Purple Heron, Spoonbill, Red Kite, Hen Harrier, Pectoral Sandpiper, Long-eared Owl, Black Redstart, and Wood Lark. *All year:* Common ducks and waterfowl, many resident passerines, including Tree Sparrow. *April-June:* Passage waders include Curlew, Ringed Plover, Dunlin, Redshank, Green and Common Sandpipers, and both godwits. Passage Black Tern. Breeding Oystercatcher, Little Ringed Plover, Lapwing, warblers, hirundines. *July-September:* Return wader passage from late July can include

Little Stint, Greenshank, Green, Wood, Curlew and Common Sandpipers, and possible unusual species such as Pectoral Sandpiper. *October-March:* Occasional wintering Bittern, Tundra and Whooper Swans (both scarce). Geese include occasional White-fronted. Ducks include Wigeon, Teal, Pintail, Shoveler, Pochard, Goosander (up to 50 in evening roosts) and occasional Goldeneye. Water Rail, vagrant raptors and owls, winter thrushes and large passerine flocks including Lesser Redpoll, Linnet, Tree Sparrow, Reed Bunting and Yellowhammer.
Contact: For full detail about Venus Pool, visit: www.shropshirebirds.com

7. WOOD LANE

Shropshire Wildlife Trust.
Location: SJ 421 331. Turn off A528 at Spurnhill, 1 mile SE of Ellesmere. Car park is three quarter miles down on R.

Access: Open at all times. Apply to Trust for permit to use hides. Reserve accessible to people of all abilities.
Facilities: Car parks clearly signed. Hides (access by permit).
Public transport: None.
Habitat: Gravel pit restored by Tudor Griffiths.
Key birds: *Summer:* 168 species recorded since 1999. Breeding Sand Martin, Lapwing, Little Ringed Plover and Tree Sparrow. Osprey platforms erected to tempt over-flying birds. Popular staging post for waders (inc. Redshank, Greenshank, Ruff, Dunlin, Little Stint, Green and Wood Sandpiper).
Winter: Large flocks of Lapwing, plus Curlew and common wildfowl.
Other notable flora and fauna: Hay meadow plants.
Contact: Trust HQ, 01743 284 280. www.shropshirewildlifetrust.org.uk

Somerset

1. BREAN DOWN

National Trust (North Somerset).
Location: ST 290 590. 182 map. Juts into Bristol Channel five miles N of Burnham on Sea. J22 of M5, head for Weston-super-Mare on A370 and then head for Brean at Lympsham.
Access: Open all year. Dogs on lead. Steep slope — not suitable for wheelchair-users.
Facilities: Toilets one mile before property, not NT.
Public transport: Call Tourist Information Centre for details 01934 888 800 (bus services differ in winter/summer).
Habitat: Limestone and neutral grassland, scrub and steep cliffs.
Key birds: *All year:* Peregrine, Raven. *Summer:* Blackcap, Garden Warbler, Whitethroat, Stonechat. *Winter:* Curlew, Shelduck, Dunlin on mudflat. Migrants.
Other notable flora and fauna: Chalkhill blue, marbled white and commoner butterflies. Extremely rare white rock rose in June. Somerset hair grass, dwarf sedge.
Contact: The National Trust, Barton Rocks, Barton, Winscombe, North Somerset BS25 1DU. 01934 844 518.

2. BRIDGWATER BAY NATIONAL NATURE RESERVE

Natural England (Dorset and Somerset Team)
Location: ST 270 470. Five kilometres N of Bridgwater and extends to Burnham-on-Sea. Take J23 or 24 off M5. Turn N off A39 at Cannington.

Access: Hides open every day except Christmas Day. Permits needed for Steart Island (by boat only). Dogs on leads to protect grazing animals/nesting birds. Disabled access to hides by arrangement, other areas accessible.
Facilities: Car park, interpretive panels and leaflet dispenser at Steart. Footpath approx 0.5 miles to tower and hides.
Public transport: Train and bus stations in Bridgwater. First Group buses on A39 stop at Stockland Bristol, 2km SW of Steart. www.firstgroup.com
Habitat: Estuary, intertidal mudflats, saltmarsh.
Key birds: *All*

year: Approx 190 species recorded on this Ramsar and SPA site. Wildfowl includes large population of Shelduck and nationally important numbers of Wigeon. Internationally important numbers of Whimbrel and Black-tailed Godwit.Resident Curlews and Oystercatchers joined by many other waders on passage. Good for birds of prey. *Spring/autumn*: Passage migrants, including occasiobnal vagrants.
Other notable flora and fauna: Saltmarsh flora. Rare invertebrates include great silver water beetle, aquatic snail and hairy dragonfly.
Contact: Natural England, 0300 060 2570. www.naturalengland.org.uk

3. CATCOTT LOWS

Somerset Wildlife Trust.
Location: ST 400 415. Approx one mile N of Catcott village (off A39 from J23 of M5).
Access: Open at all times.
Facilities: River Parrett Trail passes through reserve.
Public transport: None.
Habitat: Wet meadows with winter flooding and summer grazing.
Key birds: *Winter*: Wigeon, Teal, Pintail, Shoveler, Gadwall, Bewick's Swan, Peregrine. *Spring*: Little Egret, passage waders, breeding Lapwing, Snipe, Redshank, Yellow Wagtail.
Contact: David Reid, SWT, Fyne Court, Broomfield, Bridgwater, Somerset, TA5 2EQ. 01823 451 587.

4. CHEW VALLEY LAKE

Avon Wildlife Trust/Bristol Water Plc.
Location: ST 570 600. Reservoir (partly a Trust reserve) between Chew Stoke and West Harptree, crossed by A368 and B3114, nine miles S of Bristol.
Access: Permit for access to hides (five at Chew, two at Blagdon). Best roadside viewing from causeways at Herriott's Bridge (nature reserve) and Herons Green Bay. Day, half-year and year permits from Bristol Water, Recreation Department, Woodford Lodge, Chew Stoke, Bristol BS18 8SH. Tel/Fax 01275 332 339. Parking for coaches available.
Facilities: Hides.
Public transport: Traveline, 0870 6082 608.
Habitat: Reservoir.
Key birds: *Autumn/winter*: Concentrations of wildfowl (inc. Bewick's Swan, Goldeneye, Smew, Ruddy Duck), gull roost (inc. regular Mediterranean, occasional Ring-billed). Migrant waders and terns (inc. Black). Recent rarities inc. Blue-winged Teal, Spoonbill, Alpine Swift, Citrine Wagtail, Little Bunting, Ring-necked Duck, Kumlien's Gull.
Contact: Avon Wildlife Trust HQ or Bristol Water Recreation Dept, Woodford Lodge, Chew Stoke, Bristol, BS40 8XH. 01275 332 339.
e-mail: mail@avonwildlifetrust.org.uk
www.avonwildlifetrust.org.uk

5. GREYLAKE

RSPB (South West England Office).
Location: ST 399 346. Off A361 Taunton to Glastonbury road between Othery and Greinton.

Access: Open all year, dawn to dusk, free admission. No dogs, apart from guide-dogs. Wheelchair users can access a 700 metre-long boardwalk and viewing hide.
Facilities: Surfaced nature trail, interpretive signs. No toilets on site.
Public transport: Bus No 29 (First Group). Nearest stop is one mile along main road at Greinton phone box, but drivers may stop at reserve on request.
Habitat: A large wet grassland reserve bought by RSPB in 2003. Formerly arable farmland.
Key birds: *Spring/summer*: Breeding Snipe, Lapwing, Sky Lark, Yellow Wagtail, Kingfisher. Grey Heron, Little Egret. *Autumn*: Large Starling roost, Green Sandpiper, waders on passage. *Winter*: Wildfowl, waders, Peregrine.
Other notable flora and fauna: Roe deer, water vole, otter, dragonflies including four-spotted chaser.
Contact: RSPB, 01392 432 691.
www.rspb.org.uk/reserves

6. HAM WALL

RSPB (South West England Office).
Location: ST 449 397. W of Glastonbury. From A39 turn N in Ashcott and follow road onto the moor. After three miles pass Church Farm Horticultural building. Shortly after, at metal bridge, reserve is opposite side of road to Shapwick Heath NNR.
Access: Open all year. 2m height restriction on car park. Coach parking available at Peat Moors Centre, Shapwick Road. Dogs only on public footpaths and disused railway line. Wheelchair users can access viewing areas from main track. Other rougher tracks cover 3.8 miles.
Facilities: Two open-air viewing platforms, four roofed viewing screens. Part-time education officer available for school visits.
Public transport: By bus: Service 668 to Peat Moors Centre at Westhay village, approx I mile or St Mary's Road, Meare (approx 1.2 miles from reserve entrance).
Habitat: Recently-created 200-plus hectare wetland, including region's largest reedbed.
Key birds: *Spring/summer*: Cetti's Warbler, Water Rail. Bittern, warblers, Hobby, Barn Owl. *Autumn*: Migrant thrushes, Lesser Redpoll, Siskin, Kingfisher, Bearded Tit. *Winter*: Millions of Starlings roost, plus large flocks of ducks, Bittern, Little Egret, Peregrine, Merlin, Short-eared Owl.
Other notable flora and fauna: Otter, water vole, dragonflies, butterflies.
Contact: RSPB, 01392 432 691.

7. HORNER WOOD

National Trust
Location: SS 897 454. From Minehead, take A39 W to a minor road 0.8km E of Porlock signed to Horner. Park in village car park.
Access: Open all year. Car parking in Horner village, extensive footpath system.
Facilities: Tea-room and toilets. Walks leaflets available from Holnicote Estate office and Porlock visitor centre. Interpretation boards in car parks.

Public transport: Bus: Porlock.
Habitat: Oak woodland, moorland.
Key birds: *Spring/summer*: Wood Warbler, Pied Flycatcher, Redstart, Stonechat, Whinchat, Tree Pipit, Dartford Warbler possible. *All year*: Dipper, Grey Wagtail, woodpeckers, Buzzard, Sparrowhawk.
Other notable flora and fauna: Silver-washed fritillary in July.
Contact: National Trust, Holnicote Estate, Selworthy, Minehead, Somerset TA24 8TJ. 01643 862 452.
e-mail: holnicote@nationaltrust.org.uk
www.nationaltrust.org.uk

8. SHAPWICK HEATH NATIONAL NATURE RESERVE

Natural England (Dorset and Somerset Team)
Location: ST 426 415. Situated between Shapwick and Westhay, near Glastonbury. The nearest car park is 400 metres away at the Peat Moors Centre, south of Westhay.
Access: Open all year. Disabled access to displays, hides. No dogs.
Facilities: Network of paths, hides, elevated boardwalk. Toilets, leaflets and refreshments available at the Peat Moors Centre.
Public transport: None.
Habitat: Traditionally managed herb-rich grassland, ferny wet woodland, fen, scrub, ditches, open water, reedswamp and reedbed.
Key birds: *All year*: Ducks and waders. *Summer*: Bittern, Hobby, Cuckoo, Cetti's Warbler. *Winter*: Starling roost, large flocks of wildfowl.
Other notable flora and fauna: Wetland plants, otter and roe deer.
Contact: Senior Reserves Manager, Natural England, Riverside Chambers, Castle Street, Taunton, Somerset TA1 4AS. 0300 060 2570. www.naturalengland.org.uk

9. SHAPWICK MOOR

Hawk and Owl Trust
Location: ST417 398. On the Somerset Levels. Take A39 between Bridgwater and Glastonbury and turn N, signposted Shapwick, on to minor road, straight over crossroads and through Shapwick village, turn L at T-junction following signs for 'Peat Moors Centre'. The reserve is less than a mile north of village.
Access: Open all year. Access only along public footpaths and permissive path (closed on Christmas Day). Dogs must be kept on leads.
Facilities: Information panels. No toilets on site but at nearby Peat Moors Centre.

Public transport: Train to Bridgwater, then First Bus (01278 434 574) No 375 Bridgwater-Glastonbury, to Shapwick village. Sustrans National Route 3 passes through Shapwick village.
Habitat: A new wet grassland reserve being created from arable farmland as part of the Avalon Marshes project. Grazing pasture with rough grass edges, fen, open ditches (known as rhynes), pollard willows and hedges.
Key birds: *Spring/summer*: Hobby, Barn Owl, Reed Bunting, and Cetti's Warbler. Waders on passage. Sky Lark. Passerines such as Bullfinch and Yellowhammer. *Autumn/winter*: Flocks of finches, Snipe, Shoveler, Gadwall, Stonechat, Brambling. Peregrine and harriers may fly over. *All the year*: Buzzard, Kestrel, Sparrowhawk, Kingfisher, Lapwing, Grey Heron.
Other notable flora and fauna: Roe deer, brown hare, badger, otter and water vole.
Contact: Hawk and Owl Trust, PO Box 400, Taunton, Somerset TA4 2NR. 0844 984 2824; e-mail enquiries@hawkandowl.org www.hawkandowl.org

10. STEEP HOLM ISLAND

Kenneth Allsop Memorial Trust.
Location: ST 229 607. Small island in Severn River, five miles from Weston-super-Mare harbour.
Access: Scheduled service depending on tides, via Knightstone Pier ferry. Advance booking necessary to ensure a place, contact Mrs Joy Wilson (01934 522 125). No animals allowed. Not suitable for disabled.
Facilities: Visitor centre, toilets, trails, basic refreshments and sales counter, postal service. Guidebook available, indoor exhibition area.
Public transport: None.
Habitat: Limestone grassland, scrub, rare flora, small sycamore wood.
Key birds: Important breeding station for Greater and Lesser Black-backed and Herring Gulls, largest colony of Cormorants in England. On migration routes.
Other notable flora and fauna: Rare plants include Steep Holm peony, henbane and many herbal/medicinal species. Butterflies are often abundant, dragonflies in migratory season and moths, particularly lackey and brown-tail larva/caterpillars. Muntjac deer roam wild.
Contact: For direct bookings: Mrs Joy Wilson, 01934 522 125. For enquiries and general information: Mrs Joan Rendell, Stonedale, 11 Fairfield Close, Milton, Weston-super-Mare, BS22 8EA. 01934 632 307.
www.steepholm.org.uk

Staffordshire

1. BELVIDE RESERVOIR

British Waterways Board and West Midland Bird Club.
Location: SJ865102. Near Brewood, 7 miles NW of Wolverhampton.
Access: Access only by permit from the West Midland Bird Club.

Facilities: Hides.
Public transport: Bus to Kiddermore Green (eight minute walk to reserve). Traveline - 0870 6082608.
Habitat: Canal feeder reservoir with marshy margins and gravel islands.
Key birds: Important breeding, moulting and wintering ground for wildfowl), including Ruddy

NATURE RESERVES - ENGLAND

Duck, Goldeneye and Goosander), passage terns and waders. Night roost for gulls.
Contact: Barbara Oakley, 147 World's End Lane, Quinton, Birmingham B32 1JX;
e-mail: permit@westmidlandbirdclub.com
www.westmidlandbirdclub.com/belvide

2. BLITHFIELD RESERVOIR

South Staffs Waterworks Co.
Location: SK 058 237. View from causeway on B5013 (Rugeley/Uttoxeter).
Access: Access to reservoir and hides by permit from West Midland Bird Club.
Facilities: None.
Public transport: None.
Habitat: Large reservoir.
Key birds: *Winter*: Good populations of wildfowl (inc. Bewick's Swan, Goosander, Goldeneye, Ruddy Duck), large gull roost (can inc. Glaucous, Iceland). Passage terns (Common, Arctic, Black) and waders, esp. in autumn (Little Stint, Curlew Sandpiper, Spotted Redshank regular).
Contact: Permit sec Barbara Oakley, 147 World's End Lane, Quinton, Birmingham B32 1JX;
e-mail: permit@westmidlandbirdclub.com
www.westmidlandbirdclub.com/belvide

3. BRANSTON WATER PARK

East Staffordshire Borough Council.
Location: SK 217 207. Follow brown tourist sign from A38 N. No access from A38 S — head to the Barton-under-Needwood exit and return N. The park is 0.5 miles S of A5121 Burton-upon-Trent exit.
Access: Open all year, flat, wheelchair-accessible stone path all round the lake.
Facilities: Disabled toilets, picnic area (some wheelchair accessible tables), modern children's play area.
Public transport: Contact ESBC Tourist information 01283 508 111.
Habitat: Reedbed, willow carr woodland, scrub, meadow area.
Key birds: *Spring/summer*: Reed Warbler, Cuckoo, Reed Bunting. Important roost for Swallow and Sand Martin. *Winter*: Waders, Little Ringed Plover occasionally, Pied Wagtail roost.
Other notable flora and fauna: Wide range of butterflies and dragonflies.
Contact: East Staffordshire Borough Council, Midland Grain Warehouse, Derby Street, Burton-on-Trent DE14 2JJ. 01283 508 657; Fax 01283 508 571.

4. CASTERN WOOD

Staffordshire Wildlife Trust.
Location: SK 119 537. E of Leek. Unclassified road SE of Wetton, seven miles NW of Ashbourne.
Access: Use parking area at end of minor road running due SE from Wetton.
Facilities: None.
Public transport: None.
Habitat: Limestone grassland and woodland, spoil

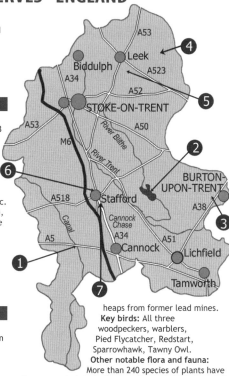

heaps from former lead mines.
Key birds: All three woodpeckers, warblers, Pied Flycatcher, Redstart, Sparrowhawk, Tawny Owl.
Other notable flora and fauna: More than 240 species of plants have been recorded, including cowslips and violets, several species of orchids, small scabious, ladies mantle and salad burnet, plus good numbers of woodland flowers and ferns. Five species of bats have been known to over-winter.
Contact: Trust HQ, 01889 880 100. e-mail: staffswt@cix.co.uk   www.staffs-wildlife.org.uk

5. COOMBES VALLEY

RSPB (Midlands Regional Office).
Location: SK 005 530. Four miles from Leek along A523 between Leek and Ashbourne and 0.5 miles down unclassified road — signposted.
Access: Open daily — no charge. Free parking. Coach groups welcome by prior arrangement. No dogs allowed. Most of the trails are unsuitable for disabled visitors.
Facilities: Visitor centre, toilets, two miles of nature trail, one hide.
Public transport: Contact local bus company First Potteries on 01782 207 999.
Habitat: Sessile oak woodland, unimproved pasture and meadow.
Key birds: *Spring*: Pied Flycatcher, Redstart, Wood Warbler. Jan-Mar: Displaying birds of prey.
Other notable flora and fauna: Bluebells, various butterflies.
Contact: Jarrod Sneyd, Six Oaks Farm, Bradnop, Leek ST13 7EU. 01538 384 017. www.rspb.org.uk

193

NATURE RESERVES - ENGLAND

6. DOXEY MARSHES

Staffordshire Wildlife Trust.
Location: SJ 903 250. In Stafford. Parking 0.25 miles off M6 J14/A513 Eccleshall Road or walk from town centre.
Access: Open at all times. Dogs on leads. Disabled access being improved. Coach and car parking off Wooton Drive.
Facilities: One hide, three viewing platforms, two are accessible to wheelchairs.
Public transport: Walk from town centre via Sainsbury's.
Habitat: Designated SSSI for wet meadow habitats. Marsh, pools, reedbeds, hedgerows, reed sweet-grass swamp.
Key birds: *Spring/summer*: Breeding Snipe, Lapwing, Redshank, Little Ringed Plover, Oystercatcher, warblers, buntings, Sky Lark, Water Rail. *Winter*: Snipe, wildfowl, thrushes, Short-eared Owl. Passage waders, vagrants.
Other notable flora and fauna: Otter, noctule bat, musk beetle.
Contact: Trust HQ, 01889 880 100. e-mail: staffswt@cix.co.uk www.staffs-wildlife.org.uk

7. RADFORD MEADOWS

Staffordshire Wildlife Trust.
Location: SJ 938 216. South of Radford Bridge on A34, Stafford and alongside Staffs & Worcs Canal.
Access: View reserve from canal towpath only (access from A34 between bridge and BMW garage or via Hazelstrine Lane (over canal bridge). On-site visits restricted to special events only. No formal carpark.
Facilities: Trust intends to erect information boards along towpath.
Public transport: Site is close to National Cycle Network routes (www.sustrans.co.uk).
Habitat: 104 acres of lowland wet grassland, forming part of River Penk floodplain.
Key birds: Largest heronry in county (more than 20 pairs of Grey Heron). Breeding Sky Lark, Lapwing, Snipe and Reed Bunting. *Winter*: Wildfowl, Kingfisher, Buzzard.
Other notable flora and fauna: Several veteran black poplar trees.
Contact: Staffordshire Wildlife Trust, 01889 880 100. e-mail: staffswt@cix.co.uk www.staffs-wildlife.org.uk Leaflet about birding the Trent Valley available on request.

Suffolk

1. BOYTON MARSHES

RSPB (Eastern England Office).
Location: TM 387 475. Approx. seven miles E of Woodbridge. Follow B1084 to village of Butley. Turn R and follow road through to Capel St. Andrew. Turn L and follow road towards Boyton village. Approximately 0.25 mile (400 m) before village, bear L down concrete track on sharp right-hand turn.
Access: Open at all times. Entrance free but donations welcome. Public footpath on site not suited to wheelchair use.
Facilities: Car park too small for coaches. No toilets or hides.
Public transport: None.
Habitat: 57 ha of coastal grazing marsh. Also saltmarsh.
Key birds: *Spring*: Breeding waders and wildfowl, such as Lapwing, Redshank, Shoveler and Gadwall. Spring migrants inc Yellow Wagtail and Whitethroat. Barn and Little Owls. *Autumn*: Wintering wildfowl such as Teal and Wigeon. Migrating waders inc Whimbrel, Black-tailed Godwit and Greenshank. *Winter*: Wintering wildfowl and wading birds, including Pintail, Curlew, Dunlin and Redshank. Fieldfare, Redwing and Mistle Thrush.
Other notable flora and fauna: Grassland butterflies such as skippers, wall and meadow browns and dragonflies.
Contact: RSPB Havergate,Unit 3, Richmond Old Dairy, Gedgrave,Woodbridge, Suffolk IP12 2BU. 01394 450 732. www.rspb.org.uk/reserves/

2. BRADFIELD WOODS NATIONAL NATURE RESERVE

Suffolk Wildlife Trust.
Location: TL 935 581. W of Stowmarket. From J46 on A14 take road through Beyton and Hessett towards Felsham. Turn R on Felsham road towards Cargate. Wood and parking is on L.
Access: Often wet and muddy, Wheelchair/pushchair accessible in parts, please phone 01449 737 996. Dogs on leads only.
Facilities: Visitor centre (open at weekends, no toilets), local pubs. Three coloured trails of different lengths, trail guide available.
Habitat: Broadleaved woodland.
Key birds: Good range of woodland birds and migrant warblers.
Other notable flora and fauna: 24 species of butterfly including white admiral and purple emperor. More than 370 varieties of plants. Mammals include stoat, yellow-necked mouse, dormouse, deer and badger.
Contact: Trust HQ 01473 890 089. e-mail: info@suffolkwildlife.cix.co.uk www.wildlifetrust.org.uk/suffolk

3. CASTLE MARSHES

Suffolk Wildlife Trust.
Location: TM 471 904. Head E on the A146 from

194

NATURE RESERVES - ENGLAND

Beccles to Lowestoft. Take the first L turn after Three Horseshoes pub. Continue on the minor road which bends round to the R. Carry straight on — the road bends to the R again. The car park is on the L just after White Gables house.
Access: Public right of way. Unsuitable for wheelchairs. Stiles where path leaves the reserve. Unmanned level crossing is gated.
Facilities: None.
Public transport: Bus: nearest bus route is on the A146 Lowestoft to Beccles road. Tel: 0845 958 3358. Train: Beccles and Oulton Broad South on the Ipswich to Lowestoft line.
Habitat: Grazing marshes, riverbank.
Key birds: *Spring/summer*: Marsh Harrier, Cetti's Warbler, occasional Grasshopper Warbler. *Winter*: Hen Harrier, wildfowl, Snipe.
Contact: Trust HQ, 01473 890 089.
e-mail: info@suffolkwildlife.cix.co.uk
www.wildlifetrust.org.uk/suffolk

4. DINGLE MARSHES

Suffolk Wildlife Trust/RSPB.
Location: TM 48 07 20. Eight miles from Saxmundham. Follow brown signs from A12 to Minsmere and continue to Dunwich. Forest car park (hide) TM 467 710. Beach car park TM 479 707. The reserve forms part of the Suffolk Coast NNR.
Access: Open at all times. Access via public rights of way and permissive path along beach. Dogs on lead please. Coaches can park on beach car park.
Facilities: Toilets at beach car park, Dunwich. Hide in Dunwich Forest overlooking reedbed, accessed via Forest car park. Circular trail waymarked from car park.
Public transport: Via Coastlink, Dial-a-ride service to Dingle (01728 833 546) links to buses and trains.
Habitat: Grazing marsh, reedbed, shingle beach and saline lagoons
Key birds: *All year*: In reedbed, Bittern, Marsh Harrier, Bearded Tit. *Winter*: Hen harrier, White-fronted Goose, Wigeon, Snipe, Teal on grazing marsh. *Summer*: Lapwing, Avocet, Snipe, Black-tailed Godwit, Hobby. Good for passage waders.
Other notable flora and fauna: The site is internationally important for starlet sea anemone — the rarest sea anemone in Britain. Otter and water vole.
Contact: Alan Miller, Suffolk Wildlife Trust,

Moonrakers, Back Road, Wenhaston, Halesworth, Suffolk IP16 4AP. www.suffolkwildlife.co.uk
e-mail: alan.miller@suffolkwildlifetrust.org

5. HAVERGATE ISLAND

RSPB (Eastern England Office).
Location: TM 425 496. Part of the Orfordness-Havergate Island NNR on the Alde/Ore estuary. Orford is 17km NE of Woodbridge, signposted off the A12.
Access: Open Apr-Aug (1st & 3rd weekends and every Thu), Sep-Mar (1st Sat every month). Book in advance through Minsmere RSPB visitor centre, tel 01728 648 281. Park in Orford at the large pay and display car park next to the quay.
Facilities: Toilets, picnic area, five birdwatching hides, viewing platform, visitor trail (approx 2km).
Public transport: Orford served by local buses (route 160). For timetable info call 0870 608 2608. Bus stop is 0.25 miles from quay. Boat trips from Orford (one mile)
Habitat: Shallow brackish water, lagoons with islands, saltmarsh, shingle beaches.
Key birds: *Summer*: Breeding gulls, terns, Avocet, Redshank and Oystercatcher. *Winter*: Wildfowl and waders.
Contact: RSPB Havergate Reserves, Unit 3, Richmond Old Dairy, Cedgrave, Woodbridge, Suffolk IP12 2BU. 01394 450 732.

6. HEN REEDBED

Suffolk Wildlife Trust.
Location: TM 470 770. Three miles from Southwold. Turn off A12 at Blythburgh and follow along A1095 for two miles where brown signs guide you to the car park. Not suitable for coaches. The reserve forms part of the Suffolk Coast NNR.

Access: Open at all times.
Facilities: Two hides and two viewing platforms on waymarked trails.
Public transport: Bus service between Halesworth and Southwold.
Habitat: Reedbed, grazing marsh, scrape and estuary.
Key birds: *Spring/summer*: Marsh Harrier, Bittern, Bearded Tit, Hobby, Lapwing, Snipe, Avocet, Black-tailed and Bar-tailed Godwits. *Passage*: Wood and Green Sandpipers. *Winter*: Large flocks of waders on estuary, inc Golden and Grey Plovers, Bar and Black-tailed Godwits, Avocet and Dunlin.
Other notable flora and fauna: Otters and water voles frequently seen. Hairy dragonfly, occasional Norfolk hawker. Brown argus butterfly colony close to car park.
Contact: Alan Miller, Suffolk Wildlife Trust, e-mail: alan.miller@suffolkwildlifetrust.org www.suffolkwildlife.co.uk

7. LACKFORD LAKES

Suffolk Wildlife Trust.
Location: TL 803 708. Via track off N side of A1101 (Bury St Edmunds to Mildenhall road), between Lackford and Flempton. Five miles from Bury.
Access: Visitor centre open winter (10am-4pm), summer (10am-5pm) Wed to Sun (closed Mon and Tues). Tea and coffee facilities, toilets. Visitor centre and 4 hides with wheelchair access.
Facilities: Visitor centre with viewing area upstairs. Tea and coffee facilities, toilets. Eight hides. Coaches should pre-book.
Public transport: Bus to Lackford village (Bury St Edmunds to Mildenhall service) — walk from church.
Habitat: Restored gravel pit with open water, lagoons, islands, willow scrub, reedbeds.
Key birds: *Winter*: Bittern, Water Rail, Bearded Tit. Large gull roost. Wide range of waders and wildfowl (inc. Goosander, Pochard, Tufted Duck, Shoveler). *Spring/autumn*: Migrants, inc. raptors. Breeding Shelduck, Little Ringed Plover and reedbed warblers.
Other notable flora and fauna: 17 species of dragonfly including hairy and emperor. Early marsh and southern orchid.
Contact: Lackford Lakes Visitor Centre, Lackford Lakes, Lackford, Bury St Edmunds, Suffolk IP28 6HX. 01284 728 706. www.suffolkwildlifetrust.org e-mail: lackford@suffolkwildlifetrust.org

8. LAKENHEATH FEN

RSPB (Eastern England Office).
Location: TL722 864. W of Thetford, straddling the Norfolk/Suffolk border. From A11, head N on B1112 to Lakenheath and then two miles further. Entrance is 200 metres after level crossing.
Access: Dawn to dusk, year round. Group bookings welcome. Visitor centre accessible to wheelchair users and a few points on the reserve.
Facilities: Visitor centre, toilets (inc disabled). Coach parking (must book). Hard and grass paths. Viewpoints. Picnic area with tables. Events programme.

Public transport: Limited weekend stops at Lakenheath train station.
Habitat: Reedbed, riverside pools, poplar woods.
Key birds: Principally a site for nesting migrants but ducks and some wild swans in winter.
Spring: Marsh Harrier, Crane. *Summer*: Bittern, Golden Oriole, Hobby, Reed and Sedge Warblers.
Autumn: Harriers, Bearded Tit.
Winter: Ducks, swans, Peregrine.
Other notable flora and fauna: More than 15 species of dragonflies and damselflies, inc hairy dragonfly and scarce chaser. Range of fenland plants e.g. water violet, common meadow rue and fen ragwort. Roe deer, otter and water vole.
Contact: Becky Pitman (Information Officer), Visitor Centre, RSPB Lakenheath Fen, Lakenheath, Norfolk IP27 9AD. 01842 863 400. e-mail: lakenheath@rspb.org.uk www.rspb.org.uk/reserves/

9. LANDGUARD BIRD OBSERVATORY

Landguard Conservation Trust
Location: TM 283 317. Road S of Felixstowe to Landguard Nature Reserve and Fort.
Access: Visiting by appointment.
Facilities: Migration watch point and ringing station.
Public transport: Call for advice.
Habitat: Close grazed turf, raised banks with holm oak, tamarisk, etc.
Key birds: Unusual species and common migrants.
Other notable flora and fauna: 18 species of dragonfly and 29 species of butterfly have been recorded on the site. Several small mammal species plus sightings of cetaceans and seals off-shore.
Contact: The Warden, Landguard Bird Observatory, View Point Road, Felixstowe, Suffolk IP11 3TW. 01394 673 782. e.mail: landguardbo@yahoo.co.uk www.lbo.co.uk

10. MINSMERE

RSPB (Eastern England Regional Office)
Location: TM 452 680. Six miles NE of Saxmundham. From A12 at Yoxford or Blythburgh. Follow brown tourist signs via Westleton village. Car park is two miles from the village.
Access: Open every day except Dec 25/26. Visitor centre open 9am-5pm (9am-4pm Nov-Jan). Shop and tea-room open from 10am. Free entry to visitor centre. Nature trails free to RSPB/Wildlife Explorer members, otherwise £5 adults, £1.50 children, £3 concession. Site partially accessible to wheelchairs.
Facilities: Car park, hides, toilets (inc disabled and nappy changing), visitor centre with RSPB shop and tearoom. Family activity packs. Volunteer guides. Guided walks and family events (see website for details). Educational programme. Coaches by appointment only (max two per day, not bank holidays).
Public transport: Train to Saxmundham or Darsham (6 miles) then Coastlink (book in advance on 01728 833 526).
Habitat: Coastal lagoons, 'the scrape', freshwater

NATURE RESERVES - ENGLAND

reedbed, grazing marsh, vegetated dunes, heathland, arable reversion and woodland.

Key birds: *All year:* Marsh Harrier, Bearded Tit, Bittern, Cetti's and Dartford Warblers, Little Egret, Green and Great Spotted Woodpeckers. *Summer:* Breeding Hobby, Avocet, Lapwing, Redshank, Common and Little Terns, Mediterranean Gull, Sand Martin, warblers, Nightingale, Nightjar, Wood Lark, Redstart (scarce). *Winter:* Wildfowl inc White-fronted Goose, Bewick's Swan, Smew, Hen Harrier (scarce), Water Pipit, Siskin.
Autumn/spring: Passage waders inc Black-tailed Godwit, Spotted Redshank, Ruff. Regular Wryneck, Red-backed Shrike, Yellow-browed Warbler.
Other notable flora and fauna: Red and muntjac deer, otter, water vole, badger. Dragonflies inc emperor, Norfolk hawker and small red-eyed damselfly. Butterflies inc purple and green hairstreaks, brown argus, silver-studded blue. Adder. Antlion. Marsh mallow, southern marsh orchid. Shingle flora.
Contact: RSPB Minsmere Nature Reserve, Westleton, Saxmundham, Suffolk, IP17 3BY. 01728 648 281.
e-mail: minsmere@rspb.org.uk
www.rspb.org.uk/minsmere

11. NORTH WARREN & ALDRINGHAM WALKS

RSPB (Eastern England Office).
Location: TM 468 575. Directly N of Aldeburgh on Suffolk coast. Use signposted main car park on beach.
Access: Open at all times. Please keep dogs under close control. Beach area suitable for disabled.
Facilities: Three nature trails, leaflet available from Minsmere RSPB. Toilets in Aldeburgh and Thorpeness. Three spaces for coaches at Thorpeness beach car park.
Public transport: Bus service to Aldeburgh. First Eastern Counties (08456 020 121). Nearest train station is Saxmundham.
Habitat: Grazing marsh, lowland heath, reedbed, woodland.
Key birds: *Winter:* White-fronted Goose, Tundra Bean Goose, Wigeon, Shoveler, Teal, Gadwall, Pintail, Snow Bunting. *Spring/summer:* Breeding Bittern, Marsh Harrier, Hobby, Nightjar, Wood Lark, Nightingale, Dartford Warbler.
Other notable flora and fauna: Hairy dragonfly, Norfolk hawker and red-eyed damselfly, green and purple hairstreak butterflies and southern marsh orchid.
Contact: Dave Thurlow, RSPB Minsmere, Westleton, Saxmundham, Suffolk IP17 3BY. 01728 648 701.
e-mail: dave.thurlow@rspb.org.uk

12. REDGRAVE AND LOPHAM FENS

Suffolk Wildlife Trust.
Location: TM 05 07 97. Five miles from Diss, signposted and easily accessed from A1066 and A143 roads.
Access: Open all year (10am - 5pm summer, 10am - 4pm winter), dogs strictly on short leads only. Visitor centre open all year at weekends and bank holidays:

call for details on 01379 688 333.
Circular trails can be muddy after rain (not wheelchair accessible).
Facilities: Visitor centre with café, gift shop, toilets, including disabled toilet, car park with coach space. Bike parking area, wheelchair access to visitor centre and viewing platform/short boardwalk. Regular events and activities — call for details or look on website.
Public transport: Buses and trains to Diss — Coaches to local villages of Redgrave and South Lopham from Diss. Simonds Coaches 01379 647 300 and Galloway Coaches 01449 766 323.
Habitat: Calcareous fen, wet acid heath, river corridor, scrub and woodland
Key birds: *All year:* Water Rail, Snipe, Teal, Shelduck, Gadwall, Woodcock, Sparrowhawk, Kestrel, Great Spotted and Green Woodpeckers, Tawny, Little and Barn Owls, Kingfisher, Reed Bunting, Bearded Tit, Willow and Marsh Tits, Linnet.
Summer: Reed, Sedge and Grasshopper Warblers, Willow Warbler, Whitethroat, Hobby plus large Swallow and Starling roosts.
Winter/ occasionals on passage: Marsh Harrier, Greenshank, Green Sandpiper, Shoveler, Pintail, Garganey, Jack Snipe, Bittern, Little Ringed Plover, Oystercatcher, Wheatear, Stonechat.
Other notable flora and fauna: Otter, water vole, roe, muntjac and Chinese water deer, stoat, pipistrelle and Natterer's bats. Great crested newts, grass snake, adder, slow worm, common lizard. More than 270 flowering plants inc water violet, saw sedge, black bog-rush and bladderwort. 19 species of dragonfly inc emperor, hairy dragonfly, black-tailed skimmer and emerald damselfly. Visit website for more species information.
Contact: Bev Blackburn (visitor centre co-ordinator), Redgrave and Lopham Fens, Low Common Road, South Lopham, Diss, Norfolk IP22 2HX. 01379 688 333.
e-mail: redgrave.centre@suffolkwildlifetrust.org
www.suffolkwildlife.co.uk

13. WESTLETON HEATH

Natural England (Suffolk team)
Location: Lies either side of Dunwich-Westleton minor road, E of A12.
Access: Open all year — please keep dogs on leads between March-August breeding season.
Facilities: Car park next to minor road.
Public transport: Train station in Darsham, 5km to W, served by One Railway. First Group bus services on A12 (also 5km distance).
Habitat: Lowland heath with heather-burning regime.
Key birds: Breeding Tree Pipit, Stonechat, Dartford Warbler and Nightjar on open heathland, Nightingale in woods.
Other notable flora and fauna: Silver-studded blue and white admiral butterflies, solitary bees and wasps, adder.
Contact: Natural England, 110 Northgate Street, Bury St Edmunds, Suffolk IP33 1HP. 01284 762 218.
E-mail: enquiries.east@naturalengland.org.uk

Surrey

1. BRENTMOOR HEATH LOCAL NATURE RESERVE

Surrey Wildlife Trust.
Location: SU 936 612. The reserve runs along the A322 Guildford to Bagshot road, at the intersection with the A319/B311 between Chobham and Camberley. Best access is by Brentmoor Road, which runs W from West End past Donkey Town.
Access: Open all year.
Facilities: Local buses, nos 34, 590 and 591 stop less than half a miles away.
Public transport: None.
Habitat: Heathland, woodland, grassland, ponds.
Key birds: *Spring/summer*: Stonechat, Nightjar, Hobby. *All year*: usual woodland birds.
Contact: Surrey Wildlife Trust, School Lane, Pirbright, Woking, Surrey, GU24 0JN. 01483 795 440.
e-mail: surreywt@cix.co.uk
www.surreywildlifetrust.org.uk

2. FARNHAM HEATH

RSPB (South East Region Office).
Location: SU 859 433. S of Farnham. Take the B3001 south from Farnham. Take the right hand fork, signposted Tilford, immediately past level crossing. Keep to that road. Just outside Tilford village it is signed to the Rural Life Centre. Follow those signs. Entrance is on the right after 0.5 mile.
Access: Reserve open at all times. Car park opens 9.30 am weekdays and 10.30 am weekends. Parking lay-bys on adjacent roads outside those hours. Rural Life Centre open Wed-Fri and Sundays all year. Open on Saturdays April-September. Tea room opens at 11 am.
Facilities: Large grass car park, shared with Rural Life Centre. No height barrier, but gates may be locked outside opening hours. No bike racks. Toilets (including disabled), picnic area,

refreshments. Group bookings accepted, guided walks available. Good for walking, pushchair friendly.
Public transport: Bus route is number 19 (Farnham to Hindhead service). Nearest stop is in Millbridge village, outside entrance to Pierrepont House. Reserve is a mile away, along Reeds Road (follow signs to the Rural Life Centre).
Habitat: Heathland and pine woodland.
Key birds: *Spring*: Blackcap, Tree Pipit, Woodcock, Wood Lark. *Summer*: Woodcock and Nightjar, woodland birds, including Stock Dove and Green and Great Spotted Woodpeckers. *Winter*: Crossbills in the pine woods, winter finches, including Brambling around the feeders, winter thrushes.
Other notable flora and fauna: Fungi - more than 150 species. Bats in summer.
Contact: Mike Coates, c/o The Rural Life Centre, Reeds Road, Tilford, Surrey GU10 2DL. 01252 795 571.

3. FRENSHAM COMMON & COUNTRY PARK

Waverley BC and National Trust.
Location: SU 855 405. Common lies on either side of A287 between Farnham and Hindhead.
Access: Open at all times. Car park (locked 9pm-9am). Keep to paths.
Facilities: Information rooms, toilets and refreshment kiosk at Great Pond.
Public transport: Call Trust for advice.
Habitat: Dry and humid heath, woodland, two large ponds, reedbeds.
Key birds: *Summer*: Dartford Warbler, Wood Lark, Hobby, Nightjar, Stonechat. *Winter*: Wildfowl (inc. occasional Smew), Bittern, Great Grey Shrike.
Other notable flora and fauna: Tiger beetle, purple hairstreak and silver-studded blue butterflies, sand lizard, smooth snake.
Contact: Steve Webster, Rangers Office, Bacon Lane, Churt, Surrey, GU10 2QB. 01252 792 416.

4. LIGHTWATER COUNTRY PARK

Surreyheath Council
Location: SU 921 622. From J3 of M3, take the A322 and follow brown Country Park signs. From the Guildford Road in Lightwater, turn into The Avenue. Entrance to the park is at the bottom of the road.
Access: Open all year, dawn-dusk.
Facilities: Car park, toilets, waymarked trails with leaflets available.
Public transport: Train: Bagshot two miles. Tel SW

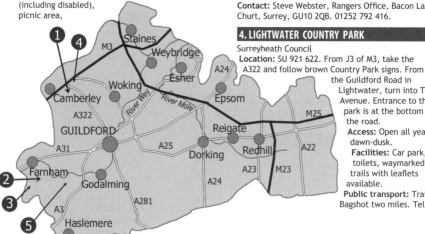

Trains 0845 6000 650. Arriva Bus: No 34. Tel: 01483 306 397.
Habitat: Heathland, woodland, three ponds and meadows.
Key birds: *All year:* Dartford Warbler on heath, all three woodpeckers, Goldcrest in woods, Grey Heron and Kingfisher on ponds. *Summer:* Nightjar, Willow and Garden Warblers. *Winter:* Fieldfare, Redwing, Siskin.
Other notable flora and fauna: Flora includes ox-eye daisies, knapweed and common spotted orchid in meadow, three heathers and two gorse species on heath. Good range of dragonflies and butterflies.
Contact: Surreyheath Ranger Service, Lightwater Country Park, The Avenue, Lightwater, Surrey GU18 5RG. 01276 479 582. www.surreyheath.gov.uk

5. THURSLEY COMMON

Natural England (Sussex & Surrey Team).
Location: SU 900 417. From Guildford, take A3 SW to B3001 (Elstead/Churt road).

Use the Moat car park, S of Elstead village.
Access: Open access. Parties must obtain prior permission.
Facilities: Boardwalk in wetter areas.
Public transport: None.
Habitat: Wet and dry heathland, woodland, bog.
Key birds: *Winter:* Hen Harrier and Great Grey Shrike. *Summer:* Hobby, Wood Lark, Dartford Warbler, Stonechat, Curlew, Snipe, Nightjar.
Other notable flora and fauna: Large populations of silver-studded blue, grayling and purple emperor butterflies can be seen here, alongside 26 recorded dragonfly species. Sandier sites on the reserve provide homes for many species of solitary bees and wasps. Damp areas support carnivorous plants such as sundew and bladderwort. Bog asphodel and marsh orchid may also be seen.
Contact: Simon Nobes, Natural England, The Barn, Heathhall Farm, Bowlhead Green, Godalming, Surrey GU8 6NW. 01483 307 703.
e-mail: enquiries.southeast@naturalengland.org.uk
www.naturalengland.org.uk

Sussex, East

1. CASTLE WATER, RYE HARBOUR

Sussex Wildlife Trust.
Location: TQ 942 189. Reserve is one mile SE of Rye along Harbour Road.
Access: Open at all times, entry is free. Information centre at Limekiln Cottage open every day 10am-4pm. The site is quite flat with some wheelchair access to all four hides, although there are stiles where the sheep are grazing the fields.
Facilities: Information centre, large car park at Rye Harbour with nearby toilets.
Habitat: Intertidal, saltmarsh, marsh, drainage ditches, shingle ridges, pits, sand, scrub, woodland.

Key birds: Many birds occur here in nationally important numbers, such as Shoveler and Sanderling in the winter and breeding Little Tern and Mediterranean Gull. Nesting Black-headed Gull colony, Common and Sandwich Terns and a good range of waders and ducks. Barn and Short-eared Owls.
Other notable flora and fauna: The saltmarsh supports such unusual plants as sea-heath and marsh mallow, and even highly specialised insects including the star-wort moth and saltmarsh bee.
Contact: Sussex Wildlife Trust, Woods Mill, Henfield, West Sussex BN5 9SD. 01273 492 630.
e-mail: enquiries@sussexwt.org.uk
www.sussexwt.org.uk

2. ERIDGE ROCKS RESERVE

Sussex Wildlife Trust.
Location: Located at Eridge Green 4 miles S of Tunbridge Wells. Car park at TQ 555 355. From A26, turn into Warren Farm Lane, next to a church and small printing works.
Access: Open all year.
Facilities: Car park.
Public transport: Bus stop on A26. Call Traveline on 0871 200 2223. Nearest railway station at Eridge (one mile).
Habitat: Sandstone rock outcrop, mixed woodland.
Key birds: *All year:* Range of common woodland

NATURE RESERVES - ENGLAND

birds. *Spring/summer:* Warblers.
Other notable flora and fauna: Mosses and liverworts on the rocks. Good for general woodland butterflies, inc white admiral.
Contact: Trust HQ, 01273 492 630.
e-mail: enquiries@sussexwt.org.uk
www.sussexwt.org.uk

3. FORE WOOD

RSPB (South East Region Office).
Location: TQ 758 123. From the A2100 (Battle/ Hastings) take lane to Crowhurst at Crowhurst Park Caravan Park. Park at Crowhurst village hall and walk up Forewood Lane for 500 yards. Look for the finger post on L and follow the public footpath across farmland to reserve entrance.
Access: Open all year. No disabled facilities. No dogs. No coaches.
Facilities: Two nature trails.
Public transport: Station at Crowhurst, about 0.5 mile walk. Charing Cross/Hastings line. No buses within one mile.
Habitat: Semi-natural ancient woodland.
Key birds: A wide range of woodland birds. *Spring:* Chiffchaff, Greater Spotted Woodpecker, Nuthatch, Treecreeper. *Summer:* Blackcap, Bullfinch, Mistle Thrush, Green Woodpecker. *Autumn:* Goldcrest, Jay, Marsh Tit. *Winter:* Fieldfare, Rook, Redwing.
Other notable flora and fauna: Rare ferns, bluebells, wood anemonies, purple orchid. Butterflies including silver-washed fritillary and white admiral.
Contact: Martin Allison, RSPB Broadwater Warren, Unit 10, Sham Farm Business Units, Eridge Green, Tunbridge Wells, Kent TN3 9JA.

4. LULLINGTON HEATH

Natural England (Sussex & Surrey Team).
Location: TQ 525 026. W of Eastbourne, between Jevington and Litlington, on northern edge of Friston Forest.
Access: Via footpaths and bridleways. Site open for access on foot as defined by CROW Act 2000.
Facilities: None. Nearest toilets/refreshmenst at pubs in Jevington, Litlington or Seven Sisters CP, 2km to S.
Public transport: Nearest bus stop is Seven Sisters Country Park. Phone Brighton & Hove services on 01273 886 200 or visit: www.buses.co.uk/bustimes/
Habitat: Grazed chalk downland and heath, with mixed scrub and gorse.
Key birds: *Summer:* Breeding Nightingale, Turtle Dove, Nightjar and diverse range of grassland/scrub-nesting species.Passage migrants include Wheatear, Redstart, Ring Ouzel. *Winter:* Raptors (inc. Hen Harrier), Woodcock.
Other notable flora and fauna: Bell heather, ling and gorse on chalk heath; orchid species in grassland.
Contact: Senior Reserve Manager, East Sussex NNRs, Natural England, Phoenix House, 33 North Street, Lewes, E Sussex BN7 2PH. 01273 476 595; Fax 01273 483 063; www.natural-england.org.uk
e-mail sussex.surrey@natural-england.org.uk

5. PEVENSEY LEVELS

Natural England (Sussex & Surrey Team).
Location: TQ 665 054. A small reserve of 12 fields, within the 3,500 ha SSSI/Ramsar site of Pevensey Levels. NE of Eastbourne. S of A259, one mile along minor road from Pevensey E towards Norman's Bay.
Access: Please view from road to avoid disturbance to summer nesting birds and sheltering flocks in winter. Access on foot allowed at Rockhouse Bank (TQ 675 057) — panoramic view of whole reserve.
Facilities: None. Nearest toilets at Star Inn (TQ 687 062) or petrol station (TQ 652 052).
Public transport: Nearest railway stations: Pevensey Bay or Cooden Beach. Eastbourne buses to Pevensey Bay — call 01323 416416.
Habitat: Freshwater grazing marsh with extensive ditch system, subject to flooding.
Key birds: *Summer:* Breeding Reed and Sedge Warblers, Yellow Wagtail, Snipe, Redshank, Lapwing. Raptors include Peregrine and Hobby. Passage migrants include Whimbrel, Curlew, Brent Geese. *Winter:* Flocks of wildfowl and waders, Short-eared Owl, Merlin and other raptors.
Other notable flora and fauna: Variable damselfly, many rare snails and other molluscs, the most important site in the UK for fen raft spider. Unusual wetland plants.
Contact: Site Manager, Natural England, 01273 476 595; e-mail sussex.surrey@natural-england.org.uk; www.natural-england.org.uk

6. RYE HARBOUR

Rye Harbour Local Nature Reserve Management Committee.
Location: TQ 941 188. One mile from Rye off A259 signed Rye Harbour. From J10 of M20 take A2070 until it joins A259.
Access: Open at all times by footpaths. Organised groups please book.
Facilities: Car park in Rye Harbour village. Information kiosk in car park. Shop, two pubs, toilets and disabled facilities near car park, four hides (wheelchair access), information centre open most days (10am-4pm) by volunteers.
Public transport: Train (08457 484 950), bus (0870 608 2608), tourist information (tel: 01797 226 696).
Habitat: Sea, sand, shingle, pits and grassland.
Key birds: *Spring:* Passage waders, especially roosting Whimbrel. *Summer:* Turtle Dove, terns (3 species), waders (7 species), gulls (6 species), Garganey, Shoveler, Cetti's Warbler, Bearded Tit. *Winter:* Wildfowl, Water Rail, Bittern, Smew.
Other notable flora and fauna: Good shingle flora including sea kale, sea pea, least lettuce and stinging hawksbeard. Excellent range of dragonflies including breeding red-veined darter and scarce emerald damselfly.
Contact: Barry Yates, (Manager), 2 Watch Cottages, Winchelsea, East Sussex, TN36 4LU. 01797 223 862.
e-mail: rhnr.office@eastsussex.gov.uk
www.wildrye.info
See also www.rxwildlife.org.uk for latest sightings

Sussex, West

1. ARUNDEL

The Wildfowl & Wetlands Trust.
Location: TQ 020 081. Clearly signposted from Arundel, just N of A27.
Access: Summer (9.30am-5.30pm) winter (9.30am-4.30pm). Closed Christmas Day. Approx 1.5 miles of level footpaths, suitable for wheelchairs. No dogs except guide dogs. Admission charges for non-WWT members.
Facilities: Visitor centre, restaurant, shop, hides, picnic area, seasonal nature trails. Eye of The Wind Wildlife Gallery. Corporate hire facilities.
Public transport: Arundel station, 15-20 minute walk. Tel: 01903 882 131.
Habitat: Lakes, wader scrapes, reedbed.
Key birds: *Summer*: Nesting Redshank, Lapwing, Oystercatcher, Common Tern, Sedge, Reed and Cetti's Warblers, Peregrine, Hobby. *Winter*: Teal, Wigeon, Reed Bunting, Water Rail, Cetti's Warbler and occasionally roosting Bewick's Swan.
Contact: James Sharpe, Mill Road, Arundel, West Sussex BN18 9PB. 01903 883 355.
e-mail: info.arundel@wwt.org.uk www.wwt.org.uk

2. PAGHAM HARBOUR

West Sussex County Council.
Location: SZ 857 966. Five miles S of Chichester on B2145 towards Selsey.
Access: Open at all times, dogs must be on leads, disabled trail with accessible hide. All groups and coach parties must book in advance.
Facilities: Visitor centre open at weekends (10am-4pm), toilets (including disabled), three hides, one nature trail.
Public transport: Bus stop by visitor centre.
Habitat: Intertidal saltmarsh, shingle beaches, lagoons and farmland.
Key birds: *Spring*: Passage migrants. *Autumn*: Passage waders, other migrants. *Winter*: Brent Goose, Slavonian Grebe, wildfowl. *All year*: Little Egret.
Other notable flora and fauna: Wide range of grasses, butterflies and dragonflies.
Contact: Sarah Patton, Pagham Harbour LNR, Selsey Road, Sidlesham, Chichester, West Sussex PO20 7NE. 01243 641 508. e-mail: pagham.nr@westsussex.gov.uk

3. PULBOROUGH BROOKS

RSPB (South East Region Office).
Location: TQ 054 170. Signposted on A283 between Pulborough (via A29) and Storrington (via A24). Two miles SE of Pulborough.

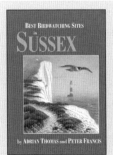

Best Birdwatching Sites *SUSSEX*

by Adrian Thomas and Peter Francis

For full details on 57 great Sussex birdwatching reserves, try our highly acclaimed guide. See what the reviewers say:

"First impression of this guide – brilliant. On closer inspection – brilliant! I cannot think of any way to improve upon this formula, content or presentation – it is the yardstick by which other guides must now be measured." Fatbirder.com

List price £14.50 (including P&P)

Contact: Buckingham Press Ltd, 55 Thorpe Park Road, Peterborough, PE3 6LJ. 01733 561739.
e-mail: admin@buckinghampress.com www.buckinghampress.co.uk

NATURE RESERVES - ENGLAND

Access: Open daily. Visitor centre open 9.30am-5pm (tea-room 4.30pm), closed Christmas Day and Boxing Day. Nature trail and hides (9am-9pm or sunset), closed Christmas Day. Admission fee for nature trail (free to RSPB members). No dogs.
All four hides accessible to wheelchair users, though strong helper is needed.
Facilities: Visitor centre (incl RSPB shop, tea room with terrace, displays, toilets). Nature trail, four hides and additional viewpoints. Large car park including coach area. Play and picnic areas. An electric buggy is available for free hire, for use on trail.
Public transport: Two miles from Pulborough train station. Connecting bus service regularly passes reserve entrance (not Sun). Compass Travel (01903 690 025). Cycle stands.
Habitat: Lowland wet grassland (wet meadows and ditches). Hedgerows and woodland.
Key birds: *Winter*: Wintering waterbirds, Bewick's Swan. *Spring*: Breeding wading birds and songbirds (incl Lapwing and Nightingale).
Summer: Butterflies and dragonflies, warblers.
Autumn: Passage wading birds, Redstart, Whinchat.
Contact: Pulborough Brooks Nature Reserve, Upperton's Barn, Wiggonholt, Pulborough, West Sussex RH20 2EL. 01798 875 851.
e-mail: pulborough.brooks@rspb.org.uk

4. THORNEY/PILSEY

RSPB (South East Region Office).
Location: SW of Chichester. Park in Emsworth and walk over sea walls to view both Thorney and Pilsey islands.
Access: No vehicle access to Thorney Island, viewing from footpaths only. Pilsey Island can also be viewed from coastal path (the Sussex Border Path) that runs around the Thorney Island MoD base. Long, exposed walk.
Facilities: Footpath.
Public transport: None.
Habitat: Intertidal sandflats and mudflats, fore dunes and yellow dunes, bare and vegetated shingle and saltmarsh.
Key birds: The reserve, together with the adjacent area of Pilsey Sand, forms one of the most important pre-roost and roost site for passage and wintering waders in the area.
Contact: Tim Callaway, RSPB Pulborough Brooks, Wiggonholt, Pulborough, West Sussex RH20 2EL. 01798 875 851.

5. WARNHAM LOCAL NATURE RESERVE

Horsham District Council.
Location: TQ 167 324. One mile from Horsham town centre, just off A24 'Robin Hood' roundabout on B2237.
Access: Open every day, all year, including bank holidays (10am-6pm or dusk if earlier). Day permits: Adults £1, children under 16 free. Annual permits also available.

No dogs or cycling allowed. Good wheelchair access over most of the Reserve.
Facilities: Visitor centre and café open every day except Christmas Day and Boxing Day (10am-5.30pm). Also new Stag Beetle Loggery.
Ample car park – coaches by request. Toilets (including disabled), two hides, reserve leaflets, millpond nature trail, bird feeding station, boardwalks, benches and hardstanding paths.
Public transport: From Horsham Railway Station it is a mile walk along Hurst Road, with a R turn onto Warnham Road. Buses from 'CarFax' in Horsham Centre stop within 150 yards of the reserve. Travel line, 0870 608 2608.
Habitat: 17 acre millpond, reedbeds, marsh, meadow and woodland (deciduous and coniferous).
Key birds: *Summer*: Breeding Common Tern, Kingfisher, woodpeckers, Mandarin Duck, Little Owl, Marsh Tit, Goldcrest, hirundines, Hobby, warblers. *Winter*: Cormorant, gulls, Little Grebe, Water Rail, Brambling, Siskin, Lesser Redpoll, thrushes and wildfowl. *Passage*: Waders, pipits, terns and Sand Martin.
Other notable flora and fauna: Extensive invertebrate interest, including 33 species of butterfly and 25 species of dragonfly. Mammals including harvest mouse, water vole and badger. More than 450 species of plant, including broad-leaved helleborine and common spotted orchid.
Contact: Sam Bayley, Countryside Warden, Leisure Services, Park House Lodge, North Street, Horsham, W Sussex, RH12 1RL. 01403 256 890.
e-mail: sam.bayley@horsham.gov.uk
www.horshamdistrictcountryside.org

6. WOODS MILL

Sussex Wildlife Trust.
Location: TQ 218 138. Located NW of Brighton, one mile S of Henfield on A2037.
Access: Open every day except Christmas week. All-weather surface nature trail suitable for wheelchairs. HQ of Sussex Wildlife Trust.
Facilities: Toilets (including disabled), nature trail, car parking and parking for two coaches.
Public transport: Bus route 100 stops outside. Compass Travel 01903 690 025.
Habitat: Wetland, woodland and meadow habitats.
Key birds: General woodland birds and Kingfisher all year. *Summer*: Warblers (Reed and Garden Warblers, Blackcap, Whitethroat, Lesser Whitethroat) and Nightingales.
Other notable flora and fauna: Dragon and damselflies including beautiful demoiselle, red and ruddy darter and the rare scarce chaser.
Wide range of water, woodland and meadow plants. Spring flowers include bluebells, wood anemones and common spotted orchids.
Contact: Woods Mill, 01273 492 630.
www.sussexwt.co.uk

NATURE RESERVES - ENGLAND

Tyne & Wear

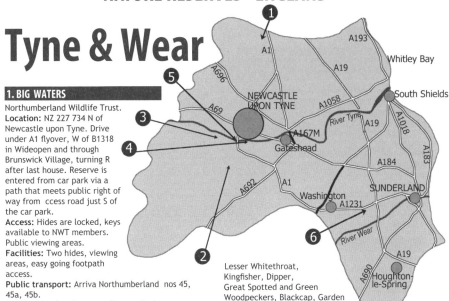

1. BIG WATERS

Northumberland Wildlife Trust.
Location: NZ 227 734 N of
Newcastle upon Tyne. Drive
under A1 flyover, W of B1318
in Wideopen and through
Brunswick Village, turning R
after last house. Reserve is
entered from car park via a
path that meets public right of
way from ccess road just S of
the car park.
Access: Hides are locked, keys
available to NWT members.
Public viewing areas.
Facilities: Two hides, viewing
areas, easy going footpath
access.
Public transport: Arriva Northumberland nos 45,
45a, 45b.
Habitat: Pond with surrounding reedbed.
Key birds: Wintering wildfowl including Teal, Tufted
Duck and Shoveler. Breeding species include Great
Crested and Little Grebe and Coot. Tree Sparrow,
Yellowhammer and Great Spotted Woodpecker use
feeding station all year.
Other notable flora and fauna: Otters are frequently
seen from the hide. The small pond on site is used by
dragonflies, while woodland edges and fields are used
by a variety of butterflies, including large skipper and
small copper.
Contact: Trust HQ, 01912 846 884; www.nwt.org.uk
e-mail: mail@northwt.org.uk

2. DERWENT WALK COUNTRY PARK & DERWENTHAUGH PARK

Gateshead Council.
Location: NZ 178 604. Along River Derwent, four
miles SW of Newcastle and Gateshead. Several car
parks along A694.
Access: Site open all times. Thornley visitor centre
open weekends and Bank Holidays (12-5pm). Keys
for hides available from Thornley Woodlands Centre.
Swalwell visitor centre open daily (9am-5pm).
Facilities: Toilets at Thornley and Swalwell visitor
centres. Hides at Far Pasture Ponds and Thornley
feeding station.
Public transport: 45, 46, 46A, 47/47A/47B buses
from Newcastle/Gateshead to Swalwell/Rowlands
Gill. Bus stop Thornley Woodlands Centre. (Regular
bus service from Newcastle).
Information from Nexus Travel Information, 0919 203
3333. www.nexus.org.uk
Habitat: Mixed woodland, river, ponds, meadows.
Key birds: *Summer:* Red Kite, Grasshopper Warbler,

Lesser Whitethroat,
Kingfisher, Dipper,
Great Spotted and Green
Woodpeckers, Blackcap, Garden
Warbler, Nuthatch. *Winter:* Teal,
Tufted Duck, Brambling, Marsh Tit,
Bullfinch, Great Spotted Woodpecker, Nuthatch,
Goosander, Kingfisher.
Contact: Trevor Weston, Thornley Woodlands Centre,
Rowlands Gill, Tyne & Wear NE39 1AU. 01207 545
212. e-mail: countryside@gateshead.gov.uk
www.gatesheadbirders.co.uk www.gateshead.gov.uk

3. RYTON WILLOWS

Gateshead Council.
Location: NZ 155 650. Five miles W of Newcastle.
Access along several tracks running N from Ryton.
Access: Open at all times.
Facilities: Nature trail and free leaflet.
Public transport: Regular service to Ryton from
Newcastle/Gateshead. Information from Nexus
Traveline on 0191 232 5325.
Habitat: Deciduous woodland, scrub, riverside, tidal
river.
Key birds: *Winter:* Goldeneye (now rare), Goosander,
Green Woodpecker, Nuthatch, Treecreeper. *Autumn:*
Greenshank. *Summer:* Lesser Whitethroat, Sedge
Warbler, Yellowhammer, Linnet, Reed Bunting,
Common Sandpiper.
Other notable flora and fauna: Invertebrate species
associated with acid grassland.
Contact: See Derwent Country Park.

4. SHIBDON POND

Gateshead Council.
Location: NZ 192 628. E of Blaydon, S of Scotswood
Bridge, close to A1. Car park at Blaydon swimming
baths. Open access from B6317 (Shibdon Road).
Access: Open at all times. Disabled access to hide.

Facilities: Hide in SW corner of pond. Free leaflet available.
Public transport: At least six buses per hour from Newcastle/Gateshead to Blaydon (bus stop Shibdon Road). Information from Nexus Travel Line (0191 232 5325).
Habitat: Pond, marsh, scrub and damp grassland.
Key birds: *Winter:* Wildfowl, Water Rail, occasional white-winged gulls. *Summer:* Reed Warbler, Sedge Warbler, Lesser Whitethroat, Grasshopper Warbler, Water Rail. *Autumn:* Passage waders and wildfowl, Kingfisher.
Other notable flora and fauna: 18 species of butterfly, inc dingy skipper. Dragonflies inc ruddy darter, migrant hawker, occasional emperor and vagrants.
Contact: Brian Pollinger, Thornley Woodlands Centre, Rowlands Gill, Tyne & Wear NE39 1AU. 1209 545 212. e-mail: countryside@gateshead.gov.uk
www.gatesheadbirders.co.uk

5. TYNE RIVERSIDE COUNTRY PARK & THE REIGH

Newcastle City Council
Location: NZ 158 658 in Newburn. From the Newcastle to Carlisle by-pass on the A69(T) take the A6085 into Newburn. The park is signposted along the road to Blaydon. 0.25 miles after this junction, turn due W (the Newburn Hotel is on the corner) and after 0.5 miles the parking and information area is signed just beyond the Newburn Leisure Centre.
Access: Open all year.
Facilities: Car park. Leaflets and walk details available.
Habitat: River, pond with reed and willow stands, mixed woodland, open grassland.
Key birds: *Spring/summer:* Swift, Swallow, Whitethroat, Lesser Whitethroat. *Winter:*

Sparrowhawk, Kingfisher, Little Grebe, finches, Siskin, Fieldfare, Redwing, Goosander. *All year:* Grey Partridge, Green and Great Spotted Woodpecker, Bullfinch, Yellowhammer.
Contact: Newcastle City Council, The Riverside Country Park, Newburn, Newcastle upon Tyne, NE15 8BW.

6. WASHINGTON

The Wildfowl & Wetlands Trust.
Location: NZ 331 566. In Washington. On N bank of River Wear, W of Sunderland. Signposted from A195, A19, A1231 and A182.
Access: Open 9.30am-5pm (summer), 9.30am-4pm (winter). Free to WWT members. Admission charge for non-members. No dogs except guide dogs. Good access for people with disabilities.
Facilities: Visitor centre, toilets, parent and baby room, range of hides. Shop and café.
Public transport: Buses to Waterview Park (250 yards walk) from Washington, from Sunderland, Newcastle-upon-Tyne, Durham and South Shields. Tel: 0845 6060 260 for details.
Habitat: Wetlands, woodland and meadows.
Key birds: *Spring/summer:* Nesting colony of Grey Heron, other breeders include Common Tern, Oystercatcher, Lapwing. *Winter:* Bird-feeding station visited by Great Spotted Woodpecker, Bullfinch, Jay and Sparrowhawk. Goldeneye and other ducks.
Other notable flora and fauna: Wildflower meadows - cuckoo flower, bee orchid and yellow rattle. Dragonfly and amphibian ponds.
Contact: Dean Heward, (Conservation Manager), Wildfowl & Wetlands Trust, Pottinson, Washington, NE38 8LE. 01914 165 454 ext 231. www.wwt.org.uk e-mail: dean.heward@wwt.org.uk

Warwickshire

1. ALVECOTE POOLS

Warwickshire Wildlife Trust.
Location: SK 253 034. Located alongside River Anker E of Tamworth. Access via Robey's Lane (off B5000) just past Alvecote Priory car park. Also along towpath via Pooley Hall visitor centre, also number of points along towpath.
Access: Some parts of extensive path system are accessible to wheelchair-users. Park Alvecote Priory car park.
Facilities: Nature trail.
Public transport: Within walking distance of the Alvecote village bus stop.
Habitat: Marsh, pools (open and reedbeds) and woodland.
Key birds: *Spring/summer:* Breeding Oystercatcher, Common Tern and Little Ringed Plover. Common species include Great Crested Grebe, Tufted Duck

and Snipe. Important for wintering, passage and breeding wetland birds.
Other notable flora and fauna: *Spring:* Dingy skipper, frog, toad, great crested newt, grass snake. *Summer:* Southern marsh orchid, hairy dragonfly, damselflies, purple hairstreak butterfly and elephant hawkmoth.
Contact: Reserves Team, Brandon Marsh Nature Centre, Brandon Lane, Brandon, Coventry, CV3 3GW. 02476 302 912. e-mail: enquiries@wrwt.org.uk
www.warwickshire-wildlife-trust.org.uk

2. BRANDON MARSH

Warwickshire Wildlife Trust.
Location: SP 386 762. Three miles SE of Coventry, 200 yards SE of A45/A46 junction (Tollbar End). Turn E off A45 into Brandon Lane. Reserve entrance 1.25 miles on R.

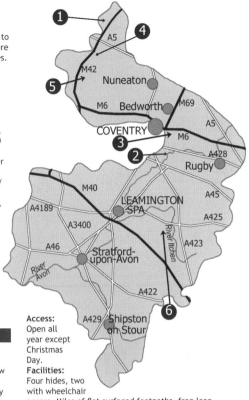

Access: Open weekdays (9am-4.30pm), weekends (10am-4pm). Entrance charge currently £2.50 (free to Wildlife Trust members). Wheelchair access to nature trail and Wright hide. No dogs. Parking for 2 coaches.

Facilities: Visitor centre, toilets, tea-room (open daily 10am-3pm weekdays, 10am-4pm weekends), nature trail, seven hides.

Public transport: Bus service from Coventry to Tollbar End then 1.25 mile walk. Tel Travel West Midlands 02476 817 032 for bus times.

Habitat: Ten pools, together with marsh, reedbeds, willow carr, scrub and small mixed woodland in 260 acres, designated SSSI in 1972.

Key birds: *Spring/summer*: Garden and Grasshopper Warblers, Whitethroat, Lesser Whitethroat, Hobby, Little Ringed Plover, Whinchat, Wheatear. *Autumn/winter*: Bittern (last two winters), Dunlin, Ruff, Snipe, Greenshank, Green and Common Sandpipers, Wigeon, Shoveler, Pochard, Goldeneye, Siskin, Redpoll. *All year*: Cetti's Warbler, Kingfisher, Water Rail, Gadwall, Little Grebe, Buzzard.

Other notable flora and fauna: More than 20 species of butterfly and 18 species of dragonfly recorded. Almost 500 plants species listed on www.brandonbirding.co.uk

Contact: Ken Bond, Hon. Sec. Brandon Marsh Voluntary Conservation Team, 54 Wiclif Way, Stockingford, Nuneaton, Warwickshire CV10 8NF. 02476 328 785.

3. COOMBE COUNTRY PARK

Coventry City Council

Location: CV3 2AB. SP 402 795. Five miles E of Coventry city centre, on B4027 Coventry to Brinklow road.

Access: Park open every day, 7.30am to dusk. Entry by foot is free with pay and display system for vehicles. Paths mainly hard surfaces accessible for wheelchairs. £5 hire charge for manual wheelchair.

Facilities: Information centre, toilets, including disabled, café. Manual wheelchairs available for £5 returnable deposit. Bird hide.

Public transport: By rail: To Coventry City Centre followed by a 20 minute bus journey (see below). By bus: No-585 Mike de Courcey Travel (for timetable please ring 02476 302 656).

Habitat: Parkland, lake and woodland.

Key birds: Large heronry with more than 50 pairs, plus many Cormorants. Lesser Spotted Woodpecker and Marsh Tit top the list of woodland species.

Other notable flora and fauna: More than 250 species of plant, inc lesser celandine, foxglove, bluebell, red campion and herb robert. Mammals inc wood mouse, Muntjac deer.

Contact: Coombe Country Park, Brinklow Road, Binley, Nr Coventry CV3 2AB. 024 7645 3720. e-mail: Coombe.countrypark@coventry.gov.uk

4. KINGSBURY WATER PARK

Warwickshire County Council.

Location: SP 203 960. Signposted `Water Park' from J9 M42, A4097 NE of Birmingham.

Access: Open all year except Christmas Day.

Facilities: Four hides, two with wheelchair access. Miles of flat surfaced footpaths, free loan scheme for mobility scooters. Cafes, Information Centre with gift shop.

Public transport: Call for advice.

Habitat: Open water; numerous small pools, some with gravel islands; gravel pits; silt beds with reedmace, reed, willow and alder; rough areas and grassland.

Key birds: *Summer*: Breeding warblers (nine species), Little Ringed Plover, Great Crested and Little Grebes. Shoveler, Shelduck and a thriving Common Tern colony. Passage waders (esp. spring). *Winter*: Wildfowl, Short-eared Owl.

Contact: Paula Cheesman, Kingsbury Water Park, Bodymoor Heath Lane, Sutton Coldfield, West Midlands B76 0DY. 01827 872 660; e-mail parks@warwickshire.gov.uk www.warwickshire.gov.uk/countryside.

5. MARSH LANE

Packington Estate Enterprises Limited.

Location: SP 217 804. Equidistant between Birmingham and Coventry, both approx 7-8 miles away. Off A452 between A45 and Balsall Common, S of B4102/A452 junction. Turn R into Marsh Lane and immediately R onto Old Kenilworth Road (now a public footpath), to locked gate. Key required for access.

Access: Only guide dogs allowed. Site suitable for disabled. Access by day or year permit only. Contact reserve for membership rates. Day permits: adult £4, OAP £3.50, children (under 16) £3 obtained from Golf Professional Shop, Stonebridge Golf Centre, Somers Road, off Hampton Lane, Meriden, (tel 01676 522 442),which is open Mon-Sun (7am-7pm). Golf Centre, four minutes' car journey from site, open to non-members for drinks and meals. £33 deposit required for key. Site readily accessible for coaches.

Facilities: No toilets or visitor centre. Four hides and hard tracks between hides. Car park behind locked gates.

Public transport: Hampton-in-Arden railway station within walking distance on footpath loop. Bus no 194 stops at N end of Old Kenilworth Road, one mile from reserve gate.

Habitat: Two large pools with islands, three small areas of woodland crops for finches and buntings as winter feed.

Key birds: 177 species. *Summer*: Breeding birds include Little Ringed Plover, Common Tern, most species of warbler including Grasshopper. Good passage of waders in Apr, May, Aug and Sept. Hobby and Buzzard breed locally.

Other notable flora and fauna: The woodlands also contain a diversity of wild flowers including lesser celandine, foxglove, bluebell, red campion, herb robert and many more, making the woodlands very attractive during spring and summer.

Contact: Nicholas P Barlow, Packington Hall, Packington Park, Meriden, Nr Coventry CV7 7HF. 01676 522 020. www.packingtonestate.net

6. UFTON FIELDS

Warwickshire Wildlife Trust.

Location: SP 378 615. Located SE of Leamington Spa off A425. At South Ufton village, take B4452.

Access: Open at all times. Access via Ufton Fields Lane, South Ufton village.

Facilities: Two hides, nature trail.

Public transport: Within walking distance of Ufton village bus stop.

Habitat: Grassland, woodland, pools with limestone quarry.

Key birds: Usual species for pools/woodland/grassland including Willow Tit, Goldcrest, Green Woodpecker, Little Grebe and up to nine warbler species.

Contact: Reserves Team, Brandon Marsh Nature Centre, Brandon Lane, Brandon, Coventry, CV3 3GW. 02476 302 912. e-mail: reserves@warkswt.cix.co.uk www.warwickshire-wildlife-trust.org.uk

West Midlands

1. LICKEY HILLS COUNTRY PARK

Birmingham County Council.

Location: Eleven miles SW of Birmingham City Centre.

Access: Open all year, (10am-7pm in summer; 10am-4.30pm in winter). Land-Rover tours can be arranged for less able visitors.

Facilities: Car park, visitor centre with wheelchair pathway with viewing gallery, picnic site, toilets, café, shop.

Public transport: Bus: West Midlands 62 Rednal (20 mins walk to visitor centre. Rail: Barnt Green (25 mins walk through woods to the centre).

Habitat: Hills covered with mixed deciduous woodland, conifer plantations and heathland.

Key birds: *Spring/summer*: Warblers, Tree Pipit, Redstart. *Winter*: Redwing, Fieldfare. *All year*: Common woodland species.

Contact: The Visitor Centre, Lickey Hills CP, Warren Lane, Rednal, Birmingham, B45 8ER. 01214 477 106. e-mail: lickey.hills@birmingham.gov.uk

2. ROUGH WOOD CHASE

Walsall Metropolitan Borough Council

Location: SJ 987 012. From M6 (Jt 10) head for Willenhall and A462. Turn right into Bloxwich Road North and right again into Hunts Lane. Park by site entrance.

Access: Open all year. Circular nature trail.

Facilities: None.

Public transport: WMT bus 341 from Walsall.

Habitat: 70 acres of oakwood, significant for West Midlands. Also meadows, ponds, marshes and scrubland.

Key birds: Great Crested and Little Grebes on pools. Breeding Jay and Sparrowhawk. Common woodland species all year and warblers in summer.

Other notable flora and fauna: Great crested and smooth newts, water vole, various dragonfly species, purple hairstreak, brimstone and small heath butterflies.

Contact: Countryside Services, Walsall Metropolitan Borough Council, Dept of Leisure & Community Services, PO box 42, The Civic Centre, Darwall Street, Walsall WS1 1TZ. 01922 650 000; www.walsall.gov.uk

3. SANDWELL VALLEY COUNTRY PARK

Sandwell Metropolitan Borough Council.

Location: Entrances at SP 012 918 & SP 028 992. Located approx. 1 mile NE of West Bromwich town centre. Main entrance off Salters Lane or Forge Lane.

Access: Car parks open 8am to sunset. Wheelchair access to Priory Woods LNR, Forge Mill Lake LNR and

other parts of the country park.
Facilities: 1,700 acre site. Visitor centre, toilets, café at Sandwell Park Farm (10am-4.30pm). Good footpaths around LNRs and much of the country park. Coach parking by appointment. Also 20 acre RSPB reserve (see below).
Public transport: West Bromwich bus station West Bromwich central metro stop. (Traveline 0871 200 2233).
Habitat: Pools, woodlands, grasslands, including three local nature reserves.
Key birds: Wintering wildfowl including regular flock of Goosander, small heronry. *All year*: Grey Heron, Great Crested Grebe, Lapwing, Reed Bunting, Great Spotted and Green Woodpecker, Sparrowhawk, Kestrel. *Spring*: Little Ringed Plover, Oystercatcher, up to 8 species of warber breeding, passage migrants. *Autumn*: Passage migrants. *Winter*: Goosander, Shoveler, Teal, Wigeon, Snipe.
Other notable flora and fauna: Common spotted and southern marsh orchid. Ringlet butterfly. Water vole, weasel.
Contact: Senior Countryside Ranger, Sandwell Park Farm, Salters Lane, West Bromwich, W Midlands B71 4BG. 01215 530 220 or 2147.

4. SANDWELL VALLEY
RSPB (Midlands Regional Office).
Location: SP 035 928. Great Barr, Birmingham.

Follow signs S from M6 J7 via A34. Take R at 1st junction onto A4041. Take 4th L onto Hamstead Road (B4167), then R at 1st mini roundabout onto Tanhouse Avenue.
Access: 800 metres of paths accessible to assisted and powered wheelchairs with some gradients (please ring centre for further information), centre fully accessible.
Facilities: Visitor centre and car park (open Tue-Fri 9am-5pm, Sat-Sun 10am-5pm. Closes at dusk in winter), with viewing area, small shop and hot drinks, four viewing screens, one hide. Phone centre for details on coach parking.
Public transport: Bus: 16 from Corporation Street (Stand CJ), Birmingham City Centre (ask for Tanhouse Avenue). Train: Hamstead Station, then 16 bus for one mile towards West Bromwich from Hamstead (ask for Tanhouse Avenue).
Habitat: Open water, wet grassland, reedbed, dry grassland and scrub.
Key birds: *Summer*: Lapwing, Little Ringed Plover, Reed Warbler, Whitethroat, Sedge Warbler, Willow Tit. *Passage*: Sandpipers, Yellow Wagtail, chats, Common Tern. *Winter*: Water Rail, Snipe, Jack Snipe, Goosander, Bullfinch, woodpeckers and wildfowl.
Contact: Lee Copplestone, 20 Tanhouse Avenue, Great Barr, Birmingham, B43 5AG. 0121 3577 395.

Wiltshire

1. FYFIELD DOWNS NATIONAL NATURE RESERVE
Natural England (Wiltshire team).
Location: On the Marlborough Downs. From the A345 at N end of Marlborough a minor road signed Broad Hinton, bisects the downs, dipping steeply at Hackpen Hill to the A361 just before Broad Hinton. From Hackpen Hill walk S to Fyfield Down.
Access: Open all year but avoid the racing gallops. Keep dogs on leads.
Facilities: Car park. **Public transport:** None.
Habitat: Downland.
Key birds: *Spring*: Ring Ouzel possible on passage, Wheatear, Cuckoo, Redstart, common warblers. *Summer*: Possible Quail. *Winter*: Occasional Hen Harrier, possible Merlin, Golden Plover, Short-eared Owl, thrushes. *All year*: Sparrowhawk, Buzzard, Kestrel, partridges, Green and Great Spotted Woodpeckers, Goldfinch, Corn Bunting.
Contact: Natural England, Prince Maurice Court, Hambleton, Devizes, Wiltshire SN10 2RT. 01380 726 344. email: wiltshire@naturalengland.org.uk

2. LANGFORD LAKES
Wiltshire Wildlife Trust.
Location: SU 037 370. Nr Steeple Langford, S of

A36, approx eight miles W of Salisbury. In the centre of the village, turn S into Duck Street, signposted Hanging Langford. Langford Lakes is the first turning on the L just after a small bridge across River Wylye.
Access: Opened to the public in Sept 2002. Main gates opening the during the day – ample parking. Advance notice required for coaches. No dogs allowed on this reserve.
Facilities: Four hides, all accessible to wheelchairs. Cycle stands provided (250m from Wiltshire Cycleway between Great Wishford and Hanging Langford).
Public transport: Nearest bus stop 500m - X4 Service between Salisbury and Warminster.
Habitat: Three former gravel pits, with newly created islands and developing reed fringes. 12 ha (29 acres) of open water; also wet woodland, scrub, chalk river.
Key birds: *Summer*: Breeding Coot, Moorhen, Mallard Tufted Duck, Pochard, Gadwall, Little Grebe, Great Crested Grebe. Also Kingfisher, Common Sandpiper, Grey Wagtail, warblers (8 species). *Winter*: Wildfowl, sometimes also Wigeon, Shoveler, Teal, Water Rail, Little Egret, Bittern. *Passage*: Sand Martin, Green Sandpiper, waders, Black Tern.
Contact: Wiltshire Wildlife Trust, 01722 790 770. e-mail: admin@wiltshirewildlife.org
www.wiltshirewildlife.org

NATURE RESERVES - ENGLAND

3. RAVENSROOST WOOD

Wiltshire Wildlife Trust.
Location: SU 023 877. NW of Swindon. Take B4696
Ashton Keynes road N from Wootton Bassett. After
two miles take second turn L to Minety. Go straight
on when main road turns R. Go straight over next
crossroads and Ravensroost Wood car park is one R
after 1/4 mile.
Access: Open at all times.
Facilities: Small car park, small shelter.
Habitat: Woodland, both coppice and high oak forest,
and ponds.
Key birds: Willow Warblers, Blackcap, Chiffchaff
and Garden Warblers. In winter mixed flocks of
Nuthatches, tits and Treecreepers move noisily
through the wood and Woodcock can be flushed from
wet, muddy areas.
Other notable flora and fauna: Butterflies include
silver-washed fritillary and white admiral, plus
meadow brown, gatekeeper and peacock. Trees
include small-leaved lime and wild service tree (rare
for Wiltshire). Good display of spring bluebells, wood
anemone, wood sorrel, sanicle, violet and primrose.
In summer, common spotted, early purple and
greater butterfly orchids, hemp agrimony and betony.
Contact: Wiltshire Wildlife Trust, 01722 790 770.
e-mail: admin@wiltshirewildlife.org
www.wiltshirewildlife.org

4. SAVERNAKE FOREST

Savernake Estate Trustees.
Location: From Marlborough the A4 Hungerford road
runs along the N side of the forest. Two pillars mark
the Forest Hill entrance, 1.5 miles E of the A346/A4
junction. The Grand Avenue leads straight through
the middle of the woodland to join a minor road from
Stibb Green on the A346 N of Burbage to the A4 W of
Froxfield.
Access: Privately owned but open all year to public.
Facilities: Car park, picnic site at NW end by A346.
Fenced-off areas should not be entered unless there
is a footpath.
Public transport: None.
Habitat: Ancient woodland, with one of the largest
collections of veteran trees in Britain.
Key birds: *Spring/summer*: Garden Warbler,
Blackcap, Willow Warbler, Chiffchaff, Wood Warbler,
Redstart, occasional Nightingale, Tree Pipit, Spotted
Flycatcher. *Winter*: Finch flocks possibly inc Siskin
Redpoll, Brambling. *All year*: Sparrowhawk, Buzzard,
Woodcock, owls, all three woodpeckers, Marsh Tit,
Willow Tit, Jay and other woodland birds.
Contact: Forest Enterprise, Postern Hill Lodge,
Marlborough SN8 4ND. 01672 512 520.
e-mail: admin@wiltshirewildlife.org
www.wiltshirewildlife.org

5. SWILLBROOK LAKES

Wiltshire Wildlife Trust.
Location: SU 018 934. NW of Swindon, one mile S
of Somerford Keynes on Cotswold Water Park spine
road; turn off down Minety Lane (parking).
Access: Open at all times.
Facilities: Footpath along N and E sides of lakes.
Public transport: None.
Habitat: Gravel pits with shallow pools, rough
grassland and scrub around edges.
Key birds: *Winter*: Wildfowl (inc. Gadwall, Pochard,
Smew, Goosander). *Summer*: Breeding Nightingale,
Garden, Reed and Sedge Warblers; one of the best
sites for Hobby and Nightingale in Cotswold WP.
Other notable flora and fauna: 18 species of
dragonfly including downy emerald and lesser
emperor in recent years.
Contact: Wiltshire Wildlife Trust, 01722 790 770.
e-mail: admin@wiltshirewildlife.org
www.wiltshirewildlife.org

Worcestershire

1. BEACONWOOD/THE WINSEL

Worcestershire Wildlife Trust.
Location: SO 974 759. N of Bromsgrove. Entrance
near Lydiate Ash, three miles north of Bromsgrove,
at end of cul-de-sac of Old Birmingham Road. Take
public footpath along metalled track going N and
enter reserve through a metal gate on L after about
20 yards.
Access: The reserve is open throughout the year but
please keep to the footpaths.
Facilities: None.
Public transport: Nearest station – Longbridge (three
miles). Nearest bus stops in Rubery (1 mile).
Habitat: Mixed woodlands.
Key birds: Buzzard, Kestrel, Sparrowhawk, Tawny
Owl, Little Owl, Great Spotted Woodpecker, Spotted
Flycatcher, Nuthatch, Treecreeper and many other
woodland birds are resident. *Summer*: Pied and
Spotted Flycatcher, warblers.
Other notable flora and fauna: In May there is an
unbroken sea of bluebells over 5 acres. Good variety
of trees including the Great Oak, probably 250 years
old.
Contact: Worcestershire Wildlife Trust, Lower Smite
Farm, Smite Hill, Hindlip, Worcester, WR3 8SZ. 01905
754 919. www.worcswildlife.co.uk
e-mail: enquiries@worcestershirewildlifetrust.org

2. BROADWAY GRAVEL PIT

Worcestershire Wildlife Trust.
Location: SP 087 379. Approx. half mile NW of Broadway on the N side of the Broadway to Childswickham road and E of the old disused railway line.
Access: Open access at all times. Disabled access to hide only. Parts of circular path sometimes flooded but hide is usually clear.
Facilities: 1 hide. Cafes and toilets in Broadway. Very limited car parking (2-3 cars), no room for a coach. Large car park within half mile in Broadway.
Public transport: No rail connection. Buses to Broadway from Evesham etc. Check the timetable.
Habitat: Open water, wet woodland, dry scrub.
Key birds: As this is a very small site (1.6ha), it does not hold great numbers of bird species. Wintering Chiffchaff with tit and crest flocks, finches and buntings. Whitethroat, Blackcap, Chiffchaff, Cuckoo in spring/summer.
Other notable flora and fauna: A good dragonfly site for commoner species. Butterflies in dryer, grassy areas. Mare's tail (unusual in Worcestershire wetland sites) found in abundance in June and August.
Contact: Trust HQ, 01905 754 919.

3. GWEN FINCH WETLAND

Worcestershire Wildlife Trust.
Location: SO 937 421. W of Evesham. Take B4080 S off A4104. Turn L at Eckington. Park where available and view reserve from road.
Access: Due to its sensitive nature, access to this reserve is restricted to special open days or guided walks. The whole site can be viewed from the minor road between Nafford and Eckington at grid reference SO 937 417, where you can park. A footpath leads down to Nafford Lock. From here a footpath leads to Birlingham village, the first part of which passes alongside part of the Gwen Finch reserve.
Facilities: None.
Habitat: Recently created wetland with pools and marshes.
Key birds: Redshank, Water Rail and Reed Warbler breed here and, Green Sandpiper and other waders are regular passage visitors. The pools attract hundreds of House Martins and Swallows, which feed on insects over the reeds and pools before heading south on migration.
Other notable flora and fauna: Dragonflies and damselflies are abundant along the margins of the river and the pools. Regular haunt for otters.
Contact: Trust HQ, 01905 754 919.

4. KNAPP AND PAPERMILL

Worcestershire Wildlife Trust.
Location: SO 749 522. Take A4103 SW from Worcester; R at Bransford roundabout then L towards Suckley and reserve is approx three miles (do not turn off for Alfrick). Park at Bridges Stone layby (SO 751 522), cross road and follow path to the Knapp House.
Access: Open daily. Large parties should contact Warden
Facilities: Nature trail, small information centre, wildlife garden, Kingfisher viewing screen.
Public transport: None.
Habitat: Broadleaved woodland, unimproved grassland, fast stream, old orchard in Leigh Brook Valley.
Key birds: *Summer*: Breeding Grey Wagtail, Kingfisher, Spotted Flycatcher nests in warden's garden, all three woodpeckers. Buzzard, Sparrowhawk and Redstart also occur.
Other notable flora and fauna: Otters have returned recently. Good numbers of dragonflies and butterflies on all three meadows include holly blue, purple hairstreak and white admiral. Bluebells, green-winged and spotted orchids.
Contact: The Warden, Knapp and Papermill Reserve, The Knapp, Alfrick, Worcester, WR6 5HR. 01886 832 065.

5. TIDDESLEY WOOD

Worcestershire Wildlife Trust.
Location: SO 929 462. Take B4084 from Pershore to Worcester. Turn L towards Besford and Croome near town boundary just before the summit of the hill. Entrance is on L after about 0.75 miles.
Access: Open all year except Christmas Day. Cycles and horses only allowed on the bridleway. Please keep dogs fully under control. Military firing range at the SW corner of wood, so do not enter the area marked by red flags. The NE plot is private

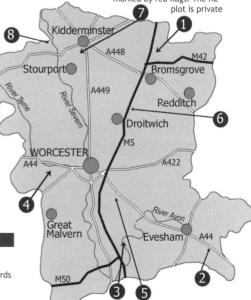

property and visitors should not enter the area. Main ride stoned, with some potholes. Small pathways difficult if wet. Coach parking by appointment.
Facilities: Information board. May find numbered posts around the reserve which were described in an old leaflet. Circular trail around small pathways.
Public transport: First Midland Red services (see above).
Habitat: Ancient woodland, conifers.
Key birds: *All year*: Crossbill, Coal Tit, Goldcrest, Sparrowhawk, Willow Tit, Marsh Tit. *Spring*: Chiffchaff, Blackcap, Cuckoo. *Winter*: Redwing, Fieldfare.
Other notable flora and fauna: Dragonflies including club-tailed and white-legged damselflies. Good for butterflies, including white admiral, peacock and gatekeeper. Important invertebrates, include nationally rare noble chafer beetle which has been recorded here for many years. Plants include uncommon violet helleborine and herb paris, greater butterfly orchid and twayblade.
Contact: Trust HQ, 01905 754 919.

6. UPTON WARREN
Worcestershire Wildlife Trust.
Location: SO 936 675. Two miles S of Bromsgrove on A38. Leave M5 at junction 5.
Access: Christopher Cadbury Wetland Resere divided into two parts — Moors Pools and Flashes Pools. Always open except Christmas Day. Trust membership gives access, or day permit from sailing centre. Disabled access to hides at Moors Pools only. No dogs.
Facilities: Seven hides, maps at entrances, paths can be very muddy. Coach parking at sailing centre by previous booking.
Public transport: Birmingham/Worcester bus passes reserve entrance.
Habitat: Fresh and saline pools with muddy islands, some woodland and scrub.
Key birds: *Winter*: Wildfowl. *Spring/autumn*: Passage waders. *Summer*: Breeding Avocet, Redshank, Little Ringed Plover, Oystercatcher, Common Tern, Sedge, Reed, Grasshopper and Cetti's Warblers. Hobby nearby.
Other notable flora and fauna: Saltmarsh plants, dragonflies.
Contact: A F Jacobs, 3 The Beeches, Upton Warren, Bromsgrove, Worcs B61 7EL. 01527 861 370.

7. WILDEN MARSH
Worcestershire Wildlife Trust.
Location: SO 825 730 and SO 829 735. S of Kidderminster. Take A449 S from Kidderminster. At junction with A442 go straight across roundabout into Wilden Lane. This is a very busy road with few parking spaces so park carefully. There are gated entrances off Wilden Lane.
Access: Parts of reserve accessed by gated entrances are open at all times. Visitors to the more northerly part of the reserve should obtain a permit from the Trust's office. This reserve is complex and new visitors should consult a map. Cattle will be on the

reserve at all times so ensure that all gates are secured after use. Parts of this reserve are dangerous with boggy areas, steep banks by the River Stour and deep ditches.
Facilities: None
Public transport: Nearest bus stop at Wilden, half mile from reserve.
Habitat: Dry and marshy fields with small alder and willow woods, reed beds and many drainage ditches.
Key birds: 192 bird species have been recorded since 1968 and about 70 breed, including Yellow Wagtail, nine species of warblers and Redshank. It is one of the few wintering places for Water Pipits in Worcestershire, though numbers have declined recently.
Other notable flora and fauna: Plants include southern marsh orchids, marsh cinquefoil, marsh arrow-grass, marsh pennywort and lesser water parsnip.
Contact: Trust HQ. 01905 754 919.
www.worcswildlifetrust.co.uk
e-mail: enquiries@worcestershirewildlifetrust.org

8. WYRE FOREST
Natural England/Worcs Wildlife Trust.
Location: SO 750 760. Half a mile NW of Bewdley (on the A456) and four and a half miles W of Kidderminster.
Access: Observe reserve signs and keep to paths. Forestry Commission visitor centre at Callow Hill. Fred Dale Reserve is reached by footpath W of B4194 (parking at SO 776 763).
Facilities: Toilet and refreshment facilities at Wyre Forest Visitor Centre (near the Discovery Centre) at Callow Hill. Several waymarked trails in the Forest (some suitable for wheelchair users) as well as regular guided walks, also family cycle routes through the reserve. The Visitor Centre and Discovery Centre provide facilities for disabled visitors.
Public transport: The nearest train station is in Bewdley, served by the Severn Valley Railway (01299 403 816) although service is seasonal and sometimes infrequent. Also Central Trains to Kidderminster (0121 634 2040) and local bus services between Bewdley and Kidderminster.
Habitat: Oak forest, conifer areas, birch heath, lowland grassland, stream.
Key birds: Breeding birds include Redstart, Pied Flycatcher, Wood Warbler, Buzzard and Raven, with Dipper, Grey Wagtail and Kingfisher found on the larger streams.
Other notable flora and fauna: Mammals include, fallow, roe and muntjac deer, polecat, otter and mink, yellow neck mouse, dormouse, voles and water shrew. Several bat species including pipistrelle and Daubenton's. Important site for invertebrates including England's largest colony of pearl-bordered fritillary butterflies.
Contact: Tim Dixon, Natural England, Block B, Government Buildings, Whittington Road, Worcester WR5 2LQ. 01905 763 355; e-mail: herefordshire. worcestershire@naturalengland.org.uk.

Yorkshire, East

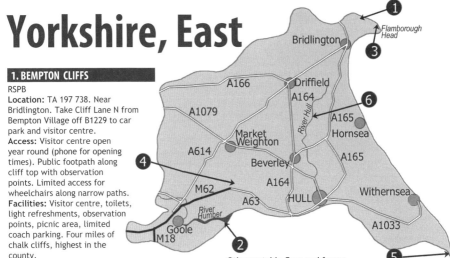

1. BEMPTON CLIFFS

RSPB
Location: TA 197 738. Near Bridlington. Take Cliff Lane N from Bempton Village off B1229 to car park and visitor centre.
Access: Visitor centre open year round (phone for opening times). Public footpath along cliff top with observation points. Limited access for wheelchairs along narrow paths.
Facilities: Visitor centre, toilets, light refreshments, observation points, picnic area, limited coach parking. Four miles of chalk cliffs, highest in the county.
Public transport: Bempton railway station (limited service) 1.5 miles — irregular bus service to village 1.25 miles.
Habitat: Seabird nesting cliffs, farmland, coastal scrub.
Key birds: Breeding seabirds from March to October, peak in May to July. Largest mainland Gannet colony in England. Also Kittiwake, Puffin, Guillemot, Razorbill. Nesting Tree Sparrow and Corn Bunting. Passage skuas, shearwaters, terns and passerine migrants.
Other notable flora and fauna: Harbour porpoise regularly offshore. Also bee and northern marsh orchid occur.
Contact: Site Manager, RSPB, Bempton Cliffs Nature Reserve, 11 Cliff Lane, Bempton, Bridlington, E Yorks, YO15 1JF. 01262 851 179.

2. BLACKTOFT SANDS

RSPB (North of England Office).
Location: SE 843 232. Eight miles E of Goole on minor road between Ousefleet and Adlingfleet.
Access: Open 9am-9pm or dusk if earlier. RSPB members free, £3 permit for non-members, £2 concessionary, £1 children, £6 family.
Facilities: Car park, toilets, visitor centre (open 9am to 5pm April to Oct and weekends between Nov and March), six hides, footpaths suitable for wheelchairs.
Public transport: Goole/Scunthorpe bus (Sweynes' Coaches stops outside reserve entrance). Bus timetable on main RSPB website (see Blacktoft Reserve details).
Habitat: Reedbed, saline lagoons, lowland wet grassland, willow scrub.
Key birds: *Summer:* Breeding Avocet, Marsh Harrier, Bittern, Bearded Tit, passage waders (exceptional list inc many rarities). *Winter:* Hen Harrier, Merlin, Peregrine, wildfowl.

Other notable flora and fauna:
Good place to see water vole. Small number of dragonflies and damselflies including black-tailed skimmer, four-spotted chaser, large red damselfly. Marsh sow thistle easily seen from footpaths in summer.
Contact: Mike Andrews, Visitor Development Officer Blacktoft Sands RSPB reserve, Hillcrest, Whitgift, Nr Goole, E Yorks DN14 8HL. 01405 704 665.
e-mail: michael.andrews@rspb.org.uk

3. FLAMBOROUGH CLIFFS

Yorkshire Wildlife Trust
Location: TA 240 722. The reserve is part of the Flamborough headland, approx 4 miles NE of Bridlington. From Bridlington take B1255 to Flamborough and follow the signs for the North Landing.
Access: Open all year. Public pay and display car park at North Landing gives access to both parts of the reserve. Paths not suitable for wheelchairs.
Facilities: Car park (pay and display), trails, refreshments available at café at North Landing (open Apr-Oct 10am-5pm), toilets.
Public transport: Flamborough is served by buses from Bridlington and Bempton. Phone 01482 222 222 for details.
Habitat: Coastal cliffs, rough grassland and scrub, farmland.
Key birds: *Summer:* Puffin, Guillemot, Razorbill, Kittiwake, Shag, Fulmar, Sky Lark, Meadow Pipit, Linnet, Whitethroat, Yellowhammer, Tree Sparrow, occasional Corn Bunting. *Passage migrants:* Fieldfare, Redwing and occasional rarities such as Wryneck and Red-backed Shrike.
Contact: Yorkshire Wildlife Trust, 1 St George's Place, York, YO24 1GN. 01904 659 570.
www.ywt.org.uk e-mail: info@ywt.org.uk

4. NORTH CAVE WETLANDS

Yorkshire Wildlife Trust
Location: SE 887 328. At NW of North Cave village, approx 10 miles W of Hull. From junction 28 of M62, follow signs to North Cave on B1230. In village, turn L and follow road to next crossroads where you go L, then take next L onto Dryham Lane. Alternatively, from N, follow minor road direct from Market Weighton. After the turning for Hotham, take the next R (Dryham Lane), which is one mile further down the road.
Access: Open all year with car parking on Dryham Lane. Some of the footpaths are suitable for all abilities.
Facilities: Three bird-viewing hides, two accessible to wheelchair users. Nearest toilet and refreshment facilities in North Cave, one mile away.
Public transport: Buses serve North Cave from Hull and Goole: telephone 01482 222 222 for details.
Habitat: Six former gravel pits have been converted into various lagoons for wetland birds, including one reedbed. There are also grasslands, scrub and hedgerows.
Key birds: More than 150 different species have been recorded including Great Crested Grebe, Gadwall, Pochard, Sparrowhawk, Avocet, Ringed Plover, Golden Plover, Dunlin, Ruff, Redshank, Green Sandpiper, Common Sandpiper and Tree Sparrow.
Contact: Trust HQ, 01904 659 570. www.ywt.org.uk e-mail: info@ywt.org.uk

5. SPURN NATIONAL NATURE RESERVE

Yorkshire Wildlife Trust.
Location: Entrance Gate TA 417 151. 26 miles from Hull. Take A1033 from Hull to Patrington then B1445 from Patrington to Easington and unclassed roads on to Kilnsea and Spurn Head.
Access: Normally open at all times. Vehicle admission fee (at present £3). No charge for pedestrians. No dogs allowed under any circumstances, not even in cars. Coaches by permit only (must be in advance).
Facilities: Centre open weekends, Bank Holidays, school holidays. Three hides. Cafe at point open weekends Apr to Oct 10am to 5pm. Public toilets in Blue Bell car park.
Public transport: Nearest bus service is at Easington (3.5 miles away).
Habitat: Sand dunes with marram and sea buckthorn scrub. Mudflats around Humber Estuary.
Key birds: *Spring*: Many migrants on passage and often rare birds such as Red-backed Shrike, Bluethroat etc. *Autumn*: Passage migrants and rarities such as Wryneck, Pallas's Warbler. *Winter*: Waders and Brent Goose.
Other notable flora and fauna: Unique habitats and geographical position make Spurn the most important site in Yorkshire for butterflies (25 species recorded) and moths.
Contact: Spurn Reserves Officer, Spurn NNR, Blue Bell, Kilnsea, Hull HU12 0UB.
e-mail: spurnywt@ukonline.co.uk

6. TOPHILL LOW

Yorkshire Water.
Location: TA 071 482. Nine miles SE of Driffield and ten miles NE of Beverley. Signposted from village of Watton on A164.
Access: Open Wed-Sun and Bank Holiday Mon. Apr-Oct (9am-6pm). Nov-Mar (9am-4pm). Charges: £2.50 per person. £1 concessions. No dogs allowed. Provision for disabled visitors (paths, ramps, hides, toilet etc). Coaches welcome.
Facilities: Visitor Centre with toilets open every weekend/ most week days. Disabled toilet open at all times.. 12 hides (five with access for wheelchairs), good paths and sightings board.
Public transport: None.
Habitat: Open water (two reservoirs), marshes, wader scrapes, woodland and thorn scrub.
Key birds: 160 to 170 species each year. *Winter:* SSSI for wildfowl numbers, plus one of the UK's largest Black-head and Common Gull roosts. Active feeding station with Brambling. Water Rail and Woodcock. *Spring/early summer:* Passage waders, Black Tern and Black-necked Grebe. Breeding Little Ringed Plover, Common Tern, Kingfisher and Barn Owl with a diverse variety of warblers. *Late summer/autumn:* Up to 20 species of passage wader.
Other notable flora and fauna: Specialist grassland and wetland flora including orchids. Fauna includes red-eyed damselfly, marbled white and brown argus butterflies, grass snake, otter, water vole and roe deer.
Contact: Richard Hampshire, Tophill Low Nature Reserve, Watton Carrs, Driffield YO25 9RH. 01377 270 690. e-mail: richard.hampshire@yorkshirewater.co.uk

Yorkshire, North

1. BOWESFIELD

Tees Valley Wildlife Trust.
Location: NZ 440 160. SE of Stockton on Tees. From A66 take A135 to Yarm. At first roundabout turn L along Concord Way. At next roundabout go straight onto the new Bowesfield Industrial Estate, the reserve is on the floodplain below the development.
Access: Public footpaths around the site open at all times.
Facilities: None. **Public transport:** None.
Habitat: New wetland reserve on the edge of the River Tees.
Key birds: The reserve is home to a growing number of birds including Reed Bunting, Stonechat, Water Rail, Lapwing and Curlew which roost and feed in the

rich, wet grassland and lakes found on the site.
Other notable flora and fauna: The reserve offers opportunities to see otter, harvest mouse and roe deer.
Contact: Steve Ashton,
Tees Valley Wildlife Trust,
Margrove Heritage Centre,
Margrove Park, Boosbeck,
Saltburn TS12 3BZ.
01287 636 382; Fax
01287 636 383. e-mail:
info@teeswildlife.org
www.teeswildlife.org

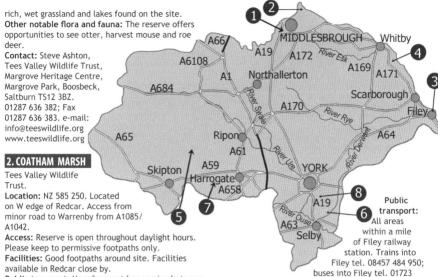

2. COATHAM MARSH

Tees Valley Wildlife
Trust.
Location: NZ 585 250. Located on W edge of Redcar. Access from minor road to Warrenby from A1085/A1042.
Access: Reserve is open throughout daylight hours. Please keep to permissive footpaths only.
Facilities: Good footpaths around site. Facilities available in Redcar close by.
Public transport: Very frequent bus service between Middlesbrough and Redcar. Nearest stops are in Coatham 0.25 mile from reserve (Arriva tel 0871 200 2233). Redcar Central Station one mile from site. Frequent trains from Middlesbrough and Darlington.
Habitat: Freshwater wetlands, lakes, reedbeds.
Key birds: *Spring/autumn*: Wader passage (including Wood Sandpiper and Greenshank). *Summer*: Passerines (including Sedge Warbler, Yellow Wagtail). *Winter*: Ducks (including Smew). *Occasional rarities*: Water Rail, Great White Egret, Avocet, Bearded Tit and Bittern.
Other notable flora and fauna: The lime-rich soil allows wildflower meadows to grow around the site, including northern marsh orchid. Also good for insects incuding migrant hawker dragonfly.
Contact: Trust HQ, 01287 636 382;
e-mail: info@teeswildlife.org www.teeswildlife.org

3. FILEY BRIGG ORNITHOLOGICAL GROUP BIRD OBSERVATORY

FBOG/Yorkshire Wildlife Trust (The Dams).
Location: TA 10 68 07. Two access roads into Filey from A165 (Scarborough to Bridlington road). Filey is ten miles N of Bridlington and eight miles S of Scarborough.
Access: Opening times – no restrictions. Dogs only in Parish Wood and The Old Tip (on lead). Coaches welcome. Park in the North Cliff Country Park.
Facilities: No provisions for disabled at present. Two hides at The Dams, one on The Brigg (open most weekends from late Jul-Oct, key can be hired from Country Park café). Toilets in Country Park (Apr-Nov 1) and town centre. Nature trails at The Dams, Parish Wood/Old Tip. Cliff top walk for seabirds along Cleveland Way.

Public transport: All areas within a mile of Filey railway station. Trains into Filey tel. 08457 484 950; buses into Filey tel. 01723 503 020
Habitat: The Dams — two freshwater lakes, fringed with some tree cover and small reedbeds. Parish Wood — a newly planted wood which leads to the Old Tip, the latter has been fenced (for stock and crop strips) though there is a public trail. Carr Naze has a pond and can produce newly arrived migrants.
Key birds: The Dams: Breeding and wintering water birds, breeding Sedge Warbler, Reed Warbler and Tree Sparrow. The Tip: Important for breeding Sky Lark, Meadow Pipit, common warblers and Grey Partridge. *Winter*: Buntings, including Lapland. Seawatch Hide: *Jul-Oct*. All four skuas, shearwaters, terns. *Winter*: Divers and grebes. Totem Pole Field: A new project should encourage breeding species and wintering larks, buntings etc. Many sub-rare/rare migrants possible at all sites.
Contact: Craig Thomas, Recorder, 16 Scarborough Road, Filey, N Yorks YO14 9NU. 01723 513 055. e-mail: recorder@fbog.co.uk www.fbog.co.uk

4. FYLINGDALES MOOR CONSERVATION AREA

Strickland Estate/Hawk and Owl Trust
Location: NZ 947 003. Off A171 S of Whitby. On eastern side of North York Moors National Park, stretching between Sneaton High Moor (Newton House Plantation) and the coast at Ravenscar. Crossed by A171 Scarborough to Whitby road.
Access: Open access. Parking (inc for coaches) available at Jugger Howe Layby (OS NZ 947 003) on A171 Scarborough to Whitby road.
Facilities: Numerous footpaths including the Lyke Wake Walk and Robin Hood's Bay Road.
Public transport: Half-hourly bus service (No. 93 and X93) between Scarborough and Whitby, nearest stop at Flask Inn (approx. 1 mile N of Jugger Howe

Layby). Services run by Arriva (0191 281 1313) www.arrivabus.co.uk

Habitat: About 6,800 acres (2,750 hectares) of heather moorland (former grouse moor), with scattered trees and wooded valleys and gulleys. Managed exclusively for wildlife and archaeological remains, the moor is an SSSI and SPA (Merlin and Golden Plover) and a special area of conservation.

Key birds: As well as more than 80 more common bird species, rare and endangered breeding birds include harriers, Merlin, Golden Plover, Red Grouse, Curlew, Wheatear, Stonechat, Whinchat, Sky Lark, Marsh Tit, Willow Tit, Linnet, Bullfinch, Reed Bunting and Yellowhammer. The moor is also home to Kestrel, Lapwing, Snipe, Cuckoo, Meadow Pipit, Grey Wagtail and Wood Warbler and visited by Peregrine.

Other notable flora and fauna: Mammals include otter, roe deer, brown hare, stoat, weasel and badger. Important for water vole. Three species of heather, plus cranberry, cowberry, moonwort and, in wetter parts, bog myrtle, lesser twayblade, bog asphodel, butterwort, marsh helleborine, and sundews can be found. Also rare orchids and sedges. Insect species include large heath and small pearl-bordered fritillary butterflies and emperor moth.

Contact: Professor John Edwards, The Hawk and Owl Trust. 01751 417 398. www.hawkandowl.org e-mail: john.edwards@wildfylingdales.co.uk

5. GOUTHWAITE RESERVOIR

Yorkshire Water.

Location: SE 12 69. 2.5miles NW of Pately Bridge on the B6265.

Access: Open all hours, all year.

Facilities: Three viewing areas on edge of reservoir.

Public transport: Nidderdale Rambler route 24/25 (summer Sundays and bank holidays). Harrogate and District Travel 01423 566 061.

Habitat: Reservoir, deciduous woodland shoreline, moors.

Key birds: Green Woodpecker, Nuthatch, Merlin and Buzzard all year. Summer warblers with passage Osprey. *Winter:* Goosander, Goldeneye and Whooper Swan.

Contact: Geoff Lomas, Catchment & Recreation Officer, PO Box 52, Bradford BD6 2LZ. www.yorkshirewater.co.uk (turn to recreation page).

6. LOWER DERWENT VALLEY

Natural England (Yorkshire and Humber Region)/Yorkshire Wildlife Trust/Countryside Trust.

Location: Six miles SE of York, stretching 12 miles S along the River Derwent from Newton-on-Derwent to Wressle and along the Pocklington Canal. Visitor facilities at Bank Island (SE 691 448), Wheldrake Ings YWT (SE 691 444 see separate entry), Thorganby (SE 692 418) and North Duffield Carrs (SE 697 367).

Access: Open all year. No dogs. Disabled access at North Duffield Carrs.

Facilities: Bank Island — two hides, viewing tower. Wheldrake Ings — four hides. Thorganby — viewing

platform. North Duffield Carrs — two hides and wheelchair access. Car parks at all sites, height restriction of 2.1m at Bank Island and North Duffield Carrs. Bicycle stands in car parks at Bank Island and North Duffield Carrs.

Public transport: Bus from York/Selby — contact First (01904 622 992).

Habitat: Hay meadow and pasture, swamp, open water and alder/willow woodland.

Key birds: *Spring/summer:* Breeding wildfowl and waders, incl. Garganey, Snipe and Ruff. Barn Owl and warblers. *Winter/spring:* 20,000-plus waterfowl including Whooper Swan, wild geese, Teal and Wigeon. Large gull roost, incl. white-winged gulls. Also passage waders, incl. Whimbrel.

Other notable flora and fauna: A walk alongside the Pocklington Canal is particularly good for a wide range of aquatic plants and animals.

Contact: Senior Reserve Manager, Natural England Yorkshire and Humber Region, 01904 435 500. email: york@naturalengland.org.uk www.naturalengland.org.uk Pocklington Canal: www.pocklington.gov.uk/pcas

7. TIMBLE INGS

Yorkshire Water.

Location: SE 15 53. West of Harrogate, north of Otley. Off the A59 south of Blubberhouses, near Timble village.

Access: Open at all times, all year.

Facilities: Toilets, cafes, pubs, coach parking all nearby. Hard forest tracks.

Habitat: Woodland and nearby reservoir.

Key birds: Bradford OG species list stands at 134. Habitat management work by Yorkshire Water makes site attractive to Long-eared and Tawny Owls, Nightjars and Tree Pipits. Buzzards now nest and Red Kites seen regularly. Goshawk numbers in decline. *Summer:* Breeding species inc Redpoll, Siskin, Crossbill, Woodcock, Redstart and Grasshopper Warbler. Short-eared Owls hunt adjacent moorland. *Winter:* Fieldfare, Redwing, Brambling, occasional Waxwings and Hawfinches.

Other notable flora and fauna: Roe deer, badger, brown hare, shrew, vole and mouse species (all detected from owl pellets). New ponds attractive to amphibians and dragonflies, inc broad-bodied chaser, emperor and black darter.

Contact: Geoff Lomas Catchment & Recreation Officer, Yorkshire Water, Western House, Halifax Road, Bradford BD6 2LZ. www.yorkshirewater.co.uk (turn to recreation page).

8. WHELDRAKE INGS (LOWER DERWENT VALLEY NATIONAL NATURE RESERVE)

Yorkshire Wildlife Trust.

Location: From York ring-road head S onto A19 Selby road. After one mile turn L, signed Wheldrake and Thorganby. Continue through Wheldrake towards Thorganby. After a sharp R bend, turn L after 0.5 miles onto an unsigned tarmac track. Look for two stone gateposts with pointed tops. Car park is about

0.25 miles down the track. To reach the reserve, cross the bridge over river and turn R over a stile.
Access: Open all year. Please keep to the riverside path. From Apr-Sep.
Facilities: Car park, four hides.
Habitat: Water meadows, river, scrub, open water.

Key birds: *Spring/summer*: Duck species, Grey Partridge, Turtle Dove, some waders, Spotted Flycatcher, warblers. *Winter*: Occasional divers and scarce grebes. wildfowl inc. Pintail, Pochard, Goshawk, Hen Harrier, Water Rail, Short-eared Owl, thrushes, good mix of other birds.
Contact: Trust HQ, 01904 659 570.

Yorkshire, South & West

1. BOLTON INGS (DEARNE VALLEY)

RSPB North West Office
Location: SE 425 020. Lies SE of Barnsley. From M1 take A61 in direction of Barnsley and continue on A6195 for four miles. After Morrisons superstore, follow A6195 and brown signs for RSPB Old Moor.
Access: Dearne Way footpath and Trans-Pennine Trail open at all times, but not suitable for wheelchair users.
Facilities: None. Old Moor site close by.
Public transport: Nearest train stations at Wombwell and Swinton both 3m from reserve. Buses run to Old Moor reserve from Barnsley, Doncaster and Meadowhall – call Traveline on 01709 515 151 for details. Trans-Pennine Way runs along southern edge of reserve.
Habitat: 43 hectares of reedbed.
Key birds: *All year*: Kingfisher, Little Egret, Stonechat, Reed Bunting. *Spring/summer*: Breeding waders and warblers, Cuckoo, Garganey. *Autumn*: Passage waders including Greenshank, Green Sandpiper, Golden Plover. *Winter*: Wildfowl, including Goosander, Wigeon and Teal. Rarer species include Spoonbill and Avocet.
Other notable flora and fauna: Dragonflies inc

banded demoiselle, roe deer.
Contact: RSPB Old Moor, Old Moor Lane, Wombwell, Barnsley, S Yorks S73 0YF. 01226 751 593 or e-mail: old.moor@rspb.org

2. DENABY INGS

Yorkshire Wildlife Trust.
Location: Reserve on A6023 from Mexborough. Look for L fork, signed Denaby Ings Nature Reserve. Proceed along Pastures Road for 0.5 miles and watch for a 2nd sign on R marking entrance to car park. From car park, walk back to the road to a set of concrete steps on R leading to a small visitor centre and a hide.
Access: Open all year.
Facilities: Car park, visitor centre, hide, nature trail.
Public transport: None.
Habitat: Water, deciduous woodland, marsh, willows.
Key birds: *Spring/summer*: Waterfowl, Little Ringed Plover, Turtle Dove, Cuckoo, Little Owl, Tawny Owl, Sand Martin, Swallow, Whinchat, possible Grasshopper Warbler, Lesser Whitethroat, Whitethroat, other warblers, Spotted Flycatcher, Red-legged and Grey Partridges, Kingfisher. *Passage*: Waders, Common, Arctic and Black Terns, Redstart, Wheatear. *Winter*: Whooper Swan, wildfowl, Jack Snipe, waders, Grey Wagtail, Short-eared Owl, Stonchat, Fieldfare, Redwing, Brambling, Siskin. *All year*: Corn Bunting, Yellowhammer, all three woodpeckers, common woodland birds, possible, Willow Tit.
Contact: Trust HQ. 01904 659 570. www.ywt.org.uk

3. FAIRBURN INGS

RSPB (North of England Office).
Location: SE 452 277. 12 miles from Leeds, six miles from Pontefract, three miles from Castleford, situated next to A1246 from J42 of A1.
Access: Reserve and hides open every day except Dec 25/26. Centre and shop open each day (9am-5pm). Dogs on leads welcome. Boardwalks leading to Pickup Pool, feeding station and Kingfisher viewpoint are all wheelchair-friendly.
Facilities: Five hides open at all times. Toilets open 9am-5pm. Disabled toilets

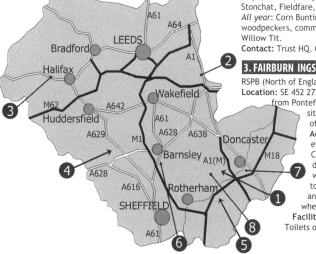

215

and baby-changing facilities. Hot and cold drinks, snacks available. Wildlife garden, pond-dipping and mini beast areas, plus duck feeding platform. Coach parking for club visits.
Public transport: Nearest train stations are Castleford, Micklefield and Garforth. No bus service.
Habitat: Open water, wet grassland, marsh and fen scrub, reedbed, reclaimed colliery spoil heaps.
Key birds: *All year:* Tree Sparrow, Willow Tit, Green Woodpecker, Bullfinch. *Winter:* Smew. Goldeneye, Goosander, Wigeon, Peregrine. *Spring:* Osprey, Little Gull, Wheatear, five species of tern inc annual Black Tern. *Summer:* Nine species of breeding warbler, Grey Heron, Gadwall, Little Ringed Plover.
Other notable flora and fauna: Brown hare, harvest mouse, roe deer, Leisler's and Daubenton's bats, 28 species of butterfly and 20 species of dragonfly.
Contact: Laura Bentley, Visitor Services Manager, Fairburn Ings Visitor Centre, Newton Lane, Fairburn, Castleford WF10 2BH. 01977 628 191.

3. HARDCASTLE CRAGS

National Trust.
Location: From Halifax, follow A646 W for five miles to Hebden Bridge and pick up National Trust signs in town centre to the A6033 Keighley Road. Follow this for 0.75 miles. Turn L at the National Trust sign to the car parks. Alternate pay-and-display car park at Clough Hole, Widdop Road, on R above Gibson Mill.
Access: Open all year. NT car park charges: £2.50 up to 3 hours, £3 all day weekdays, £4 at weekends and bank holidays. No charge for NT members and disabled badge holders.
Facilities: 2 small pay car parks, cycle racks and several way-marked trails. Gibson Mill has toilets, café, exhibitions. Not connected to any mains services, in extreme conditions the mill may be closed for health and safety reasons.
Public transport: Good public transport links. Trains to Hebden Bridge from Manchester or Leeds every 30 minutes. Call 08457 484 950. Weekday buses every 30 minutes to Keighley Road, then 1 mile walk to Midghole. Summer weekend bus 906 Widdop-Hardcastle Crags leaves Hebden Bridge rail station every 90 minutes 9.20am-6.05pm. Tel: 0113 245 7676.
Habitat: Wooded valleys, ravines, streams, hay meadows and moorland edge.
Key birds: *Spring/summer:* Cuckoo, Redstart, Lesser Whitethroat, Garden Warbler, Blackcap, Wood Warbler, Chiffchaff, Spotted Flycatcher, Pied Flycatcher, Curlew, Lapwing, Meadow Pipit. *All year:* Sparrowhawk, Kestrel, Green and Greater Spotted Woodpeckers, Tawny Owl, Barn Owl, Little Owl, Jay, Coal Tit and other woodland species.
Contact: National Trust, Hardcastle Crags, Hollin Hall Office, Hebden Bridge, West Yorks, HX7 7AP. 01422 844 518.

4. INGBIRCHWORTH RESERVOIR

Yorkshire Water.
Location: Leave the M1 at J37 and take the A628 to Manchester and Penistone. After five miles you reach a roundabout. Turn R onto the A629 Huddersfield road. After 2.5 miles you reach Ingbirchworth. At a sign for The Fountain Inn, turn L. Pass a pub. The road bears L to cross the dam, proceed straight forward onto the track leading to the car park.
Access: Open all year. One of the few reservoirs in the area with footpath access.
Facilities: Car park, picnic tables.
Habitat: Reservoir, small strip of deciduous woodland.
Key birds: *Spring/summer:* Whinchat, warblers, woodland birds, House Martin. *Spring/autumn passage:* Little Ringed Plover, Ringed Plover, Dotterel, other waders, Common Tern, Arctic Tern, Black Tern, Yellow Wagtail, Wheatear. *Winter:* Wildfowl, Golden Plover, waders, occasional rare gull such as Iceland or Glaucous, Grey Wagtail, Fieldfare, Redwing, Brambling, Redpoll.
Other notable flora and fauna: Woodland wildflowers, inc bluebells.
Contact: Yorkshire Water, PO Box 52, Bradford, BD6 2LZ. www.yorkshirewater.co.uk (recreation page).

6. OLD MOOR (DEARNE VALLEY)

RSPB (North of England Office).
Location: SE 422 022. From M1 J36, take A61 towards Barnsley, then A6195 towards Doncaster. From A1 J37, then A635 and A6195 – follow brown signs.
Access: Open Apr 1-Oct 31 (Wed-Sun 9am-5pm), Nov 1-Mar 31 (Wed/Thu/Sat/Sun 10am-4pm). Members free. Non-member adults £2.50. Concessions £2. Wheelchair and electric scooter for hire. Disabled parking bays 100m from visitor centre.
Facilities: Toilets (including disabled), large visitor centre, tearoom and shop, five superb hides fully accessible for disabled. Two trails suitable for wheelchairs.
Public transport: Buses from Barnsley, Doncaster, Meadowhall, Wombwell and Swinton stop near reserve – information Traveline 01709 515 151.
Habitat: Lakes and flood meadows, wader scrape and reedbeds.
Key birds: *All year:* Kingfisher, Little Owl. *Winter:* Large numbers of wildfowl, spectacular flocks of Lapwing and Golden Plover, Peregrine, Tree Sparrow in garden feeding area. *Summer:* Breeding waders, inc drumming Snipe, and wildfowl. Rare vagrants recorded annually.
Contact: The Warden, RSPB Old Moor, Old Moor Lane, Wombwell, Barnsley, South Yorkshire, S73 0YF. 01226 751 593 Fax: 01226 341 078. www.rspb.org.uk

7. POTTERIC CARR

Yorkshire Wildlife Trust.
Location: SE 589 007. From M18 junction 3 take A6182 (Doncaster) and at first roundabout take third exit; entrance and car park are on R after 50m.
Access: Access by permit only. Parties must obtain prior permission.
Facilities: Field Centre (hot and cold drinks, snacks

and meals, toilet) open 9.30am-4pm Thursdays to Sundays all year round. Bank Holiday Mondays open, also Tues 9.30am-1.30pm. Approx 12 km of footpaths including 8km suitable for disabled unaided. Twelve new/refurbished hides, 10 suitable for wheelchairs. See website for more details and events programme.
Public transport: Buses from Doncaster to new B&Q store travel within easy reach of entrance.
Habitat: Reed fen, subsidence ponds, artificial pools, grassland, woodland.
Key birds: 96 species have bred. Nesting waterfowl (inc. Shoveler, Gadwall, Pochard), Water Rail, Kingfisher, all three woodpeckers, Lesser Whitethroat, Reed and Sedge Warblers, Willow Tit. *Passage/winter*: Bittern, Marsh Harrier, Black Tern, waders, wildfowl.
Other notable flora and fauna: 20 species of dragonfly recorded, 28 species of butterfly including purple hairstreak and dingy skipper.
Palmate and great crested newt.
Contact: Yorkshire Wildlife Trust, 1 St George's Place, York YO24 1GN. 01904 659 570.
e-mail: info@ywt.org.uk   www.ywt.org.uk
www.potteric-carr.org.uk

8. SPROTBOROUGH FLASH & THE DON GORGE

Yorkshire Wildlife Trust.
Location: From A1, follow A630 to Rotherham 4.8km W of Doncaster. After 0.8km, turn R at traffic lights to Sprotborough. After approx 1.6km the road drops down the slopes of the Gorse. Cross a bridge over river, then another over a canal, turn immediately L. Park in a small roadside parking area 45m on L beside canal. Walk along canal bank, past The Boat Inn to reserve entrance approx 90m further on.
Access: Open all year.
Facilities: Three hides, footpaths.
Public transport: River bus from Doncaster in summer months.
Habitat: River, reed, gorge, woodland.
Key birds: *Summer*: Turtle Dove, Cuckoo, hirundines, Lesser Whitethroat, Whitethroat, Garden Warbler, Blackcap, Chiffchaff, Willow Warbler, Spotted Flycatcher. *Spring/autumn passage*: Little Ringed Plover, Dunlin, Greenshank, Green Sandpiper, waders, Yellow Wagtail.
Winter/all year: Wildfowl, Water Rail, Snipe, Little Owl, Tawny Owl, all three woodpeckers, thrushes, Siskin, possible Corn Bunting.
Contact: Trust HQ. 01904 659 570.

ISLE OF MAN

CALF OF MAN BIRD OBSERVATORY

Manx National Heritage.
Location: SC 15 65. Small island off the SW of the Isle of Man.
Access: Landings by private craft all year. No dogs, fires, camping or climbing.
Facilities: Accommodation for 8 people, plus 2 volunteers sharing, from Apr-Sept. Bookings: at contact address. Bird ringers welcome to join in ringing activities with prior notice.
Public transport: Local boat from Port Erin (Apr-Sept) or Port St Mary (all year).
Habitat: Heather/bracken moor and seabird cliffs.
Key birds: *All year*: Hen Harrier, Peregrine and Chough. Breeding seabirds including Shag, Razorbill, Manx Shearwater etc. Excellent spring and autumn migration, seabird passage best in autumn.
Contact: Ben Jones, (Warden), Manx National Heritage, Douglas, Isle of Man IM1 3LY.

CLOSE SARTFIELD

Manx Wildlife Trust.
Location: SC 361 956. From Ramsey drive W on A3. Turn on to B9, take third R and follow this road for nearly a mile. Reserve entrance is on R.
Access: Open all year round. No dogs. Path and boardwalk suitable for wheelchairs from car park

through wildflower meadow and willow scrub to hide.
Facilities: Car park, hide, reserve leaflet (50p, available from office) outlines circular walk.
Public transport: None.
Habitat: Wildflower-rich hay meadow, marshy grassland, willow scrub/developing birch woodland, bog.
Key birds: *Winter*: Large roost of Hen Harrier.
Summer: Corn Crake, Curlew, warblers.
Contact: Manx Wildlife Trust, 01624 801 985.
e-mail: manxwt@cix.co.uk
www.wildlifetrust.org.uk/manxwt

CRONK Y BING

Manx Wildlife Trust.
Location: NX 381 017. Take A10 coast road N from Jurby. Approx two miles along there is a sharp R hand turn over a bridge. Before the bridge there is a track to the L. A parking area is available at end of track.
Access: Open all year round. Dogs to be kept on a lead. Not suitable for the disabled.
Facilities: None.
Public transport: None.
Habitat: Open dune and dune grassland.
Key birds: *Summer*: Terns. *Winter*: Divers, grebes, skuas, gulls.
Contact: Manx Wildlife Trust, 01624 801 985.
e-mail: manxwt@cix.co.uk
www.wildlifetrust.org.uk/manxwt

SCOTLAND
Border Counties
Borders

1. DUNS CASTLE

Scottish Wildlife Trust.
Location: NT 778 550. Located N of the centre of Duns (W of Berwick upon Tweed).
Access: Access from Castle Street or at N end of reserve from B6365.
Facilities: None
Public transport: None.
Habitat: Loch and woodland.
Key birds: Woodland birds, waterfowl.
Other notable flora and fauna: Occasional otter.
Contact: SWT headquarters 132 312 7765.

2. GUNKNOWE LOCH AND PARK

Scottish Borders Council.
Location: NT 518 345. 3.2km from Galashiels on the A6091. Park at Gunknowe Loch.
Access: Open all year. Surfaced paths suitable for wheelchair use.
Facilities: Car park, paths.
Public transport: Tweedbank is on the Melrose to Peebles bus route.
Habitat: River, parkland, scrub, woodland.
Key birds: *Spring/summer*: Grey Wagtail, Kingfisher, Sand Martin, Blackcap, Sedge and Grasshopper Warblers. *Passage*: Yellow Wagtail, Whinchat, Wheatear. *Winter*: Thrushes, Brambling, Wigeon, Tufted Duck, Pochard, Goldeneye. *All year*: Great Spotted and Green Woodpeckers, Redpoll, Goosander, possible Marsh Tit.
Contact: Scottish Borders Council Ranger Service, Planning Dept, Council HQ, Newtown, St Boswells TD6 0SA. 01835 825 060. www.scotborders.gov.uk

3. ST ABB'S HEAD

National Trust for Scotland.
Location: NT 914 693. Lies five miles N of Eyemouth. Follow A1107 from A1.
Access: Reserve open all year. Keep dogs under control. Viewpoint at Starney accessible for disabled visitors. Coach parking at Northfield Farm by prior arrangement.
Facilities: Visitor centre and toilets open daily Apr-Oct.
Public transport: Nearest rail station is Berwick-upon-Tweed. Bus service from Berwick, tel 01289 308 719.

Habitat: Cliffs, coastal grasslands and freshwater loch.
Key birds: Apr-Aug: Seabird colonies with large numbers of Kittiwake, auks, Shag, Fulmar, migrants. *Apr-May and Sept-Oct*: Good autumn seawatching.
Other notable flora and fauna: Northern brown argus butterfly. Rock-rose, purple milk-vetch, spring sandwort.
Contact: Kevin Rideout, Rangers Cottage, Northfield, St Abbs, Borders TD14 5QF. 0844 493 2256.
e-mail: krideout@nts.org.uk www.nts.org.uk

4. THE HIRSEL

The Estate Office, The Hirsel.
Location: NT 827 403. Signed off the A698 on the outskirts of Coldstream.
Access: Open all year. Private estate so please stick to the public paths. Coaches by appointment.
Facilities: Car parks, visitor centre, toilets, hide, walks, café.
Public transport: Bus: Coldstream, Kelso, Berwick-upon-Tweed, Edinburgh.
Habitat: Freshwater loch, reeds, woods.
Key birds: *Spring/summer*: Redstart, Garden Warbler, Blackcap, flycatchers, possible Water Rail, wildfowl. *Autumn*: Wildfowl, Goosander, possible Green Sandpiper. *Winter*: Whooper Swan, Pink-footed Goose, Wigeon, Goldeneye, Pochard, occasional Smew, Scaup, Slavonian Grebe.
Contact: The Managing Factor, Roger Dodd, The Hirsel, Bridge Street, Kelso, TD5 7JD. 01573 224 144.

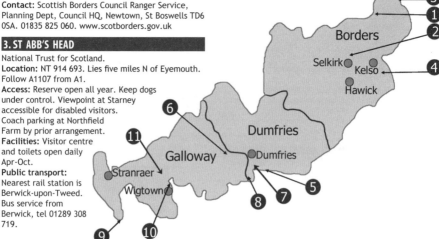

Dumfries & Galloway

5. CAERLAVEROCK WETLAND CENTRE

The Wildfowl & Wetlands Trust.
Location: NY 051 656. Overlooks the Solway. From Dumfries take B725 towards Bankend.
Access: Open daily (10am-5pm), except Christmas Day.
Facilities: 20 hides, heated observatory, four towers, Salcot Merse Observatory, sheltered picnic area. Self-catering accommodation and camping facilities. Nature trails in summer. Old Granary visitor building with fair-trade coffee shop serving light meals and snacks; natural history bookshop; binoculars & telescopes for sale. Theatre/conference room. Binoculars for hire. Parking for coaches.
Public transport: Bus 371 from Dumfries stops 30 mins walk from reserve. Stagecoach 01387 253 496.
Habitat: Saltmarsh, grassland, wetland.
Key birds: *Winter*: Wildfowl esp. Barnacle Geese (max 30,000) and Whooper Swans. *Summer*: Osprey, Barn Owl, Sky Lark.
Other notable flora and fauna: Natterjack toads. Northern marsh, common spotted and twayblade orchids.
Contact: The Wildfowl & Wetlands Trust, Eastpark Farm, Caerlaverock, Dumfries DG1 4RS. 01387 770 200.

6. KEN/DEE MARSHES

RSPB (South & West Scotland Office).
Location: NX 699 684. Six miles from Castle Douglas — good views from A762 and A713 roads to New Galloway.
Access: From car park at entrance to farm Mains of Duchrae. Open during daylight hours. No dogs.
Facilities: Hides, nature trails. Three miles of trails available, nearer parking for elderly and disabled, but phone warden first. Part of Red Kite trail.
Public transport: None.
Habitat: Marshes, woodlands, open water.
Key birds: *All year*: Mallard, Grey Heron, Buzzard, Nuthatch, Willow Tit. *Spring/summer*: Pied Flycatcher, Redstart, Tree Pipit, Sedge Warbler. *Winter*: Greenland White-fronted and Greylag Geese, birds of prey (Hen Harrier, Peregrine, Merlin, Red Kite).
Other notable flora and fauna: Red squirrel.
Contact: Gus Keys, RSPB Scotland, WRDC Business Centre, 608 Queen Street, Newton Stewart, Dumfries DG8 6JL. 01671 404 975.

7. KIRKCONNELL MERSE

RSPB (South & West Scotland Office).
Location: NX990 690. Lies between Dumfries and Glencaple (B725) on banks of River Nith.
Access: None. View reserve from B725 on east side of River Nith.
Facilities: None. **Public transport:** None.
Habitat: Saltmarsh, inter-tidal sand flats and grassland.

Key birds: *Winter*: Whooper Swan, Pink-footed and Barnacle Geese, Pintail, waders.
Contact: Dave Fairlamb, RSPB Scotland, Mersehead Reserve, Southwick, Dumfries DG2 8AH. 01387 780 579.

8. MERSEHEAD

RSPB (South & West Scotland Office).
Access: Open at all times.
Facilities: Hide, nature trails, information centre and toilets. **Public transport:** None.
Habitat: Wet grassland, arable farmland, saltmarsh, inter-tidal mudflats.
Key birds: *Winter*: Up to 9,500 Barnacle Geese, 4,000 Teal, 2,000 Wigeon, 1,000 Pintail, waders (inc. Dunlin, Knot, Oystercatcher). *Summer*: Breeding birds include Lapwing, Redshank, Sky Lark.
Contact: Eric Nielson, Mersehead, Southwick, Mersehead, Dumfries DG2 8AH. 01387 780 298.

9. MULL OF GALLOWAY

RSPB (South & West Scotland Office).
Location: NX 156 304. Most southerly tip of Scotland — five miles from village of Drummore, S of Stranraer.
Access: Open at all times. Access suitable for disabled. Disabled parking by centre. Centre open summer only (Apr-Oct).
Facilities: Visitor centre, toilets, nature trails, CCTV on cliffs.
Public transport: None.
Habitat: Sea cliffs, coastal heath.
Key birds: *Spring/summer*: Guillemot, Razorbill, Kittiwake, Black Guillemot, Puffin, Fulmar, Raven, Wheatear, Rock Pipit, Twite. Migrating Manx Shearwater. *All year*: Peregrine.
Contact: RSPB Scotland, 01671 404 975.

10. WIGTOWN BAY LOCAL NATURE RESERVE

Dumfries & Galloway Council.
Location: NX 465 545. Between Wigtown and Creetown, S of Newton Stewart. It is the largest LNR in Britain at 2,845 ha. The A75 runs along E side with A714 S to Wigtown and B7004 providing superb views of the LNR.
Access: Reserve open at all times. The hide is disabled-friendly. Main accesses: Roadside lay-bys on A75 near Creetown and parking at Martyr's Stake and Wigtown Harbour. All suitable for coaches. Visitor Centre in Wigtown County Building has coach parking and welcomes groups. It has full disabled access, including lift and toilets.
Facilities: Hide at Wigtown Harbour overlooking River Bladnoch, saltmarsh and fresh water wetland has disabled access from harbour car park. Walks and interpretation in this area. Visitor centre has a commanding view of the bay. CCTV of Ospreys breeding in Galloway during summer and wetland birds in winter. Open Mon-Sat (10am-5pm, later some days). Sun (2pm-5pm).
Public transport: Travel Information Line 08457 090 510 (local rate 9am-5pm Mon-Fri). Bus No 415 for Wigtown and W side. Bus No 431 or 500 X75 for

Creetown and E side.

Habitat: Estuary with extensive saltmarsh/merse and mudflats with developed fresh water wetland at Wigtown Harbour.

Key birds: *Winter*: Internationally important for Pink-footed Goose, nationally important for Curlew, Whooper Swan and Pintail, with major gull roost and other migratory coastal birds. *Summer*: Breeding waders and duck.

Other notable flora and fauna: Fish including smelt and shad. Lax-flowered sea-lavender, thrift, sea aster.

Contact: Elizabeth Tindal, Countryside Ranger, Wigtown Bay Visitor Centre, Wigtown, Dumfries & Galloway DG8 9JH01988 402 401, mobile 07702 212 728. e-mail: wblnr@dumgal.gov.uk www.dgcommunity.net/wblr

11. WOOD OF CREE

RSPB (South & West Scotland Office).

Location: NX 382 708. Four miles N of Newton Stewart on minor road from Minnigaff, parallel to A714.

Access: Open during daylight hours. Dogs on lead. Not suitable for disabled.

Facilities: Nature trails.

Public transport: None.

Habitat: Oak woodland, marshes, river.

Key birds: *Spring/summer:* Pied Flycatcher, Wood Warbler, Tree Pipit, Redstart, Buzzard, Great Spotted Woodpecker.

Other notable flora and fauna: Red squirrel, otter, Leisler's bat, carpet of bluebells and other spring wildflowers.

Contact: RSPB Scotland 01671 404 975.

Central Scotland

Argyll

1. COLL RESERVE

RSPB (South & West Scotland Office).

Location: NM 167 563. By ferry from Oban to island of Coll. Take the B8070 W from Arinagour for five miles. Turn R at Arileod. Continue for about one mile. Park at end of the road. Reception point at Totronald.

Access: Open all year. A natural site with unimproved paths not suitable for wheelchairs. Please avoid walking through fields and crops.

Facilities: Car park, information bothy at Totronald, guided walks in summer. Corn Crake viewing bench.

Public transport: None.

Habitat: Sand dunes, beaches, machair grassland, moorland, farmland.

Key birds: *Spring:* Gt Northern Diver offshore. Corn Crake arrive in late April. Displaying waders, inc Redshank, Lapwing, Snipe. *Summer:* Auks offshore, plus Gannet, shearwaters and terns. *Autumn:* Barnacle and Greenland White-fronted Geese arrive, thrushes on passage. Waders inc Purple Sandpiper. *Winter:* Long-tailed Duck, divers offshore. Hunting Hen Harrier and Merlin. Twite.

Other notable flora and fauna: Good for ceteceans and basking shark. Otter, 300-plus machair wildflowers inc rare orchids, great yellow bumblebee.

Contact: RSPB Coll Nature Reserve, Totronald, Isle of Coll, Argyll, PA78 6TB, 01879 230 301.

2. LOCH GRUINART, ISLAY

RSPB (South & West Scotland Office).

Location: NR 275 672. Sea loch on N coast of Islay, seven miles NW from Bridgend.

Access: Hide open all hours, visitor centre open (10am-5pm), disabled access to hide, viewing area and toilets. Assistance required for wheelchair users. Coach parking at visitor centre only. No dogs.

Facilities: Toilets (inc disabled), visitor centre (offers hot drinks), hide, trail. Two car parks — the one opposite the viewpoint is level and made from rolled stone. Group bookings accepted.

Public transport: Nearest bus stops 3 miles from reserve.

Habitat: Lowland wet grasslands, sea loch, moorland.

Key birds: *Oct-Apr:* Large numbers of Barnacle and White-fronted Geese, plus other wildfowl and waders. *May-Aug:* Breeding and displaying waders and Corn Crake. *Sept-Nov:* Many passage migrants and arriving wildfowl. Birds of prey are present all year, esp Hen Harrier and Peregrine, while Chough can be seen feeding in nearby fields. *Spring:* Displaying Snipe, Lapwing, Curlew and Redshank.

Other notable flora and fauna: Good chance of seeing otter, red and roe deer. Marsh fritillary butterflies during May and June. Herb-rich meadows.

Contact: Liz Hathaway, RSPB Scotland, Bushmills Cottage, Gruinart, Isle of Islay PA44 7PP. 01496 850 505. e-mail: loch.gruinart@rspb.org.uk www.rspb.org.uk/scotland

3. MACHRIHANISH SEABIRD OBSERVATORY

(sponsored by SNH and Leader)

John McGlynn, Nancie Smith and Eddie Maguire.

Location: NR 628 209. Southwest Kintyre, Argyll. Six miles W of Campbeltown on A83, then B843.

Access: Daily April-Oct. Wheelchair access. Dogs welcome. Parking for three cars. Digiscoping facilities include electricity and monitor.

Facilities: Seawatching hide, toilets in nearby village. Coach parking.

Public transport: Regular buses from Campbeltown (West Coast Motors, tel 01586 552 319).

Habitat: Marine, rocky shore and upland habitats.

Key birds: *Summer:* Golden Eagle, Peregrine, Storm Petrel and Twite. *Autumn:* Passage seabirds and waders. On-shore gales often produce inshore

NATURE RESERVES - SCOTLAND

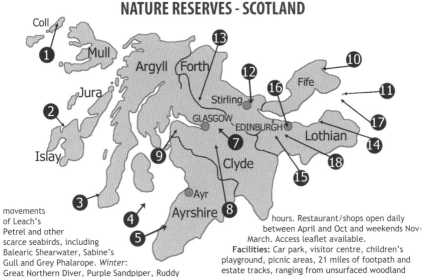

movements of Leach's Petrel and other scarce seabirds, including Balearic Shearwater, Sabine's Gull and Grey Phalarope. *Winter*: Great Northern Diver, Purple Sandpiper, Ruddy Turnstone with occasional Glaucous and Iceland Gulls.
Other notable flora and fauna: Grey and common seals, otter, wild goat.
Contact: Eddie Maguire, Warden, Seabird & Wildlife Observatory, Lossit Park, Machrihanish, SW Kintyre, Argyll PA28 6PZ. 07919 660 292.
e-mail: machrihanishbirds@btinternet.com
www.machrihanishbirds.org.uk

Ayrshire

4. AILSA CRAIG

RSPB (South & West Scotland Office).
Location: NX 020 998. Island is nine miles offshore, nearest town on mainland is Girvan.
Access: Accessible only by boat - no landing possible. Boat trips on the MFV Glorious (tel: 01465 713 219) or Kintyre Express (tel: 01294 270 160) from Girvan during the summer period. Also from Campbeltown by Mull of Kintyre Seatours' fast rib (Tel: 07785 542 811).
Facilities: None
Public transport: None.
Habitat: Dramatic seacliffs.
Key birds: Ailsa Craig is the third largest gannetry in the UK and supports 73,000 breeding seabirds, including Guillemont, Razorbill, Puffin, Black Guillemot, Kittiwake and up to 36,000 pairs of Gannets. Twite can also be found here.
Other notable flora and fauna: Slow worm.
Contact: RSPB South & West Scotland Office, 10 Park Quadrant, Glasgow, G3 6BS. 0141 331 0993.
e-mail: glasgow@rspb.org.uk

5. CULZEAN CASTLE & COUNTRY PARK

National Trust for Scotland.
Location: NS 234 103. 12 miles SW of Ayr on A719.
Access: Country Park open all year during daylight hours. Restaurant/shops open daily between April and Oct and weekends Nov-March. Access leaflet available.
Facilities: Car park, visitor centre, children's playground, picnic areas, 21 miles of footpath and estate tracks, ranging from unsurfaced woodland paths to metalled roads.
Public transport: Stagecoach bus No 60 (Ayr to Girvan) stops at site entrance. One mile walk downhill to visitor centre and castle.
Habitat: Shoreline, parkland, woodland, gardens, streams, ponds.
Key birds: *All year*: Good populations of common woodland species, inc Jay, Great Spotted Woodpecker and thrushes. *Spring/summer*: Arriving migrants, esp Blackcap, Chiffchaff and Willow Warbler. Nesting Raven and Gannet on cliffs, Gannet and terns offshore. *Autumn/winter*: Regular flocks of Redwing and Fieldfare, Waxwing, crossbills. Wildfowl on pond inc Little Grebe, Tufted Duck, Goldeneye. Offshore divers and Eider.
Other notable flora and fauna: The high diversity of flora and fauna due to range of habitats merits site being listed as SWT Wildlife Site. Roe deer, otter, water vole, several species of bat. Shoreline SSSI rich in rock pool life.
Contact: The Ranger Service, Culzean Castle & CP, Maybole, Ayrshire KA19 8LE. 0844 493 2148.

Clyde

7. BARON'S HAUGH

RSPB (South & West Scotland Office).
Location: RSPB NS 756 553. On SW edge of Motherwell, overlooking River Clyde. Via Adele Street, then lane off North Lodge Avenue.
Access: Open all year. Most paths suitable for wheelchairs, except circular nature trail, which has some steep sections.
Facilities: Four hides, information board in car park.
Public transport: None.
Habitat: Marshland, flooded areas, woodland, parkland, meadows, scrub, river.
Key birds: *Summer*: Breeding Gadwall, warblers (inc. Garden, Grasshopper); Whinchat, Common Sandpiper,

221

Kingfisher, Sand Martin. *Autumn:* Excellent for waders (22 species). *Winter:* Whooper Swan, Pochard, Wigeon, Sparrowhawk.
Contact: RSPB South & West Scotland Office,10 Park Quadrant, Glasgow, G3 6BS. 01413 30 993.

8. FALLS OF CLYDE

Scottish Wildlife Trust.
Location: NS 88 34 14. Approx one mile S of Lanark. Directions from Glasgow – travel S on M74 until J7 then along A72, following signs for Lanark and New Lanark.
Access: Open during daylight hours all year. Disabled access limited.
Facilities: Visitor centre open 11am-5pm Mar-Dec, 12-4pm Jan-Feb. Toilets and cafeteria on site. Seasonal viewing facility for Peregrines. Numerous walkways and ranger service offers comprehensive guided walks programme.
Public transport: Scotrail trains run to Lanark (0845 7484 950). Local bus service from Lanark to New Lanark.
Habitat: River Clyde gorge, waterfalls, mixed woodland and broadleaved riparian gorge, meadow, pond.
Key birds: More than 100 species of bird recorded on the reserve, including unrivalled views of breeding Peregrine. Others include Tawny Owl, Kingfisher, Dipper, Great Spotted Woodpecker, Spotted Flycatcher and Goosander.
Contact: Miss Lindsay Cook, The Falls of Clyde Reserve & Visitor Centre, New Lanark, South Lanark ML11 9DB. 01555 665 262.
e-mail: fallsofclyde@swt.co.uk www.swt.org.uk

9. LOCHWINNOCH

RSPB (South & West Scotland Office).
Location: NS 358 582. 18 miles SW of Glasgow, adjacent to A760.
Access: Open every day except Christmas and Boxing Day, Jan 1 and Jan 2. (10am-5pm).
Facilities: Special facilities for schools and disabled. Refreshments available. Visitor centre, hides.
Public transport: Rail station adjacent, bus services nearby.
Habitat: Shallow lochs, marsh, mixed woodland.
Key birds: *Winter:* Wildfowl (esp. Whooper Swan, Wigeon, Goosander, Goldeneye). Occasional passage migrants inc. Whimbrel, Greenshank. *Summer:* Breeding Great Crested Grebe, Water Rail, Sedge and Grasshopper Warblers, Reed Bunting.
Contact: RSPB Nature Centre, Largs Road, Lochwinnoch, Renfrewshire PA12 4JF. 01505 842 663; Fax 01505 843 026; e-mail lochwinnoch@rspb.org.uk.

Fife

10. EDEN ESTUARY

Fife Council.
Location: 470 195 (centre of site). The Local Nature Reserve can be accessed from Guardbridge, St Andrews (one mile) on A91, and from Leuchars via Tentsmuir Forest off A919 (four miles). Use Outhead at St Andrews off West Sands beach to access Balgove Bay. Tentsmuir Forest car park best for northern access and Guardbridge village best for the River Eden section of reserve. Coble Shore southern access at GR 467 188.
Access: Eden Estuary Centre, Guardbridge: open (9am-5pm) all days except Dec 25, Jan 1 and Leuchars Airshow day. Evans Hide: at GR 483 183, parking at Pilmuir Links golf course car park. Combination number required from ranger service.
Facilities: Visitor centre at Guardbridge. Information panels at Outhead. Hide at Balgove Bay (key from Ranger Service).
Public transport: Leuchars train station (1.5 miles), regular bus service from Cupar and Dundee. Tel 08457 484 950.
Habitat: Intertidal mudflats, saltmarsh, river, reed, sand dunes and wetland.
Key birds: *Winter and passage:* Significant numbers of waders and wildfowl. Outer estuary is good place for sea duck such as scoter, Eider and Long-tailed Duck,plus Gannet, terns and skuas. Mudflats ideal for godwits, plovers, sandpipers, Redshank and Shelduck. River good for Kingfisher, Common Sandpiper and Goosander. Surrounding area is good for Short and Long-eared Owl, Peregrine, Marsh Harrier and Merlin. Osprey are regular visitors, daily throughout the season.
Other notable flora and fauna: Northern marsh orchid, dune grasses, herbs, maiden pink, saltmarsh grasses and reed systems. Common harbour seal, bottle-nosed dolphin, porpoise, brown hare, stoat. Butterflies include comma, grayling, small pearl-bordered, dark green fritilliary, painted lady and orange tip.
Contact: Ranald Strachan, Fife Ranger Service, Harbourmaster House, Hot Pot Wynd, Dysart, KY1 2TQ. 01592 656 080, mobile: 07985 707 593; e-mail: Ranald.Strachan@fife.gov.uk

11. ISLE OF MAY NATIONAL NATURE RESERVE

Scottish Natural Heritage.
Location: NT 655 995. This small island lying six miles off Fife Ness in the Firth of Forth is a National Nature Reserve.
Access: Boats run from Anstruther and North Berwick. Contact SNH for details 01334 654038. Keep to paths. Fishing boat from Anstruther arranged for those using Observatory accommodation. Delays are possible, both arriving and leaving, because of weather.
Facilities: No dogs; no camping; no fires. Prior permission required if scientific work or filming is to be carried out.
Public transport: Regular bus service to Anstruther and North Berwick harbour.
Habitat: Sea cliffs, rocky shoreline.
Key birds: Early *Summer:* Breeding auks and terns, Kittiwake, Shag, Eider, Fulmar. Over 68,000 pairs of Puffins. *Autumn/spring:* Weather-related migrations include rarities each year.

NATURE RESERVES - SCOTLAND

Contact: For Observatory accomodation: David Thorne, Craigurd House, Blyth Bridge, West Linton, Peeblesshire EH46 7AH. For all other enquiries: SNH, 46 Crossgate, Cupar, Fife KY15 5HS.

Forth

12. CAMBUS POOLS

Scottish Wildlife Trust.
Location: NS 846 937. Take A907 from Stirling towards Alloa, then Station Road to Cambus village. Park by river in village.
Access: Cross River Devon by bridge at NS 853 940 and walk down stream on R bank past bonded warehouses. Open all year.
Facilities: Bench on S side of western pool.
Public transport: None.
Habitat: Wet grassland with two salty pools.
Key birds: Used extensively by migrants in spring and autumn, inc. wildfowl and waders such as Black-tailed Godwit and Greenshank. Gadwall have bred here and Kingfisher is seen regularly.
Other notable flora and fauna: Brown hare, stoat, short-tailed vole, 115 species of vascular plants. Harbour porpoise seen in Forth.
Contact: SWT headquarters 01313 127 765.

13. INVERSNAID

RSPB (South & West Scotland Office).
Location: NN 337 088. On E side of Loch Lomond. Via B829 W from Aberfoyle, then along minor road to car park by Inversnaid Hotel.
Access: Open all year.
Facilities: New car park and trail at Garrison Farm (NN 348 095).
Public transport: None.
Habitat: Deciduous woodland rises to craggy ridge and moorland.
Key birds: *Summer:* Breeding Black Grouse, Snipe, Cuckoo, Wheatear and Twite. Raven, Grey Wagtail, Dipper, Wood Warbler, Redstart, Pied Flycatcher, Tree Pipit. The loch is on a migration route, especially for wildfowl and waders. Look for Red-throated and Black-throated Divers in spring. *Winter:* Hen Harrier and thrushes.
Other notable flora and fauna: Pine marten, slow worm, 17 species of butterfly inc small pearl-bordered fritillary on nature trail at Inversaid. Wilson's and Tunbridge filmy ferns on boulders through woodland.
Contact: RSPB South & West Scotland Office, 10 Park Quadrant, Glasgow, G3 6BS. 01413 310 993.

Lothian

14. ABERLADY BAY

East Lothian Council (LNR).
Location: NT 472 806. From Edinburgh take A198 E to Aberlady. Reserve is 1.5 miles E of Aberlady village.

Access: Open at all times. Please stay on footpaths to avoid disturbance. Disabled access from reserve car park. No dogs please.
Facilities: Small car park and toilets. Notice board with recent sightings at end of footbridge.
Public transport: Edinburgh to N Berwick bus service stops at reserve (request), service no 124. Railway 4 miles away at Longniddry.
Habitat: Tidal mudflats, saltmarsh, freshwater marsh, dune grassland, scrub, open sea.
Key birds: *Summer:* Breeding birds include Shelduck, Eider, Reed Bunting and up to eight species of warbler. Passage waders inc. Green, Wood and Curlew Sandpipers, Little Stint, Greenshank, Whimbrel, Black-tailed Godwit. *Winter:* Divers (esp. Red-throated), Red-necked and Slavonian Grebes and geese (large numbers of Pink-footed roost); sea-ducks, waders.
Contact: John Harrison, Reserve Warden, Landscape & Countryside Management, East Lothian Council, Council Buildings, East Lothian EH41 3HA. 01875 870 588. email: jharrison@eastlothian.gov.uk www.aberlady.org

15. ALMONDELL & CALDERWOOD COUNTRY PARK

West Lothian Council.
Location: NT 091 697. North entrance, the closest to the visitor centre is signposted off A89, two miles S of Broxburn.
Access: Open all year. Parking available at N entrance. S entrance at East Calder. Mid Calder and Oakbank on A71 (furthest from visitor centre). Disabled car park at visitor centre. Coach parking available with prior notice.
Facilities: Car park, picnic area, hot and cold drinks, toilets, pushchair access, partial access for wheelchairs, visitor centre (open every day), gift shop, countryside ranger service.
Habitat: Woodland, river.
Key birds: *Spring/summer:* Woodcock, Tawny Owl, Grasshopper Warbler, Yellowhammer, Blackcap, Garden Warbler. *Winter:* Goldcrest, Redpoll, Willow Tit. *All year:* Dipper, Grey Wagtail, Sparrowhawk.
Contact: Head Ranger, Almondell and Calderwood Country Park Visitor Centre, Broxburn, West Lothian EH52 5PE, 01506 882 254.
e-mail: almondell&calderwood@westlothian.gov.uk www.beecraigs.com

16. BAWSINCH AND DUDDINGSTON LOCH

Scottish Wildlife Trust/Historic Scotland
Location: NT 284 725. Centre of Edinburgh, below Arthur's Seat. Use car park on Duddingston Road West and Holyrood Park Gate.
Access: Open access to north shore of loch and Cavalry ground to SE.
Remainder of site and hide by prior arrangement with C.McLean, 88 Gilmore Place, Edinburgh.
Facilities: Hide with bird and plant lists.
Public transport: Call SWT on 0131 312 7765 for advice.
Habitat: Reedbed, marsh, loch, ponds, mixed

223

woodland, flower meadow and scrub. Developed from former waste area.

Key birds: Heronry. Loch has breeding swans, geese, ducks and grebes. Summer migrants, winter-roosting wildfowl.

Key flora and fauna: Fox and otter. Damselfly, four species of amphibian.

Contact: Trust HQ, 0131 312 7765.

17. BASS ROCK

Location: NT 605 875. Island NE of North Berwick.

Access: Private property. Regular daily sailings from N Berwick around Rock; local boatman has owner's permission to land individuals or parties by prior arrangement. For details contact 01620 892 838 or The Scottish Seabird Centre 01620 890 202; www.seabird.org

Facilities: None.

Habitat: Sea cliffs.

Key birds: The spectacular cliffs hold a large Gannet colony, (up to 9,000 pairs), plus auks, Kittiwake, Shag and Fulmar.

18. GLADHOUSE RESERVOIR

Scottish Water.

Location: NT 295 535. S of Edinburgh off the A703.

Access: Open all year although there is no access to the reservoir itself. Most viewing can be done from the road (telescope required).

Facilities: Small car park on north side. Not suitable for coaches.

Habitat: Reservoir, grassland, farmland.

Key birds: *Spring/summer*: Oystercatcher, Lapwing, Curlew. Possible Black Grouse. *Winter*: Geese, including Pinkfeet, Twite, Brambling, Hen Harrier.

Contact: Scottish Water, PO Box 8855, Edinburgh, EH10 6YQ, 084 6 018 855.

e-mail: customer.service@scottishwater.co.uk
www.scottishwater.co.uk

Eastern Scotland

Angus & Dundee

1. BALGAVIES LOCH

Scottish Wildlife Trust.

Location: NO523 516. From car park on A932, four miles E of Forfar.

Access: All areas apart from hide restricted. Groups should apply in advance.

Facilities: Hide, path.

Public transport: None.

Habitat: Loch, fen and woodland.

Key birds: *Winter*: Wildfowl and wetland breeding birds.

Contact: Montrose Basin Wildlife Centre, 01674 676 336. www.rspb.org

2. LOCH OF LINTRATHEN

Scottish Wildlife Trust.

Location: NO 278 550. Seven miles W of Kirriemuir. Take B951 and choose circular route on unclassified roads round loch.

Access: Two public hides (one wheelchair-accessible) open 24 hours a day. Rest of reserve is private, but good viewing is possible from several places along unclassified roads.

Facilities: Viewpoint can accommodate five cars.

Public transport: None.

Habitat: Mesotrophic loch designated a Ramsar site because of its value to waterbirds. Surrounded by mainly coniferous woodland.

Key birds: *Summer*: Grey Heron, Great Crested Grebe and other water birds. Osprey. *Winter*: Internationally-important numbers of Icelandic Greylag Geese, plus Goosander, Whooper Swan, Wigeon, Teal and other wildfowl.

Other notable flora and fauna: Red squirrel.

Contact: Robert Potter, SWT, Gardener's Cottage, Balhary Estate, Alyth PH11 8LT. 07920 468 568.

e-mail: rpotter@swt.org.uk

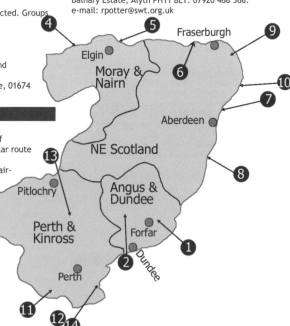

Moray & Nairn

4. CULBIN SANDS

RSPB (North Scotland Office).
Location: NH 900 576. Approx ½ mile NE of Nairn, overlooking Moray Firth. Access to parking at East Beach car park, signed off A96.
Access: Open at all times. 750m path to Minster's Pool suitable for all abilities.
Facilities: Toilets (inc disabled) and bike racks at car park. Track along dunes and saltmarsh.
Public transport: Buses stop in St Ninian's Road, Nairn, half mile W of site. Call Rapsons on 0870 608 2608 or Stagecoach on 01862 892 683. Train station in Nairn three-quarters mile W of reserve.
Habitat: Saltmarsh, sandflats, dunes.
Key birds: *Winter*: Flocks of Common Scoter, Long-tailed Duck, Knot, Bar-tailed Godwit, Red-breasted Merganser. Raptors including Peregrine, Merlin and Hen Harrier attracted by wader flocks. Roosting geese, Snow Bunting flocks. *Spring*: Tern flock, esp Sandwich, passage waders. *Summer*: Breeding Eider, Ringed Plover, Oystercatcher. Osprey on passage.
Other notable flora and fauna: Dolphins in Firth. Otters sometimes seen.
Contact: RSPB North Scotland Office, Etive House, Beechwood Park, Inverness IV2 3BW. 01463 715 000. e-mail: nsro@rspb.org.uk www.rspb.org.uk

5. SPEY BAY

Scottish Wildlife Trust.
Location: NJ 335 657. Eight miles NE of Elgin. From Elgin take A96 and B9015 to Kingston. Reserve is immediately E of village. Car parks at Kingston and Tugnet.
Access: Open all year.
Facilities: Car park, information board.
Public transport: None.
Habitat: Shingle, rivermouth and coastal habitats.
Key birds: *Summer*: Osprey, waders, wildfowl. *Winter*: Seaduck and divers offshore, esp. Long-tailed Duck, Common and Velvet Scoters, Red-throated Diver.
Other notable flora and fauna: Otter, plus dolphin offshore. Good range of dragonflies.
Contact: Robert Potter, Gardener's Cottage, Balhary Estate, Alyth, PH11 8LT. 07920 468 568. e-mail: rpotter@swt.org.uk

6. TROUP HEAD

RSPB (East Scotland).
Location: NJ 825 672. Troup Head is between Pennan and Gardenstown on B9031, E along coast from Macduff. It is signposted off B9031. Look for small RSPB signs which direct you past the farm buildings to car park.
Access: Unrestricted, but not suitable for wheelchair users.
Facilities: Parking for small number of cars. Not suitable for coaches. Live pictures are beamed from the reserve to the Macduff Marine Aquarium

during the summer. Boat trips run from Macduff (contact Puffin Cruises 07900 920 445) and Banff or Gardenstown (contact North 580 01261 819 900).
Public transport: None.
Habitat: Sea cliffs, farmland.
Key birds: Spectacular seabird colony, including Scotland's only mainland nesting Gannets. Bonxies linger in summer. Migrants occur during spring/autumn.
Other notable flora and fauna: Impressive common flower assemblage in spring. Ceteceans possible offshore in summer including minke whale. Brown hare common.
Contact: RSPB Troup Head Warden, c/o Starnafin Farmhouse, Crimond, Fraserburgh AB43 8QN. 01346 532 017. E-mail: troup@rspb.org.uk

NE Scotland

7. FORVIE NATIONAL NATURE RESERVE

Scottish Natural Heritage.
Location: NK 034 289. 12 miles N of Aberdeen. Through Newburgh off A975 road.
Access: Reserve open at all times but ternery closed Apr 1 to end of Aug annually. Stevenson Forvie Centre open every day (Apr-Sept) and, outside these months when staff are available. Centre and short trail are wheelchair-accessible.
Facilities: Interpretive display and toilets at Stevenson Forvie Centre. Bird hide, waymarked trails. Coach parking at Waterside car park and Stevenson Forvie Centre.
Public transport: Bluebird No 263 to Cruden Bay. Ask for the Newburgh or Collieston Crossroads stop. Tel: 01224 591 381.
Habitat: Estuary, dunes, coastal heath.
Key birds: *Spring/summer*: Breeding Eider and terns. Migrant waders and seabirds offshore. *Autumn*: Pink-footed Goose, migrant seabirds, waders and passerines inc occasional scarce species or rarity. *Winter*: Waders and wildfowl, inc Whooper Swan, Long-tailed Duck and Golden Plover.
Other notable flora and fauna: Occasional ceteceans offshore, esp in summer.
Contact: Annabel Drysdale (Reserve Manager), Scottish Natural Heritage, Stevenson Forvie Centre, Little Collieston Croft, Collieston, Aberdeenshire AB41 8RU. 01358 751 330.
www.snh.org.uk

8. FOWLSHEUGH

RSPB
Location: NO 879 80. Cliff top path N from Crawton, signposted from A92, three miles S of Stonehaven.
Access: Unrestricted. Not suitable for wheelchair users.
Facilities: Car park with 12 spaces, 200 yards from reserve.
Public transport: Request bus stop (Stonehaven to Johnshaven route). Mile walk to reserve entrance.

Habitat: Sea cliffs.
Key birds: Spectacular 130,000-strong seabird colony, mainly Kittiwake and Guillemot plus Razorbill, Fulmar and Puffin. Gannet, Eider and skuas offshore, inc Bonxies lingering in summer. *Autumn:* Red-throated Diver on sea, terns on passage.
Other notable flora and fauna: Grey and common seals, bottle-nosed dolphin regular, white-beaked dolphin and minke whale occasional in summer. Spring flowers, common butterflies and moths.
Contact: RSPB Fowlsheugh Warden , c/o Starnafin Farmhouse, Crimond, Fraserburgh AB43 8QN. 01346 532 017. e-mail: strathbeg@rspb.org.uk www.rspb.org.uk

9. LOCH OF STRATHBEG

RSPB.
Location: NK 057 581. Britain's largest dune loch is near Crimond on the A90, nine miles S of Fraserburgh.
Access: Visitor Centre open daily 8am-6pm. Tower Pool, Bay and Fen Hides open dawn-dusk. Visitor centre wheelchair accessible. Coach parking available – book in advance.
Facilities: Visitor centre, with toilets and coffee machine. Tower Pool hide accessible via 700 metre footpath. Two hides overlooking Loch accessed via drive to Airfield. Wildlife garden, indoor children's area – kid's backpacks available to borrow.
Public transport: Access to whole reserve difficult without vehicle. Buses from Fraserburgh and Peterhead to Crimond, one mile from centre. Details at www.travelinescotland.com.
Habitat: Dune loch with surrounding marshes, reedbeds, grasslands and dunes.
Key birds: Breeding wetland species, passage waders, internationally important numbers of wintering wildfowl. Scarcities year round. *Winter:* Pink-footed and Barnacle Geese, Whooper Swan, large numbers of duck. Snow Goose and Smew annual. Raptors including Hen and Marsh Harriers. Great Northern Diver offshore. *Summer:* Common Tern, Water Rail, Corn Bunting. *Spring/autumn:* Little Egret, Spoonbill, Avocet, Marsh Harrier, Garganey, Little Gull, occasional Pectoral Sandpiper.
Other notable flora and fauna: Otter, badger, stoat, roe deer. Early purple, butterfly and northern marsh orchids, dark green fritillary butterfly.
Contact: RSPB Loch of Strathbeg, Starnafin, Crimond, Fraserburgh, AB43 8QN. 01346 532 017.
e-mail: strathbeg@rspb.org.uk
www.rspb.org.uk/reserves/guide/l/lochofstrathbeg

10. LONGHAVEN CLIFFS

Scottish Wildlife Trust.
Location: NK 116 394. 3.8 miles S of Peterhead. Take A952 S from Peterhead and then A975 to Bullers of Buchan (gorge).
Access: Access from car park at Blackhills quarry or Bullers of Buchan.
Facilities: Leaflet available. Parking.
Habitat: Rugged red granite cliffs and cliff-top vegetation.

Key birds: : Nine species of breeding seabird, including Kittiwake, Shag, Guillemot, Razorbill, Puffin.
Other notable flora and fauna: Unusual form of coastal heath has developed, with plants such as bell heather, crowberry, devil's-bit scabious and grass-of-Parnassus. Grey seals in sheltered inlets. Porpoise, dolphin and minke whale occasionally seen.
Contact: SWT headquarters 0131 312 7765.

Perth & Kinross

11. DOUNE PONDS

Stirling Council.
Location: NN 726 019. Take A820 Dunblane road E from the junction with the A84 Callander-Stirling road. Turn L onto Moray Street just before Doune Church.
Access: Open all year.
Facilities: Information board, nature trail, hides. Wheelchair access to both hides. Leaflet from local tourist information offices, local library.
Public transport: Bus: from Stirling and Callander to Doune. Traveline 0870 608 2608.
Habitat: Pools, scrape, plantations, birch woodlands.
Key birds: *All year:* Grey Heron, Buzzard, Snipe, Goldcrest, Siskin, Red Kite. *Spring/summer:* Common Sandpiper, Whitethroat, warblers.
Contact: Stirling Council Countryside Ranger Service, Viewforth, Stirling FK8 2ET. 0845 2777 000.

12. LOCH LEVEN NATIONAL NATURE RESERVE

SNH/Loch Leven Laboratory.
Location: NO 150 010. Head S from Perth and leave M90 at exit 6, Kinross.
Access: Traditional access areas at three stretches of shoreline. New local access guidance is in place at the site. See www.snh.org.uk for details or pick up leaflet locally. New paths are in place between Kinross and Burleigh Sands.
Facilities: Hides and paths along the west shore. Café and toilets at Kinross harbout. Observation room, café, shop and toilets at Vane Farm.
Public transport: Bus from Perth or Edinburgh to Kinross.
Habitat: Lowland loch with islands.
Key birds: *Winter:* Flocks of geese (more than 20,000 Pinkfeet), huge numbers of the full range of ducks, Whooper Swan. *Summer:* Greatest concentration of inland breeding ducks in Britain (10 species), Osprey and grebes. *Passage:* Waders (Golden Plover flocks up to 500).
Contact: Paul Brooks, SNH, Loch Leven Laboratory, The Pier, Kinross KY13 8UF. 01577 864 439.
www.snh.org.uk

13. LOCH OF THE LOWES

Scottish Wildlife Trust.
Location: NO 042 435. Sixteen miles N of Perth, two miles NE of Dunkeld, just off A923 (signposted).
Access: Visitor centre open Apr-Sept inclusive (10am-

5pm). Observation hide open all year during daylight hours. No dogs allowed. Full access for wheelchairs.
Facilities: Visitor centre with toilets, observation hide.
Public transport: Railway station at Birnam/Dunkeld, three miles from reserve. Bus from Dunkeld two miles from reserve.
Habitat: Freshwater loch with fringing woodland.
Key birds: Breeding Ospreys (Apr-end Aug). Nest in view, 200 metres from hide. Wildfowl and woodland birds. Greylag roost (Oct-Mar).
Contact: Peter Ferns, (Manager), Scottish Wildlife Trust, Loch of the Lowes, Visitor Centre, Dunkeld, Perthshire PH8 0HH. 01350 727 337.

14. VANE FARM

RSPB Scotland
Location: NT 160 990. Part of Loch Leven National Nature Reserve. Seven miles from Cowdenbeath, signposted two miles E of J5 from M90 onto B9097. Drive for approx two miles. The nature centre car park is on R.
Access: Open daily (10am-5pm) except Christmas Day, Boxing Day, Jan 1 and Jan 2. Cost £3 adults, £2 concessions, 50p children, £6 family. Free to members. Disabled access to shop, coffee shop, observation room and toilets. Coach parking available for up to two coaches. Free car parking.

Facilities: Shop, coffee shop and observation room with five telescopes overlooking Loch Leven and the reserve. There is a 1.25 mile hill trail through woodland and moorland. Wetland trail with three observation hides. Toilets, including disabled. binoculars can be hired from shop.
Public transport: Trains to Cowdenbeath (7 miles), but no bus service from here. Limited bus service (204) runs to the reserve from Kinross (4 miles) on Wednesdays, Saturdays and Sundays. Contact Stagecoach Fife on 01383 511911 for further details. Eight-mile cycle path around loch.
Habitat: Wet grassland and flooded areas by Loch Leven. Arable farmland. Native woodland and heath moorland.
Key birds: *Spring/summer:* Breeding and passage waders (including Lapwing, Redshank, Snipe, Curlew). Farmland birds (including Sky Lark and Yellowhammer), Tree Pipit. *Autumn:* Migrating waders on exposed mud. *Winter:* Whooper Swan, Bewick's Swan, Pink-footed Goose, finch and tit flocks.
Other notable flora and fauna: 237 butterfly and moth species. 25 mammal species including pipstrelle bat and roe deer.
Contact: Uwe Stoneman, Business Manager, Vane Farm Nature Centre, Kinross, Tayside KY13 9LX. 01577 862 355. e-mail: vanefarm@rspb.co.uk

Highlands & Islands

Highlands, Caithness and Sutherland

1. BEINN EIGHE

Scottish Natural Heritage.
Location: NG 990 620. By Kinlochewe, Wester Ross, 50 miles from Inverness and 20 miles from Gairloch on A832.
Access: Reserve open at all times, no charge. Visitor centre open Easter-Oct (10am-5pm).
Facilities: Visitor centre, toilets, woodland trail and mountain trail (self-guided with leaflets from visitor centre). Trails suitable for all abilities.
Public transport: Very limited.
Habitat: Caledonian pine forest, dwarf shrub heath, mountain tops, freshwater loch shore.
Key birds: *All year:* Golden Eagle, Scottish Crossbill, Ptarmigan, Red Grouse, Siskin. *Summer:* Black-throated Diver, Redwing, Snow Bunting.
Other notable flora and fauna: Wide range of dragonflies, including golden ringed and common hawker.
Contact: Eoghain Maclean, Reserve Manager, Scottish

Natural Heritage, Anancaun, Kinlochewe, Ross-shire IV22 2PD. 01445 760 254.
e-mail: eoghain.maclean@snh.gov.uk

2. CORRIMONY

RSPB (North Scotland Office).
Location: NH 379 304. Lies SW of Inverness between Glen Affric and Loch Ness, off A 831.
Access: Open at all times. Unimproved paths, so terrain may not be suitable for disabled visitors.
Facilities: Way-marked trail (8.5 miles long) passes through farm. Please leave gates as you find them. Guided minibus safaris to see Black Grouse leks in April and May.
Public transport: No 17 bus from Inverness to Cannich stops 1.5 miles from reserve.
Habitat: Pine woodland, moorland, blanket bog.
Key birds: Black Grouse, Crested Tit, crossbill species, occasional Golden Eagle and Osprey. Breeding Greenshank, Red Grouse, Black-throated Diver. *Autumn:* Whooper Swan, Pinkfooted Goose, Woodcock.
Other notable flora and fauna: Red deer, pine marten. Many orchids in July.
Contact: RSPB North Scotland Office, Etive House, Beechwood Park, Inverness IV2 3BW. 01463 715 000.
e-mail: nsro@rspb.org.uk

3. FAIRY GLEN

RSPB (North Scotland Office).
Location: NH 732 580. On the Black Isle, by Rosemarkie on the A832.
Access: Open all year.
Facilities: Car park, nature trail. Coach parking available.
Public transport: Buses between Inverness and Cromarty stops in reserve car park. Bus info contact: Rapsons on 0870 608 2608.
Habitat: Broadleaved woodland in a steep-sided valley, stream, waterfalls.
Key birds: *All year:* Large rookery, Dipper, Buzzard, Grey Wagtail, usual woodland species. Migrant warblers in spring/summer.
Other notable flora and fauna: Roe deer. Range of dragonflies, pipistrelle bat, bluebells and other spring woodland plants.
Contact: RSPB North Scotland Office, Etive House, Beechwood Park, Inverness IV2 3BW. 01463 715 000.
e-mail: nsro@rspb.org.uk

4. FORSINARD

RSPB (North Scotland Office).
Location: NC 890 425. 30 miles SW of Thurso on A897. Turn off at Helmsdale from S (24 miles) or A836 at Melvich from N coast road (14 miles).
Access: Open at all times. Contact reserve office during breeding season (mid-Apr to end Jul) and during deerstalking season (Jul 1 to Feb 15) for advice. Families welcome. Self-guided trail open all year, requested no dogs, no suitable for wheelchairs.
Facilities: Visitor centre open Apr 1 to Oct 31 (9am-5.30pm), seven days per week. Static and AV displays, Hen Harrier nest CCTV. Wheelchair access to centre and toilet. Guided walks Tue and Thu afternoon, May-Aug. Hotel and B&B nearby.
Public transport: Train from Inverness and Thurso (08457 484 950). RSPB visitor centre is in former Forsinard Station building.
Habitat: Blanket bog, upland hill farm.
Key birds: The best time to visit for birds is May-July. Join a guided walk for the best chance of views of Red-throated Diver, Golden Plover, Greenshank, Dunlin, Hen Harrier, Merlin, Short-eared Owl. Few birds between Sep-Feb.
Other notable flora and fauna: Red deer, azure hawker dragonfly, emperor moth.
Contact: RSPB, Forsinard Flows Reserve, Forsinard, Sutherland KW13 6YT. 01641 571 225.
e-mail: forsinard@rspb.org.uk

5. HANDA

Scottish Wildlife Trust.
Location: NC 138 480. Island accessible by boat from Tarbet, near Scourie — follow A894 N from Ullapool 40 miles. Continue another three miles, turn L down single track road another three miles to Tarbet.
Access: Open April-Sept. Boats leave 9.30am-2pm (last boat back 5pm). Dogs not allowed. Visitors are asked for a contribution of £2 towards costs. Not suitable for disabled due to uneven terrain.
Facilities: Three mile circular path, shelter (no toilets on island — use those in Tarbet car park). Visitors are given introductory talk and a leaflet with map on arrival.
Public transport: Post bus to Scourie (tel 01549 402 357 Lairg Post Office). Train to Lairg (tel 0845 484 950 National Train enquiries). No connecting public transport between Scourie and Tarbet.
Habitat: Sea cliffs, blanket bog.
Key birds: *Spring/summer:* Biggest Guillemot and Razorbill colony in Britain and Ireland. Also nationally important for Kittiwakes, Arctic and Great Skuas. Puffin, Shag, Fulmar and Common and Arctic Terns also present.
Contact: Mark Foxwell, Conservation Manager, Unit 4A, 3 Carsegate Road North, Inverness IV3 8PU. 01463 714 746. Charles Thomson (Boatman) 01971 502 347.
e-mail: mfoxwell@swt.org.uk
www.swt.org.uk

6. INSH MARSHES

RSPB (North Scotland Office).
Location: NN 775 998. In Spey Valley, two miles NE of Kingussie on B970 minor road.
Access: Open at all times. No disabled access. Coach parking available along access road to car park.
Facilities: Information viewpoint, two hides, three nature trails. Not suitable for disabled. No toilets.
Public transport: Nearest rail station and bus stop at Kingussie (two miles).
Habitat: Marshes, woodland, river, open water.
Key birds: *Spring/summer:* Waders (Lapwing, Curlew, Redshank, Snipe), wildfowl (including Goldeneye and Wigeon), Osprey, Wood Warbler, Redstart, Tree Pipit. *Winter:* Hen Harrier, Whooper Swan, other wildfowl.
Other notable flora and fauna: Black and highland darter dragonflies along Invertromie trail plus northern brown argus butterflies. Five species of orchid in Tromie Meadow. Roe deer.
Contact: Pete Moore, Ivy Cottage, Insh, Kingussie, Inverness-shire PH21 1NT. 01540 661 518.
e-mail: pete.moore@rspb.org.uk
www.visitkincraig.com

7. ISLE OF EIGG

Scottish Wildlife Trust.
Location: NM 38 48. Small island S of Skye, reached by ferry from Mallaig or Arisaig (approx 12 miles).
Access: Ferries seven days per week (weather permitting) during summer. Four days per week (weather permitting) between Sept-Apr. Coach parties would need to transfer to ferries for visit to Eigg. Please contact ferry companies prior to trip. Mix of roads, hardcore tracks and rough paths on island.
Facilities: Pier centre: shop/post office, tea-room, craftshop, toilets.
Public transport: Train service from Glasgow, via Arisaig to Mallaig. Cal-Mac (01687 462 403) ferries (no sailing Wed and sun), MV Sheerwater (no sailing Thurs, tel: 01687 450 224). Island minibus/taxi usually available at the pier.

Habitat: Moorland (leading to Sgurr pitchstone ridge), extensive woodland and scrub, marshland,and bog, hay meadows, sandy bays and rocky shorelines.
Key birds: *All year*: Resident species include Red-throated Diver, Golden Eagle, Hen Harrier, Woodcock and Raven. *Summer*: Cuckoo, Wheatear, Whitethroat, Whinchat, Sedge and Willow Warblers, Twite. Large numbers of Manx Shearwaters offshore with Storm-petrels regularly seen from boats between June-Sept.
Other notable flora and fauna: 17 species of butterfly recorded, including green hairstreak, small pearl-bordered and dark green fritillaries. Nine species of damsel/dragonfly occur with golden ringed, common hawker and highland darter the most numerous. Approx 500 species of 'higher' plants listed, including 12 species of orchid, and alpine/arctic species such as mountain aven and moss campion. Carpet of primroses, bluebells and wild garlic in spring. Otters not uncommon and minke whales, bottle-nosed and common dolphins and harbour porpoises regularly recorded offshore. Basking sharks can be quite numerous in early summer.
Contact: John Chester, Millers Cottage, Isle of Eigg, Small Isles PH42 4RL. 01687 482 477. www.isleofeigg.org

8. ISLE OF RUM

Scottish Natural Heritage
Location: NM 370 970. Island lying S of Skye. Passenger ferry from Mallaig, take A830 from Fort William.
Access: Contact Reserve Office for details of special access arrangements relating to breeding birds, deer stalking and deer research.
Facilities: Kinloch Castle Hostel, 01687 462 037, Lea Cottage B&B, 01687 462 036. General store and post office, Kinloch Castle tea shop and bar. Guided walks in summer.
Public transport: The Shearwater boat from Arisaig — 01687 450 224, also Caledonian MacBrayne ferry from Mallaig, 01687 450224, www. arisaig.co.uk
Habitat: Coast, moorland, woodland restoration, montane.
Key birds: *Summer*: Unique mountain-top Manx Shearwater colony (a third of the world population). Seabird breeding colony including auks, Kittiwake, Fulmar, Eider, Shag. Gull colonies including Common, Herring, Lesser and Greater Black-backed. Upland breeding species including Golden Plover, Wheatear, Merlin, Kestrel. *Late autumn/spring*: Thrush passage. *Winter*: Greylag Geese, Oystercatcher, Red-breasted Merganser.
Other notable flora and fauna: Butterflies including small white, green veined, large white, green hairstreak, small copper, common blue, red admiral, small tortoiseshell, dark green fritillary, peacock etc. Various dragonflies. Heath spotted orchid. Feral goat, red deer, otter, Rhum highland pony, palmate newt, lizard.
Contact: SNH Reserve Office, Isle of Rum, PH43 4RR01687 462 026; Fax 01687 462805.

9. LOCH FLEET

Scottish Wildlife Trust.
Location: NH 794 965. Site lies two miles S of Golspie on the A9 and five miles N of Dornoch. View across tidal basin from A9 or unclassified road to Skelbo.
Access: Park at Little Ferry or in lay-bys around the basin.
Facilities: Guided walks in summer. Interpretive centre.
Public transport: None.
Habitat: Tidal basin, sand dunes, shingle, woodland, marshes.

Key birds: *Winter:* Important feeding place for ducks and waders. The sea off the mouth of Loch Fleet is a major wintering area for Long-tailed Duck, Common and Velvet Scoters, Eider Duck. In pine wood off minor road S from Golspie to Little Ferry: Crossbill, occasional Crested Tit.
Contact: SWT headquarters 01313 127 765.

10. LOCH RUTHVEN

RSPB (North Scotland Office).
Location: NH 638 280. From Inverness, take A9 SE to junction with B851. Head SW until the minor road NE at Croachy (reserve is signposted); car park one mile.
Access: Open at all times.
Facilities: Hide, car park.
Public transport: Nearest bus-stop at Croachy (one mile from reserve). Service is not frequent.
Habitat: Freshwater loch and woodland.
Key birds: Best breeding site in Britain for Slavonian Grebe, which arrive in late March. *Spring/summer:* Red-throated Diver and Osprey. Teal, Wigeon and other wildfowl breed. Peregrine, Buzzard often seen.
Other notable flora and fauna: Toad (mid-April).
Contact: RSPB North Scotland Office. Etive House, Beechwood Park, Inverness IV2 3BW, 01463 715 000. e-mail: nsro@rspb.org.uk

11. UDALE BAY

RSPB (North Scotland Office).
Location: NH 712 651. On the Black Isle, one mile W of Jemimaville on the B9163.
Access: Open all year. View wader roost from lay-by. Nearest adapted unisex toilet in Allen Street, Cromarty (one mile away).
Facilities: Hide, large lay-by. No coach parking.
Public transport: No 26 bus stops in Jemimaville six times a day (approx 5 min walk to reserve). Bus Info contact: Rapsons, 0870 608 2608 or Stagecoach on 01862 892 683.
Habitat: Mudflat, saltmarsh and wet grassland.
Key birds: *Spring/summer:* 10,000 Pinkfeet on passage each year, other wildfowl, Oystercatcher, Redshank, waders. Possible Osprey fishing. *Autumn/winter:* Large flocks of wildfowl (approx 10,000 Wigeon), geese, waders.
Contact: RSPB North Scotland Office, Etive House, Beechwood Park, Inverness IV2 3BW. 01463 715 000. e-mail: nsro@rspb.org.uk

Orkney

12. BRODGAR

RSPB (East Scotland).
Location: HY 296 134. Reserve surrounds the Ring of Brodgar, part of the Heart of Neolithic Orkney World Heritage Site on the B9055 off the Stromness-Finstown Road.
Access: Open all year.
Facilities: Footpath, circular route approx one mile.
Public transport: Orkney Coaches. Service within

0.5 mile of reserve. Tel: 01856 870 555. Occasional service past reserve.
Habitat: Wetland and farmland including species-rich grassland, loch shores.
Key birds: *Spring/summer:* Breeding waterfowl on farmland and nine species of waders breed here. The farmed grassland is suitable for Corn Crake and provides water, food and shelter for finches, larks and buntings. *Winter:* large numbers of Golden Plover, Curlew and Lapwing.
Other notable flora and fauna: A hotspot for great yellow bumblebee in August. Possibility of otter, while common seals haul out nearby on Loch of Stenness.
Contact: The Warden, 12/14 North End Road, Stromness, Orkney KW16 3AG. 01856 850 176. e-mail: orkney@rspb.org.uk www.rspb.co.uk

13. COPINSAY

RSPB (East Scotland).
Location: HY 610 010. Small island accessed by private boat or hire boat from mainland Orkney.
Access: Open all year round.
Facilities: House on island open to visitors, but no facilities. No toilets or hides.
Public transport: None.
Habitat: Sea cliffs, farmland.
Key birds: *Summer:* Stunning seabird-cliffs with breeding Kittiwake, Guillemot, Black Guillemot, Puffin, Razorbill, Shag, Fulmar, Rock Dove, Eider, Twite, Raven and Greater Black-backed Gull, Great Skua (new breeding species in recent years). Passage migrants esp. during periods of E winds.
Other notable flora and fauna: The island is a key breeding location for Atlantic grey seals from Oct-Dec. 2,385 pups counted in 2006.
Contact: The Warden, 12/14 North End Road, Stromness, Orkney KW16 3AG. 01856 850 176. e-mail: orkney@rspb.org.uk
www.rspb.co.uk
S Foubisher (boatman) 01856 741252 — boat cannot sail if wind is in the east

14. HOBBISTER

RSPB (East Scotland).
Location: HY 396 070 or HY 381 068. Near Kirkwall.
Access: Open access between A964 and the sea. Dogs on leads please.
Facilities: A council-maintained footpath to Waulkmill Bay, two car parks. New circular walk from RSPB car park along cliff top and Scapa Flow.
Public transport: Orkney Coaches. Tel: 01856 877 500.
Habitat: Orkney moorland, bog, fen, saltmarsh, coastal cliffs, scrub.
Key birds: *Summer:* Breeding Hen Harrier, Merlin, Short-eared Owl, Red Grouse, Red-throated Diver, Eider, Merganser, Black Guillemot. Wildfowl and waders at Waulkmill Bay. *Autumn/winter:* Waulkmill for sea ducks, divers, auks and grebes (Long-tailed Duck, Red-throated, Black-throated and Great Northern Divers, Slavonian Grebe).

Other notable flora and fauna: Otter occasionally seen from the Scapa trail. Grey and common seal both possible from footpath looking towards Scapa Flow.
Contact: The Warden, 12/14 North End Road, Stromness, Orkney KW16 3AG. 01856 850 176. e-mail: orkney@rspb.org.uk www.rspb.co.uk

15. MARWICK HEAD

RSPB (East Scotland).
Location: HY 229 242. On W coast of mainland Orkney, near Dounby. Path N from Marwick Bay, or from council car park at Cumlaquoy at HY 232 252.
Access: Open all year. Rough terrain not suitable for wheelchairs.
Facilities: Cliff top path.
Public transport: Orkney Coaches (01856 877 500), nearest stop one mile from reserve.
Habitat: Rocky bay, sandstone cliffs. Beach path good place for great yellow bumblebee in Aug.
Key birds: May-Jul best. Huge numbers of Kittiwakes and auks, inc. Puffins, also nesting Fulmar, Rock Dove, Raven, Rock Pipit.
Other notable flora and fauna: Cetaceans are a possibility from Marwick with porpoise and minke whale occasionally seen.
Contact: The Warden, 12/14 North End Road, Stromness, Orkney KW16 3AG. 01856 850 176. e-mail: orkney@rspb.org.uk www.rspb.co.uk

16. NORTH HILL, PAPA WESTRAY

RSPB (East Scotland).
Location: HY 496 538. Small island lying NE of Westray, reserve at N end of island's main road.
Access: Access at all times. During breeding season report to summer warden at Rose Cottage, 650 yards S of reserve entrance (Tel 01857 644 240) or use trail guide.
Facilities: Nature trails, hide/info hut.
Public transport: Orkney Ferries (01856 872 044), Loganair (01856 872 494).
Habitat: Sea cliffs, maritime heath.
Key birds: *Summer*: Close views of colony of Puffin, Guillemot, Razorbill and Kittiwake. Black Guillemot nest under flagstones around reserve's coastline. One of UK's largest colonies of Arctic Tern, also Arctic Skua.
Other notable flora and fauna: North Hill is one of the best areas to see 'Scottish primrose' (*primula scotica*) which have two flowering periods that just overlap (May-Aug).
Contact: (In summer) The Warden at Rose Cottage, Papa Westray DW17 2BU. 01857 644 240.
(Other times) RSPB Orkney Office12/14 North End Road, Stromness, Orkney KW16 3AG. 01856 850 176. e-mail: orkney@rspb.org.uk www.rspb.co.uk

17. NORTH RONALDSAY BIRD OBSERVATORY

Location: HY 64 52. 35 miles from Kirkwall, Orkney mainland.
Access: Open all year except Christmas.
Facilities: Three star guest house and hostel

accommodation, restaurant, cafe, fully licenced, croft walk.
Public transport: Daily subsidised flights from Kirkwall (Loganair 01856 872 494). Once weekly ferry from Kirkwall (Fri or Sat), Tuesday and some Sunday sailings in summer (Orkney Ferries Ltd 01856 872 044).
Habitat: Crofting island with a number of eutrophic and oligotrophic wetlands. Coastline has both sandy bays and rocky shore. Walled gardens concentrate passerines.
Key birds: *Spring/Autumn*: Prime migration site including regular BBRC species. Wide variety of breeding seabirds, wildfowl and waders. *Winter*: Waders and wildfowl include Whooper Swan and hard weather movements occur.
Contact: Alison Duncan, North Ronaldsay Bird Observatory, Twingness, North Ronaldsay, Orkney KW17 2BE. 01857 633 200.
e-mail: alison@nrbo.prestel.co.uk
www.nrbo.f2s.com

Outer Hebrides

18. BALRANALD

RSPB (North Scotland Office).
Location: NF 705 707. From Skye take ferry to Lochmaddy, North Uist. Drive W on A865 for 20 miles to reserve. Turn off main road three miles NW of Bayhead at signpost to Houghharry.
Access: Open at all times, no charge. Dogs on leads. Circular walk not suitable for wheelchairs.
Facilities: Visitor Centre and toilets (disabled access). Marked nature trail. Group bookings welcome.
Public transport: Post bus service (tel 01876 560 244).
Habitat: Freshwater loch, machair, coast and croft lands.
Key birds: *Spring*: Skuas and divers at sea, Purple Sandpiper and other waders on shore. Dotterel. *Summer*: Corn Crake, Corn Bunting, Lapwing, Oystercatcher, Dunlin, Ringed Plover, Redshank, Snipe, terns. *Autumn*: Hen Harrier, Peregrine, Greylag Goose. *Winter*: Twite, Snow Bunting, Whooper Swan, Greylag Goose, Wigeon, Teal, Shoveler, sightings of Golden and White-tailed Eagles becoming commoner. *Passage*: Barnacle Goose, Pomarine Skua, Long-tailed Skua.
Other notable flora and fauna: Blanket bog and machair plants reach their peak in July.
Contact: Jamie Boyle, 9 Grenitote, Isle of North Uist, H56 5BP. 01876 560 287.
e-mail: james.boyle3@btinternet.com

19. LOCH DRUIDIBEG NATIONAL NATURE RESERVE

SNH (Western Isles Area).
Location: NF 782 378. Reserve of 1,577 ha on South Uist. Turn off A865 at B890 road for Loch Sgioport. Track to reserve is 1.5 miles further on — park at side of road.

Access: Open all year. Several tracks and one walk covering a range of habitats — most not suitable for wheelchair use. Stout footwear essential. Observe Scottish Outdoor Access Code in all areas with livestock. View E part of reserve from public roads but parking and turning areas for coaches is limited.
Facilities: None.
Public transport: Regular bus service stops at reserve. Hebridean Coaches 01870 620 345, MacDonald Coaches 01870 620 288. Large print timetable — call 01851 709 592.
Habitat: Range of freshwater lochs and marshes, machair, coast and moorland.
Key birds: *Summer*: Breeding waders, Corn Crake, wildfowl, terns and raptors. *Spring and autumn*: Migrant waders and wildfowl. *Winter*: Waders, wildfowl and raptors.
Contact: SNH Office Stilligarry, 01870 620 238; e-mail: western.isles@snh.gov.uk
www.nnr-scotland.org.uk

Shetland

20. FAIR ISLE BIRD OBSERVATORY

Fair Isle Bird Observatory.
Location: HZ 2172. Famous island for rarities located SE of mainland Shetland.
Access: Open from end Apr-end Oct. No access restrictions.
Facilities: Public toilets at Airstrip and Stackhoull Stores (shop). Accommodation at Fair Isle Bird Observatory (phone/e-mail: for brochure/details). Guests can be involved in observatory work and get to see birds in the hand. Slide shows, guided walks through Ranger Service.
Public transport: Tue, Thurs, Sat — ferry (12 passengers) from Grutness, Shetland. Tel: Neil or Pat Thomson on 01595 760 363. Mon, Wed, Fri, Sat — air (7 seater) from Tingwall, Shetland. Tel: Direct Flight 01595 840 246.
Habitat: Heather moor and lowland pasture/crofting land. Cliffs.
Key birds: Large breeding seabird colonies (auks, Gannet, Arctic Tern, Kittiwake, Shag, Arctic Skua and Great Skua). Many common and rare migrants Apr/May/early Jun, late Aug-Nov.
Other notable flora and fauna: Northern marsh, heath spotted and frog orchid, lesser twayblade, small adders tongue, oyster plant. Orcas, minke whale, white-backed, white-sided and Risso's dolphins. Endemic field mouse.
Contact: Deryk Shaw (Warden), Hollie Shaw (Administrator), Fair Isle Bird Observatory, Fair Isle, Shetland ZE2 9JU. 01595 760 258.
e-mail: fairisle.birdobs@zetnet.co.uk
www.fairislebirdobs.co.uk

21. FETLAR

RSPB Scotland
Location: HU 603 917. Small island lying E of Yell. Take car ferry from Gutcher, N Yell. Booking advised. Tel: 01957 722 259.
Access: Apart from the footpath to Hjaltadance circle, Vord Hill, the Special Protection Area is closed mid May to end July. Entry during this period is only by arrangement with warden. Hide at Mires of Funzie open Apr-Nov.
Facilities: Hide at Mires of Funzie. Toilets and payphone at ferry terminal, interpretive centre at Houbie, campsite, shop.
Public transport: None.
Habitat: Serpentine heath, rough hill lane, upland mire.
Key birds: *Summer*: Breeding Red-throated Diver, Eider, Shag, Whimbrel, Golden Plover, Dunlin, skuas, Manx Shearwater, Storm Petrel. Red-necked Phalarope on Loch of Funzie (HU 655 899) viewed from road or RSPB hide overlooking Mires of Funzie.
Other notable flora and fauna: Heath spotted orchid and autumn gentian. Otters are common, harbour and grey seals breed.
Contact: RSPB North Isles Warden, Bealance, Fetlar, Shetland ZE2 9DJ. Tel/Fax: 01957 733 246.
e-mail: malcolm.smith@rspb.org.uk

22. NOSS NATIONAL NATURE RESERVE

Scottish Natural Heritage (Shetland Office).
Location: HU 531 410. Take car ferry to Bressay from Lerwick and follow signs for Noss (5km). At end of road walk to shore (600 mtrs) where inflatable ferry (passenger only) to island will collect you (if red flag is flying, island is closed due to sea conditions). Freephone 0800 107 7818 for daily ferry information.
Access: Access (Tue, Wed, Fri, Sat, Sun) 10am-5pm, late Apr-late Aug. Access by zodiac inflatable. Sorry, no dogs allowed on ferry. Steep rough track down to ferry. Groups or anyone requiring assistance to board ferry should contact SNH as far in advance as possible.
Facilities: Visitor centre, toilets. Bike rack/car park on Bressay side. Parking for small coaches.
Public transport: None. Post bus available, phone Royal Mail on 01595 820 200. Cycle hire in Lerwick.
Habitat: Dune and coastal grassland, moorland, heath, blanket bog, sea cliffs.
Key birds: *Spring/summer*: Breeding Fulmar, Shag, Gannet, Arctic Tern, Kittiwake, Herring and Great Black-backed Gull, Great Skua, Arctic Skua, Guillemot, Razorbill, Puffin, Black Guillemot, Eider, Lapwing, Dunlin, Snipe, Wheatear, Twite plus migrant birds at any time.
Other notable flora and fauna: Grey and common seals, otter porpoise regularly seen, killer whales annual in recent years.
Contact: Simon Smith, Scottish Natural Heritage, 01595 693 345. e-mail: noss_nnr@snh.gov.uk

WALES
Eastern Wales

1. BAILEY EINON LOCAL NATURE RESERVE

Radnorshire Wildlife Trust.
Location: SO 083 613. From Llandrindod Wells, take the Craig Road leading to Cefnllys Lane. Down this road is Shaky Bridge with a car park and picnic site. A kissing-gate downstream from the picnic site marks the reserve entrance. Please do not park in front of the kissing-gate.
Access: Open all year.
Facilities: Car park, picnic site, waymarked trail.
Public transport: None.
Habitat: Woodland, river.
Key birds: *Spring/summer*: Pied Flycatcher, Redstart, Wood Warbler. *All year*: Great Spotted Woodpecker, Buzzard, usual woodland birds.
Other notable flora and fauna: Orange tip and ringlet buterflies. Red campion, yellow archangel.
Contact: Radnorshire Wildlife Trust, Warwick House, High Street, Llandrindod Wells, Powys, LD1 6AG, 01597 823 298.e-mail: info@rwtwales.org www.radnorshirewildlifetrust.org.uk

2. BRECHFA POOL

Brecknock Wildlife Trust.
Location: SO 118 377. Travelling NE from Brecon look for lane off A470, 1.5 miles SW of Llyswen; on Brechfa Common, pool is on R after cattle grid.
Access: Open dawn to dusk. Road runs around three-quarters of pool, giving good access.
Facilities: None.
Public transport: None.
Habitat: Marshy grassland, large shallow pool.
Key birds: Good numbers of wintering wildfowl are replaced by breeding gulls and commoner waterfowl. Species recorded inc Teal, Gadwall, Tufted Duck, Shoveler, Wigeon, Little Grebe, Black-headed Gull, Lapwing, Dunlin, Redshank, Kestrel.
Other notable flora and fauna: Rare pillwort around pond margins, plus crowfoot, penny royal and orange foxtail.
Contact: Trust HQ, Lion House, Bethel Square, Brecon, Powys LD3 7AY. 01874 625 708. e-mail: enquiries@bricknockwildlifetrust.org.uk www.brecknockwildlifetrust.org.uk

3. CARNGAFALLT

RSPB Wales
Location: SN 935 653. From Rhayader take the B4518 W to Elan village. Turn into village and carry on over bridge into Elan village. Continue through village to cattle grid where nature trail starts.
Access: The nature trail is open at all times.
Facilities: Nature trail.
Public transport: None.

Habitat: Ancient oak woodland, grassland and moorland. Spectacular upland scenery.
Key birds: Red Kite, Buzzard, Sparrowhawk, Peregrine, Raven, Green Woodpecker, Grey Wagtail and Marsh Tit are joined in the summer by Pied Flycatcher, Spotted Flycatcher, Wood Warbler, Redstart, Tree Pipit and Cuckoo.
Other notable flora and fauna: Golden-ringed dragonfly, silver-washed, small pearl-bordered and dark-green fritillaries and purple hairstreak butterflies.
Contact: RSPB Ynys-Hir Reserve, Eglwys-fach, Machynlleth, Powys SY20 8TA. 01654 700 222. e-mail: ynyshir@rspb.org.uk

4. ELAN VALLEY

Dwr Cymru /Welsh Water.
Location: SN 928 646 (visitor centre). Three miles SW of Rhayader, off B4518.
Access: Mostly open access.
Facilities: Visitor centre and toilets (open between mid Mar-end Oct), nature trails all year and hide at SN 905 617.

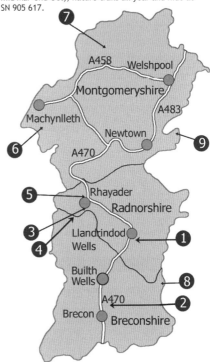

Public transport: Local bus service discontinued.
Habitat: 45,000 acres of moorland, woodland, river and reservoir.
Key birds: *Spring/summer*: Birds of prey, upland birds including Golden Plover and Dunlin. Woodland birds include Redstart and Pied Flycatcher.
Other notable flora and fauna: Internationally important oak woodlands. More than 3,000 species of flora and fauna recorded.
Contact: Pete Jennings, Rangers Office, Elan Valley Visitor Centre, Rhayader, Powys LD6 5HP. 01597 810 880. e-mail: pete@elanvalley.org.uk
www.elanvalley.org.uk

5. GILFACH

Radnorshire Wildlife Trust.
Location: SN 952 714. Two miles NW from Rhayader/Rhaeadr-Gwy. Take minor road to St Harmon from A470 at Marteg Bridge.
Access: Open every day, all year.
Facilities: Visitor centre opening times may vary — contact Trust for details.
Public transport: None.
Habitat: Upland hill farm, river, oak woods, meadows, hill-land.
Key birds: *Spring/summer*: Pied Flycatcher, Redstart. *All year*: Dipper, Red Kite.
Other notable flora and fauna: Green hairstreak, wall brown and ringlet butterflies, mountain pansy, bloody-nosed beetle.
Contact: Reserve manager, St Harmon, Gilfach, St Harmon, Rhaeadr-Gwy, Powys LD6 5LF. 01597 823 298. e-mail: info@rwtwales.org
www.radnorshirewildlifetrust.org.uk

6. GLASLYN, PLYNLIMON

Montgomeryshire Wildlife Trust.
Location: SN 826 941. Nine miles SE of Machynlleth. Off minor road between the B4518 near Staylittle and the A489 at Machynlleth. Go down the track for about a mile to the car park.
Access: Open at all times — dogs on lead at all times.
Facilities: Footpath.
Public transport: None.
Habitat: Heather moorland and upland lake.
Key birds: Red Grouse, Short-eared Owl, Meadow Pipit, Sky Lark, Wheatear and Ring Ouzel, Red Kite, Merlin, Peregrine. Goldeneye occasional.
Contact: Montgomeryshire Wildlife Trust, Collot House, 20 Severn Street, Welshpool, Powys SY21 7AD. 01938 555 654. e-mail: info@montwt.co.uk
www.wildlifetrust.org.uk/montgomeryshire
www.montwt.co.uk

7. LAKE VYRNWY

RSPB (North Wales Office).
Location: SJ 020 193. Located WSW of Oswestry. Nearest village is Llanfyllin on A490. Take B4393 to lake.
Access: Reserve open all year. Visitor centre open Apr-Dec (10.30am-4.30pm), Dec-Apr weekends only

(10.30am-4.30pm).
Facilities: Toilets, visitor centre, hides, nature trails, coffee shop, RSPB shop, craft workshops.
Public transport: Train and bus Welshpool (25 miles away).
Habitat: Heather moorland, woodland, meadows, rocky streams and large reservoir.
Key birds: Dipper, Kingfisher, Pied Flycatcher, Wood Warbler, Redstart, Peregrine and Buzzard.
Other notable flora and fauna: Mammals include otter, mink, brown hare. Golden-ringed dragonflies frequent in summer.
Contact: Centre Manager,, RSPB Lake Vyrnwy Reserve, Bryn Awel, Llanwddyn, Oswestry, Salop SY10 0LZ. 01691 870 278.
e-mail: lake.vyrnwy@rspb.org.uk

8. PWLL-Y-WRACH

Brecknock Wildlife Trust.
Location: SO 165 326. From Talgarth town centre take Bell Street and then Hospital Road. After 1.5 miles, reserve is on the right.
Access: Reserve open all year. Please keep to footpaths. Level wheelchair-friendly path runs half way into site. Elsewhere, paths can be muddy and there are steps in places.
Facilities: No facilities.
Public transport: No local services.
Habitat: 8.5 hectares of ancient woodland, river and spectacular waterfall.
Key birds: Large variety of resident woodland birds, with migrant boost in spring. Dipper, Kingfisher, Pied Wagtail, Great Spotted Woodpecker, Chiffchaff, Wood Warbler, Pied Flycatcher, Mistle and Song Thrushes, Nuthatch.
Other notable flora and fauna: Otter, dormouse, bats, common lizard. Early purple and birds' nest orchids, herb paris, bluebell, wood anemone.
Contact: Brecknock Wildlife Trust, Lion House, Bethel Square, Brecon, Powys LD3 7AY. 01874 625 708 .
e-mail: enquiries@brecknockwildlifetrust.org.uk
www.brecknockwildlifetrust.org.uk

9. ROUNDTON HILL

Montgomeryshire Wildlife Trust.
Location: SO 293 947. SE of Montgomery. From Churchstoke on A489, take minor road to Old Churchstoke, R at phone box, then first R.
Access: Open access. Tracks rough in places. Dogs on lead at all times.
Facilities: Car park. Waymarked trails.
Public transport: None.
Habitat: Ancient hill grassland, woodland, streamside wet flushes, scree, rock outcrops.
Key birds: Buzzard, Raven, Wheatear, all three woodpeckers, Tawny Owl, Redstart, Linnet, Goldfinch.
Contact: Trust HQ, 01938 555 654.
e-mail: info@montwt.co.uk
www.wildlifetrust.org.uk/montgomeryshire
www.montwt.co.uk

North Wales

1. BARDSEY BIRD OBSERVATORY

Bardsey Bird Observatory.

Location: SH 11 21. Private 444 acre island. Twenty minute boat journey from Aberdaron.

Access: Mar-Nov. No dogs. Visitor accommodation in 150-year-old farmhouse (two single, two double, one x four bed dorm). To stay at the Observatory contact Alicia Normand (tel 01626 773 908) e-mail bookings@bbfo.org.uk). Day visitors by Bardsey Ferries (07971 769 895).

Facilities: Public toilets available for day visitors. Three hides, one on small bay, two seawatching. Gift shops and payphone.

Public transport: Trains from Birmingham to Pwllheli. Tel: 0345 484 950. Arriva bus from Bangor to Pwllheli. Tel: 0870 6082 608.

Habitat: Sea-birds cliffs viewable from boat only. Farm and scrubland, Spruce plantation, willow copses and gorse-covered hillside.

Key birds: *All year*: Chough, Peregrine. *Spring/summer*: Manx Shearwaters 16,000 pairs, other seabirds. Migrant warblers, chats, Redstart, thrushes. *Autumn*: Many rarities including Eye-browed Thrush, Lanceolated Warbler, American Robin, Yellowthroat, Summer Tanager.

Other notable flora and fauna: Autumn ladies' tresses.

Contact: Steven Stansfield, Cristin, Ynys Enlli (Bardsey), off Aberaron, via Pwllheil, Gwynedd LL53 8DE. 07855 264 151. e-mail: warden@bbfo.org.uk www.bbfo.org.uk

2. CEMLYN

North Wales Wildlife Trust.

Location: SH 329 936 and SH 336 932. Cemlyn is signposted from Tregele on A5025 between Valley and Amlwch on Anglesey.

Access: Open all the time. Dogs on leads. No wheelchair access. During summer months walk on seaward side of ridge and follow signs.

Facilities: Car parks at either end of reserve.

Public transport: None within a mile.

Habitat: Brackish lagoon, shingle ridge, salt marsh, mixed scrub.

Key birds: Wintering wildfowl and waders, breeding terns, gulls and warblers, pipits and passing migrants. *Spring*: Wheatear, Whitethroat, Sedge Warbler, Manx Shearwater, Sandwich Tern, Whimbrel, Dunlin, Knot and Black-tailed Godwit. *Summer*: Breeding Arctic, Common and Sandwich Terns, Black-headed Gull, Oystercatcher and Ringed Plover. *Autumn*: Golden Plover, Lapwing, Curlew, Manx Shearwater, Gannet, Kittiwake, Guillemot. *Winter*: Little and Great Crested Grebes, Shoveler, Shelduck, Wigeon, Red-breasted Merganser, Coot, Turnstone, Purple Sandpiper.

Other notable flora and fauna: 20 species of butterfly recorded. Sea kale, yellow horned poppy, sea purselane, sea beet, glasswort. Grey seal, harbour porpoise, bottlenose dolphin.

Contact: Chris Wynne, Conservation Officer, North Wales Wildlife Trust, 376 High Street, Bangor, Gwynedd LL57 1YE. 01248 351 541. e-mail: nwwt@wildlifetrustswales.org www.wildlifetrust.org.uk/northwales

3. CONNAHS QUAY POWER STATION

Deeside Naturalists' Society and E.ON UK.

Location: SJ 275 715. From England: Take A550 from Liverpool/N Wirral or A5117 from Ellesmere Port/M56, follow road to Queensferry. 200 metres after junction of A550 and A5117, turn L at A548 and follow signs to Flint. Cross Dee Bridge and turn off dual carriageway at B5129, signed Connah's Key. Turn R under A548 then L, following signs to power station. From Flint: Take A548 towards Connah's Quay/Queensferry. After 2.5 miles, take B5129 (Connah's Quay exit). Turn L following signs to power station. From Connah's Quay: Take B5129 towards Flint. Go under A548, turn L following signs to power station.

Access: Advance permit required (group bookings only). Wheelchair access. Public welcome on open days — see website for details.

Facilities: Field studies centre, five hides.

Public transport: Contact Arriva Cymru on 01745 343 492.

Habitat: Saltmarsh, mudflats, grassland scrub, open water, wetland meadow.

Key birds: *Summer*: Small roosts of non-breeding estuarine birds. *Winter*: High water roosts of waders and wildfowl including, Black-tailed Godwit, Oystercatcher, Redshank, Spotted Redshank, Curlew, Lapwing, Teal, Pintail and Wigcon.

Contact: Secretary, Deeside Naturalist's Society, 21 Woodlands Court, Hawarden, Deeside, Flintshire CH5 3NB. 01244 537 440. www.deesidenaturalists.org.uk email: deenaturalists@btinternet.com

4. CONWY

RSPB (North Wales Office).

Location: SH 799 773. On E bank of Conwy Estuary. Access from A55 at exit 18 signed to Conwy and Deganwy. Footpath and cycleway accessed from Conway Cob.

Access: Open daily (9.30am-5pm). Closed for Christmas Day. Ample parking for coaches. Toilets, buildings and trails accessible to pushchairs and wheelchairs.

Facilities: Visitor centre, gift shop, coffee shop, toilets including disabled. Four hides (accessible to wheelchairs) two viewing screens. Trails firm and level, though a little rough in places and wet in winter.

Public transport: Train service to Llandudno Junction, 10 minute walk. Bus service to Tesco supermarket, Llandudno Junction 5 minutes walk. Tel: 0871 200 2233.
Habitat: Lagoons, islands, reedbed, scrub, estuary.
Key birds: Wildfowl and waders in winter, warblers and wetland breeding birds in summer. *Spring*: Passage waders, hirundines and wagtails. *Summer*: Lapwing, waterbirds and warblers. *Winter*: Kingfisher, Goldeneye, Water Rail, Red-breasted Merganser, wildfowl, huge Starling roost.
Other notable flora and fauna: Common butterflies through summer, especially common blues. Great display of cowslips in March, bee orchids in summer. Otters seen early mornings.
Contact: Conwy RSPB Nature Reserve, Llandudno Junction, Conwy, North Wales LL31 9XZ. 01492 584 091.

5. GORS MAEN LLWYD

North Wales Wildlife Trust.
Location: SH 975 580. Follow A5 to Cerrigydrudion (seven miles S of site), then take B4501 and go past the Llyn Brennig Visitor Centre. Approx two miles beyond centre, turn R (still on B4501). First car park on R approx 300 yards after the cattle grid.
Access: Open all the time. Dogs on leads. Keep to the paths. Rare breeding birds on the heather so keep to paths.
Facilities: In second car park by lake shore there are toilets and short walk to bird hide. Paths are waymarked, but can be very wet and muddy in poor weather.
Public transport: None.
Habitat: Heathland. Heather and grass overlooking large lake.
Key birds: *Summer*: Red and Black Grouse, Hen Harrier, Merlin, Sky Lark, Curlew. *Winter*: Wildfowl on lake.
Contact: Neil Griffiths, Reserves Officer, NWWT, 376 High Street, Bangor, Gwynedd LL57 1YE. 01248 351 541. e-mail: nwwt@wildlifetrustswales.org www.wildlifetrust.org.uk/northwales

6. LLYN ALAW

Welsh Water/United Utilities.
Location: SH 390 865. North Anglesey, SW of Amlwch. Signposted from J5 of A55. Main car park at SH375 856.
Access: Open all year. No dogs to hides or sanctuary area but dogs allowed (maximum two per adult) other areas. Limited wheelchair access. Coach parking in main car park (SH 373 856).
Facilities: Visitor centre, Toilets (including disabled), earth paths, boardwalks. Two hides, car parks, network of mapped walks, picnic sites, information boards. Coach parking at main car park.
Public transport: Not to within a mile.
Habitat: Large area of standing water, shallow reedy bays, hedges, scrub, woodland, marsh, grassland.
Key birds: *Winter*: Wildfowl and thrushes, breeding warblers/waterfowl. *Summer*: Lesser Whitethroat,

Sedge and Grasshopper Warblers, Little and Great Crested Grebes, Tawny Owl, Barn Owl, Buzzard. *Winter*: Whooper Swan, Goldeneye, Hen Harrier, Short-eared Owl, Redwing, Fieldfare, Peregrine, Raven. *All year*: Bullfinch, Siskin, Redpoll, Goldfinch, Stonechat. *Passage waders*: Ruff, Spotted Redshank, Curlew Sandpiper, Green Sandpiper.
Other notable flora and fauna: Bee and northern marsh orchid, royal fern, skullcap, needle spikerush. Migrant hawker, hairy, four-spotted chaser dragonflies, banded demoiselle, wall brown, gatekeeper, clouded yellow and orange tip butterflies. Brown hare, water vole.
Contact: The Warden, Llyn Alaw, Llantrisant, Holyhead LL65 4TW. 01407 730 762.

7. LLYN CEFNI

Welsh Water/Forestry Commission/United Utilities.
Location: Entrance at Bodffordd SH 433 775 and Rhosmeirch SH 451 783. A reservoir located two miles NW of Llangefni, in central Anglesey. Follow B5111 or B5109 from the village.
Access: Open at all times. Dogs allowed except in sanctuary area. Good footpath (wheelchair accessible) for most of the site, bridges over streams.
Facilities: Two picnic sites, good footpath, coach parking at Rhosmeirch car prk SH451 783.
Public transport: Bus 32, 4 (44 Sun only, 52 Thu only). Tel 0871 200 2233 for information.
Habitat: Large area of open water, reedy bays, coniferous woodland, scrub, carr.
Key birds: *Summer*: Sedge and Grasshopper Warblers, Whitethroat, Buzzard, Tawny Owl, Little Grebe, Gadwall, Shoveler, Kingfisher. *Winter*: Waterfowl (Whooper Swan, Goldeneye), Crossbill, Redpoll, Siskin, Redwing. *All year*: Stonechat, Treecreeper, Song Thrush.
Other notable flora and fauna: Northern marsh orchid, rustyback fern, needle spikerush. Banded demoiselle, migrant hawker, golden ringed dragonfly, emerald damselfly. Ringlet, gatekeeper, clouded yellow and wall butterflies. Bloody nose beetle.
Contact: The Warden, Llyn Alaw, Llantrisant, Holyhead LL65 4TW. 01407 730 762.

8. MAWDDACH VALLEY

RSPB (North Wales Office).
Location: Coed Garth Gell (SH 688 192) is adjacent to the main Dolgellau to Barmouth road (A496) near Taicynhaeaf. No reserve parking is available but lay-bys are found close to the reserve's entrances. Arthog Bog (SH630138) is off the main Dolgellau to Tywyn road (A493) west of Arthog. Parking is available near by at the Morfa Mawddach station.
Access: Nature trails are open at all times.
Facilities: Nature trails and information boards.
Public transport: A regular bus service runs between Dolgellau and Barmouth and stops close to the reserve entrance at Coed Garth Gell. The Arthog Bog part of the reserve is served by the Dolgellau to Tywyn bus services which stops close by at Arthog. The Arthog Bog reserve is a short distance from the

Morfa Mawddach railway station.
Habitat: Oak woodland, bracken and heathland at Coed Garth Gell. Willow and alder scrub and raised bog at Arthog bog.
Key birds: At Coed Garth Gell: Buzzard, Sparrowhawk, Peregrine, Raven, Lesser Spotted Woodpecker, Grey Wagtail, Dipper and Hawfinch are joined in the summer by Pied Flycatcher, Spotted Flycatcher, Wood Warbler, Redstart, Tree Pipit and Cuckoo. At Arthog bog Buzzard, Sparrowhawk, Peregrine, Raven are resident. Summer migrants include Tree Pipits, Grasshopper Warbler and Cuckoo. In winter flocks of Redpolls and Siskins are common and Red-breasted Merganser, Pintail and Little Egrets are on the nearby estuary.
Other notable flora and fauna: Coed Garth Gell has Tunbridge filmy and beech ferns and a wide variety of butterflies. Golden-ringed dragonflies are regular at both reserves.
Contact: RSPB Ynys-Hir Reserve, Eglwys-fach, Machynlleth, Powys SY20 8TA. 01654 700 222.
e-mail: ynyshir@rspb.org.uk

9. MORFA HARLECH NATIONAL NATURE RESERVE

Countryside Council for Wales (North West Area).
Location: SH 574 317, NW of Harlech. On the A496 Harlech road.
Access: Open all year.
Facilities: Car park. Disabled parking bays and three coach parking spaces.
Public transport: The site is served by both bus and train. Train stations are at Harlech and Ty Gwyn (Ty Gwyn is near the saltmarsh wintering birds.) Contact Arriva for details (0844 8004 411).
Habitat: Shingle (no shingle at Harlech), coast, marsh, dunes. Also forestry plantation, grassland, swamp.
Key birds: *Spring/summer*: Whitethroat, Spotted Flycatcher, Grasshopper Warbler, migrants. *Passage*: Waders, Manx Shearwater, ducks. *Winter*: Divers, Whooper Swan, Wigeon, Teal, Pintail, Scaup, Common Scoter, Hen Harrier, Merlin, Peregrine, Short-eared Owl, Little Egret, Water Pipit, Snow Bunting, Twite. *All year/breeding*: Redshank, Lapwing, Ringed Plover, Snipe, Curlew, Shelduck, Oystercatcher, Stonechat, Whinchat, Wheatear, Linnet, Reed Bunting, Sedge Warbler. Also Red-breasted Merganser, Kestrel, gulls.

Other notable flora and fauna: Sand lizard, otter, water vole.
Contact: Countryside Council for Wales North West Wales, Maes y Ffynnon, Ffordd, Bangor, Gwynedd, LL57 2DN, 0845 1306 229.
e-mail: enquiries@ccw.gov.uk www.ccw.gov.uk

10. NEWBOROUGH WARREN & YNYS LLANDDWYN NATIONAL NATURE RESERVE

CCW (North Region).
Location: SH 406 670/430 630. In SE corner of Anglesey. From Menai Bridge head SW on A4080 to Niwbwrch or Malltraeth.
Access: Permit required for places away from designated routes. Disabled access from main car park in Newborough Forest.
Facilities: Toilets and shop in village. Bird hide in Llyn Rhosddu.
Public transport: Arriva Wales bus service.
Habitat: Sandhills, estuaries, saltmarshes, dune grasslands, rocky headlands.
Key birds: Wildfowl and waders at Malltraeth Pool (visible from road), Braint and Cefni estuaries (licensed winter shoot on marked areas of Cefni estuary administered by CCW); waterfowl at Llyn Rhosddu (public hide). Key site for Raven, also Curlew and other waders.
Other notable flora and fauna: Spectacular display of orchids, inc early marsh and northern marsh, plus marsh helleborine. A patch of dune helleborine is located near Newborough Forest car park. Other plants inc dune pansy, yellow wort and grass of Parnassus.
Contact: CCW North Region, Llys y bont, Ffordd y Parc, Parc Menai, Bangor, Gwynedd LL57 4BH. 0845 1306 229. e-mail: enquiries@ccw.gov.uk www.ccw.gov.uk

11. SOUTH STACK CLIFFS

RSPB (North Wales Office).
Location: RSPB Car Park SH 211 818, Ellins Tower information centre SH 206 820. Follow A55 to W end in Holyhead, proceed straight on at roundabout, continue straight on through traffic lights. After another half mile turn L and follow the Brown Tourist signs for RSPB Ynys Lawd/South Stack.
Access: RSPB car park with disabled parking, 'Access for all' track leading to a viewing area overlooking the lighthouse adjacent to Ellins Tower Visitor centre. Access to Ellins Tower gained via staircase. Reserve covered by an extensive network of paths, some of which are steep and uneven. Coach parking by prior arrangement at The South Stack Kitchen Tel: 01407 762 181 (privately owned).
Facilities: Free access to Ellins Tower which has windows overlooking main auk colony open daily (10am-5.30pm Easter-Sep).
Public transport: Mainline station Holyhead. Infrequent local bus service, Holyhead-South Stack. Tel. 0870 608 2608.
Habitat: Sea cliffs, maritime grassland, maritime heath, lowland heath.
Key birds: Peregrine, Chough, Fulmar, Puffin, Guillemot, Razorbill, Rock Pipit, Sky Lark, Stonechat, Linnet, Shag, migrant warblers and passage seabirds.
Contact: Dave Bateson, Plas Nico, South Stack, Holyhead, Anglesey LL65 1YH. 01407 764 973. www.rspb.org.uke

12. VALLEY WETLANDS

RSPB (North Wales Office).
Location: Off A5 on Anglesey, two miles S of Caergeilliog.
Access: Open all year.
Facilities: Nature trail.
Public transport: Bus: Maes Awyr/RAF Valley daily from Bangor and Holyhead. Train: Valley (four miles)/ Rhosneigr (seven miles).
Habitat: Reed-fringed lakes, small rocky outcrops.
Key birds: *All year:* Grebes, ducks, geese, rails, Cetti's Warbler. *Summer:* Reed, Sedge and Grasshopper Warblers. *Winter:* Bittern recorded most years, but hard to see.
Other notable flora and fauna: Several species of dragonfly inc hairy dragonfly and variable damselfy.
Contact: RSPB (Cymru), Maes Y Ffynnon, Penrhosgarnedd, Bangor, Gwynedd, 01248 363 800.

South Wales

1. CWM CLYDACH

RSPB Wales
Location: SN 684 026. N of Swansea. Three miles N of J45 on M4, through the village of Clydach on B4291 to car park in Craig Cefn Parc.
Access: Open at all times along public footpaths and waymarked trails. Not suitable for wheelchairs. Coach parking not available.
Facilities: Two nature trails, car park, information boards.
Public transport: Hourly buses from Swansea stop at reserve entrance. Nearest railway station is in Swansea.
Habitat: Oak woodland on steep slopes lining the banks of the fast-flowing Lower Clydach River.
Key birds: Red Kite, Sparrowhawk, Buzzard, Peregrine, Raven, Green Woodpecker, Dipper, Grey Wagtail and Marsh Tit are joined in the summer by Pied Flycatcher, Spotted Flycatcher, Wood Warbler, Redstart and Cuckoo. In winter Siskins and Lesser Redpolls are regular.
Other notable flora and fauna: Wood sorrel, silver-washed fritillary and speckled wood butterflies. Good range of fungi.
Contact: RSPB Ynys-Hir Reserve, Eglwys-fach, Machynlleth, Powys SY20 8TA. 01654 700 222. e-mail: ynyshir@rspb.org.uk

2. CWM COL-HUW

The Wildlife Trust of South and West Wales.
Location: SS 957 674. SE from Bridgend, site includes Iron Age fort, overlooking Bristol Channel. From Bridgend take B4265 S to Llanwit Major. Follow beach road from village.
Access: Park in seafront car park. Climb steps. Open all year.
Facilities: All year toilets and café. Information boards.
Public transport: None.
Habitat: Unimproved grassland, woodland, scrub and Jurassic blue lias cliff.
Key birds: Cliff-nesting House Martin colony, breeding Fulmar, Grasshopper Warbler. Large autumn passerine passage. Peregrine. Seawatching vantage point. Occasional Chough.
Contact: Trust HQ, 01656 724 100. e-mail: information@wtsww.cix.co.uk

3. KENFIG NATIONAL NATURE RESERVE

Bridgend County Borough Council.
Location: SS 802 811. Seven miles W of Bridgend. From J37 on M4, drive towards Porthcawl, then North Cornelly, then follow signs.
Access: Open at all times. Unsurfaced sandy paths, not suitable for wheelchairs. Flooding possible in

winter and spring. Coach parking available.
Facilities: Toilets, hides, free car parking and sign-posted paths. Visitor centre open weekends and holidays (10am-4.30pm), weekdays (2pm-4.30pm).
Public transport: Local bus service: contact reserve for details.
Habitat: 1,300 acre sand dune system, freshwater lake with reeds, numerous wet dune slacks, sandy coastline with some rocky outcrops.
Key birds: *Summer*: Warblers including Cetti's, Grasshopper, Sedge, Reed and Willow Warbler, Blackcap and Whitethroat. *Winter*: Wildfowl, Water Rail, Bittern, grebes.
Other notable flora and fauna: 16 species of orchid, hairy dragonfly, red-veined and ruddy darters, small blue, dark green fritillary, grayling, brown argus butterflies.
Contact: David Carrington, Ton Kenfig, Bridgend, CF33 4PT. 01656 743 386.
e-mail: david.carrington@bridgend.gov.uk

4. MAGOR MARSH

Gwent Wildlife Trust.
Location: ST 427 867. Magor can be reached from junctions 23 and 23A of the M4 motorway. Reserve lies to S of Magor. Leave M4 at exit 23, turning R onto B4245. Follow signs for Redwick in Magor village. Take first L after railway bridge. Reserve entrance is half mile further on R.
Access: Open all year. Keep to path. Wheelchair access to bird hide..
Facilities: Hide. Car park, footpaths and boardwalks.
Public transport: Bus service to Magor village. Reserve is approx 10 mins walk along Redwick road.
Habitat: Sedge fen, reedswamp, willow carr, damp hay meadows and open water.
Key birds: Important for wetland birds. *Spring*: Reed, Sedge and Grasshopper Warblers, occasional Garganey and Green Sandpiper on passage, Hobby. *Winter*: Teal, Peregrine, Jack Snipe, Snipe, occasional Shoveler and Gadwall, Bittern records in two recent years. *All year*: Little Egret, Little Grebe, Reed Bunting, Cetti's Warbler and Water Rail.
Contact: Gwent Wildlife Trust, Seddon House, Dingestow, Monmouth NP25 4DY. 01600 740 358; Fax 01600 740 299. e-mail: info@gwentwildlife.co.uk www.gwentwildlife.org

5. NEWPORT WETLANDS NATIONAL NATURE RESERVE

CCW/ RSPB/ Newport City Council.
Location: ST 334 834. SW of Newport. Reserve car park on West Nash Road, just before entrance to Uskmouth power station. From M4 J 24 take the A48 to Newport Retail Park, turn towards steelworks and follow brown 'duck' signs to the reserve car park.
Access: Free entry 9am to 5pm each day apart from Dec 25. Six disabled parking bays. All nature trails are accessible by wheelchair. Dogs only on perimeter footpath.
Facilities: Information centre, tea-rooms, shop, toilets (inc disabled), viewing screens.
Public transport: No 65 bus from Queensway bus station in Newport stops at West Nash Community Hall, a 15 min walk from reserve. Contact Newport bus services, tel: 01633 263 600. Nearest train station: Newport.
Habitat: 438 hectares of wet meadows, saline lagoons, reedbed, scrub and mudflats on Severn estuary.
Key birds: *Spring/ summer*: Breeding waders such as Lapwing and Oystercatcher, Bearded Tit, Cetti's Warbler, Cuckoo and regular migrants on passage. *Autumn*: Large numbers of migrating wildfowl and waders arrive at the reserve — regulars include Curlew, Dunlin, Ringed Plover, Shoveler. *Winter*: Massive Starling roost (up to 50,000 birds). Bittern, nationally important numbers of Black-tailed Godwit, Shoveler and Dunlin.
Other notable flora and fauna: Badger, wood mouse, otter. Great crested newt. Orchids in spring, 16 species of dragonfly, 23 species of butterfly and around 200 species of moth.
Contact: Newport Wetlands Reserve, West Nash Road, Newport, Gwent NP18 2BZ. RSPB visitor centre — 01633 636 363.

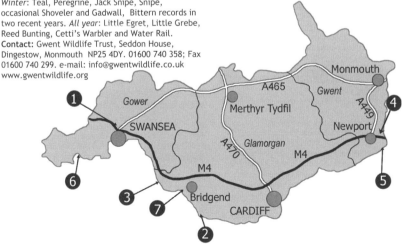

6. OXWICH NATIONAL NATURE RESERVE

CCW (Swansea Office).
Location: SS 872 773. 12 miles from Swansea, off A4118.
Access: NNR open at all times. No permit required for access to foreshore, dunes, woodlands and facilities.
Facilities: Private car park, summer only. Toilets summer only. Marsh boardwalk and marsh lookout. No visitor centre, no facilities for disabled visitors.
Public transport: Bus service Swansea/Oxwich. First Cymru, tel 01792 580 580.
Habitat: Freshwater marsh, saltmarsh, foreshore, dunes, woodlands.
Key birds: *Summer*: Breeding Reed, Sedge and Cetti's Warblers, Treecreeper, Nuthatch, woodpeckers. *Winter*: Wildfowl.
Contact: Countryside Council for Wales, RVB House, Llys Tawe, King's Road, Swansea SA1 8PG. 01792 634 960. e-mail: enquiries@ccw.gov.uk www.ccw.gov.uk

7. PARC SLIP NATURE PARK

The Wildlife Trust of South and West Wales.
Location: SS 880 840. Tondu, half mile W of Aberkenfig. From Bridgend take A4063 N, turning L onto B4281 after passing M4. Reserve is signposted from this road.
Access: Open dawn to dusk. Space for coach parking.
Facilities: Three hides, nature trail, interpretation centre.
Public transport: None.
Habitat: Restored opencast mining site, wader scrape, lagoons.
Key birds: *Summer*: Breeding Tufted Duck, Lapwing, Sky Lark. Migrant waders (inc. Little Ringed Plover, Green Sandpiper), Little Gull. Kingfisher, Green Woodpecker.
Contact: Trust HQ, 01656 724 100.
e-mail: information@wtsww.cix.co.uk

Western Wales

1. CASTLE WOODS

The Wildlife Trust of South and West Wales.
Location: SN 615 217. About 60 acres of woodland overlooking River Tywi, W of Llandeilo town centre.
Access: Open all year by footpath from Tywi Bridge, Llandeilo (SN 627 221).
Facilities: Call for advice.
Public transport: None.
Habitat: Old mixed deciduous woodlands.
Key birds: All three woodpeckers, Buzzard, Raven, Sparrowhawk. *Summer*: Pied and Spotted Flycatchers, Redstart, Wood Warbler. *Winter*: On water meadows below, look for Teal, Wigeon, Goosander, Shoveler, Tufted Duck and Pochard.
Contact: Area Officer, 35 Maesquarre Road, Betws, Ammanford, Carmarthenshire SA18 2LF. 01269 594 293. e-mail: information@wtsww.cix.co.uk www.wildlifetrust.org.uk/wtsww

2. CORS CARON NATIONAL NATURE RESERVE

CCW (West Wales Area).
Location: SN 692 625 (car park). Reached from B4343 N of Tregaron.
Access: Open access to S of car park along the railway to boardwalk (which is wheelchair accessible), out to SE bog. Access to rest of the reserve by permit. Dogs on lead. Access for coaches.
Facilities: New car park with toilets and picnic space. Bird hide along boardwalk. Riverside walk is open access. For access to the rest of the reserve please contact the reserve manager.
Public transport: None.
Habitat: Raised bog, river, fen, wet grassland, willow woodland, reedbed.

Key birds: *Summer*: Lapwing, Redshank, Curlew, Red Kite, Hobby, Grasshopper Warbler, Whinchat. *Winter*: Teal, Wigeon, Whooper Swan, Hen Harrier, Red Kite.
Other notable flora and fauna: Small red damselfy among the abundant dragonflies which can be seen from boardwalk.
Contact: CCW, Neuaddlas, Tregaron, Ceredigion. 01974 298 480. www.ccw.gov.uk
e-mail: p.culyer@ccw.gov.uk

3. GWENFFRWD & DINAS

RSPB Wales
Location: SN 788 471. North of Llandovery.From A483 take B road signposted to Llyn Brianne Reservoir.
Access: Public nature trail at Dinas open at all times.
Facilities: Nature trail including a board walk. Other parts of the trail are rugged. Car park and information board at start of trail. Coach parking can be arranged.
Public transport: Nearest station at Llandovery, 10 miles away.
Habitat: Hillside oak woods, streams and bracken slopes. Spectacular upland scenery.
Key birds: Upland species such as Red Kite, Buzzard, Peregrine, Raven, Goosander, Dipper and Grey Wagtail are joined in the summer by Pied Flycatcher, Spotted Flycatcher, Wood Warbler, Redstart, Tree Pipit, Common Sandpiper And Cuckoo. Marsh Tit and all three woodpecker species are present.
Other notable flora and fauna: Golden-ringed dragonfly, purple hairstreak, silver-washed fritillary and Wilson's filmy fern.
Contact: RSPB Ynys-Hir Reserve, Eglwys-fach, Machynlleth, Powys SY20 8TA. 01654 700 222.
e-mail: ynyshir@rspb.org.uk

4. DYFI

CCW (West Wales Area).
Location: SN 610 942. Large estuary area W of
Machynlleth. Public footpaths off A493 E of Aberdyfi,
and off B4353 (S of river); minor road from B4353 at
Ynyslas to dunes and parking area.
Access: Ynyslas dunes and the estuary have
unrestricted access. No access to Cors Fochno (raised
bog) for casual birdwatching; permit required for
study and research purposes. Good views over the
bog and Aberleri marshes from W bank of Afon Leri.
Facilities: Public hide overlooking marshes beside
footpath at SN 611 911.
Public transport: None.
Habitat: Sandflats, mudflats, saltmarsh, creeks,
dunes, raised bog, grazing marsh.
Key birds: *Winter*: Greenland White-fronted Goose,
wildfowl, waders and raptors. *Summer*: Breeding
wildfowl and waders (inc. Teal, Shoveler, Merganser,
Lapwing, Curlew, Redshank).
Contact: CCW Warden, Plas Gogerddan, Aberystwyth,
Ceredigion SY23 3EE. 01970 821 100.

5. NATIONAL WETLANDS CENTRE WALES

The Wildfowl & Wetlands Trust.
Location: SS 533 984. Overlooks the Burry Inlet.
Leave M4 at junction 48. Signposted from A484, E of
Llanelli.
Access: Open daily 9.30am-5pm, except Christmas
Eve and Christmas Day. Grounds are open until
6pm in summer. The centre is fully accessible with
disabled toilets. Mobility scooters and wheelchairs
are free to hire.
Facilities: Visitor centre with toilets, hides,
restaurant, shop, education facilities, free car and
coach parking. The centre has level access and hard-
surfaced paths.
Public transport: Bus from Llanelli to Lllwydhendy,
approx 1 mile from the centre. Telephone Traveline
Cymru 0871 200 2233 (7am-10pm daily).
Habitat: Inter-tidal mudflats, reedbeds, pools, marsh,
waterfowl collection.
Key birds: Large flocks of Curlew, Oystercatcher,
Redshank on saltmarsh. *Winter*: Pintail, Wigeon,
Teal. Also Little Egret, Short-eared Owl, Peregrine.
Other notable flora and fauna: Bee and southern
marsh orchids, yellow bartisa. Damselflies and
dragonflies, water voles and otters.
Contact: Centre Manager, WWT
National Wetlands Centre Wales,
Llwynhendy, Llanelli SA14 9SH.
01554 741 087; Fax 01554 744
101. www.wwt.org.uk
e-mail: info.llanelli@wwt.org.uk

6. RAMSEY ISLAND

RSPB Wales.
Location: SM 706 237. One mile
offshore from St Justinians slipway,
two miles W of St Davids.
Access: Open every day, Easter-Oct

31. No wheelchair access. Coach parking available at
St Justinians. For boat bookings contact: Thousand
Island Expeditions, 01437 721 721;
e-mail. sales@thousandislands.co.uk
Facilities: Toilets, small RSPB shop, tuck shop, hot
drinks and snacks, self-guiding trail.
Public transport: Trains to Haverfordwest Station.
Hourly buses to St Davids.
Habitat: Acid grassland, maritime heath, seacliffs.
Key birds: *Spring/summer*: Cliff-nesting auks
(Guillemot, Razorbill). Kittiwake, Lesser, Great
Black-backed and Herring Gulls, Shag, Wheatear,
Stonechat. *All year*: Peregrine, Raven, Chough,
Lapwing.
Other notable flora and fauna: Grey seal, red deer,
porpoise seen most days.
Contact: Warden: 07836 535 733.
www.rspb.org.uk/reserves

7. SKOKHOLM ISLAND

The Wildlife Trust of South and West Wales.
Location: SM 735 050. Island lying S of Skomer.
Access: Occasional day visits, also 3 or 4 night stays
available. Weekly accomm. Apr-Sep, tel 01239 621
212 for details and booking.
Facilities: Call for details.
Public transport: None.
Habitat: Cliffs, bays and inlets.
Key birds: *Summer*: Large colonies of Razorbill,
Puffin, Guillemot, Manx Shearwater, Storm Petrel,
Lesser Black-backed Gull. Migrants inc. rare species.
Contact: 01239 621 212.

8. SKOMER ISLAND

The Wildlife Trust of South
and West Wales.
Location: SM 725 095.
Fifteen miles from
Haverfordwest.
Take B4327 turn-
off for Marloes,
embarkation point
at Martin's

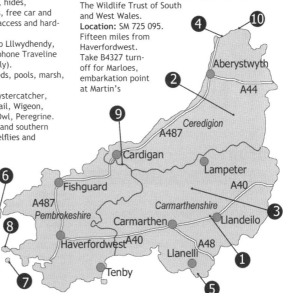

Haven, two miles past village.
Access: Apr 1-Oct 31. Boats sail at 10am, 11am and noon every day except Mon (Bank Holidays excluded). Closed four days beginning of Jun for seabird counts. Not suitable for infirm (steep landing steps and rough ground).
Facilities: Information centre, toilets, two hides, wardens, booklets, guides, nature trails.
Public transport: None.
Habitat: Maritime cliff, heathland, freshwater ponds.
Key birds: Largest colony of Manx Shearwater in the world (overnight). Puffin, Guillemot, Razorbill (Apr-end Jul). Kittiwake (until end Aug), Fulmar (absent Oct), Short-eared Owl (during day Jun and Jul), Chough, Peregrine, Buzzard (all year), migrants.
Contact: Skomer Island, Marloes, Pembs SA62 2BJ. 07971 114 302. e-mail: skomer@wtww.co.uk

9. WELSH WILDLIFE CENTRE

The Wildlife Trust of South and West Wales.
Location: SN 188 451. Two miles SE of Cardigan. River Teifi is N boundary. Sign-posted from Cardigan to Fishguard road.
Access: Open 10.30am-5pm all year. Free parking for WTSWW members, £3 non-members. Dogs on leads welcome. Disabled access to visitor centre, paths, four hides.
Facilities: Visitor centre, restaurant, network of paths and seven hides.
Public transport: Train station, Haverfordwest (23 miles). Bus station in Cardigan. Access on foot from Cardigan centre, ten mins.
Habitat: Wetlands, marsh, swamp, reedbed, open water, creek (tidal), river, saltmarsh, woodland.
Key birds: Cetti's Warbler, Kingfisher, Water Rail, Greater Spotted Woodpecker, Dipper, gulls, Marsh Harrier, Sand Martin, Hobby, Redstart, occasional Bittern and Red Kite.
Contact: The Welsh Wildlife Centre, Cilgerran,

Cardigan SA43 2TB. 01239 621 212.
e-mail: wwc@welshwildlife.org
www.welshwildlife.org

10. YNYS-HIR

RSPB (Wales).
Location: SN 68 29 63. Off A487 Aberystwyth - Machynlleth road in Eglwys-fach village. Six miles SW of Machynlleth.
Access: Open every day (9am-9pm or dusk if earlier) except Christmas Day. Visitor centre open daily Apr-Oct (10am-5pm), Wed-Sun Nov-Mar (10am-4pm). Coaches welcome but please call for parking information. Sorry, no dogs allowed.
Facilities: Visitor centre and toilets. Numerous trails, six hides, drinks machine.
Public transport: Bus service to Eglwys-fach from either Machynlleth or Aberystwyth, tel. 01970 617 951. Rail service to Machynlleth.
Habitat: Estuary, freshwater pools, woodland and wet grassland.
Key birds: Large numbers of wintering waders, wildfowl and birds of prey on the estuary are replaced with breeding woodland birds in spring and summer. *All year*: Red Kite, Buzzard, Little Egret, Lapwing, Teal. *Spring*: Wood Warbler, Redstart, Pied Flycatcher, nine species of warbler. *Winter*: Greenland white-fronted Goose, Barnacle Goose, Wigeon, Hen Harrier.
Other notable flora and fauna: Sixteen species of dragonfly and damselfly include small red damselfly and golden-ringed dragonfly. Butterflies include dark green fritillary, brimstone and speckled wood. Otters and brown hares are resident though the former are rarely seen.
Contact: RSPB Ynys-Hir Reserve, Eglwys-fach, Machynlleth, Powys SY20 8TA. 01654 700 222.
e-mail: ynyshir@rspb.org.uk

NORTHERN IRELAND

Antrim

BOG MEADOWS

Ulster Wildlife Trust.
Location: J 315 726. UNESCO award-winning reserve accessed from Milltown Row, signposted from the Falls Road, West Belfast. (OS map 15).
Access: Open at all times. Coach parties welcome. Suitable for wheelchair users.
Facilities: Car park, network of paths (contact warden for toilets and bird hide access arrangements).
Public transport: Bus service from Belfast city along

Falls Road. For more details contact Translink on 028 9066 6630.
Habitat: 47 acres of woodland, unimproved grassland, scrub, ponds, reedbeds.
Key birds: *Summer*: Passage waders, Grey Wagtail, Stonechat, Sedge and Grasshopper Warblers, Reed Bunting. *Winter*: Water Rail, Snipe, Teal.
Other notable flora and fauna: Leisler's bat, hawker dragonflies.
Contact: Deborah McLaughlin, Bog Meadows Warden, Belfast UWT office, 163 Stewartstown Road, Dunmurry, Belfast BT19 9EP. 028 9062 8647.
e-mail: info@ulsterwildlifetrust.org
www.ulsterwildlifetrust.org

NATURE RESERVES - NORTHERN IRELAND

ECOS NATURE RESERVE

Ballymena Borough Council/Ulster Wildlife Trust.
Location: D 118 036. 0.5 miles NE of Ballymena town centre. Signposted off M2 (OS map 9).
Access: Open at all times. Coaches welcome. Suitable for wheelchair users.
Facilities: Environmental centre (028 2566 4400), car park, toilets, bird hide, network of paths.
Public transport: Bus from Ballymena town centre or within easy walking distance. For more details contact Translink on 028 9066 6630.
Habitat: 24ha of damp and dry grassland, lake edge, willow coppice, scrub.
Key birds: *Summer*: Breeding Snipe, Sedge Warbler, Grasshopper Warbler, Reed Bunting. *Winter*: Teal, Goldeneye, Lapwing, Curlew. Rarities have included, White-winged Black Tern, Yellow Wagtail and Hoopoe in recent years.
Other notable flora and fauna: Otter, Irish hare and Leisler's bat. Notable for orchids, inc Irish lady's tresses, butterflies and dragonflies.
Contact: Cliff Henry, Ecos Warden, Ulster Wildlife Trust, 3 New Line, Crossgar, Co Down BT19 9EP. 028 4483 0282. e-mail: info@ulsterwildlifetrust.org www.ulsterwildlifetrust.org

GLENARM

Ulster Wildlife Trust.
Location: D 301 132, OS 1:50 000 sheet 9. On Glenarm Estate. Gate by B97 Ballymena Road half mile SW of Glenarm, 15 miles from Ballymena.
Access: Wildlife Trust members only. Not suitable for coaches. Parts of reserve accessible for wheelchair users.
Facilities: Forest tracks.
Public transport: Ulsterbus – from Ballymena. For more details contact Translink on 028 9066 6630.
Habitat: Species-rich grassland, mature oaks and hazel coppiced woodland.
Key birds: *Summer*: Breeding Blackcap, Garden Warbler, Wood Warbler, Redpoll, Buzzard, Dipper, Jay, Common Crossbill, Grey Wagtail, Raven.
Other notable flora and fauna: Fungi, bluebell, wild garlic, toothwort and other woodland plants. Red squirrel and Irish hare.
Contact: Reserves Manager, Ulster Wildlife Trust. 028 9062 8647. e-mail: info@ulsterwildlifetrust.org www.ulsterwildlifetrust.org

ISLE OF MUCK

Ulster Wildlife Trust.
Location: D 464 024 (OS Map 9). Situated off NE tip of Island Magee, Co Antrim. Take the B150 from Whitehead and after 7 miles, take unclassified road at Mullaghnoy, signposted to Portmuck.
Access: Wildlife Trust members only. UWT Permit required for boat landings. Not suitable for disabled, but island can be viewed from mainland.
Facilities: None on island. Toilets in Portmuck.
Public transport: None.

Habitat: Offshore island with cliffs and stack
Key birds: *Summer*: Third largest colony of cliff-nesting seabirds in Northern Ireland, with Kittiwake, Guillemot, Fulmar and Razorbill all breeding and Peregrine Falcons commonly hunting over the island. Also look for Manx Shearwater, terns, Black Guillemot, Puffin. *Winter*: Red-throated Diver at sea. Occasional Glaucous and Iceland Gulls.
Other notable flora and fauna: Harbour porpoise offshore.
Contact: Reserves Manager, Ulster Wildlife Trust, 028 9062 8647. e-mail: info@ulsterwildlifetrust.org www.ulsterwildlifetrust.org

LAGAN MEADOWS

Ulster Wildlife Trust.
Location: J 335 703 (OS map 15). Located within Lagan Valley Regional Park, signposted off Malone Road, 2 miles S of Belfast city centre.
Access: Open at all times. On-street parking, maps and information available at Knightsbridge Park entrance. Suitable for coach parties. Disabled parking at Sharman Road entrance. Suitable for wheelchair users along Lagan towpath.
Facilities: Network of paths.
Public transport: Bus service from Belfast city centre along Malone/Stranmillis Roads. For more details contact Translink on 028 9066 6630.
Habitat: Species-rich meadows, marsh, pond and scrub.
Key birds: *All year*: Kingfisher, Bullfinch, Goldcrest. *Summer*: Sedge and Grasshopper Warblers, Blackcap and Reed Bunting. *Winter*: Water Rail, Snipe, Redpoll and Siskin.
Other notable flora and fauna: Pink meadow waxcap fungus, devil's bit scabious, Real's wood white butterfly, banded demoiselle damselfly.
Contact: Reserves Manager, Ulster Wildlife Trust, 028 9062 8647. e-mail: info@ulsterwildlifetrust.org www.ulsterwildlifetrust.org

RATHLIN ISLAND SEABIRD CENTRE

RSPB (Northern Ireland Office).
Location: NR 282 092. Nearest town on mainland is Ballycastle from where ferry to Rathlin departs. From Rathlin Harbour, it is a further four miles to the Seabird Centre. Private minibus service and bicycle hire available on the island.
Access: 11am-3pm daily (Apr -mid Sep). Seabird Centre accessed by 89 steps down cliffside, so access may not be suitable for all visitors. Contact the reserve or regional office for advice. Four mile trail to viewpoint.
Facilities: Car park with limited parking and limited vehicle access via ferry, cycle racks available. Binocular hire, group bookings accepted, remote location that is good for walking.
Public transport: Minibus service on island.
Habitat: Coastal.
Key birds: *Spring/summer*: Large numbers of breeding Puffin, Guillemot, Razorbill, Fulmar,

Kittiwake and Gannet from mid-April. First chicks in mid-June. Eiders in harbour. Peregrine, Wheatear and Stonechat. At Roonivoolin at island's southern end look for Chough, Corn Crake, Snipe and breeding Lapwing.
Other notable flora and fauna: Orchids and Irish hares possible close to reserve. Dolphin and porpoise offshore.
Contact: Seabird Centre (02820 760 062), RSPB Northern Ireland HQ (02890 491 547).

Co. Armagh

OXFORD ISLAND NATIONAL NATURE RESERVE

Craigavon Borough Council.
Location: J 061 608. On shores of Lough Neagh, 2.5 miles from Lurgan, Co Armagh. Signposted from J10 of M1.
Access: Site open at all times. Car parks locked at varying times (see signs). Coach parking available. Lough Neagh Discovery Centre open every day Apr-Sept (10am-5pm Mon-Sat, 10am-7pm Sun), Oct-Mar (10am-5pm every day). Closed Christmas Day. Dogs on leads please. Most of site and all of Centre accessible for wheelchairs. Wheelchairs and mobility scooters available for visitors.
Facilities: Public toilets, Lough Neagh Discovery Centre with loop system for hard-of-hearing, shop, café and conference facilities. Four miles of footpaths, five birdwatching hides, children's play areas, trails, picnic tables, public jetties, museum. Guided walks and boat trips available (pre-booking essential). Varied programme of events.
Public transport: Ulsterbus Park'n Ride at Lough Road, Lurgan is 0.5 miles from reserve entrance. Tel 02890 333 000. Lurgan Railway Station, 3 miles from reserve entrance.
Habitat: Freshwater lake, ponds, wet grassland, reedbed, woodland.
Key birds: *Winter*: Large flocks of wildfowl, especially Pochard, Tufted Duck, Goldeneye and Scaup (mainly Dec/Jan). Whooper and Bewick's Swans and Greylag Geese (Oct-Apr). Tree Sparrows. *Summer*: Sedge Warbler, Grasshopper Warbler and Great Crested Grebe.
Other notable flora and fauna: Discovery Centre pond has interesting variety of pond weeds. Real's white butterfly (May-Jun). Rare Irish moiled cattle and Dexter cattle are used for conservation grazing.
Contact: Marcus Malley, Conservation Officer, Lough Neagh Discovery Centre, Oxford Island NNR, Lurgan, Co Armagh, N Ireland BT66 6NJ. 02838 322 205.
e-mail: oxford.island@craigavon.gov.uk
www.oxfordisland.com

PORTMORE LOUGH

RSPB (Northern Ireland Office).
Location: NW 222 280. Eight miles from Lurgan. Leave M1 at J9 (Moira roundabout) and head N on A26. Take road to Aghalee village, from where reserve is signposted.

Access: Open every day, unmanned. Hide on main trail and meadows not suitable for wheelchairs, but the information shelter affords good views of reserve for all visitors.
Facilities: Remote site. Car park, toilets, information shelter and one hide.
Public transport: None.
Habitat: Lowland wet grassland, scrub and reedbed.
Key birds: *Spring/summer*: Breeding wildfowl, terns and waders, inc Curlew, Snipe, Lapwing, warblers, inc Grasshopper and Sedge. Tree Sparrows nest along woodland edge. *Autumn*: Hen Harrier, Buzzard and incoming winter thrushes. *Winter*: Greylag Goose, Whooper Swan and a variety of wildfowl. Large flocks of Golden Plover and Lapwing, also Tree Sparrow and Linnet.
Other notable flora and fauna: Dragonflies inc common hawker, four-spotted chaser, ruddy, red-coloured and common darters. Green-veined white butterfly and many varieties of meadow plants.
Contact: RSPB Northern Ireland HQ. 02890 491 547. e-mail: john.scovell@rspb.org.uk

Co. Down

BELFAST LOUGH

RSPB (Northern Ireland Office).
Location: NW 488 307. Take A2 N from Belfast and follow signs to Belfast Harbour Estate. Both entrances to reserve have Harbour checkpoints. From Dee Street entrance it is two miles to reserve, from Tillysburn entrance, one mile.
Access: Viewpoints open dawn to dusk. Observation room closed Sunday morning and Monday and Dec 25/26. Other days open 9m to 5pm.
Facilities: Lagoon overlooked by observation room (see opening hours above), two other viewpoints.
Public transport: Translink's metro bus stops close to reserve, service 26A and 27 (Translink 028 9066 6630).
Habitat: Mudflats, wet grassland, freshwater lagoon.
Key birds: Noted for Black-tailed Godwit numbers and excellent variety of waterfowl in spring, autumn and winter, with close views. Rarities have included Buff-breasted, Pectoral, White-rumped and Semi-palmated Sandpipers, Spotted Crake, American Wigeon, Laughing Gull.
Contact: RSPB Northern Ireland HQ, 02890 491 154.

CASTLE ESPIE

The Wildfowl & Wetlands Trust.
Location: J 474 672. On Strangford Lough 10 miles E of Belfast, signposted from A22 in the Comber area.
Access: Open daily except Christmas Day (10.30am Mon-Sat, 11.30am Sun).
Facilities: Visitor centre, educational facilities, views over lough, three hides, woodland walk.
Public transport: Call for advice.
Habitat: Reedbed filtration system with viewing facilities.
Key birds: *Winter*: Wildfowl esp. pale-bellied Brent

Goose, Scaup. *Summer*: Warblers. Wader scrape has attracted Little Egret, Ruff, Long-billed Dowitcher, Killdeer.
Contact: James Orr, Centre Manager, The Wildfowl & Wetlands Trust, Castle Espie, Ballydrain Road, Comber, Co Down BT23 6EA. 02891 874 146.

COPELAND BIRD OBSERVATORY

Location: Situated on a 40-acre island on outer edge of Belfast Lough, four miles N of Donaghadee.
Access: Access is by chartered boat from Donaghadee.
Facilities: Observatory open Apr-Oct most weekends and some whole weeks. Hostel-type accommodation for up to 20. Daily ringing, bird census, sea passage recording. General bookings: Neville McKee, 67 Temple Rise, Templepatrick, Co. Antrim BT39 0AG (tel 028 9443 3068).
Public transport: None.
Habitat: Grassy areas, rock foreshore.
Key birds: Large colony of Manx Shearwaters; Black Guillemot, Eider, Water Rail also nest. Summer: Visiting Storm Petrels. Moderate passage of passerine migrants.
Contact: Bookings Secretary: Neville McKee, 028 9443 3068. e-mail: Neville.McKee@btinternet.com

MURLOUGH NATIONAL NATURE RESERVE

National Trust.
Location: J 394 338. Ireland's first nature reserve, between Dundrum and Newcastle, close to Mourne Mountains.
Access: Permit needed except on marked paths.
Facilities: Visitor centre.
Public transport: Local bus service from Belfast-Newcastle passes reserve entrances.
Habitat: Sand dunes, heathland.
Key birds: Waders and wildfowl occur in Inner Dundrum Bay adjacent to the reserve; divers and large numbers of scoter (inc. regular Surf Scoter) and Red-breasted Merganser in Dundrum Bay.
Contact: Head Warden, Murlough NNR, The Stable Yard, Keel Point, Dundrum, Newcastle, Co Down BT33 0NQ. Tel/Fax 02843 751 467; e-mail umnnrw@smtp.ntrust.org.uk.

NORTH STRANGFORD LOUGH

National Trust.
Location: J 510 700. View from adjacent roads and car parks; also from hide at Castle Espie (J 492 675).
Access: Call for advice.
Facilities: Hide.
Public transport: Bus service from Newtownards to Portaferry.
Habitat: Extensive tidal mudflats, limited saltmarsh.
Key birds: Major winter feeding area for pale-bellied Brent Goose, also Pintail, Wigeon, Whooper Swan. Waders (inc. Dunlin, Knot, Oystercatcher, Bar-tailed Godwit). During the summer months, Strangford's many islands provide the perfect breeding sites for thousands of gulls, terns and other waterfowl.

Other notable flora and fauna: Stranford Lough is an important refuge for substantial common and grey seal populations. Otters and porpoises are also regularly seen.
Contact: Head Warden, National Trust, Strangford Lough Wildlife Centre, Castle Ward, Strangford, Co Down BT30 7LS. Tel/Fax 02844 881 411; e-mail uslwcw@smtp.ntrust.org.uk. e-mail: strangford@nationaltrust.org.uk

SLIEVENACLOY

Ulster Wildlife Trust.
Location: J 255 712 (OS map 14,15). Situated in the Belfast Hills, W of Belfast. Access from Flowbog Road after taking Ballycolin Road off A501.
Access: There is pedestrian and wheelchair access all year round from the main entrance and through kissing gates on the Flowbog Road. Cars can be parked along Flowbog Road. On-site car parking only available during events or by prior arrangement with the warden. Please phone 028 4483 0282 for more information.
Facilities: Information leaflets on site about various way-marked trails.
Public transport: Bus service from Belfast to Glenavy. For more details contact Translink on 028 9066 6630.
Habitat: Unimproved grassland, scrub.
Key birds: *Summer*: Snipe, Curlew, Sky Lark, Grey Wagtail, Stonechat, Wheatear, Grasshopper Warbler and Reed Bunting. *Winter*: Hen Harrier, Merlin, Fieldfare and Snow Bunting.
Other notable flora and fauna: Irish hare, bitter vetchling, bilberry, waxcap fungi, orchids, small heath butterfly.
Contact: Ulster Wildlife Trust, 028 4483 0282. e-mail: info@ulsterwildlifetrust.org www.ulsterwildlifetrust.org

Co. Londonderry

LOUGH FOYLE

RSPB (Northern Ireland Office).
Location: NV 714 858. Large sea lough NE of Londonderry. Take minor roads off Limavady-Londonderry road to view-points (choose high tide) at Longfield Point, Ballykelly, Faughanvale.
Access: Open all year. No permit, but keep to trails.
Facilities: None.
Public transport: Nearest bus stop in Ballykelly.
Habitat: Beds of eel-grass, mudflats, surrounding agricultural land.
Key birds: Staging-post for migrating wildfowl (eg. 15,000 Wigeon, 4,000 Pale-bellied Brent Geese in Oct/Nov). *Winter*: Slavonian Grebe, divers, Bewick's and Whooper Swans, Bar-tailed Godwit, Golden Plover, Snow Bunting. *Autumn*: Waders (inc. Ruff, Little Stint, Curlew Sandpiper, Spotted Redshank).
Other notable species: Otters near Roe estuary.
Contact: RSPB N Ireland HQ, 02890 491 547

Co Tyrone

BLESSINGBOURNE

Ulster Wildlife Trust.
Location: H448487. Situated immediately NE of Fivemiletown (OS Map 18)
Access: Open at all times. Not suitable for coach parties. Unsuitable for wheelchair users.
Facilities: Paths

Public transport: For more details contact Translink on 028 9066 6630
Habitat: lake, reedbeds, mixed woodland
Key birds: *Summer*: Water Rail, Kingfisher, Sedge Warbler, Grasshopper Warbler, Blackcap.
Contact: Ulster Wildlife Trust, 028 4483 0282.
e-mail: info@ulsterwildifetrust.org
www.ulsterwildlifetrust.org

CHANNEL ISLANDS

COLIN McCATHIE RESERVE

La Société Guernesiaise.
Location: Perry's Island Guide for Guernsey (page 6 B5).
Access: Open at all times.
Facilities: Hide on road to Vale Church must be used.
Public transport: Hourly bus service 7/7A (island circular), tel: 01481 720 210.
Habitat: Brackish tidal pond, reed fringes.
Key birds: Passage waders. *Summer*: Breeding Reed Warbler, Moorhen, Coot. *Winter*: Wildfowl, Water Rail, Little Egret, Snipe, Kingfisher.
Contact: Vic Froome, La Cloture, Courtil de Bas Lane, St Sampson's, Guernsey GY2 4XJ. 01481 254 841.
www.societe.org.gg

LA CLAIRE MARE

La Société Guernesiaise.
Location: Perry's Island Guide for Guernsey (page 12 C5).
Access: Open at all times.
Facilities: Hide down concrete track off the Rue de la Rocque Road then footpath to second hide.
Public transport: Hourly bus service 7/7A (island circular), tel: 01481 720 210.

Habitat: Reedbeds, pasture, willow thickets, scrape.
Key birds: Passage waders and passerines. *Summer*: Breeding Reed Warbler, Moorhen, Coot, Kestrel. *Winter*: Wildfowl, Water Rail, Snipe, Kingfisher.
Contact: Vic Froome, La Cloture, Courtil de Bas Lane, St Sampson's, Guernsey GY2 4XJ. 01481 254 841.
www.societe.org.gg

PLEINMONT

La Société Guernesiaise.
Location: Perry's Island Guide for Guernsey (Page 32 B3).
Access: Open at all times.
Facilities: Public footpath around reserve.
Public transport: Hourly bus service 7/7A (island circular) 0.5 miles from Imperial Hotel, tel 01481 720 210.
Habitat: Cliff-top headland of scrub, remnant heathland and small fields.
Key birds: Passage passerines. *Summer*: Breeding Shag, Fulmar, gulls, Dartford Warbler, Whitethroat, Stonechat and Linnet.
Contact: Vic Froome, La Cloture, Courtil Le Bas Lane, St Sampson's, Guernsey GY2 4XT. 01481 254 841.
www.societe.org.gg

EDITOR'S NOTE

It is the *Yearbook's* editorial policy to provide widespread geographical coverage for the Bird Reserves section and we welcome suggestions from readers about new sites they feel should be included in future editions.

While every care is taken to provide accurate and up-to-date information about sites, it is inevitable that some details may change between the date of publication and your visit. Again, we welcome feedback about any significant differences, to help in updating the next edition. Please e-mail your comments to: editor@buckinghampress.com

COUNTY DIRECTORY

This striking image of a Mute Swan family by Mike Smith was commended in the Berkshire Ornithological Society's annual photo competition.

ENGLAND

THE INFORMATION in the directory has been obtained either from the persons listed or from the appropriate national or other bodies. In some cases, where it has not proved possible to verify the details directly, alternative responsible sources have been relied upon. When no satisfactory record was available, previously included entries have sometimes had to be deleted. Readers are requested to advise the editor of any errors or omissions.

AVON

See Somerset.

BEDFORDSHIRE

Bird Atlas/Avifauna
An Atlas of the Breeding Birds of Bedfordshire 1988-92 by R A Dazley and P Trodd (Bedfordshire Natural History Society, 1994).

Bird Recorders
Steve Blain, 34 Southill Road, Broom, Bedfordshire SG18 9NN. 07979 606 300;
e-mail: recorder@bedsbirdclub.org.uk

Bird Report
BEDFORDSHIRE BIRD REPORT (1946-), from Mary Sheridan, 28 Chestnut Hill, Linslade, Leighton Buzzard, Beds LU7 2TR. 01525 378 245;
e-mail: mary.sheridansec@talktalk.net.

BTO Regional Representative
RR. Nigel Willits, Orchard Cottage, 68 High Street, Wilden, Beds MK44 2QD. 01234 771 948;
e-mail: willits1960@hotmail.com

Club
BEDFORDSHIRE BIRD CLUB. (1992; 300). Miss Sheila Alliez, Flat 61 Adamson Court, Adamson Walk, Kempston, Bedford MK42 8QZ.
e-mail: alliezsec@peewit.
freeserve.co.uk
www.bedsbirdclub.org.uk
Meetings: 8.00pm, last Tuesday of the month (Sep-Mar), Maulden Village Hall, Maulden, Beds.

Ringing Groups
IVEL RG. Graham Buss, 11 Northall Close, Eaton Bray, Dunstable, LU6 2EB. 01525 221 023;
e-mail: g1j2buss@yahoo.co.uk

RSPB. WB Kirby. e-mail: will.kirby@rspb.org.uk

RSPB Local Groups
BEDFORD. (1970; 80). Bob Montgomery, 36 Princes Road, Bromham, Beds MK43 8QD. 01234 822 035;
www.rspb.org.uk/groups/bedford/
Meetings: 7.30pm, 3rd Thursday of the month, A.R.A. Manton Lane, Bedford.

LUTON AND SOUTH BEDFORDSHIRE. (1973; 120+).
Mick Price, 120 Common Road, Kensworth, Beds LU6 3RG. 01582 873 268.
Meetings: 7.45pm, 2nd Wednesday of the month, Houghton Regis Social Centre, Parkside Drive, Houghton Regis, Beds LU5 5QN.

Wetland Bird Survey Organiser
BEDFORDSHIRE. Richard Bashford. 6 Brook Road, Eaton Ford, St Neots, Cambridgeshire PE19 7AX. e-mail: richard.bashford@rspb.org.uk

Wildlife Trust
See Cambridgeshire,

BERKSHIRE

BirdAtlas/Avifauna
The Birds of Berkshire by P E Standley et al (Berkshire Atlas Group/Reading Ornithological Club, 1996).

Bird Recorder
RECORDER (Records Committee and rarity records). Chris DR Heard, 3 Waterside Lodge, Ray Mead Road, Maidenhead, Berkshire SL6 8NP. 01628 633 828;
e-mail: chris.heard@virgin.net

Bird Reports
BERKSHIRE BIRD BULLETIN (Monthly, 1986-), from Brian Clews, 118 Broomhill, Cookham, Berks SL6 9LQ. 01628 525 314;
e-mail: brian.clews@btconnect.com

BIRDS OF BERKSHIRE (1974-), from Secretary of the Berkshire Ornithological Club,
e-mail: renton.righelato@berksoc.org.uk

BIRDS OF THE THEALE AREA (1988-), from Secretary, Theale Area Bird Conservation Group.

NEWBURY DISTRICT BIRD REPORT (1959-) - covering West Berkshire (approx 12 miles from centre of Newbury), plus parts of north Hants, south Oxon, from The Secretary, Newbury District Ornithological Club.

BTO Regional Representatives
RR. Sarah Priest and Kent White, 01635 268 442;
e-mail: btoberks.ken.sarah@googlemail.com

ENGLAND

Clubs
BERKSHIRE BIRD BULLETIN GROUP. (1986; 100).
Berkshire Bird Bulletin Group, PO Box 680,
Maidenhead, Berks, SL6 9ST. 01628 525 314;
e-mail: brian.clews@btconnect.com

NEWBURY DISTRICT ORNITHOLOGICAL CLUB. (1959;
110). Mrs Lesley Staves, Hell Corner Farm, Kintbury,
Hungerford, Berkshire RG17 9SX. 01488 668 482;
e-mail: info1@ndoc.org.uk www.ndoc.org.uk

BERKSHIRE ORNITHOLOGICAL CLUB. (1947; 320).
Renton Righelato, 63 Hamilton Road, Reading RG1
5RA. 0787 981 2564;
e-mail: renton.righelato@berksoc.org.uk
www.berksoc.org.uk
Meetings: 8pm, alternate Wednesdays (Oct-Mar).
University of Reading.

THEALE AREA BIRD
CONSERVATION GROUP. (1988;
75). Catherine McEwan. 0118
941 5792; e-mail: catherine_j_
mcewan@fsmail.net
www.freewebs.com/tabcg/index.htm
Meetings: 8pm, 1st Tuesday of the month, Englefield
Social Club.

Ringing Groups
NEWBURY RG. J Legg, 31 Haysoms Drive, Greenham,
Nr Newbury, Berks RG19 8EY.
e-mail: janlegg@btinternet.com
www.newburyrg.co.uk

RUNNYMEDE RG. D G Harris, 22 Blossom Waye,
Hounslow, TW5 9HD.
e-mail: daveharris@tinyonline.co.uk

RSPB Local Groups
EAST BERKSHIRE. (1974; 200). Gerry Studd, 5 Cherry
Grove, Holmer Green, High Wycombe, Bucks HP15
6RG. 01494 715 609;
e-mail: gerrystudd@aol.com
www.eastberksrspb.org.uk
Meetings: 7.30pm, Thursdays (Sept-April), Methodist
Church Hall, High Street, Maidenhead.

READING. (1986; 80). Carl Feltham. 0118 941 1713;
e-mail: carl.feltham@talktalk.net
www.reading-rspb.org.uk
Meetings: 2nd Tues of each month at Pangbourne
village hall (8pm start).

WOKINGHAM & BRACKNELL. (1979; 200). Les Blundell,
Folly Cottage, Buckle Lane, Warfield, RG42 5SB.
01344 861 964;
e-mail: lesblundell@ymail.com
www.rspb.org.uk/groups/wokinghamandbracknell
Meetings: 8.00pm, 2nd Tuesday of the month (Sep-
Jun), Finchampstead Memorial Hall, Wokingham,
RG40 4JU.

Wildlife Hospitals
LIFELINE. Wendy Hermon, Treatment Centre Co-
ordinator, Swan Treatment Centre, Cuckoo Weir

Island, South Meadow Lane, Eton, Windsor, Berks SL4
6SS. 01753 859 397; (Fax) 01753 622 709;
e-mail: wendyhermon@aol.com
www.swanlifeline.org.uk
Registered charity. Thames Valley 24-hour swan
rescue and treatment service. Veterinary support and
hospital unit. Operates membership scheme.

Wildlife Trust
Director, See Oxfordshire,

BUCKINGHAMSHIRE

BirdAtlas/Avifauna
The Birds of Buckinghamshire ed by P Lack and D
Ferguson (Buckinghamshire Bird Club, 1993). Now out
of print.

Bird Recorder
Andy Harding, 93 Deanshanger Lane, Old Stratford,
MK19 6AX. e-mail: a.v.harding@open.ac.uk

Bird Reports
*AMERSHAM BIRDWATCHING CLUB ANNUAL REPORT
(1975-)*, from Secretary,

BUCKINGHAMSHIRE BIRD REPORT (1980-), from John
Gearing, Valentines, Dinton, Aylesbury, Bucks HP17
8UW. e-mail: john_gearing@hotmail.com

NORTH BUCKS BIRD REPORT (12 pa), from Recorder.

**BTO Regional Representative & Regional
Development Officer**
RR. David Lee. 01844 347 576;
e-mail: oldfield51@btinternet.com

RDO. Peter Hearn, 160 High Street, Aylesbury, Bucks
HP20 1RE. 01296 424 145; (Fax)01296 581 520.

Clubs
BUCKINGHAMSHIRE BIRD
CLUB. (1981; 340). Neill
Foster, Secretary. 01296
748 597;
e-mail: Secretary@bucksbirdclub.co.uk
www.bucksbirdclub.co.uk
Meetings: 1st Thurs of month (Oct
to Apr) at Wendover Memorial Hall, Wharf Road,
Wendover (7.45pm start). Non-members welcome (£2
admission).

NORTH BUCKS BIRDERS. (1977; 40). Andy Harding,
15 Jubilee Terrace, Stony Stratford, Milton Keynes,
MK11 1DU. H:01908 565896; W:01908 653328; e-mail:
a.v.harding@open.ac.uk
Meetings: Last Tuesday of the month (Nov, Jan, Feb,
Mar), The Cock, High Street, Stony Stratford.

RSPB Local Groups
See also Herts: Chorleywood.

AYLESBURY. (1981; 220). Ann Wallington. 01295 253
330, e-mail: Jenny.wallington@btinternet.com
Meetings: Mondays (Oct to May) at Prebendal Farm
Community Centre, Fowler Road, Aylesbury (7.30pm).

ENGLAND

NORTH BUCKINGHAMSHIRE. (1976; 440). Chris Ward, 41 William Smith Close, Woolstone, Milton Keynes, MK15 0AN. 01908 669 448;
e-mail: cwphotography@hotmail.com
www.rspb.org.uk/groups/northbucks
Meetings: 8.00pm, 2nd Thursday of the month, Cruck Barn, City Discovery Centre, Bradwell Abbey MK13 9AP.

Wetland Bird Survey Organiser
BUCKINGHAMSHIRE. Graeme Taylor. Field House, 54 Halton Lane, Wendover, Nr. Aylesbury, Buckinghamshire HP22 6AU.

Wildlife Hospitals
WILDLIFE HOSPITAL TRUST. St Tiggywinkles, Aston Road, Haddenham, Aylesbury, Bucks, HP17 8AF. 01844 292 292 (24hr helpline);
e-mail: mail@sttiggywinkles.org.uk
www.sttiggywinkles.org.uk
Registered charity. All British species. Veterinary referrals and helpline for vets and others on wild bird treatments. Full veterinary unit and staff. Pub: *Bright Eyes* (free to members - sae).

Wildlife Trust
Director, See Oxfordshire,

CAMBRIDGESHIRE

BirdAtlas/Avifauna
An Atlas of the Breeding Birds of Cambridgeshire (VC 29) PMM Bircham et al (Cambridge Bird Club, 1994).

The Birds of Cambridgeshire: checklist 2000 (Cambridge Bird Club)

Bird Recorders
CAMBRIDGESHIRE. Mark Hawkes, 7 Cook Drive, Eynesbury, St Neots, Cambs PE19 2JU. 01480 215 305;
e-mail: marklhawkes@yahoo.co.uk

Bird Reports
CAMBRIDGESHIRE BIRD REPORT (1925-), from Bruce Martin, 178 Nuns Way, Cambridge, CB4 2NS. 01223 700 656; e-mail: bruce.s.martin@ntlworld.com

PETERBOROUGH BIRD CLUB REPORT (1999-), from Secretary, Peterborough Bird Club.

BTO Regional Representatives
CAMBRIDGESHIRE RR. Position vacant.

HUNTINGDON & PETERBOROUGH. Phillip Todd. 01733 810 832.

Clubs
CAMBRIDGESHIRE BIRD CLUB. (1925; 329). John Harding, 3 Cotton's Field, Dry Drayton, Cambs CB23 8DG.
e-mail: johnharding44@googlemail.com
Meetings: 2nd Friday of the month, St John's Church Hall, Hills Road, Cambridge/Milton CP Visitors Centre, Milton, Cambridge.

PETERBOROUGH BIRD CLUB. (1999; 210). Trevor Williams, The Old Rectory, Market Deeping, PE6 8DA. 01778 345 711; www.pbc.codehog.co.uk
e-mail: Trevor@oldrectory.screaming.net
Meetings: Last Tuesday each month (Sep-Nov and Jan -Apr) at 7.30pm at Post Office Social Club, Bourges Boulevard, Peterborough. Outdoor meetings monthly throughout most of year. Non-members welcome.

THE FRIENDS OF PAXTON PITS. (1995; 2,200+). Trevor Gunton, 15 St James Road, Little Paxton, St Neots, Cambs, PE19 6QW; (tel/fax)01480 473 562.
www.paxton-pits.org.uk
Meetings: No set days or venues - visit website for details.

Ringing Group
WICKEN FEN RG. Dr C J R Thorne, 17 The Footpath, Coton, Cambs CB23 7PX. 01954 210 566;
e-mail: cjrt@cam.ac.uk

Wetland Bird Survey Organisers
CAMBRIDGESHIRE (including Huntingdonshire). Bruce Martin, 178 Nuns Way, Cambridge, CB4 2NS. (H)01223 700 656; e-mail: bruce.s.martin@ntlworld.com

NENE WASHES. Charlie Kitchin, RSPB Nene Washes, 21a East Delph, Whittlesey, Cambs PE7 1RH. 01733 205 140; e-mail: charlie.kitchin@rspb.org.uk

RSPB Local Groups
CAMBRIDGE. (1977; 150). Melvyn Smith. 01799 500 482; e-mail: mel_brensmith@hotmail.co.uk
www.RSPB.org.uk/groups/cambridge
Meetings: 3rd Wednesday every month (Jan-May and Sept-Dec) 8pm. Chemistry Labs, Lensfield Road, Cambridge.

HUNTINGDONSHIRE. (1982; 180). Rick Harrison, 23 Willow Green, Needingworth, St Ives, PE27 4SW. 01480 465 885;
e-mail: richardharrison1@btinternet.com
www.rspb.org.uk/groups/huntingdon
Meetings: Last Wednesday of month (Sep-Apr), Free Church, St Ives (7.30pm).

Wildlife Trust
THE WILDLIFE TRUST FOR BEDFORDSHIRE, CAMBRIDGESHIRE, NORTHAMPTONSHIRE AND PETERBOROUGH. (1990; 33,000). The Manor House, Broad Street, Great Cambourne, Cambridgeshire CB23 6DH. 01954 713 500; (Fax)01954 710 051;
e-mail: cambridgeshire@wildlifebcnp.org
www.wildlifebcnp.org

CHESHIRE

BirdAtlas/Avifauna.
Birds in Cheshire and Wirral - A Breeding and Wintering Atlas 2004-2007 by Professor David Norman, Liverpool University Press, Autumn 2008.

250

ENGLAND

The Birds of Sandbach Flashes 1935-1999 by Andrew Goodwin and Colin Lythgoe (The Printing House, Crewe, 2000).

Bird Recorder (inc Wirral)
CHESHIRE & WIRRAL. Hugh Pulsford, 6 Buttermere Drive, Great Warford, Alderley Edge, Cheshire SK9 7WA. 01565 880 171; e-mail: countyrec@cawos.org

Bird Report
CHESHIRE & WIRRAL BIRD REPORT (1969-), from Peter Mathews, Hordern Farm Pottery, Buxton New Road, Macclesfield SK11 0AN.

SOUTH EAST CHESHIRE ORNITHOLOGICAL SOCIETY BIRD REPORT (1985-), from Secretary, South East Cheshire Ornithol Soc. 01270 582 642.

BTO Regional Representatives & Regional Development Officer
MID RR. Paul Miller.
01928 787 535; e-mail: huntershill@worldonline.co.uk

NORTH & EAST RR. Mark Eddowes, 59 Westfield Drive, Knutsford, Cheshire WA16 0BH. 01565 621 683; e-mail: mark.eddowes@esrtechnology.com

SOUTH RR & RDO. Charles Hull, Edleston Cottage, Edleston Hall Lane, Nantwich, Cheshire CW5 8PL. 01270 628 194; e-mail: edleston@yahoo.co.uk

Clubs
CHESHIRE & WIRRAL ORNITHOLOGICAL SOCIETY. (1988; 375). Dr Ted Lock, 2 Bourne Street, Wilmslow, Cheshire SK9 5HD. 01625 540 466; e-mail: secretary@cawos.org
CAWOS
www.cawos.org
Meetings: 7.45pm, 1st Friday of the month, Knutsford Civic Centre.

KNUTSFORD ORNITHOLOGICAL SOCIETY. (1974; 45). Derek A Pike, 2 Lilac Avenue, Knutsford, Cheshire, WA16 0AZ. 01565 653 811; www.10x50.com
Meetings: 7.30pm, 4th Friday of the month (not Dec), Jubilee Hall, Stanley Road, Knutsford.

LANCASHIRE & CHESHIRE FAUNA SOCIETY. (1914; 140). Dave Bickerton, 64 Petre Crescent, Rishton, Blackburn, Lancs, BB1 4RB. 01254 886257; e-mail: bickertond@aol.com
www.lacfs.org.uk

LYMM ORNITHOLOGY GROUP. (1975; 60). Mrs Ann Ledden, 4 Hill View, Widnes, WA8 9AL. 0151 424 0441; e-mail: secretary-log@tiscali.co.uk
Meetings: 8.00pm, last Friday of the month (Aug-May), Lymm Village Hall.

MID-CHESHIRE ORNITHOLOGICAL SOCIETY. (1963; 80). Paul Kenyon, 196 Chester Road, Hartford, Northwich, Cheshire CW8 1LG. 01606 779 60; e-mail: contact@midcheshireos.co.uk
www.midcheshireos.co.uk
Meetings: 7.30pm, 2nd Friday of the month (Oct-Mar), Hartford Village Hall.

SOUTH EAST CHESHIRE ORNITHOLOGICAL SOCIETY. (1964; 140). Colin Lythgoe, 11 Waterloo Road, Haslington, Crewe, CW1 5TF. 01270 582 642. www.secos.org.uk
Meetings: 2nd Friday each month (Sept-Apr), 7.30pm, St Matthew's Church Hall, Elworth.

WILMSLOW GUILD BIRDWATCHING GROUP. (1965; 67). Tom Gibbons, Chestnut Cottage, 37 Strawberry Lane, Wilmslow, Cheshire SK9 6AQ. 01625 520317.
Meetings: 7.30pm last Friday of the month, Wilmslow Guild, Bourne St, Wilmslow.

Ringing Groups
MERSEYSIDE RG. Bob Harris, 3 Mossleigh, Whixalll, Whitchurch, Shropshire SY13 2SA. Work; 0151 706 4311; e-mail: harris@liv.ac.uk

SOUTH MANCHESTER RG. Mr N.B. Powell, e-mail: neville.powell@tiscali.co.uk

RSPB Local Groups
CHESTER. (1988; 220). Liz McClure. 01829 782 237; e-mail: chester1RSPB@btinternet.com
www.rspb.org.uk/groups/chester
Meetings: 7.30pm, 3rd Wednesday of the month (Sep-Apr), St Mary's Centre, Chester.

MACCLESFIELD. (1979; 394). Anne Bennett. 01260 271 231; e-mail: ks.bennett@virgin.net
www.macclesfieldrspb.org.uk
Meetings: 7.45pm, 2nd Tuesday of the month, Senior Citizens Hall, Duke Street, Macclesfield, Cheshire SK11 6UR.

NORTH CHESHIRE. (1976; 100). Paul Grimmet.
01925 268 770;
e-mail: paulwtwitcher@hotmail.com
www.rspb.org.uk/groups/north_cheshire
Meetings: 7.45pm, 3rd Friday (Jan-April and Sept-Nov), Appleton Parish Hall, Dudlow's Green Road, Appleton, Warrington.

Wetland Bird Survey Organiser
CHESHIRE SOUTH. David Cookson.
e-mail: cheshireswans@aol.com

Wildlife Hospitals
RSPCA STAPELEY GRANGE WILDLIFE CENTRE. London Road, Stapeley, Nantwich, Cheshire, CW5 7JW. 0300 123 0722. All wild birds. Oiled bird wash facilities and pools. Veterinary support.

Wildlife Trust
CHESHIRE WILDLIFE TRUST. (1962; 13,100). Bickley Hall Farm, Bickley, Malpas, Cheshire SY14 8EF. 01948 820 728; (Fax) 0709 2888 469
e-mail: cheshirewt@cix.co.uk
www.cheshirewildlifetrust.co.uk

251

ENGLAND

CLEVELAND

Bird Atlas/Avifauna
The Breeding Birds of Cleveland. Teesmouth Bird Club, 2008.

Bird Recorder
CLEVELAND. Tom Francis.
E-mail: mot.francis@ntlworld.com

Bird Report
CLEVELAND BIRD REPORT (1974-), from Mr J Fletcher, 43 Glaisdale Avenue, Middlesbrough TS5 7PF. 01642 818 825.

BTO Regional Representative
CLEVELAND RR. Vic Fairbrother, 8, Whitby Avenue, Guisborough, Cleveland, TS14 7AP. 01287 633 744; e-mail: vic.fairbrother@ntlworld.com

Club
TEESMOUTH BIRD CLUB. (1960; 425). Chris Sharp (Hon Sec.), 20 Auckland Way, Hartlepool, TS26 0AN.
01429 865 163.
www.teesmouthbc.com
Meetings: 7.30pm, 1st Monday of the month (Sep-Apr), Stockton Library, Church Road, Stockton.

Ringing Groups
TEES RG. E Wood, Southfields, 16 Marton Moor Road, Nunthorpe, Middlesbrough, Cleveland TS7 0BH. 01642 323 563.

SOUTH CLEVELAND RG. W Norman, 2 Station Cottages, Grosmont, Whitby, N Yorks YO22 5PB. 01947 895226; e-mail: wilfgros@lineone.net

RSPB Local Group
CLEVELAND. (1974; 200). Terry Reeve.
e-mail: ClevelandRSPB@googlemail.com
www.rspb.org.uk/groups/cleveland
Meetings: 7.00 for 7.30pm, 2nd Monday of each month (Sep-Apr), Nature's World, Ladgate Lane, Middlesbrough, Cleveland

Wetland Bird Survey Organiser
CLEVELAND (EXCL. TEES ESTUARY). Chris Sharp. 20 Auckland Way, Hartlepool TS26 0AN.
e-mail: chrisandlucia@ntlworld.com

TEES ESTUARY. Mike Leakey, c/o Natural England, British Energy, Tees Road, Hartlepool TS25 2BZ. 01429 853 325;
e-mail: mike.leakey@naturalengland.org.uk

Wildlife Trust
TEES VALLEY WILDLIFE TRUST. (1979; 5,000). Margrove Heritage Centre, Margrove Park, Boosbeck, Saltburn-by-the-Sea, TS12 3BZ. 01287 636 382; (Fax)01287 636 383; e-mail: info@teeswildlife.org www.teeswildlife.org

CORNWALL

Bird Recorders
CORNWALL. Darrell Clegg, 55 Lower Fore Street, Saltash, Cornwall PL12 6JQ.
E-mail: darrell@bluetail.fsnet.co.uk

Bird Atlas/Avifauna
The Essential Guide to Birds of The Isles of Scilly 2007 by RL Flood, N Hudson and B Thomas, published by authors.

ISLES OF SCILLY. Nigel Hudson, Post Office Flat, Hugh Street, St Mary's, Isles of Scilly TR21 0JE. 01720 422267; e-mail: nigel-hudson1@tiscali.co.uk

Bird Reports
BIRDS IN CORNWALL (1931-), from CBWPS Treasurer; Gary Lewis, 40 Podfield Road, Saltash PL12 4UA. £11.00 (UK), cheque payable to CBWPS.

ISLES OF SCILLY BIRD REPORT and NATURAL HISTORY REVIEW 2000 (1969-), from The Secretary, Lyonnesse Guest House, The Strand, St Mary's, Isles of Scilly TR21 0PS. e-mail: scillybirding@scilly-birding.co.uk www.scilly-birding.co.uk

BTO Regional Representative
CORNWALL. Stephen Jackson, 2, Trelawney Cottages, Falmouth, Cornwall TR11 3NY. 01326 313 533; e-mail: stephen.f.jackson@btinternet.com

ISLES OF SCILLY RR & RDO. Will Wagstaff, 42 Sally Port, St Mary's, Isles of Scilly, TR21 0JE. 01720 422 212; e-mail: will@islandwildlifetours.co.uk

Clubs
CORNWALL BIRDWATCHING & PRESERVATION SOCIETY. (1931; 990). Tony Bertenshaw, (Honorary Secretary), Hantergantick, St. Breward, Cornwall PL30 4NH. 01208 850 419; www.cbwps.org.uk e-mail:secretary@cbwps.org.uk

CORNWALL WILDLIFE TRUST PHOTOGRAPHIC GROUP. (40). David Chapman, 41 Bosence Road, Townshend, Nr Hayle, Cornwall TR27 6AL. 01736 850 287; e-mail: david@ruralimages.freeserve.co.uk www.ruralimages.freeserve.co.uk
Meetings: Mixture of indoor and outdoor meetings, please phone for details.

ISLES OF SCILLY BIRD GROUP. (2000; 510). The Group leader, Lyonnesse Guest House, The Strand, St Mary's, Isles of Scilly TR21 0PS.
www.scilly-birding.co.uk

Ringing Group
SCILLONIA SEABIRD GROUP. Peter Robinson, Secretary, 19 Pine Park Road, Honiton, Devon EX14 2HR. (Tel/fax)01404 549 873; (M)07768 538 132; e-mail: pjrobinson2@aol.com www.birdexpertuk.com

ENGLAND

RSPB Local Group
CORNWALL. (1972; 450). Roger Hooper. 01209 820
610; e-mail: rogerhooper@talktalk.net
www.rspbcornwall.org.uk
Meetings: Indoor meetings (Sep-Apr), Chacewater
Village Hall, Nr Truro, Cornwall.

Wetland Bird Survey Organiser
TAMAR COMPLEX. Gladys Grant, 18 Orchard Crescent,
Oreston, Plymouth, PL9 7NF. 01752 406 287;
e-mail: gladysgrant@talktalk.net

Wildlife Hospital
MOUSEHOLE WILD BIRD HOSPITAL & SANCTUARY
ASSOCIATION LTD. Raginnis Hill, Mousehole,
Penzance, Cornwall, TR19 6SR. 01736 731 386.
All species. No ringing.

Wildlife Trust
CORNWALL WILDLIFE TRUST. (1962; 14,000). Five
Acres, Allet, Truro, Cornwall, TR4 9DJ. 01872 273
939; (Fax)01872 225 476;
e-mail: info@cornwt.demon.co.uk
www.cornwallwildlifetrust.org.uk

THE ISLES OF SCILLY WILDLIFE TRUST. (1986; 462).
Carn Thomas, Hugh Town, St Marys, Isles of Scilly
TR21 0PT.01720 422 153; (Fax) 01720 422 153;
e-mail: enquiries@ios-wildlifetrust.org.uk
www.www.ios-wildlifetrust.org.uk

CUMBRIA

BirdAtlas/Avifauna
The Breeding Birds of Cumbria by Stott, Callion,
Kinley, Raven and Roberts (Cumbria Bird Club, 2002).

Bird Recorders
CUMBRIA. Colin Raven, 18 Seathwaite Road, Barrow-
in-Furness, Cumbria, LA14 4LX.
e-mail: colin@walneyobs.fsnet.co.uk

NORTH WEST (Allerdale & Copeland). Derek McAlone,
88 Whinlatter Road, Mirehouse, Whitehaven, Cumbria
CA28 8DQ. 01946 691 370;
e-mail: derek@derekmcalone3.wanadoo.co.uk

SOUTH (South Lakeland & Furness). Ronnie Irving.
e-mail:ronnie@wsi-sign.co.uk

Bird Reports
BIRDS AND WILDLIFE IN CUMBRIA (1970-), from Dave
Shackleton, 8 Burnbanks, Penrith, Cumbria CA10
2RW; e-mail: dave.shack@care4free.net

WALNEY BIRD OBSERVATORY REPORT, from Warden,
see Reserves.

BTO Regional Representatives
CUMBRIA. Clive Hartley, Undercragg, Charney Well
La, Grange Over Sands, Cumbria LA11 6DB. 01539 532
856; e-mail: clive.hartley@tiscali.co.uk

Clubs
ARNSIDE & DISTRICT NATURAL HISTORY SOCIETY.
(1967; 221). Jane Phillips. 01524 782 582.
Meetings: 7.30pm, 2nd Tuesday of the month (Sept-
Apr). WI Hall, Arnside. (Also summer walks).

CUMBRIA BIRD CLUB. (1989; 230). Dave Piercy,
Secretary, Derwentwater Youth Hostel,
Borrowdale, Keswick CA12 5UR.
01768 777 909; e-mail:
daveandkathypiercy@tiscali.co.uk
Meetings: Various evenings
and venues (Oct-Mar) check on
website for further details. £2 for
non-members.

CUMBRIA RAPTOR STUDY GROUP. (1992). P N Davies,
Snowhill Cottage, Caldbeck, Wigton, Cumbria CA7
8HL. 01697 371 249;
e-mail: pete.caldbeck@virgin.net

Ringing Groups
EDEN RG. G Longrigg, 1 Spring Cottage, Heights,
Appleby-in-Westmorland, Cumbria CA16 6EP.

WALNEY BIRD OBSERVATORY. K Parkes, 176 Harrogate
Street, Barrow-in-Furness, Cumbria, LA14 5NA. 01229
824 219.

RSPB Local Groups
CARLISLE. (1974; 400). Bob Jones, 130 Greenacres,
Wetheral, Carlisle, 01225 561 684;
e-mail: bob@onethirty.force9.co.uk
www.rspb.org.uk/groups/carlisle
Meetings: 7.30pm, Wednesday monthly, Tithe Barn,
(Behind Marks And Spencer's), West Walls, Carlisle,
Cumbria CA3.

SOUTH LAKELAND. (1973; 305). Mr Martin Baines, 101
Serpentine Road, Kendal, Cumbria LA9 4PD. 01539
732 214.
Meetings: Contact above.

WEST CUMBRIA. (1986; 270). Marjorie Hutchin,
3 Camerton Road, Gt Broughton, Cockermouth,
Cumbria CA13 0YR. 01900 825 231;
e-mail: majorie.hutchin@btinternet.com
www.rspb.org.uk/groups/westcumbria
Meetings: 7.30pm, 1st Tuesday each month
(Sept-Apr), United Reformed Church, Main St,
Cockermouth.

Wetland Bird Survey Organiser
CUMBRIA (EXCL. ESTUARIES). Dave Shackleton. 8
Burnbanks, Bampton, Penrith, Cumbria CA10 2RW.
e-mail: dave.shack@care4free.net

DUDDON ESTUARY. Rosalyn Gay, 8 Victoria Street,
Millom, Cumbria LA18 5AS. 01229 773 820;
e-mail: colinathodbarrow@aol.com

IRT/MITE/ESK ESTUARY. Mike Douglas. Cumbria
Wildlife Trust, Plumgarths, Crook Road, Kendal,
Cumbria LA14 3YQ. 01539 816300;
e-mail: miked@cumbriawildlifetrust.org.uk

ENGLAND

MORECAMBE BAY (NORTH). Clive Hartley. Undercragg, Charney Well Lane, Grange-over-Sands, Cumbria LA11 6DB. 01539 536 824;
e-mail: clive.hartley304@btinternet.com

SOLWAY ESTUARY - SOUTH. Norman Holton. North Plain Farm, Bowness on Solway, Carlisle, Cumbria, CA7 5AG. 01697 351 330;
e-mail: norman.holton@rspb.org.uk

Wildlife Trust
CUMBRIA WILDLIFE TRUST. (1962; 15,000). Plumgarths, Crook Road, Kendal, Cumbria LA8 8LX. 01539 816 300; (Fax)01539 816 301;
e-mail: mail@cumbriawildlifetrust.org.uk
www.cumbriawildlifetrust.org.uk

DERBYSHIRE

The Birds of Derbyshire, ed. RA Frost (in preparation).

Bird Recorders
1. JOINT RECORDER. Roy A Frost, 66 St Lawrence Road, North Wingfield, Chesterfield, Derbyshire S42 5LL. 01246 850 037;
e-mail: frostra66@btinternet.com

2. Records Committee & rarity records. Rodney W Key, 3 Farningham Close, Spondon, Derby, DE21 7DZ. 01332 678571; e-mail: r_key@sky.com

3. JOINT RECORDER. Richard MR James, 10 Eastbrae Road, Littleover, Derby, DE23 1WA. 01332 771 787;
e-mail: rmrjames@yahoo.co.uk

Bird Reports
CARSINGTON BIRD CLUB ANNUAL REPORT, from Secretary.

DERBYSHIRE BIRD REPORT (1954-), from Bryan Barnacle, Mays, Malthouse Lane, Froggatt, Hope Valley, Derbyshire S32 3ZA. 01433 630 726;
e-mail: barney@mays1.demon.co.uk

OGSTON BIRD CLUB REPORT (1970-), from contact for Ogston Bird Club below.

BTO Regional Representatives
NORTH RR. Dave Budworth, 121 Wood Lane, Newhall, Swadlincote, Derbys DE11 0LX. 01283 215 188;
e-mail: dbud01@aol.com

SOUTH RR. Dave Budworth, 121 Wood Lane, Newhall, Swadlincote, Derbys DE11 0LX. 01283 215 188; e-mail: dbud01@aol.com

Clubs
BAKEWELL BIRD STUDY GROUP. (1987; 80). Ken Rome, View Cottage, Wensley, Matlock, Derbys DE4 2LH. www.bakewellbirdstudygroup.co.uk
Meetings: 7.30pm, 2nd Monday of the month, Friends Meeting House, Bakewell.

BUXTON FIELD CLUB. (1946; 68). B Aries, 1 Horsefair Avenue, Chapel-en-le-Frith, High Peak, Derbys SK23 9SQ. 01298 815291;
e-mail: brian.aries@btinternet.com
Meetings: 7.30pm, Saturdays fortnightly (Oct-Mar), Methodist Church Hall, Buxton.

CARSINGTON BIRD CLUB. (1992; 257). Maria Harwood/Pat Wain, Joint Membership Secretary, 2 Yokecliffe Avenue, Wirksworth, Derbyshire DE4 4DJ. 01629 823 693; e-mail: membership@carsingtonbirdclub.co.uk
www.carsingtonbirdclub.co.uk
Meetings: 3rd Tuesday of the month (Sep-Mar), Hognaston Village Hall, (Apr-Aug), outdoors.

DERBYSHIRE ORNITHOLOGICAL SOCIETY. (1954; 550). Steve Shaw, 84 Moorland View Road, Walton, Chesterfield, Derbys S40 3DF. 01246 236 090;
e-mail: steveshaw84mrr@btinternet.com
www.derbyshireOS.org.uk
Meetings: 7.30pm, last Friday of the winter months, various venues.

OGSTON BIRD CLUB. (1969; 1,126). Malcolm Hill, 2 Sycamore Avenue, Glapwell, Chesterfield, S44 5LH. 01623 812 159. www.ogstonbirdclub.co.uk

SOUTH PEAK RAPTOR STUDY GROUP. (1998; 12). M E Taylor, 76 Hawksley Avenue, Newbold, Chesterfield, Derbys S40 4TL. 01246 277 749.

Ringing Groups
DARK PEAK RG. W M Underwood, Ivy Cottage, 15 Broadbottom Road, Mottram-in-Longdendale, Hyde, Cheshire SK14 6JB.
e-mail: w.m.underwood@talk21.com

SORBY-BRECK RG. Dr Geoff P Mawson, Moonpenny Farm, Farwater Lane, Dronfield, Sheffield S18 1RA.
e-mail: moonpenny@talktalk.net
www.sorbybreckringinggroup.co.uk

SOUDER RG. Dave Budworth, 121 Wood Lane, Newhall, Swadlincote, Derbys DE11 0LX.
e-mail: dbud01@aol.com

RSPB Local Groups
CHESTERFIELD. (1987; 274). Barry Whittleston. 01246 819 667;
e-mail: barrymavis@whittleston.fsnet.co.uk
www.rspb.org.uk/groups/chesterfield
Meetings: 7.15pm, usually 3rd Monday of the month, Winding Wheel, New Exhibition Centre, 13 Holywell Street, Chesterfield.

DERBY LOCAL GROUP. (1973; 400). Chris Hunt, 38 Spenbeck Drive, Allestree, Derby, DE22 2UH. 01332 551 701; e-mail: chris.hunt42@ntlworld.com
www.rspb.org.uk/groups/derby
Meetings: 7.30pm, 2nd Wednesday of the month (Sep-Apr), Broughton Suite, Grange Banqueting Suite, 457 Burton Road, Littleover, Derby DE23 6FL.

254

HIGH PEAK. (1974; 175). Jim Jeffery. 0161 494 5367; e-mail: henrygordon@live.co.uk
www.rspb.org.uk/groups/highpeak
Meetings: 7.30pm, 3rd Monday of the month (Sep-May), Marple Senior Citizens Hall, Memorial Park, Marple, Stockport SK6 6BA.

Wetland Bird Survey Organiser
DERBYSHIRE. Chris Burnett. 23 The Potlocks, Willington, Derbyshire, DE65 6YA.
e-mail: Tweetyburnett@aol.com

Wildlife Trust
DERBYSHIRE WILDLIFE TRUST. (1962; 14,000). East Mill, Bridge Foot, Belper, Derbyshire DE56 1XH. 01773 881 188; (Fax)01773 821 826;
e-mail: enquiries@derbyshirewt.co.uk
www.derbyshirewildlifetrust.org.uk

DEVON

BirdAtlas/Avifauna
Tetrad Atlas of Breeding Birds of Devon by H P Sitters (Devon Birdwatching & Preservation Society, 1988).

The Birds of Lundy by Tim Davis and Tim Jones 2007. Available from R M Young (Bookseller) on 01769 573 350 (see www.birdsoflundy.org.uk for further details)

Bird Recorder
Mike Langman, 38 Brantwood Drive, Paignton, Devon TQ4 5HZ. 01803 528 008;
e-mail: devon-birdrecorder@lycos.com

Bird Reports
DEVON BIRD REPORT (1971) Previous annual reports since 1929, from DBWPS, PO Box 71, Okehampton, Devon EX20 1WF.

LUNDY FIELD SOCIETY ANNUAL REPORT (1946-). £3 each inc postage, check website for availability, from Frances Stuart, 3 Lower Linden Road, Clevedon, North Somerset BS21 7SU.
e-mail: lfssec@hotmail.co.uk

BTO Regional Representative
Position vacant.

Clubs
DEVON BIRD WATCHING & PRESERVATION SOCIETY. (1928; 1200). Mrs Joy Vaughan, 28 Fern Meadow, Okehampton, Devon, EX20 1PB. 01837 53360;
e-mail: joy.vaughan411.freeserve.co.uk
www.devonbirds.org

KINGSBRIDGE & DISTRICT NATURAL HISTORY SOCIETY. (1989; 130). Martin Catt, Migrants Rest, East Prawle, Kingsbridge, Devon TQ7 2DB. 01548 511 443; e-mail: martin.catt@btinternet.com
Meeting: 4th Monday of Sept-Apr, 7.30pm phone for venue.

LUNDY FIELD SOCIETY. (1946; 450). Mr Paul James, Hibernia, New Road, Pamber Green, Tadley RG26 3AG. e-mail: lfssec@hotmail.co.uk
www.lundy.org.uk
Meeting: AGM 1st Saturday in March, 1.45pm, Exeter University.

TOPSHAM BIRDWATCHING & NATURALISTS' SOCIETY. (1969; 140). Mrs M Heal, 5 Majorfield Road, Topsham, Exeter, EX3 0ES. e-mail: tbnsociety@hotmail.com
www.topsham.org/tbns
Meetings: 7.30pm, 2nd Friday of the month (Sep-May), Matthews Hall, Topsham.

Ringing Groups
AXE ESTUARY RINGING GROUP. Mike Tyler, The Acorn, Shute Road, Kilmington, Axminster EX13 7ST. 01297 34958; e-mail: mwtyler2@googlemail.com

DEVON & CORNWALL WADER RG. R C Swinfen, 72 Dunraven Drive, Derriford, Plymouth PL6 6AT. 01752 704 184.

LUNDY FIELD SOCIETY. A M Taylor, 26 High Street, Spetisbury, Blandford, Dorset DT11 9DJ. 01258 857 336; e-mail: ammataylor@yahoo.co.uk

SLAPTON BIRD OBSERVATORY. R C Swinfen, 72 Dunraven Drive, Derriford, Plymouth PL6 6AT. 01752 704 184.

RSPB Local Groups
EXETER & DISTRICT. (1974; 466). Roger Tucker. 01392 860 518; e-mail: parrog@aol.com
www.exeter-rspb.org.uk
Meetings: 7.30p, various evenings, Southernhay United Reformed Church Rooms, Dix's Field, Exeter.

PLYMOUTH. (1974; 600). Mrs Eileen Willey, 11 Beverstone Way, Roborough, Plymouth, PL6 7DY. 01752 208 996. E-mail: edward.willey@sky.com
Meetings: Trinity United Reform Church, Tor Lane, Plymouth PL3 5TH.

TORBAY AND SOUTH DEVON TEAM. John Allan 01626 821 344; e-mail: john@morsey.f2s.com
www.rspb.org.uk/groups/torbayandsouthdevon
Meetings: Run events and walks throughout Torbay and South Devon.

Wetland Bird Survey Organiser
DEVON. Peter Reay, 10 Devon House, Bovey Tracey, Devon TQ13 9HB. 01626 834 486;
e-mail: peter.p.j.reay@btinternet.com

TAW/TORRIDGE ESTUARY. Terry Chaplin. Little Orchard, Braunton Road, Barnstaple, Devon EX31 1GA. 01271 342 590;
e-mail: terry@chaplin.eclipse.co.uk

TAMAR COMPLEX. Gladys Grant, 18 Orchard Crescent, Oreston, Plymouth, PL9 7NF. 01752 406 287;
e-mail: gladysgrant@talktalk.net

Wildlife Hospitals
BIRD OF PREY CASUALTY CENTRE. Mrs J E L Vinson,

ENGLAND

Crooked Meadow, Stidston Lane, South Brent, Devon, TQ10 9JS. 01364 72174.
Birds of prey, with emergency advice on other species. Aviaries, rehabilitation facilities. Veterinary support.

Wildlife Trust
DEVON WILDLIFE TRUST. (1962; 33,000). Cricklepit, Commercial Road, Exeter, EX2 4AB. 01392 279244; (Fax)01392 433 221;
e-mail: contactus@devonwildlifewt.org
www.devonwildlifetrust.org

DORSET

BirdAtlas/Avifauna
Dorset Breeding Bird Atlas (working title). In preparation.

The Birds of Dorset by Dr George Green (Christopher Helm 2004).

Bird Recorder
Kevin Lane, e-mail: kevin@broadstoneheath.co.uk

Bird Reports
DORSET BIRDS (1977-), from Neil Gartshore, Moor Edge, 2 Bere Road, Wareham, Dorset BH20 4DD. 01929 552 560; e-mail: enquiries@callunabooks.co.uk.

THE BIRDS OF CHRISTCHURCH HARBOUR (1956-), from Ian Southworth, 1 Bodowen Road, Burton, Christchurch, Dorset BH23 7JL.
e-mail: ianbirder@aol.com

PORTLAND BIRD OBSERVATORY REPORT, from Warden, see Reserves,

BTO Regional Representatives
Mike Pleasants, 10 Green Lane, Bournemouth, BH10 5LB. 07751 555 033 or 01202 593 500;
e-mail: mike@btorepdorset.org
www.btorepdorset.org

Clubs
CHRISTCHURCH HARBOUR ORNITHOLOGICAL GROUP. (1956; 225). Mr. I.H. Southworth, Membership Secretary, 1 Bodowen Road, Burton, Christchurch, Dorset BH23 7JL. 01202 478 093. www.chog.org.uk.

DORSET BIRD CLUB. (1987; 525). Mrs Diana Dyer, The Cedars, 30 Osmay Road, Swanage, Dorset BH19 2JQ. 01929 421 402; e-mail: richarddiana@tiscali.com
www.dorsetbirdclub.org.uk

DORSET NATURAL HISTORY & ARCHAEOLOGICAL SOCIETY. (1845; 2188). Dorset County Museum. High West Street, Dorchester, Dorset DT1 1XA. 01305 262 735; e-mail: secretary@dorsetcountymuseum.org
www.dorsetcountymuseum.org

Ringing Groups
CHRISTCHURCH HARBOUR RS. E C Brett, 3 Whitfield Park, St Ives, Ringwood, Hants, BH24 2DX.
e-mail: ed_brett@lineone.net

PORTLAND BIRD OBSERVATORY. Martin Cade, Old Lower Light, Portland Bill, Dorset DT5 2JT. 01305 820553; e-mail: obs@btinternet.com
www.portlandbirdobs.org.uk

STOUR RG. R Gifford, 62 Beacon Park Road, Upton, Poole, Dorset BH16 5PE.

RSPB Local Groups
BLACKMOOR VALE. (1981; 130). Alison Rymell, Group Leader, 01985 844 819;
www.rspb.org.uk/groups/blackmoorvale
Meetings: 7.30pm, 3rd Friday in the month, Gillingham Primary School.

EAST DORSET. (1974; 435). Kenneth Baxter. 01202 474 204; e-mail: kenangela@ntlworld.com
www.rspb.org.uk/groups/eastdorset
Meetings: 7.30pm, 2nd Wednesday of the month, St Mark's Church Hall, Talbot Village, Wallisdown, Bournemouth.

POOLE. (1982; 305). John Derricott, 49 Medbourne Close, Blandford, Dorset DT11 7UA. 01258 450 927; e-mail: jd461@btinternet.com
www.rspb.org.uk/groups/poole
Meetings: 7.30pm, Upton Community Centre, Poole Road, Upton.

SOUTH DORSET. (1976; 422). Andrew Parsons. 01305 772 678; e-mail: andrew_parsons_141@yahoo.co.uk
www.rspb.org.uk/groups/southdorset
Meetings: 3rd Thursday of each month (Jan-Apr 2010) St Georges Church Hall, Fordington, Dorchester.

Wetland Bird Survey Organiser
POOLE HARBOUR. Harold Lilley. 3 Willow Drive, Wimborne, Dorset, BH21 2RA. 01202 889633;
e-mail: halilley@tiscali.co.uk

THE FLEET & PORTLAND HARBOUR. Steve Groves, Abbotsbury Swannery, New Barn Road, Abbotsbury, Dorset DT3 4JG. (W)01305 871 684;
e-mail: swannery@gotadsl.co.uk

RADIPOLE & LODMOOR. Nick Tomlinson, RSPB Visitor Centre, Swannery Carpark, Weymouth, Dorset DT4 7TZ. 01305 778 313.
e-mail: nick.tomlinson@rspb.org.uk

Wildlife Hospital
SWAN RESCUE SANCTUARY. Ken and Judy Merriman, The Wigeon, Crooked Withies, Holt, Wimborne, Dorset BH21 7LB. 01202 828 166;
www.swan.jowebdesign.co.uk
24 hr rescue service for swans. Large sanctuary of 40 ponds and lakes. Hospital and intensive care. Veterinary support. Free advice and help line. Three fully equipped rescue ambulances. Rescue water craft for all emergencies. Viewing by appointment only.

Wildlife Trust
DORSET WILDLIFE TRUST. (1961; 25,000). Brooklands Farm, Forston, Dorchester, Dorset, DT2 7AA. 01305 264 620; (Fax)01305 251 120;
e-mail: enquiries@dorsetwildlife.co.uk
www.dorsetwildlife.co.uk

DURHAM

BirdAtlas/Avifauna
*A Summer Atlas of Breeding Birds of County Durham*by Stephen Westerberg/Kieth Bowey. (Durham Bird Club, 2000)

Bird Recorders
Mark Newsome, 69 Cedar Drive, Jarrow, NE32 4BF.
e-mail: mvnewsome@hotmail.com

Bird Reports
BIRDS IN DURHAM (1971-), from D Sowerbutts, 9 Prebends Fields, Gilesgate, Durham, DH1 1HH. 0191 386 7201; e-mail: d16lst@tiscali.co.uk

BTO Regional Representatives
David L Sowerbutts, 9 Prebends Field, Gilesgate Moor, Durham, DH1 1HH. 0191 386 7201;
e-mail: david.sowerbutts@dunelm.org.uk

Clubs
DURHAM BIRD CLUB. (1975; 280). Paula Charlton, Secretary, 14 Bywell Road, Cleadon SR6 7QT. 0191 537 3178; e-mail: barryandpaula@tiscali.co.uk
www.durhambirdclub.org
Meetings: Monthly indoor meetings (Sept-Apr), in Durham and Sunderland.

SUMMERHILL (HARTLEPOOL) BIRD CLUB. (2000; 75). Paul Grinter, 11 Hawkridge Close, Hartlepool, TS26 8SA. 01429 422 313.
www.summerhillbirdclub.co.uk
Meetings: 7pm, 2nd Tuesday of the month (Sept-May), Summerhill Visitors Centre, Catcote Road, Hartlepool.

Ringing Groups
NORTHUMBRIA RG. Mr B. Galloway, 34 West Meadows, Stamfordham Road, Westerhope, Newcastle upon Tyne NE5 1LS.

DURHAM DALES RG. J R Hawes, Fairways, 5 Raby Terrace, Willington, Crook, Durham DL15 0HR.

RSPB Local Group
DURHAM. (1974; 125). David Gibson. 0191 386 9793; www.durham-rspb.org.uk
Meetings: 7.30pm, 2nd Tuesday of the month (Oct-Mar), Room CG83, adjacent to Scarborough Lecture Theatre, University Science Site, Stockton Road entrance.

Wildlife Trust
DURHAM WILDLIFE TRUST. (1971; 4,000). Rainton Meadows, Chilton Moor, Houghton-le-Spring, Tyne &

Wear, DH4 6PU. 0191 5843 112; (Fax)0191 584 3934;
e-mail: info@durhamwt.co.uk
www.durhamwildlifetrust.org.uk

ESSEX

Bird Atlas/Avifauna
The Birds of Essex by Simon Wood (A&C Black, August 2007).

The Breeding Birds of Essex by M K Dennis (Essex Birdwatching Society, 1996).

Bird Recorder
Les Steward, 6 Creek View, Basildon, Essex SS16 4RU. 01268 551 464; e-mail: les.steward@btinternet.com

Bird Report
ESSEX BIRD REPORT (inc Bradwell Bird Obs records) (1950-), from Peter Dwyer, Sales Officer, 48 Churchill Avenue, Halstead, Essex CO9 2BE.
01787 476 524;
e-mail: petedwyer@petedwyer.plus.com

BTO Regional Representatives
NORTH-EAST RR. Position vacant.

NORTH-WEST RR. Graham Smith. 01277 354 034;
e-mail: silaum.silaus@tiscali.co.uk

SOUTH RR. Lynn Parr.
e-mail: lynnparr99@hotmail.co.uk

Club
ESSEX BIRDWATCHING SOCIETY. (1949; 700). Carol O'Leary, 24 Horseshoe Crescent, The Garrison, Shoeburyness, Essex SS3 9WL. e-mail: carol@carololeary.wanadoo.co.uk
www.essexbirdwatchsoc.co.uk
Meetings: 1st Friday of the month (Oct-Mar), Friends' Meeting House, Rainsford Road, Chelmsford.

Ringing Groups
ABBERTON RG. C P Harris, Wylandotte, Seamer Road, Southminster, Essex, CM0 7BX.

BRADWELL BIRD OBSERVATORY. C P Harris, Wyandotte, Seamer Road, Southminster, Essex, CM0 7BX.

RSPB Local Groups
CHELMSFORD AND CENTRAL ESSEX. (1976; 7500 in catchment area). Mike Logan Wood, Highwood, Ishams Chase, Wickham Bishops, Essex, CM8 3LG. 01621 892045; e-mail: mike.lw@tiscali.co.uk
www.rspb.org.uk/groups/chelmsford
Meetings: 8pm, Thursdays, eight times a year. The Cramphorn Theatre, Chelmsford.

COLCHESTER. (1981; 250). Mr R Leavett, 10 Grove Road, Brantham, CO11 1TX.
Meetings: 7.45pm, 2nd Thursday of the month (Sep-Apr), Shrub End Community Hall, Shrub End Road, Colchester.

SOUTH EAST ESSEX. (1983; 200). Graham Mee, 34 Park View Drive, Leigh on Sea, Essex SS9 4TU. 01702 525 152; e-mail: grahamm@southendrspb.co.uk www.southendrspb.co.uk
Meetings: 7.30pm, usually 1st Tuesday of the month (Sep-May), Belfairs School Hall, School Way, Leigh-on-Sea SS9 4HX.

Wetland Bird Survey Organiser
CROUCH/ROACH ESTUARY AND SOUTH DENGIE. Peter Mason. e-mail: Petermason32@waitrose.com

HAMFORD WATER. Julian Novorol. The Brents, Harwich Road, Great Oakley, Harwich, Essex CO12 5AD.

LEE VALLEY. Cath Patrick. Myddelton House, Bulls Cross, Enfield, Herts EN2 9HG. 01992 717 711; e-mail: cpatrick@leevalleypark.org.uk

SOUTH BLACKWATER AND NORTH DENGIE. Anthony Harbott. 5 Allnutts Road, Epping, Essex, CM16 7BD. 01992 575 213;
e-mail: anthonyharbott@talktalk.net

STOUR ESTUARY. Rick Vonk, RSPB, Unit 13 Court Farm, 3 Stutton Road, Brantham Suffolk CO11 1PW. (D)01473 328 006; e-mail:rick.vonk@rspb.org.uk

THAMES ESTUARY - FOULNESS. Chris Lewis. 166 Kings Road, Westcliff-on-Sea, Essex, SS0 8PP.
e-mail: cpm.lewis@ukonline.co.uk

Wildlife Trust
ESSEX WILDLIFE TRUST. (1959; 36,000). The Joan Elliot Visitor Centre, Abbots Hall Farm, Great Wigborough, Colchester, CO5 7RZ. 01621 862 960; (Fax)01621 862 990; e-mail: admin@essexwt.org.uk www.essexwt.org.uk

GLOUCESTERSHIRE

Bird Atlas/Avifauna
Atlas of Breeding Birds of the North Cotswolds. (North Cotswold Ornithological Society, 1990)

Birds of Gloucestershire CM Swaine (Alan Sutton 1982 - now out of print)

Birds of The Cotswolds (Liverpool University Press 2009).

Bird Recorder
GLOUCESTERSHIRE EXCLUDING S.GLOS (AVON). Richard Baatsen. E-mail: baatsen@surfbirder.com

Bird Reports
CHELTENHAM BIRD CLUB BIRD REPORT (1998-2001) - (no longer published) old issues from Secretary.

GLOUCESTERSHIRE BIRD REPORT (1953-). £7.50 including postage, from David Cramp, 2 Ellenor Drive, Alderton, Tewkesbury, GL20 8NZ.
e-mail: djcramp@btinternet.com

NORTH COTSWOLD ORNITHOLOGICAL SOCIETY ANNUAL REPORT (1983-), from T Hutton, 15 Green Close, Childswickham, Broadway, Worcs, WR12 7JJ. 01386 858 511.

BTO Regional Representative
Mike Smart, 143 Cheltenham Road, Gloucester, GL2 0JH. Home/work 01452 421 131;
e-mail: smartmike@btinternet.com

Clubs
CHELTENHAM BIRD CLUB. (1976; 94). Mr Peter Ridout, 64 Prestbury Road, Cheltenham, GL52 2DA. 01242 517 424; www.cheltenhambirdclub.org.uk
Meetings: 7.15pm, Mondays (Oct-Mar), Bournside School, Warden Hill Road, Cheltenham.

DURSLEY BIRDWATCHING & PRESERVATION SOCIETY. (1953; 350). Jennifer Rogers, 15 Shadwell, Uley, Dursley, Glos GL11 5BW. 01453 860 128. email: j.rogers1@btinternet.com
www.dursleybirdwatchers.btik.com
Meetings: 7.45pm, 2nd and 4th Monday (Sept-Mar), Dursley Community Centre.

GLOUCESTERSHIRE NATURALISTS' SOCIETY. (1948; 500). Mike Smart, 143 Cheltenham Road, Gloucester, GL2 0JH. 01452 421 131;
e-mail: smartmike@btinternet.com
www.glosnats.org.uk

NORTH COTSWOLD ORNITHOLOGICAL SOCIETY. (1982; 70). T Hutton, 15 Green Close, Childswickham, Broadway, Worcs WR12 7JJ. 01386 858 511.
Meetings: Monthly field meetings, usually Sunday 9.30pm.

Ringing Groups
COTSWOLD WATER PARK RG. John Wells, 25 Pipers Grove, Highnam, Glos, GL2 8NJ.
e-mail: john.wells2@btinternet.com

SEVERN ESTUARY GULL GROUP. M E Durham, 6 Glebe Close, Frampton-on-Severn, Glos, GL2 7EL. 01452 741 312.

SEVERN VALE RG. John Wells, 25 Pipers Grove, Highnam, Glos, GL2 8NJ.
e-mail: john.wells2@btinternet.com

WILDFOWL & WETLANDS TRUST. Richard Hearn, Wildfowl & Wetlands Trust, Slimbridge, Glos, GL2 7BT. e-mail: richard.hearn@wwt.org.uk

RSPB Local Group
GLOUCESTERSHIRE. (1972; 600). David Cramp, 2 Ellenor Drive, Alderton, Tewkesbury, GL20 8NZ. 01242 620 281; www.rspbgloucestershire.co.uk
Meetings: 7.30pm, 3rd Tuesday of the month, Gala Club, Longford, Gloucester.

Wildlife Hospital
VALE WILDLIFE RESCUE (WILDLIFE HOSPITAL & REHABILITATION CENTRE). Any staff member, Station

Road, Beckford, Tewkesbury, Glos GL20 7AN. 01386
882 288; (Fax)01386 882 299; e-mail: info@vwr.org.uk
website: www.vwr.org.uk
All wild birds. Intensive care. Registered charity.
Veterinary support.

Wetland Bird Survey Organisers
GLOUCESTERSHIRE. Mike Smart, 143 Cheltenham
Road, Gloucester, GL2 0JH. 01452 421 131;
e-mail: smartmike@btinternet.com

COTSWOLD WATER PARK. Gareth Harris, Cotswold
Water Park Society, Cotswold House, Down Ampney
Estate, Cirencester, Glos GL7 5QF. 01793 752 413;
e-mail: gareth.harris@waterpark.org
www.waterpark.org

Wildlife Trust
GLOUCESTERSHIRE WILDLIFE TRUST. (1961; 23,000).
Conservation Centre, Robinswood Hill Country Park,
Reservoir Road, Gloucester, GL4 6SX. 01452 383 333;
(Fax)01452 383 334;
e-mail: info@gloucestershirewildlifetrust.co.uk
www.gloucestershirewildlifetrust.co.uk

HAMPSHIRE

Bird Atlas/Avifauna
Birds of Hampshire by J M Clark and J A Eyre
(Hampshire Ornithological Society, 1993).

Bird Recorder
ASSISTANT RECORDER. Keith Betton.
E-mail: keithbetton@hotmail.com

RECORDER. John Clark, 4 Cygnet Court, Old Cove
Road, Fleet, Hants, GU51 2RL. (Tel/fax)01252 623
397; e-mail johnclark50@sky.com

Bird Reports
HAMPSHIRE BIRD REPORT (1955-). 2007 edition £11.80
inc postage, from Mrs Margaret Boswell, 5 Clarence
Road, Lyndhurst, Hants, SO43 7AL. 023 8028 2105;
e-mail: mag_bos@btinternet.com

BTO Regional Representative
RR. Glynne C Evans, Waverley, Station Road,
Chilbolton, Stockbridge, Hants SO20 6AL. H:01264 860
697; e-mail: hantsbto@hotmail.com

Clubs
HAMPSHIRE ORNITHOLOGICAL SOCIETY.
(1979; 1200). John Shillitoe, Hon Sec, Westerly,
Hundred Acres Road, Wickham, Hampshire PO17 6HY.
01329 833 086; www.hos.org.uk
e-mail: john@shillitoe.freeserve.co.uk

SOUTHAMPTON & DISTRICT
BIRD GROUP. (1994; 52). Dave
Holloway, 73 Ampthill Road,
Freemantle, Southampton,
SO15 8LN. e-mail: david.
holloway@solent.ac.uk
Meetings: Programme available.

Ringing Groups
FARLINGTON RG. D A Bell, 38 Holly Grove, Fareham,
Hants, PO16 7UP.

ITCHEN RG. W F Simcox, 10 Holdaway Close,
Kingsworthy, Winchester, SO23 7QH.
e-mail: wsimcox@sparsholt.ac.uk

RSPB Local Groups
BASINGSTOKE. (1979; 90). Peter Hutchins, 35
Woodlands, Overton, Whitchurch, RG25 3HN. 01256
770 831; e-mail: fieldfare@jaybry.gotadsl.co.uk
www.rspb.org.uk/groups/basingstoke
Meetings: 7.30pm. 3rd Wednesday of the month
(Sept-May), The Barn, Church Cottage, St Michael's
Church, Church Square, Basingstoke.

NORTH EAST HAMPSHIRE. (1976; 215). The Group
leader, 4 Buttermer Close, Farnham, Surrey, GU10
4PN. 01252 724 093.
www.northeasthantsrspb.org.uk
Meetings: See website.

PORTSMOUTH. (1974; 210). Gordon Humby, 19
Charlesworth Gardens, Waterlooville, Hants, PO7
6AU. 02392 353 949.
Meetings: 7.30pm, 4th Saturday of every month.
Colmans' Church Hall, Colman's Ave, Cosham.
Programme and newsletter issued to paid-up
members of the group who must be RSPB members.

WINCHESTER & DISTRICT. (1974; 175). Maurice
Walker, Jesmond, 1 Compton Way, Olivers Battery,
Winchester, SO22 4EY. 01962 854 033; e-mail:
Rogerclark33@btinternet.com
www.rspb.org.uk/groups/winchester
Meetings: 7.30pm, 1st Wednesday of the month (not
Jul or Aug), Shawford Parish Hall, Pearson Lane,
Shawford.

Wetland Bird Survey Organisers
AVON VALLEY. John Clark, 4 Cygnet Court, Old Cove
Road, Fleet, Hants GU51 2RL. 01252 623 397;
e-mail johnclark50@sky.com

CHICHESTER HARBOUR. Edward Rowsell. Conservation
Officer, Chichester Harbour Conservancy, Harbour
Office, Itchenor, Chichester, West Sussex PO20 7AW.
01243 510 985 ;
e-mail: edward@conservancy.co.uk

HAMPSHIRE (Inland - excluding Avon Valley). Keith
Wills, 51 Peabody Road, Farnborough, GU14 6EB.
(H)01252 548408;
e-mail: keithb.wills@ukgateway.net

HAMPSHIRE (ESTUARIES/COASTAL). John Shillitoe.
Westerly, Hundred Acres Road, Wickham, Hampshire,
PO17 6HY. e-mail: john@shillitoe.freeserve.co.uk

Wildlife Trust
HAMPSHIRE & ISLE OF WIGHT WILDLIFE TRUST. (1960;
27,000). Beechcroft House, Vicarage Lane, Curdridge,
Hampshire SO32 2DP. 01489 774 400; (Fax)01489 774
401; e-mail: feedback@hwt.org.uk
www.hwt.org.uk

ENGLAND

HEREFORDSHIRE

Bird Recorder
Steve Coney, 5 Springfield Road, Withington,
Hereford, HR1 3RU. 01432 850 068;
e-mail: coney@bluecarrots.com

Bird Report
THE BIRDS OF HEREFORDSHIRE (2008 -), from Mr WJ
Marler, Cherry Tree House, Walford, Leintwardine,
Craven Arms, Shropshire SY7 0JT.

THE YELLOWHAMMER - Herefordshire Ornithological
Club annual report, (1951-), from Mr I Evans, 12
Brockington Drive, Tupsley, Hereford, HR1 1TA. 01432
265 509; e-mail: iforelanine@tiscali.co.uk

BTO Regional Representative
Steve Coney, 5 Springfield Road, Withington,
Hereford, HR1 3RU. 01432 850 068;
e-mail: coney@bluecarrots.com

Club
HEREFORDSHIRE ORNITHOLOGICAL CLUB. (1950; 439).
TM Weale, Foxholes, Bringsty Common, Worcester,
WR6 5UN. 01886 821 368;
e-mail: weale@tinyworld.co.uk
www.herefordshirebirds.org
Meetings: 7.30pm, 2nd Thursday of the month
(autumn/winter), Holmer Parish Centre, Holmer,
Hereford.

Ringing Group
LLANCILLO RG. Dr G R Geen, 6 The Copse, Bannister
Green, Felsted, Dunmow, Essex CM6 3NP. 01371 820
189; e-mail: graham.geen@gsk.com

Wetland Bird Survey Organiser
HEREFORDSHIRE. Steve Coney. 5 Springfield Road,
Withington, Hereford, HR1 3RU. 01432 850 068; e-
mail: coney@bluecarrots.com

Wildlife Trust
HEREFORDSHIRE NATURE TRUST. (1962; 2,535). Lower
House Farm, Ledbury Road, Tupsley, Hereford, HR1
1UT. 01432 356 872; (Fax)01432 275 489;
e-mail: enquiries@herefordshirewt.co.uk
www.herefordshirewt.org

HERTFORDSHIRE

Bird Atlas/Avifauna
Birds at Tring Reservoirs by R Young et al
(Hertfordshire Natural History Society, 1996).

Mammals, Amphibians and Reptiles of Hertfordshire
by Hertfordshire NHS in association with Training
Publications Ltd, 3 Finway Court, Whippendell Road,
Watford WD18 7EN, (2001).

The Breeding Birds of Hertfordshire by K W Smith et
al (Herts NHS, 1993). Purchase from HNHS at £5 plus
postage. E-mail: herts.naturalhistorysociety@aol.com

Bird Recorder
Tony Blake, 9 Old Forge Close, Stanmore, Middx HA7
3EB. E-mail: recorder@hertsbirdclub.org.uk

Bird Report
HERTFORDSHIRE BIRD REPORT (1908-2006), from
Linda Smith, 24 Mandeville Road, Welwyn Garden
City, Herts AL8 7JU.
e-mail: herts.naturalhistorysociety@ntlworld.com
www.hnhs.org and www.hertsbirdclub.org.uk

**BTO Regional Representative & Regional
Development Officer**
Chris Dee, 26 Broadleaf Avenue, Thorley Park,
Bishop's Stortford, Herts, CM23 4JY. H:01279 755
637; e-mail: hertsbto@hotmail.com

Clubs
FRIENDS OF TRING RESERVOIRS.
(1993; 350). Membership Secretary,
PO Box 1083, Tring HP23 5WU. 01442
822 471; e-mail: keith@fotr.org.uk
www.fotr.org.uk
Meetings: See website.

HERTFORDSHIRE BIRD CLUB. (1971; 330) Part of
Hertfordshire NHS. Ted Fletcher, Beech House,
Aspenden, Buntingford, Herts SG9 9PG. 01763 272
979. www.hertsbirdclub.org.uk

HERTFORDSHIRE NATURAL HISTORY SOCIETY. (1875;
320) Linda Smith, 24 Mandeville Rise, Welwyn
Garden City, Herts, AL8 7JU. 01707 330 405; e-mail:
secretary@hnhs.org
www.hnhs.org and www.hertsbirdclub.org.uk
Meetings: Saturday afternoon, Nov and Mar (date and
venue varies).

Ringing Groups
MAPLE CROSS RG. P Delaloye.
e-mail: pdelaloye@tiscali.co.uk

RYE MEADS RG. Chris Dee, 26 Broadleaf Avenue,
Thorley Park, Bishop's Stortford, Herts CM23 4JY.
H:01279 755 637;
e-mail: ringingsecretary@rmrg.org.uk

TRING RG. Mick A'Court, 6 Chalkshire Cottages,
Chalkshire road, Butlers Cross, Bucks HP17 0TW.
H:01296 623610; W:01494 462246;
e-mail: mick@focusrite.com
a.arundinaceous@virgin.net

RSPB Local Groups
CHORLEYWOOD & DISTRICT. (1977; 142). Carol Smith,
24 Beacon Way, Rickmansworth, Herts WD3 7PE.
01923 897 885;
e-mail: carolsmithuk@hotmail.com
www.rspb.org.uk/groups/chorleywood
Meetings: 8pm, last Thursday of the month (Sept-
May), Russell School, Brushwood Drive, Chorleywood.

HARPENDEN. (1974; 1000). Geoff Horn, 41 Ridgewood
Drive, Harpenden, Herts AL5 3LJ. 01582 765443;
e-mail: geoffrhorn@yahoo.co.uk

ENGLAND

Meetings: 8pm, 2nd Thursday of the month (Sept-June), All Saint's Church Hall, Station Road, Harpenden.

HEMEL HEMPSTEAD. (1972; 150). Paul Green, 207 Northridge Way, Hemel Hempstead, Herts, HP1 2AU. 01442 266 637;
e-mail: paul@310nrwhh.freeserve.co.uk
www.hemelrspb.org.uk
Meetings: 8pm, 1st Monday of the month (Sep-Jun), The Cavendish School.

HITCHIN & LETCHWORTH. (1973; 100). Dr Martin Johnson, 1 Cartwright Road, Royston, Herts SG8 9ET. 01763 249 459;
e-mail: martinrjspc@hotmail.com
Meetings: 7.30pm, 1st Friday of the month, The Settlement, Nevells Road, Letchworth SG6 4UB.

POTTERS BAR & BARNET. (1977; 1800). Stan Bailey, 23 Bowmans Close, Potters Bar, Herts, EN6 5NN. 01707 646 073.
Meetings: 2.00pm, 2nd Wednesday of the month, St Johns URC Hall, Mowbray Road, Barnet. Evening meetings, 3rd Friday of the month (not Jul, Aug or Dec) 7.45pm, Potters Bar United Reform Church, Tilbury Hall, Darkes Lane, Potters Bar, EN6 1BZ.

ST ALBANS. (1979; 1550 in catchment area). Peter Antram, 6 Yule Close, Bricket Wood, St Albans, Herts AL2 3XZ. 01923 678 534;
www.rspb.org.uk/groups/stalbans
Meetings: 8pm, 2nd Tuesday of the month (Sep-May), St Saviours Church Hall, Sandpit Lane, St Albans.

SOUTH EAST HERTS. (1971; 2,400 in catchment area). Terry Smith, 31 Marle Gardens, Waltham Abbey, Essex, EN9 2DZ. 01992 715 634;
e-mail: se_herts_rspb@yahoo.co.uk
www.rspb.org.uk/groups/southeasthertfordshire
Meetings: 7.30pm, usually last Tuesday of the month (Sept-June), URC Church Hall, Mill Lane, Broxbourne EN10 7BQ.

STEVENAGE. (1982; 1,300 in the catchment area). Mrs Ann Collis, 16 Stevenage Road, Walkern, Herts, 01483 861 547.
Meetings: 7.30pm, 3rd Tuesday of the month, Friends Meeting House, Cuttys Lane, Stevenage.

WATFORD. (1974; 590). Janet Reynolds. 01923 249 647; e-mail: janet.reynolds@whht.nhs.uk
www.rspb.org.uk/groups/watford
Meetings: 7.30pm, 2nd Wednesday (Sep-Jun), St Thomas' Church Hall, Langley Road, Watford.

Wetland Bird Survey Organiser
HERTFORDSHIRE (EXCL. LEE VALLEY). Jim Terry. 46 Manor Way, Boreham Wood, Herts, WD6 1QY.
e-mail: jim@jayjoy.wanadoo.co.uk

LEE VALLEY. Cath Patrick. Myddelton House, Bulls Cross, Enfield, Herts EN2 9HG. 01992 717 711;
e-mail: cpatrick@leevalleypark.org.uk

Wildlife Trust
HERTS & MIDDLESEX WILDLIFE TRUST. (1964; 18,500). Grebe House, St Michael's Street, St Albans, Herts, AL3 4SN. 01727 858 901; (Fax)01727 854 542;
e-mail: info@hmwt.org
www.wildlifetrust.org.uk/herts/

ISLE OF WIGHT

Bird Recorder
G Sparshott, Leopards Farm, Main Road, Havenstreet, Isle of Wight, PO33 4DR. 01983 882 549;
e-mail: grahamspa@aol.com

Bird Reports
ISLE OF WIGHT BIRD REPORT (1986-) (Pre-1986 not available), from Mr DJ Hunnybun, 40 Churchill Road, Cowes, Isle of Wight, PO31 8HH. 01983 292 880;
email: davehunnybun@hotmail.com

BTO Regional Representative
James C Gloyn, 3 School Close, Newchurch, Isle of Wight, PO36 0NL. 01983 865 567;
e-mail: gloynjc@yahoo.com

Clubs
ISLE OF WIGHT NATURAL HISTORY & ARCHAEOLOGICAL SOCIETY. (1919; 500). The Secretary, Salisbury Gardens, Dudley Road, Ventnor, Isle of Wight PO38 1EJ. 01983 855 385. www.iwnhas.org

ISLE OF WIGHT ORNITHOLOGICAL GROUP. (1986; 155). Mr DJ Hunnybun, 40 Churchill Road, Cowes, Isle of Wight, PO31 8HH. 01983 292 880; e-mail: davehunnybun@hotmail.com

Wetland Bird Survey Organiser
ISLE OF WIGHT. James Gloyn.
e-mail: gloynjc@yahoo.com

Wildlife Trust
Director, See Hampshire,

KENT

Bird Atlas/Avifauna
Birding in Kent by D W Taylor et al 1996. Pica Press

Bird Recorder
Barry Wright, 6 Hatton Close, Northfleet, Kent DA11 8SD. 01474 320 918; (M)07789 710 555;
e-mail: barrybirding@tiscali.co.uk

Bird Reports
DUNGENESS BIRD OBSERVATORY REPORT (1989-), from Warden, see Reserves.

KENT BIRD REPORT (1952-), from Dave Sutton, 61 Alpha Road, Birchington, Kent, CT7 9ED. 01843 842 541.

SANDWICH BAY BIRD OBSERVATORY REPORT, from Warden, see Reserves,

ENGLAND

BTO Regional Representative
RR. Sally Hunter. 01304 612 425; e-mail: sally.
hunter@tesco.net

Club

KENT ORNITHOLOGICAL SOCIETY.
(1952; 650). Mrs Ann Abrams, 4
Laxton Way, Faversham, Kent,
ME13 8LJ. 01795 533 453; e-mail:
annie@chrisabrams.plus.com
www.kentos.org.uk
Meetings: Indoor: October-April
at various venues; AGM in April
at Grove Green community Hall, Grovewood Drive,
Maidstone ME14 5TQ. See website for details: www.
kentos.org.uk

Ringing Groups
DARTFORD RG. PE Jones.
e-mail: philjones@beamingbroadband.com

DUNGENESS BIRD OBSERVATORY. David Walker,
Dungeness Bird Observatory, Dungeness, Romney
Marsh, Kent TN29 9NA. 01797 321 309;
e-mail: dungeness.obs@tinyonline.co.uk
www.dungenessbirdobs.org.uk

RECULVER RG. Chris Hindle, 42 Glenbervie Drive,
Herne Bay, Kent, CT6 6QL. 01227 373 070;
e-mail: christopherhindle@hotmail.com

SANDWICH BAY BIRD OBSERVATORY. Mr KB Ellis, 6
Alderney Gardens, St Peters, Broadstairs, Kent CT10
2TN. 01304 617 341;
e-mail: keithjulie@talktalk.net

SWALE WADER GROUP. Rod Smith, 67 York Avenue,
Chatham, Kent, ME5 9ES. 01634 865 836;
www.swalewaders.co.uk

RSPB Local Groups
CANTERBURY. (1973; 216). Chris Sproul. 01227 450
655; e-mail: cyasproul@yahoo.co.uk
www.rspb.org.uk/groups/canterbury
Meetings: 8.00pm, 2nd Tuesday of the month
(Sept-Apr), Chaucer Social Club, Off Chaucer Drive,
Canterbury, CT1 1YW.

GRAVESEND & DISTRICT. (1977; 278). Malcolm
Jennings, 206 Lower Higham Road, Gravesend, Kent,
DA12 2NN. 01474 322 171;
e-mail: malcolm.chalkland@btinternet.com
www.rspbgravesend.org.uk
Meetings: 7.45pm, 2nd Wednesday of the month
(Sep-May), St Botolph's Hall, North Fleet, Gravesend.

MAIDSTONE. (1973; 250). Dick Marchese, 11 Bathurst
Road, Staplehurst, Tonbridge, Kent TN12 0LG. 01580
892 458; e-mail: marchese8@aol.com
http://maidstone.localrspb.org.uk/
Meetings: 7.30pm, 3rd Thursday of the month, Grove
Green Community Hall, Penhurst Close, Grove Green,
(opposite Tesco's).

MEDWAY. (1974; 230). Des Felix. 01634 261 484;
e-mail: descar@72marshallroad.freeserve.co.uk
www.medway-rspb.pwp.blueyonder.co.uk
Meetings: 7.45pm 3rd Tuesday of the month (except
Aug), Strood Library, Bryant Road, Strood.

SEVENOAKS. (1974; 265). Bernard Morris, New House,
Kilkhampton, Bude, Cornwall EX23 9RZ. 01288 321
727; or 07967 564 699;(Fax)01288 321 838;
e-mail: bernard.morris5@btinternet.com
www.rspb.org.uk/groups/sevenoaks
Meetings: 7.45pm 1st Thursday of the month, Otford
Memorial Hall.

THANET. (1975; 119). Peter Radclyffe, Cottage of St
John, Caterbury Road, Sarre, Kent CT7 0JY. 01843
847 345.
Meetings: 7.30pm last Tuesday of the month (Jan-
Nov), Portland Centre, Hopeville Avenue, Broadstairs.

TONBRIDGE. (1975; 150 reg attendees/1,700 in
catchment). Ms Gabrielle Sutcliffe, 1 Postern Heath
Cottages, Postern Lane, Tonbridge, Kent TN11 0QU.
01732 365 583.
Meetings: 7.45pm 3rd Wednesday of the month (Sept-
Apr), St Phillips Church, Salisbury Road.

Wetland Bird Survey Organisers
DUNGENESS AREA. David Walker. Dungeness Bird
Observatory, 11 RNSSS, Dungeness, Kent, TN29 9NA.
01797 321 309;
e-mail: dungeness.obs@tinyonline.co.uk

EAST KENT. Ken Lodge, 14 Gallwey Avenue,
Birchington, Kent CT7 9PA. 01843 843 105;
e-mail: lodge9pa@btinternet.com

MEDWAY ESTUARY & NORTH KENT MARSHES. Sally
Jennings, RSPB, Bromhey Farm, Cooling, Rochester,
Kent ME3 8DS. 01634 222 480.

PEGWELL BAY. Pete Findley. Contact via WeBS Office,
BTO, The Nunnery, Thetford, Norfolk IP24 2PU.
e-mail: webs@bto.org

SWALE ESTUARY. Sally Jennings, RSPB, Bromhey
Farm, Cooling, Rochester, Kent ME3 8DS.
01634 222 480.

WEST KENT. Grant Hazlehurst.
e-mail: granthazlehurst@msn.com

Wildlife Hospital
RAPTOR CENTRE. Eddie Hare, Ivy Cottage,
Groombridge Place, Groombridge, Tunbridge Wells,
Kent TN3 9QG. 01892 861 175;
www.raptorcentre.co.uk
Birds of prey. Veterinary support. 24hr rescue service
for sick and injured birds of prey that covers the
South-East.

Wildlife Trust
KENT WILDLIFE TRUST. (1958; 10,500). Tyland Barn,
Sandling, Maidstone, Kent, ME14 3BD. 01622 662 012;
(Fax)01622 671 390; e-mail: info@kentwildlife.org.uk
www.kentwildlifetrust.org.uk

ENGLAND

LANCASHIRE

Bird Atlas/Avifauna
An Atlas of Breeding Birds of Lancaster and District by Ken Harrison (Lancaster & District Birdwatching Society, 1995).

Birds of Lancashire and North Merseyside by White, McCarthy and Jones (Hobby Publications 2008).

Breeding Birds of Lancashire and North Merseyside (2001), sponsored by North West Water. Contact: Bob Pyefinch, 12 Bannistre Court, Tarleton, Preston PR4 6HA.

Bird Recorder
(See also Manchester).

LANCASHIRE (inc North Merseyside). Steve White, 102 Minster Court, Crown Street, Liverpool, L7 3QD. 0151 707 2744; e-mail: stephen.white2@tesco.net

Bird Reports
EAST LANCASHIRE ORNITHOLOGISTS' CLUB BIRD REPORT (1982-), from The Secretary, 01282 612 870; e-mail: john.plackett@eastlancsornithologists.org.uk
www.eastlancsornithologists.org.uk

CHORLEY AND DISTRICT NATURAL HISTORY SOCIETY ANNUAL REPORT (1979 -), published on website www.chorleynats.org.uk

BLACKBURN & DISTRICT BIRD CLUB ANNUAL REPORT (1992-), from Doreen Bonner, 6 Winston Road, Blackburn, BB1 8BJ. 01254 261 480; www.blackburnbirdclub.co.uk
e-mail: webmaster@blackburnbirdclub.co.uk

FYLDE BIRD REPORT (1983-), from Paul Ellis, 18 Staining Rise, Blackpool, FY3 0BU.
www.fyldebirdclub.org

LANCASHIRE BIRD REPORT (1914-), from Secretary, Lancs & Cheshire Fauna Soc.

ROSSENDALE ORNITHOLOGISTS' CLUB BIRD REPORT (1977-) from Secretary, Rossendale Ornithologists Club, 25 Church St, Newchurch, Rossendale, Lancs BB4 9EX.

BTO Regional Representatives
EAST RR. Tony Cooper, 28 Peel Park Avenue, Clitheroe, Lancs, BB7 1ET. 01200 424 577; e-mail: tony.cooper@eastlancsornithologists.org.uk

NORTH & WEST RR. Jean Roberts. 01524 770 295; e-mail: JeanRbrts6@aol.com

SOUTH RR. Stephen Dunstan.
E-mail: stephen-dunstan@tiscali.co.uk

Clubs
BLACKBURN & DISTRICT BIRD CLUB. (1991; 134). Jim Bonner, 6 Winston Road, Blackburn, BB1 8BJ. 01254 261 480; e-mail: webmaster@blackburnbirdclub.co.uk
www.blackburnbirdclub.co.uk
Meetings: Normally 7.30pm, 1st Monday of the month, (Sept-Apr), Church Hall, Preston New Road. Check website for all indoor and outdoor meetings.

CHORLEY & DISTRICT NATURAL HISTORY SOCIETY. (1979; 170). Phil Kirk, Millend, Dawbers Lane, Euxton, Chorley, Lancs PR7 6EB. 01257 266783; e-mail: secretary@chorleynats.org.uk
www.chorleynats.org.uk
Meetings: 7.30pm, 3rd Thursday of the month (Sept-Apr), St Mary's Parish Centre, Chorley.

EAST LANCASHIRE ORNITHOLOGISTS' CLUB. (1955; 40). Dr J Plackett, 71 Walton Lane, Nelson, Lancs BB9 8BG. 01282 612 870; e-mail: john.plackett@eastlancsornithologists.org.uk
www.eastlancsornithologists.org.uk
Meetings: 7.30pm, 1st Monday of the month (Check website or local press), St Anne's Church Hall, Fence, Nr Burnley.

FYLDE BIRD CLUB. (1982; 110). Paul Ellis, 18 Staining Rise, Blackpool, FY3 0BU. 01253 891 281; e-mail: paul.ellis24@btopenworld.com
or kinta.beaver@man.ac.uk
www.fyldebirdclub.org
Meetings: 7.45pm, 4th Tuesday of the month, River Wyre Hotel, Breck Road, Poulton le Fylde.

FYLDE NATURALISTS' SOCIETY. (1946; 140). Julie Clarke, 7 Cedar Avenue, Poulton-le-Fylde, Blackpool, FY6 8DQ. 01253 883 785;
e-mail: secretary@fyldenaturalists.co.uk
www.fyldenaturalists.co.uk
Meetings: 7.30pm, fortnightly (Sep-Mar), Fylde Coast Alive, Church Hall, Raikes Parade, Blackpool unless otherwise stated in the Programme.

LANCASHIRE & CHESHIRE FAUNA SOCIETY. (1914; 150). Dave Bickerton, 64 Petre Crescent, Rishton, Lancs, BB1 4RB. 01254 886 257;
e-mail: bickertond@aol.com
www.lacfs.org.uk

LANCASTER & DISTRICT BIRD WATCHING SOCIETY. (1959; 200). Kevin Briggs, The Bramblings, 1 Washington Drive, Warton LA5 9RA.
e-mail: ldbws@yahoo.co.uk
Meetings: 7.30pm, last Monday of the month (Sep-Nov, Feb-Mar), Bare Methodist Church Hall, St Margarets Road, Morecambe; (Jan and Apr) the Hornby Institute, Hornby.

ROSSENDALE ORNITHOLOGISTS' CLUB. (1976; 35). Ian Brady, 25 Church St, Newchurch, Rossendale, Lancs BB4 9EX. 01706 222 120.
Meetings: 7.30pm, 3rd Monday of the month, Weavers Cottage, Bacup Road, Rawtenstall.

ENGLAND

Ringing Groups

MORECAMBE BAY WADER RG. J Sheldon, 140 Oxford Street, Barrow-in-Furness, Cumbria LA14 5PJ.

NORTH LANCS RG. John Wilson BEM, 40 Church Hill Avenue, Warton, Carnforth, Lancs LA5 9NU. E-mail: johnwilson711@btinternet.com

SOUTH WEST LANCASHIRE RG. I H Wolfenden, 35 Hartdale Road, Thornton, Liverpool, Merseyside L23 1TA. 01519 311 232.

RSPB Local Groups

BLACKPOOL. (1983; 170). Alan Stamford, 6 Kensington Road, Cleveleys, FY5 1ER. 01253 859 662; e-mail: alanstamford140@msn.com
Meetings: 7.30pm, 2nd Friday of the month (Sept-June), Frank Townend Centre, Beach Road, Cleveleys.

LANCASTER. (1972; 176). Jill Blackburn, 13 Coach Road, Warton, Carnforth, Lancs LA5 9PR. e-mail: jill.blackburn@dsl.pipex.com
www.rspb.org.uk/localgroups/lancaster

Wetland Bird Survey Organisers

NORTH LANCASHIRE (Inland). Pete Marsh, Leck View Cottage, Ashley's farm, High Tatham, Lancaster LA2 8PH. 01524 264 944; e-mail: pbmarsh@btopenworld.com

RIVER LUNE. Jean Roberts. 3 Claughton Terrace, Claughton, Lancaster, LA2 9JZ. 07815 979856; e-mail: JeanRbrts6@aol.com

Wildlife Trust

THE WILDLIFE TRUST FOR LANCASHIRE, MANCHESTER AND NORTH MERSEYSIDE. (1962; 18,000). Peter Mallon, Communications Officer, The Barn, Berkeley Drive, Bamber Bridge, Preston PR5 6BY. 01772 324 129; fax: 01772 628 849; e-mail: info@lancswt.org.uk
www.lancswt.org.uk

LEICESTERSHIRE & RUTLAND

The Birds of Leicestershire and Rutland by Rob Fray et al. (A&C Black, due August 2009)

Bird Recorder

Steve Lister, 6 Albert Promenade, Loughborough, Leicestershire LE11 1RE. 01509 829 495; e-mail: stevelister@surfbirder.com

Bird Reports

LEICESTERSHIRE & RUTLAND BIRD REPORT (1941-), from Mrs S Graham, 5 Lychgate Close, Cropston, Leicestershire LE7 7HU. 0116 236 6474.

RUTLAND NAT HIST SOC ANNUAL REPORT (1965-), from Secretary, 01572 747302.

BTO Regional Representative

LEICESTER & RUTLAND RR. Tim Grove, 35 Clumber Street, Melton Mowbray, Leicestershire LE13 0ND. 01664 850 766; e-mail: k.grove1@ntlworld.com

Clubs

BIRSTALL BIRDWATCHING CLUB. (1976; 50). KJ Goodrich, 6 Riversdale Close, Birstall, Leicester, LE4 4EH. 0116 267 4813.
Meetings: 7.30pm, 2nd Tuesday of the month (Oct-Apr), The Rothley Centre, Mountsorrel Lane, Rothley, Leics LE7 7PR.

BURBAGE BIRDERS. Ken Reeves (kenreeves@shorelarks.freeserve.co.uk)
Meetings:7.30pm, 2nd Monday of each month, Burbage Common visitor centre.

LEICESTERSHIRE & RUTLAND ORNITHOLOGICAL SOCIETY. (1941; 580). Mrs Marion Vincent, 48 Templar Way, Rothley, Leicester, LE7 7RB. 0116 230 3405. www.lros.org.uk
Meetings: 7.30pm, 1st Friday of the month (Oct-May), Oadby Methodist Church, off Central Car Park, alternating with The Rothley Centre, Mountsorrel Lane, Rothley. Additional meeting at Rutland Water Birdwatching Cntr.

SOUTH LEICESTER BIRDWATCHERS. (2006; 60). Paul Seaton, 76 Roehampton Drive, Wigston, Leics, LE18 1HU. 07969 387 914; e-mail: paul.lseaton@btinternet.com
Meetings: 7.30 pm, 2nd Wednesday of the month (Sep-Jun), County Scout Centre, Winchester Road, Blaby, Leicester LE8 4HN.

RUTLAND NATURAL HISTORY SOCIETY. (1964; 256). Mrs L Worrall, 6 Redland Close, Barrowden, Oakham, Rutland, LE15 8ES. 01572 747 302.
www.rnhs.org.uk
Meetings: 7.30pm, 1st Tuesday of the month (Oct-Apr), Oakham CofE School, Burley Road, Oakham.

Ringing Groups

STANFORD RG. John Cranfield, 41 Main Street, Fleckney, Leicester, LE8 8AP. 0116 240 4385; e-mail: JacanaJohn@talktalk.net

RSPB Local Groups

LEICESTER. (1969; 1600 in catchment area). Chris Woolass, 136 Braunstone Lane, Leicester, LE3 2RW. 0116 2990078; e-mail: j.woolass1@ntlworld.com
www.rspb.org.uk/groups/leicester
Meetings: 7.30pm, 3rd Friday of the month (Sep-May), Trinity Methodist Hall, Harborough Road, Oadby, Leicester, LE2 4LA.

LOUGHBOROUGH. (1970; 300). Robert Orton, 12 Avon Road, Barrow-on-Soar, Leics, LE12 8LE. 077 4887 6798. www.rspb.org.uk/loughborough
Meetings: Monthly Friday nights, Loughborough University.

Wetland Bird Survey Organisers

LEICESTERSHIRE & RUTLAND (excl Rutland Water. Tim Grove, 35 Clumber Street, Melton Mowbray, Leics

LE13 0ND. 01664 850 766;
e-mail: k.grove1@ntlworld.com

Wildlife Trust
LEICESTERSHIRE & RUTLAND WILDLIFE TRUST. (1956; 14,000). Brocks Hill Environment Centre, Washbrook Lane, Oadby, Leicestershire LE2 5JJ. 0116 272 0444; (Fax)0116 272 0404; e-mail: info@lrwt.org.uk
www.lrwt.org.uk

LINCOLNSHIRE

Bird Recorders
Steve Keightley, Redclyffe, Swineshead Road, Frampton Fen, Boston PE20 1SG. 01205 290 233; e-mail: steve.keightley@btinternet.com

Bird Reports
LINCOLNSHIRE BIRD REPORT (1979-1996 - 1990 is now sold out), from Bill Sterling, Newlyn, 5 Carlton Avenue, Healing, NE Lincs DN41 7PW.
e-mail: wbsterling@hotmail.com.

LINCOLNSHIRE RARE AND SCARCE BIRD REPORT (2000-2002), from Bill Sterling (see above).

SCUNTHORPE & NORTH WEST LINCOLNSHIRE BIRD REPORT (1973-), from Secretary, Scunthorpe Museum Society, Ornithological Section, (Day)01724 402 871; (Eve)01724 734 261.

BTO Regional Representatives and Regional Development Officer
EAST RR. Position vacant.

NORTH RR. Chris Gunn. 01777 707 888;
e-mail: chris@cgtraining.co.uk

SOUTH RR. Richard & Kay Heath, 56 Pennytoft Lane, Pinchbeck, Spalding, Lincs PE11 3PQ. 01775 767 055; e-mail: heathsrk@ukonline.co.uk

WEST RR. Peter Overton, Hilltop Farm, Welbourn, Lincoln, LN5 0QH. Work 01400 273 323; e-mail: nyika@biosearch.org.uk

RDO. Nicholas Watts, Vine House Farm, Deeping St Nicholas, Spalding, Lincs PE11 3DG. 01775 630 208.

Club
LINCOLNSHIRE BIRD CLUB. (1979; 220). Janet Eastmead, 3 Oxeney Drive, Langworth, Lincoln, LN3 5DD. 01522 754 522; e-mail: janet.eastmead02@btinternet.com
www.lincsbirdclub.co.uk
Meetings: Local groups hold winter evening meetings (contact Secretary for details).

SCUNTHORPE MUSEUM SOCIETY (Ornithological Section). (1973; 50). Keith Parker, 7 Ryedale Avenue, Winterton, Scunthorpe, Lincs DN15 9BJ.
Meetings: 7.15pm, 3rd Monday of the month (Sep-Apr), Scunthorpe Museum, Oswald Road.

Ringing Groups
GIBRALTAR POINT BIRD OBSERVATORY. M.R. Briggs. e-mail: mbriggs@gibobs.fsworld.co.uk

MID LINCOLNSHIRE RG. J Mawer, 2 The Chestnuts, Owmby Road, Searby, Lincolnshire DN38 6EH. 01652 628 583.

WASH WADER RG. P. L. Ireland, 27 Hainfield Drive, Solihull, W Midlands, B91 2PL. 0121 704 1168; e-mail: enquiries@wwrg.org.uk

RSPB Local Groups
GRIMSBY AND CLEETHORPES. (1986; 2,200 in catchment area). Terry Whalin. 0845 1580 183; e-mail: terence@terencewhalin.wanadoo.co.uk
www.rspb.org.uk/groups/grimsby
Meetings: 7.30pm, 1st Monday of the month (Sept-May), Corpus Christi Church Hall, Grimsby Road, Cleethorpes, DN35 7LJ.

LINCOLN. (1974; 250). Peter Skelson, 26 Parksgate Avenue, Lincoln, LN6 7HP. 01522 695747; e-mail: peter.skelson@lincolnrspb.org.uk
www.lincolnrspb.org.uk
Meetings: 7.30pm, 2nd Thursday of the month (not Jun, Jul, Aug, Dec), The Lawn, Union Road, Lincoln.

SOUTH LINCOLNSHIRE. (1987; 350). Anne Algar. 01529 460 877; e-mail: algar@talktalk.net
www.southlincsrspb.org.uk
Meetings: Contact group.

Wetland Bird Survey Organiser
HUMBER ESTUARY - OUTER SOUTH. John Walker. 3 Coastguard Cottage, Churchill Lane, Theddlethorpe, Lincs, LN12 1PQ. 01507 338 038, (M)07970 838 421; e-mail: dunewalker@btopenworld.com

SOUTH LINCOLNSHIRE/PETERBOROUGH (INLAND). Robert Titman. 28 Eastgate, Deeping St James, Peterborough, PE6 8HJ. 01733 583 254; e-mail: titman@nildram.co.uk

Wildlife Trust
LINCOLNSHIRE WILDLIFE TRUST. (1948; 26,000). Banovallum House, Manor House Street, Horncastle, Lincs, LN9 5HF. 01507 526 667; (Fax)01507 525 732; e-mail: info@lincstrust.co.uk
www.lincstrust.org.uk

LONDON, GREATER

Bird Atlas/Avifauna
The Breeding Birds Illustrated magazine of the London Area, 2002. ISBN 0901009 121 ed Jan Hewlett(London Natural History Society).

Two Centuries of Croydon's Birds by John Birkett (RSPB Croydon Local Group 2007).

Bird Recorder (see also Surrey)
Andrew Self, 16 Harp Island Close, Neasden, London, NW10 0DF. 07889 761 828; e-mail: a-self@sky.com
http://editthis.info/londonbirders/Main_Page

ENGLAND

Bird Report
CROYDON BIRD SURVEY (1995), from Secretary,
Croydon RSPB Group, 020 8640 4578;
e-mail: johndavis.wine@care4free.net
www.croydon-rspb.org.uk.

LONDON BIRD REPORT (20-mile radius of St Paul's
Cath) (1936-), from Catherine Schmitt, Publications
Sales, London Natural History Society, 4 Falkland
Avenue, London N3 1QR.

BTO Regional Representatives
LONDON, NORTH. Ian Woodward, 245 Larkshall Road,
Chingford, London E4 9HY. 07947 321 889;
e-mail: ianw_bto_nlon@hotmail.co.uk

LONDON, SOUTH. Richard Arnold. 020 8224 1135;
e-mail: bto@thomsonecology.com

Clubs

LONDON NATURAL HISTORY
SOCIETY (Ornithology Section).
(1858; 1000). Mrs Angela
Linnell, 20 Eleven Acre Rise,
Loughton, Essex, IG10 1AN.
020 8508 2932; e-mail: angela.
linnell@phonecoop.coop
www.lnhs.org.uk
Meetings: See website.

MARYLEBONE BIRDWATCHING SOCIETY. (1981; 95).
Lester Hunt, East Wing, The Old Hall, South Grove,
London N6 6BP. E-mail: birdsmbs@yahoo.com
www.birdsmbs.org.uk
Meeting: 2nd Friday of month (Sept-May), 7.15pm
Gospel Oak Methodist Chapel, Lisburne Road, London
NW3 2NR.

Ringing Groups
LONDON GULL STUDY GROUP - (SE including
Hampshire, Surrey, Sussex, Berkshire and
Oxfordshire). No longer active but still welcomes
sightings/recoveries of ringed birds. (Also
includes Hampshire, Surrey, Sussex, Berkshire and
Oxfordshire). No longer active but able to give
information on gulls. Mark Fletcher, 24 The Gowans,
Sutton-on-the-Forest, York, YO61 1DJ.
e-mail: fletcher548@btinternet.com

RUNNYMEDE RG. DG Harris, 22 Blossom Way,
Hounslow, TW5 9HD.
e-mail: daveharris@tinyonline.co.uk

RSPB Local Groups
BEXLEY. (1979; 180). Tony Banks, 15 Boundary Road,
Sidcup, Kent DA15 8SS. 020 8859 3518;
e-mail: tonybanks@fsmail.net
www.bexleyrspb.org.uk
Meetings: 7.30pm, 3rd Friday of the month,
Hurstmere School Hall, Hurst Road, Sidcup.

BROMLEY. (1972; 285). Val Bryant, 11 Hastings Road,
Bromley, Kent BR2 8NZ. 0208 462 6330.
e-mail: valbryant5@gmail.comt
www.bromleyrspb.org.uk

Meetings: 2nd Wednesday of the month (Sep-Jun),
Large Hall, Bromley Central Library Building, Bromley
High Street.

CENTRAL LONDON. (1974; 330). Margaret Blackburn.
020 8866 5853; e-mail: mblackburn@tesco.net
www.janja.dircon.co.uk/rspb
Meetings: 2nd Thursday of the month (Sep-May), St
Columba's Church Hall, Pont St, London SW1.

CROYDON. (1973; 4,000 in catchment area). John
Davis, 9 Cricket Green, Mitcham, CR4 4LB. 020 8640
4578; e-mail: johndavis.wine@care4free.net
www.croydon-rspb.org.uk
Meetings: 2nd Monday of each month at 2pm-4pm
and again at 8pm-10pm at Old Whitgiftian Clubhouse,
Croham Manor Road, South Croydon.

ENFIELD. (1971; 2,700 in catchment area). Norman G
Hudson, 125 Morley Hill, Enfield, Middx, EN2 0BQ. 020
8363 1431. www.rspb.org.uk/groups/enfield
Meetings: 8pm, 1st Thursday of the month, St
Andrews Hall, Enfield Town.

HAVERING. (1972; 270). David Coe, 11 Freshfields
Avenue, Upminster, Essex, RM14 2BY. 01708 220 710.
www.rspb.org.uk/groups/havering/about
Meetings: 8pm, 2nd Friday of the month, Hornchurch
Library, North Street, Hornchurch.

NORTH EAST LONDON. David Littlejohns
0208 989 4746; e-mail: NelondonRSPB@yahoo.co.uk
www.rspb.org.uk/groups/northeastlondon
Meetings: 7.30pm, 2nd Tuesday of every month,
Snaresbrook Primary School, Meadow Walk, South
Woodford, London E18 2EN.

NORTH WEST LONDON. (1983; 2,000 in catchment
area). Bob Husband, The Firs, 49 Carson Road,
Cockfosters, Barnet, Herts EN4 9EN. 020 8441 8742;
e-mail: bobhusband@hotmail.co.uk
www.rspb.org.uk/groups/nwlondon
Meetings: 8pm, last Tuesday of the month (Sept-Apr),
Retail Trust, Marshall Estate, Hammers Lane, Mill
Hill, London NW7 4DQ

PINNER & DISTRICT. (1972; 300). Dennis Bristow, 118
Crofts Road, Harrow, Middx HA1 2PJ. 020 8863 5026.
www.rspb.org.uk/groups/pinner
Meetings: 8pm, 2nd Thursday of the month (Sept-
May), Church Hall, St John The Baptist Parish Church,
Pinner HA5 3AS.

RICHMOND & TWICKENHAM. (1979; 285). Jenny
Shalom, 49 Sheen Court, Richmond TW10 5DG. 0208
392 9938; e-mail jennyrshalom@hotmail.com
www.rspb.org.uk/groups/richmond
Meetings: 8.00pm, 1st Wednesday of the month, York
House, Twickenham.

Wetland Bird Survey Organiser
GREATER LONDON (EXCL. THAMES ESTUARY). Helen
Baker. 60 Townfield, Rickmansworth, Hertfordshire
WD3 7DD. 02072 385 687;
e-mail: helen.baker60@tiscali.co.uk

ENGLAND

LEE VALLEY. Cath Patrick. Myddelton House, Bulls Cross, Enfield, Herts EN2 9HG. 01992 717 711; e-mail: cpatrick@leevalleypark.org.uk

Wildlife Trust
LONDON WILDLIFE TRUST. (1981; 7500). Skyline House, 200 Union Street, London, SE1 0LX. 0207 261 0447; (Fax)0207 633 0811; e-mail: enquiries@wildlondon.org.uk www.wildlondon.org.uk

MANCHESTER, GREATER

Bird Atlas/Avifauna
Breeding Birds in Greater Manchester by Philip Holland et al (1984).

Bird Recorder
RECORDER AND REPORT EDITOR. Mrs A Judith Smith, 12 Edge Green Street, Ashton-in-Makerfield, Wigan, WN4 8SL. 01942 712 615; e-mail: judith@gmbirds.freeserve.co.uk www.manchesterbirding.com

ASSISTANT RECORDER (Rarities). Ian McKerchar, 42 Green Ave, Astley, Manchester M29 7EH. 01942 701 758; e-mail: ian@mckerchar1.freeserve.co.uk

ASSISTANT RECORDER (Database). Steve Atkins, 33 King's Grove, Wardle, Rochdale OL12 9HR. 01706 645 097; e-mail: steveatkins@tiscali.co.uk

Bird Reports
BIRDS IN GREATER MANCHESTER (1976-). Year 2001 onwards from County Recorder.

LEIGH ORNITHOLOGICAL SOCIETY BIRD REPORT (1971-), from Mr D Shallcross, 28 Surrey Avenue, Leigh, Lancs, WN7 2NN. E-mail: chairman@leighos.org.uk www.leighos.org.uk.

BTO Regional Representative
RR. Steve Suttill, 94 Manchester Road, Mossley, Ashton-under-Lyne, Lancashire OL5 9AY. 01457 836 360; e-mail: suttill.parkinson@virgin.net

ASSISTANT RR. Steve Atkins, 33 King's Grove, Wardle, Rochdale OL12 9HR 01706 645 097; e-mail: steveatkins@tiscali.co.uk

Clubs
MANCHESTER ORNITHOLOGICAL SOCIETY. (1954; 66). Dr R Sandling, School of Mathematics, Manchester University, Manchester M13 9PL. e-mail: rsandling@manchester.ac.uk
Meetings: 7.30pm, 1st Tuesday (Oct-Apr), St James Church Hall, off Church Street, Gatley.

GREATER MANCHESTER BIRD RECORDING GROUP. (2002; 40) Restricted to contributors of the county bird report. Mrs A Judith Smith. 01942 712 615; e-mail: judith@gmbirds.freeserve.co.uk www.manchesterbirding.com

HALE ORNITHOLOGISTS. (1968; 63). Mrs E Hall, Flat 22, Shirley Court, Wardle Road, Sale M33 3DQ. **Meetings:** 7.30pm, 2nd Wednesday of the month (Sept-July), St Peters Assembly Rooms, Hale.

LEIGH ORNITHOLOGICAL SOCIETY. (1971; 118). Mr D Shallcross, 28 Surrey Avenue, Leigh, Lancs, WN7 2NN. E-mail: chairman@leighos.org.uk www.leighos.org.uk **Meetings:** 7.15pm, Fridays, Leigh Library (check website for details).

ROCHDALE FIELD NATURALISTS' SOCIETY. (1970; 90). Mrs D Francis, 20 Hillside Avenue, Shaw, Oldham OL2 8HR. 01706 843 685; www.rochdalefieldnaturalistssociety.co.uk **Meetings:** 7.30pm (Sept-Apr) at Cutgate Baptist Church, Edenfield Rd, Rochdale. Yearly syllabus (out after AGM in Sept) states dates of lectures and outings.

STOCKPORT BIRDWATCHING SOCIETY. (1972; 80). Dave Evans, 36 Tatton Road South, Stockport, Cheshire SK4 4LU. 0161 432 9513; e-mail: windhover@ntlworld.com **Meetings:** 7.30pm, last Wednesday of the month, Tiviot Dale Church.

Ringing Groups
LEIGH RG. A J Gramauskas, 21 Elliot Avenue, Golborne, Warrington, WA3 3DU. 0151 929 215.

SOUTH MANCHESTER RG. Mr N.B.Powell. e-mail: neville.powell@tiscali.co.uk

RSPB Local Groups
BOLTON. (1978; 320). Mr Barry Shore, 6 Martin Drive, Darwen, Lancs BB3 2HW. 01254 772 089. **Meetings:** 7.30pm, Thursdays (dates vary), Main Hall, Smithills School, Smithills Dean Road, Bolton.

MANCHESTER. (1972; 3,600 in catchment area). Peter Wolstenholme, 31 South Park Road, Gatley, Cheshire, SK8 4AL. 0161 428 2175. **Meetings:** 7.30 pm, St James Parish Hall, Gatley Green, Church Road, Gatley, Cheadle.

STOCKPORT LOCAL GROUP. (1979; 200). Gay Crossley, 5 Broadhill Close, Bramhall, Stockport, Cheshire SK7 3BY. 0161 439 3210. www.rspb.org.uk/groups/stockport **Meetings:** 7.30pm, 2nd Monday of the month (Sep-Apr), Stockport College of Technology, Lecture Theatre A.

WIGAN. (1973; 80). Neil Martin. 01695 624 860; e-mail: neimaz07@yahoo.co.uk www.rspb.org.uk/groups/wigan **Meetings:** 7.45pm. St Anne's Parish Hall, Church Lane, Shevington, Wigan, Lancashire, WN6 8BD.

Wildlife Hospital
THREE OWLS BIRD SANCTUARY AND RESERVE. Trustee,

ENGLAND

Nigel Fowler, Wolstenholme Fold, Norden, Rochdale, OL11 5UD. 01706 642162; Emergency helpline 07973 819 389; e-mail: info@threeowls.co.uk
www.threeowls.co.uk
Registered charity. All wild birds. Rehabilitation and release on Sanctuary Reserve. Open every Sunday (12pm-4pm), otherwise by appointment. Quarterly newsletter. Veterinary support.

Wetland Bird Survey Organiser
GREATER MANCHESTER. Adrian Dancy.
0161 278 5381; e-mail: a.dancy@ntlworld.com

Wildlife Trust
Director, See Lancashire,

MERSEYSIDE & WIRRAL

Bird Atlas see Cheshire

Bird Recorders see Cheshire; Lancashire

Bird Reports see also Cheshire
HILBRE BIRD OBSERVATORY REPORT, from Warden, see Reserves.

NORTHWESTERN BIRD REPORT (1938- irregular), from Secretary, Merseyside Naturalists' Assoc.

BTO Regional Representatives
MERSEYSIDE RR and RDO. Bob Harris, 3 Mossleigh, Whixalll, Whitchurch, Shropshire SY13 2SA. (Work)0151 706 4311; e-mail: harris@liv.ac.uk

WIRRAL RR. Paul Miller. 01928 787 535; e-mail: huntershill@worldonline.co.uk

Clubs
MERSEYSIDE NATURALISTS' ASSOCIATION. (1938; 150). John Clegg, MNA Membership Secretary, 29 Barlow Lane, Liverpool, L4 3QP. www.geocities.com/mnahome
Meetings: 3rd Saturday afternoon (winter only), Bootle Cricket Club. Coach outings throughout the year.

WIRRAL BIRD CLUB. (1977; 150). The Secretary. E-mail: info@wirralbirdclub.com
www.wirralbirdclub.com

Ringing Groups
MERSEYSIDE RG. Bob Harris, 3 Mossleigh, Whixalll, Whitchurch, Shropshire SY13 2SA. (Work)0151 706 4311; e-mail: harris@liv.ac.uk

SOUTH WEST LANCASHIRE RG. I H Wolfenden, 35 Hartdale Road, Thornton, Liverpool, Merseyside L23 1TA. 01519 311 232.

RSPB Local Groups
LIVERPOOL. (1966; 162). Chris Tynan, 10 Barker Close, Huyton, Liverpool, L36 0XU. 0151 480 7938; e-mail: christtynan@aol.com
www.rspbliverpool.org.uk

Meetings: 7pm for 7.30pm, 3rd Monday of the month (Sep-Apr), Mossley Hill Parish Church, Junc. Rose Lane and Elmswood Rd.

SOUTHPORT. (1974; 300). Alan Toms. 01704 871 540; e-mail: tomox@talktalk.net
Meetings: 7.45pm, Lord Street West Church Hall, Duke Street, Southport.

WIRRAL. (1982; 120). Jeremy Bradshaw. 0151 632 2364; email: Info@wirralRSPB.org.uk
www.rspb.org.uk/groups/wirral
Meetings: 7.30pm, 1st Thursday of the month, Bromborough Civic Centre, 2 Bromborough Village Road, Wirral.

Wetland Bird Survey Organiser
ALT ESTUARY. Steve White. 102 Minster Court, Crown Street, Liverpool, L7 3QD.
e-mail: swhite@lancswt.org.uk

DEE ESTUARY. Colin Wells, Burton Farm Point, Station Road, Nr Neston, South Wirral CH64 5SB. 01513 367 681; e-mail: colinwells@rspb.org.uk

MERSEY ESTUARY. Graham Thomason. 110 Coroners Lane, Widnes, Cheshire, WA8 9HZ.

RIBBLE ESTUARY. Ribble RSPB Team.
e-mail: k.abram@btinternet.com

Wildlife Trust
Director, See Lancashire,

NORFOLK

Bird Atlas/Avifauna
The Birds of Norfolk by Moss Taylor, Michael Seago, Peter Allard & Don Dorling (Pica Press, 1999).

Bird Recorder
JOINT COUNTY RECORDERS. Dave and Jacquie Bridges, 27 Swan Close, Hempstead Road, Holt, Norfolk NR25 6DP. 01263 713 249; e-mail: dnjnorfolkrec@aol.com

Bird Reports
CLEY BIRD CLUB 10-KM SQUARE BIRD REPORT (1987-), from Peter Gooden, 45 Charles Road, Holt, Norfolk, NR25 6DA. 01263 712 368.

NAR VALLEY ORNITHOLOGICAL SOCIETY ANNUAL REPORT (1976-), from The Secretary, Ian Black.

NORFOLK BIRD & MAMMAL REPORT (1953-), from DL Paull, 8 Lindford Drive, Eaton, Norwich NR4 6LT

NORFOLK ORNITHOLOGISTS' ASSOCN ANNUAL REPORT (1961-), from Secretary.

WENSUM VALLEY BIRDWATCHING SOCIETY (2003-)
from e-mail: admin@wvbs.co.uk
www.wvbs.co.uk

ENGLAND

BTO Regional Representatives
NORTH-EAST RR. Chris Hudson, Cornerstones, 5 Ringland Road, Taverham, Norwich, NR8 6TG. 01603 868 805; (M)07771 635 844;
e-mail: Chris697@btinternet.com

NORTH-WEST RR. Allan Hale. 01366 328 421;
e-mail: allan@ajhale.plus.com

SOUTH-EAST RR. Rachel Warren. 01603 593 912;
e-mail: campephilus@btinternet.com

SOUTH-WEST RR. Vince Matthews, Rose's Cottage, The Green, Merton, Thetford, Norfolk IP25 6QU.

Clubs
CLEY BIRD CLUB. (1986; 500). Peter Gooden, 45 Charles Road, Holt, Norfolk, NR25 6DA. 01263 712368. **Meetings:** 8pm, Wednesdays, monthly (Dec-Feb), White Horse Hotel, Blakeney.

GREAT YARMOUTH BIRD CLUB. (1989; 30). Keith R Dye, 104 Wolseley Road, Great Yarmouth, Norfolk, NR31 0EJ. 01493 600 705; www.gybc.org.uk
Meetings: 7.45pm, 4th Monday of the month, Rumbold Arms, Southtown Road.

NAR VALLEY ORNITHOLOGICAL SOCIETY. (1976; 125). Ian Black, Three Chimneys, Tumbler Hill, Swaffham, Norfolk, PE37 7JG. 01760 724092;
e-mail: ian_a_black@hotmail.com
www.accessbs.com/narvos
Meetings: 7.30pm, last Tuesday of the month (Jul-Nov and Jan-May), Barn Theatre, Convent of The Sacred Heart, Mangate Street, Swaffham, PE37 7QW.

NORFOLK & NORWICH NATURALISTS' SOCIETY. (1869; 630). DL Paull. 8 Lindford Drive, Eaton, Norwich NR4 6LT. 01603 457 270; www.NNNS.org.uk
Meetings: 7.30pm, 3rd Tuesday of the month (Oct-Mar), St Andrew's Church Hall, Church Lane, Norwich.

NORFOLK ORNITHOLOGISTS' ASSOCIATION. (1962; 1,100). Jed Andrews, Broadwater Road, Holme-next-Sea, Hunstanton, Norfolk PE36 6LQ. 01485 525 406;
e-mail: info@noa.org.uk www.noa.org.uk

WENSUM VALLEY BIRDWATCHING SOCIETY. (2003; 125). Colin Wright, 7 Hinshalwood Way, Old Costessey, Norwich, Norfolk NR8 5BN. 01603 740548;
e-mail: admin@wvbs.co.uk
www.wvbs.co.uk
Meetings: 7.30pm, 3rd Thursday of the month, Weston Longville village hall.

Ringing Groups
BTO NUNNERY RG. Kate Risely, c/o BTO, The Nunnery, Thetford, Norfolk IP24 2PU.
e-mail: kate.risely@bto.org

NORTH NORFOLK FARMLAND STUDY & RINGING GROUP. Keith Herber, Laleham, 60 Dale End, Brancaster Staithe, King's Lynn PE31 8DA. 01485 210 980; e-mail: keith.herber@btinternet.com

NORTH WEST NORFOLK RG. JL Middleton, 8 Back Lane, Burnham Market, Norfolk PE31 8EY.
E-mail: middleton@bmarket.freeserve.co.uk

RSPCA. K Leighton.
e-mail: kev.leighton@O2.co.uk

SHERINGHAM RG. D Sadler, 26 Abbey Road, Sheringham, Norfolk, NR26 8NN. 01263 821 904.

WASH WADER RG. PL Ireland, 27 Hainfield Drive, Solihull, W Midlands, B91 2PL. 0121 704 1168;
e-mail: enquiries@wwrg.org.uk

RSPB Local Groups
NORWICH. (1971; 360). Robert Pindar. 01692 582 689;
e-mail: r.pindar@yahoo.com.
www.rspb.org.uk/groups/norwich
Meetings: 7.30pm, 2nd Monday of the month (except Aug), Hellesdon Community Centre, Middletons Lane, Hellesdon, Norwich (entrance of Woodview Road).

WEST NORFOLK. (1977; 247). Ken Bayliss, 23 Church Lane, Roydon, King's Lynn, Norfolk PE32 1AR. 01485 600 446; e-mail: ken.bayliss3@btopenworld.com
www.rspb-westnorfolk.org
Meetings: 7.30pm, 3rd Wednesday of the month (Sep-Apr), South Wootton Village Hall, Church Lane, South Wootton, King's Lynn.

Wetland Bird Survey Organisers
INLAND. Tim Strudwick, RSPB Strumpshaw Fen, Staithe Cottage, Low Road, Strumpshaw Norfolk NR13 4HS. 01603 715 191.

NORTH NORFOLK COAST. Michael Rooney, English Nature, Hill Farm Offices, Main Road, Well-next-the -Sea Norfolk NR23 1AB. 01328 711 631;
e-mail: michael.rooney@naturalengland.org.uk

THE WASH. Jim Scott. RSPB Snettisham Site Manager, Barn A , Home Farm Barns , Snettisham , Kings Lynn Norfolk PE31 7PD. 01485 545261;
e-mail: jim.scott@rspb.org.uk

Wildlife Trust
NORFOLK WILDLIFE TRUST. (1926; 35,000). Bewick House, 22 Thorpe Road, Norwich, Norfolk NR1 1RY. 01603 625 540; (Fax)01603 598 300;
e-mail: info@norfolkwildlifetrust.org.uk
www.norfolkwildlifetrust.org.uk

NORTHAMPTONSHIRE

Bird Recorder
Position vacant. Enquiries to Mike Alibone, 25 Harrier Park, East Hunsbury, Northants NN4 0QG.
E-mail: northantsbirds@ntlworld.com

Bird Report
NORTHAMPTONSHIRE BIRD REPORT (1969-), from John Coleman, 2 Marsons Drive, Crick, Northants NN6 7TD. 01788 822 905.

ENGLAND

NORTHUMBERLAND

ENGLAND

Registered charity. All categories of wildlife. Pools for swans and other waterfowl. Veterinary support.

Wildlife Trust
NORTHUMBERLAND WILDLIFE TRUST. (1962; 13,000). The Garden House, St Nicholas Park, Jubilee Road, Gosforth, Newcastle upon Tyne, NE3 3XT. 0191 284 6884; (Fax)0191 284 6794; www.nwt.org.uk
e-mail: mail@northwt.org.uk

NOTTINGHAMSHIRE

Bird Recorders
Andy Hall, E-mail: andy.h11@ntlworld.com

Bird Reports
BIRDS OF NOTTINGHAMSHIRE (1943-). £4 for previous issues, plus p&p, from Ms Jenny Swindells, 21 Chaworth Road, West Bridgford, Nottingham NG2 7AE. 0115 9812 432; www.nottsbirders.net
e-mail: j.swindells@btinternet.com

LOUND BIRD REPORT (1990-) latest 2007 report £4, from Gary Hobson, 18 Barnes Avenue, Wrenthorpe, Wakefield, WF1 2BH. 01924 384 419;
e-mail: gary.lbc1@tiscali.co.uk.

NETHERFIELD WILDLIFE GROUP ANNUAL REPORT (1990-). £5 inc postage, from Mr N Matthews, 4 Shelburne Close, Heronridge, Nottingham, NG5 9LL.

BTO Regional Representative
RR. Mrs Lynda Milner, 6 Kirton Park, Kirton, Newark, Notts NG22 9LR. 01623 862 025;
e-mail: lyndamilner@hotmail.com

Clubs
ATTENBOROUGH BIRD CLUB. (1996; 45). John Ellis, 67 Springfield Avenue, Sandiacre, Nottingham, NG10 5NA. E-mail: jellis@trent83.freeserve.co.uk

LOUND BIRD CLUB. (1991; 50). Gary Hobson, 18 Barnes Avenue, Wrenthorpe, Wakefield, WF1 2BH. 01924 384 419;
e-mail: gary.lbc1@tiscali.co.uk
www.loundbirdclub.piczo.com
Meetings: Various walks and talks throughout the year, see website for details.

NETHERFIELD WILDLIFE GROUP. (1999; 130). Philip Burnham, 57 Tilford Road, Newstead Village, Nottingham, NG15 0BU. 01623 401 980; e-mail: philip.burnham1@ntlworld.com.

NOTTINGHAMSHIRE BIRDWATCHERS. (1935; 370). Ms Jenny Swindells, 21 Chaworth Road, West Bridgford, Nottingham, NG2 7AE. 0115 9812 432;
e-mail: j.swindells@btinternet.com
www.nottsbirders.net
Meetings and events: Please see website for details.

WOLLATON NATURAL HISTORY SOCIETY. (1976; 86). Mrs P Price, 33 Coatsby Road, Hollycroft, Kimberley, Nottingham NG16 2TH. 0115 938 4965.
Meetings: 7.30pm, 3rd Wednesday of the month, St Leonards Community Centre, Wollaton Village, HG8 2ND.

Integrated Population Monitoring Group
TRESWELL WOOD INTEGRATED POPULATION MONITORING GROUP. Chris du Feu, 66 High Street, Beckingham, Notts, DN10 4PF.
e-mail: chris@chrisdufeu.force9.co.uk

Ringing Groups
BIRKLANDS RG. A Ashley, 39 Winkburn Road, Mansfield, Notts NG19 6SJ. 07794 179 494;
e-mail: andyashley39@googlemail.com

NORTH NOTTS RG. Adrian Blackburn, Willows End, 27 Palmer Road, Retford, Notts DN22 6SS. 01777 706 516; (M)07718 766 873:
e-mail: adrian.blackburn@sky.com

SOUTH NOTTINGHAMSHIRE RG. K J Hemsley, 8 Grange Farm Close, Toton, Beeston, Notts NG9 6EB.
e-mail: k.hemsley@ntlworld.com

RSPB Local Groups
MANSFIELD LOCAL GROUP. (1986; 200). John Barlow, 240 Southwell Road West, Mansfield, Notts NG18 4LB. 01623 626 647.
Meetings: 7pm, 1st Wednesday of the month (Sep-Jun), Bridge St Methodist Church, Rock Valley, Mansfield.

NOTTINGHAM. (1974; 395). Andrew Griffin, Lindholme, New Hill, Walesby, Newark, Notts NG22 9PB. 01623 860 529; www.notts-rspb.org.uk
e-mail: amg1963@btinternet.com
Meetings: 7.30pm, 1st Wednesday of the month, Nottingham Mechanics, North Sherwood Street, Nottingham.

Wetland Bird Survey Organiser
Gary Hobson, 18 Barnes Avenue, Wrenthorpe, Wakefield, WF1 2BH. 01924 384 419;
e-mail: gary.lbc1@tiscali.co.uk.

Wildlife Trust
NOTTINGHAMSHIRE WILDLIFE TRUST. (1963; 4,300). The Old Ragged School, Brook Street, Nottingham, NG1 1EA. 0115 958 8242; (Fax)0115 924 3175;
e-mail: info@nottswt.co.uk
www.nottinghamshirewildlife.org.uk

OXFORDSHIRE

Bird Atlas/Avifauna
Birds of Oxfordshire by J W Brucker et al (Oxford, Pisces, 1992).

The New Birds of the Banbury Area by T G Easterbrook (Banbury Ornithological Society, 1995).

Bird Recorder
Ian Lewington, 119 Brasenose Road, Didcot, Oxon,
OX11 7BP. 01235 819 792;
e-mail: ian@recorder.fsnet.co.uk

Bird Reports
BIRDS OF OXFORDSHIRE (1921-), from Barry Hudson,
Pinfold, 4 Bushy Row, Bampton, Oxon OX18 2JU.
01865 775 632.

*BANBURY ORNITHOLOGICAL SOCIETY ANNUAL
REPORT (1952-)*. £5 each including postage, from
MJ Lewis, Old Mill Cottage, Avon Dassett, Southam,
Warwickshire, CV47 2AE. 01295 690 643;
e-mail: mikelewisad@hotmail.com.

**BTO Regional Representatives & Regional
Development Officer**
NORTH. Frances Buckel, Witts End, Radbones Hill,
Over Norton, Chipping Norton, Oxon OX7 5RA. 01608
644 425; e-mail: fran.buckel@btinternet.com

SOUTH RR & RDO. Mr John Melling, 17 Lime Grove,
Southmoor, Nr Abingdon, Oxon OX13 5DN.
e-mail: bto-rep@oos.org.uk

Clubs
BANBURY ORNITHOLOGICAL SOCIETY. (1952; 100).
Frances Buckel, Witts End, Radbones Hill, Over
Norton, Chipping Norton, Oxon OX7 5RA. 01608 644
425; e-mail: fran.buckel@btinternet.com
www.banburyornithologicalsociety.org.uk
Meetings: 7.30pm, 2nd Monday of the month,
Freemason's Hall, Marlborough Road, Banbury.

OXFORD ORNITHOLOGICAL SOCIETY. (1921;
330). Barry Hudson, Pinfold, 4 Bushy
Row, Bampton, Oxon OX18
2JU. 01993 852 028; e-mail:
secretary@oos.org.uk
www.oos.org.uk
Meetings: 7.45pm, various
dates, Stratfield Brake,
Kidlington.

Ringing Group
EDWARD GREY INSTITUTE. Dr A G Gosler, c/o Edward
Grey Institute, Department of Zoology, South Parks
Road, Oxford OX1 3PS. 01865 271 158;
e-mail: andrew.gosler@zoo.ox.ac.uk

RSPB Local Groups
OXFORD. (1977; 100). Ian Kilshaw, 6 Queens Court,
Bicester, Oxon, OX26 6JX. 01869 601 901;
e-mail: ian.kilshaw@ntlworld.com
www.rspb-oxford.org.uk
Meetings: 7.45pm, normally 1st Thursday of the
month, Sandhills Primary School, Terret Avenue,
Headington, Oxford (opposite Thornhill park-and-
ride).

VALE OF WHITE HORSE. (1977; 330). Philip Morris.
01367 710 285; e-mail: Philip.P.Morris@tesco.net
www.rspb-vwh.org.uk

Meetings: 7.30pm, 3rd Monday of the month (Sep-
May). Didcot Civic Hall.

Wetland Bird Survey Organiser
OXFORDSHIRE (NORTH). Sandra Bletchly. 11 Orchard
Grove, Bloxham, Banbury, Oxfordshire, OX15 4NZ.
e-mail: sandra@banornsoc.fsnet.co.uk

OXFORDSHIRE (SOUTH). Ian Lees. 16 Dove House
Close, Upper Wolvercote, Oxford, OX2 8BG. 01865
311104; e-mail: ian.photography@virgin.net

Wildlife Trust
BBOWT. (1959; 24,000). The Lodge, 1 Armstrong
Road, Littlemore, Oxford, OX4 4XT. 01865 775 476;
(Fax)01865 711 301; e-mail: info@bbowt.org.uk
www.bbowt.org.uk

SHROPSHIRE

Bird Atlas/Avifauna
Atlas of the Breeding Birds of Shropshire (Shropshire
Ornithological Society, 1995).

Bird Recorder
Geoff Holmes, 22 Tenbury Drive, Telford Estate,
Shrewsbury, SY2 5YF. 01743 364 621;
e-mail: geoff.holmes.4@btinternet.com

Bird Report
SHROPSHIRE BIRD REPORT (1956-) Annual, from Helen
Griffiths (Hon Secretary), 104 Noel Hill Road, Cross
Houses, Shrewsbury SY5 6LD. 01743 761507;
e-mail: helen.griffiths@english-nature.org.uk
www.shropshirebirds.com

BTO Regional Representative
RR. Allan Dawes, Rosedale, Chapel Lane, Trefonen,
Oswestry, Shrops SY10 9DX. 01691 654 245;
e-mail: allandawes@btinternet.com

Club
SHROPSHIRE ORNITHOLOGICAL SOCIETY. (1955; 800).
Helen Griffiths, 104 Noel Hill Road, Cross Houses,
Shrewsbury, SY5 6LD. 01743 761 507;
e-mail: helen.griffiths@english-nature.org.uk
www.shropshirebirds.com
Meetings: 7.15pm, 1st Thursday of month (Oct-Apr),
Shirehall, Shrewsbury.

RSPB Local Group
SHROPSHIRE. (1992; 320). Roger M Evans, 31 The
Wheatlands, Bridgnorth, WV16 5BD. 01746 766 042;
e-mail: r.evans441@btinternet.com
www.rspb.org.uk/groups/shropshire
Meetings: 7.30pm, 4th Wednesday of the month (Sep-
Apr), Council Chamber, Shirehall, Shrewsbury.

SOUTH SHROPSHIRE. Alan Botting (Group Leader).
01547 540 176; e-mail: Christinelbateman@yahoo.
com www.rspbsouthshropshire.co.uk
Meetings: 7.30pm (Sep-Apr), Shropshire Hills
Discovery Centre (Secret Hills), Craven Arms.

ENGLAND

Wetland Bird Survey Organiser
SHROPSHIRE. Michael Wallace. 75 Larkhill Road,
Copthorne, Shrewsbury, Shropshire, SY3 8XJ.
01743 369 035;
e-mail: michael@wallace7536.freeserve.co.uk

Wildlife Trust
SHROPSHIRE WILDLIFE TRUST. (1962; 10,000). 193
Abbey Foregate, Shrewsbury, Shropshire SY2 6AH.
01743 284 280; (Fax)01743 284 281;
e-mail: shropshirewt@cix.co.uk
www.shropshirewildlifetrust.org.uk

SOMERSET & BRISTOL

Bird Atlas/Avifauna
Atlas of Breeding Birds in Avon 1988-91 by R L Bland
and John Tully (John Tully, 6 Falcondale Walk,
Westbury-on-Trym, Bristol BS9 3JG, 1992).

Bristol Ornithology no. 29 by Robin Prytherch (Bristol
Ornithological Club 2008).

The Birds of Exmoor and the Quantocks by DK
Ballance and BD Gibbs. (Isabelline Books, 2 Highbury
House, 8 Woodland Crescent, Falmouth TR11 4QS.
2003).

Bird Recorders
SOMERSET. Brian D Gibbs, 23 Lyngford Road, Taunton,
Somerset, TA2 7EE. 01823 274 887;
e-mail: brian.gibbs@virgin.net
www.somersetbirds.net

BRISTOL, S. GLOS, BATH AND NE SOMERSET, NORTH
SOMERSET. John Martin, 34 Cranmore Green, Pilning,
Bristol BS35 4QF. 01454 633 040;
e-mail: avonbirdrecorder@googlemail.com

Bird Reports
AVON BIRD REPORT (1977-), from Harvey Rose, 12
Birbeck Road, Bristol, BS9 1BD. 0117 968 1638;
e-mail: h.e.rose@bris.ac.uk

EXMOOR NATURALIST (1974-), from Secretary,
Exmoor Natural History Society.

SOMERSET BIRDS (1912-) £8.50 inc p&p, from David
Ballance, Flat 2, Dunboyne, Bratton Lane, Minehead.
TA24 8SQ. www.somersetbirds.net

BTO Regional Representatives
AVON RR. Richard L Bland, 11 Percival Road, Bristol,
BS8 3LN. Home/W:01179 734 828;
e-mail: richardbland@blueyonder.co.uk

AVON ASST REGIONAL REPRESENTATIVE. John Tully,
6 Falcondale Walk, Westbury-on-Trym, Bristol, BS9
3JG. 0117 950 0992; e-mail: johntully4@aol.com

SOMERSET RR. Eve Tigwell, Hawthorne Cottage, 3
Friggle Street, Frome, Somerset BA11 5LP. 01373
451630; e-mail: eve.tigwell@zen.co.uk

Clubs
BRISTOL NATURALISTS' SOCIETY (Ornithological
Section). (1862; 550). Becky Coffin, 33 London Street,
Kingswood, Bristol, BS15 1RA. 01179 610 222; 07773
188 286; e-mail: beckycoffin@yahoo.com
www.bristolnats.org.uk
Meetings: 7.30pm, 2nd Wednesday in the month
(check for dates, Oct-Mar), Westmorland Hall,
Westmorland Road, Bristol

BRISTOL ORNITHOLOGICAL CLUB. (1966; 670). Mrs
Judy Copeland, 19 St George's Hill, Easton-in-
Gordano, North Somerset, BS20 0PS. Tel/fax 01275
373554; e-mail: judy.copeland@ukgateway.net
www.boc-bristol.org.uk
Meetings: 7.30pm, 3rd Thursday of the
month, Newman Hall,
Grange Court Road,
Westbury-on-Trym.

CAM VALLEY WILDLIFE
GROUP. (1994: 356). André Fournier, 1 Boomfield
Lane, Paulton, Bristol BS39 7QU. 01761 418 153.
e-mail: andre.fournier@btinternet.com
www.somersetmade.co.uk/cvwg/

EXMOOR NATURAL HISTORY SOCIETY. (1974; 480).
Miss Caroline Giddens, 12 King George Road,
Minehead, Somerset, TA24 5JD. 01643 707624;
e-mail: carol.enhs@virgin.net
www.enhs.org.uk
Meetings: 7.30pm, 1st Wednesday of the month (Oct-
Mar), Methodist Church Hall, The Avenue, Minehead.

SOMERSET ORNITHOLOGICAL SOCIETY. (1974; 350).
Mr JA Hazell, Membership Secretary, 9 Hooper Road,
Street, Somerset BA16 0NP. 01458 443 780;
e-mail: jeffreyhazell@ymail.com
www.somersetbirds.net
Meetings: 7.30pm, various Thursdays (Oct-Apr),
Ruishton Village Hall, Taunton.

Ringing Groups
CHEW VALLEY RS. Mr A Ashman.
e-mail: alan.ashman@talktalk.net

GORDANO VALLEY RG. Lyndon Roberts, 20 Glebe
Road, Long Ashton, Bristol, BS41 9LH. 01275 392 722;
e-mail: mail@lyndonroberts.com

STEEP HOLM RS. A J Parsons, Barnfield, Tower Hill
Road, Crewkerne, Somerset, TA18 8BJ. 01460 73640.

RSPB Local Groups
BATH AND DISTRICT. (1989; 220). Alan Barrett. 01225
310 905; e-mail: alan_w_h_barrett@yahoo.co.uk
www.rspb.org.uk/groups/bath
Meetings: 7.30pm, 3rd Wednesday of the month
(Sep-Mar), Bath Society Meeting Room, Green Park
Station, Bath.

CREWKERNE & DISTRICT. (1979; 320). Denise
Chamings, Daniels Farm, Lower Stratton, South
Petherton, Somerset TA13 5LP. 01460 240 740;
e-mail: denise.chamings@talktalk.net

rspb.org.uk/groups/crewkerne
Meetings: 7.30pm, 3rd Thursday of the month (Sep-Apr), The Henhayes Centre, Crewkerne.

TAUNTON. (1975; 148). Frances Freeman. 01823 674 182; e-mail: francesfreeman@yahoo.com
www.rspb.org.uk/groups/taunton
Meetings: 7.30pm, last Friday of the month, Trull Memorial Hall, Church Road, Trull, Taunton TA3 7JZ.

WESTON-SUPER-MARE (N SOMERSET). (1976; 215). Don Hurrell, Freeways, Star, Winscombe, BS25 1PS. 01934 842 717; e-mail: hurrell@cpsmail.co.uk
www.rspb.org.uk/groups/westonsupermare
Meetings: 7.45pm, 1st Thursday of the month (Sep-Apr), St Paul's Church Hall, Walliscote Road, Weston-Super-Mare.

Wetland Bird Survey Organisers
SEVERN ESTUARY - SOUTHERN COAST. Harvey Rose, 12 Birbek Road, Stoke Bishop, Bristol, BS9 1BD. 0117 968 1638; e-mail: h.e.rose@bris.ac.uk

SOMERSET LEVELS. Steve Meen, RSPB West Sedgemoor, Dewlands Farm, Redhill, Curry Rivel, Langport Somerset TA10 0PH. 01458 252 805; e-mail: steve.meen@rspb.org.uk

SOMERSET (OTHER SITES) AND SOUTH AVON (INLAND). Keith Fox, Vernwood, 32 Ash Hayes Road, Nailsea, Avon, BS48 2LW. e-mail: keith@kfox.wanadoo.co.uk

Wildlife Trusts
AVON WILDLIFE TRUST. (1980; 7,000). The Old Police Station, 32 Jacobs Wells Road, Bristol, BS8 1DR. 0117 917 7270; (Fax)0117 929 7273; e-mail: mail@avonwildlifetrust.org.uk
www.avonwildlifetrust.org.uk

SOMERSET WILDLIFE TRUST. (1964; 19,500). Tonedale Mill, Tonedale, Wellington, Somerset TA21 0AW. 01823 652 400; (Fax)01823 652 411; e-mail: enquiries@somersetwildlife.org
www.somersetwildlife.org

STAFFORDSHIRE

Bird Recorder
Nick Pomiankowski, 22 The Villas, West End, Stoke ST4 5AQ; 01782 849 682; e-mail: staffs-recorder@westmidlandbirdclub.com

Bird Report See West Midlands

BTO Regional Representatives
NORTH EAST. Gilly Jones, 4 The Poplars, Lichfield Road, Abbots Bromley, Rugeley Staffs WS15 3AA. 01283 840 555; e-mail: g.n.jones@wlv.ac.uk

SOUTH & CENTRAL. Gilly Jones, 4 The Poplars, Lichfield Road, Abbots Bromley, Rugeley Staffs WS15 3AA. 01283 840 555; e-mail: g.n.jones@wlv.ac.uk

WEST. Gilly Jones, 4 The Poplars, Lichfield Road, Abbots Bromley, Rugeley Staffs WS15 3AA. 01283 840 555; e-mail: g.n.jones@wlv.ac.uk

Clubs
SOUTH PEAK RAPTOR STUDY GROUP. (1998; 12). M E Taylor, 76 Hawksley Avenue, Newbold, Chesterfield, Derbys S40 4TL. 01246 277 749.

WEST MIDLAND BIRD CLUB (STAFFORD BRANCH). Gerald Ford. 01630 673 409; e-mail: gerald.ford@westmidlandbirdclub.com
www.westmidlandbirdclub.com/stafford
Meetings: 7.30pm, 2nd Friday of the month (Oct-Mar),The Centre for The Blind, North Walls, Stafford.

WEST MIDLAND BIRD CLUB (TAMWORTH BRANCH). (1992). Barbara Stubbs, 19 Alfred Street, Tamworth, Staffs, B79 7RL. 01827 57865; e-mail: tamworth@westmidlandbirdclub
www.westmidlandbirdclub.com/tamworth
Meetings: 7.30pm, 3rd Friday of the month (Sep-Apr), Phil Dix Centre, Corporation Street, Tamworth.

RSPB Local Groups
BURTON-ON-TRENT AND SOUTH DERBYSHIRE. (1973; 50). Dave Lummis, 121 Wilmot Road, Swadlincote, Derbys, DE11 9BN. 01283 219 902.
www.basd-rspb.co.uk
Meetings: 7.30pm 1st Wednesday of the month, All Saint's Church, Branston Road, Burton.

LICHFIELD & DISTRICT. (1977; 1,150). Bob Russon, 108 Walsall Road, Lichfield, Staffs, WS13 8AF. 01543 252 547; e-mail: bob@russon.co.uk
Meetings: 7.30pm, 2nd Tuesday of the month (Jan-May, Sept-Dec), St Mary's Centre, Lichfield.

NORTH STAFFS. (1982; 198). John Booth, 32 St Margaret Drive, Sneyd Green, Stoke-on-Trent, ST1 6EW. 01782 262 082;
www.rspb.org.uk/groups/northstaffordshire
Meetings: 7.30pm, normally 3rd Wednesday of the month, North Staffs Conference Centre (Medical Institute).

SOUTH WEST STAFFORDSHIRE. (1972; 172). Mrs Theresa Dorrance, 39 Wilkes Road, Codsall, Wolverhampton, WV8 1RZ. 01902 847 041; e-mail: stevedorrance@googlemail.com
Meetings: 8.00pm, 2nd Tuesday of the month (Sep-May), Codsall Village Hall.

Wildlife Hospitals
BRITISH WILDLIFE RESCUE CENTRE. Alfred Hardy, Amerton Working Farm, Stowe-by-Chartley, Stafford, ST18 0LA. 01889 271 308; e-mail: joyce.hardy351@ntlworld.com
www.britishwildliferescue.co.uk.
On A518 Stafford/Uttoxeter road. All species, including imprints and permanently injured. Hospital,

large aviaries and caging. Open to the public every day. Veterinary support.

GENTLESHAW BIRD OF PREY HOSPITAL. Jenny Smith, Gentleshaw Wildlife Centre, Fletcher's Country Garden Centre, Stone Road, Eccleshall, Staffs ST21 6JY. 01785 850 379; www.gentleshawwildlife.co.uk. e-mail: info@gentleshawwildlife.co.uk Registered charity. All birds of prey (inc. owls). Hospital cages and aviaries; release sites. Veterinary support. Also GENTLESHAW BIRD OF PREY AND WILDLIFE CENTRE, Fletchers Country Garden Centre, Stone Road, Eccleshall, Stafford. 01785 850379 (1000-1700).

Wildlife Trust
STAFFORDSHIRE WILDLIFE TRUST. (1969; 14,000). The Wolseley Centre, Wolseley Bridge, Stafford, ST17 0WT. 01889 880 100; (Fax)01889 880 101; e-mail: staffs-wildlife.org.uk www.staffs-wildlife.org.uk

SUFFOLK

Bird Atlas/Avifauna
Birds of Suffolk by S H Piotrowski (February 2003) Quatermelon.

Bird Recorders
SOUTH EAST (inc. coastal region from Slaughden Quay southwards). Eddie Marsh. e-mail: marshharrier@btinternet.com

WEST (whole of Suffolk W of Stowmarket, inc. Breckland). Colin Jakes, 7 Maltward Avenue, Bury St Edmunds, Suffolk IP33 3XN. 01284 702 215; e-mail: colin.jakes@stedsbc.gov.uk

Bird Report
SUFFOLK BIRDS (inc Landguard Bird Observatory Report) (1950-), from Ipswich Museum, High Street, Ipswich, Suffolk.

BTO Regional Representative
Mick T Wright, 15 Avondale Road, Ipswich, IP3 9JT. 01473 710 032; e-mail: micktwright@btinternet.com

Clubs
LAVENHAM BIRD CLUB. (1972; 54). Mr G Pattrick, Brights Farmhouse, Brights Lane, Lavenham, Suffolk CO10 9PH. 01787 248 128.
Meetings: 7.30pm, normally 3rd Saturday (Sep-Mar, except Dec), Lavenham Guildhall.

SUFFOLK ORNITHOLOGISTS' GROUP. (1973; 650). Paul Gowen, 14 Two Acres, Capel St Mary, Ipswich, Suffolk IP9 2XP. 01473 311 263.
Meetings: Last Thursday of the month (Jan-Mar, Oct-Nov), Holiday Inn, Ipswich.

Ringing Groups
DINGLE BIRD CLUB. Dr D Pearson, 4 Lupin Close, Reydon, Southwold, Suffolk IP18 6NW. 01502 722 348.

LACKFORD RG. Dr Peter Lack, 11 Holden Road, Lackford, Bury St Edmunds, Suffolk IP28 6HZ. e-mail: peter.diane@tinyworld.co.uk

LANDGUARD RG. Landguard Ringing Group, Landguard Bird Observatory, View Point Road, Felixstowe, Suffolk, IP11 3TW. 01394 673 782; e-mail: landguardbo@yahoo.co.uk www.lbo.co.uk

MARKET WESTON RG. Dr R H W Langston, Walnut Tree Farm, Thorpe Street, Hinderclay, Diss, Norfolk IP22 1HT. e-mail: rlangston@wntfarm.demon.co.uk

RSPB Local Groups
BURY ST EDMUNDS. (1982; 150). John Sharpe. 01359 230 045; e-mail: sharpix@tiscali.co.uk www.rspb.org.uk/groups/burystedmunds
Meetings: 7.30pm, 3rd Tuesday of the month (Sep-May), County Upper School, Beetons Way, Bury St Edmunds.

IPSWICH. (1975; 275). Mr Chris Courtney, St Elmo, 19 Marlborough Road, Ipswich, Suffolk IP4 5AT. 01473 423 213; e-mail: chrisc.courtney@yahoo.co.uk www.ipswichrspb.org.uk.
Meetings: 7.30pm, 2nd Thursday of the month (Sep-Apr), Sidegate Lane Primary School, Sidegate Lane, Ipswich.

LOWESTOFT & DISTRICT. (1976; 130). Mrs E Beaumont, 52 Squires Walk, Lowestoft, Suffolk, NR32 4LA. 01502 560 126; e-mail: embeaumont@supanet.com www.rspb.org.uk/groups/lowestoft
Meetings: Friday 7.15pm 1st Monday in the month, St Marks Church Hall, Oulton Broad.

WOODBRIDGE. (1987; 450). Malcolm Key, Riverside, Parham, Suffolk, IP13 9LZ. 01728 723 155; e-mail: malcolm.key@btopenworld.com
Meetings: 7.30pm, 1st Thursday of the month (Oct-May), Woodbridge Community Hall.

Wetland Bird Survey Organisers
ALDE COMPLEX. Ian Castle. 5 Chapelfield, Orford, Woodbridge, Suffolk, IP12 2HW. 01394 450 188; e-mail: ic.pda@the-pda.com

ALTON WATER. John Glazebrook. e-mail: johnglazebrook@btopenworld.com

DEBEN ESTUARY. Nick Mason, 8 Mallard Way, Hollesley, Nr Woodbridge, Ipswich IP12 3QJ. (H)01359 411 150; e-mail: nick.mason4@btinternet.com

ORWELL ESTUARY. Mick Wright. 15 Avondale Road, Ipswich, Suffolk, IP3 9JT. 01473 710 032; e-mail: micktwright@btinternet.com

STOUR ESTUARY. Rick Vonk, RSPB, Unit 13 Court Farm, 3 Stutton Road, Brantham Suffolk CO11 1PW. (D)01473 328 006; e-mail:rick.vonk@rspb.org.uk

ENGLAND

SUFFOLK (other sites). Alan Miller, Suffolk Wildlife Trust, Moonrakers, Back Lane, Wenhaston, Halesworth, Suffolk, IP19 9DY.
e-mail: alan.miller@suffolkwildlifetrust.org

Wildlife Trust
SUFFOLK WILDLIFE TRUST. (1961; 25,000). Brooke House, The Green, Ashbocking, Ipswich, IP6 9JY. 01473 890 089; (Fax)01473 890 165;
e-mail: info@suffolkwildlifetrust.org
www.suffolkwildlifetrust.org

SURREY

Bird Atlas/Avifauna
Birds of Surrey by Jeffery Wheatley (Surrey Bird Club 2007).

Bird Recorder (inc London S of Thames and E to Surrey Docks)
SURREY (includes Greater London south of the Thames and east to the Surrey Docks, excludes Spellthorne). Jeffery Wheatley, 9 Copse Edge, Elstead, Godalming, Surrey, GU8 6DJ. 01252 702 450;
e-mail: j.j.wheatley@btinternet.com.

Bird Report
SURBITON AND DISTRICT BIRD WATCHING SOCIETY (1972-), from Thelma Caine, 21 More Lane, Esher, Surrey KT10 8AJ.

SURREY BIRD REPORT (1952-), from J Gates, 5 Hillside Road, Weybourne, Farnham, Surrey GU9 9DW. 01252 315 047;e-mail: jeremygates@live.com

BTO Regional Representative
RR. Hugh Evans. 01932 227 781;
e-mail: hugh.evans31@tiscali.co.uk

Clubs
SURBITON & DISTRICT BIRDWATCHING SOCIETY. (1954; 140). Gary Caine, 21 More Lane, Esher, Surrey, KT10 8AJ. 01372 468 432; e-mail: sdbws@encief.co.uk www.encief.co.uk/sdbws
Meetings: 7.30pm, 3rd Tuesday of the month, Surbiton Library Annex.

SURREY BIRD CLUB. (1957; 350). Penny Williams, Bournbrook House, Sandpit Hall Lane, Chobham, Surrey GU24 8HA. 01276 857 736; e-mail: penny@waxwing.plus.com www.surreybirdclub.org.uk
Meetings: See website for details.

Ringing Groups
HERSHAM RG. A J Beasley, 29 Selbourne Avenue, New Haw, Weybridge, Surrey KT15 3RB.
e-mail: abeasley00@hotmail.com

RUNNYMEDE RG. DG Harris, 22 Blossom Waye, Hounslow, TW5 9HD.
e-mail: daveharris@tinyonline.co.uk

RSPB Local Groups
DORKING & DISTRICT. (1982; 280). John Burge, Broughton Norrels Drive, East Horsley, Leatherhead, KT24 5DR. 01483 283 803;
e-mail: burgejs@googlemail.com
Meetings: 8pm, Fridays each month (Sep-Apr), Christian Centre, next to St Martin's Church, Dorking.

EAST SURREY. (1984; 150-200). Brian Hobley, 26 Alexandra Road, Warlingham, Surrey, CR6 9DU. 01883 625 404;
e-mail: brianhobley@btinternet.com
www.eastsurreyrspb.co.uk
Meetings: 8pm, 2nd Wednesday of the month (Sep-Jul), Whitehart Barn, Godstone.

EPSOM & EWELL. (1974; 168). Janet Gilbert, 78 Fairfax Avenue, Ewell, Epsom, Surrey KT17 2QQ. 0208 394 0405;
e-mail: janetegilbert@btinternet.com
www.rspb.org.uk/groups/epsom
Meetings: 7.45pm, 2nd Friday of the month, All Saints Church Hall, Fulford Road, West Ewell.

GUILDFORD AND DISTRICT. (1974; 600). Roger Beck, 14 Overbrook, West Horsley, KT24 6BH. 01483 282 417; e-mail: rogerbeck@beck40.fsnet.co.uk
www.rspb.org.uk/groups/guildford
Meetings: 2.15pm 2nd Thursday and 7.45pm 4th Wednesday (Oct-Apr), Onslow Village Hall, Guildford.

NORTH WEST SURREY. (1973; 150). Ms Mary Braddock, 20 Meadway Drive, New Haw, Surrey, KT15 2DT. 01932 858 692;
e-mail: mary@braddock3.wanadoo.co.uk
www.nwsurreyrspb.org.uk
Meetings: 7.45pm, 4th Wednesday of the month (not Dec, Jul, Aug), Sir William Perkin's School, Chertsey KT16 9BN.

Wetland Bird Survey Organiser
SURREY (includes Greater London south of the Thames and east to the Surrey Docks, excludes Spellthorne). Jeffery Wheatley, 9 Copse Edge, Elstead, Godalming, Surrey GU8 6DJ. 01252 702 450;
e-mail: j.j.wheatley@btinternet.com

Wildlife Hospitals
THE SWAN SANCTUARY. See National Directory

WILDLIFE AID. Randalls Farm House, Randalls Road, Leatherhead, Surrey, KT22 0AL. 01372 377 332; 24-hr emergency line 09061 800 132 (50p/min); (Fax)01372 375183; e-mail: wildlife@pncl.co.uk
www.wildlifeaid.com
Registered charity. Wildlife hospital and rehabilitation centre helping all native British species. Special housing for birds of prey. Membership scheme and fund raising activities. Veterinary support.

Wildlife Trust
SURREY WILDLIFE TRUST. (1959; 25,700). School Lane, Pirbright, Woking, Surrey, GU24 0JN. 01483 795

440; (Fax)01483 486 505;
e-mail: info@surreywt.org.uk
www.surreywildlifetrust.org

SUSSEX

Bird Atlas/Avifauna
The Birds of Selsey Bill and the Selsey Peninsula (a checklist to year 2000) From: O Mitchell, 21 Trundle View Close, Barnham, Bognor Regis, PO22 0JZ.

Birds of Sussex ed by Paul James (Sussex Ornithological Society, 1996).

Fifty Years of Birdwatching, a celebration of the acheivements of the Shoreham District OS from 1953 onwards. From Shoreham District Ornithological Society, 7 Berberis Court, Shoreham by Sea, West Sussex BN43 6JA. £15 plus £2.50 p&p.

Henfield Birdwatcher Reports 2000 and 2005 ed Mike Russell et al, Henfield Birdwatch

Bird Recorder
CW Melgar, The Penthouse, Broadway Court, Brighton Road, Lancing, West Sussex BN15 8JT. 01903 765 511; e-mail: cwmelgar@yahoo.com

Bird Reports
BIRDS OF RYE HARBOUR NR ANNUAL REPORT (1977-published every 5 years), from Dr Barry Yates, see Clubs.

PAGHAM HARBOUR LOCAL NATURE RESERVE ANNUAL REPORT, from Warden, see Reserves,

SHOREHAM DISTRICT ORNITHOLOGICAL SOCIETY ANNUAL REPORT (1952-) - back issues available, from Mrs. Shena Maskell, SDOS Membership Administrator, 41 St. Lawrence Avenue, Worthing, West Sussex BN14 7JJ. E-mail: avianadventures@tiscali.co.uk
www.sdos.org

SUSSEX BIRD REPORT (1963-), from J E Trowell, Lorrimer, Main Road, Icklesham, Winchelsea, E Sussex, TN36 4BS. e-mail: membership@sos.org.uk
www.sos.org.uk

BTO Regional Representative
Dr Helen Crabtree, 01444 441 687;
e-mail: hcrabtree@gmail.com.

Clubs
FRIENDS OF RYE HARBOUR NATURE RESERVE. (1973; 1800). Dr Barry Yates, 2 Watch Cottages, Nook Beach, Winchelsea, E Sussex TN36 4LU. 01797 223 862; e-mail: rhnr.office@eastsussex.gov.uk
www.wildrye.info
Meetings: Monthly talks in winter, monthly walks all year.

HENFIELD BIRDWATCH. (1999; 135). Mike Russell, 31 Downsview, Small Dole, Henfield, West Sussex BN5 9YB. 01273 494311;
e-mail: mikerussell@sussexwt.org.uk

SHOREHAM DISTRICT ORNITHOLOGICAL SOCIETY. (1953; 150). Mrs. Shena Maskell, SDOS Membership Administrator, 41 St. Lawrence Avenue, Worthing, West Sussex BN14 7JJ.
E-mail: avianadventures@tiscali.co.uk
www.sdos.org
Meetings: 7.30pm, 1st Tuesday of the month (Oct-Apr), St Peter's Church Hall, Shoreham-by-Sea. (7 indoor meetings, 16 field outings)

SUSSEX ORNITHOLOGICAL SOCIETY. (1962; 1,600). Nigel Bowie, 55 Rochester Street, Brighton, BN2 0EJ. 01273 571 266; e-mail:secretary@sos.org.uk
www.sos.org.uk

Ringing Groups
BEACHY HEAD RS. RDM Edgar, 32 Hartfield Road, Seaford, E Sussex BN25 4PW.

CUCKMERE RG. Tim Parmenter, 18 Chapel Road, Plumpton Green, East Sussex, BN7 3DD. 01273 891 881.

RYE BAY RG. P Jones,
e-mail: philjones@beamingbroadband.com

STEYNING RG. BR Clay, Meghana, Honeysuckle Lane, High Salvington, Worthing, West Sussex BN13 3BT. e-mail: brian.clay@ntlworld.com

RSPB Local Groups
BATTLE. (1973; 80). Miss Lynn Jenkins, 61 Austen Way, Guestling, Hastings, E Sussex TN35 4JH. 01424 432 076; e-mail: Lynn.jenkins@battlerspb.org.uk
www.battlerspb.org.uk
Meetings: 7.30pm, 4th Tuesday of the month, Battle and Langton Primary School, Battle.

BRIGHTON & DISTRICT. (1974; 350). Ian Booth. 01273 588 288; e-mail: Ian@batatzes.fsnet.co.uk
www.rspb.org.uk/groups/brighton
Meetings: 7.30pm, 4th Tuesday of the month, All Saints Church Hall, Eaton Road, Hove.

CHICHESTER & SW SUSSEX. (1979; 245). David Hart, Heys Bridle Rd, Slindon Common, Arundel, BN18 0NA. 01243 814 497;
e-mail: heather.dave1@tiscali.co.uk
www.rspb.org.uk/groups/chichester
Meetings: 7.30 pm, 2nd Thursday of each month, Newell Centre, Newell Centre, Tozer Way, St Pancras, Chichester.

CRAWLEY & HORSHAM. (1978; 148). Andrea Saxton, 104 Heath Way, Horsham, W Sussex, RH12 5XS. 01403 242 218; e-mail: Andrea.saxton@sky.com
www.rspb.org.uk/groups/crawley
Meetings: 8pm, 3rd Wednesday of the month (Sept-Apr), The Friary Hall, Crawley.

EAST GRINSTEAD. (1998; 185). Nick Walker, 14 York Avenue, East Grinstead, W Sussex RH19 4TL. 01342

ENGLAND

315 825; e-mail: gnwalker@tiscali.co.uk
www.rspb.org.uk/groups/egrinstead
Meetings: 8pm, last Wednesday of the month, Large
Parish Hall, De La Warr Road, East Grinstead.

EASTBOURNE & DISTRICT. (1993; 520). Ian Muldoon.
01273 476852; e-mail: ian1muldoon@yahoo.co.uk
www.rspb.org.uk/groups/eastbourne
Meetings: 2.15 pm and 7.30 pm, 1st Wednesday
of the month (Sep-Jun), St. Wilfrid's Church Hall,
Eastbourne Road, Pevensey Bay.

HASTINGS & ST LEONARDS. (1983; 110). Susan
Neighbour, 9 Gainsborough Road, Bexhill on Sea, E
Sussex TN40 2UL. 01424 211 140;
e-mail: s92neighbour@tesco.net
Meetings: 7.30pm, 3rd Friday of the month, Taplin
Centre, Upper Maze Hill.

Wetland Bird Survey Organiser
SUSSEX (OTHER SITES). Richard Bown. 49 Long Beach
View, Sovereign Harbour North, Eastbourne, East
Sussex, BN23 5NB.
e-mail: hr.bown@btinternet.com

Wildlife Hospital
BRENT LODGE BIRD & WILDLIFE TRUST. Penny Cooper,
Brent Lodge, Cow Lane, Sidlesham, Chichester,
West Sussex, PO20 7LN. 01243 641 672 (emergency
number); www.brentlodge.org.
All species of wild birds and small mammals.
Full surgical and medical facilities (inc. X-ray) in
conjunction with veterinary support. Purpose-built
oiled bird washing unit. Veterinary support.

Wildlife Trust
SUSSEX WILDLIFE TRUST. (1961; 26,000). Woods Mill,
Shoreham Road, Henfield, W Sussex, BN5 9SD. 01273
492630; (Fax)01273 494500;
e-mail: enquiries@sussexwt.org.uk
www.sussexwt.org.uk

TYNE & WEAR

Bird Recorders
See Durham; Northumberland.

Bird Report See Durham; Northumberland.

Clubs
NATURAL HISTORY SOCIETY OF NORTHUMBRIA. (1829;
900). The Natural History Society of Northumbria,
Hancock Museum, Barras Bridge, Newcastle upon
Tyne, NE2 4PT. 0191 232 6386;
e-mail: nhsn@ncl.ac.uk
www.NHSN.ncl.ac.uk
Meetings: 7pm, every Friday (Oct-Mar), Percy
Building, Newcastle University.

NORTHUMBERLAND &
TYNESIDE BIRD CLUB.
(1958; 270). Alan Watson,
Secretary, 3 Green
Close, Whitley Bay,

Northumberland NE25 9SH. 0191 252 2744;
e-mail: apusx@blueyonder.co.uk
www.ntbc.org.uk

RSPB Local Groups
NEWCASTLE UPON TYNE. (1969; 250). Brian
Moorhead. 07903 387 429;
e-mail: ncastlerspbgroup@btinternet.com
www.rspb.org.uk/groups/newcastle
Meetings: 7pm, (Mar, Jun, Sep, Nov), Northumbria
University, Ellison Place, Newcastle upon Tyne.

WARWICKSHIRE

Bird Recorder
Jonathan Bowley, 17 Meadow Way, Fenny Compton,
Southam, Warks CV47 2WD. 01295 770069;
e-mail: warks-recorder@westmidlandbirdclub.com

Bird Report See West Midlands.

BTO Regional Representatives
WARWICKSHIRE. Mark Smith. 01926 735 398;
e-mail: mark.smith36@ntlworld.com

RUGBY. Position vacant.

Clubs
NUNEATON & DISTRICT
BIRDWATCHERS' CLUB. (1950;
78). Alvin K Burton, 23 Redruth
Close, Horeston Grange, Nuneaton,
Warwicks CV11 6FG. 024 7664 1591.
www.ndbwc.btik.com
Meetings: 7.30pm, 3rd Thursday of
the month (Sep-Jun), Hatters Space
Community Centre, Upper Abbey Street, Nuneaton.

Ringing Groups
ARDEN RG. Roger J Juckes, 24 Croft Lane, Temple
Grafton, Alcester, Warks B49 6PA. 01789 778748.

BRANDON RG. David Stone, Overbury, Wolverton,
Stratford-on-Avon, Warks CV37 0HG. 01789 731488.

RSPB Local Group
See West Midlands.

Wildlife Trust
WARWICKSHIRE WILDLIFE TRUST. (1970; 13,000).
Brandon Marsh Nature Centre, Brandon Lane,
Coventry, CV3 3GW. 024 7630 2912; (Fax)024 7663
9556; e-mail: enquiries@wkwt.org.uk
www.warwickshire-wildlife-trust.org.uk

WEST MIDLANDS

Bird Atlas/Avifauna
The New Birds of the West Midlands edited by
Graham and Janet Harrison (West Midland Bird Club,
2005). Available from 147 Worlds End Lane, Quinton,
Birmingham B32 1JX.

ENGLAND

Bird Recorder
Kevin Clements, 26 Hambrook Close, Dunstall Park, Wolverhampton, West Midlands WV6 0XA. e-mail: west-mids-recorder@westmidlandbirdclub.com

Bird Reports
THE BIRDS OF SMESTOW VALLEY AND DUNSTALL PARK (1988-), from Secretary, Smestow Valley Bird Group.

WEST MIDLAND BIRD REPORT (inc Staffs, Warks, Worcs and W Midlands) (1934-), from Barbara Oakley, 147 Worlds End, Quinton, Birmingham B32 1JX. e-mail: secretary@westmidlandbirdclub.com westmidlandbirdclub.com.

BTO Regional Representative
BIRMINGHAM & WEST MIDLANDS.
Steve Davies. 07882 891 726;
e-mail:stevendavies907@btinternet.com

Clubs
SMESTOW VALLEY BIRD GROUP. (1988; 44). Frank Dickson, 11 Bow Street, Bilston, Wolverhampton, WV14 7NB. 01902 493 733.

WEST MIDLAND BIRD CLUB. (1929; 2000). Barbara Oakley. e-mail: secretary@westmidlandbirdclub.com www.westmidlandbirdclub.com
Meetings: Check website for details of the different branches and their events.

WEST MIDLAND BIRD CLUB (BIRMINGHAM BRANCH). (1995; 800). Andy Mabbett.
e-mail: birmingham@westmidlandbirdclub.com www.westmidlandbirdclub.com/birmingham
Meetings: 7.30pm, usually last Tuesday (Oct-Apr), Birmingham Medical Institute, in Harborne Road, Edgbaston, near Five Ways.

WEST MIDLAND BIRD CLUB (SOLIHULL BRANCH). Raymond Brown, The Spinney, 63 Grange Road, Dorridge, Solihull B93 8QS. 01564 772 550;
e-mail: solihull@westmidlandbirdclub www.westmidlandbirdclub.com/solihull
Meetings: 7.30pm, Fridays (usually 1st of month), Guild House, Knowle, Solihull, West Midlands B93 0LN.

Ringing Groups
MERCIAN RG (Sutton Coldfield). Mr DJ Clifton. 59 Daisybank Crescent, Walsall, WS5 3BH. 01922 628 572.

RSPB Local Groups
BIRMINGHAM. (1975; 100). John Bailey, 52 Gresham Road, Hall Green, Birmingham, B28 0HY. 0121 777 4389; e-mail: jvbailey@btinternet.com www.rspb-birmingham.org.uk
Meetings: 7.30pm, 3rd Thursday of the month (Sep-Jun), Salvation Army Citadel, St Chads, Queensway, Birmingham.

COVENTRY & WARWICKSHIRE. (1969; 130). Ron Speddings. 01926 428 365;
e-mail: Ron@speddings.spacomputers.com www.rspb.org.uk/groups/coventryandwarwickshire
Meetings: 7.30pm, 4th Friday of the month, (Sep-May unless otherwise stated), Warwick Arts Centre And Baginton Village Hall.

SOLIHULL. (1983; 2600). John Roberts, 115 Dovehouse Lane, Solihull, West Midlands, B91 2EQ. 0121 707 3101; e-mail: johnbirder@care4free.net www.rspb.org.uk/groups/solihull
Meetings: 7.30pm, usually 2nd Tuesday of the month (Sep-Apr), Oliver Bird Hall, Church Hill Road, Solihull.

STOURBRIDGE. (1978; 150). David Ackland. 01384 293 090; e-mail: davidackland@blueyonder.co.uk www.rspb.org.uk/groups/stourbridge
Meetings: 2nd Wednesday of the month (Sep-May), Woollaston Suite, Stourbridge Town Hall, Crown Centre, Stourbridge, West Midlands, DY8 1YE.

SUTTON COLDFIELD. (1986; 250). Martin Fisher. 0121 308 4400; e-mail: martinjfisher@care4free.net www.rspb.org.uk/groups/suttoncoldfield
Meetings: 7.30pm, 1st Monday of the month, Bishop Vesey's Grammar School, Sutton Coldfield.

WALSALL. (1970). Mike Pittaway, 2 Kedleston Close, Bloxwich, Walsall, WS3 3TW. 01922 710568;
e-mail: chair@rspb-walsall.org.uk www.rspb-walsall.org.uk
Meetings: 7.30pm, 3rd Wednesday of the month, St Mary's School, Jesson Road, Walsall.

WOLVERHAMPTON. (1974; 110). Barry Proffitt. 07900 431 820;
e-mail: RSPBwolverhampton@hotmail.co.uk www.rspb.org.uk/groups/wolverhampton
Meetings: 7.30pm, 2nd Wednesday of the month (Sept-Apr), The Newman Centre, Haywood Drive, Tettenhall, Wolverhampton. Also monthly field-trips (Sep-Jun).

Wildlife Trust
THE WILDLIFE TRUST FOR BIRMINGHAM AND THE BLACK COUNTRY. (1980; 5,500). 28 Harborne Road, Edgbaston, Birmingham, B15 3AA. 0121 454 1199; (Fax)0121 454 6556; e-mail: info@bbcwildlife.org.uk www.bbcwildlife.org.uk

WILTSHIRE

Bird Atlas/Avifauna
Birds of Wiltshire by James Ferguson-Lees 2007, Wiltshire Ornithological Society

Bird Recorder
Rob Turner, 14 Ethendun, Bratton, Westbury, Wilts, BA13 4RX. 01380 830 862;
e-mail: robt14@btopenworld.com

ENGLAND

Bird Report
Published in Hobby (journal of the Wiltshire OS)
(1975-), from John Osborne, 4 Fairdown Avenue,
Westbury, Wiltshire BA13 3HS. 01373 864 598,

BTO Regional Representatives
NORTH. Bill Quantrill. 01225 866 245;
e-mail: william.quantrill@btinternet.com

SOUTH. Bill Quantrill. 01225 866 245;
e-mail: william.quantrill@btinternet.com

Clubs
SALISBURY & DISTRICT NATURAL HISTORY SOCIETY.
(1952; 146). Elisabeth Richmond, 15 Chantry Road,
Wilton, Salisbury, SP2 0LT. 01722 742 755; e-mail:
erichmond@madasafish.com.
Meetings: 7.30pm, 3rd Thursday of the month (Sept-
Apr), Lecture Hall, Salisbury Museum, Kings House,
The Close, Salisbury.

WILTSHIRE ORNITHOLOGICAL
SOCIETY. (1974; 450). Phil
Deacon, 12 Rawston Close,
Nythe, Swindon, Wilts SN3
3PW. 01793 528 930; e-mail:
phil.deacon@ntlworld.com
www.wiltshirebirds.co.uk
Meetings: See website for
details.

Ringing Group
COTSWOLD WATER PARK RG. John Wells, 25 Pipers
Grove, Highnam, Glos, GL2 8NJ.
e-mail: john.wells2@btinternet.com

WEST WILTSHIRE RG. Mr M.J. Hamzij, 13 Halfway
Close , Trowbridge, Wilts BA14 7HQ.
e-mail: m.hamzij@btinternet.com

RSPB Local Groups
NORTH WILTSHIRE. (1973; 115). Derek Lyford, 9
Devon Road, Swindon, SN2 1PQ. 01793 520997; e-
mail: derek.lyford@virgin.net
www.rspb.org.uk/groups/northwiltshire
Meetings: 7.30pm, 1st Tuesday of the month (Sep-
Jun), Even Swindon Community Centre, Jennings St,
Swindon SU 137 849.

SOUTH WILTSHIRE. (1986; 800). Tony Goddard,
Clovelly, Lower Road, Charlton All Saints, Salisbury,
SP5 4HQ. 01725 510309.
Meetings: 7.30pm, Tuesday evenings (monthly),
Salisbury Arts Centre, Salisbury.

Wetland Bird Survey Organiser
COTSWOLD WATER PARK. Gareth Harris, Keynes
Country Park, Spratsgate Lane, Shorncote, Glos GL7
6DF. e-mail: gareth.harris@waterpark.org

WILTSHIRE. Julian Rolls. 110 Beanacre, Nr Melksham,
Wilts, SN12 7PZ. 01225 790 495.

Wildlife Trust
WILTSHIRE WILDLIFE TRUST. (1962;
18,000). Elm Tree Court, Long
Street, Devizes, Wilts, SN10 1NJ.
01380 725 670; (Fax)01380 729 017;
e-mail: info@wiltshirewildlife.org
www.wiltshirewildlife.org

WORCESTERSHIRE

Bird Recorder
Brian Stretch, 13 Pitmaston Road, Worcester WR2
4HY. 01905 423 417;
e-mail: worcs-recorder@westmidlandbirdclub.com
www.westmidlandbirdclub.com

Bird Report See West Midlands.

BTO Regional Representative
G Harry Green MBE, Windy Ridge, Pershore Road,
Little Comberton, Pershore, Worcs, WR10 3EW. 01386
710 377; e-mail: harrygreen_worcs@yahoo.co.uk or
zen130501@zen.co.uk

Club
WEST MIDLAND BIRD CLUB (KIDDERMINSTER BRANCH).
Celia Barton, 28A Albert Street, Wall Heath,
Kingswinford, DY6 0NA. 01384 839 838;
e-mail: kidderminster@westmidlandbirdclub.com
Meetings: 7.30pm, 4th Wednesday of the month
(Sep-Apr), St Oswald's Church Centre, Broadwaters,
Kidderminster.

Ringing Group
WYCHAVON RG. J R Hodson, 15 High Green, Severn
Stoke, Worcester, WR8 9JS. 01905 754 919(day),
01905 371 333(eve);
e-mail: hodson77@btinternet.com

RSPB Local Group
WORCESTER & MALVERN. (1980; 300). Garth Lowe,
Sunnymead, Old Storridge, Alfrick, Worcester WR6
5HT. 01886 833 362.
Meetings: 7.30pm, 2nd Wednesday in month (Sept-
May), Powick Village Hall.

Wetland Bird Survey Organiser
WORCESTERSHIRE. Andrew Warr. 14 Bromsgrove
Street, Barbourne, Worcester, WR3 8AR.
e-mail: andrew.warr3@btopenworld.com

Wildlife Hospital
VALE WILDLIFE RESCUE (WILDLIFE HOSPITAL &
REHABILITATION CENTRE). Any staff member, Station
Road, Beckford, Tewkesbury, Glos GL20 7AN. 01386
882 288; (Fax)01386 882 299;
e-mail: info@vwr.org.uk www.vwr.org.uk
All wild birds. Intensive care. Registered charity.
Veterinary support.

Wildlife Trust
WORCESTERSHIRE WILDLIFE TRUST. (1968; 9,000).
Lower Smite Farm, Smite Hill, Hindlip, Worcester,
WR3 8SZ. 01905 754 919; (Fax)01905 755 868;

ENGLAND

e-mail: enquiries@worcestershirewildlifetrust.co.uk
www.worcswildlifetrust.co.uk
Charity no. 256618.

YORKSHIRE

Bird Atlas/Avifauna
Atlas of Breeding Birds in the Leeds Area 1987-1991
by Richard Fuller et al (Leeds Birdwatchers' Club,
1994).

*The Birds of Halifax*by Nick Dawtrey (only 20 left), 14
Moorend Gardens, Pellon, Halifax, W Yorks, HX2 0SD.

The Birds of Yorkshire by John Mather (Croom Helm,
1986).

*An Atlas of the Breeding Birds of the Huddersfield
Area, 1987-1992.*by Brian Armitage et al (2000) - very
few copies left.

Birds of Barnsley by Nick Addey (Pub by author, 114
Everill Gate Lane, Broomhill, Barnsley S73 0YJ, 1998).

Birds of The Huddersfield Area by Paul and Betty Bray
(Huddersfield Birdwatchers Club 2008).

Breeding Bird Atlas for Barnsley in preparation.

Vice County Bird Recorders
VC61 (East Yorkshire) and Editor of *Yorkshire Bird
Report*. Geoff Dobbs, 1 Priory Road, Beverley, East
Yorkshire HU17 0EG. 07778 559 763;
e-mail: geoffdobbs@aol.com

VC62 (North Yorkshire East). Alistair Forsyth.
e-mail: birdsvc62@gmail.com

VC63 (South & West Yorkshire). Covering the
following groups - Barnsley Bird Study, Blacktoft
Sands RSPB, Doncaster and District OS, Rotherham
and District OS, Sheffield Bird Study and SK58 Birders.
John Wint, 9 Yew Tree Park, Whitley, Goole, DN14
0NZ. 01977 662 826;
e-mail: john.wint@tiscali.co.uk

VC64 (West Yorkshire)/Harrogate & Craven. Phil
Bone, 11 Dorrington Close, Pocklington, York, YO42
2GS. 0788 084 6905;
e-mail: p.bone@fera.gsi.gov.uk

VC65 (North Yorkshire West). Steve Worwood, 18
Coltsgate Hill, Ripon, HG4 2AB. 01765 602 518;
e-mail: steve@worwood.entadsl.com

Bird Reports
*BARNSLEY & DISTRICT BIRD STUDY GROUP REPORT
(1971-)*, from Waxwing Books, Sunnybank Cottage,
Ruston Parva, Driffield YO25 4DG.

*YORKSHIRE NATURALISTS' UNION: BIRD REPORT
(1940-)*. 2007 edition £12 including postage, from Jill
Warwick, Sharow Grange, Sharow, Ripon, HG4 5BN.
01765 602 832.

BRADFORD NATURALISTS' SOCIETY ANNUAL REPORT,
from Mr I Hogg, 23 St Matthews Road, Bankfoot,
Bradford, BD5 9AB. 01274 727 902.

*BRADFORD ORNITHOLOGICAL
GROUP REPORT
(1987-)* - after the 2008 issue,
this report will only be available
to paid-up members of the
group. From Jenny Barker,
3 Chapel Fold, Slack Lane,
Oakworth, Keighley, BD22 0RQ.

DONCASTER BIRD REPORT (1955-), from Mr M Roberts,
8 Sandbeck court, Rossington, Doncaster, DN11 0FN.
01302 326 265.

FILEY BRIGG BIRD REPORT (1976-), from Mr C Court,
12 Pinewood Avenue, Filey, YO14 9NS.

*HARROGATE & DISTRICT NATURALISTS' ORNITHOLOGY
REPORT (1996-)*, from Secretary.

HULL VALLEY WILDLIFE GROUP REPORT (2000-)
covering Hull Valley. from Roy Lyon, 670 Hotham
Road South, Hull, HU5 5LE. 07754 439 496.

BIRDS IN HUDDERSFIELD (1966-), from Mr M Wainman,
2 Bankfield Avenue, Taylor Hill, Huddersfield HD4
7QY.01484 305054;
e-mail: brian.armitage@ntlworld.com

*LEEDS BIRDWATCHERS' CLUB ANNUAL REPORT
(1949-)*, from Peter Murphy, 12 West End Lane,
Horsforth, Leeds LS18 5JP.

*BIRDS OF ROTHERHAM (1975-) - cost £2.50 inc
p&p, cheque payable to R.D.O.S.*, from Duncan
Bye, 12 Hall Grove, Rotherham S60 2BS. www.
rotherhambirds.co.uk (check website for current
publication details).

BIRDS IN THE SHEFFIELD AREA (1973-), from Margaret
Miller, 14 Worcester Close, Sheffield, S10 4JF. e-mail:
margmiller@talktalk.net
www.sbsg.org

THE BIRDS OF SK58 (1993-), from Secretary, SK58
Birders. e-mail: recorder@sk58birders.com
www.sk58birders.com

SORBY RECORD (1962-), from A.Brackenbury, 76
Crawford Road, Sheffield S8 9BU.
SPURN BIRD OBSERVATORY ANNUAL REPORT, from
Warden, see Reserves.

*SWILLINGTON INGS BIRD GROUP - ANNUAL REPORT
AND TWENTY YEAR REVIEW - 2008*, from Chris
Robinson, 43 Northfield Road, Sprotbrough,
Doncaster, DN5 8AY. 07534 271 254;
e-mail: GBFShrike@hotmail.com

WINTERSETT AREA ANNUAL REPORT (1988-), from
Steve Denny, 13 Rutland Drive, Crofton, Wakefield,
WF4 1SA. 01924 864 487.

**BTO Regional Representatives & Regional
Development Officers**
NORTH-EAST RR. Michael Carroll. 01751 476 550.

ENGLAND

NORTH-WEST RR. Gerald Light. 01756 753 720;
e-mail: gerald@uwlig.plus.com

SOUTH-EAST AND SOUTH-WEST RR. David Gains. 28
Raleigh Road, Sheffield, S2 3AZ.
E-mail: bto-rep@fireflyuk.net

EAST RR. Position vacant.

BRADFORD RR & RDO. Mike L Denton, 77 Hawthorne
Terrace, Crosland Moor, Huddersfield, HD4 5RP.
01484 646 990.

YORKSHIRE (HARROGATE) RR. Mike Brown, 48 Pannal
Ash Drive, Harrogate, N Yorks, HG2 0HU. 01423 567
382; e-mail: mike@thebrownsathome.plus.com

HULL RR. Martin Chadwick. 01482 653 391;
e-mail: martin_chadwick@hotmail.com

LEEDS & WAKEFIELD RR & RDO. Position vacant.

RICHMOND RR. John Edwards, 7 Church Garth, Great
Smeaton, Northallerton, N Yorks DL6 2HW. H:01609
881 476; e-mail: john@jhedwards.plus.com

YORK RR. Rob Chapman, 12 Moorland Road, York,
YO10 4HF. 01904 633 558;
e-mail: robert.chapman@tinyworld.co.uk

Clubs

BARNSLEY BIRD STUDY GROUP. (1970; 35). Graham
Speight, 58 Locke Avenue, Barnsley, South Yorkshire
S70 1QH. 01226 321 300.
Meetings: 7.15pm, 1st Thursday in the month (Nov-
Mar), RSPB Old Moor, Barnsley.

BRADFORD ORNITHOLOGICAL GROUP. (1987; 180).
Shaun Radcliffe, 8 Longwood Avenue, Bingley, W
Yorks, BD16 2RX. 01274 770 960;
www.bradfordbirding.org
Meetings: 1st Tuesday of the month - see website for
details.

CASTLEFORD & DISTRICT NATURALISTS' SOCIETY.
(1956; 16). Michael J Warrington, 31 Mount Avenue,
Hemsworth, Pontefract, W Yorks WF9 4QE. 01977 614
954; e-mail: michaelwarrington@talktalk.net
Meetings: 7.30pm, Tuesdays monthly (Sep-Mar),
Castleford College, Glasshoughton. Check website
for dates.

DONCASTER & DISTRICT
ORNITHOLOGICAL SOCIETY.
(1955; 40). Dave Ward,
Membership Secretary, 11
Newstead Road, Scawthorpe,
Doncaster DN5 9JS.
www.birdingdoncaster.org.uk
Meetings: 7.15pm, last
Thursday of the month (Jan-
May and Sep-Nov), Parklands
Sports and social club,
Wheatley Hall Road.

FILEY BRIGG ORNITHOLOGICAL GROUP. (1977; 100).
Sue Hull. 01723 515 042;
e-mail:secretary-at-fbog.co.uk
www.fbog.co.uk

HARROGATE & DISTRICT NATURALISTS' SOCIETY.
(1947; 350). Mrs Pat Cook, General Secretary, 1
Millbank Terrace, Shaw Mills, Harrogate, 01423 772
953; e-mail: gensec.hdns@talktalk.net
www.knaresborough.co.uk/hdns/index.html
Meetings: 7.45pm, St. Roberts Centre, 2/3 Robert
Street, Harrogate. The programme of meetings is sent
out to members in September.

HORNSEA BIRD CLUB. (1967; 35). John Eldret, 44
Rolston Road, Hornsea, HU18 1UH. 01964 532 854.
Meetings: 7.30pm, 3rd Friday of the month (Sep-
Mar), Hornsea Library. Monthly visits to local bird
reserves.

HUDDERSFIELD BIRDWATCHERS' CLUB. (1966; 80).
Chris Abell, 57 Butterley Lane, New Mill, Holmfirth,
HD9 7EZ. 01484 681 499;
e-mail: cdabell@gmail.com
www.huddersfieldbirdwatchersclub.org.uk
Meetings: 7.30pm, Tuesday's fortnightly (Sep-May),
Children's Library (section), Huddersfield Library and
Art Gallery, Princess Alexandra Walk, Huddersfield.

HULL VALLEY WILDLIFE GROUP. (1997; 175). The
Secretary, 29 Beech View, Cranswick, East Yorkshire
YO25 9QQ. 01377 270 957.
www.hullvalleywildlifegroup.org.uk

LEEDS BIRDWATCHERS' CLUB. (1949; 60). Peter
Murphy, 12 West End lane, Horsforth, Leeds, LS18
5JP. 0113 293 0188;
e-mail: pandbmurphy@ntlworld.com
Meetings: 7.15pm Monday fortnightly, Quaker
Meeting House, Woodhouse Lane, Leeds.

ROTHERHAM & DISTRICT ORNITHOLOGICAL SOCIETY.
(1974; 80). Malcolm Taylor, 18 Maple Place,
Chapeltown, Sheffield, S35 1QW. 0114 246 1848;
e-mail: rdos@hotmail.co.uk
www.rotherhambirds.co.uk
Meetings: 7.30pm, 2nd Friday of the month, United
Reform church hall, Herringthorpe.

SCARBOROUGH BIRDERS. (1993; 21). R.N.Hopper
(Membership Secretary), 10A Ramshill Road,
Scarborough, N Yorkshire YO11 2QE. 01723 369 537.
www.scarboroughbirding.co.uk
Meetings: 3rd Thursday of the month (Sep-Nov) and
(Jan-Apr). Check website for details.

SHEFFIELD BIRD STUDY GROUP. (1972; 160). Richard
Dale, 109 Main Road, Wharncliffe Side, Sheffield, S35
0DP. e-mail: richarddale9@hotmail.com
www.sbsg.org
Meetings: 7.15pm, 2nd Wednesday of the month
(Sep-Jun), Lecture Theatre 5, Sheffield University
Arts Tower.

ENGLAND

SK58 BIRDERS. (1993; 66). Andy Hirst, 15 Hunters Drive, Dinnington, Sheffield, S25 2TG. 07947 068 125; e-mail: contact@skbirders.com
Chair: Mick Clay, 2 High St, S.Anston, Sheffield. 01909 566 000. www.sk58birders.com
Meetings: 7.30pm, last Wednesday of the month (except July and Aug), Upstairs Room, Loyal Trooper pub, South Anston.

SOUTH PEAK RAPTOR STUDY GROUP. (1998; 12). ME Taylor, 76 Hawksley Avenue, Newbold, Chesterfield, Derbys S40 4TL. 01246 277 749.

SORBY NHS (ORNITHOLOGICAL SECTION). (1918; 400). The Secretary, c/o 100 Bole Hill Lane, Sheffield S10 1SD, e-mail: ornithology@sorby.org.uk
www.sorby.org.uk

SWILLINGTON INGS BIRD GROUP. (1989; 83). Chris Robinson, 43 Northfield Road, Sprotbrough, Doncaster, DN5 8AY. 07534 271 254; e-mail: GBFShrike@hotmail.com
Meetings: 7.30pm, 1st Thursday of even months with informal social evenings 1st Thursday of odd months (please phone for details of venue).

WAKEFIELD NATURALISTS' SOCIETY. (1851; 35). Michael Warrington, 31 Mount Avenue, Hemsworth, Pontefract, W Yorks WF9 4QE. 01977 614 954; e-mail: michaelwarrington@talktalk.net
Meetings: 7.30pm, 2nd Tuesday of the month (Sep-Apr), Friends Meeting House, Thornhill Street, Wakefield.

YORK ORNITHOLOGICAL CLUB. (1967; 80). Linda Newton, 5 Fairfields Drive, Skelton, York YO30 1YP, 01904 471 446; e-mail: secretary@yorkbirding. org.uk
www.yorkbirding.org.uk
Meetings: 7.30pm, 1st Tuesday of the month, Friends' Meeting House, Friargate, York (see website).

YORKSHIRE NATURALISTS' UNION (Ornithological Section). (1875; 500). Jim Pewtress, 31 Piercy End, Kirbymoorside, York, YO62 6DQ. 01751 431 001; e-mail: trivialis@operamail.com

Ringing Groups

BARNSLEY RG. M C Wells, 715 Manchester Road, Stocksbridge, Sheffield, S36 1DQ. 0114 288 4211; e-mail: barnsleybsg.plus.com

SOUTH CLEVELAND RG. W Norman, 2 Station Cottages, Grosmont, Whitby, N Yorks YO22 5PB. 01947 895226; e-mail: wilfgros@lineone.net

DONCASTER RG. D Hazard, 41 Jossey Lane, Scawthorpe, Doncaster, S Yorks DN5 9DB. 01302 788 044; e-mail: dave.hazard@tiscali.co.uk

EAST DALES RG. P. Bone, 11 Dorrington Close, Pocklington, York, YO42 2GS.
E-mail: p.bone@fera.gsi.gov.uk

EAST YORKS RG. Peter J Dunn, 43 West Garth Gardens, Cayton, Scarborough, N Yorks YO11 3SF. 01723 583149; e-mail: pjd@fbog.co.uk

SORBY-BRECK RG. Geoff P Mawson, Moonpenny Farm, Farwater Lane, Dronfield, Sheffield S18 1RA. e-mail: moonpenny@talktalk.net

SPURN BIRD OBSERVATORY (ringing group and migration watchpoint). Paul Collins, Kew Villa, Seaside Road, Kilnsea, Hull HU12 0UB. 01964 650 479; e-mail: pcnfa@hotmail.com

WINTERSETT RG. P Smith, 16 Templar Street, Wakefield, W Yorks, WF1 5HB. 01924 375 082.

RSPB Local Groups

AIREDALE AND BRADFORD. (1972; 3,500 in catchment area). Ruth Porter.
e-mail: AbRSPB@blueyonder.co.uk
www.rspb.org.uk/groups/airedaleandbradford
Meetings: 7.30pm, monthly on Fridays, Room 3, Shipley Library.

CRAVEN & PENDLE. (1986; 300). Colin Straker. 01756 751 888;
e-mail: colin.straker@btinternet.com
www.cravenandpendlerspb.org
Meetings: 7.30pm 2nd Wednesday of the month (Sep-May), St Andrews Church Hall, Newmarket Street, Skipton.

DONCASTER. (1984; 100). Sue Clifton, West Lodge, Wadworth Hall Lane, Wadworth, Doncaster, DN11 9BH. Tel/fax 01302 854 956;
e-mail: sue.cl.@waitrose.com
www.rspb.org.uk/groups/doncaster
Meetings: 7.30pm, 2nd Wednesday of the month (Sept-May), Salvation Army Community Church, Lakeside.

EAST YORKSHIRE. (1986; 110). Trevor Malkin, 49 Taylors Field, Driffield, E Yorks, YO25 6FQ. 01377 257 325;
e-mail: EastyorksRSPB@yahoo.co.uk
www.rspb.org.uk/groups/eastyorkshire
Meetings: 7.30pm, North Bridlington Library, Martongate, Bridlington (check website for details).

HUDDERSFIELD & HALIFAX. (1981; 140). David Hemingway, 267 Long Lane, Dalton, Huddersfield, HD5 9SH. 01484 301920;
e-mail: d.hemingway@ntlworld.com
www.rspb.org.uk/groups/huddersfieldand halifax
Meetings: 7.30pm, Huddersfield Methodist Mission, 3-13 Lord Street, HUDDERSFIELD, HD1 1QA.

HULL & DISTRICT. (1983; 334). Betty Hilton. 01482 849 503; e-mail: betty_hilton@hotmail.com
Meetings: 7.30pm, Tuesdays (Sept-May), United Reformed Church, Southella Way, Kirkella, Hull. (£1.50 for Local Group Members and £2.00 for Non Members).

LEEDS. (1974; 450). Ian Willoughby.
e-mail: RSPBleeds@googlemail.com
www.rspb.org.uk/groups/leeds
Meetings: 7.30pm, 3rd Wednesday of the month (Sep-Apr), Lecture Theatre B, School of Mechanical Engineering, University of Leeds.

RICHMONDSHIRE & HAMBLE (2005). Carl Watts. 01748 812 392; e-mail: rhRSPB@pigeonpost.plus.com
www.communigate.co.uk/ne/rhrspb
Meetings: Check website.

SHEFFIELD. (1981; 500). Malcolm Dyke, Flat 5, 648 Abbeydale Road, Sheffield, S7 2BB. 07947 605.959; www.rspb-sheffield.org.uk
Meetings: 7.30pm 1st Thursday of the month (Sept-May), Central United Reformed Church, Norfolk St, Sheffield.

WAKEFIELD. (1987; 150). Duncan Stokoe, 12 New Road, Horbury, Wakefield, West Yorkshire WF4 5LR.
e-mail: duncanstokoe@talktalk.net
www.rspb.org.uk/groups/wakefield
Meetings: 7.30pm, 4th Thursday of the month (Sep-Apr), Ossett War Memorial Community Centre, Prospect Road, Ossett, WF5 8AN.

WHITBY. (1977; 120). Sec Maureen Osborne. 01947 605 141; e-mail: mfogso@yahoo.co.uk
www.rspb.org.uk/groups/whitby
Meetings: 7.15pm, 2nd Wednesday of the month, St John Ambulance Hall, St Hilda's Terrace, Whitby.

YORK. (1973; 600). Chris Lloyd, 7 School Lane, Upper Poppleton, York YO26 6JS. 01904 794 865;
e-mail: rspb.calyork@btinternet.com
www.yorkrspb.org.uk

Meetings: 7.30pm, Tues, Wed or Thurs, Temple Hall, York St John College, Lord Mayors Walk, York.

Wetland Bird Survey Organiser
EAST YORKSHIRE AND SCARBOROUGH (EXCL. HUMBER). Shirley Pashby. 10 Ambrey Close, Hunmanby, Filey, North Yorks YO14 0LZ.

HARROGATE AND YORKSHIRE DALES. William Haines. 3 Rosemount Road, London W13 0HJ. 07870 8289788; e-mail: bill.haines@tiscali.co.uk

LEEDS AREA. Paul Morris.
e-mail: pmorris@wyjs.org.uk

Wildlife Hospital
ANIMAL HOUSE WILDLIFE WELFARE. Mrs C Buckroyd, 14 Victoria Street, Scarborough, YO12 7SS. 01723 371 256 (please leave a message on the answer machine and callers will be contacted as soon as possible); e-mail: cynthiabuckroyd@talktalk.net or cindybuckroyd@hotmail.com.
All species of wild birds. Oiled birds given treatment before forwarding to cleaning stations. Incubators, hospital cages, heat pads, release sites. Birds ringed before release. Prior telephone call requested. Collection if required. Veterinary support. Charity shop at 127 Victoria Road.

Wildlife Trusts
SHEFFIELD WILDLIFE TRUST. (1985; 4,450). 37 Stafford Road, Sheffield, S2 2SF. 0114 263 3335; (Fax)0114 263 4345; e-mail: mail@wildsheffield.com
www.wildsheffield.com

YORKSHIRE WILDLIFE TRUST. (1946; 21,500). 1 St George's Place,Tadcaster Road, York YO24 1GN. 01904 659 570; (Fax)01904 613 467; e-mail: info@ywt.org.uk
www.ywt.org.uk

SCOTLAND

Bird Report
SCOTTISH BIRD REPORT from The SOC, The Scottish
Birdwatching Resource Centre, Waterston House,
Aberlady, East Lothian, EH32 0PY.

Club
See Scottish Ornithologists' Club in National
Directory.

ANGUS & DUNDEE

Bird Recorder
ANGUS & DUNDEE. John Ogilvie, 23 Church Street,
Brechin, Angus DD9 6HB. 01356 662 672;
e-mail: johncogilvie@aol.com

Bird Report
ANGUS & DUNDEE BIRD REPORT (1974-), from The
Secretary, Angus & Dundee Bird Club.

BTO Regional Representative
ANGUS RR. Ken Slater, Braedownie Farmhouse, Glen
Clova, Kirriemuir, Angus, DD8 4RD. 01575 550 233;
e-mail: rec_glendoll@angus.sol.co.uk

Clubs
ANGUS & DUNDEE BIRD
CLUB. (1997; 220). Bob
McCurley, 22 Kinnordy
Terrace, Dundee,DD4 7NW.
01382 462 944; e-mail:
lunanbay2@btinternet.com
www.angusbirding.com
Meetings: 7.30pm,
Tuesdays, Montrose Basin
Wildlife Centre.

SOC TAYSIDE BRANCH. (145). Brian Boag, Birch Brae,
Knapp, Inchture, Perthshire PH14 9SW. 01828 686
669. www.the-soc.org.uk

Ringing Group
TAY RG. Ms S Millar, Edenvale Cottage, 1 Lydox
Cottages, Dairsie, Fife KY15 4RN.
e-mail: shirley@edenecology.co.uk

RSPB Members' Groups
DUNDEE. (1972; 110). Graham Smith, 01382 532 461;
e-mail: grahamnjen@hotmail.com
www.RSPB.org.uk/groups/dundee
Meetings: 7.30 pm, monthly on a Wednesday
(Sep-Mar), Methodist Church, 20, West Marketgait,
Dundee. Admission £1.00 for all, including
refreshments.

ARGYLL

Birds of Argyll (Argyll Bird Club 2007, £45 inc
postage), available from Bob Furness, The Cnoc,

Tarbert, Arrochar, Dunbartonshire G83 7DG. 01301
702 603.

Bird Recorder
ARGYLL. Paul Daw, Tigh-na-Tulloch, Tullochgorm,
Minard, Argyll PA32 8YQ. 01546 886 260; e-mail:
monedula@globalnet.co.uk

Bird Reports
ARGYLL BIRD REPORT (1984-), from Dr Bob Furness,
The Cnoc, Tarbet, Dumbartonshire G83 7DG. 01301
702 603; e-mail: r.furness@bio.gla.ac.uk

ISLE OF MULL BIRD REPORT (2004-), from Mr Alan
Spellman, Maridon, Lochdon, Isle of Mull, Argyll PA64
6AP. 01680 812 448. www.mullbirds.com

MACHRIHANISH SEABIRD OBSERVATORY REPORT
(1992-), from the Observatory.

BTO Regional Representatives
ARGYLL (MULL, COLL, TIREE AND MORVERN).
Sue Dewar, 01680 812 594;
e-mail: sue.dewar@btconnect.com

ARGYLL SOUTH, BUTE, GIGHA AND ARRAN.
Richard Allen, e-mail: r.allan13@btinternet.com

ISLAY, JURA, COLONSAY RR. John S Armitage, Airigh
Sgallaidh, Portnahaven, Isle of Islay, PA47 7SZ. 01496
860 396; e-mail: jsa@ornquest.plus.com
www.islaybirder.blogspot.com

Club
ARGYLL BIRD CLUB. (1983; 270). Sue Furness, The
Cnoc, Tarbet, Argyll, G83 7DG. 01301 702 603;
www.argyllbirdclub.org

ISLE OF MULL BIRD CLUB. (2001;160), Mrs Janet T
Hall, Membership Secretary, Druim Mhor, Craignure,
Isle of Mull, Argyll PA65
6AY.01680 812 441;
e-mail: oystercatcher@dee-emm.
co.uk
www.mullbirdclub.org.uk
Meetings: 7 for 7.30pm start, 3rd
Friday of the month (Oct-Apr),
Craignure Village Hall.

Ringing Group
TRESHNISH AUK RG. Robin Ward,
e-mail: robin.ward807@ntlworld.com

RSPB Members' Groups
HELENSBURGH. (1975; 62). Steve Chadwin, 01436
670 158.
Meetings: The Guide Halls, Lower John Street,
Helensburgh.

SCOTLAND

Wetland Bird Survey Organisers
ARGYLL MAINLAND. Paul Daw, Tigh-Na-Tullock, Minard, Inveraray, Argyll PA32 8YQ. 01546 886 260; e-mail: monedula@globalnet.co.uk

MULL. Paul Daw, Tigh-Na-Tullock, Minard, Inveraray, Argyll PA32 8YQ. 01546 886 260; e-mail: monedula@globalnet.co.uk

TIREE & COLL. John Bowler, e-mail: john.bowler@rspb.org.uk

Wildlife Hospital
WINGS OVER MULL. Richard and Sue Dewar, Auchnacroish House, Torosay, Craignure, Isle of Mull PA65 6AY. Tel/fax: 01680 812 594; email: dewars@wingsovermull.com www.wingsovermull.com

AYRSHIRE

Bird Recorder
AYRSHIRE. Fraser Simpson, 4 Inchmurrin Drive, Kilmarnock, Ayrshire KA3 2JD. e-mail: recorder@ayrshire-birding.org.uk

Bird Reports
AYRSHIRE BIRD REPORT (1976-), from The Recorder (see above) or Dr RG Vernon, 29 Knoll Park, Ayr KA7 4RH. e-mail: rgv_mcv@tiscali.co.uk

BTO Regional Representatives
AYRSHIRE RR. Brian Broadley, 01290 424 241; e-mail: brianbroadley@onegreendoor.com

Club
SOC AYRSHIRE. (1962; 154). Duncan Watt, Wildings Studio, 28 Greenbank, Dalry, Ayrshire KA24 5AY. 01294 832 361; www.ayrshire-birding.org.uk www.the-soc.org.uk
Meetings: 7.30pm, Tuesdays monthly, Monkton Community Church, Monkton by Prestwick.

RSPB Members' Groups
CENTRAL AYRSHIRE LOCAL GROUP. (1978; 85). Ronnie Coombes (Group Leader), 12 Johnstone Drive, Mossblown, Ayrshire KA6 5DP. 01292 521 522; e-mail: ronnie.coombes@tesco.net www.ayrshire-birding.org.uk
Meetings: 7.40pm, 3rd Monday of the month (Sep-Apr), Carnegie Library, Main Street, Ayr.

NORTH AYRSHIRE. (1976; 180). Duncan Watt, 28 Greenbank, Dalry, Ayrshire, KA24 5AY. 01294 832 361; e-mail: duncan@spectrus.co.uk www.narspb.org.uk
Meetings: 7.30pm, various Fridays (Aug-Apr), Argyll Centre, Donaldson Avenue, SALTCOATS, Ayrshire, KA21 5AG.

Wetland Bird Survey Organiser
AYRSHIRE. Mr David Grant, e-mail: david.grant@sac.ac.uk

ARRAN. Jim Cassels, Kilpatrick Kennels, Kilpatrick, Blackwaterfoot, Isle of Arran KA27 8EY. e-mail: james.cassels@virgin.net

Wildlife Hospital
HESSILHEAD WILDLIFE RESCUE CENTRE. Gay & Andy Christie, Gateside, Beith, Ayrshire KA15 1HT. 01505 502 415; e-mail: info@hessilhead.org.uk www.hessilhead.org.uk
All species. Releasing aviaries. Veterinary support. Visits only on open days please.

BORDERS

Bird Atlas/Avifauna
The Breeding Birds of South-east Scotland, a tetrad atlas 1988-1994 by R D Murray et al. (Scottish Ornithologists' Club, 1998).

Bird Recorder
Ray Murray, 4 Bellfield Crescent, Eddleston, Peebles, EH45 8RQ. 01721 730 677; e-mail: raymurray1@tiscali.co.uk

Bird Report
BORDERS BIRD REPORT (1979-), from Malcolm Ross, Westfield Cottage, Smailholm, Kelso TD5 7PN. 01573 460 699; e-mail: eliseandmalcolm@btinternet.com

BTO Regional Representative
RR. Graham Pyatt, The Schoolhouse, Manor, Peebles EH45 9JN. 01721 740 319; e-mail: d.g.pyatt@btinternet.com

Club
SOC BORDERS BRANCH. (100). Graham Pyatt, The Schoolhouse, Manor, Peebles EH45 9JN. 01721 740 319. www.the-soc.org.uk
Meetings: 7.30pm, 2nd Monday of the month, George & Abbotsford Hotel, Melrose.

Ringing Group
BORDERS RG. (1991; 10) Dr T W Dougall, 38 Leamington Terrace, Edinburgh EH10 4JL. (Office) 0131 344 2600.

RSPB Members' Group
BORDERS. (1995; 94). John Marshall, 01896 850 564; e-mail: n-jmarshall@tiscali.co.uk
Meetings: 7.30pm, 3rd Wednesday of the month, The Corn Exchange, Market Square, Melrose.

Wetland Bird Survey Organisers
FIFE (excluding estuaries). Allan Brown, 61 Watts Gardens, Cupar, Fife KY15 4UG; e-mail: swans@allanwbrown.co.uk

BORDERS. Andrew Bramhall, 2 Abbotsferry Road, Tweedbank, Galashiels, Scottish Borders TD1 3RX; e-mail: andrew@atbramhall.go-plus.net

GREY GOOSE COUNT ORGANISER for Fife, Lothians and Borders. Allan Brown, 61 Watts Gardens, Cupar, Fife KY15 4UG; e-mail: swans@allanwbrown.co.uk

SCOTLAND

CAITHNESS

Bird Recorders
CAITHNESS. Stan Laybourne, Old Schoolhouse, Harpsdale, Halkirk, Caithness KW12 6UN. 01847 841244; e-mail:stanlaybourne@talk21.com

Bird Reports
CAITHNESS BIRD REPORT (1983-97). Now incorporated into *The Highland Bird Report*, from Julian Smith, St John's, Brough, Dunnet, Caithness KW14 8YD; e-mail: designsmith@madasafish.com

BTO Regional Representative
CAITHNESS. D Omand, 9 Skiall, Shebster, Thurso, Caithness KW14 7YD. 01847 811 403; e-mail: achreamie@yahoo.co.uk

Clubs
SOC CAITHNESS BRANCH. (51). Stan Laybourne, Old Schoolhouse, Harpsdale, Halkirk, Caithness, KW12 6UN. 01847 841 244; www.the-soc.org.uk e-mail:stanlaybourne@talk21.com

CLYDE

Bird Atlas/Avifauna
A Guide to Birdwatching in the Clyde Area (2001) by Cliff Baister and Marin Osler (Scottish Ornithologists' Club, Clyde branch).

Clyde Breeding Bird Atlas (working title). In preparation.

Bird Recorder
CLYDE ISLANDS (ARRAN, BUTE & CUMBRAES). Bernard Zonfrillo, 28 Brodie Road, Glasgow G21 3SB. e-mail:b.zonfrillo@bio.gla.ac.uk

CLYDE. Iain P Gibson, 8 Kenmure View, Howwood, Johnstone, Renfrewshire, PA9 1DR. 01505 705 874; e-mail: iain.gibson@land.glasgow.gov.uk

Bird Reports
CLYDE BIRDS (1973-), from Valerie Wilson, 76 Laigh Road, Newton Mearns, Glasgow, G77 5EQ. e-mail: jim.val@btinternet.com

BTO Regional Representative
LANARK, RENFREW, DUMBARTON. John Knowler, 0141 584 9117; e-mail: john.knowler@ntlworld.com

Club
SOC CLYDE BRANCH. (300). Hayley Douglas, Top Right, 35 Church Street, Lochwinnoch PA12 4AE. 07715 634 079. www.the-soc.org.uk

Ringing Groups
CLYDE RG. (1979; 18) I Livingstone, 57 Strathview Road, Bellshill, Lanarkshire, ML4 2UY. 01698 749 844; e-mail: iainlivcrg@googlemail.com

RSPB Members' Groups
GLASGOW. (1972;141). Roger Adams. 0141 942 6920; e-mail: r.adams855@btinternet.com www.rspb.org.uk/groups/glasgow
Meetings: 7.30pm, generally 1st Wednesday of the month (Sep-Apr), Woodside Halls, Clarendon Street, off Maryhill Road, GLASGOW, G20 7QD.

HAMILTON. (1976;90). Jim Lynch, 0141 583 1044; e-mail: birder45a@yahoo.co.uk www.baronshaugh.co.uk
Meetings: 7.30pm, 3rd Thursday of the month (Sept-May), Watersports Centre, Motherwell (next to Strathclyde Loch).

RENFREWSHIRE. (1986; 200). Iain Smeaton. e-mail: RenfrewRSPB@hotmail.co.uk www.rspb.org.uk/groups/renfrewshire
Meetings: 1st Friday of the month (Sep-Apr), The McMaster Centre, 2a Donaldson Drive, Renfrew.

Wetland Bird Survey Organisers
CLYDE ESTUARY. Valerie Wilson, 76 Laigh Road, Newton Mearns, Glasgow G77 5EQ. (H)0141 639 2516; e-mail: Jim.Val@btinternet.com

GLASGOW/RENFREWSHIRE/LANARKSHIRE/ DUNBARTONSHIRE. Valerie Wilson, 76 Laigh Road, Newton Mearns, Glasgow G77 5EQ. (H)0141 639 2516; e-mail: Jim.Val@btinternet.com

BUTE. Ian Leslie Hopkins, 2 Eden Place, 179 High Street, Rothesay, Isle of Bute PA20 9BS. 01700 504 042; e-mail: ian@hopkins0079.freeserve.co.uk

DUMFRIES & GALLOWAY

Bird Recorder
Paul Collin, Gairland, Old Edinburgh Road, Minnigaff, Newton Stewart, DG8 6PL. 01671 402 861; e-mail: pncollin@live.co.uk

Bird Report
DUMFRIES & GALLOWAY REGION BIRD REPORT (1985-), from Duncan Irving, 12 Great Eastern Drive, Glancaple, Dumfries, DG1 4QZ. e-mail: duncanirving@btinternet.com

BTO Regional Representatives
DUMFRIES RR. Edmund Fellowes, 01387 262 094; e-mail: edmundfellowes@aol.com

KIRKCUDBRIGHT RR and Atlas Co-ordinator. Andrew Bielinski, 41 Main Street, St Johns Town of Dalry, Castle Douglas, Kirkcudbright, DG7 3UP. 01644 430 418 (evening); e-mail: andrewb@bielinski.fsnet.co.uk

WIGTOWN RR. Geoff Sheppard, The Roddens, Leswalt, Stranraer, Wigtownshire DG9 0QR. 01776 870 685; e-mail: geoff.roddens@btinternet.com

SCOTLAND

Clubs

SOC DUMFRIES BRANCH. (1961; 105). Mrs Pat Abery, East Daylesford, Colvend, Dalbeattie, Dumfries DG5 4QA. 01556 630 483. www.the-soc.org.uk
Meetings: 7.30pm, 2nd Wednesday of the month (Sept-Apr), Cumberland St Day Centre.

SOC STEWARTRY BRANCH. (1976; 80). Miss Joan Howie, 60 Main Street, St Johns Town of Dalry, Castle Douglas, Kirkcudbrightshire, DG7 3UW. 01644 430 226 www.the-soc.org.uk
Meetings: 7.30pm, usually 2nd Thursday of the month (Sep-Apr), Kells School, New Galloway.

SOC WEST GALLOWAY BRANCH. (1975; 50). Geoff Sheppard, The Roddens, Leswalt, Stranraer, Wigtownshire, DG9 0QR. 01776 870 685;
e-mail: geoff.roddens@btinternet.com
www.the-soc.org.uk
Meetings: 7.30pm, 2nd Tuesday of the month (Oct-Mar), Stranraer Library.

Ringing Group

NORTH SOLWAY RG. Geoff Sheppard, The Roddens, Leswalt, Stranraer, Wigtownshire DG9 0QR. 01776 870 685; e-mail: geoff.roddens@btinternet.com

RSPB Members' Group

GALLOWAY. (1985; 150). Cynthia Douglas, Midpark, Balmaclellan, Castle Douglas, DG7 3PX. 01644 420 605; www.rspb.org.uk/groups/galloway
Meetings: 7.30pm 3rd Tuesday in the month, Castle Douglas High School.

Wetland Bird Survey Organisers

AUCHENCAIRN. Euan MacAlpine, Auchenshore, Auchencairn, Castle Douglas, Galloway DG7 1QZ . 01556 640 244; e-mail: js.eamm@sky.com

FLEET BAY. David Hawker. 01556 610 086;
e-mail: dheco@dsl.pipex.com

LOCH RYAN. Geoff Shepherd, The Roddens, Leswalt, Stranraer, Wigtonshire DG9 0QR. 01776 870 685;
e-mail: geoff.roddens@btinternet.com

ROUGH FIRTH. Judy Baxter, Saltflats Cottage, Rockcliffe, Dalbeattie, DG5 4QQ. 01556 630 262;
e-mail: Jbaxter@nts.org.uk

WIGTOWN. Paul Collin, Gairland, Old Edinburgh Road, Minnigaff, Newton Stewart, DG8 6PL. 01671 402 861; e-mail: pncollin@live.co.uk

DUMFRIES AND GALLOWAY (OTHER SITES). Andy Riches, 07792 142 446; e-mail: slioch69@aol.com

SOLWAY ESTUARY - NORTH. Andy Riches, 07792 142 446; e-mail: slioch69@aol.com

FIFE

Bird Atlas/Avifauna

The Fife Bird Atlas 2003 by Norman Elkins, Jim Reid, Allan Brown, Derek Robertson & Anne-Marie Smout.

Available from Allan W. Brown (FOAG), 61 Watts Gardens, Cupar, Fife KY15 4UG, Tel. 01334 656 804, email: swans@allanwbrown.co.uk

Bird Recorders

FIFE REGION INC OFFSHORE ISLANDS (NORTH FORTH). Rab Shand. e-mail: rabshand@blueyonder.co.uk

ISLE OF MAY BIRD OBSERVATORY. Iain English, 19 Nethan Gate, Hamilton, S Lanarks, ML3 8NH.
e-mail: i.english@talk21.com

Bird Reports

FIFE BIRD REPORT (1988-) (FIFE & KINROSS BR 1980-87), from Willie McBay, 41 Shamrock Street, Dunfermline, Fife, KY12 0JQ. 01383 723 464;
e-mail: wmcbay@aol.com

ISLE OF MAY BIRD OBSERVATORY REPORT (1985-), from Jonathan Osborne, The Shieling, Halcombe Crescent, Earlston, Berwickshire TD4 6DA.

BTO Regional Representative

FIFE & KINROSS RR. Norman Elkins, 18 Scotstarvit View, Cupar, Fife KY15 5DX. 01334 654 348;
e-mail: jandnelkins@btinternet.com

Clubs

FIFE BIRD CLUB. (1985; 250). Willie McBay, 41 Shamrock Street, Dunfermline, Fife KY12 0JQ.
01383 723 464;
www.fifebirdclub.org
Meetings: 7.30pm, (various evenings), Dean Park Hotel, Chapel Level, Kirkcaldy.

LOTHIANS AND FIFE SWAN & GOOSE STUDY GROUP. (1978) Allan & Lyndesay Brown, 61 Watts Gardens, Cupar, Fife, KY15 4UG.
e-mail: swans@allanwbrown.co.uk

SOC FIFE BRANCH. (1956;170). Robert Armstrong, Struan House, Old St Andrews Road, Guardbridge, Fife KY16 0UD. 01334 838 279. www.the-soc.org.uk
Meetings: 7.30pm, 2nd Wednesday of the month (Sep-Apr), St Andrews Town Hall.

Ringing Groups

ISLE OF MAY BIRD OBSERVATORY. David Grieve, 50 Main Street, Symington, Biggar, South Lanarkshire ML12 6LJ. 01899 309 176.

TAY RG. Ms S Millar, Edenvale Cottage, 1 Lydox Cottages, Dairsie, Fife, KY15 4RN.
e-mail: shirley@edenecology.co.uk

Wetland Bird Survey Organisers

FIFE (excluding estuaries). Allan Brown, 61 Watts Gardens, Cupar, Fife KY15 4UG;
e-mail: swans@allanwbrown.co.uk

FORTH ESTUARY (North). Alastair Inglis, 5 Crowhill Road, Dalgety Bay, Fife KY11 5LJ.
e-mail: aandjinglis@hotmail.com

SCOTLAND

EDEN ESTUARY. Norman Elkins, 18 Scotstarvit View, Cupar, Fife KY15 5DX. 01334 654 348; e-mail: jandnelkins@btinternet.com

GREY GOOSE COUNT ORGANISER. Allan Brown, 61 Watts Gardens, Cupar, Fife KY15 4UG; e-mail: swans@allanwbrown.co.uk

TAY ESTUARY. Norman Elkins, 18 Scotstarvit View, Cupar, Fife KY15 5DX. 01334 654 348; e-mail: jandnelkins@btinternet.com

Wildlife Hospital
SCOTTISH SPCA WILDLIFE REHABILITATION CENTRE. Middlebank Farm, Masterton Road, Dunfermline, Fife, KY11 8QN. 01383 412 520
All species. Open to visitors, groups and school parties. Illustrated talk on oiled bird cleaning and other aspects of wildlife rehabilitation available. Veterinary support.

FORTH

Bird Recorder
UPPER FORTH (Does not include parts of Stirling in Loch Lomondside/Clyde Basin). Chris Pendlebury, 3 Sinclair Street, Dunblane, FK5 0AH. 07798 711 134; e-mail: chris@upperforthbirds.co.uk

Bird Report
FORTH AREA BIRD REPORT (1975-) - enlarged report published annually in The Forth Naturalist and Historian, University of Stirling. From Dr Roy Sexton, 22 Alexander Drive, Bridge of Allan, Stirling FK9 4QB. 01786 833 409.

BTO Regional Representative
CENTRAL RR. Neil Bielby, 56 Ochiltree, Dunblane, Perthshire FK15 0DF. 01786 823 830; e-mail: n.bielby@sky.com

Club
SOC CENTRAL SCOTLAND BRANCH. (1968; 101). RL Gooch, The Red House, Dollarfield, Dollar, Clacks FK14 7LX. 01259 742 326; www.the-soc.org.uk
Meetings: 7.30pm, 1st Thursday of month (Sep-Apr), Smith Art Gallery and Museum, Dumbarton Road, Stirling.

RSPB Members' Group
FORTH VALLEY. (1995; 150). Tam Craig, 53 The Braes, Tullibody, Perthshire FK10 2TT. 01259 211 550; e-mail: tam_craig@btinternet.com
www.forthrspb.org.uk
Meetings: 7.30pm, 3rd Thursday of the month (Sept-Apr), Hill Park Centre, Stirling.

Wetland Bird Survey Organiser
CENTRAL (excl Forth Estuary). Neil Bielby, 56 Ochiltree, Dunblane, Perthshire FK15 0DF. 01786 823 830; e-mail: n.bielby@sky.com

FORTH ESTUARY (INNER). Michael Bell, 48 Newton Crescent, Dunblane, Perthshire FK15 0DZ. 01786

73171; e-mail: mvbell34@tiscali.co.uk

HIGHLAND

Bird Atlas/Avifauna
The Birds of Sutherland by Alan Vittery (Colin Baxter Photography Ltd,1997).

Birds of Skye by Andrew Currie. In preparation.

Bird Recorders
ROSS-SHIRE, INVERNESS-SHIRE, SUTHERLAND. Alastair McNee, Liathach, 4 Balnafettack Place, Inverness IV3 8TQ. 01463 220 493; (M)07763 927 814; e-mail: aj.mcnee@care4free.net

Bird Reports
HIGHLAND BIRD REPORT (1991-), from The Recorder. 2007 edition £8, 2009 £9.50 including p&p.

BTO Regional Representatives & Regional Development Officer
INVERNESS & SPEYSIDE RR & RDO. Hugh Insley, 1 Drummond Place, Inverness, IV2 4JT. 01463 230 652; e-mail: hugh.insley@btinternet.com

RUM, EIGG, CANNA & MUCK RR & RDO. Bob Swann, 14 St Vincent Road, Tain, Ross-shire IV19 1JR. 01862 894 329; e-mail: robert.swann@homecall.co.uk

ROSS-SHIRE RR. Simon Cohen, e-mail: saraandsimon@hotmail.com

SUTHERLAND. Position vacant.

SKYE. Bob McMillan, 01471 866 305; e-mail: bob@skye-birds.com

Clubs
EAST SUTHERLAND BIRD GROUP. (1976; 100). Tony Mainwood, 13 Ben Bhraggie Drive, Golspie, Sutherland KW10 6SX. 01408 633 247; e-mail: tony.mainwood@btinternet.com
Meetings: 7.30pm, Last Monday of the month (Oct, Nov, Jan, feb, Mar), Golspie Community Centre.

SOC HIGHLAND BRANCH. (1955; 151). Ann Sime, Drumrunie House, Myrtlefield Lane, Westhill, Inverness IV2 5UE. 01463 790 249
www.the-soc.org.uk
Meetings: 7.45pm, 1st Tuesday of the month (Sep-Mar), Culloden Library.

Ringing Groups
HIGHLAND RG. Bob Swann, 14 St Vincent Road, Tain, Ross-shire, IV19 1JR.
e-mail: robert.swann@homecall.co.uk

RSPB Local Group
HIGHLAND. (1987; 214). Doreen Manson, Muirton Lodge, Urray, Muir of Ord, Ross-shire IV6. 01997 433 283; e-mail: john@jmanson.wanadoo.co.uk
www.rspb.org.uk/groups/highland

289

Meetings: 7.30pm, last Thursday of the month (Sep-Apr), Kingsmill Hotel, Culcabock Road, Inverness.

Wetland Bird Survey Organisers
BADENOCH AND STRATHSPEY. Keith Duncan, Scottish Natural Heritage, Achantoul, Aviemore, Inverness-Shire PH22 1QD. 01479 810 477; e-mail: keith.duncan@snh.gov.uk

LOCHABER. John Dye. e-mail: john.dye@virgin.net

LOSSIE ESTUARY. Bob Proctor, 78 Marleon Field, Silvercrest, Bishopmill, Elgin IV30 4GE. 07976 456 657; e-mail: bobandlouise@proctor8246.fsnet.co.uk

SKYE & LOCHALSH. Bob McMillan, 11 Elgol, Nr Broadford, Isle of Skye IV49 9BL. 01471 866 305; e-mail: bob@skye-birds.com

LOTHIAN

Bird Atlas/Avifauna
The Breeding Birds of South-east Scotland, a tetrad atlas 1988-1994 by R D Murray et al. (Scottish Ornithologists' Club, 1998).

Bird Recorder
David J Kelly, 01875 6140 72; e-mail: dj_kelly@btinternet.com

Bird Reports
LOTHIAN BIRD REPORT (1979-), from the Lothian SOC Branch Secretary.

BTO Regional Representative
RR. Alan Heavisides, 9 Addiston Crescent, Balerno, Edinburgh, EH14 7DB. 0131 449 3816; e-mail: a.heavisides@napier.ac.uk

Clubs
EDINBURGH NATURAL HISTORY SOCIETY. (1869; 200). Mrs Joan McNaughton, 14 Relugas Road, Edinburgh EH9 2ND. 0131 477 0270. www.edinburghnaturalhistorysoc iety.org.uk

LOTHIANS AND FIFE MUTE SWAN STUDY GROUP. (1978; 12) Allan & Lyndesay Brown, 61 Watts Gardens, Cupar, Fife, KY15 4UG. e-mail: swans@allanwbrown.co.uk

LOTHIAN SOC. (1936; 450). Doreen and James Main; e-mail: doreen.main@yahoo.com www.the-soc.org.uk
Meetings: 7.30pm, 2nd Tuesday (Sep-Dec and Jan-Apr), Lounge 2, Meadowbank Sports Stadium.

Ringing Group
LOTHIAN RG. Mr M Cubitt, 12 Burgh Mills Lane, Linlithgow,West Lothian EH49 7TA.

RSPB Members' Group
EDINBURGH. (1974;480). Mark Stephen, 25 Newcroft Drive, Glasgow G44 5RT. 07796 538 837;

e-mail: markbirder@googlemail.com
www.rspb.org.uk/groups/edinburgh/
Meetings: 7.30pm, 3rd Tuesday or Wednesday of the month (Sep-Apr), Napier University, Craiglockhart Campus, Edinburgh.

Wetland Bird Survey Organisers
FORTH ESTUARY (Outer South). Duncan Priddle, 19c High Street, Haddington, East Lothian EH41 3ES. 01620 827 459; e-mail: dpriddle@eastlothian.gov.uk

GREY GOOSE COUNT ORGANISER for Fife, Lothians and Borders. Allan Brown, 61 Watts Gardens, Cupar, Fife KY15 4UG; e-mail: swans@allanwbrown.co.uk

LOTHIAN (excl estuaries). Joan Wilcox, 18 Howdenhall Gardens, Edinburgh, Midlothian EH16 6UN. (H)0131 664 8 893; e-mail: webs@bto.org

TYNINGHAME ESTUARY. R Anderson, John Muir Country Park, Town House, Dunbar, East Lothian EH42 1ER. (W)01368 863 886; e-mail: randerson@eastlothian.gov.uk

MORAY & NAIRN

Bird Atlas/Avifauna *The Birds of Moray and Nairn* by Martin Cook (Mercat Press), 1992.

Bird Recorder
NAIRN. Martin J H Cook, Rowanbrae, Clochan, Buckie, Banffshire, AB56 5EQ. 01542 850 296; e-mail: martin.cook99@btinternet.com

MORAY. Martin J H Cook, Rowanbrae, Clochan, Buckie, Banffshire, AB56 5EQ. 01542 850 296; e-mail: martin.cook99@btinternet.com

Bird Reports
BIRDS IN MORAY AND NAIRN (1999-), from the Moray Recorder, 01542 850 296; e-mail: martin.cook99@btinternet.com

MORAY & NAIRN BIRD REPORT (1985-1998), from the Moray Recorder, 01542 850 296; e-mail: martin.cook99@btinternet.com

BTO Regional Representatives
NAIRN RR. Bob Proctor, 78 Marleon Field, Elgin, Moray, IV30 4GE. e-mail: bobandlouise@proctor8246.fsnet.co.uk

MORAY RR. Bob Proctor, 78 Marleon Field, Elgin, Moray, IV30 4GE. e-mail: bobandlouise@proctor8246.fsnet.co.uk

Wetland Bird Survey Organisers
LOSSIE ESTUARY. Bob Proctor, 78 Marleon Field, Silvercrest, Bishopmill, Elgin, IV30 4GE; e-mail: bobandlouise@proctor8246.fsnet.co.uk

MORAY & NAIRN (Inland). David Law, Hollybrae, South Darkland, Elgin, Moray IV30 8NT.

SCOTLAND

MORAY BASIN COAST. Bob Swann, 14 St Vincent Road, Tain , Ross-Shire IV19 1JR. 01862 894 329; e-mail: robert.swann@homecall.co.uk

NORTH-EAST SCOTLAND

Bird Atlas/Avifauna
The Birds of North East Scotland by S T Buckland, M V Bell & N Picozzi (North East Scotland Bird Club, 1990).

Bird Recorder
NORTH-EAST SCOTLAND. Hywel Maggs, 4 Merlin Terrace, Newburgh, Ellon, Aberdeenshire AB41 6FA.01358 788 106; e-mail: hywelmaggs@hotmail.com

Bird Reports
NORTH-EAST SCOTLAND BIRD REPORT (1974-), from Dave Gill, Drakemyre Croft, Cairnorrie, Methlick, Aberdeenshire AB41 7JN. 01651 806 252; e-mail: david@gilldavid1.orangehome.co.uk

NORTH SEA BIRD CLUB ANNUAL REPORT (1979-), from Andrew Thorpe, Ocean Laboratory and Centre for Ecology, Aberdeen University, Newburgh, Ellon, Aberdeenshire AB41 6AA. 01224 274 428; e-mail: nsbc@abdn.ac.uk

BTO Regional Representatives
ABERDEEN. Paul Doyle, 01358 751 365; e-mail: paul@albaecology.co.uk

KINCARDINE & DEESIDE. Graham Cooper, Westbank, Beltie Road, Torphins, Banchory, Aberdeen, AB31 4JT. 01339 882 706; e-mail: grm.cooper@btinternet.com

Clubs
SOC GRAMPIAN BRANCH. (1956; 110). Graham Cooper, Westbank, Beltie Road, Torphins, Banchory, Aberdeen, AB31 4JT. 01339 882 706; e-mail: grm.cooper@btinternet.com
www.the-soc.org.uk
Meetings: 7.30pm, usually 1st Monday of the month (Sep-Apr), Sportsmans's Club, 11 Queens Road, Aberdeen.

Ringing Groups
ABERDEEN UNIVERSITY RG. Andrew Thorpe, Ocean Laboratory and Centre for Ecology, Aberdeen University, Newburgh, Ellon, Aberdeenshire, AB41 6AA. 01224 274 428; e-mail: nsbc@abdn.ac.uk

GRAMPIAN RG. R Duncan, 86 Broadfold Drive, Bridge of Don, Aberdeen, AB23 8PP.
e-mail: Raymond@waxwing.fsnet.co.uk

RSPB Members' Group
ABERDEEN. (1975; 210). Rodney Payne, 2 Arbuthnott Court, Stonehaven,AB39 2GW. 01569 763 742; e-mail: rodney_payne@btopenworld.com
www.rspb.org.uk/groups/aberdeen.
Meetings: 7.30pm, monthly in the winter, Lecture Theatre, Zoology Dept, Tillydrone Av, Aberdeen. Two

birding trips monthly throughout the year.

Wildlife Hospital
GRAMPIAN WILDLIFE REHABILITATION TRUST. 40 High Street, New Deer, Turriff, Aberdeenshire, AB53 6SX. 01771 644 489; (M)07803 235 383; e-mail: laurence.brain@btconnect.com
Veterinary surgeon. Access to full practice facilities. Will care for all species of birds.

ORKNEY

Bird Atlas/Avifauna
The Birds of Orkney by CJ Booth et al (The Orkney Press, 1984).

Bird Recorder
EJ Williams, Fairholm, Finstown, Orkney, KW17 2EQ. e-mail: jim@geniefea.freeserve.co.uk

Bird Report
ORKNEY BIRD REPORT (inc North Ronaldsay Bird Report) (1974-), from EJ Williams, Fairholm, Finstown, Orkney, KW17 2EQ. e-mail: jim@geniefea.freeserve.co.uk

BTO Regional Representative
Colin Corse, Garrisdale, Lynn Park, Kirkwall, Orkney, KW15 1SL. 01856 874 484; e-mail: ccorse@aol.com

Club
SOC ORKNEY BRANCH. (1993; 15). Colin Corse, Garrisdale, Lynn Park, Kirkwall, Orkney, KW15 1SL. H:01856 874 484; e-mail: ccorse@aol.com
www.the-soc.org.uk

Ringing Groups
NORTH RONALDSAY BIRD OBSERVATORY. Ms A E Duncan, Twingness, North Ronaldsay, Orkney, KW17 2BE. e-mail: alison@nrbo.prestel.co.uk
www.nrbo.co.uk

ORKNEY RG. Colin Corse, Garrisdale, Lynn Park, Kirkwall, Orkney, KW15 1SL. H:01856 874 484; e-mail: ccorse@aol.com

SULE SKERRY RG. Dave Budworth, 121 Wood Lane, Newhall, Swadlincote, Derbys, DE11 0LX. 01283 215 188.

RSPB Members' Group
ORKNEY. (1985; 300 in catchment area). Mrs Pauline Wilson, Sunny Bank, Deerness, Orkney KW17 2QQ. 01856 741 382; e-mail: p.wilson410@btinternet.com
Meetings: Meetings advertised in newsletter and local press, held at St Magnus Centre, Kirkwall.

Wetland Bird Survey Organiser
ORKNEY. Eric Meek, Smyril, Stenness, Stromness, Orkney KW16 3JX. 01856 850 176; e-mail: eric.meek@smyril.fsnet.co.uk.

OUTER HEBRIDES

SCOTLAND

Bird Recorder
OUTER HEBRIDES AND WESTERN ISLES. Brian Rabbitts, 6 Carinish, Isle of North Uist HS6 5HL. 01876 580 328; e-mail: rabbitts@hebrides.net

Bird Report
OUTER HEBRIDES BIRD REPORT (1989-), from The Recorder, 6 Carinish, Isle of North Uist HS6 5HL. 01876 580 328; e-mail: rabbitts@hebrides.net

BTO Regional Representative
BENBECULA & THE UISTS. Position vacant.

LEWIS & HARRIS RR. Chris Reynolds, 11 Reef, Isle of Lewis, HS2 9HU. 01851 672 376; e-mail: cmreynolds@btinternet.com

Ringing Group
SHIANTS AUK RG. David Steventon, Welland House, 207 Hurdsfield Road, Macclesfield, Cheshire, SK10 2PX. 01625 421 936. Group Secretary, Jim Lennon, The Dovecote, Main Street, Fintham, Newark NG23 5LA. 01636 525 963.

Wetland Bird Survey Organiser
UISTS AND BENBECULA. Brian Rabbitts, 6 Carinish, Isle of North Uist HS6 5HL. 01876 580 328; e-mail: rabbitts@hebrides.net

ISLAY, JURA AND COLONSAY. John Armitage, Airigh Sgallaidh, Portnahaven, Isle of Islay PA47 7SZ. 01496 860 396; e-mail: jsa@ornquest.plus.com
www.islaybirder.blogspot.com/

PERTH & KINROSS

Bird Recorder
PERTH & KINROSS. Ron Youngman, Blairchroisk Cottage, Ballinluig, Pitlochry, Perthshire, PH9 0NE. 01796 482 324; e-mail: blairchroisk@aol.com

Bird Report
PERTH & KINROSS BIRD REPORT (1974-), from the Recorder.

BTO Regional Representative
PERTHSHIRE RR. Richard Paul. 01882 632 212; e-mail: richard@rannoch.biz
www.perthshire-birds.org.uk

Clubs
PERTHSHIRE SOCIETY OF NATURAL SCIENCE (Ornithological Section). (1964; 29). Miss Esther Taylor, 23 Verena Terrace, Perth PH2 0BZ. 01738 621 986; www.psns.org.uk
Meetings: 7.30pm, Wednesdays monthly (Oct-Mar), Perth Museum. Summer outings.

Wetland Bird Survey Organiser
LOCH LEVEN. Jeremy Squire, 93 South Street, Milnathort, Kinross, KY13 9XB. e-mail: jeremy.squire@snh.gov.uk

PERTHSHIRE. Ron Youngman, Blairchroisk Cottage,

Ballinluig, Pitlochry, Perthshire PH9 0NE. e-mail: blairchroisk@aol.com

TAY ESTUARY. Norman Elkins, 18 Scotstarvit View, Cupar, Fife KY15 5DX. 01334 654 348; e-mail: jandnelkins@rapidial.co.uk

SHETLAND

Bird Recorders
FAIR ISLE. Deryk Shaw, Bird Observatory, Fair Isle, Shetland, ZE2 9JU. e-mail: fairisle.birdobs@zetnet.co.uk

SHETLAND. Mark Chapman, 55 Leaside, firth, Mossbank, Shetland ZE2 9TF. 01806 242 401; e-mail: msc.l@btinternet.com

Bird Reports
FAIR ISLE BIRD OBSERVATORY REPORT (1949-), from Scottish Ornithologists' Club, 21 Regent Terrace, Edinburgh, EH7 5BT. 0131 556 6042

SHETLAND BIRD REPORT (1969-) no pre-1973 available. From Russ Haywood, Lamnaberg, Wester Quarff, Shetland ZE2 9EZ. e-mail: haywood712@btinternet.com

BTO Regional Representative
Dave Okill, Heilinabretta, Cauldhame, Trondra, Shetland, ZE1 0XL. 01595 880 450.

Club
SHETLAND BIRD CLUB. (1973; 200). Russ Haywood, Lamnaberg, Wester Quarff, Shetland ZE2 9EZ. 01950 477 471;
e-mail:

haywood712@btinternet.com
www.nature-shetland.co.uk

Ringing Groups
FAIR ISLE BIRD OBSERVATORY. Deryk Shaw, Bird Observatory, fair Isle, Shetland, ZE2 9JU. e-mail: fairisle.birdobs@zetnet.co.uk

SHETLAND RG. Dave Okill, Heilinabretta, Cauldhame, Trondra, Shetland, ZE1 0XL. H:01595 880450; W:01595 696926.

Wetland Bird Survey Organiser
Paul Harvey, Shetland Biological Records Centre, Shetland Amenity Trust, 22-24 North Road, Lerwick, Shetland, ZE1 3NG. (Day)01595 694 688; e-mail: shetamenity.trust@zetnet.co.uk

WALES

Bird Report
See Welsh Ornithological Society in National Directory.

BTO Honorary Wales Officer
BTO WALES OFFICER. John Lloyd, Cynghordy Hall, Cynghordy, Llandovery, Carms SA20 OLN.
e-mail: the_lloyds@dsl.pipex.com

Club
See Welsh Ornithological Society in National Directory.

EASTERN WALES

Bird Atlas/Avifauna
Birds of Radnorshire. In preparation, due spring 2005.

The Gwent Atlas of Breeding Birds by Tyler, Lewis, Venables & Walton (Gwent Ornithological Society, 1987).

Bird Recorders
BRECONSHIRE. Andrew King, Heddfan, Pennorth, Brecon, Powys LD3 7EX. 01874 658 351;
e-mail: andrew.king53@virgin.net

GWENT. Chris Jones.
e-mail: countyrecorder@gwentbirds.org.uk

MONTGOMERYSHIRE. Brayton Holt, Scops Cottage, Pentrebeirdd, Welshpool, Powys SY21 9DL. 01938 500 266; e-mail: brayton.wanda@virgin.net

RADNORSHIRE, Pete Jennings, Penbont House, Elan Valley, Rhayader, Powys LD6 5HS. (H)01597 811 522; (W)01597 810 880;
e-mail: petejelanvalley@hotmail.com

Bird Reports
BRECONSHIRE BIRDS (1962-), from Brecknock Wildlife Trust.

GWENT BIRD REPORT (1964-), from Jerry Lewis, Y Bwthyn Gwyn, Coldbrook, Abergavenny, Monmouthshire NP7 9TD. (H)01873 855 091; (W)01633 644 856

MONTGOMERYSHIRE BIRD REPORT (1981-82-), from Montgomeryshire Wildlife Trust.

RADNOR BIRDS (1987/92-), from Radnorshire Recorder.

BTO Regional Representatives
BRECKNOCK RR. John Lloyd, Cynghordy Hall, Cynghordy, Llandovery, Carms, SA20 OLN.
e-mail: the_lloyds@dsl.pipex.com

GWENT RR. Jerry Lewis, Y Bwthyn Gwyn, Coldbrook, Abergavenny, Monmouthshire NP7 9TD. (H)01873 855 091; (W)01633 644 856

MONTGOMERY RR. Jane Kelsall, Holly Bank, Moel y Garth, Welshpool, Powys SY21 9JA. 01938 556 438; e-mail: janekelsall@phonecoop.coop

RADNORSHIRE RR. Brian Jones.
e-mail: jones.brn10@virgin.net

Clubs
THE GWENT ORNITHOLOGICAL SOCIETY. (1964; 420). T J Russell. 01600 716 266;
e-mail: secretary@GwentBirds. org.uk
www.gwentbirds.org.uk
Meetings: 7.30pm, alternate Saturdays (Sept-Apr), Goytre Village Hall.

MONTGOMERYSHIRE FIELD SOCIETY. (1946; 190). Maureen Preen, Ivy House, Deep Cutting, Pool Quay, Welshpool, Powys SY21 9LJ.
Tel: Mary Oliver, 01686 413 518.
Meetings: 2.30pm, 2nd Saturday of the month (Nov, Jan, Feb, Mar), Methodist Church Hall, Welshpool. Field trips (Apr-Oct) weekdays.

MONTGOMERYSHIRE WILDLIFE TRUST BIRD GROUP. (1997; 110). A M Puzey, Four Seasons, Arddleen, Llanymynech, Powys SY22 6RU. 01938 590 578.
Meetings: 7.30pm, 3rd Wednesday of the month (Jan-Mar) and (Sep-Dec), Welshpool Methodist Hall.

Ringing Groups
GOLDCLIFF RG. RM Clarke.
e-mail: chykembro2@aol.com.

LLANGORSE RG. (1987; 15). Jerry Lewis, Y Bwthyn Gwyn, Coldbrook, Abergavenny, Monmouthshire NP7 9TD. (H)01873 855 091; (W)01633 644 856.

Wetland Bird Survey Organisers
BRECONSHIRE. Andrew King, Heddfan, Pennorth, Brecon LD3 7EX. e-mail: andrew.king53@virgin.net

GWENT. Chris Jones, 22 Walnut Drive, Caerleon, Newport, Gwent NP18 3SB. 01633 232 806;
e-mail: chrisj22@talktalk.net

RADNORSHIRE. Peter Jennings, Pentbont House, Elan Valley, Rhayader, Powys LD6 5HS. (H)01597 811 522; (W)01597 810 880;
e-mail: petejelanvalley@hotmail.com

Wildlife Trusts
BRECKNOCK WILDLIFE TRUST. (1963; 650). Lion House, Bethel Square, Brecon, Powys LD3 7AY. 01874 625 708;
e-mail: enquiries@brecknockwildlifetrust.org.uk
www.brecknockwildlifetrust.org.uk

WALES

GWENT WILDLIFE TRUST. (1963; 7,800). Seddon House, Dingestow, Monmouth, NP25 4DY. 01600 740 358; (Fax)01600 740 299; e-mail: info@gwentwildlife.org www.gwentwildlife.org

MONTGOMERYSHIRE WILDLIFE TRUST. (1982; 1,000). Collot House, 20 Severn Street, Welshpool, Powys, SY21 7AD. 01938 555 654; (Fax)01938 556 161; e-mail: info@montwt.co.uk www.montwt.co.uk

RADNORSHIRE WILDLIFE TRUST. (1987; 878). Warwick House, High Street, Llandrindod Wells, Powys LD1 6AG. 01597 823 298; (Fax)01597 823 274; e-mail:info@rwtwales.org www.radnorshirewildlifetrust.org.uk

NORTH WALES

Bird Atlas/Avifauna
The Birds of Caernarfonshire by John Barnes (1998, from Lionel Pilling, 51 Brighton Close, Rhyl LL18 3HL).

Bird Recorders
ANGLESEY. Stephen Culley, 22 Cae Derwydd, Cemaes Bay, Anglesey, LL67 0LP. 01407 710 542; e-mail: SteCul10@aol.com

CAERNARFONSHIRE. John Barnes, Fach Goch, Waunfawr, Caernarfon, LL55 4YS. 01286 650 362.

DENBIGHSHIRE & FLINTSHIRE. Ian Spence, 43 Blackbrook, Sychdyn, Mold, Flintshire CH7 6LT. 01352 750 118; www.cbrg.org.uk e-mail: ianspence.cr@btinternet.com.

MEIRIONNYDD. Jim Dustow, Afallon, 7 Glan y Don, Rhiwbryfdir, Blaenau Ffestiniog, Gwynedd LL41 3LW. e-mail: Jim.Dustow@rspb.org.uk

Bird Reports
BARDSEY BIRD OBSERVATORY ANNUAL REPORT, from the Warden, see Reserves.

CAMBRIAN BIRD REPORT (sometime Gwynedd Bird Report) (1953-), from Stephen Culley, 22 Cae Derwydd, Cemaes Bay, Anglesey, LL67 0LP. 01407 710 542; e-mail: SteCul10@aol.com

NORTH-EAST WALES BIRD REPORT (2004-), formerly *Clwyd Bird Report (2002-2003)*, from Ian M Spence, Ty'r Fawnog, 43 Blackbrook, Sychdyn, Mold, Flintshire CH7 6LT. 01352 750 118; e-mail: ianspence.cr@btinternet.com

MEIRIONNYDD BIRD REPORT, published in *Cambrian Bird Report (above)*.

WREXHAM BIRDWATCHERS' SOCIETY ANNUAL REPORT (1982-), from The Secretary, Wrexham Birdwatchers' Society.

BTO Regional Representatives
ANGLESEY RR. Tony White. 01407 710 137; e-mail: wylfor@treg5360.freeserve.co.uk

CAERNARFON RR. Geoff Gibbs. 01248 681 936; e-mail: geoffkate.gibbs@care4free.net

CLWYD EAST RR. Dr Anne Brenchley, Ty'r Fawnog, 43 Black Brook, Sychdyn, Mold, Flints CH7 6LT. 01352 750 118; e-mail: anne.brenchley@btinternet.com

CLWYD WEST RR. Mel ab Owain, 31 Coed Bedw, Abergele, Conwy, LL22 7EH. 01745 826 528; e-mail: melabowain@btinternet.com

MEIRIONNYDD RR. David Anning. 01654 761 481; e-mail: davidanning@freeuk.com

Clubs
BANGOR BIRD GROUP. (1947; 100). Jane Prosser, 15 Victoria Street, Bangor, Gwynedd LL57 2HD. 01248 364 632.
Meetings: 7.30pm, Semester terms, Bramble Building, University of Bangor.

CAMBRIAN ORNITHOLOGICAL SOCIETY. (1952; 190) . Geoff Gibbs. 01248 681 936; e-mail: geoffkate.gibbs@care4free.net
Meetings: 7.30pm, 1st Friday of the month, Pensychnant Centre, Sychnant Pass.

CLWYD BIRD RECORDING GROUP (committee that produces the Bird Report). e-mail: julie.s.rogers@talktalk.net

CLWYD ORNITHOLOGICAL SOCIETY. (1956; 45). Ms J Irving, 45, Plas Uchaf Avenue, Prestatyn, LL19 9NR. 01745 854 132; e-mail: jacqui970irving@btinternet.com
Meetings: 7.30pm (Sep-Apr), Farmers Arms, Waen, St. Asaph.

DEE ESTUARY CONSERVATION GROUP. (1973; 25 grps). e-mail: decg@deeestuary.co.uk www.deeestuary.co.uk/decg.htm

DEESIDE NATURALISTS' SOCIETY. (1973; 1,000). Secretary, 21 Woodlands Court, Hawarden, Deeside, Flints CH5 3NB. 01244 537 440;  e-mail: deenaturalists@btinternet.com www.deesidenaturalists.org.uk

WREXHAM BIRDWATCHERS' SOCIETY. (1974; 90). Miss Marian Williams, 10 Lake View, Gresford, Wrexham, Clwyd LL12 8PU. 01978 854 633.
Meetings: 7.30pm, 1st Friday of the month (Sep-Apr), Gresford Memorial Hall, Gresford.

WALES

Ringing Groups
BARDSEY BIRD OBSERVATORY. Steven Stansfield, Bardsey Island, off Aberdaron, Pwllheli, Gwynedd LL53 8DE. 07855 264 151;
e-mail: warden@bbfo.org.uk

MERSEYSIDE RG. Bob Harris, 3 Mossleigh, Whixalll, Whitchurch, Shropshire SY13 2SA. (Work)0151 706 4311; e-mail: harris@liv.ac.uk

SCAN RG. Dr D. Moss.
e-mail: dorian@dorianmoss.com

RSPB Local Group
NORTH WALES. (1986; 80). Maureen Douglas, 57 Penrhyn Beach East, Penrhyn Bay, Llandudno, Conwy LL30 3RW. 01492 547 768.
Meetings: 7.30pm, 3rd Friday of the month (Sep-Apr), St Davids Church Hall, Penrhyn Bay, Llandudno, Gwynedd, LL30 3EJ.

Wetland Bird Survey Organisers
ANGLESEY (other sites). Ian Sims, RSPB Malltraeth Marsh, Tai'r Gors, Pentre Berw, Gaerwen, Anglesey, LL60 6LB.. e-mail: ian.sims@rspb.org.uk

CAERNARFONSHIRE (excl Traeth Lafan). Rhion Pritchard, Pant Afonig, Hafod Lane, Bangor, Gwynedd LL57 4BU. (H)01248 671 301;
e-mail: rhion678pritchard@btinternet.com

CLWYD (Coastal). Mr Peter Wellington, 4 Cheltenham Avenue, Rhyl, Clwyd LL18 4DN. (H)01745 3542 32; e-mail: webs@bto.org.

ARTRO/MAWDDACH/TRAETH BACH/DYSYNNI ESTUARY. Jim Dustow, Afallon, 7 Glan y Don, Rhiwbryfdir, Blaenau Ffestiniog, Gwynedd LL41 3LW. e-mail: Jim.Dustow@rspb.org.uk.

MEIRIONNYDD (other sites). Trefor Owen, Crochendy Twrog, Maentwrog, Blaenau Ffestiniog, LL41 3YU. (H)01766 590 302.

DEE ESTUARY. Colin Wells, Burton Point Farm, Station Road, Burton, Nr Neston, South Wirral CH64 5SB. 0151 336 7681.

FORYD BAY, Simon Hugheston-Roberts, Oakhurst, St David's Road, Caernarfon, LL55 1EL.
e-mail: sm.roberts@ccw.gov.uky

Wildlife Trust
NORTH WALES WILDLIFE TRUST. (1963; 3,433). 376 High Street, Bangor, Gwynedd, LL57 1YE. 01248 351 541; (Fax)01248 353 192;
e-mail: nwwt@wildlifetrustswales.org
www.northwaleswildlifetrust.org.uk

SOUTH WALES

Bird Atlas/Avifauna
An Atlas of Breeding Birds in West Glamorgan by David M Hanford et al (Gower Ornithological Society, 1992).

Birds of Glamorgan by Clive Hurford and Peter Lansdown (Published by the authors, c/o National Museum of Wales, Cardiff, 1995)

Bird Recorders
GLAMORGAN (EAST). Geri Thomas, 9 Julian's Close, Gelligaer, Glamorgan CF82 8DT. (H) 01443 836 949; (M) 07984 591 983;
e-mail: merlinbiosurveys@btinternet.com

GLAMORGAN (GOWER). Robert Taylor, 285 Llangyfelach Road, Brynhyfryd, Swansea, SA5 9LB. 01792 464 780; (M) 07970 567 007;
e-mail: rob@birding.freeserve.co.uk

Bird Reports
EAST GLAMORGAN BIRD REPORT (title varies 1963-95) 1996-2007, from John D Wilson, 122 Westbourne Road, Penarth, Vale of Glamorgan, CF64 3HH. 029 2033 9424; e-mail: johndw@ntllworld.com

GOWER BIRDS (1965-) - covers Swansea, Neath and Port Talbot counties, from Heather Coats, 3 Brynawel Close, Crynant, Neath, SA10 8TG.
e-mail: gowerbirdsf@hotmail.com
www.glamorganbirds.org.uk

BTO Regional Representatives
EAST GLAMORGAN (former Mid & South Glam) RR. Wayne Morris, 8 Hughes Street, Penygraig, Rhondda, CF40 1LX. e-mail: waynemorris@tiscali.co.uk

WEST RR. Bob Howells, Ynys Enlli, 14 Dolgoy Close, West Cross, Swansea SA3 5LT.
e-mail: bobhowells31@hotmail.com

Clubs
CARDIFF NATURALISTS' SOCIETY. (1867; 225). Stephen R Howe, National Museum of Wales, Cardiff, CF10 3NP. e-mail: steve.howe@museumwales.ac.uk
www.cardiffnaturalists.org.uk
Meetings: 7.30pm, various evenings, Llandaff Campus Uwic, Western Avenue, Cardiff.

GLAMORGAN BIRD CLUB.
(1990; 290). Richard May, Hon Secretary, 36 Greenway Court, Barry, CF63 2FE. 0774 086 7384; e-mail: richardmay1984@hotmail.co.uk
www.glamorganbirds.org.uk
Meetings: 7.30pm, 2nd Tuesday of winter months, Kenfig Reserve Centre.

GOWER ORNITHOLOGICAL SOCIETY. (1956; 120). Peter Douglas-Jones, 28 Brynfield Road, Langland, Swansea, SA3 4SX. 01792 360 287;
e-mail: gowerbirdsf@hotmail.com
www.glamorganbirds.org.uk
Meetings: 7.15pm, last Friday of the month (Sep-Mar), The Environment Centre, Pier Street, Swansea.

WALES

Ringing Groups
FLAT HOLM RG. Brian Bailey, Tamarisk House, Wards Court, Frampton-on-Severn, Glos, GL2 7DY.
e-mail: brian.bailey@sandbservices.eclipse.co.uk

KENFIG RG. D.G. Carrington, 44 Ogmore Drive, Nottage, Porthcawl, Mid Glamorgan CF36 3HR.

RSPB Local Groups
CARDIFF & DISTRICT. (1973). Peter Elkington, 25 Wolfs Castle Avenue, Llanishen, Cardiff, CF14 5JS. 02920 752 5231; www.RSPB.org.uk/groups/cardiff.
Meetings: 7.30pm, various Fridays (Sept-May), Llandaff Parish Hall, Llandaff, Cardiff.

WEST GLAMORGAN. (1985; 346). Maggie Cornelius. 01792 229 244;
e-mail: RSPBwglamgrp@googlemail.com
www.rspb.org.uk/groups/westglamorgan
Meetings: 7.30pm, Environment Centre, Pier Street, Swansea, SA1 1RY

Wetland Bird Survey Organisers
EAST GLAMORGAN (former Mid & South Glam), Wayne Morris, 8 Hughes Street, Penygraig, Rhondda, CF40 1LX. e-mail: waynemorris@tiscali.co.uk

SEVERN ESTUARY, Niall Burton, c/o BTO, The Nunnery, Thetford, Norfolk, IP24 2PU.
e-mail: niall.burton@bto.org

WEST GLAMORGAN, Bob Howells, Ynys Enlli, 14 Dolgoy Close, West Cross, Swansea SA3 5LT. 01792 405 363; e-mail: bobhowells31@hotmail.com

Wildlife Hospital
GOWER BIRD HOSPITAL. Karen Kingsnorth and Simon Allen, Valetta, Sandy Lane, Pennard, Swansea, SA3 2EW. 01792 371 630;
e-mail: info@gowerbirdhospital.org.uk
www.gowerbirdhospital.org.uk
All species of wild birds, also hedgehogs and small mammals. Prior phone call essential. Gower Bird Hospital cares for sick, injured and orphaned wild birds and animals with the sole intention of returning them to the wild. Post-release radio-tracking projects, ringing scheme.
Contact hospital for more information.

Wildlife Trust
WILDLIFE TRUST OF SOUTH AND WEST WALES. (2002; 6,000). Nature Centre, Parc Slip, Fountain Road, Tondu, Bridgend CF32 0EH. 01656 724 100; fax 01656 726 980; e-mail: info@welshwildlife.org
www.welshwildlife.org

WESTERN WALES

Bird Atlas/Avifauna
The Birds of Carmarthenshire by John Lloyd (in preparation)

Birds of Pembrokeshire by Jack Donovan and Graham Rees (Dyfed Wildlife Trust, 1994).

Bird Recorders
CARMARTHENSHIRE. Derek Moore, Rowan Howe, Gors Road, Salem, Llandeilo, Carmarthenshire SA19 7LY. 01558 823 708; e-mail: DerekBirdBrain@aol.com

CEREDIGION. Russell Jones, Bron y Gan, Talybont, Ceredigion, SY24 5ER. 07753 774 891;
e-mail: russell.jones@rspb.org.uk

PEMBROKESHIRE 1. Stephen Berry, Teifi House, Dolbadau Road, Cilgerran, Pembrokeshire SA43 2SS. 01239 621 610.

PEMBROKESHIRE 2. Jon Green, Crud Yr Awel, Bowls Road, Blaenporth, Ceredigion SA43 2AR. 01239 811 561; e-mail: jonrg@tiscali.co.uk

Bird Reports
WELSH BIRD REPORT (2007-), from Jon Green, Crud Yr Awel, Bowls Road, Blaenporth, Ceredigion SA43 2AR. 01239 811 561;
e-mail: jonrg@tiscali.co.uk

CARMARTHENSHIRE BIRD REPORT (1982-), from Wendell Thomas, 48 Gleve Road, Loughor, Swansea, SA4 6QD.

CEREDIGION BIRD REPORT (biennial 1982-87; annual 1988-), from Wildlife Trust West Wales.

PEMBROKESHIRE BIRD REPORT (1981-), from Ms Barbara Priest, The Pines, Templeton, Pembs SA67 8RT. e-mail: barbara.priest@tiscali.co.uk

BTO Regional Representatives
CARDIGAN RR. Moira Convery, 41 Danycoed, Aberystwyth SY23 2HD. 01970 612 998;
e-mail: moira.convery@dsl.pipex.com

CARMARTHEN RR. Position vacant.

PEMBROKE RR. Annie and Bob Haycock, 1 Rushmoor, Martletwy, Pembrokeshire, SA67 8BB. 01834 891 667; e-mail: rushmoor1@tiscali.co.uk

Clubs
CARMARTHENSHIRE BIRD CLUB.(2003; 120). Owen Harris, 2 Marine Cottages, Water Street, Ferryside, SA17 5SB. www.carmarthenshirebirds. co.uk
Meetings: Winter evenings at WWT Penclacwydd (check website for details).

LLANELLI NATURALISTS. (1971; 100). Richard Pryce, Trevethin, School Road, Pwll, Llanelli, Carmarthenshire SA15 4AL.
e-mail: Contact@llanellinaturalists.org.uk
www.llanellinaturalists.org.uk
Meetings: 1st Thursday of the month, YWCA Llanelli (see programme in local libraries).

WALES

PEMBROKESHIRE BIRD GROUP. (1993; 60). Ms Barbara Priest, The Pines, Templeton, Pembs SA67 8RT. e-mail: barbara.priest@tiscali.co.uk.
Meetings: 7.30pm, 1st Tuesday of the month (Oct-Apr), The Patch, Furzy Park, Haverfordwest.

Ringing Group
PEMBROKESHIRE RG. J Hayes, 3 Wades Close, Holyland Road, Pembroke, SA71 4BN. 01646 687 036; e-mail: hayesj@chevron.com.

Wetland Bird Survey Organisers
DYFI ESTUARY, Dick Squires, Cae'r Berllan, Eglwysfach, Machynlleth, Powys SY20 8TA. e-mail: dick.squires@rspb.org.uk

CARDIGAN, Dick Squires, Cae'r Berllan, Eglwysfach, Machynlleth, Powys SY20 8TA. e-mail: dick.squires@rspb.org.uk

CARMARTHEN, BAY AND INLAND. Ian Hainsworth, 23 Rhyd y Defaid Drive, Swansea, SA2 8AJ. 01792 205 693; e-mail: ian.hains@ntlworld.com

PEMBROKESHIRE, Annie Haycock, 1 Rushmoor, Martletwy, Pembrokeshire SA67 8BB. e-mail: rushmoor1@tiscali.co.uk

Wildlife Hospitals
NEW QUAY BIRD HOSPITAL. Jean Bryant, Penfoel, Cross Inn, Llandysul, Ceredigion, SA44 6NR. 01545 560 462.
All species of birds. Fully equipped for cleansing oiled seabirds. Veterinary support.

Wildlife Trust
See South Wales.

ISLE OF MAN

Bird Atlas/Avifauna
Manx Bird Atlas. 5-yr BBS and Winter Atlas research completed. (Liverpool University 2007). Contact: Chris Sharpe (see below, BTO Representative).

Bird Recorder
Dr Pat Cullen, Troutbeck, Cronkbourne, Braddan, Isle of Man, IM4 4QA. Home: 01624 623 308; Work 01624 676 774; e-mail: bridgeen@mcb.net

Bird Reports
MANX BIRD REPORT (1947-), published in *Peregrine*. Mrs A C Kaye, Cronk Ny Ollee, Glen Chass, Port St Mary, Isle of Man, IM9 5PL.

CALF OF MAN BIRD OBSERVATORY ANNUAL REPORT, from The Secretary, Manx National Heritage, Manx Museum, Douglas, Isle of Man, IM1 3LY.

BTO Regional Representative & Regional Development Officer
RR. Dr Pat Cullen, as above, 01624 623 308.

RDO. Chris Sharpe, 33 Mines Road, Laxey, Isle of Man, IM4 7NH. 01624 861 130; e-mail: chris@manxbirdatlas.org.uk

Club
MANX ORNITHOLOGICAL SOCIETY. (1967; 150). Mrs A C Kaye, Cronk Ny Ollee, Glen Chass, Port St Mary, Isle of Man, IM9 5PL. 01624 834 015
Meetings: 1st Tues in month, 7.30pm, Union Mills Hall.

Ringing Group
MANX RINGING GROUP. Mr K. N. Scott. e-mail: kev@manxbroadband.com

Wetland Bird Survey Organiser
Pat Cullen, Troutbeck, Cronkbourne, Braddan, Isle of Man, IM4 4QA. (H)01624 623 308; (W)01624 676 774; e-mail: bridgeen@mcb.net

Wildlife Trust
MANX WILDLIFE TRUST. (1973; 900). The Courtyard, Tynwald Mills, St Johns, Isle of Man IM4 3AE. 01624 801 985; (Fax) 01624 801 022; e-mail: manxwt@cix.co.uk www.wildlifetrust.org.uk/manxwt/

CHANNEL ISLANDS

ALDERNEY

Bird Recorder
Mark Atkinson. E-mail: atkinson@cwgsy.net

Bird Report
ALDERNEY SOCIETY ORNITHOLOGY REPORT (1992-), from the Recorder.

BTO Regional Representative
Philip Alexander. 01481 726 173;
e-mail: alybru@cwgsy.net

Wildlife Trust
ALDERNEY WILDLIFE TRUST (2002; 460). Alderney
Information Centre, 34 Victoria Street, St Anne
Alderney GY9 3AA. 01481 822 935; (Fax) 01481 822
935; e-mail: info@alderneywildlife.org
www.alderneywildlife.org

GUERNSEY

Bird Atlas/Avifauna
Birds of the Bailiwick of Guernsey (working title). In
preparation.

Bird Recorder
Mark Lawlor; e-mail: mplawlor@cwgsy.net

Bird Report
*REPORT & TRANSACTIONS OF LA SOCIETE
GUERNESIAISE (1882-)*, from the Recorder.

BTO Regional Representative
Philip Alexander. 01481 726 173;
e-mail: alybru@cwgsy.net

Clubs
LA SOCIÉTIÉ GUERNESIAISE
(Ornithological Section). (1882; 30).
The Secretary,
e-mail: societe@cwgsy.net
www.societe.org.gg
Meetings: First Thurs of month,
8pm, Candie Gardens lecture theatre.

RSPB Local Group
GUERNSEY. (1975; 350+). Michael Bairds, Les Quatre
Vents, La Passee, St Sampsons, Guernsey, GY2 4TS.
01481 255 524; e-mail: mikebairds@cwgsy.nett
www.rspbguernsey.co.uk

Wetland Bird Survey Organiser
GUERNSEY COAST. Mary Simmons, Les Maeures, Mont
d'Aval, Castel, Guernsey, GY5 7UQ. 01481 256 016;
e-mail: msim@cwgsy.net

Wildlife Hospital
GUERNSEY. GSPCA ANIMAL
SHELTER. Mrs Jayne Le
Cras, Rue des Truchots, Les
Fiers Moutons, St Andrews,

Guernsey, Channel Islands, GY6 8UD. 01481 257 261;
e-mail: jaynelecras@gspca.org.gg
All species. Modern cleansing unit for oiled seabirds.
24-hour emergency service. Veterinary support.

JERSEY

Bird Recorder
Tony Paintin, 16 Quennevais Gardens, St Brelade,
Jersey, Channel Islands, JE3 8FQ. 01534 741 928;
e-mail: cavokjersey@hotmail.com

Bird Report
JERSEY BIRD REPORT, from La Société Jersiaise, 7
Pier Road, St Helier, Jersey JE2 4XW.
e-mail: societe@societe-jersiaise.org

BTO Regional Representative
Tony Paintin, 16 Quennevais Gardens, St Brelade,
Jersey, Channel Islands, JE3 8FQ. 01534 741 928;
e-mail: cavokjersey@hotmail.com

Club
SOCIÉTIÉ JERSIAISE (Ornithological Section). (1948;
40). C/O La Société Jersiaise, 7 Pier Road, St Helier,
Jersey JE2 4XW. 01534 758 314;
e-mail: societe@societe-jersiaise.org
www.societe-jersiaise.org
Meetings: 8.00pm, alternate Thursdays throughout
the year, Museum in St.Helier.

Wildlife Hospital
JERSEY. JSPCA ANIMALS' SHELTER. The Manager, 89
St Saviour's Road, St Helier, Jersey, JE2 4GJ. 01534
724 331; (Fax) 01534 871797;
e-mail: info@jspca.org.je
www.jspca.org.je All species. Expert outside support
for owls and raptors. Oiled seabird unit. Veterinary
surgeon on site. Educational Centre.

NORTHERN IRELAND

Bird Recorder
George Gordon, 2 Brooklyn Avenue, Bangor,
Co Down, BT20 5RB. 028 9145 5763; e-mail:
gordon@ballyholme2.freeserve.co.uk

Bird Reports
NORTHERN IRELAND BIRD REPORT, from Secretary,
Northern Ireland, Birdwatchers' Association (see
National Directory).

IRISH BIRD REPORT, Included in Irish Birds,,
BirdWatch Ireland in National Directory..

COPELAND BIRD OBSERVATORY REPORT, from see
Reserves.

BTO Regional Representatives
BTO IRELAND OFFICER. Shane Wolsey. 028 9146
7947; e-mail: shane@swolsey.biz

ANTRIM & BELFAST. Position vacant.

ARMAGH. David W A Knight, 23 Richmond Drive,
Ballymore Road, Tandragee, Co Armagh BT62 2JJ.
028 38 840 658; e-mail: david.knight@niwater.com

DOWN. Position vacant.

FERMANAGH. Position vacant.

LONDONDERRY. Charles Stewart, Bravallen,
18 Duncrun Road, Bellarena, Limavady, Co
Londonderry BT49 0JD. 028 7775 0468; e-mail:
charles.stewart2@btinternet.com

TYRONE. Position vacant.

Clubs
NORTHERN IRELAND BIRDWATCHERS' ASSOCIATION
See National Directory.

NORTHERN IRELAND ORNITHOLOGISTS' CLUB See
National Directory.

CASTLE ESPIE BIRDWATCHING CLUB (COMBER).
(1995; 60). Dot Blakely, 8 Rosemary Park, Bangor,
Co Down, BT20 3EX. 028 9145 0784.

Ringing Groups
COPELAND BIRD OBSERVATORY. C W Acheson, 28
Church Avenue, Dunmurry, Belfast, BT17 9RS.

NORTH DOWN RINGING GROUP. Mr D C Clarke.
07774 780 750; e-mail: declan.clarke@homecall.
co.uk

RSPB Local Groups
ANTRIM. (1977; 23). Brenda Campbell . 02893 323
657; e-mail: brendacampbell@supanet.com

www.rspb.org.uk/groups/antrim
Meetings: 8pm, 2nd Monday of the month,
College of Agriculture Food & Rural Enterprise, 22
Greenmount Road, ANTRIM

BANGOR. (1973; 25). Fulton Somerville. E-mail:
fultonsomerville@yahoo.co.uk
Meetings: Trinity Presbyterian Church Hall, Main
Street, BANGOR, County Down.

BELFAST. (1970; 130). Ron Houston. 028 9079 6188.
Meetings: Cooke Centenary Church Hall, Cooke
Centenary Church Hall, Ormeau Rd, BELFAST

COLERAINE. (1978; 45). Peter Robinson,
34 Blackthorn Court, Coleraine, Co
Londonderry, BT52 2EX. 028 7034 4361; e-mail:
robinson493@btinternet.com
Meetings: 7.30pm, third Monday of the month
(Sept-Apr), St Patricks Church, Minor Church Hall,
Corner of Brook St and Circular Road, Coleraine

FERMANAGH. (1977; 28). Barbara Johnston. 028
6634 1708; e-mail: johnston.cb@googlemail.com
Meetings: 7.30pm, 4th Tuesday of the month, St
Macartans Church Hall.

LARNE. (1974; 35). Jimmy Christie, 314 Coast Road,
Ballygally, Co Antrim, BT40 2QZ. 028 2858 3223;
e-mail: candjchristie@btinternet.com
Meetings: 7.30pm, 1st Wednesday of the month,
Larne Grammar School.

LISBURN. (1978; 30). Peter Galloway. 028 9266
1982; e-mail: peter.dolly@virgin.net
www.rspblisburn.com
Meetings: 7.30pm, 4th Monday of the month,
Friends Meeting House, 4 Magheralave Road,
LISBURN

Wetland Bird Survey Organisers
LARNE LOUGH. Doreen Hilditch.
e-mail:18brae@btinternet.com

BELFAST LOUGH. Shane Wolsey, 25 Ballyholme
Esplanade, Bangor, County Down, BT20 5LZ. 02891
467947; e-mail: shane@swolsey.biz

DUNDRUM BAY. Malachy Martin, Murlough NNR,
Keel Point, Dundrum, Co. Down, BT33 0NQ. 028
4375 1467; E-mail: Malachy.Martin@nationaltrust.
org.uk

BANN ESTUARY. Hill Dick, 02870 329 720;
e-mail: webs@bto.org

LOUGH FOYLE. Matthew Tickner, RSPB, Belvoir Park Forest, Belfast, Co Antrim, BT8 7QT. 028 491 547(c/o Belfast RSPB); e-mail: matthew.tickner@rspb.org.uk

Wildlife Hospital
TACT WILDLIFE CENTRE. Mrs Patricia Nevines, 2 Crumlin Road, Crumlin, Co Antrim, BT29 4AD. Tel/fax 028 9442 2900;
e-mail: tactwildlife@btinternet.com
www.tactwildlifecentre.org.uk.
All categories of birds treated and rehabilitated;

released where practicable, otherwise given a home. Visitors (inc. school groups and organisations) welcome by prior arrangement. Veterinary support.

Wildlife Trust
ULSTER WILDLIFE TRUST. (1978; 7.500). 3 New Line, Crossgar, Co Down, BT30 9EP. 028 4483 0282; fax 028 4483 0888;
e-mail: info@ulsterwildlifetrust.org
www.ulsterwildlifetrust.org

REPUBLIC OF IRELAND

Bird Recorders
BirdWatch Ireland, P.O. Box 12, Greystones, Co. Wicklow, Ireland. 353 (0)1 2819 878 (Fax) 353 (0)1 2810 997; e-mail: info@birdwatchireland.ie
www.birdwatchireland.ie

Rarities. Paul Milne, 100 Dublin Road, Sutton, Dublin 13, +353 (0)1 832 5653;
e-mail: paul.milne@oceanfree.net

CLARE. John Murphy;
e-mail: jemurphy@esatclearie

CORK. Mark Shorten; e-mail: mshorten@indigo.ie

DONEGAL. Ralph Sheppard;
e-mail: rsheppard@eircom.net

DUBLIN, LOUTH, MEATH AND WICKLOW. Declan Murphy; e-mail: dmurphy@birdwatchireland.ie

Dick Coombes;
e-mail: rcoombes@birdwatchireland.ie

GALWAY. Tim Griffin; 74 Monalee Heights, Knocknacarra.

KERRY. Edward Carty; 3 The Orchard, Ballyrickard, Tralee.

LIMERICK. Tony Mee; Ballyorgan, Kilfinane, Co. Limerick.

MAYO. Tony Murray; National Parks and Wildlife, Lagduff More, Ballycroy, Westport

MID-SHANNON. Stephen Heery;
e-mail: sheery@eircom.net

MONAGHAN. Joe Shannon;
e-mail: joeshan@eircom.net

WATERFORD. Paul Walsh;
e-mail: pmwalsh@waterfordbirds.com

WEXFORD. Wexford Wildfowl Reserve, North Slob

Bird Reports
IRISH BIRD REPORT, contact BirdWatch Ireland in National, Directory).

CAPE CLEAR BIRD OBSERVATORY ANNUAL REPORT, from the observatory.

CORK BIRD REPORT (1963-71; 1976-), Cork Bird Report Editorial Team, Long Strand, Castlefreke, Clonakilty, Co. Cork; e-mail: cbr@corkecology.net

EAST COAST BIRD REPORT (1980-), Contact BirdWatch Ireland.

BirdWatch Ireland Branches
Branches may be contacted in writing via BirdWatch Ireland HQ (see entry in National Directory).

Ringing Groups
CAPE CLEAR B.O, Mr M.E. O'Donnell, Barnlands, Killinieran, Gorey, Co Wexford;
e-mail: micealodonnell@eircom.net

GREAT SALTEE RINGING STATION, Mr O J Merne, 20 Cuala Road, Bray, Co Wicklow, Ireland,
e-mail: omerne@eircom.net

MUNSTER RG, Mr K.P.C. Collins, Ballygambon, Lisronagh, Clonmel, County Tipperary,
e-mail: kcsk@eircom.net

ARTICLES IN BIRD REPORTS

Ayrshire Bird Report 2007
- The birds of the Hunterston Area – The early years of county ornithology to 1968 by M McGinty and James TM Towill
- Ayrshire's historical rookeries by Kevin Waite
- Kestrel in Ayrshire 2007 by Gordon Riddle
- Sparrowhawk breeding details 2007 Ian Todd
- Ayrshire butterfly report 2007 by Fraser S Simpson

Bedfordshire Bird Report 2005
- The Great Reed Warbler at Willington, 2005 by Mark Thomas
- Visible migration at Pegsdon Hills, 16th October 2005 by Graham White
- The increase of Peregrine Falcons in Bedfordshire by Dave Odell
- The Hawfinch influx, winter 2005/6 by Richard Bashford
- The Waxwing influx in 2005 by Barry Nightingale
- Breeding bird population changes in Potton Wood 1986-2005 by C.James Cadbury
- Changes affecting species on the Bedfordshire list by Barry Nightingale

Bedfordshire Bird Report 2006
- Bearded Tit -A new breeding bird for Bedfordshire - Graham White
- Looking Back by 1956
- Alpine Swift at Stewartby Lake, April 2006 by Graham White
- Red-footed Falcon at MVCP, June 2006 by John Lynch
- Looking Back by 1981
- Visible Migration by Steve Blain and Tim Sharrock
- Roof-nesting Gulls in Bedfordshire by Barry Nightingale
- RSPB Heathland Restoration at The Lodge, Sandy by Peter Bradley

Bedfordshire Bird Report 2007
- Looking back …1957
- Barnacle Geese on the move by Errol Newman
- Caspian Tern at Marston Vale CP by Steven Northwood
- Looking back …1992
- Snow Bunting at Rookery Clay-pit by Steven Northwood
- Breeding *Charadrius* plovers in Bedfordshire by Nigel Willits
- When are rare birds found in Bedfordshire? by Barry Nightingale

The Birds of Berkshire 2005
- Heathlake by Ian Twyford
- Feral Barnacle and Snow Geese in the Upper Loddon and Blackwater Valleys by John Clark
- The Laughing Gull at Reading by Rob Laughton
- Cetti's Warbler in West Berkshire by Jan Legg
- The Berkshire Kingfisher Survey 2005; Chris Robinson
- Sparrowhawk eye Colour by Jan Legg
- Whiskered Tern at Moor Green Lakes by Bruce Archer
- Survey of Theale and Burghfield 2005 by Richard Crawford
- Ringing and Nestbox highlights 2005 by Brian Clews
- Study of Tree Pipits in West Berkshire by Jon Wilding

Carmarthenshire Birds 2007
- The Carmarthenshire county bird list by Rob Hunt
- National Westland Centre ringing report by HF Coates
- Dotterel passage sites on Mynydd Du by Coling Richards
- The BTO Little Ringed Plover survey 2007 by Julian Friese

Birds and Wildlife in Cumbria 2007
- Gazetteer of Cumbrian Sites
- Wetland Bird Survey (WeBS) coverage 2007
- The results of the Non-Estuarine Waterbird Survey January 2007
- The Cumbria Bird Club Records Panel - past, present and future.

Derbyshire Bird Report 2007
- A long-term study of bird populations at Scarcliffe Woods by Roy Frost

Devon Birds – Volume 61 No. 1 (April 2008)
Incorporating the *Devon Bird Report*
- The story of Pied Flycatchers breeding in Devon Peter Goodfellow
- The Heronries Census in Devon: 1928-2007 David Rogers
- "Just William" Elaine Hurrell
- That tricky accipiter Mark Darlaston
- The status and distribution of three Dartmoor birds, following a major survey in 2006 Helen Booker & Peter Slader
- The Canary Islands' special birds Peter Goodfellow
- Aspects of warbler migration and ringing at South Milton Ley Vic Tucker
- The Norfolk Blackbird that winters in Devon – Part 2 Robin & Anne Woods
- My flycatchers Peter Ellicott

301

ARTICLES IN BIRD REPORTS

- Little Owls Ann Wells
- My best birds Robert Kempster
- South West Ringers' Conference Judith Read
- Book reviews Nick Dymond & Roger Smaldon

Essex Bird Report 2007
- Old Hall Marshes RSPB 2007 by Paul Charlton
- 2007 survey of breeding Corn Buntings in Essex by Chris Tyas

The Hertfordshire Bird Report 2007
- A Review of first and last dates for migrant birds in Hertfordshire - Part 2
- Nest recording in Hertfordshire in 2007
- Little Ringed Plover *Charadrius dubius*, Ringed Plover *C. hiaticula* and other gravel pit breeding waders in Hertfordshire in 2007
- Wintering Green Sandpipers in Herfordshire in 2006/07
- A possible Siberian Chiffchaff wintering at Wilstone Reservoir 2006/07
- Little Bunting *Emberiza pusilla* at Amwell Nature Reserve
- Cetti's Warblers *Cettia cetti* at Tring Reservoirs

Isle of May Bird Observatory Annual Report 2006
- Systematic list of Birds recorded in 2006
- Report on bird ringing in 2006
- Seabird breeding on the Isle of May in 2006
- Calandra Lark - first record for the Isle of May by Mark Newell
- The Little Auk influx of November 2006
- Evidence of bird species amongst the archeological remains on the Isle of May by Mike Martin
- Bryophyte records on the Isle of May 2-5 September 2006 by DF Chamberlain

Kent Bird report 2006
- Storm Petrels in Kent, May 2006 by A Henderson and D Walker
- Zitting Cisticola: a new species for Kent by R Heading

Birds in Moray and Nairn 2007
- Birds of the Moray moors - a re-survey of the Lodder Hills area 2007 by Ian Francis
- Problems with NE Scottish Common Gulls by WRP Bourne
- Boneparte's Gull at Loch Spynie - new to Moray and Nairn by Duncan Gibson
- Great Shearwater at Lossiemouth - new to Moray and Nairn by Bob Proctor

North East Scotland Bird Report 2007
- Brunnich, Guillemot at Girdle Ness by A Whitehouse

- Aberdeen Red Kites by J Lennon
- Seasonal distribution and population trends of waterfowl on Loch of Skene by J Wills
- Birds in mid-Deeside 1970-2008 by D Jenkins and P Chapman
- New additons and taxonomic changes that affect the NES list: A brief review (1996-2007) by I Phillips

Northants Birds 2004-5
- Barn Owl breeding population in Northamptonshire by The Hawk and Owl Trust
- A Future for breeding waders of wet grassland in Northamptonshire? By Steve Brayshaw
- Stanford Reservoir ringing report by Stanford Ringing and Conservation Group
- East Midlands Red Kite report 2005 by Derek Holman and Karl Ivens

Orkney Bird Report 2008
- Wintering sea fowl in Wide Firth, Shapinsay Sound and Deer Sound - 2007/8
- Birds in a Kirkwall garden 2004-2008
- The North Ronaldsay Bird Observatory Report 2008
- Ringing Report 2008

Pembrokeshire Bird Report 2008
- Blackpoll Warbler at Marloes by M.Spirito
- Black Duck at Marloes by DJ Astins
- Ringing report by S Sutcliffe
- Survey report by B and A Haycock

Sussex Bird Report 2007
- Sussex ringing report for 2007 by RDM Edgar and S McKenzie
- The West Sussex Red Kite study area, 2004-7 by Dr M Kalcher et al
- Fluctuations in the numbers of auks recorded off the Sussex coast by D.Howey
- Sussex results from the non-estuarine coastal waterbird sruvey 2006-7 by Dr H Crabtree and Dr J Newnham
- The first record in the UK fof a fertile mating between a wild female Peregrine and a hybrid male falcon of domestic origin by P Everitt and J Franklin
- Changes in breeding populations on a Sussex estate 1982-2006 by C Banfield et al

Hobby 2007 (Wiltshire Ornithological Society)
- Great Bustard Reintroduction: 2007 summary by Al Davies
- The breeding bird survey 1994-2007 by Bill Quantrill
- Cotswold Water Park Breeding waterbird surveys 2007 by Nick Adams and Gareth Harris
- Species new to Wiltshire - Lesser Scaup at Cotswold Water Park by Stephen Edwards
- Birds of Wiltshire: Corrigenda and Addenda by Peter Cranswick et al

302

NATIONAL DIRECTORY

David Cromack

Red-throated Diver, now a rare breeding species in Britain, relies on its camouflage for protection when incubating its eggs.

NATIONAL ORGANISATIONS

After the title of each organisation you will see (in brackets) the year the group was founded and, where known, the current membership figure.

ARMY ORNITHOLOGICAL SOCIETY (1960; 200)

Open to serving and retired MoD employees who have an interest in their local MoD estate. Activities include field meetings, expeditions, the preparation of checklists of birds on Ministry of Defence property, conservation advice and an annual bird count. Annual journal *Adjutant*.

Contact: The Secretary, Army Ornithological Society, JAMES Project Team, Battlesbury Brks, Warminster BA12 9DT. 01985 223 682; e-mail: secretary@aos.org.uk
www.aos-uk.com

ASSOCIATION FOR THE PROTECTION OF RURAL SCOTLAND (1926)

Works to protect Scotland's countryside from unnecessary or inappropriate development, recognising the needs of those who live and work there and the necessity of reconciling these with the sometimes competing requirements of recreational use.

Contact: Association for the Protection Rural Scotland, Gladstone's Land, 3rd Floor, 483 Lawnmarket, Edinburgh EH1 2NT. 0131 225 7012; e-mail: info@ruralscotland.org
www.ruralscotland.org

ASSOCIATION OF COUNTY RECORDERS AND EDITORS (1993; 120)

Administered by a Google group called ACRE - for County Recorders and allies. The basic aim is to promote best practice in the business of producing county bird reports, in the work of Recorders and in problems arising in managing record systems and archives. Access is limited to County Recorders, editors and others with a legitimate interest — for further clarification please contact the webmaster; e-mail: countyrec@cawos.org

BARN OWL TRUST (1988)

Registered charity. Aims to conserve the Barn Owl and its environment through conservation, education, research and information. Free leaflets on all aspects of Barn Owl conservation. Educational material inc. video and resource pack. Book *Barn Owls on Site*, a guide for planners and developers. Works with and advises landowners, farmers, planners, countryside bodies and others. Currently providing training for ecological consultants via a one-day 'Barn Owl Ecology, Surveys and Signs' training course. Open to phone calls Mon-Fri (9am-5pm). Send SAE for information.

Contact: Barn Owl Trust, Waterleat, Ashburton, Devon TQ13 7HU. 01364 653 026; e-mail: info@barnowltrust.org.uk
www.barnowltrust.org.uk

BIRD OBSERVATORIES COUNCIL (1970)

Aims to provide a forum for establishing closer links and co-operation between individual observatories and to help co-ordinate the work carried out by them. All accredited bird observatories affiliated to the Council undertake a ringing programme and provide ringing experience to those interested. Most also provide accommodation for visiting birdwatchers.

Contact: Peter Howlett, Bird Observatories Council, c/o Dept of Biodiversity, National Museum Wales, Cardiff CF10 3NP. 0292 057 3233; (Fax)0292 023 9009; e-mail: info@birdobscouncil.org.uk
www.birdobscouncil.org.uk

BIRD STAMP SOCIETY (1986; 220)

Quarterly journal *Flight* contains philatelic and ornithological articles. Lists all new issues and identifies species. Runs a quarterly Postal Auction; number of lots range from 400 to 800 per auction. UK subs £14 per annum from 1st August.

Contact: Mrs R Bradley, Bird Stamp Society, 31 Park View, Crossway Green, Chepstow NP16 5NA. 01291 625412; e-mail: bradley666@lycos.co.uk
www.bird-stamps.org

BIRDWATCH IRELAND (1968; 10,000)

The trading name of the Irish Wildbird Conservancy, a voluntary body founded by the amalgamation of the Irish Society for the Protection of Birds, the Irish Wildfowl Conservancy and the Irish Ornithologists' b. Now the BirdLife International partner in Ireland with 21 voluntary branches. Conservation policy is based on formal research and surveys of birds and their habitats. Owns or manages an increasing number of reserves to protect threatened species and habitats. Publishes *Wings* quarterly and *Irish Birds* annually, in addition to annual project reports and survey results.

Contact: BirdWatch Ireland, PO Box 12, Greystones, Co. Wicklow, Ireland. +353 (0)1 2819878; (Fax)+353 (0)1 2819763; e-mail: info@birdwatchireland.org
www.birdwatchireland.ie

BRITISH BIRDS RARITIES COMMITTEE (1959)

The Committee adjudicates records of species of rare occurrence in Britain (marked `R' in the Log Charts) and publishes its annual report in *British Birds*. The BBRC also assesses records from the Channel Islands. In the case of rarities trapped for ringing, records should be sent to the Ringing Office of the British Trust for Ornithology, who will in turn forward them to the BBRC.

Contact: Mr N Hudson, Hon Secretary, British Birds Rarities Committee, Post Office Flat, Hugh Street, St Mary's, Isles of Scilly TR21 0JE TR21 0JE; e-mail: secretary@bbrc.org.uk
www.bbrc.org.uk

BRITISH DRAGONFLY SOCIETY (1983; 1,604)

The BDS aims to promote the conservation and study of dragonflies. Members receive two issues of *Dragonfly News* and *BDS Journal* each year in spring and autumn. There are countrywide field trips, an annual members day and training is available on aspects of dragonfly ecology.
Contact: Mr H Curry, Hon Secretary, British Dragonfly Society, 23 Bowker Way, Whittlesey, Cambs PE7 1PY.
e-mail: bdssecretary@dragonflysoc.org.uk
www.dragonflysoc.org.uk

BRITISH FALCONERS' CLUB (1927; 1,200)

Largest falconry club in Europe, with regional branches. Its aim is to encourage responsible falconers and conserve birds of prey by breeding, holding educational meetings and providing facilities, guidance and advice to those wishing to take up the sport. Publishes *The Falconer* annually and newsletter twice yearly.
Contact: British Falconers' Club, Westfield, Meeting Hill, Worstead, North Walsham, Norfolk NR28 9LS. 01692 404 057;
e-mail: admin@britishfalconersclub.co.uk
www.britishfalconersclub.co.uk

BRITISH MUSEUM (NAT HIST) see Walter Rothschild Zoological Museum

British Museum (Natural History),

BRITISH NATURALISTS ASSOCIATION (1905)

The association, a registered charity, was founded to promote the interests of nature lovers and bring them together. Today, it encourages and supports schemes and legislation for the protection of the country`s natural resources. It organises meetings, field weeks, lectures and exhibitions to help popularise the study of nature. BNA publishes two magazines and copies of *Country- Side* are available to non-members at some libraries.
Contact: General Secretary, BNA, PO Box 5682, Corby, Northants NN17 2ZW. 01536 262 977;
e-mail: info@bna-naturalists.org
www.bna-naturalists.org

BRITISH ORNITHOLOGISTS' CLUB (1892; 450)

A registered charity, the Club's objects are `the promotion of scientific discussion between members of the BOU, and others interested in ornithology, and to facilitate the publication of scientific information in connection with ornithology'. The Club maintains a special interest in avian systematics, taxonomy and distribution. About eight dinner meetings are held each year. Publishes the Bulletin of the British Ornithologists' Club quarterly, also (since 1992) a continuing series of occasional publications.
Contact: BOC Office, British Ornithologists' Club, PO Box 417, Peterborough, PE7 3FX. (Tel/Fax) 01733 844 820; e-mail: boc.admin@bou.org.uk
www.boc-online.org

BRITISH ORNITHOLOGISTS' UNION (1858; 1,250)

The BOU is one of the world's oldest and most respected ornithological societies. It aims to promote ornithology within the scientific and birdwatching communities, both in Britain and around the world. This is largely achieved by the publication of its quarterly international journal, *Ibis* (1859-), featuring work at the cutting edge of our understanding of the world's birdlife. It also publishes an ongoing series of country/island group 'checklists' (24 titles to date - see BOU website for details) and operates an active programme of meetings, seminars and conferences. Work being undertaken around the world can include research projects that have received financial assistance from the BOU's ongoing programme of Ornithological Research Grants. Copies of journals and offprints received and books reviewed in *Ibis* are held as part of the Alexander Library in the Zoology Department of the University of Oxford (see Edward Grey Institute) The BOU Records Committee maintains the official British List (see below)
Contact: Steve Dudley, British Ornithologists' Union, PO Box 417, Peterborough, PE7 3FX. (Tel/Fax) 01733 844 820; e-mail: bou@bou.org.uk
www.ibis.ac.uk and www.bouproc.net

BRITISH ORNITHOLOGISTS' UNION RECORDS COMMITTEE

A standing committee of the British Ornithologists' Union, the BOURC's function is to maintain the British List, the official list of birds recorded in Great Britain. The up-to-date list can be viewed on the BOU website. Where vagrants are involved it is concerned only with those which relate to potential additions to the British List (ie first records) In this it differs from the British Birds Rarities Committee (qv) In maintaining the British List, it also differs from the BBRC in that it examines, where necessary, important pre-1950 records, monitors introduced species for possible admission to or deletion from the List, and reviews taxonomy and nomenclature relating to the List. BOURC reports are published in *Ibis* and are also available via the BOU website. Decisions which affect the List are also announced direct to the birdwatching public via e-groups, web forums and the popular birdwatching press.

Contact: Steve Dudley, BOURC, PO Box 417, Peterborough, PE7 3FX. (Tel/Fax) 01733 844 820; e-mail: bourc@bou.org
www.bou.org.uk

BRITISH TRUST FOR ORNITHOLOGY (1933; 13,200)

A registered charity governed by an elected Council, BTO has a rapidly growing membership and enjoys the support of a large number of county and local birdwatching clubs and societies through the BTO/

Bird Clubs Partnership. Its aims are: `To promote and encourage the wider understanding, appreciation and conservation of birds through scientific studies using the combined skills and enthusiasm of its members, other birdwatchers and staff.' Through the fieldwork of its members and other birdwatchers, the BTO is responsible for the majority of the monitoring of British birds, British bird population and their habitats. BTO surveys include the National Ringing Scheme, the Nest Record Scheme, the Breeding Bird Survey (in collaboration with JNCC and RSPB), and the Waterways Breeding Bird Survey, which all contribute to an integrated programme of population monitoring. The BTO also runs projects on the birds of farmland and woodland, also (in collaboration with WWT, RSPB and JNCC) the Wetland Bird Survey, in particular Low Tide Counts. Garden BirdWatch, which started in 1995, now has more than 14,000 participants. The Trust has 140 voluntary regional representatives (see County Directory) who organise fieldworkers for the BTO's programme of national surveys. The results of these co-operative efforts are communicated to government departments, local authorities, industry and conservation bodies for effective action. For details of current activities see National Projects. Members receive *BTO News* six times a year and have the option of subscribing to the thrice-yearly journal, *Bird Study* and twice yearly *Ringing & Migration*. Local meetings are held in conjunction with bird clubs and societies; there are regional and national birdwatchers' conferences, and specialist courses in bird identification and modern censusing techniques. Grants are made for research, and members have the use of a lending and reference library at Thetford and the Alexander Library at the Edward Grey Institute of Field Ornithology (qv)

Contact: British Trust for Ornithology, The Nunnery, Thetford, Norfolk IP24 2PU. 01842 750 050; (Fax)01842 750 030; e-mail: info@bto.org
www.bto.org

BTO SCOTLAND (2000; 989)

BTO Scotland's main functions are to promote the work of the Trust and develop wider coverage for surveys in Scotland, by encouraging greater participation in survey work. It also seeks to develop contract research income within Scotland. BTO Scotland ensures that the work the Trust does is not just related to the priorities of the UK as a whole but is also focused on the priorities of Scotland, with a landscape and wildlife so different from the rest of the UK.

Contact: BTO Scotland, British Trust for Ornithology, School of Biological and Environmental Sciences, Cottrell Building, University of Stirling, Stirling FK9 4LA. 01786 466 560 (Fax)01786 466 561; e-mail: scot.info@bto.org
www.bto.org

BRITISH LIBRARY SOUND ARCHIVE - WILDLIFE SOUNDS (1969)

(Formerly BLOWS - British Library of Wildlife Sounds) The most comprehensive collection of bird sound recordings in existence: over 150,000 recordings of more than 8,000 species of birds worldwide, available for free listening. Copies or sonograms of most recordings can be supplied for private study or research and, subject to copyright clearance, for commercial uses. Contribution of new material and enquiries on all aspects of wildlife sounds and recording techniques are welcome. Publishes *Bioacoustics* journal, CD guides to bird songs and other wildlife, including ambience titles. Comprehensive catalogue available on-line at http://cadensa.bl.uk/uhtbin/cgisirsi/x/x/0/49/

Contact: Cheryl Tipp, Curator, Wildlife Sounds, The British Library Sound Archive, 96 Euston Road, London NW1 2DB. 020 7412 7403; (Fax)020 7412 7441; e-mail: wildlifesound@bl.uk
www.bl.uk/reshelp/findhelprestype/sound/wildsounds/wildlife.html

BRITISH WATERFOWL ASSOCIATION

The BWA is an association of enthusiasts interested in keeping, breeding and conserving all types of waterfowl, including wildfowl and domestic ducks and geese. It is a registered charity, without trade affiliations, dedicated to educating the public about waterfowl and the need for conservation as well as to raising the standards of keeping and breeding ducks, geese and swans in captivity.

Contact: Mrs Sue Schubert, British Waterfowl Association, PO Box 163, Oxted, RH8 0WP. 01892 740 212; e-mail: info@waterfowl.org.uk
www.waterfowl.org.uk

BRITISH WILDLIFE REHABILITATION COUNCIL (1987)

Promoting the care and rehabilitation of wildlife casualties through the exchange of information between people such as rehabilitators, zoologists and veterinary surgeons who are active in this

NATIONAL ORGANISATIONS

field. Organises an annual symposium or workshop. Publishes a regular newsletter. Supported by many national bodies including the Zoological Society of London, the British Veterinary Zoological Society, the RSPCA, the SSPCA, and the Vincent Wildlife Trust.
Contact: To make a contribution - Janet Peto, BWRC, PO Box 8686, Grantham, Lincolnshire NG31 0AG. www.bwrc.org.uk

BTCV (formerly British Trust for Conservation Volunteers) (1959)
BTCV's mission is to create a more sustainable future by inspiring people and improving places. Between 2004 and 2008 it aims to enrich the lives of one million people, through volunteering opportunities, employment, improved health, and life skills development; to Improve the biodiversity and local environment of 20,000 places and to support active citizenship in 5,000 community-based groups. BTCV currently supports 140,000 volunteers to take practical action to improve their urban and rural environments. Publishes a quarterly magazine, *Roots*, a series of practical handbooks and a wide range of other publications.
Contact: BTCV, Sedum House, Mallard Way, Potteric Carr, Doncaster DN4 8DB. 01302 388 883; e-mail: Information@btcv.org.uk
www.btcv.org.uk

BTCV CYMRU
The Conservation Centre, BTCV Cymru, Forest Farm Road, Whitchurch, Cardiff, CF14 7JJ. 029 2052 0990; (Fax) 029 2052 2181; e-mail: wales@btcv.org.uk
www.btcvcymru.org

BTCV SCOTLAND
Runs 7-14 day Action Breaks in Scotland during which participants undertake conservation projects; weekend training courses in environmental skills; midweek projects in Edinburgh, Glasgow, Aberdeen, Stirling and Inverness.
Contact: BTCV Scotland, Balallan House, 24 Allan Park, Stirling FK8 2QG. 01786 479697; (Fax)01786 465359; e-mail: scotland@btcv.org.uk
www2.btcv.org.uk/display/btcv_scotland

BTCV NORTHERN IRELAND (1983)
Conservation Volunteers Northern Ireland, Beech House, 159 Ravenhill Road, Belfast BT6 0BP. 028 9064 5169; (Fax)028 9064 4409; e-mail: CVNI@btcv.org.uk
www.cvni.org

BUGLIFE – THE INVERTEBRATE CONSERVATION TRUST (2000)
The first organisation in Europe devoted to the conservation of all invertebrates, actively engaged in halting the extinction of Britain's rarest slugs, snails, bees, wasps,

ants, spiders, beetles and many more. It is working to achieve this through practical conservation projects; promoting the environmental importance of invertebrates and raising awareness about the challenges to their survival; assisting in the development of helpful legislation and policy and encouraging and supporting invertebrate conservation initiatives by other organisations in the UK, Europe and worldwide.
Contact: Buglife (ICT), 1st Floor, 90 Bridge Street, Peterborough PE1 1DY. 01733 201 210.
www.buglife.org.uk

CAMPAIGN FOR THE PROTECTION OF RURAL WALES (1928; 2,800)
Its aims are to help the conservation and enhancement of the landscape, environment and amenities of the countryside, towns and villages of rural Wales and to form and educate opinion to ensure the promotion of its objectives. It gives advice and information upon matters affecting protection, conservation and improvement of the visual environment.
Contact: CPRW, Tŷ Gwyn, 31 High Street, Welshpool, Powys SY21 7YD. 01938 552525/556212; (Fax)552741; www.cprw.org.uk

CENTRE FOR ECOLOGY & HYDROLOGY (CEH)
The work of the CEH, a component body of the Natural Environment Research Council, includes a range of ornithological research, covering population studies, habitat management and work on the effects of pollution. The CEH has a long-term programme to monitor pesticide and pollutant residues in the corpses of predatory birds sent in by birdwatchers, and carries out detailed studies on affected species. The Biological Records Centre (BRC), which is part of the CEH, is responsible for the national biological data bank on plant and animal distributions (except birds).
Contact: Centre for Ecology & Hydrology, Maclean Building, Crowmarsh Gifford, Wallingford, Oxfordshire OX10 8BB. 01491 692 371.
E-mail: enquiries@ceh.ac.uk www.ceh.ac.uk

CONSERVATION FOUNDATION (1982)
Created by David Bellamy and David Shreeve to provide a means for people in public, private and not-for-profit sectors to collaborate on environmental causes. Over the years its programme

NATIONAL ORGANISATIONS

has included award schemes, conferences, promotions, special events, field studies, school programmes, media work, seminars and workshops etc. The Conservation Foundation has created and managed environmental award schemes of all kinds including the Ford European Awards, The Trust House Forte Community Chest, The PA Golden Leaf Awards, The Co-op Save Our Species Awards, the Pollution Abatement Technology Awards and many others. For information about how to apply for current award schemes visit the website at: www.conservationfoundation.co.uk
Contact: Conservation Foundation, 1 Kensington Gore, London SW7 2AR. 020 7591 3111; e-mail: info@conservationfoundation.co.uk

COUNTRY LAND AND BUSINESS ASSOCIATION (1907; 36,000)
The CLA is at the heart of rural life and is the voice of the countryside for England and Wales, campaigning on issues which directly affect those who live and work in rural communities. Its members, ranging from some of the largest landowners, with interests in forest, moorland, water and agriculture, to some with little more than a paddock or garden, together manage 50% of the countryside.
Contact: Country Land and Business Association, 16 Belgrave Square, London, SW1X 8PQ. 020 7235 0511;(Fax) 020 7235 4696; e-mail: mail@cla.org.uk www.cla.org.uk

COUNTRYSIDE AGENCY
This is now part of Natural England.

COUNTRYSIDE COUNCIL FOR WALES
The Government's statutory adviser on wildlife, countryside and maritime conservation matters in Wales and the executive authority for the conservation of habitats and wildlife. CCW champions the environment and landscapes of Wales and its coastal waters as sources of natural and cultural riches, as a foundation for economic and social activity, and as a place for leisure and learning opportunities.
Contact: Countryside Council for Wales, Maes-y-Ffynnon, Penrhosgarnedd, Bangor, Gwynedd LL57 2DL. 01248 385 500; (Fax)01248 355 782; (Enquiry unit) 0845 1306229; e-mail: enquiries@ccw.gov.uk www.ccw.gov.uk

CPRE (formerly Council for the Protection of Rural England) (1926; 60,000)

Patron HM The Queen. CPRE now has 43 county branches and 200 local groups. It highlights threats to the countryside and promotes positive solutions. In-depth research supports active campaigning, and through reasoned argument and lobbying, CPRE seeks to influence public opinion and decision-makers at every level. Membership open to all.
Contact: CPRE National Office, 128 Southwark Street, London SE1 0SW. 020 7981 2800; (Fax)020 7981 2899; e-mail: info@cpre.org.uk www.cpre.org.uk

DEPARTMENT OF THE ENVIRONMENT FOR NORTHERN IRELAND
Responsible for the declaration and management of National Nature Reserves, the declaration of Areas of Special Scientific Interest, the administration of Wildlife Refuges, the classification of Special Protection Areas under the EC Birds Directive, the designation of Special Areas of Conservation under the EC Habitats Directive and the designation of Ramsar sites under the Ramsar Convention. It administers the Nature Conservation and Amenity Lands (Northern Ireland) Order 1985, the Wildlife (Northern Ireland) Order 1985, the Game Acts and the Conservation (Natural Habitats, etc) Regulations (NI) 1995 and the Environment (Northern Ireland) Order 2002.
Contact: Environment and Heritage Service, Klondyke Building, Cromac Avenue, Gasworks Business Park, Lower Ormeau Road, Belfast BT7 2JA. 0845 302 0008; (pollution hotline; 0800 807 060);
e-mail: nieaplan@doeni.gov.uk www.ehsni.gov.uk

DISABLED BIRDER'S ASSOCIATION (2000; 700)
The DBA is a registered charity and international movement, which aims to promote access to reserves and other birding places and to a range of services, so that people with different needs can follow the birding obsession as freely as able-bodied people. Membership is currently free and new members are needed to help give a stronger message across to those who own and manage nature reserves to improve access when they are planning and improving facilities. DBA also seeks to influence those who provide birdwatching services and equipment. The DBA also runs overseas trips. Chairman, Bo Beolens.
Contact: The Membership Secretary, Margaret Read MBE, Disabled Birder's Association, 121 Lavernock Road, Pengarth, Vale of Glamorgan CF64 3QG. e-mail: bo@fatbirder.com www.disabledbirdersassociation.co.uk

NATIONAL ORGANISATIONS

EARTHWATCH INSTITUTE (1971)

Earthwatch developed the innovative idea of engaging the general public into the scientific process by bringing together individual volunteers and scientists on field research projects, thereby providing an alternative means of funding, as well as a dedicated labour force for field scientists. Last year, more than 3,500 volunteers had worked on Earthwatch projects, which have grown to 140 projects in over 50 countries around the world. **Contact:** Earthwatch Institute (Europe), Mayfield House, 256 Banbury Road, Oxford OX2 7DE. 01864 318 838; e-mail: info@earthwatch.co.uk

EDWARD GREY INSTITUTE OF FIELD ORNITHOLOGY (1938)

The EGI takes its name from Edward Grey, first Viscount Grey of Fallodon, a life-long lover of birds and former Chancellor of the University of Oxford, who gave his support to an appeal for its foundation capital. The Institute now has a permanent research staff; it usually houses some 12-15 research students, five or six senior visitors and post-doctoral research workers. Field research is carried out mainly in Wytham Woods near Oxford and on the island of Skomer in West Wales. In addition there are laboratory facilities and aviary space for experimental work. The Institute houses the Alexander Library, one of the largest collections of 20th Century material on birds in the world and which is supported by the British Ornithologists Union which provides much of the material. It also houses the British Falconers Club library. The Library is open to members of the BOU and Oxford Ornithological Society; other bona fide ornithologists may use the library by prior arrangement.
Contact: Clare Harvey, PA to Prof. Sheldon, Edward Grey Institute, Department of Zoology, South Parks Road, Oxford OX1 3PS. 01865 271274, Alexander Library 01865 271143; e-mail: lynne. bradley@zoology.oxford.ac.uk; e-mail:clare. rowsell@zoo.ox.ac.uk web-site, EGI: http:// egizoosrv.zoo.ox.ac.uk/EGI/EGIhome.htm web-site library http://users.ox.ac.uk/~zoolib/

ENVIRONMENT AGENCY

A non-departmental body that aims to protect and improve the environment and to contribute towards the delivery of sustainable development through the integrated management of air, land and water. Functions include pollution prevention and control, waste minimisation, management of water resources, flood defence, improvement of salmon and freshwater fisheries, conservation of aquatic species, navigation and use of inland and coastal waters for recreation. Sponsored by the Department of the Environment, Transport and the Regions, MAFF and the Welsh Office.
Contact: Environment Agency, National Customer Contact Centre, PO Box 544, Rotherham S60 1BY. General enquiries; 08708 506 506 (Mon-Fri, 8am - 6pm); e-mail: enquiries@environment-agency. gov.uk
www.environment-agency.gov.uk
Pollution hotline - 0800 807 060.

FARMING AND WILDLIFE ADVISORY GROUP (FWAG) (1969)

An independent UK-registered charity led by farmers and supported by government and leading countryside organisations. Its aim is to unite farming and forestry with wildlife and landscape conservation. Active in most UK counties. There are 120 Farm Conservation Advisers who give practical advice to farmers and landowners to help them integrate environmental objectives with commercial farming practices.

Contact:
English Head Office, FWAG, National Agricultural Centre, Stoneleigh, Kenilworth, Warwickshire CV8 2RX. 02476 696 699; (Fax)02476 696 699; e-mail: info@fwag.org.uk www.fwag.org.uk

Northern Ireland, FWAG, National Agricultural Centre, 46b Rainey Street, Magherafelt, Co. Derry BT45 5AH. 028 7930 0606; (Fax)028 7930 0599; e-mail: n.ireland@fwag.org.uk

Scottish Head Office, FWAG Scotland, Algo Business Centre, Glenearn Road, Perth PH2 ONJ. 01738 450 500; (Fax)01738 450 495; e-mail: steven.hunt@fwag.org.uk

Wales Head Office. FWAG Cymru, c/o Countryside Council For Wales, Eden House, Ithon Road, Llandrindod Wells, Powys LD1 6AS. 01341 421 456; (Fax) 01341 422 757; e-mail: helen.barnes@fwag.org.uk.

FIELD STUDIES COUNCIL (1943)

Manages Centres where students from schools, universities and colleges, as well as individuals of all ages, can stay to study various aspects of the environment under expert guidance. Courses include many for birdwatchers, providing opportunities to study birdlife on coasts, estuaries, mountains and islands. Others demonstrate bird ringing and others are for members of the BTO. Research workers and naturalists wishing to use the records and resources are welcome.
Contact: Field Studies Council, Preston Montford, Montford Bridge, Shrewsbury SY4 1HW. 01743 852 100; (Fax)01743 852 101; e-mail: fsc.headoffice@field-studies-council.org www.field-studies-council.org

Centres:
Amersham Field Centre, Mop End, Amersham, Bucks

NATIONAL ORGANISATIONS

HP7 0QR. 01494 721 054; (Fax)01494 726 893;
e-mail: enquiries.am@field-studies-council.org

Blencathra Field Centre, Threlkeld, Keswick, Cumbria CA12 4SG, 01768 77 9601;
e-mail: enquiries.bl@field-studies-council.org

Brockhole Centre, L.D.N.P.A. Education Service, The Lake District Visitor Centre, Brockhole, Windermere, Cumbria LA23 1LJ. 01539 440 800; (Fax)015394 455 555; e-mail: education@lake-district.gov.uk

Castle Head Field Centre, Grange-over-Sands, Cumbria LA11 6QT, 0845 330 7364;
e-mail: enquiries.ch@field-studies-council.org

Dale Fort Field Centre, Haverfordwest, Pembs SA62 3RD, 0845 330 7365;
e-mail: enquiries.df@field-studies-council.org

Derrygonnelly Field Centre, Tir Navar, Creamery St, Derrygonnelly, Co Fermanagh, BT93 6HW. 028 686 41673;
e-mail: enquiries.dg.@field-studies-council.org

Epping Forest Field Centre, High Beach, Loughton, Essex, IG10 4AF, 020 8502 8500;
e-mail: enquiries.ef@field-studies-council.org

Flatford Mill Field Centre, East Bergholt, Suffolk, CO7 6UL, 0845 330 7368;
-mail: enquiries.fm@field-studies-council.org

Juniper Hall Field Centre, Dorking, Surrey, RH5 6DA, 0845 458 3507;
e-mail: enquiries.jh@field-studies-council.org

Kindrogan Field Centre, Enochdhu, Blairgowrie, Perthshire PH10 7PG. 01250 870 150;
e-mail: admin.kd@field-studies-council.org

Malham Tarn Field Centre, Settle, N Yorks, BD24 9PU, 01729 830 331;
e-mail: fsc.malham@ukonline.co.uk

Margam Park Field Centre, Port Talbot SA13 2TJ. 01639 8956 36; e-mail: margam_sustainable_centre@hotmail.com

Nettlecombe Court, The Leonard Wills Field Centre, Williton, Taunton, Somerset, TA4 4HT, 01984 640 320; e-mail: enquiries.nc@field-studies-council.org

Orielton Field Centre, Pembroke, Pembs,SA71 5EZ, 0845 330 7372;
e-mail: enquiries.or@field-studies-council.org

Preston Montford Field Centre, Montford Bridge, Shrewsbury, SY4 1DX, 0845 330 7378;
e-mail: enquiries.pm@field-studies-council.org

Rhyd-y-creuau, the Drapers' Field Centre Betws-y-coed, Conwy, LL24 0HB, 01690 710 494;
e-mail: enquiries.rc@field-studies-council.org

Slapton Ley Field Centre, Slapton, Kingsbridge, Devon, TQ7 2QP, 01548 580 466;
e-mail: enquiries.sl@field-studies-council.org

FIELDFARE TRUST
A registered charity, Fieldfare works with people with disabilities and countryside managers to improve access to the countryside for everyone. It provides advice and training services to countryside management teams, supported by its research into national standards for accessibility under the BT Countryside  for All Project. For members of the public it runs projects which can enable them to take action locally, provide information on accessible places to visit and run events like the Fieldfare Kielder Challenge which encourages young people to get active in the countryside.
Contact: Fieldfare Trust, Volunteer House, 69 Crossgate, Cupar, Fife KY15 5AS. 01334 657 708;
e-mail: info@fieldfare.org.uk; www.fieldfare.org.uk

FORESTRY COMMISSION OF GREAT BRITAIN
The government department responsible for the protection and expansion of Britain's forests and woodlands, it runs from national offices in England, Wales and Scotland, working to targets set by Commissioners and Ministers in each of the three countries. Its objectives are to protect Britain's forests and resources, conserve and improve the biodiversity, landscape and cultural heritage of forests and woodlands, develop opportunities for woodland recreation and increase public understanding and community participation in forestry.
Contact: *Forestry Commission GB Functions*, 231 Corstorphine Road, Edinburgh EH12 7AT. 0131 334 0303; (Fax) 0131 334 3047,
e-mail: enquiries@forestry.gsi.gov.uk
www.forestry.gov.uk

Forestry Commission England, Great Eastern House, Tenison Road, Cambridge CB1 2DU. 01223 314 546; (Fax) 01223 460 699;
e-mail: fcengland@forestry.gsi.gov.uk

Forestry Commission Scotland, 231 Corstorphine Road, Edinburgh EH12 7AT. 0131 334 0303, Fax : 0131 314 6152;
e-mail: fcscotland@forestry.gsi.gov.uk

Forestry Commission Wales, Victoria Terrace, Aberystwyth, Ceredigion, SY23 2DQ. 0845 604 0845; Fax : 01970 625 282;
e-mail: fcwenquiries@forestry.gsi.gov.uk

NATIONAL ORGANISATIONS

FRIENDS OF THE EARTH (1971; 100,000)
The largest international network of environmental groups in the world, represented in 68 countries. In the UK it has a unique network of campaigning local groups, working in 200 communities in England, Wales and Northern Ireland. It is largely funded by supporters with more than 90% of income coming from individual donations, the rest from special fundraising events, grants and trading.
Contact: Friends of the Earth, 26-28 Underwood Street, London, N1 7JQ. 020 7490 1555; (Fax)020 7490 0881; e-mail: info@foe.co.uk
www.foe.co.uk

GAME CONSERVANCY TRUST (1933; 22,000)
A registered charity which researches the conservation of game and other wildlife in the British countryside. More than 60 scientists are engaged in detailed work on insects, pesticides, birds (30 species inc. raptors), mammals (inc. foxes), and habitats. The results are used to advise government, landowners, farmers and conservationists on practical management techniques which will benefit game species, their habitats, and wildlife. Each June the *Annual Review* lists about 50 papers published in the peer-reviewed scientific press.
Contact: Game Conservancy Trust, Fordingbridge, Hampshire, SP6 1EF. 01425 652 381; (Fax)01425 655 848; e-mail: info@gct.org.uk www.gct.org.uk

GAY BIRDERS CLUB (1994; 300+)
A voluntary society for lesbian, gay and bisexual birdwatchers, their friends and supporters, over the age of consent, in the UK and worldwide. The club has a network of regional contacts and organises day trips, weekends and longer events at notable birding locations in the UK and abroad; about 200+ events in a year. Members receive a quarterly newletter *Out Birding* with details of all events. There is a Grand Get-Together every 18 months. Membership £12 waged and £5 unwaged.
Contact: Gay Birders Club, GeeBeeCee, BCM-Mono, London WC1N 3XX. www.gbc-online.org.uk
e-mail: contact@gbc-online.org.uk

GOLDEN ORIOLE GROUP (1987; 15)
Organises censuses of breeding Golden Orioles in parts of Cambridgeshire, Norfolk and Suffolk. Maintains contact with a network of individuals in other parts of the country where Orioles may or do breed. Studies breeding biology, habitat and food requirements of the species.
Contact: Jake Allsop, Golden Oriole Group, 5 Bury Lane, Haddenham, Ely, Cambs CB6 3PR. 01353 740 540; www.goldenoriolegroup.org.uk

HAWK AND OWL TRUST (1969)

Registered charity dedicated to the conservation and appreciation of wild birds of prey and their habitats. Publishes a newsletter *Peregrine* and educational materials for all ages.The Trust achieves its major aim of creating and enhancing nesting, roosting and feeding habitats for birds of prey through projects which involve practical research, creative conservation and education, both on its own reserves and in partnership with landowners, farmers and others. Members are invited to take part in fieldwork, population studies, surveys, etc. The Trust manages three main reserves: Sculthorpe Moor in Norfolk; Shapwick Moor on the Somerset Levels; and Fylingdales Moor conservation area in North Yorkshire. Its Sculthorpe reserve near Fakenham, Norfolk and Conservation and Education Centre at Chiltern Open Air Museum near Chalfont St Giles, Buckinghamshire, offer schools and other groups cross-curricular environmental activities
Contact: Hawk and Owl Trust, PO Box 400, Bishops Lydeard, Taunton TA4 3WH Tel: 0844 984 2824
E-mail: enquiries@hawkandowl.org
www.hawkandowl.org

INTERNATIONAL CENTRE FOR BIRDS OF PREY (1967)
Formerly the National Bird of Prey Centre, it is once again under the direction of founder Jemima Parry-Jones MBE. Seeks to deliver conservation of birds of prey through captive breeding, rescue and rehabilitation, and research. The Centre is home to some 170 birds of prey and has an active captive breeding programme of many of its residents and also contributes to the rescue, and rehabilitation of the many species brought into the Centre each year. Open all year 10.30am-5.30pm (or dusk if earlier) Closed Christmas and Boxing Day.
Contact: International Centre for Birds of Prey, Newent, Glos, GL18 1JJ. 0870 990 1992;
e-mail: kb@nbpc.org www.nbpc.co.uk

IRISH RARE BIRDS COMMITTEE (1985)

Assesses records of species of rare occurrence in the Republic of Ireland. Details of records accepted and rejected are incorporated in the *Irish Bird Report*, published annually in *Irish Birds*. In the case of rarities trapped for ringing, ringers in the Republic of Ireland are required to send their schedules initially to the National Parks and Wildlife Service, 51 St Stephen's Green, Dublin 2. A copy is then taken before the schedules are sent to the British Trust for Ornithology.

NATIONAL ORGANISATIONS

Contact: Paul Milne, Hon Secretary, Irish Rare Birds Committee, 100 Dublin Road, Sutton, Dublin 13. +353 (0)1 832 5653; e-mail: pjmilne@hotmail.com www.irbc.ie

JOINT NATURE CONSERVATION COMMITTEE (1990)
A committee of the three country agencies (English Nature, Scottish Natural Heritage and the Countryside Council for Wales), together with independent members and representatives from Northern Ireland and the Countryside Agency. Supported by specialist staff, its statutory responsibilities include the establishment of common standards for monitoring, the analysis of information and research; advising Ministers on the development and implementation of policies for or affecting nature conservation; and the undertaking and commissioning of research relevant to these functions. JNCC additionally has the UK responsibility for relevant European and wider international matters. The Species Team, located at the HQ address is responsible for terrestrial bird conservation.
Contact: Joint Nature Conservation Committee, Monkstone House, City Road, Peterborough PE1 1JY. 01733 562 626; (Fax)01733 555 948; e-mail: comment@jncc.gov.uk www.jncc.gov.uk

LINNEAN SOCIETY OF LONDON (1788, 2,000)
Named after Carl Linnaeus, the 18th Century Swedish biologist, who created the modern system of scientific biological nomenclature, the Society promotes all aspects of pure and applied biology. It houses Linnaeus' collection of plants, insects and fishes, library and correspondence. The Society has a major reference library of some 100,000 volumes. Publishes the Biological, Botanical and Zoological Journals, and the *Synopses of the British Fauna*.
Contact: Linnean Society of London, Burlington House, Piccadilly, London W1J 0BF. 020 7434 4479; (Fax)020 7287 9364; e-mail: info@linnean.org www.linnean.org

MAMMAL SOCIETY (1954; 2,500)
The Mammal Society is the only organisation solely dedicated to the study and conservation of all British mammals. It seeks to raise awareness of mammal ecology and conservation needs, to survey British mammals and their habitats to identify the threats they face and to to promote mammal studies in the UK and overseas.

Contact: The Mammal Society, 2B Inworth Street, London SW11 3EP. 020 7350 2200; (Fax)020 7350 2211; e-mail: enquiries@mammal.org.uk
The Mammal Society, 3 The Carronades, New Road, Southampton SO14 0AA. 0238 0237 874; (Fax)0238 0634 726. www.mammal.org.uk

MANX ORNITHOLOGICAL SOCIETY see County Directory

MANX WILDLIFE TRUST see County Directory

MARINE CONSERVATION SOCIETY (1983)
MCS is the UK charity that campaigns for clean seas and beaches around the British coastline, sustainable fisheries, and protection for all marine life. MCS is consulted on a wide range of marine issues and provides advice primarily to government. but also to industry, on topics ranging from offshore wind and oil and gas to marine strategies and fisheries reform. It provides advice to ensure that further action is taken to conserve our seas and reduce the effect of marine activities on marine habitats and species. It has an extensive programme for volunteers, ranging from fund-raising and an annual clean-up of UK beaches to surveys of species such as basking shark.
Contact: Marine Conservation Society, Unit 3 Wolf Business Park, Alton Road, Ross-on-Wye, Herefordshire HR9 5NB. 01989 566 017. www.mcsuk.org

NATIONAL TRUST (1895; 3.5 million)
Charity that works for the preservation of places of historic interest or natural beauty in England, Wales and Northern Ireland. It relies on 3.5 million members, 49,000 volunteers, 500,000 school children and millions of visitors, donors and supporters. The Trust protects and opens to the public more than 300 historic houses and gardens, 49 industrial monuments and mills, plus more than 617,500 acres of land and 700 miles of coast. About 10% of SSSIs and ASSIs in England, Wales and Northern Ireland are wholly or partially owned by the Trust, as are 63 NNRs (e.g. Blakeney Point, Wicken Fen, Murlough and Dinefwr Estate), 33% of Ramsar sites include Trust land as do 45% of SPAs.
Contact: National Trust, PO Box 39, Warrington, WA5 7WD. 0844 800 1895; (Fax)0844 800 4642; e-mail: enquiries@thenationaltrust.org.uk www.nationaltrust.org.uk

NATIONAL TRUST FOR SCOTLAND (1931; 310,000)
The conservation charity that protects and promotes Scotland's natural and cultural heritage for present and future generations to enjoy. Its 128 properties open to the public are described in its annual *Scotland For You* guide.
Contact: National Trust for Scotland, Wemyss House, 28 Charlotte Square, Edinburgh, EH2 4ET. 0844 493 2100; (Fax)0131 243 9301; e-mail: information@nts.org.uk www.nts.org.uk

NATURAL ENGLAND
Natural England has been formed by bringing together English Nature, the landscape, access and recreation elements of the Countryside Agency and

the environmental land management functions of the Rural Development Service.
Natural England is working towards the delivery of four strategic outcomes:
- A healthy natural environment through conservation and enhancement.
- Encouraging more people to enjoy, understand and act to improve the natural environment, more often.
- Ensure the use and management of the natural environment is more sustainable.
- A secure environmental future.

Contact: Natural England, Northminster House, Peterborough, PE1 1UA. 0845 600 3078; (Fax)01733 455103; e-mail: enquiries@naturalengland.org.uk www.naturalengland.org.uk

NATURAL HISTORY MUSEUM AT TRING (1937)
Founded by Lionel Walter (later Lord) Rothschild, the Museum displays British and exotic birds (1,500 species) including many rarities and extinct species. Galleries open all year except 24-26 Dec. Adjacent to the Bird Group of the Natural History Museum - with over a million specimens and an extensive ornithological library, an internationally important centre for bird research.
Contact: The Natural History Museum at Tring, Akeman Street, Tring, Herts HP23 6AP. 020 7942 6171; (Fax)020 7942 6150; www.nhm.ac.uk/tring e-mail: tring-enquiries@nhm.ac.uk

NATURE PHOTOGRAPHERS' PORTFOLIO (1944; 74)
A society for photographers of wildlife, especially birds. Circulates postal portfolios of prints and transparencies and an on-line folio.
Contact: A Winspear-Cundall, Hon Secretary, Nature Photographers' Portfolio, 8 Gig Bridge Lane, Pershore, Worcs WR10 1NH. 01386 552103; www.nature-photographers-portfolio.co.uk

NORTHERN IRELAND BIRDWATCHERS' ASSOCIATION (1991; 120)
The NIBA Records Committee, established in 1997, has full responsibility for the assessment of records in N Ireland. NIBA also publishes the *Northern Ireland Bird Report* and is responsible for Flightline, a local rate telephone hotline for rare bird sightings.
Contact: Wilton Farrelly, Hon Secretary, Northern Ireland Birdwatchers' Assoc, 24 Cabin Hill Gardens, Knock, Belfast BT5 7AP. 028 9022 5818; e-mail: wilton.farrelly@ntlworld.com

NORTHERN IRELAND ORNITHOLOGISTS' CLUB (1965; 150)
Formed to focus the interests of active birdwatchers in Northern Ireland, it operates Tree Sparrow and Barn Owl nestbox schemes and a winter feeding programme for Yellowhammers. Has a regular programme of lectures and field trips for members

and organises a high quality annual photographic competition. Publishes *The Harrier* quarterly.
Contact: Mrs Carol Gillespie, Northern Ireland Ornithologists Club, 4 Demesne Gate, Saintfield, Co. Down, BT24 7BE. www.nioc.co.uk

NORTH SEA BIRD CLUB (1979; 200)
The stated aims of the Club are to: provide a recreational pursuit for people employed offshore; obtain, collate and analyse observations of all birds seen offshore; produce reports of observations, including an annual report; promote the collection of data on other wildlife offshore. Currently it holds in excess of 100,000 records of birds, cetaceans and insects reported since 1979.
Contact: Andrew Thorpe, The North Sea Bird Club, Ocean Laboratory and Culterty Field Station, University of Aberdeen, Newburgh, Aberdeenshire AB41 6AA. 01224-274 428 (Fax) 01224-274 402; e-mail: nsbc@abdn.ac.uk www.abdn.ac.uk/nsbc

PEOPLE'S DISPENSARY FOR SICK ANIMALS (1917)
Registered charity. Provides free veterinary treatment for sick and injured animals whose owners qualify for this charitable service.
Contact: PDSA, Whitechapel Way, Priorslee, Telford, Shropshire TF2 9PQ. 01952 290 999; (Fax)01952 291 035; e-mail: pr@pdsa.org.uk www. pdsa.org.uk

POND CONSERVATION
Pond Conservation is the national charity dedicated to creating and protecting ponds and the wildlife they support. It carries
out research, surveys and practical conservation, working in partnership with others, and also works to protect the wildlife of other freshwaters. Key projects include: Million Ponds Project, an ambitious scheme to dig half a million new high-quality potential ponds in the UK that will be good for biodiversity; Garden ponds survey to find out what really lives in the UK's garden ponds; Pond Habitat Action Plan, in conjunction with the Environment Agency.
Contact: Pond Conservation, c/o School of Life Sciences, Oxford Brookes University, Gipsy Lane, Headington, Oxford OX3 0BP.
e-mail: info@pondconservation.org.uk www.pondconservation.org.uk

RAPTOR FOUNDATION (1989)
Involved in the care of wild disabled birds of prey, as well as raptors rescued from breeders. The foundation is involved in research into raptor ailments and assists veterinary schools with placement of student vets at the centre. A full 24 hour rescue service is available for injured

raptors and owls and the centre assists in breed-and-release schemes to rebuild populations across Europe. Centre is open to the public (200 birds of 40 different species on display) 10am to 5pm each day apart from Jan 1 and Dec 25/26.

Contact: The Raptor Foundation, The Heath, St Ives Road, Woodhurst, Cambs PE28 3BT. 01487 741 140; e-mail: heleowl@aol.com
www.raptorfoundation.org.uk

RAPTOR RESCUE (1978)

Since inauguration, Raptor Rescue has evolved into one of the UK's foremost organisations dedicated to ensuring all sick and injured birds of prey are cared for in heated hospital units by suitably qualified people, and wherever possible, released back into the wild. Facilities include secluded aviaries, rehabilitation aviaries/flights, foster birds for rearing young to avoid imprinting. Veterinary support. Reg charity.

Contact: Raptor Rescue, Bird of Prey Rehabilitation, 28 Victoria Road, Great Sankey, Warrington, WA5 2ST. (National advice line) 0870 241 0609; e-mail: info@raptorrescue.org.uk
www.raptorrescue.org.uk

RARE BREEDING BIRDS PANEL (1973; 7)

An independent body funded by the JNCC and RSPB. Both bodies are represented on the panel, as are BTO and ACRE. It collects all information on rare breeding birds in the United Kingdom, so that changes in status can be monitored as an aid to conservation and stored for posterity. Special forms are used (obtainable free from the secretary and the website) and records should be submitted via the county and regional recorders. Since 1996 the Panel also monitors breeding by scarcer non-native species and seeks records of these in the same way. Annual report is published in *British Birds*. For details of species covered by the Panel see Log Charts and the websites.

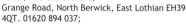

Contact: The Secretary, Rare Breeding Birds Panel, The Old Orchard, Grange Road, North Berwick, East Lothian EH39 4QT. 01620 894 037; e-mail: secretary@rbbp.org.uk www.rbbp.org.uk

ROYAL AIR FORCE ORNITHOLOGICAL SOCIETY (1965; 250)

RAFOS organises regular field meetings for members, carries out ornithological census work on MoD properties and mounts major expeditions annually to various UK and overseas locations. Publishes a Newsletter twice a year, a Journal annually, and reports on its expeditions and surveys.

Contact: General Secretary by e-mail: rafos_secretary@hotmail.com
www.rafos.org.uk

ROYAL NAVAL BIRDWATCHING SOCIETY (1946; 250 approx)

Covering all main ocean routes, the Society has a system for reporting the positions and identity of seabirds and landbirds at sea by means of standard sea report forms. Maintains an extensive worldwide seabird database. Members are encouraged to photograph birds and a library of images is maintained. Publishes a Bulletin and an annual report entitled *The Sea Swallow*. The Simpson Scholarship provides assistance to embryonic ornithologists for studies regarding seabirds and landbirds at sea.

Contact: Cdr FS Ward RN, Gen Secretary, Royal Naval Birdwatching Society, 16 Cutlers Lane, Stubbington, Fareham, Hants PO14 2JN. +44 1329 665 931; e-mail: francisward@btopenworld.com
www.rnbws.org.uk

ROYAL PIGEON RACING ASSOCIATION (1897; 39,000)

Exists to promote the sport of pigeon racing and controls pigeon racing within the Association. Organises liberation sites, issues rings, calculates distances between liberation sites and home lofts, and assists in the return of strays. May be able to assist in identifying owners of ringed birds caught or found.

Contact: David Bills, General Manager, Royal Pigeon Racing Association, The Reddings, Cheltenham, GL51 6RN. 01452 713 529; www.rpra.org
e-mail: gm@rpra.org or strays@rpra.org

ROYAL SOCIETY FOR THE PREVENTION OF CRUELTY TO ANIMALS (1824; 43,690)

In addition to its animal centres, the Society also runs a woodland study centre and nature reserve at Mallydams Wood in East Sussex and specialist wildlife rehabilitation centres at West Hatch, Taunton, Somerset TA3 5RT (0870 0101847), at Station Road, East Winch, King's Lynn, Norfolk PE32 1NR (0870 9061420), and London Road, Stapeley, Nantwich, Cheshire CW5 7JW (not open to the public) Inspectors are contacted through their National Communication Centre, which can be reached via the Society's 24-hour national cruelty and advice line: 08705 555 999.

Contact: RSPCA Headquarters, RSPCA, Willberforce Way, Horsham, West Sussex RH13 9RS. 0300 1234 555; (Fax)0303 123 0284. 24-hour cruelty and advice line: 0300 1234 999. www.rspca.org.uk

NATIONAL ORGANISATIONS

ROYAL SOCIETY FOR THE PROTECTION OF BIRDS (1899 1,000,000+)

UK Partner of BirdLife International, and Europe's largest voluntary wildlife conservation body. The RSPB, a registered charity, is governed by an elected body (see also RSPB Phoenix and RSPB Wildlife Explorers) Its work in the conservation of wild birds and habitats covers the acquisition and management of nature reserves; research and surveys; monitoring and responding to development proposals, land use practices and pollution which threaten wild birds and biodiversity; and the provision of an advisory service on wildlife law enforcement.

Work in the education and information field includes formal education in schools and colleges, and informal activities for children through Wildlife Explorers; publications (including *Birds*, a quarterly magazine for members); displays and exhibitions; and the development of membership activities through Members' Groups.

The RSPB currently manages 200 nature reserves in the UK, covering almost 130,00 hectares and home to 80% of Britain's rarest or most threatened bird species. The aim is to conserve a countrywide network of reserves with all examples of the main bird communities and with due regard to the conservation of plants and other animals.

Current national projects include extensive work on agriculture, and conservation and campaigning for the conservation of the marine environment and to halt the illegal persecution of birds of prey. Increasingly, there is involvement with broader environmental concerns such as climate change and transport.

The RSPB's International Dept works closely with Birdlife International and its partners in other countries and is involved with numerous projects overseas, especially in Europe and Asia.

Contact: RSPB, The Lodge, Sandy, Beds SG19 2DL. Membership enquiries: 01767 693 680. Wildlife enquiries: 01767 693 690; (Fax)01767 692 365; e-mail: (firstname.name)@rspb.org.uk www.rspb.org.uk

Regional Offices:
ENGLAND
Eastern England Regional Office, Stalham House, 65 Thorpe Road, Norwich, Norfolk, NR1 1UD. 01603 661 662.
Covers: Beds, Cambs, Essex, Herts, Lincs, Norfolk, Suffolk.

London Office, RSPB London Office, 2nd Floor, 65 Petty France, London, SW1H 9EU. 0207 808 1240.

Midlands Regional Office, 46 The Green, South Bar, Banbury, Oxfordshire, OX16 9AB. 01295 253 330.
Covers: Bucks, Derbys, Herefordshire, Leicestershire, Northants, Notts, Oxon, Rutland, Shropshire, Staffs, Warwickshire, West Midlands, Worcestershire.

Northern England Regional Office, Denby Dale Office, Westleigh Mews, Wakefield Road, Denby Dale, Huddersfield, HD8 8QD. 01484 861 148.
Covers: Cheshire, Cleveland, Cumbria, East Riding of Yorkshire, Greater Manchester, Lancashire, Merseyside, Middlesbrough, North, South and West Yorkshire, North East and North Lincolnshire, Northumberland, Tyne and Wear.

South East Regional Office, 2nd Floor, 42 Frederick Place, Brighton, East Sussex, BN1 4EA. 01273 775 333.
Covers: East Sussex, Hampshire, Isle of Wight, Kent, Surrey, West Berkshire, West Sussex.

South West Regional Office, Keble House, Southernhay Gardens, Exeter, Devon, EX1 1NT. 01392 432 691.
Covers: Bristol, Cornwall, Devon, Dorset, Somerset, Gloucs, Wiltshire.

SCOTLAND
Scotland Headquarters, Dunedin House, 25 Ravelston Terrace, Edinburgh, EH4 3TP. 0131 311 6500.
e-mail: rspb.scotland@rspb.org.uk

East Scotland Regional Office, 10 Albyn Terrace, Aberdeen, Aberdeenshire, AB10 1YP. 01224 624 824.
Covers: Aberdeen, Aberdeenshire, Angus, Moray, Perth and Kinross.

North Scotland Regional Office, Etive House, Beechwood Park, Inverness, IV2 3BW. 01463 715 000; e-mail: nsro@rspb.org.uk
Covers: Eilean Siar, Highland.

South and West Scotland Regional Office, 10 Park Quadrant, Glasgow, G3 6BS. 0141 331 0993; e-mail: glasgow@rspb.org.uk
Covers: Argyll and Bute, Clackmannanshire, Dumfries and Galloway, East Ayrshire, East Lothian, East Dunbartonshire, East Renfrewshire, Midlothian, North Ayrshire, North Lanarkshire, Renfrewshire, Scottish borders, South Ayrshire, South Lanarkshire, Stirling, West Dunbartonshire, West Lothian.

WALES
RSPB Wales, Sutherland House, Castlebridge, Cowbridge Road East, Cardiff CF11 9AB. 029 2035 3000.

NORTHERN IRELAND
Northern Ireland Headquarters, Belvoir Park Forest, Belfast, BT8 7QT. 028 9049 1547.
Covers: County Antrim,County Armagh, County Down, County Fermanagh, County Londonderry, County Tyrone.

RSPB WILDLIFE EXPLORERS and RSPB PHOENIX (formerly YOC) (1965; 168,000)

Junior section of the RSPB. There are more than 100 groups run by 300 volunteers. Activities include projects, holidays, roadshows, competitions, and local events for children, families and teenagers. Phoenix members (13 years and over) receive *BirdLife* magazine every two months, plus *Wingbeat* - the only environmental magazine written by teenagers for teenagers - four times a year.
Contact: The Youth Manager, RSPB Youth and Education Dept, The Lodge, Sandy, Beds SG19 2DL. 01767 680 551; e-mail: explorers@rspb.org.uk and phoenix@rspb.org.uk
www.rspb.org.uk/youth

SAVE OUR SEABIRDS CHARITABLE TRUST (1988)

Founded following an oil spill which resulted in oiled birds being washed ashore in SE England, it now has two functions:1) to rescue and support the rescue of seabirds injured by pollution and 2) to raise awareness of the pollution that damages them. The Trust has built up a network of concerned people and carers along the South-East coast organised in five geographical areas: Medway to Folkestone; Rye to Bexhill; Pevensey Bay to Cuckmere; Newhaven to Hove; and Shoreham to Chichester. In practical terms, its members act to get injured seabirds to carers as quickly as possible; advise people who report casulaties how best to help; keep carers in touch with each other and up-to date with the best methods of care for various injuries; and run money-raising events.
Contact: Save Our Seabirds Charitable Trust, 22 Pearl Court, Courtfield Terrace, Eastbourne, East Sussex BN21 4AA. E-mail: stanleysec@aol.com
www.saveourseabirdscharitabletrust.org.uk/

SCOTTISH BIRDS RECORDS COMMITTEE (1984; 7 members, plus secretary)

Set up by the Scottish Ornithologists' Club to ensure that records of species not deemed rare enough to be considered by the British Birds Rarities Committee, but which are rare in Scotland, are fully assessed; also maintains the official list of Scottish birds.
Contact: Angus Hogg, Secretary, Scottish Birds Records Committee, 11 Kirkmichael Road, Crosshill, Maybole, Ayrshire KA19 7RJ.
e-mail: dcgos@globalnet.co.uk
www.the-soc.org.uk

SCOTTISH ORNITHOLOGISTS' CLUB (1936; 2,250)

The Club has 14 branches (see County Directory), each with a programme of winter meetings and field trips throughout the year. The SOC organises an annual weekend conference in the autumn and a joint SOC/BTO one-day birdwatchers' conference in spring. In August 2009 it re-launched its magazine, *Scottish Birds*, which is now published quarterly and incorporates the *Scottish Bird News* and the scarce sightings journal *Birding Scotland*. The SOC is based in a large resource centre which offers panoramic views of Aberlady Bay and houses the George Waterston Library. Details can be found on the website.
Contact: The Scottish Birdwatching Resource Centre, The SOC, Waterston House, Aberlady, East Lothian EH32 0PY. 01875 871 330; (Fax)01875 871 035;
e-mail: mail@the-soc.org.uk www.the-soc.org.uk

SCOTTISH NATURAL HERITAGE (1991)

SNH is the Scottish Executive's statutory advisor in respect to the conservation, enhancement, enjoyment, understanding and sustainable use of the natural heritage.
Contact: Scottish Natural Heritage, Great Glen House, Inverness IV3 8NW. 01463 725000;
e-mail: enquiries@snh.gov.uk
www.snh.org.uk

SCOTTISH SOCIETY FOR THE PREVENTION OF CRUELTY TO ANIMALS (1839; 45,000 supporters)

Represents animal welfare interests to Government, local authorities and others. Educates young people to realise their responsibilities. Maintains an inspectorate to patrol and investigate and to advise owners about the welfare of animals and birds in their care. Maintains welfare centres, two of which include oiled bird cleaning centres. Bird species, including birds of prey, are rehabilitated and where possible released back into the wild.
Contact: Scottish SPCA, Braehead Mains, 603 Queensferry Road, Edinburgh EH4 6EA. 03000 999 999; (Fax)0131 339 4777;
e-mail: enquiries@scottishspca.org
www.scottishspca.org

SCOTTISH WILDLIFE TRUST (1964; 35,000)

The Trust aims to re-establish: "a network of healthy and resilient ecosystems supporting expanding communities of native species across large areas of Scotland's land, water and seas." Its main activities focus on managing 123 wildlife reserves and undertaking practical conservation tasks; influencing and campaigning for better wildlife-related policy and action; and, inspiring people to enjoy and find out more about wildlife. Member of The Wildlife Trusts partnership and organises Scottish Wildlife Week. Publishes *Scottish Wildlife* three times a year.
Contact: Scottish Wildlife Trust, Cramond House, Cramond Glebe Road, Edinburgh EH4 6NS. 0131 312 7765; (Fax)0131 312 8705; www.swt.org.uk
e-mail: enquiries@swt.org.uk

NATIONAL ORGANISATIONS

SEABIRD GROUP (1966; 350)

Concerned with conservation issues affecting seabirds. Co-ordinates census and monitoring work on breeding seabirds; has established and maintains the Seabird Colony Register in collaboration with the JNCC; organises triennial conferences on seabird biology and conservation topics. Small grants available to assist with research and survey work on seabirds. Publishes the *Seabird Group Newsletter* every four months and the journal *Atlantic Seabirds* quarterly, in association with the Dutch Seabird Group.
Contact: Linda Wilson, JNCC, Dunnet House, 7 Thistle Place, Aberdeen, AB10 1UZ;
e-mail: linda.wilson@jncc.gov.uk
www.seabirdgroup.org.uk

SOCIETY OF WILDLIFE ARTISTS (1964; 69 Members, 68 Associates)

Registered charity that seeks to generate an appreciation of the natural world through all forms of fine art. Annual exhibition held in Sept/Oct at the Mall Galleries, London. Through bursary schemes (sponsored by Capmark Europe) the Society has been able to help young artists with awards of up to £1,000 towards travel, education or the cost of materials.
Contact: The Secretary, Society of Wildlife Artists, Federation of British Artists, 17 Carlton House Terrace, London SW1Y 5BD. 020 7930 6844;
e-mail: info@mallgalleries.com
www.swla.co.uk

SWAN SANCTUARY (2005)

Founded by Dorothy Beeson BEM. A registered charity which operates nationally. Has a fully equipped swan hospital with an operating theatre, X-ray facilities and a veterinary surgeon. New site has several nursing ponds and a four acre rehabilitatin lake where around 4,000 swans and the same number of other forms of wildlife are treated. 24-hour service operated, with volunteer rescuers on hand to recover victims of oil spills, vandalism etc. Reg. charity number 1002582.
Contact: The Swan Sanctuary, Felix Lane, Shepperton, Middlesex TW17 8NN. Emergency number: 01932 240 790;
e-mail: swans@swanuk.org.uk
www.swanuk.org.uk

UK400 CLUB (1981)

Serves to monitor the nation's leading twitchers and their life lists, and to keep under review contentious species occurrences. Publishes a bi-monthly magazine *Rare Birds*. Membership open to all.
Contact: LGR Evans, UK400 Club, 8 Sandycroft Road, Little Chalfont, Amersham, Bucks HP6 6QL. 01494 763 010; e-mail: LGREUK400@aol.com
www.uk400clubonline.co.uk

ULSTER WILDLIFE TRUST see County Directory

Ulster Wildlife Trust.

WADER STUDY GROUP (1970; 600)

An association of wader enthusiasts, both amateur and professional, from all parts of the world. The Group aims to maintain contact between them, to help in the organisation of co-operative studies, and to provide a vehicle for the exchange of information. Publishes the *Wader Study Group Bulletin* three times a year and holds annual meetings throughout Europe.
Contact: The General Secretary, Wader Study Group, The National Centre for Ornithology, The Nunnery, Thetford, Norfolk IP24 2PU.
www.waderstudygroup.org

WELSH KITE TRUST (1996; 1,200)

A registered charity that undertakes the conservation and annual monitoring of Red Kites in Wales. It attempts to locate all the breeding birds, to compile data on population growth, productivity, range expansion etc. The Trust liaises with landowners, acts as consultant on planning issues and with regard to filming and photography, and represents Welsh interests on the UK Kite Steering Group. Provides a limited rescue service for injured kites and eggs or chicks at risk of desertion or starvation. Publishes a newsletter *Boda Wennol* twice a year, sent free to subscribing Friends of the Welsh Kite and to all landowners with nesting kites.

Contact: Tony Cross, Project Officer, Welsh Kite Trust, Samaria, Nantmel, Llandrindod Wells, Powys LD1 6EN. 01597 825 981;
e-mail: tony.cross@welshkitetrust.org
www.welshkitetrust.org

WELSH ORNITHOLOGICAL SOCIETY (1988; 250)

Promotes the study, conservation and enjoyment of birds throughout Wales. Runs the Welsh Records Panel which adjudicates records of scarce species in Wales. Publishes the journal *Welsh Birds* twice a year, along with newsletters, and organises an annual conference.
Contact: Membership details from Welsh Ornithological Society, Alan Williams, Treasurer WOS, 30 Fairfield, Penperlleni, Pontypool, NP4 0AQ. e-mail: alan.williams6@virgin.net
http://welshos.org.uk

WETLAND TRUST

Set up to encourage conservation of wetlands and develop study of migratory birds, and to foster international relations in these fields. Destinations for recent expeditions inc. Brazil, Senegal, The

Gambia, Guinea-Bissau, Nigeria, Kuwait, Thailand, Greece and Jordan. Large numbers of birds are ringed each year in Sussex and applications are invited from individuals to train in bird ringing or extend their experience.
Contact: Phil Jones, Wetland Trust, Elms Farm, Pett Lane, Icklesham, Winchelsea, E Sussex TN36 4AH. 01797 226374; e-mail: phil@wetlandtrust.org

WILDFOWL & WETLANDS TRUST (1946; 130,000 members and 4,700 bird adopters)

Registered charity founded by the late Sir Peter Scott to conserve wetlands and their biodiversity. WWT has nine centres with reserves (see Arundel, Caerlaverock, Castle Espie, Llanelli, Martin Mere, Slimbridge, Washington, Welney, and The London Wetland Centre in Reserves and Observatories section) The centres are nationally or internationally important for wintering wildfowl. Programmes of walks and talks are available for visitors with varied interests - resources and programmes are provided for school groups. Centres, except Caerlaverock and Welney, have wildfowl from around the world, inc. endangered species. Research Department works on population dynamics, species management plans and wetland ecology. The Wetland Advisory Service (WAS) undertakes contracts, and Wetland Link International promotes the role of wetland centres for education and public awareness.
Contact: Wildfowl and Wetlands Trust, Slimbridge, Glos, GL2 7BT. 01453 891 900; (Fax)01453 890 827; e-mail: enquiries@wwt.org.uk
www.wwt.org.uk

WILDLIFE SOUND RECORDING SOCIETY (1968; 327)

Works closely with the Wildlife Section of the National Sound Archive. Members carry out recording work for scientific purposes as well as for pleasure. A field weekend is held each spring, and members organise meetings locally. Four CD sound magazines of members' recordings are produced for members each year, and a journal, *Wildlife Sound*, is published twice a year.
Contact: Hon Membership Secretary, WSRS, Wildlife Sound Recording Society.
e-mail: enquiries@wildlife-sound.org
www.wildlife-sound.org/

WILDLIFE TRUSTS (1995; 791,000)

Originally the Society for the Promotion of Nature Reserves, founded in 1912, now the largest UK charity exclusively dedicated to conserving all habitats and species, with a membership of more than 791,000 people including 108,000 junior members in 47 individual county trusts. Collectively, they manage more than 2,200 nature reserves spanning over 80,000 hectares. The Wildlife Trusts also lobby for better protection of the UK's natural heritage and are dedicated to

protecting wildlife for the future. Members receive *Natural World* magazine three times a year. See also Wildlife Watch.
Contact: The Wildlife Trusts, The Kiln, Waterside, Mather Road, Newark NG24 1WT. 01636 677 711; (Fax) 01636 670 001; www.wildlifetrusts.org
e-mail: enquiry@wildlifetrusts.org

WILDLIFE WATCH (1977; 108.000)

The junior branch of The Wildlife Trusts (see previous entry) It supports 1,500 registered volunteer leaders running Watch groups across the UK. Publishes *Watchword* and *Wildlife Extra* for children and activity books for adults working with young people.
Contact: Wildlife Watch, The Wildlife Trusts, The Kiln, Waterside, Mather Road, Newark NG24 1WT. 01636 677 711; (Fax) 01636 670 001; e-mail: watch@wildlifewatch.org
www.wildlifewatch.org.uk

WWF-UK (1961)

WWF is the world's largest independent conservation organisation, comprising 27 national organisations. It works to conserve endangered species, protect endangered spaces, and address global threats to nature by seeking long-term solutions with people in government and industry, education and civil society. Publishes *WWF News* (quarterly magazine)
Contact: WWF-UK (World Wide Fund for Nature), Panda House, Weyside Park, Catteshall Lane, Godalming, Surrey GU7 1XR. 01483 426 444; (Fax)01483 426 409; www.wwf.org.uk

ZOOLOGICAL PHOTOGRAPHIC CLUB (1899)

Circulates black and white and colour prints of zoological interest via a series of postal portfolios.
Contact: Martin B Withers, Hon Secretary, Zoological Photographic Club, 93 Cross Lane, Mountsorrel, Loughborough, Leics LE12 7BX. 0116 229 6080.

ZOOLOGICAL SOCIETY OF LONDON (1826)

Carries out research, organises symposia and holds scientific meetings. Manages the Zoological Gardens in Regent's Park (first opened in 1828) and Whipsnade Wild Animal Park near Dunstable, Beds, each with extensive collections of birds. The Society's library has a large collection of ornithological books and journals. Publications include *the Journal of Zoology, Animal Conservation, Conservation Biology* book series, *The Symposia* and *The International Zoo Yearbook*.
Contact: Zoological Society of London, Regent's Park, London, NW1 4RY. 020 7722 3333; www.zsl.org

NATIONAL PROJECTS

National ornithological projects depend for their success on the active participation of amateur birdwatchers. In return they provide birdwatchers with an excellent opportunity to contribute in a positive and worthwhile way to the scientific study of birds and their habitats, which is the vital basis of all conservation programmes. The following entries provide a description of each particular project and a note of whom to contact for further information (full address details are in the previous section).

BARN OWL MONITORING PROGRAMME
A BTO project
Volunteers monitor nest sites to record site occupancy, clutch size, brood size and breeding success. Qualified ringers may catch and ring adults and chicks and record measurements. Volunteers must be qualified bird ringers or nest recorders with a Schedule 1 licence for Barn Owl.
Contact: Carl Barimore,
e-mail: barnowls@bto.org

BIRD ATLAS 2007-11
BTO, run in partnership with BirdWatch Ireland and the Scottish Ornithologists' Club
Atlases have provided a periodic stock-take of the birds of Britain and Ireland, and this latest Atlas will do just that, only this time in both the breeding season and in winter. It will generate range and abundance maps for all species while giving the opportunity to contrast past and present distributions and assess changes, for better or worse. Fieldwork started in earnest in November 2007 and will run for 4 winters and 4 summers. Observers can submit their records and see up-to-date results online. Mapping Britain and Ireland's birds is a major undertaking and the BTO needs your support.
Contact: birdatlas@bto.org
www.birdatlas.net

BIRDTRACK
Organised by BTO on behalf of BTO, RSPB and BirdWatch Ireland.
BirdTrack is a year-round bird recording scheme, designed to collect large numbers of lists of birds. The idea is simple – you make a note of the birds seen at each site you visit and enter your daily observations on a simple-to-use web page. Birdwatchers can also send in other types of records, including counts and casual observations. The focus of the website (www.birdtrack.net) will be spring and autumn migration, seasonal

movements and the distribution of scarce species. BirdTrack is also an ideal electronic notebook to store your own bird records, allowing queries and reports by sites and species.
Contact: Nick Moran, BTO.
E-mail: birdtrack@bto.org

BREEDING BIRD SURVEY
Supported by the BTO, JNCC and the RSPB.
Begun in 1994, the BBS is designed to keep track of the changes in populations of our common breeding birds. It is dependent on volunteer birdwatchers throughout the country who can spare about five hours a year to cover a 1x1km survey square. There are just two morning visits to survey the breeding birds each year.

Survey squares are picked at random by computer to ensure that all habitats and regions are covered. Since its inception it has been a tremendous success, with more than 3,000 squares covered and more than 200 species recorded each year.

Contact: Kate Risely, e-mail: bbs@bto.org, or your local BTO Regional Representative (see County Directory).

CONSTANT EFFORT SITES (CES) SCHEME
The CES scheme, run since 1983, coordinates standardised summer ringing at 120 sites across Britain and Ireland. This allows the BTO to monitor trends in the numbers of adults at breeding sites, annual breeding productivity and survival rates of adults for 25 common songbirds. Information from CES complements demographic information from other surveys and feeds into the BTO's Integrated Population Monitoring, highlighting the causes of changes in bird populations.

The scheme is funded by a partnership between BTO, JNCC, The National Parks & Wildlife Service (Ireland) and ringers themselves.
Contact: Mark Grantham, BTO

NATIONAL PROJECTS

GARDEN BIRD FEEDING SURVEY

A BTO project.

The Garden Bird Feeding Survey is Britain's longest-running study of garden birds. Each year 250 observers record the numbers and variety of garden birds fed by man in the 26 weeks between October and March. Gardens are selected by region and type, from city flats, suburban semis and rural houses to outlying farms.

Contact: Amy Lewis, BTO.

E-mail: amy.lewis@bto.org

BTO GARDEN BIRDWATCH

A BTO project.

Started in January 1995, this project is a year-round survey that monitors the use that birds and other types of wildlife make of gardens. Approximately 15,000 participants from all over the UK and Ireland keep a weekly log of species using their gardens. The data collected are used to monitor regional, seasonal and year-to-year changes in the garden populations of our commoner birds, mammals, butterflies, reptiles and amphibians. To cover running costs there is an annual subscription of £15. Participants receive a quarterly colour magazine and all new joiners receive a full-colour, garden bird handbook. Results and more information are available online: www.bto.org/gbw.

E-mail: gbw@bto.org

Contact: Garden Ecology Team, BTO.

GOOSE CENSUSES

A WWT project

Britain and Ireland support internationally important goose populations. During the day, many of these feed away from wetlands and are therefore not adequately censused by the Wetland Bird Survey. Additional surveys are therefore undertaken to provide estimates of population size. These primarily involve roost counts, supplemented by further counts of feeding birds.

Most populations are censused up to three times a year, typically during the autumn, midwinter, and spring. In addition, counts of the proportion of juveniles in goose flocks are undertaken to provide estimates of annual productivity. Further volunteers are always needed. In particular, counters in Scotland, Lancashire and Norfolk are sought. For more information

Contact: Richard Hearn, Programme Manager,

E-mail: richard.hearn@wwt.org.uk

T: +44 (0)1453 891 185;

e-mail: monitoring@wwt.org.uk

HERONRIES CENSUS

A BTO project.

This survey started in 1928 and has been carried out under the auspices of the BTO since 1934. It represents the longest continuous series of population data for any European breeding bird (Grey Heron). Counts of apparently occupied nests are made at as many heronries as possible each year, throughout the UK, to provide an index of current population levels; data from Scotland and Northern Ireland are scant and more contributions from these countries would be especially welcomed. Herons may be hit hard during periods of severe weather and are vulnerable to pesticides and pollution. Currently, however, population levels are relatively high. Little Egret and other incoming species of colonial waterbird such as Cattle Egret are now fully included, whether nesting with Grey Herons or on their own; counts of Cormorant nests at heronries are also encouraged.

Contact: John Marchant, BTO

IRISH WETLAND BIRD SURVEY (I-WeBS)

A joint project of BirdWatch Ireland, the National Parks & Wildlife Service of the Dept of Arts, Culture & the Gaeltacht, and WWT, and supported by the Heritage Council and WWF-UK.

Established in 1994, I-WeBS aims to monitor the numbers and distribution of waterfowl populations wintering in Ireland in the long term, enabling the population size and spatial and temporal trends in numbers to be identified and described for each species.

Methods are compatible with existing schemes in the UK and Europe, and I-WeBS collaborates closely with the Wetland Bird Survey (WeBS) in the UK. Synchronised monthly counts are undertaken at wetland sites of all habitats during the winter.

Counts are straightforward and counters receive a newsletter and full report annually. Additional help is always welcome, especially during these initial years as the scheme continues to grow.

Contact: BirdWatch Ireland;

www.birdwatchireland.ie

NEST RECORD SCHEME

A BTO Project forming part of the BTO's Integrated Population Monitoring programme carried out under contract with the JNCC.

The BTO are interested in records of any nest

found anywhere in the country, from a Blackbird in the garden to an Oystercatcher on a Scottish Loch, as long as you can count the number of eggs and/or chicks inside and preferably make several return visits. Data are submitted to the NRS on standard Nest Record Cards or electronically via the IPMR computer package. The NRS monitors changes in the nesting success and the timing of breeding of Britain's bird species. Guidance on how to record nest and visit them safely, without disturbing breeding birds, is available at www.bto.org/nrs and in the free starter pack available on request from the Nest Records Unit.
Contact: Carl Barimore;
e-mail: nest.records@bto.org

RAPTOR AND OWL RESEARCH REGISTER
A BTO project
The Register has helped considerably over the past 30 years in encouraging and guiding research, and in the co-ordination of projects. There are currently almost 500 projects in the card index file through which the Register operates.

The owl species currently receiving most attention are Barn and Tawny. As to raptors, the most popular subjects are Kestrel, Buzzard, Sparrowhawk, Hobby and Peregrine, with researchers showing increasing interest in Red Kite, and fewer large in-depth studies of Goshawk, Osprey and harriers.

Contributing is a simple process and involves all raptor enthusiasts, whether it is to describe an amateur activity or professional study. The nature of research on record varies widely – from local pellet analyses to captive breeding and rehabilitation programmes to national surveys of Peregrine, Buzzard and Golden Eagle. Birdwatchers in both Britain and abroad are encouraged to write for photocopies of cards relevant to the species or nature of their work. The effectiveness of the Register depends upon those running projects (however big or small) ensuring that their work is included.
Contact: David Glue, BTO.

RED KITE RE-INTRODUCTION PROJECT
An English Nature/SNH/RSPB project supported by Forest Enterprise, Yorkshire Water and authorities in Germany and Spain
The project involves the translocation of birds from Spain, Germany and the expanding Chilterns population for release at sites in England and Scotland.

Records of any wing-tagged Red Kites in England should be reported to Natural Engand,

Northminster House, Peterborough, PEI IUA (tel 01733 455 281). Scottish records should be sent to the RSPB's North Scotland Regional Office, Etive House, Beechwood Park, Inverness, IV2 3BW (tel 01463 715 000).

Sightings are of particular value if the letter/number code (or colour) of wing tags can be seen or if the bird is seen flying low over (or into) woodland. Records should include an exact location, preferably with a six figure grid reference.

RETRAPPING ADULTS FOR SURVIVAL (RAS) SCHEME
The RAS scheme started in 1998 and gathers information on recaptures of adult birds. Projects are chosen and run by volunteer ringers and focus on species of conservation concern that are monitored relatively poorly by CES and general ringing activity. Collection of standardised capture/recapture data allows the BTO to monitor survival rates in adult birds. Detailed information about survival helps us to understand population changes as part of the BTO's Integrated Population Monitoring. Ringers themselves choose a target species and aim to catch all the breeding adults within that area on an annual basis.

The scheme is funded by a partnership between BTO, JNCC, The National Parks & Wildlife Service (Ireland) and ringers themselves.
Contact: Mark Grantham, BTO

RINGING SCHEME
Marking birds with individually numbered metal rings allows us to study survival, productivity and movements of British and Irish birds. Nearly 2,500 trained and licensed ringers operate in Britain and Ireland, marking around 800,000 birds annually.

Training to ring, and use mist nets takes at least a year, but more often two or more years depending on the aptitude of the trainee and the amount of ringing they do. A restricted permit can usually be obtained more quickly. Anyone can contribute to the scheme by reporting any ringed or colour-ringed birds they see or find. Reports can be submitted online at www.ring.ac or direct to BTO HQ. Anyone finding a ringed bird should note the ring number, species, when and where found and, if possible, what happened to it. If the bird is dead, it may also be possible to remove the ring, which should be kept in case there is a query. Anyone reporting a ringed bird will be sent details of where and when the bird was originally ringed.

NATIONAL PROJECTS

More info: www.bto.org/ringing/
'Demog Blog' for up to date news and stories:
http://btoringing.blogspot.com/
The scheme is funded by a partnership between
BTO, JNCC, The National Parks & Wildlife Service
(Ireland) and ringers themselves.
Contact: Jacquie Clark, BTO

SWIFT CONSERVATION

Endorsed by the BTO and the RSPB, Swift
Conservation works to protect and restore
the UK's fast-diminishing Swift population, a
once-numerous species that because of changes
in building technology and design is facing
increasing difficulties in finding places to breed.
Practical information on Swift conservation is
provided to owners, architects, builders and
others via a web site, by e-mail and in person.
Swift Conservation also supports Swift populations
through a network of "Swift Champions" who
survey their localities for Swift colonies and
work to preserve and enhance them. The help of
interested bird watchers with this work is always
welcome.
Swift Conservation runs a lectures, talks
and training programme for bird clubs, local
government and building professionals. Please
contact them if you are interested in this or any
aspect of their work.
Contacts:
Edward Mayer: phone 020 7794 2098
e-mail: mail@swift-conservation.org
web site: www.swift-conservation.org/

TOOTH & CLAW

An independent
project aimed at
improving knowledge
about Britain's
predators and
promoting discussion
on the issues that
surround them.

Tooth & Claw
explores some of the complex issues surrounding
our relationship with wild predators and questions
how we really feel and why?
Through the web site, Tooth & Claw provides
a meeting place between anecdotal input and
scientific research and encourages constructive
and imaginative dialogue on predator issues.
A series of case studies led by powerful imagery
will provide insightful interviews and personal

accounts of our lives alongside the likes of eagles
and foxes with a glimpse into the future and
the return of creatures we have not known for
centuries.
Contact: Peter Cairns, Northshots, Ballintean,
Glenfeshie, Kingussie, Scotland, PH21 1NX. (44)
(0)1540 651 352;
e-mail: peter@toothandclaw.org.uk
www.toothandclaw.org.uk

WATERWAYS BREEDING BIRD SURVEY

*A BTO project, supported by the Environment
Agency*
WBBS uses transect methods like those of the
Breeding Bird Survey to record bird populations
along randomly chosen stretches of river and
canal throughout the UK. Just two survey visits
are needed during April-June. WBBS began in
1998 and has now taken over from the Waterways
Bird Survey as the main monitoring scheme for
birds in this habitat.
Contact: BTO Regional Representative (see
County Directory) to enquire if any local stretches
require coverage, otherwise John Marchant at
BTO HQ.

WETLAND BIRD SURVEY

A joint scheme of BTO, WWT, RSPB & JNCC.
The Wetland Bird Survey (WeBS) is the monitoring
scheme for non-breeding waterbirds in the UK.
The principal aims are:
1. to determine the population sizes of waterbirds
2. to determine trends in numbers and
distribution
3. to identify important sites for waterbirds
WeBS data are used to designate important
waterbird sites and protect them against adverse
development, for research into the causes of
declines, for establishing conservation priorities
and strategies and to formulate management
plans for wetland sites and waterbirds.
Monthly, synchronised Core Counts are made
at as many wetland sites as possible. Low Tide
Counts are made on about 20 estuaries each
winter to identify important feeding areas.
Counts take just a few hours and are relatively
straightforward. The 3,000 participants receive
regular newsletters and a comprehensive annual
report. New counters are always welcome.
Contacts: General Webs Enquiries - Heidi Mellan
- WeBS Office, BTO. E-mail WeBS@bto.org,
Low Tide Counts or WeBS Data Requests – Neil
Calbrade, WeBS Office, BTO. www.bto.org/webs

INTERNATIONAL DIRECTORY

A juvenile Green Heron emerges from a reedbed. This localised species lives year-round in Florida and parts of California but breeds more widely in more northerly states.

The BirdLife Partnership

BirdLife is a Partnership of non-governmental organisations (NGOs) with a special focus on conservation and birds. Each NGO Partner represents a unique geographic territory/country.

The BirdLife Network explained

Partners: Membership-based NGOs who represent BirdLife in their own territory. Vote holders and key implementing bodies for BirdLife's Strategy and Regional Programmes in their own territories.

Partners Designate: Membership-based NGOs who represent BirdLife in their own territory, in a transition stage to becoming full Partners. Non-vote holders.

Affiliates: Usually NGOs, but also individuals, foundations or governmental institutions when appropriate. Act as a BirdLife contact with the aim of developing into, or recruiting, a BirdLife Partner in their territory.

Secretariat: The co-ordinating and servicing body of BirdLife International.

Secretariat Addresses

BirdLife Global Office
BirdLife International
Wellbrook Court
Girton Road
Cambridge CB3 0NA
UNITED KINGDOM
Tel. +44 1 223 277 318
Fax +44 1 223 277 200
E-mail: birdlife@birdlife.org.uk
www.birdlife.org

Birdlife Africa Regional Office
c/o ICIPE Campus
Kasarani Road, off Thika Road
Nairobi KENYA

Postal Address
PO Box 3502
00100 GPO
Nairobi KENYA
+254 20 862246
+254 20 862246
E-mail: birdlife@birdlife.or.ke
www.birdlife.org/regional/africa/partnership

BirdLife Americas Regional Office
Birdlife International
Vicente Cárdenas 120 y Japon,
3rd Floor
Quito ECUADOR

Postal address
BirdLife International
Casilla 17-17-717
Quito ECUADOR
Tel. +593 2 453 645
Fax +593 2 459 627
E-mail: birdlife@birdlife.org.ec
www.birdlife.org/regional/americas/partnership

BirdLife Asia Regional Office
Toyo-Shinjuku Building
2nd Floor, Shinjuku 1-12-15
Shinkuju-ku
Tokyo 160-0022, JAPAN
Tel.+3 3351 9981
Fax.+3 3351 9980
E-mail: info@birdlife-asia.org
www.birdlife.org/regional/asia/partnership

BirdLife European Regional Office
Droevendaalsesteeg 3a PO Box 127, NL- 6700 AC, Wageningen
THE NETHERLANDS
Tel. +31 317 478831
Fax +31 317 478844
E-mail: birdlife@birdlife.agro.nl

European Community Office (ECO)
BirdLife International
Avenue de la Toison d'Or 67
(2nd floor), B-1060 Brussels
BELGIUM
Tel. +32 2280 08 30
Fax +32 2230 38 02
E-mail: bleco@birdlifeeco.net
www.birdlife.org/regional/europe/partnership

BirdLife Middle East Regional Office
BirdLife International - Amman
P. O. Box 2295
Amman 11953
JORDAN
Tel: +962 (6) 566-2945
Fax: +962 (6) 569-1838
E-mail: birdlife@nol.com.jo
www.birdlife.org/regional/middle_east/partnership

AFRICA

PARTNERS

Burkina Faso
Fondation des Amis de la Nature (NATURAMA), 01
B.P. 6133, Ouagadougou 01.
e-mail: naturama@fasonet.bf

Ethiopia
Ethiopian Wildlife and Natural History Society, PO
Box 13303, Addis Ababa, Pub: *Agazen; Ethiopian
Wildl. and Nat. Hist. News. (& Annual Report);
Ethiopian Wildl. and Nat. Hist. Soc. Quarterly
News (WATCH); Walia (WATCH) (Ethiopia)*.
e-mail: ewnhs@telecom.net.et
http://ewnhs.ble@telecom.net.et

Ghana
Ghana Wildlife Society, PO Box 13252, Accra, Pub:
Bongo News; NKO (The Parrots).
e-mail: wildsoc@ighmail.com

Kenya
Nature Kenya, PO Box 44486, 00100 GPO. Nairobi.
Pub: *Bulletin of the EANHS; Journal of East
African Natural; Kenya Birds.*
e-mail: office@naturekenya.org
www.naturekenya.org

Nigeria
Nigerian Conservation Foundation, PO Box 74638,
Victoria Island, Lagos. Pub: *NCF Matters/News/
Newsletter; Nigerian Conservation Foundation
Annual Report.*
e-mail: enquiries@ncf-nigeria.org
www.africanconservation.org/ncftemp/

Seychelles
Nature Seychelles, Roche Caiman, Box 1310,
Victoria, Mahe, Seychelles. Pub: *Zwazo - a BirdLife
Seychelles Newsletter.*
e-mail: nature@seychelles.net
www.nature.org.sc

Sierra Leone
Conservation Society of Sierra Leone, PO BOX
1292, Freetown. Pub: *Rockfowl Link, The.*
e-mail: cssl@sierratel.sl

South Africa
BirdLife South Africa, PO Box 515, Randburg,
Johannesburg 2125, South Africa, Pub: *Newsletter
of BirdLife South Africa; Ostrich.*
e-mail: info@birdlife.org.za
www.birdlife.org.za

Tanzania
Wildlife Conservation Society of Tanzania, PO Box
70919, Dar es Salaam, Pub: *Miombo.*
e-mail: wcst@africaonline.co.tz

Uganda
Nature Uganda, PO Box 27034, Kampala. Pub:
*Naturalist - A Newsletter of the East Africa Nat.
His. Soc.*
e-mail: nature@natureuganda.org
www.natureuganda.org/

PARTNERS DESIGNATE

Tunisia
Association "Les Amis des Oiseaux", Avenue 18
Janvier 1952, Ariana Centre, App. C209, 2080
Ariana, Tunis. Pub: *Feuille de Liaison de l'AAO;
Houbara, l'.* e-mail: aao.bird@planet.tn

Zimbabwe
BirdLife Zimbabwe, P O Box RV 100, Runiville,
Harare, Zimbabwe. Pub: *Babbler (WATCH)
(Zimbabwe); Honeyguide.*
e-mail: birds@zol.co.zw

AFFILIATES

Botswana
Birdlife Botswana, Private Bag 003 # Suite 348,
Mogoditshane, Gaborone, Botswana
e-mail: blb@birdlifebotswana.org.bw
www.birdlifebotswana.org.bw

Burundi
Association Burundaise pour la Protection des
Oiseaux, P O Box 7069, Bujumbura, Burundi
e-mail: aboburundi@yahoo.fr

Cameroon
Cameroon Biodiversity Conservation Society
(CBCS), PO Box 3055, Messa, Yaoundé.
e-mail: gdzikouk@yahoo.fr

Egypt
Sherif Baha El Din, 3 Abdala El Katib St, Dokki,
Cairo. e-mail: baha2@internetegypt.com

Rwanda
Association pour la Conservation de la Nature au
Rwanda, P O Box 4290, Kigali,
e-mail: acnrwanda@yahoo.fr

Zambia
Zambian Ornithological Society, Box 33944, Lusaka
10101, Pub: *Zambian Ornithological Society
Newsletter.* e-mail: zos@zamnet.zm
www.wattledcrane.com

INTERNATIONAL DIRECTORY

INTERNATIONAL ORGANISATIONS

PARTNERS

Argentina
Aves Argentina / AOP, 25 de Mayo 749, 2 piso, oficina 6, 1002 Buenos Aires. Pub: *Hornero; Naturaleza & Conservacion; Nuestras Aves; Vuelo de Pajaro.*
e-mail: info@avesargentinas.org.ar
www.avesargentinas.org.ar

Belize
The Belize Audubon Society, 12 Fort Street, PO Box 1001, Belize City. Pub: *Belize Audubon Society Newsletter.*
e-mail: base@btl.net
www.belizeaudubon.org

Bolivia
Asociacion Armonia, 400 Avenidad Lomas de Arena, Casilla 3566, Santa Cruz, Bolivia. Pub: *Aves en Bolivia.*
e-mail: armonia@scbbs-bo.com

Canada
Bird Studies Canada, PO Box/160, Port Rowan, Ontario N0E 1M0. Pub: *Bird Studies Canada - Annual Report; Birdwatch Canada.*
e-mail: generalinfo@bsc-eoc.org
www.bsc-eoc.org

Canada
Nature Canada, 1 Nicholas Street, Suite 606, Ottawa, Ontario, K1N 7B7. Pub: *Grass 'n Roots; IBA News Canada; Nature Canada; Nature Matters; Nature Watch News (CNF).*
e-mail: info@naturecanada.ca
www.naturecanada.ca

Ecuador
Fundación Ornithológica del Ecuador, La Tierra 203 y Av. de los Shyris, Casilla 17-17-906, Quito.
e-mail: cecia@uio.satnet.net
www.cecia.org/

Jamaica
BirdLife Jamaica, 2 Starlight Avenue, Kingston 6, Pub: *Broadsheet: BirdLife Jamaica; Important Bird Areas Programme Newsletter.*
e-mail: birdlifeja@yahoo.com
www.birdelifejamaica.com

Panama
Panama Audubon Society, Apartado 2026, Ancón, Balboa. Pub: *Toucan.*
e-mail: info@panamaaudubon.org
www.panamaaudubon.org

Venezuela
Sociedad Conservacionista Audubon de, Apartado 80.450, Caracas 1080-A, Venezuela. Pub: *Audubon (Venezuela) (formerly Boletin Audubon).*
e-mail: audubon@cantv.net

PARTNERS DESIGNATE

Mexico
CIPAMEX, Apartado Postal 22-012, D.F. 14091, Mexico. Pub: *AICA's; Cuauhtli Boletin de Cipa Mex.*
e-mail: cipamex@campus.iztacala.unam.mx
http://coro@servidor.unam.mx

Paraguay
Guyra Paraguay,, Coronel Rafael Franco 381 c/ Leandro Prieto, Casilla de Correo 1132, Asunción. Pub: *Boletin Jara Kuera.*
e-mail: guyra@guyra.org.py
or guyra@highway.com.py
www.guyra.org.py/

United States
National Audubon Society, 700 Broadway, New York, NY, 10003 -9562. Pub: *American Birds; Audubon (USA); Audubon Field Notes; Audubon Bird Conservation Newsletter.*
e-mail: audubonaction@audubon.org
www.audubon.org

Chile
Union de Ornitologis de Chile (UNORCH), Casilla 13.183, Santiago 21. Pub: *Boletin Chileno de Ornitologia; Boletin Informativo (WATCH) (Chile).*
e-mail: unorch@entelchile.net
www.geocities.com/RainForest/4372

AFFILIATES

Bahamas
Bahamas National Trust, PO Box N-4105, Nassau. Pub: *Bahamas Naturalist; Currents; Grand Bahama Update.*
e-mail: bnt@batelnet.bs
www.thebahamasnationaltrust.org/

INTERNATIONAL ORGANISATIONS

Cuba
Centro Nacional de Áreas Protegidas (CNAP). Calle 18 a, No 1441, e/ 41 y 47, Playa, Ciudad Habana, Cuba. e-mail: cnap@snap.cu
www.snap.co.cu/

El Salvador
SalvaNATURA, 33 Avenida Sur #640, Colonia Flor Blanca, San Salvador.
e-mail: salvanatura@saltel.net
www.salvanatura.org

Falkland Islands
Falklands Conservation, PO Box 26, Stanley,. or Falklands Conservation, 1 Princes Avenue, Finchley, London N3 2DA, UK. Pub: *Falklands Conservation.*
e-mail: conservation@horizon.co.fk
www.falklandsconservation.com

Honduras
Sherry Thorne, c/o Cooperación Técnica, Apdo 30289 Toncontín, Tegucigalpa.
e-mail: pilar_birds@yahoo.com

Suriname
Foundation for Nature Preservation in Suriname, Cornelis Jongbawstraat 14, PO BOX 12252, Paramaribo
e-mail: research@stinasu.sr
www.stinasu.sr

Uruguay
GUPECA, Casilla de Correo 6955, Correo Central, Montevideo. Pub: *Achara.*
e-mail: info@avesuruguay.org.uy
www.avesuruguay.org.uy/

ASIA

PARTNERS

Japan
Wild Bird Society of Japan (WBSJ), 1/F Odakyu Nishi Shinjuku Building, 1-47-1 Hatsudai Shibuya-ku, Tokyo 151-061, Japan. Pub: *Strix; Wild Birds; Wing.*
e-mail: int.center@wing-wbsj.or.jp
www.wing-wbsj.or.jp

Malaysia
Malaysian Nature Society, PO Box 10750, 50724 Kuala Lumpur. Pub: *Enggang; Suara Enggang; Malayan Nature Journal; Malaysian Naturalist.*
www.mns.org.my
e-mail: natsoc@po.jaring.my

Philippines
Haribon Foundation, Suites 401-404 Fil-Garcia Bldg, 140 Kalayaan Avenue cor. Mayaman St, Diliman, Quezon CIty 1101. Pub: *Haribon Foundation Annual Report; Haring Ibon; Philippine Biodiversity.*
e-mail: birdlife@haribon.org.ph
www.haribon.org.ph

Singapore
Nature Society (Singapore), 510 Geylang Road, #02-05, The Sunflower, 398466. Pub: *Nature News; Nature Watch (Singapore).*
e-mail: nss@nss.org.sg
www.nss.org.sg

Taiwan
Wild Bird Federation Taiwan (WBFT), 1F, No. 3, Lane 36 Jing-Long St., 116 Taipei, Taiwan, R.O.C. Pub: *Yuhina Post.*
e-mail: wbft@bird.org.tw
www.bird.org.tw

Thailand
Bird Conservation Society of Thailand, 43 Soi Chok Chai Ruam Mit 29, Vipahvadee-Rabgsit Road, Sansaen-nok, Dindaeng, Bangkok 10320 Thailand. Pub: *Bird Conservation Society of Thailand.*
e-mail: bcst@bcst.or.th
www.bcst.or.th

PARTNER DESIGNATE

India
Bombay Natural History Society, Hornbill House, Shaheed Bhagat Singh Road, Mumbai-400 023. Pub: *Buceros; Hornbill; Journal of the Bombay Natural History Society.*
e-mail: bnhs@bom4.vsnl.net.in
www.bnhs.org

AFFILIATES

Hong Kong
The Hong Kong Birdwatching Society, Room 1612 Beverley Commercial Building, 87-105 Chatham Road South, Tsim Sha Tsui, Kowloon, Hong Kong. Pub: *Hong Kong Bird Report.*
e-mail: hkbws@hkbws.org.uk
www.hkbws.org.hk

Indonesia
BirdLife Indonesia (Perhimpunan Pelestari Burung dan Habitatnya), Jl. Dadali 32, Bogor 16161, PO. Box 310/Boo, Bogor 16003, Indonesia.
e-mail: birdlife@burung.org
www.burung.org

INTERNATIONAL DIRECTORY

327

INTERNATIONAL ORGANISATIONS

Nepal
Bird Conservation Nepal, P.O.Box 12465, Lazimpat, Kathmandu, Nepal. Pub: *Bird Conservation Nepal (Danphe); Ibisbill.*
e-mail: bcn@mail.com.np
www.birdlifenepal.org

Pakistan
Ornithological Society of Pakistan, PO Box 73, 109D Dera Ghazi Khan, 32200. Pub: *Pakistan Journal of Ornithology.*
e-mail: osp@mul.paknet.com.pk

Sri Lanka
Field Ornithology Group of Sri Lanka, Dept of Zoology, University of Colombo, Colombo 03. Pub: *Malkoha - Newsletter of the Field Ornithology Group of Sri Lanka.*
e-mail: fogsl@slt.lk

EUROPE

PARTNERS

Austria
BirdLife Austria, Museumplatz 1/10/8, AT-1070 Wien. Pub: *Egretta; Vogelschutz in Osterreich.*
e-mail: office@birdlife.at
www.birdlife.at/

Belgium
BirdLife Belgium (BNVR-RNOB-BNVS), Natuurpunt, Kardinaal, Mercierplein 1, 2800 Mechelen, Belgium.
e-mail: wim.vandenbossche@natuurpunt.be
www.natuurreservaten.be

Bulgaria
Bulgarian Society for the Protection of Birds (BSPB), PO Box 50, Musagenitza Complex, Block 104, Entrance A, Floor 6, BG-1111, Sofia, Bulgaria. Pub: *Neophron (& UK).*
e-mail: bspb_hq@bspb.org
www.bspb.org

Czech Republic
Czech Society for Ornithology (CSO), Hornomecholupska 34, CZ-102 00 Praha 10. Pub: *Ptaci Svet; Sylvia; Zpravy Ceske Spolecnosti Ornitologicke.* e-mail: cso@birdlife.cz
www.birdlife.cz

Denmark
Dansk Ornitologisk Forening (DOF), Vesterbrogade 138-140, DK-1620, Copenhagen V, Denmark. Pub:

DAFIF - Dafifs Nyhedsbrev; Dansk Ornitologisk Forenings Tidsskrift; Fugle og Natur.
e-mail: dof@dof.dk
www.dof.dk

Estonia
Estonian Ornithological Society (EOU), PO Box 227, Vesti Str. 4, EE-50002 Tartu, Estonia. Pub: *Hirundo Eesti Ornitoogiauhing.*
e-mail: eoy@eoy.ee
www.eoy.ee

Finland
BirdLife SUOMI Finland, Annankatu 29 A, PO Box 1285, FI 00101, Helsinki. Pub: *Linnuston-Suojelu; Linnut; Tiira.*
e-mail: office@birdlife.fi
www.birdlife.fi

France
Ligue pour la Protection des Oiseaux (LPO), La Corderie Royale, B.P. 90263, 17305 ROCHEFORT CEDEX, France. Pub: *Lettre Internationale; Ligue Francaise Pour La Protection des Oiseaux; Oiseau, L' (LPO); Outarde infos.*
e-mail: lpo@lpo.fr
www.lpo.fr/

Germany
Naturschutzbund Deutschland, Herbert-Rabius-Str. 26, D-53225 Bonn, Germany. Pub: *Naturschutz Heute (NABU) Naturschutzbund Deutschland.*
e-mail: nabu@nabu.de
www.nabu.de

Gibraltar
Gibraltar Ornithological and Nat. History Society, Jew's Gate, Upper Rock Nature Reserve, PO Box 843, GI. Pub: *Alectoris; Gibraltar Nature News.*
e-mail: gohns@gibnet.gi
www.gibraltar.gi/gonhs

Greece
Hellenic Ornithological Society (HOS), Vas. Irakleiou 24, GR-10682 Athens, Greece. Pub: *HOS Newsletter.*
e-mail: birdlife-gr@ath.forthnet.gr
www.ornithologiki.gr

Hungary
Hungarian Orn. and Nature Cons. Society (MME), Kolto u. 21, Pf. 391, HU-1536, Budapest. Pub: *Madartani Tajekoztato; Madartavlat; Ornis Hungarica; Tuzok.*
e-mail: mme@mme.hu
www.mme.hu

Iceland
Icelandic Society for the Protection of Birds,
Fuglaverndarfélag Islands, PO Box 5069, IS-125
Reykjavik, Iceland.
e-mail: fuglavernd@fuglavernd.is
www.fuglavernd.is

Ireland
BirdWatch Ireland, Rockingham House, Newcastle,
Co. Wicklow, Eire. Pub: *Irish Birds; Wings (IWC
Birdwatch Ireland).*
e-mail: info@birdwatchireland.org
www.birdwatchireland.ie

Israel
Society for the Protection of Nature in Israel,
Hashsela 4, Tel-Aviv 66103. Pub: *SPNI News.*
e-mail: ioc@netvision.net.il
www.birds.org.il

Italy
Lega Italiana Protezione Uccelli (LIPU), Via Trento
49, IT-43100, Parma. Pub: *Ali Giovani; Ali Notizie.*
e-mail: lipusede@box1.tin.it
www.lipu.it

Latvia
Latvijas Ornitologijas Biedriba (LOB), Ak 1010, LV-
1050 Riga, Latvia. Pub: *Putni Daba.*
e-mail: putni@lob.lv
www.lob.lv

Luxembourg
Letzebuerger Natur-a Vulleschutzliga (LNVL),
Kraizhaff, rue de Luxembourg.L-1899
Kockelscheuer. Pub: *Regulus (WATCH); Regulus
Info (& Annual Report) (WATCH); Regulus
Wissenschaftliche Berichte (WATCH).*
e-mail: secretary@luxnatur.lu
www.luxnatur.lu

Malta
BirdLife Malta, 57 Marina Court, Flat 28, Triq Abate
Rigord, MT-Ta' Xbiex, MSD 12, MALTA. Pub: *Bird
Talk (WATCH) (Malta); Bird's Eye View (WATCH)
(Malta); Il-Merill.*
e-mail: info@birdlifemalta.org
www.birdlifemalta.org

Netherlands
Vogelbescherming Nederland, PO Box 925, NL-
3700 AX Zeist. Pub: *Vogelniews; Vogels.*
e-mail: info@vogelbescherming.nl
www.vogelbescherming.nl/

Norway
Norsk Ornitologisk Forening, Sandgata 30 B,

N-7012 Trondheim, Norway. Pub: *Fuglearet;
Fuglefauna; Var; Ringmerkaren.*
e-mail: nof@birdlife.no
www.birdlife.no

Poland
Ogólnopolskie Towarzystwo Ochrony Ptaków
(OTOP), Ul. Hallera 4/2, PL-80-401 Gdansk,
Poland. Pub: *Ptaki; Ptasie Ostoje.*
e-mail: office@otop.most.org.pl
www.otop.org.pl/

Portugal
Sociedade Portuguesa para o Estuda das, Aves
(SPEA), Rua da Vitoria, 53-3° Esq, 1100-618,
Lisboa. Pub: *Pardela.*
e-mail: spea@spea.pt
www.spea.pt

Romania
Romanian Ornithological Society (SOR), Str.
Gheorghe Dima 49/2, RO-3400 Cluj. Pub: *Alcedo;
Buletin AIA; Buletin de Informare Societatea
Ornitologica Romana; Milvus (Romania).*
e-mail: office@sor.ro
www.sor.ro/

Slovakia
Soc. for the Prot. of Birds in Slovakia (SOVS),
PO Box 71, 093 01 Vranov nad Topl'ou. Pub:
Spravodaj SOVS; Vtacie Spravy.
e-mail: sovs@changenet.sk
www.sovs.miesto.sk

Slovenia
BirdLife Slovenia (DOPPS), Trzaska 2, PO
Box 2990, SI-1000 Ljubljana, Slovenia. Pub:
Acrocephalus; Svet Ptic.
e-mail: dopps@dopps-drustvo.si
www.ptice.org

Spain
Sociedad Espanola de Ornitologia (SEO), C/
Melquiades Biencinto 34, E-28053, Madrid. Pub:
Ardeola; Areas Importantes para las Aves.
e-mail: seo@seo.org
www.seo.org

Sweden
Sveriges Ornitologiska Forening (SOF),
Ekhagsvagen 3, SE 104-05, Stockholm. Pub:
Fagelvarld; var; Ornis Svecica.
e-mail: birdlife@sofnet.org
www.sofnet.org

Switzerland
SVS/BirdLife Switzerland, Wiedingstrasse 78, PO

INTERNATIONAL DIRECTORY

INTERNATIONAL ORGANISATIONS

Box, CH-8036, Zurich, Switzerland. Pub: *Oiwvos Ornis; Ornis Junior; Ornithologische Beobachter; Der Ornithos; Steinadler.*
e-mail: svs@birdlife.ch
www.birdlife.ch

Turkey
Doga Dernegi, PK: 640 06445, Yenişehir, Ankarae, Turkey. Pub: *Kelaynak; Kuscu Bulteni.*
e-mail: doga@dogadernegi.org
www.dogadernegi.org/

United Kingdom
Royal Society for the Protection of Birds, The Lodge, Sandy, Bedfordshire, SG19 2DL.
e-mail: info@RSPB.org.uk
www.rspb.org.uk

PARTNERS DESIGNATE

Belarus
BirdLife Belarus (APB), PO Box 306, Minsk, 220050 Belarus. Pub: *Subbuteo - The Belarusian Ornithological Bulletin.*
e-mail: apb@tut.by
http://apb.iatp.by/

Lithuania
Lietuvos Ornitologu Draugija (LOD), Naugarduko St. 47-3, LT-2006, Vilnius, Lithuania. Pub: *Baltasis Gandras.*
e-mail: lod@birdlife.lt
www.birdlife.lt

Russia
Russian Bird Conservation Union (RBCU), Building 1, Shosse Entuziastov 60, 111123, RU-Moscow. Pub: *Newsletter of the Russian Bird Conservation Union.*
e-mail: mail@rbcu.ru
www.rbcu.ru/en/

Ukraine
Ukrainian Union for Bird Conservation (UTOP), PO Box 33, Kiev, 1103, UA. Pub: *Life of Birds.*
e-mail: utop@iptelecom.net.ua
www.utop.org.ua/

AFFILIATES

Liechtenstein
Botanish-Zoologische Gesellschaft, Im Bretscha 22, FL-9494 Schaan, Liechtenstein.
e-mail: broggi@pingnet.li or renat@pingnet.li

Andorra
Associacio per a la Defensa de la Natura, Apartado de Correus Espanyols No 96, Andora La Vella, Principat d'Andorra. Pub: *Aiguerola.*
e-mail: and@andorra.ad
www.adn-andorra.org/

Croatia
Croatian Society for Bird and Nature Protection, Gunduliceva 24, HR-10000 Zagreb, Croatia. Pub: *Troglodytes.*
e-mail: jasmina@hazu.hr

Cyprus
BirdLife Cyprus, PO Box 28076, 2090 Lefkosia, Cyprus.
e-mail: melis@cytanet.com.cy
www.birdlifecyprus.org

Faroe Islands (to Denmark)
Føroya Fuglafrødifelag (Faroese Orginithological Society) (FOS), Postssmoga 1230, FR-110 Torshavn, Faroe Islands.
e-mail: doreteb@ngs.fo

Georgia
Georgian Centre for the Conservation of Wildlife, PO Box 56, GE-Tbilisi 0160, Georgia.
e-mail: office@gccw.org
www.gccw.org/

PARTNERS

Jordan
Royal Society of the Conservation of Nature, PO Box 6354, Jubeiha-Abu-Nusseir Circle, Amman 11183. Pub: *Al Reem.*
e-mail: adminrscn@rscn.org.jo
www.rscn.org.jo

Lebanon
Society for the Protection of Nature in Lebanon, Awad Bldg, 6th Floor, Abdel Aziz Street, P.O.Box: 11-5665, Beirut, Lebanon.
e-mail: spnlorg@cyberia.net.lb
www.spnlb.org

PARTNER DESIGNATE

Palestine
Palestine Wildlife Society (PWLS), Beit Sahour, PO

Box 89. Pub: *Palestine Wildlife Society - Annual Report.* www.wildlife-pal.org
e-mail: wildlife@palnet.com

AFFILIATES

Bahrain
Dr Saeed A. Mohamed, PO Box 40266, Bahrain.
e-mail: sam53@batelco.com.bh

Iran, Islamic Republic of
Dr Jamshid Mansoori, Assistant Professor, College of Natural Resources, Tehran University, Mojtame Sabz, Golestan Shamali, Mahestan Ave, Shahrake Qarb, Phase 1, P.O.Box 14657, Tehran, I.R. of Iran.
e-mail: birdlifeiran@yahoo.com

Kuwait
Kuwait Environment Protection Society, PO Box 1896, Safat 13019, Kuwait.
e-mail: rasamhory@hotmail.com
www.keps74.com

Saudi Arabia
National Commission for Wildlife Cons & Dev, NCWDC, PO Box 61681, Riyadh 11575. Pub: *Phoenix; The.* e-mail: ncwcd@zajil.net
www.ncwcd.gov.sa/

Yemen
Yemen Society for the Protection of Wildlife (YSPW), 29 Alger Street, PO Box 19759, Sana'a, Yemen.
e-mail: wildlife.yemen@y.net.ye

PACIFIC

PARTNER

Australia
Birds Australia, 415 Riversdale Road, Hawthorn East, VIC 3123, Australia. Pub: *Australia Garcilla; Birds Australia Annual Report; Eclectus;*
Emu; Wingspan (WATCH) (Australia); from wingspan@birdsaustralia.com.au.
e-mail: mail@birdsaustralia.com.au
www.birdsaustralia.com.au

AFFILIATES

Cook Islands
Taporoporo'anga Ipukarea Society (TIS), PO Box 649, Rarotonga, Cook Islands.
e-mail: 2tis@oyster.net.ck

Fiji
Dr Dick Watling, c/o Environment Consultants Fiji, P O Box 2041, Government Buildings, Suva, Fiji.
e-mail: watling@is.com.fj
www.environmentfiji.com

French Polynesia
Société d'Ornithologie de Polynésie "Manu", B.P. 21 098, Papeete, Tahiti.
e-mail: sop@manu.pf
www.manu.pf

Palau
Palau Conservation Society, PO BOX 1811, Koror, PW96940. Pub: *Ngerel a Biib.*
e-mail: pcs@palaunet.com
www.palau-pcs.org/

Samoa
O le Si'osi'omaga Society Incorporated, O le Si'osi'omaga Society Inc., P O Box 2282, Apia, Western Samoa.
e-mail: ngo_siosiomaga@samoa.ws

New Zealand
Royal Forest & Bird Protection Society of, PO Box 631, Wellington. Pub: *Forest & Bird; Forest & Bird Annual Report; Forest & Bird Conservation News.*
e-mail: office@forestandbird.org.nz
www.forestandbird.org.nz/

SPECIAL INTEREST ORGANISATIONS

AFRICAN BIRD CLUB.
c/o Birdlife International as below.
e-mail (general): contact@africanbirdclub.org
e-mail (membership and sales):
membership@africanbirdclub.org
www.africanbirdclub.org
Pub: *Bulletin of the African Bird Club*.

BIRDLIFE INTERNATIONAL.
Wellbrook Court, Girton Road, Cambridge, CB3
ONA, +44 (0)1223 277 318; (Fax) +44 (0)1223
277 200,
Pub:*World Birdwatch*. www.birdlife.net

EAST AFRICA NATURAL HISTORY SOCIETY
see Kenya in preceding list.

EURING (European Union for Bird Ringing).
Euring Data Bank, c/o BTO, The Nunnery,
Thetford, Norfolk IP24 2PU. 01842 750 050.
www.euring.org

FAUNA AND FLORA INTERNATIONAL.
Jupiter House, 4th Floor, Station Road, Cambridge,
CB1 2JD. Call on +44 (0)1223 571 000; (Fax) +44
(0)1223 461 481. www.fauna-flora.org
e-mail: info@fauna-flora.org
Pub:*Fauna & Flora News; Oryx*.

LIPU-UK

**(the Italian League
for the Protection of
Birds).**
David Lingard, Fernwood,
Doddington Road,
Whisby, Lincs, LN6 9BX,
+44 (0)1522 689 030,
e-mail: david@lipu-
uk.org   www.lipu-uk.org
Pub:*The Hoopoe*, annually, *Ali Notizie*, quarterley.

NEOTROPICAL BIRD CLUB.
c/o The Lodge, Sandy,
Bedfordshire, SG19 2DL.
Pub:*Cotinga*.
email: secretary@neotropicalbirdclub.org
www.neotropicalbirdclub.org

ORIENTAL BIRD CLUB.
P.O.Box 324, Bedford,
MK42 0WG
Pub:*The Forktail; OBC Bulletin*.

email: mail@orientalbirdclub.org
www.orientalbirdclub.org

**ORNITHOLOGICAL SOCIETY OF THE MIDDLE
EAST (OSME).**
c/o The Lodge, Sandy, Beds, SG19 2DL.
Pub:*Sandgrouse*.
www.osme.org

**TRAFFIC International (formerly Wildlife
Trade Monitoring Unit).**
219a Huntingdon Road, Cambridge, CB3 ODL,
+44 (0)1223 277 427; (Fax) +44 (0)1223 277 237.
Pub:*TRAFFIC Bulletin*.
e-mail: traffic@traffic.org
www.traffic.org

WEST AFRICAN ORNITHOLOGICAL SOCIETY.
R E Sharland, 1 Fisher's Heron, East Mills, Hants,
SP6 2JR. Pub: *Malimbus*.
e-mail bob@sharland2002.fsnet.co.uk
http://malimbus.free.fr

WETLANDS INTERNATIONAL.
PO Box 471, 6700 AL Wageningen, Netherlands,
+31 317 485 774; (Fax) +31 317 486 770,
Pub:*Wetlands*.
e-mail: post@wetlands.org
www.wetlands.org

WORLD OWL TRUST.
The World Owl Centre, Muncaster Castle,
Ravenglass, Cumbria, CA18 1RQ, +44 (0)1229
717393; (Fax) +44 (0)1229 717107,
www.owls.org

WORLD PHEASANT ASSOCIATION.
7-9 Shaftesbury St, Fordingbridge, Hants SP6 1JF.
01425 657 129; (Fax) 01425 658 053.
Pub:*WPA News*. www.pheasant.org.uk

WORLD WIDE FUND FOR NATURE.

Panda House, Weyside
Park, Godalming
United Kingdom. +44
1483 426 444;
(Fax) +44 1483 426 409,
e-mail: supporterrelations
@wwf.org.uk
www.panda.org

QUICK REFERENCE SECTION

It's important to know the times when tides are high to ensure you have a great wader-watching experience. Our tide tables begin overleaf.

TIDE TABLES: USEFUL INFORMATION

BRITISH SUMMER TIME

In 2010 BST applies from 01:00 on March 28 to 01:00 on October 31.
Note that all the times in the following tables are GMT.

Shetland 42, 43
Orkney 44, 45

During British Summer Time one hour should be added.

Predictions are given for the times of high water at Dover throughout the year.

The times of tides at the locations shown here may be obtained by adding or subtracting their 'tidal difference' as shown opposite (subtractions are indicated by a minus sign).

Tidal predictions for Dover have been computed by the Proudman Oceanographic Laboratory. Copyright reserved.

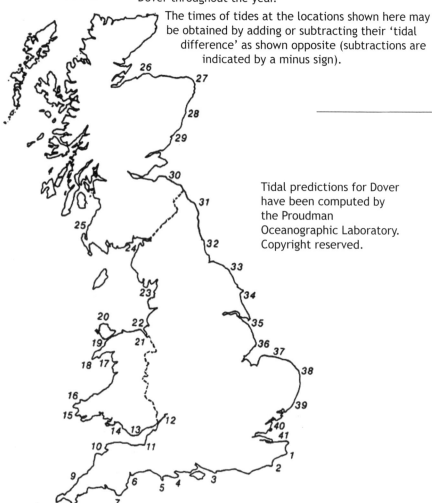

Map showing locations for which tidal differences are given on facing page.

TIDE TABLES 2009

Example 1
To calculate the time of first high water at Girvan on February 28
1. Look up the time at Dover (10 39)*
   = 10:39 am
2. Add the tidal difference for Girvan
   = 0.54
3. Therefore the time of high water at Girvan = 11.33 am

Example 2
To calculate the time of second high water at Blakeney on June 20
1. Look up the time at Dover (17 31)
   = 17:31 pm
2. Add 1 hour for British Summer Time (18 31) = 18:31 pm
3. Subtract the tidal difference for Blakeney = - 4.07
4. Therefore the time of high water at Blakeney = 14:24 pm

*All Dover times are shown on the 24-hour clock.
Following the time of each high water the height of the tide is given, in metres.

(Tables beyond April 2011 are not available at the time of going to press.)

TIDAL DIFFERENCES

1	Dover	See pp 338-341		23	Morecambe	0	20
2	Dungeness	-0	12	24	Silloth	0	51
3	Selsey Bill	0	09	25	Girvan	0	54
4	Swanage (lst H.W.Springs)	-2	36	26	Lossiemouth	0	48
5	Portland	-4	23	27	Fraserburgh	1	20
6	Exmouth (Approaches)	-4	48	28	Aberdeen	2	30
7	Salcombe	-5	23	29	Montrose	3	30
8	Newlyn (Penzance)	5	59	30	Dunbar	3	42
9	Padstow	-5	47	31	Holy Island	3	58
10	Bideford	-5	17	32	Sunderland	4	38
11	Bridgwater	-4	23	33	Whitby	5	12
12	Sharpness Dock	-3	19	34	Bridlington	5	53
13	Cardiff (Penarth)	-4	16	35	Grimsby	-5	20
14	Swansea	-4	52	36	Skegness	-5	00
15	Skomer Island	-5	00	37	Blakeney	-4	07
16	Fishguard	-3	48	38	Gorleston	-2	08
17	Barmouth	-2	45	39	Aldeburgh	-0	13
18	Bardsey Island	-3	07	40	Bradwell Waterside	1	11
19	Caernarvon	-1	07	41	Herne Bay	1	28
20	Amlwch	-0	22	42	Sullom Voe	-1	34
21	Connahs Quay	0	20	43	Lerwick	0	01
22	Hilbre Island			44	Kirkwall	-0	26
	(Hoylake/West Kirby)	-0	05	45	Widewall Bay	-1	30

NB. Care should be taken when making calculations at the beginning and end of British Summer Time. See worked examples above.

TIDE TABLES 2010

Tidal Predictions : HIGH WATERS 2010
Datum of Predictions = Chart Datum : 3.67 metres below Ordnance Datum (Newlyn)
British Summer Time : 28th March to 31st October

Units METRES

DOVER — January

Date	Day	Morning hr min	m	Afternoon hr min	m
1	F	10 59	6.7	23 31	6.8
2	Sa	11 49	6.8	** **	*
3	Su	00 22	6.9	12 41	6.8
4	M	01 10	6.9	13 34	6.7
5	Tu	01 57	6.8	14 23	6.5
6	W	02 44	6.7	15 12	6.3
7	Th	03 32	6.5	16 03	6.0
8	F	04 24	6.2	17 00	5.7
9	Sa	05 26	5.9	18 09	5.5
10	Su	06 37	5.7	19 24	5.4
11	M	07 50	5.6	20 33	5.6
12	Tu	08 56	5.7	21 21	5.8
13	W	09 50	5.9	22 12	6.0
14	Th	10 34	6.1	22 52	6.2
15	F	11 11	6.2	23 27	6.4
16	Sa	11 47	6.2	** **	*
17	Su	00 02	6.5	12 19	6.3
18	M	00 34	6.5	12 50	6.2
19	Tu	01 07	6.4	13 19	6.1
20	W	01 36	6.4	13 48	5.9
21	Th	02 03	6.3	14 17	5.8
22	F	02 34	6.2	14 54	5.6
23	Sa	03 08	6.0	15 41	5.4
24	Su	03 48	5.8	16 46	5.4
25	M	05 17	5.6	18 02	5.3
26	Tu	06 37	5.5	19 28	5.5
27	W	07 57	5.7	20 42	5.8
28	Th	09 05	6.0	21 43	6.2
29	F	10 00	6.4	22 34	6.6
30	Sa	10 50	6.7	23 21	6.8
31	Su	11 40	6.8	** **	*

DOVER — February

Date	Day	Morning hr min	m	Afternoon hr min	m
1	M	00 08	7.0	12 27	6.9
2	Tu	00 53	7.1	13 14	6.9
3	W	01 35	7.0	13 57	6.8
4	Th	02 16	6.9	14 38	6.6
5	F	02 58	6.6	15 23	6.4
6	Sa	03 46	6.2	16 13	6.1
7	Su	04 45	5.8	17 24	5.7
8	M	06 01	5.4	18 49	5.4
9	Tu	07 29	5.3	20 10	5.2
10	W	08 44	5.4	21 11	5.3
11	Th	09 39	5.7	21 56	5.6
12	F	10 21	5.9	22 34	6.0
13	Sa	10 55	5.9	23 03	6.2
14	Su	11 27	6.2	23 40	6.5
15	M	11 56	6.3	** **	*
16	Tu	00 11	6.6	12 25	6.3
17	W	00 39	6.6	13 00	6.3
18	Th	01 03	6.5	13 14	6.2
19	F	01 28	6.4	14 16	6.1
20	Sa	01 56	6.2	14 16	6.1
21	Su	02 34	6.2	15 01	5.9
22	M	03 26	5.9	16 04	5.5
23	Tu	04 41	5.5	17 30	5.3
24	W	06 15	5.4	19 12	5.3
25	Th	07 49	5.6	20 34	5.7
26	F	08 58	6.0	21 32	6.2
27	Sa	09 51	6.4	22 19	6.6
28	Su	10 39	6.7	23 03	6.9

DOVER — March

Date	Day	Morning hr min	m	Afternoon hr min	m
1	M	11 24	6.9	23 47	7.1
2	Tu	** **	*	12 08	6.9
3	W	00 29	7.1	12 50	6.8
4	Th	01 08	7.1	13 28	6.7
5	F	01 46	6.8	14 07	6.5
6	Sa	02 26	6.5	14 49	6.1
7	Su	03 12	6.1	15 40	5.7
8	M	04 11	5.6	16 45	5.3
9	Tu	05 30	5.1	18 12	5.0
10	W	07 07	5.0	19 42	5.2
11	Th	08 24	5.3	20 45	5.5
12	F	09 19	5.6	21 32	5.8
13	Sa	10 00	5.9	22 09	6.1
14	Su	10 32	6.1	22 42	6.3
15	M	11 00	6.2	23 11	6.4
16	Tu	11 27	6.4	23 40	6.5
17	W	11 52	6.4	** **	*
18	Th	00 05	6.5	12 19	6.4
19	F	00 30	6.5	12 46	6.3
20	Sa	00 57	6.4	13 15	6.3
21	Su	01 29	6.4	13 52	6.2
22	M	02 10	6.2	14 40	5.9
23	Tu	03 05	5.8	15 47	5.6
24	W	04 26	5.5	17 19	5.4
25	Th	06 11	5.4	19 01	5.4
26	F	07 42	5.6	20 17	5.8
27	Sa	08 47	6.0	21 12	6.3
28	Su	09 36	6.4	21 58	6.6
29	M	10 21	6.6	22 41	6.9
30	Tu	11 02	6.8	23 21	7.0
31	W	11 44	6.8	** **	*

DOVER — April

Date	Day	Morning hr min	m	Afternoon hr min	m
1	Th	00 02	7.0	12 23	6.8
2	F	00 41	6.9	13 03	6.6
3	Sa	01 19	6.7	13 41	6.4
4	Su	02 00	6.3	14 23	6.1
5	M	02 45	5.9	15 11	5.8
6	Tu	03 41	5.5	16 11	5.4
7	W	04 57	5.1	17 30	5.1
8	Th	06 32	5.0	18 58	5.1
9	F	07 49	5.5	20 06	5.7
10	Sa	08 44	5.5	20 55	5.6
11	Su	09 25	5.8	21 34	5.7
12	M	09 57	6.0	22 07	6.2
13	Tu	10 25	6.1	22 36	6.3
14	W	10 52	6.4	23 33	6.4
15	Th	11 21	6.4	** **	*
16	F	11 51	6.5	12 25	6.4
17	Sa	00 04	6.5	13 03	6.3
18	Su	00 37	6.5	13 46	6.2
19	M	01 17	6.3	14 41	5.9
20	Tu	02 04	5.8	15 53	5.7
21	W	03 09	5.5	17 14	5.5
22	Th	04 32	5.5	18 41	5.5
23	F	06 05	6.0	19 50	6.0
24	Sa	07 24	6.3	20 45	6.3
25	Su	08 23	6.5	21 32	6.5
26	M	09 13	6.3	22 15	6.5
27	Tu	09 57	6.5	22 57	6.7
28	W	10 39	6.6	23 40	6.8
29	Th	11 21	6.6	** **	*
30	F	** **	*	12 04	6.6

TIDE TABLES 2010

Time Zone **GMT**   Tidal Predictions : **HIGH WATERS 2010**   Units **METRES**

Datum of Predictions = Chart Datum : 3.67 metres below Ordnance Datum (Newlyn)

British Summer Time : 28th March to 31st October

DOVER — May

Date	Day	Morning hr min	m	Afternoon hr min	m
1	Sa	00 22	6.6	12 43	6.5
2	Su	01 01	6.4	13 21	6.3
3	M	01 42	6.2	14 02	6.1
4	Tu	02 26	5.9	14 44	5.9
5	W	03 16	5.5	15 39	5.6
6	Th	04 19	5.2	16 43	5.3
7	F	05 38	5.0	17 59	5.2
8	Sa	06 54	5.1	19 10	5.4
9	Su	07 52	5.3	20 04	5.6
10	M	08 37	5.6	20 48	5.8
11	Tu	09 13	5.8	21 23	6.0
12	W	09 46	6.0	21 57	6.2
13	Th	10 18	6.2	22 31	6.4
14	F	10 53	6.3	23 07	6.4
15	Sa	11 33	6.4	23 47	6.5
16	Su	** **	*.*	12 16	6.5
17	M	00 30	6.5	13 04	6.4
18	Tu	01 19	6.3	13 56	6.3
19	W	02 17	6.2	14 51	6.2
20	Th	03 20	6.0	15 51	6.0
21	F	04 29	5.9	16 59	5.9
22	Sa	05 42	5.7	18 09	5.9
23	Su	06 51	5.8	19 15	6.0
24	M	07 52	5.9	20 13	6.2
25	Tu	08 45	6.1	21 05	6.3
26	W	09 33	6.3	21 53	6.4
27	Th	10 21	6.4	22 39	6.5
28	F	11 04	6.4	23 24	6.5
29	Sa	11 47	6.4	** **	*.*
30	Su	00 06	6.4	12 26	6.4
31	M	00 46	6.3	13 05	6.3

DOVER — June

Date	Day	Morning hr min	m	Afternoon hr min	m
1	Tu	01 25	6.1	13 43	6.2
2	W	02 06	5.9	14 24	6.1
3	Th	02 49	5.7	15 08	5.9
4	F	03 39	5.4	15 55	5.6
5	Sa	04 36	5.3	16 55	5.5
6	Su	05 41	5.2	17 58	5.4
7	M	06 43	5.2	18 58	5.5
8	Tu	07 36	5.4	19 52	5.6
9	W	08 24	5.6	20 38	5.8
10	Th	09 08	5.9	21 22	6.1
11	F	09 51	6.1	22 05	6.3
12	Sa	10 35	6.3	22 50	6.3
13	Su	11 21	6.5	23 37	6.5
14	M	** **	*.*	12 11	6.6
15	Tu	00 22	6.6	13 03	6.6
16	W	01 22	6.5	13 53	6.6
17	Th	02 19	6.4	14 44	6.5
18	F	03 10	6.2	15 34	6.4
19	Sa	04 10	6.1	16 31	6.2
20	Su	05 09	5.9	17 31	6.1
21	M	06 12	5.8	18 36	6.0
22	Tu	07 18	5.7	19 42	6.0
23	W	08 18	5.8	20 42	6.1
24	Th	09 18	6.0	21 39	6.2
25	F	10 07	6.1	22 26	6.2
26	Sa	10 50	6.3	23 11	6.3
27	Su	11 31	6.4	23 51	6.4
28	M	** **	*.*	12 09	6.4
29	Tu	00 29	6.2	12 46	6.4
30	W	01 05	6.1	13 22	6.4

DOVER — July

Date	Day	Morning hr min	m	Afternoon hr min	m
1	Th	01 42	6.0	13 57	6.3
2	F	02 17	5.8	14 33	6.1
3	Sa	02 54	5.7	15 11	5.9
4	Su	03 36	5.5	15 53	5.7
5	M	04 25	5.4	16 46	5.6
6	Tu	05 24	5.3	17 48	5.5
7	W	06 32	5.3	18 56	5.3
8	Th	07 38	5.5	20 00	5.5
9	F	08 40	5.8	20 56	5.8
10	Sa	09 33	6.1	21 49	6.0
11	Su	10 22	6.4	22 38	6.2
12	M	11 11	6.6	23 23	6.5
13	Tu	11 59	6.7	** **	*.*
14	W	00 11	6.8	12 49	6.9
15	Th	01 00	6.7	13 36	6.9
16	F	01 48	6.7	14 23	6.8
17	Sa	02 45	6.4	15 08	6.6
18	Su	03 37	6.2	15 57	6.4
19	M	04 31	5.9	16 53	6.1
20	Tu	05 33	5.7	18 01	5.8
21	W	06 47	5.6	19 18	5.7
22	Th	08 03	5.8	20 31	5.7
23	F	09 05	6.0	21 31	5.9
24	Sa	09 54	6.1	22 17	6.0
25	Su	10 36	6.3	22 57	6.2
26	M	11 18	6.4	23 34	6.2
27	Tu	11 48	6.5	** **	*.*
28	W	00 08	6.3	12 23	6.5
29	Th	00 41	6.3	12 56	6.5
30	F	01 12	6.2	13 26	6.5
31	Sa	01 41	6.1	13 53	6.3

DOVER — August

Date	Day	Morning hr min	m	Afternoon hr min	m
1	Su	02 07	6.0	14 21	6.2
2	M	02 40	5.8	14 56	6.0
3	Tu	03 22	5.8	15 44	5.8
4	W	04 07	5.4	16 50	5.4
5	Th	05 37	5.3	18 11	5.3
6	F	07 21	5.4	19 35	5.4
7	Sa	08 21	5.7	20 42	5.7
8	Su	09 23	6.1	21 37	6.1
9	M	10 10	6.5	22 26	6.5
10	Tu	10 56	7.0	23 13	6.8
11	W	11 41	6.9	** **	*.*
12	Th	00 01	7.1	12 27	7.1
13	F	00 49	7.1	13 11	7.0
14	Sa	01 35	6.8	13 55	6.7
15	Su	02 19	6.5	14 37	6.5
16	M	03 03	6.4	15 23	6.4
17	Tu	03 56	5.9	16 31	6.0
18	W	05 03	5.6	17 48	5.5
19	Th	06 46	5.3	19 23	5.5
20	F	08 21	5.5	20 23	5.8
21	Sa	09 23	5.7	21 22	6.0
22	Su	10 03	6.0	22 05	6.4
23	M	10 17	6.2	22 41	6.2
24	Tu	10 52	6.4	23 11	6.4
25	W	11 24	6.6	23 42	6.3
26	Th	11 55	6.4	** **	*.*
27	F	00 39	6.6	12 25	6.6
28	Sa	01 03	6.5	12 50	6.5
29	Su	01 26	6.3	13 12	6.3
30	M	01 26	6.2	13 39	6.2
31	Tu	01 57	6.1	14 13	6.1

TIDE TABLES 2010

Time Zone **GMT**

Units **METRES**

Tidal Predictions : **HIGH WATERS 2010**

Datum of Predictions = **Chart Datum : 3.67 metres below Ordnance Datum (Newlyn)**

British Summer Time : **28th March to 31st October**

DOVER — September

Day	Morning hr min	m	Afternoon hr min	m
1 W	02 38	5.9	14 59	5.9
2 Th	03 36	5.6	16 08	5.5
3 F	04 59	5.3	17 44	5.3
4 Sa	06 43	5.4	19 21	5.5
5 Su	08 06	5.7	20 31	6.0
6 M	09 04	6.2	21 25	6.4
7 Tu	09 51	6.6	22 10	6.7
8 W	10 35	7.0	22 53	7.0
9 Th	11 17	7.2	23 37	7.0
10 F	** **	*	12 01	7.2
11 Sa	00 22	7.0	12 41	7.2
12 Su	01 04	6.8	13 22	7.0
13 M	01 45	6.6	14 04	6.7
14 Tu	02 28	6.3	14 51	6.2
15 W	03 19	5.9	15 49	5.8
16 Th	04 15	5.5	17 04	5.3
17 F	05 45	5.3	18 44	5.2
18 Sa	07 19	5.3	20 07	5.7
19 Su	08 27	5.6	21 02	6.0
20 M	09 13	6.0	21 43	6.3
21 Tu	09 51	6.2	22 17	6.4
22 W	10 25	6.4	22 46	6.5
23 Th	10 56	6.6	23 13	6.5
24 F	11 24	6.6	23 40	6.6
25 Sa	11 51	6.6	** **	*
26 Su	00 05	6.5	12 15	6.6
27 M	00 30	6.4	12 40	6.5
28 Tu	00 58	6.3	13 10	6.4
29 W	01 31	6.1	13 46	6.2
30 Th	02 14	6.0	14 34	5.9

DOVER — October

Day	Morning hr min	m	Afternoon hr min	m
1 F	03 13	5.7	15 47	5.5
2 Sa	04 42	5.4	17 31	5.4
3 Su	06 23	5.5	19 08	5.6
4 M	07 43	5.8	20 14	6.0
5 Tu	08 41	6.1	21 06	6.4
6 W	09 27	6.7	21 50	6.7
7 Th	10 11	7.1	22 31	6.9
8 F	10 52	7.1	23 13	6.9
9 Sa	11 34	7.2	23 56	6.9
10 Su	** **	*	12 15	7.1
11 M	00 37	6.8	12 57	6.8
12 Tu	01 19	6.6	13 39	6.6
13 W	02 03	6.3	14 26	6.1
14 Th	02 51	5.9	15 20	5.7
15 F	03 49	5.6	16 32	5.3
16 Sa	05 03	5.3	18 09	5.1
17 Su	06 34	5.3	19 31	5.3
18 M	07 46	5.5	20 27	5.6
19 Tu	08 38	5.8	21 11	5.9
20 W	09 19	6.1	21 46	6.1
21 Th	09 53	6.3	22 15	6.3
22 F	10 24	6.4	22 42	6.4
23 Sa	10 52	6.5	23 09	6.5
24 Su	11 19	6.5	23 37	6.5
25 M	11 47	6.6	** **	*
26 Tu	00 08	6.5	12 18	6.5
27 W	00 41	6.4	12 54	6.4
28 Th	01 22	6.3	13 36	6.2
29 F	02 10	6.1	14 25	5.9
30 Sa	03 10	5.8	15 47	5.6
31 Su	04 32	5.7	17 17	5.5

DOVER — November

Day	Morning hr min	m	Afternoon hr min	m
1 M	05 56	5.7	18 43	5.7
2 Tu	07 11	5.9	19 48	6.0
3 W	08 11	6.3	20 41	6.3
4 Th	09 04	6.6	21 11	6.5
5 F	09 46	6.8	22 11	6.7
6 Sa	10 27	6.8	22 55	6.8
7 Su	11 13	6.9	23 38	6.8
8 M	11 56	6.8	** **	*
9 Tu	00 20	6.7	12 39	6.6
10 W	01 01	6.5	13 21	6.4
11 Th	01 42	6.3	14 04	6.0
12 F	02 27	6.1	14 55	5.7
13 Sa	03 18	5.8	15 56	5.4
14 Su	04 18	5.5	17 11	5.2
15 M	05 33	5.4	18 33	5.2
16 Tu	06 49	5.6	19 36	5.4
17 W	07 48	5.8	20 26	5.6
18 Th	08 35	6.0	21 06	6.1
19 F	09 15	6.2	21 42	6.2
20 Sa	09 49	6.3	22 11	6.4
21 Su	10 19	6.4	22 42	6.4
22 M	10 52	6.4	23 17	6.5
23 Tu	11 28	6.5	23 56	6.5
24 W	** **	*	12 08	6.4
25 Th	00 39	6.5	12 51	6.3
26 F	01 25	6.4	13 41	6.1
27 Sa	02 16	6.3	14 37	5.9
28 Su	03 11	6.1	15 41	5.7
29 M	04 12	6.0	16 52	5.8
30 Tu	05 21	5.9	18 05	5.7

DOVER — December

Day	Morning hr min	m	Afternoon hr min	m
1 W	06 32	6.0	19 12	5.9
2 Th	07 35	6.1	20 13	6.0
3 F	08 33	6.3	21 06	6.2
4 Sa	09 26	6.5	21 56	6.4
5 Su	10 15	6.6	22 42	6.5
6 M	11 02	6.6	23 26	6.6
7 Tu	11 45	6.6	** **	*
8 W	00 06	6.6	12 26	6.5
9 Th	00 46	6.5	13 05	6.1
10 F	01 24	6.4	13 46	6.1
11 Sa	02 04	6.3	14 28	5.8
12 Su	02 47	6.1	15 15	5.6
13 M	03 33	5.8	16 08	5.4
14 Tu	04 28	5.6	17 13	5.2
15 W	05 31	5.4	18 25	5.3
16 Th	06 39	5.5	19 25	5.5
17 F	07 37	5.5	20 26	5.7
18 Sa	08 30	5.7	21 04	5.8
19 Su	09 13	5.9	21 43	6.0
20 M	09 54	6.2	22 22	6.3
21 Tu	10 35	6.4	23 04	6.4
22 W	11 17	6.5	23 48	6.5
23 Th	** **	*	12 39	6.6
24 F	00 33	6.7	12 50	6.7
25 Sa	01 21	6.6	13 39	6.6
26 Su	02 07	6.6	14 30	6.4
27 M	02 56	6.5	15 23	6.2
28 Tu	03 47	6.3	16 19	6.0
29 W	04 45	6.2	17 23	5.8
30 Th	05 45	6.0	18 33	5.7
31 F	07 01	5.9	19 46	5.7

Time Zone **GMT**   Tidal Predictions : **HIGH WATERS 2011**   Units **METRES**

Datum of Predictions = **Chart Datum : 3.67 metres below Ordnance Datum (Newlyn)**

British Summer Time : **27th March to 30th October**

DOVER — January

Date	Day	Morning hr min	m	Afternoon hr min	m
1	Sa	08 11	6.0	20 52	5.9
2	Su	09 15	6.1	21 47	6.1
3	M	10 08	6.2	22 34	6.3
4	Tu	10 53	6.3	23 14	6.5
5	W	11 34	6.4	23 52	6.4
6	Th	** **	*	12 12	6.4
7	F	00 29	6.6	12 42	6.3
8	Sa	01 04	6.6	13 24	6.2
9	Su	01 39	6.5	13 59	6.1
10	M	02 14	6.3	14 33	5.9
11	Tu	02 49	6.1	15 11	5.6
12	W	03 27	5.8	15 56	5.4
13	Th	04 17	5.6	16 53	5.1
14	F	05 19	5.3	18 04	5.1
15	Sa	06 33	5.3	19 21	5.2
16	Su	07 45	5.4	20 27	5.5
17	M	08 44	5.7	21 20	5.9
18	Tu	09 34	6.0	22 07	6.2
19	W	10 19	6.4	22 50	6.5
20	Th	11 04	6.6	23 34	6.8
21	F	11 49	6.8	** **	*
22	Sa	00 19	6.9	12 37	6.8
23	Su	01 04	7.0	13 24	6.8
24	M	01 49	6.9	14 10	6.6
25	Tu	02 33	6.8	14 56	6.4
26	W	03 19	6.5	15 47	6.1
27	Th	04 07	6.2	16 46	5.8
28	F	05 07	6.0	17 59	5.5
29	Sa	06 36	5.6	19 25	5.4
30	Su	08 02	5.6	20 41	5.6
31	M	09 11	5.8	21 37	5.9

DOVER — February

Date	Day	Morning hr min	m	Afternoon hr min	m
1	Tu	10 03	6.0	22 21	6.2
2	W	10 43	6.3	22 59	6.5
3	Th	11 20	6.3	23 34	6.5
4	F	11 54	6.6	** **	*
5	Sa	00 08	6.6	12 27	6.4
6	Su	00 41	6.6	12 58	6.3
7	M	01 12	6.6	13 26	6.2
8	Tu	01 39	6.4	13 52	6.1
9	W	02 04	6.3	14 21	5.9
10	Th	02 35	6.0	14 56	5.7
11	F	03 16	5.8	15 47	5.4
12	Sa	04 14	5.6	16 57	5.2
13	Su	05 35	5.2	18 30	5.1
14	M	07 07	5.3	19 56	5.4
15	Tu	08 21	5.8	20 58	5.8
16	W	09 16	6.2	21 47	6.3
17	Th	10 08	6.4	22 31	6.6
18	F	10 46	6.7	23 14	6.9
19	Sa	11 31	6.9	23 58	7.1
20	Su	** **	*	12 16	6.9
21	M	00 41	7.2	13 03	6.9
22	Tu	01 25	7.1	13 46	6.7
23	W	02 07	6.9	14 30	6.5
24	Th	02 52	6.9	15 19	6.1
25	F	03 44	6.1	16 17	5.7
26	Sa	04 50	5.7	17 30	5.4
27	Su	06 18	5.3	19 05	5.3
28	M	07 53	5.4	20 26	5.5

DOVER — March

Date	Day	Morning hr min	m	Afternoon hr min	m
1	Tu	09 02	5.6	21 20	5.8
2	W	09 51	6.2	22 03	6.3
3	Th	10 28	6.1	22 38	6.3
4	F	11 00	6.4	23 11	6.6
5	Sa	11 31	6.4	23 44	6.6
6	Su	** **	*	12 02	6.4
7	M	00 15	6.6	12 30	6.4
8	Tu	00 41	6.5	12 54	6.3
9	W	01 03	6.4	13 17	6.2
10	Th	01 26	6.3	13 43	6.1
11	F	01 56	6.1	14 19	5.9
12	Sa	02 35	5.9	15 05	5.6
13	Su	03 32	5.5	16 17	5.3
14	M	04 59	5.4	17 55	5.2
15	Tu	06 40	5.6	19 28	5.9
16	W	07 57	6.3	20 33	6.3
17	Th	08 55	6.6	21 21	6.7
18	F	09 41	6.4	22 07	7.0
19	Sa	10 25	6.7	22 50	7.1
20	Su	11 09	6.9	23 34	7.1
21	M	11 54	7.0	** **	*
22	Tu	00 18	7.2	12 39	6.9
23	W	01 01	7.0	13 24	6.7
24	Th	01 43	6.8	14 07	6.5
25	F	02 30	6.4	14 55	6.1
26	Sa	03 23	6.0	15 51	5.7
27	Su	04 29	5.5	17 03	5.4
28	M	05 59	5.2	18 36	5.2
29	Tu	07 32	5.3	19 56	5.4
30	W	08 38	5.5	20 51	5.8
31	Th	09 25	5.8	21 34	6.0

DOVER — April

Date	Day	Morning hr min	m	Afternoon hr min	m
1	F	10 03	6.0	22 11	6.3
2	Sa	10 35	6.2	22 45	6.4
3	Su	11 04	6.3	23 16	6.5
4	M	11 34	6.4	23 45	6.5
5	Tu	** **	*	12 01	6.3
6	W	00 09	6.4	12 25	6.3
7	Th	00 33	6.4	12 50	6.2
8	F	00 58	6.3	13 19	6.0
9	Sa	01 32	6.1	13 57	5.8
10	Su	02 14	5.9	14 48	5.8
11	M	03 15	5.6	16 01	5.5
12	Tu	04 42	5.4	17 31	5.4
13	W	06 16	5.7	18 56	5.6
14	Th	07 31	6.0	20 02	6.0
15	F	08 28	6.4	20 54	6.4
16	Sa	09 16	6.7	21 40	6.7
17	Su	10 01	6.7	22 24	6.9
18	M	10 46	6.8	23 09	7.0
19	Tu	11 33	6.9	23 55	7.0
20	W	** **	*	12 20	6.8
21	Th	00 41	6.6	13 05	6.7
22	F	01 26	6.6	13 49	6.7
23	Sa	02 13	6.5	14 37	6.4
24	Su	03 05	5.9	15 29	6.1
25	M	04 07	5.5	16 32	5.5
26	Tu	05 27	5.3	17 52	5.4
27	W	06 53	5.3	19 11	5.3
28	Th	07 56	5.5	20 10	5.4
29	F	08 47	5.7	20 58	5.8
30	Sa	09 27	5.9	21 37	6.1

SUNRISE AND SUNSET TIMES

Predictions are given for the times of sunrise and sunset on every Saturday throughout the year. For places on the same latitude as the following, add 4 minutes for each degree of longitude west (subtract if east).

These times are in GMT, except between 01:00 on Mar 28 and 01:00 on Oct 31, when the times are in BST (1 hour in advance of GMT).

		London		Manchester		Edinburgh	
		Rise	Set	Rise	Set	Rise	Set
Jan	2	08 06	16 03	08 25	16 01	08 44	15 51
	9	08 04	16 12	08 22	16 11	08 40	16 01
	16	07 59	16 22	08 16	16 22	08 33	16 13
	23	07 52	16 34	08 08	16 34	08 23	16 27
	30	07 42	16 46	07 58	16 48	08 11	16 42
Feb	6	07 31	16 59	07 46	17 01	07 58	16 57
	13	07 19	17 12	07 32	17 15	07 43	17 12
	20	07 05	17 25	07 17	17 29	07 27	17 27
	27	06 51	17 37	07 02	17 43	07 10	17 43
Mar	6	06 35	17 49	06 46	17 56	06 52	17 57
	13	06 20	18 02	06 29	18 09	06 34	18 12
	20	06 04	18 14	06 12	18 22	06 16	18 26
	27	05 48	18 25	05 55	18 35	05 57	18 41
Apr	3	06 32	19 37	06 38	19 48	06 39	19 55
	10	06 16	19 49	06 21	20 01	06 21	20 09
	17	06 01	20 00	06 05	20 13	06 03	20 23
	24	05 47	20 12	05 49	20 26	05 46	20 38
May	1	05 33	20 24	05 35	20 39	05 30	20 52
	8	05 20	20 35	05 21	20 51	05 14	21 06
	15	05 09	20 46	05 09	21 03	05 01	21 19
	22	05 00	20 56	04 58	21 14	04 49	21 32
	29	04 52	21 05	04 50	21 24	04 39	21 43
Jun	5	04 47	21 12	04 44	21 32	04 32	21 52
	12	04 43	21 18	04 40	21 38	04 27	21 59
	19	04 43	21 21	04 39	21 41	04 26	22 02
	26	04 45	21 22	04 41	21 42	04 28	22 03

SUNRISE AND SUNSET TIMES

		London		Manchester		Edinburgh	
		Rise	Set	Rise	Set	Rise	Set
Jul	3	04 49	21 20	04 46	21 40	04 33	22 00
	10	04 55	21 16	04 53	21 35	04 41	21 55
	17	05 03	21 10	05 01	21 28	04 51	21 46
	24	05 13	21 01	05 12	21 19	05 02	21 35
	31	05 23	20 51	05 23	21 07	05 15	21 22
Aug	7	05 33	20 39	05 34	20 54	05 28	21 08
	14	05 44	20 25	05 46	20 40	05 42	20 52
	21	05 55	20 11	05 59	20 25	05 55	20 35
	28	06 07	19 56	06 11	20 09	06 09	20 18
Sep	4	06 18	19 41	06 23	19 52	06 23	20 00
	11	06 29	19 25	06 35	19 35	06 36	19 42
	18	06 40	19 09	06 47	19 18	06 50	19 23
	25	06 51	18 53	07 00	19 01	07 04	19 04
Oct	2	07 03	18 37	07 12	18 44	07 17	18 46
	9	07 14	18 21	07 25	18 27	07 31	18 28
	16	07 26	18 06	07 38	18 11	07 46	18 10
	23	07 38	17 51	07 51	17 55	08 00	17 53
	30	07 50	17 38	08 04	17 41	08 15	17 37
Nov	6	07 03	16 25	07 17	16 27	07 30	16 22
	13	07 15	16 14	07 31	16 15	07 45	16 09
	20	07 27	16 05	07 43	16 05	07 59	15 57
	27	07 38	15 58	07 55	15 57	08 12	15 48
Dec	4	07 48	15 54	08 06	15 52	08 24	15 42
	11	07 56	15 52	08 15	15 49	08 33	15 39
	18	08 02	15 52	08 21	15 50	08 40	15 39
	25	08 06	15 56	08 25	15 54	08 44	15 42

These tables are reproduced, with permission, from data supplied by HM Nautical Almanac Office, part of the UK Hydrographic Office, Crown Copyright. The UKHO does not accept any responsibility for loss or damage arising from the use of information contained in any of its reports or in any communication about its tests or investigations.

GRID REFERENCES

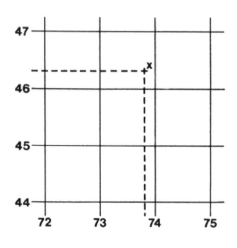

A grid reference is made up of letters and numbers. Two-letter codes are used for 100km squares on the National Grid (opposite) and single-letter codes on the Irish Grid (below).

The squares may be further subdivided into squares of 10km, 1km or 100m, allowing for increasingly specific references. On a given map the lines forming the squares are numbered in the margins, those along the top and bottom being known as 'eastings' and those along the sides as 'northings'. A reference number is made up of the relevant letter code plus two sets of figures, those representing the easting followed by the northing. According to the scale of the map they can either be read off directly or calculated by visually dividing the intervals into tenths. For most purposes three-figure eastings plus three-figure northings are adequate.

The example above, from an Ordnance Survey 'Landranger' map, illustrates how to specify a location on a map divided into lkm squares: the reference for point X is 738463. If that location lies in square SP (see map opposite), the full reference is SP738463.

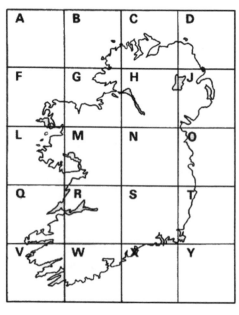

Letter codes for Irish grid 10km squares

GRID REFERENCES

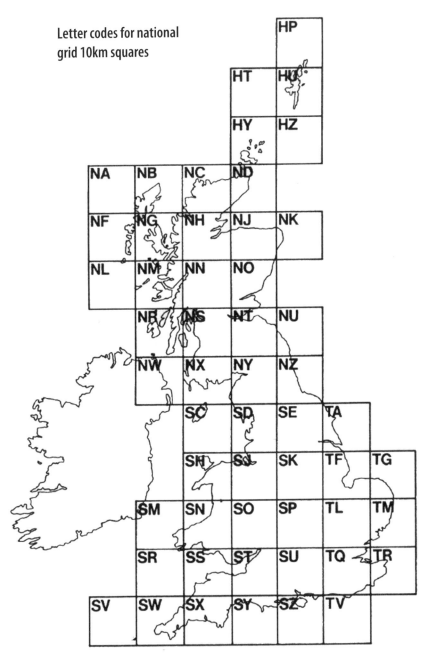

Letter codes for national
grid 10km squares

SEA AREAS

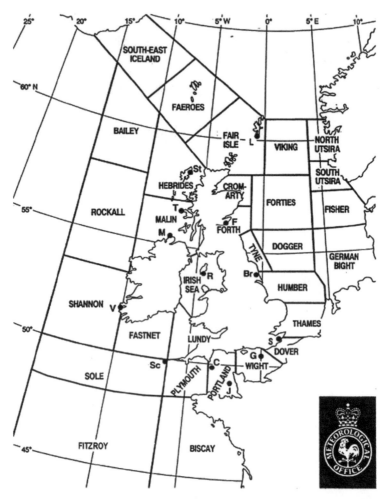

STATIONS WHOSE LATEST REPORTS ARE BROADCAST IN THE 5-MINUTE FORECASTS

Br Bridlington; C Channel Light-Vessel Automatic; F Fife Ness; G Greenwich Light-Vessel Automatic; J Jersey; L Lerwick; M Malin Head; R Ronaldsway; S Sandettie Light-Vessel Automatic; Sc Scilly Automatic; St Stornoway; T Tiree; V Valentia.

From information kindly supplied by the Meteorological Office

REVISION OF SEA AREAS

On 4 February 2002, the southern boundary of areas Plymouth and Sole, and the northern boundary of areas Biscay and Finisterre were realigned along the Metarea I/II boundary at 48°27′ North. At the same time, sea area Finisterre was renamed FitzRoy.

Did you know that the FitzRoy shipping area is named after the founder of the Met Office?

THE BIRDWATCHER'S CODE OF CONDUCT

Around three million adults go birdwatching every year in the UK. Following The birdwatchers' code is good practice, common sense and will help everybody to enjoy seeing birds.

This code puts the interests of birds first, and respects other people, whether or not they are interested in birds. It applies whenever you are watching birds in the UK or abroad. Please help everybody to enjoy birdwatching by following the code, leading by example and sensitively challenging the minority of birdwatchers who behave inappropriately.

1. The interests of the birds come first

Birds respond to people in many ways, depending on the species, location and time of year.

If birds are disturbed they may keep away from their nests, leaving chicks hungry or enabling predators to take their eggs or young. During cold weather, or when migrants have just made a long flight, repeatedly disturbing birds can mean they use up vital energy that they need for feeding.

Intentionally or recklessly disturbing some birds at or near their nest is illegal in Britain.

Whether you are particularly interested in photography, bird ringing, sound-recording or birdwatching, remember to always put the interests of the birds first.

- Avoid going too close to birds or disturbing their habitats – if a bird flies away or makes repeated alarm calls, you're too close. If it leaves, you won't get a good view of it anyway.
- Stay on roads and paths where they exist and avoid disturbing habitat used by birds.
- Think about your fieldcraft. You might disturb a bird even if you are not very close, eg a flock of wading birds on the foreshore can be disturbed from a mile away if you stand on the seawall.
- Repeatedly playing a recording of bird song or calls to encourage a bird to respond can divert a territorial bird from other important duties, such as feeding its young. Never use playback to attract a species during its breeding season.

2. Be an ambassador for birdwatching

Respond positively to questions from interested passers-by. They may not be birdwatchers yet, but good views of a bird or a helpful answer may ignite a spark of interest. Your enthusiasm could start lifetime's interest in birds and a greater appreciation of wildlife and its conservation.

Consider using local services, such as pubs, restaurants, petrol stations, and public transport. Raising awareness of the benefits to local communities of trade from visiting birdwatchers may, ultimately, help the birds themselves.

3. Know the Countryside Code, and follow it

Respect the wishes of local residents and landowners and don't enter private land without permission, unless it is open for public access on foot.

Follow the codes on access and the countryside for the place you're walking in. Irresponsible behaviour may cause a land manager to deny access to others (eg for important bird survey work). It may also disturb the bird or give birdwatching bad coverage in the media.

Access to the countryside

Legislation provides access for walkers to open country in Britain, and includes measures to protect wildlife. Note that the rules and codes are different in each part of Britain, so plan ahead and make sure you know what you can do legally.

4. The law

Laws protecting birds and their habitats are the result of hard campaigning by generations of birdwatchers. We must make sure that we don't allow them to fall into disrepute. In England, Scotland and Wales, it is a criminal offence to disturb, intentionally or recklessly, at or near the nest, a species listed on Schedule 1 of the Wildlife & Countryside Act 1981 (see www.rspb.org.uk/policy/wildbirdslaw for a full list). Disturbance could include playback of songs and calls. In Scotland, disturbing Capercaillie and Ruffs at leks is also an offence. It is a criminal offence to intentionally disturb a bird at or near the nest under the Wildlife (Northern Ireland) Order 1985.

The Government can, for particular reasons such as scientific study, issue licences to individuals that permit limited disturbance, including monitoring of nests and ringing. It is a criminal offence to destroy or damage, intentionally or recklessly, a special interest feature of a Site of Special Scientific Interest (SSSI) or to disturb the wildlife for which the site was notified.

If you witness anyone who you suspect may be illegally disturbing or destroying wildlife or habitat, phone the police immediately (ideally, with a six-figure map reference) and report it to the RSPB.

5. Rare birds

Mobile phones, telephone and pager services and the internet mean you can now share your sightings instantly. If you discover a rare bird, please bear the following in mind

- Consider the potential impact of spreading the news and make an effort to inform the landowner (or, on a nature reserve, the warden) first. Think about whether the site can cope with a large number of visitors and whether sensitive species might be at risk, such as breeding terns, flocks of wading birds or rare plants. The county bird recorder or another experienced birdwatcher can often give good advice.
- On private land, always talk to the landowner first. With a little planning, access can often be arranged.
- People coming to see a rare bird can raise money for a local reserve, other wildlife project or charity. Consider organising a voluntary collection at access points to the site.
- Rare breeding birds are at risk from egg-collectors and some birds of prey from persecution. If you discover a rare breeding species that you think is vulnerable, contact the RSPB; it has considerable experience in protecting rare breeding birds. Please also report your sighting to the county bird recorder or the Rare Breeding Birds Panel. (www.rbbp.org.uk). Also, consider telling the landowner – in most cases, this will ensure that the nest is not disturbed accidentally. If you have the opportunity to see a rare bird, enjoy it, but don't let your enthusiasm override common sense.

THE BIRDWATCHER'S CODE OF CONDUCT

In addition to the guidelines above:
- park sensibly, follow instructions and consider making a donation if requested
- don't get too close so that you can take a photograph – you'll incur the wrath of everyone else watching if you scare the bird away
- be patient if the viewing is limited, talk quietly and give others a chance to see the bird too
- do not enter private areas without permission
- not everyone likes to see an 'organised flush' and it should never be done in important wildlife habitats or where there are other nesting or roosting birds nearby. A flush should not be organised more frequently than every two hours and not within two hours of sunrise or sunset, so the bird has chance to feed and rest.

6. Make your sightings count
Add to tomorrow's knowledge of birds by sending your sightings to www.birdtrack.net This online recording scheme from the BTO, the RSPB and BirdWatch Ireland allows you to input and store all of your birdwatching records, which in turn helps to support species and site conservation. With one click, you can also have your records forwarded automatically to the relevant county recorder.

County recorders and local bird clubs are the mainstay of bird recording in the UK. Your records are important for local conservation and help to build the county's ornithological history. For a list of county bird recorders, look in the County Directory of *The Yearbook*, ask at your local library, or visit www.britishbirds.co.uk/countyrecorders

You can also get involved in a UK-wide bird monitoring scheme, such as the Breeding Bird Survey and the Wetland Bird Survey (see www.bto.org for details). If you've been birdwatching abroad, you can give your sightings to the BirdLife International Partner in that country by visiting www.worldbirds.org Your data could be vital in helping to protect sites and species in the country you've visited.

SCHEDULE 1 SPECIES

Under the provisions of the Wildlife and Countryside Act 1981 the following bird species (listed in Schedule 1 - Part I of the Act) are protected by special penalties at all times.

Avocet	Falcon, Gyr	Owl, Barn	Lark, Shore
Bee-eater	Fieldfare	Owl, Snowy	Shrike, Red-backed
Bittern	Firecrest	Peregrine	Spoonbill
Bittern, Little	Garganey	Petrel, Leach's	Stilt, Black-winged
Bluethroat	Godwit, Black-tailed	Pintail	Stint, Temminck's
Brambling	Goshawk	Phalarope, Red-necked	Swan, Bewick's
Bunting, Cirl	Grebe, Black-necked	Plover, Kentish	Swan, Whooper
Bunting, Lapland	Grebe, Slavonian	Plover, Little Ringed	Tern, Black
Bunting, Snow	Greenshank	Quail, Common	Tern, Little
Buzzard, Honey	Gull, Little	Redstart, Black	Tern, Roseate
Chough	Gull, Mediterranean	Redwing	Tit, Bearded
Crake, Corn	Harriers (all species)	Rosefinch, Scarlet	Tit, Crested
Crake, Spotted	Heron, Purple	Ruff	Treecreeper, Short-toed
Crossbills (all species)	Hobby	Sandpiper, Green	Warbler, Cetti's
Stone-curlew	Hoopoe	Sandpiper, Purple	Warbler, Dartford
Divers (all species)	Kingfisher	Sandpiper, Wood	Warbler, Marsh
Dotterel	Kite, Red	Scaup	Warbler, Savi's
Duck, Long-tailed	Merlin	Scoter, Common	Whimbrel
Eagle, Golden	Oriole, Golden	Scoter, Velvet	Lark, Wood
Eagle, White-tailed	Osprey	Serin	Wryneck

The following birds and their eggs (listed in Schedule 1 - Part II of the Act) are protected by special penalties during the close season, which is Feb 1 to Aug 31 (Feb 21 to Aug 31 below high water mark), but may be killed outside this period - Goldeneye, Greylag Goose (in Outer Hebrides, Caithness, Sutherland, and Wester Ross only), Pintail.

THE COUNTRYSIDE CODE

Launched on 12 July 2004, this Code for England has been produced through a partnership between the Countryside Agency and Countryside Council for Wales.

The Countryside Code has been revised and re-launched to reflect the introduction of new open access rights (Countryside & Rights of Way Act 2000) and changes in society over the last 20 years.

• Be safe – plan ahead
Follow any signs, even when going out locally, it's best to get the latest information about where and when you can go; for example, your rights to go onto some areas of open land may be restricted while work is carried out, for safety reasons or during breeding seasons. Follow advice and local signs, and be prepared for the unexpected.

• Leave gates and property as you find them
Please respect the working life of the countryside, as our actions can affect people's livelihoods, our heritage, and the safety and welfare of animals and ourselves.

• Protect plants and animals, and take your litter home
We have a responsibility to protect our countryside now and for future generations, so make sure you don't harm animals, birds, plants, or trees.

• Keep dogs under close control
The countryside is a great place to exercise dogs, but it's every owner's duty to make sure their dog is not a danger or nuisance to farm animals, wildlife or other people.

• Consider other people
Showing consideration and respect for other people makes the countryside a pleasant Environment for everyone – at home, at work and at leisure.

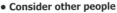

BIRDLINE NUMBERS - National and Regional

Birdline name	To obtain information	To report sightings (hotlines)
National		
Bird Information Service	09068 700 222	
www.birdingworld.co.uk		
Flightline (Northern Ireland)	028 9146 7408	
Regional		
Northern Ireland	028 9146 7408	
Scotland	09068 700 234	01292 611 994
Wales	09068 700 248	01492 544 588
East Anglia	09068 700 245	01603 763 388
Midlands	09068 700 247	01905 754 154
North East	09068 700 246	07974 358 988
North West	09068 700 249	01492 544 588
South East	09068 700 240	01845 570 444
www.southeastbirdnews.co.uk		or 08000 377 240
South West	09068 700 241	0845 4567 938

Charges
At the time of compilation, calls to premium line numbers cost 60p per minute.

Key contributors in this Edition

Authors

RICHARD FACEY

Richard Facey is a keen birder, licensed bird ringer and was a regular contributor to Birds Illustrated magazine. Richard is currently a Conservation Officer with the Countryside Council for Wales and in his spare time he studies Swallows and other migrants. His main interests are bird behaviour and the effects of weather and climate change on bird ecology.

BARBARA HALL

Barbara has worked with the Hawk and Owl Trust for more than 20 years. She is a communications consultant, specialising in environment and heritage issues, particularly helping charities and other organisations to increase awareness of their achievements. Contact her at: bmh@mycenae.co.uk

GORDON HAMLETT

Gordon is a freelance journalist living in Norfolk. As well as reviewing books and new media for magazines, he is the author of the best-selling Best Birdwatching Sites: Scottish Highlands book, published by Buckingham Press Ltd. Contact him at: gordon.hamlett@btinternet.com

Editor

DAVID CROMACK

The former editor of Bird Watching and Birds Illustrated magazines, David works with his wife Hilary as a partner in Buckingham Press Ltd, publishers of bird site guides, ID cards and for the past 30 years The Birdwatcher's Yearbook. Contact David at: editor@buckinghampress.com

HEARTFELT THANKS

The publishers would like to thank the scores of club secretaries, reserve wardens, national and international conservation groups for their continuing support of *The Birdwatcher's Yearbook*. Their willingness to take the time to update information on an annual basis ensures that the *Yearbook* remains both a pertinent and accurate resource for the greater birdwatching community.

Best Birdwatching Sites

The trusted name for accurate, accessible site information

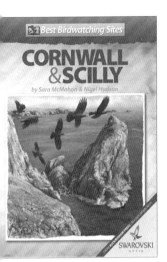

The newly-released **Best Birdwatching Sites in Cornwall & Scilly** features 52 mainland sites, plus seven routes around the key islands of Scilly. 208pp.

Price: £17.50

Extracts from the Birdguides website review, written by Cornishman Mark Golley on August 12.

"Buy this book. It's a simple as that. No fuss, no nonsense, this is a volume that anyone planning a trip to one of the very best birding areas in Britain would do well to pack in the rucksack, even if they've been to the far southwest of England on countless occasions before.

"The 208 pages that make up Best Birdwatching Sites: Cornwall & Scilly

are a "must have" .... the book is jam-packed full of useful information without ever seeming cluttered..... Everything you need to know is listed.

"Authors Sara McMahon and Nigel Hudson have done a first-class job. The word 'essential' is often rather overblown and overused — but not here. As mentioned at the start of the review: buy this book. It's as simple as that."

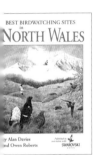

Best Birdwatching Sites in North Wales Alan Davies and Owen Roberts. Features major sites in Gwynedd and Clwyd, plus 11 smaller birding spots around Wrexham. ?2pp. **Price: £15.95**

Best Birdwatching Sites in Norfolk (2nd Edition) by Neil Glenn. Contains 83 sites (ten more than 1st Edition) – all information updated. 256pp. **Price: £16.95.**

Best Birdwatching Sites in the Scottish Highlands by Gordon Hamlett. Features 22 birding routes from John O'Groats to Pitlochry. 164 maps, 240pp. **Price: £15.95**

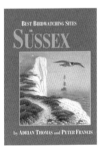

Best Birdwatching Sites in Sussex by Adrian Thomas and Peter Francis. Contains 57 sites, plus innovative migration charts. 192pp. **Price: £14.50**

For details of latest special offers on our books please contact
Buckingham Press, 55 Thorpe Park Road, Peterborough PE3 6LJ.
01733 561 739. e-mail: admin@buckinghampress.com
www.buckinghampress.co.uk (see entry on page 117).

INDEX TO RESERVES

INDEX TO RESERVES

INDEX TO RESERVES